The Apocrypha:
Including Books from the
Ethiopic Bible

Compiled by Joseph Lumpkin

Joseph B. Lumpkin

Fifth Estate Publishers,
Post Office Box 116, Blountsville, AL 35031.

First Printing, 2009

Cover Design by An Quigley

Printed on acid-free paper

Library of Congress Control No:

ISBN 10 : 1933580690
ISBN 13: 9781933580692

Fifth Estate, 2009

Joseph B. Lumpkin

Joseph B. Lumpkin

Introduction:

A Brief History of the Apocrypha

The official editions of the King James contained the books of the Apocrypha until 1796. Most printers did not clear inventories and change to the sixty-six book version we know today until the mid 1800's. Thus, most Bibles printed before 1840 still had the Apocrypha, or at least most of the Apocrypha. As it turns out, various religions have differing versions of the Bible, made up of divergent lists of books. The Protestant church has its sixty-six books, the Catholics have kept most of the Apocrypha. The Eastern Orthodox Church claims three more books than the Catholics, and the Ethiopic Church has a total of eighty-one books in its Bible.

The Etymologically of the word "apocrypha" means "things that are hidden," but why they were hidden is not clear. Some have suggested that the books were "hidden" from common use because they contained esoteric knowledge, too profound to be communicated to any except the initiated (compare 2 Esd 14.45-46). Others have suggested that such books were hidden due to their spurious or heretical teaching.

According to traditional usage "Apocrypha" has been the designation applied to the fifteen books, or portions of books, listed below. (in many earlier editions of the Apocrypha, the Letter of Jeremiah is incorporated as the final chapter of the Book of Baruch; hence in these editions there are fourteen books.)

Tobit, Judith, The Additions to the Book of Esther (contained in the Greek version of Esther), The Wisdom of Solomon, Ecclesiasticus, The Wisdom of Jesus son of Sirach, Baruch, The Letter of Jeremiah, The Prayer of Azariah, The Song of the Three Jews ,"Susanna, Bel, and the Dragon", 1 Maccabees, 2 Maccabees, 1 Esdras, The Prayer of Manasseh, and 2 Esdras.

In addition, the present expanded edition includes the following three texts that are of special interest to Eastern Orthodox readers are 3 Maccabees, 4 Maccabees, and Psalm 151.

None of these books are included in the Hebrew canon of Holy Scripture.

7

All of them, however, with the exception of 2 Esdras, are present in copies of the Greek version of the Old Testament known as the Septuagint. The Old Latin translations of the Old Testament, made from the Septuagint, also include them, along with 2 Esdras. The Eastern Orthodox Churches chose to include 1 Esdras, Psalm 151, the Prayer of Manasseh, and 3 Maccabees, and 4 Maccabees, which is placed in an appendix as a historical work.

At the end of the fourth century, Pope Damasus commissioned Jerome to prepare a standard Latin version of the Scriptures called the Latin Vulgate. Jerome wrote a note or preface, designating a separate category for the apocryphal books. However, copyists failed the include Jerome's prefaces. Thus, during the medieval period the Western Church generally regarded these books as part of the holy Scriptures.

In 1546 the Council of Trent decreed that the canon of the Old Testament includes the Apocrypha with the exception of the Prayer of Manasseh and 1 and 2 Esdras. Later, the church completed the decision by writing in its Roman Catholic Catechism, "Deuterocanonical does not mean Apocryphal, but simply 'later added to the canon.'"

But wait, there's more.

The narrow canon of the Ethiopic church contains the following Old Testament books:

Genesis
Exodus
Leviticus
Numbers
Deuteronomy
Enoch
Jubilees
Joshua
Judges

Ruth
1 Samuel
2 Samuel
1 Kings
2 Kings
1 Chronicles
2 Chronicles
Ezra
Nehemiah
3rd Ezra
4rth Ezra
Tobit
Judith
Esther (includes additions to Esther)
1 Macabees
2 Macabees
3 Macabees
Job
Psalms (+ Psalm 151)
Proverbs (Proverbs 1-24)
Täagsas (Proverbs 25-31)
Wisdom of Solomon
Ecclesiastes
Song of Solomon
Sirach (Ecclesiasticus)
Isaiah
Jeremiah
Baruch (includes Letter of Jeremiah)
Lamentations
Ezekiel
Daniel
Hosea
Amos
Micah
Joel
Obadiah
Jonah
Nahum
Habakkuk
Zephaniah
Haggai
Zecariah
Malachi

The Ethiopic Church also adds Clements and the Shepherd of Hermas to its New Testament canon. As stated before, the largest canon belongs to the Ethiopic Church, which is a part of a set of Oriental Orthodox churches. The position of Eastern and Oriental Orthodox Churches tend to have a more flexible canon of the Old Testament, and at times the list is not at all clear. For example, the Ethiopic Church has what is called a Narrow and Broad Canon.

The Broader Canon gives 46 as the total for the books of the Old Testament, made up as follows: - Octateuch (8), Judith (1), Samuel and Kings (4), Chronicles (2), 1 Esdras and the Ezra Apocalypse (2), Esther (1), Tobit (1), Maccabees (2), Job (1), Psalms (1), books of Solomon (5), Prophets (16), Ecclesiasticus (1), Pseudo-Josephus (1); Jubilees and Enoch are to be included in the number (by counting Samuel and Kings as only 2 books).

The New Testament has 35 books consisting of the Gospels (4), Acts (1), the Catholic epistles (7), the Pauline epistles (14), Revelation (1), Sinodos (4 sections), the Book of the Covenant (2 sections), Clement (1), Didascalia (1).

The Narrower Canon is made up of the Prayers of the Church and the list of the books actually printed in the large Geez and Amharic diglot, and Amharic Bibles, issued by the Emperor's command. In this, the universally accepted 39 Old Testament books are counted as 40 by the separation of Messale (Prov. 1-24) and Tägsas (Prov. 25-31), and then 14 further books are listed as equally fully canonical, namely Enoch, Jubilees, Wisdom, 1 Esdras, Ezra Apocalypse, Judith, Tobit, Ecclesiasticus, Baruch, 'the rest of Jeremiah', book of Susanna, 'the remainder of Daniel', 1 and 2 Maccabees. This brings the Old Testament total to 54, which together with the universally accepted 27 Old Testament books makes a total of 81.

The position of the Russian Orthodox Church as regards the Apocrypha appears to have changed during the centuries. The Holy Synod ruling from St. Petersburg were in sympathy with the position of the Reformers and decided to exclude the Apocrypha and since similar influences were emanating from the universities of Kiev, Moscow, Petersburg, and Kazan, the Russian Church became united in its rejection of the Apocrypha.

A full explanation of how the church of today got from the hundreds of books examined for canon to the eighty-one books of Ethiopia and finally to the mere sixty-six books of the Protestant Bible, is a matter of wide ranging discussion and varied opinions, to be taken up at another time. For now, let us simply acknowledge that the Bible many hold to with such passion and steadfastness is not the same book throughout Christendom. For now, we will simply enjoy the texts themselves.

The source of the books printed herein are in Public Domain with the exception of Enoch and Jubilees, which are my own renderings. Clements and Hermas use the J.B. Lightfoot translations as their source, but some of the archaic pronouns have been replaced. However, the "Elizabethan" sentence structure was left in place to keep the regal feel of those writings while modern pronouns assist in ease of reading.

1 Esdras

[1] Josiah kept the passover to his Lord in Jerusalem; he killed the passover lamb on the fourteenth day of the first month,

[2] having placed the priests according to their divisions, arrayed in their garments, in the temple of the Lord.

[3] And he told the Levites, the temple servants of Israel, that they should sanctify themselves to the Lord and put the holy ark of the Lord in the house which Solomon the king, the son of David, had built;

[4] and he said, "You need no longer carry it upon your shoulders. Now worship the Lord your God and serve his people Israel; and prepare yourselves by your families and kindred,

[5] in accordance with the directions of David king of Israel and the magnificence of Solomon his son. Stand in order in the temple according to the groupings of the fathers' houses of you Levites, who minister before your brethren the people of Israel,

[6] and kill the passover lamb and prepare the sacrifices for your brethren, and keep the passover according to the commandment of the Lord which was given to Moses."

[7] And Josiah gave to the people who were present thirty thousand lambs and kids, and three thousand calves; these were given from the king's possessions, as he promised, to the people and the priests and Levites.

[8] And Hilkiah, Zechariah, and Jehiel, the chief officers of the temple, gave to the priests for the passover two thousand six hundred sheep and three hundred calves. [9] And Jeconiah and Shemaiah and Nethanel his brother, and Hashabiah and Ochiel and Joram, captains over thousands, gave the Levites for the passover five thousand sheep and seven hundred calves.

[10] And this is what took place. The priests and the Levites, properly arrayed and having the unleavened bread, stood according to kindred

[11] and the grouping of the fathers' houses, before the people, to make the offering to the Lord as it is written in the book of Moses; this they did in the morning. [12] They roasted the passover lamb with fire, as required; and they boiled the sacrifices in brass pots and caldrons, with a pleasing odor,

[13] and carried them to all the people. Afterward they prepared the passover for themselves and for their brethren the priests, the sons of Aaron, [14] because the priests were offering the fat until night; so the Levites prepared it for themselves and for their brethren the priests, the sons of Aaron. [15] And the temple singers, the sons of Asaph, were in their place according to the arrangement made by David, and also Asaph,

Zechariah, and Eddinus, who represented the king. [16] The gatekeepers were at each gate; no one needed to depart from his duties, for their brethren the Levites prepared the passover for them. [17] So the things that had to do with the sacrifices to the Lord were accomplished that day: the passover was kept
[18] and the sacrifices were offered on the altar of the Lord, according to the command of King Josiah. [19] And the people of Israel who were present at that time kept the passover and the feast of unleavened bread seven days.
[20] No passover like it had been kept in Israel since the times of Samuel the prophet; [21] none of the kings of Israel had kept such a passover as was kept by Josiah and the priests and Levites and the men of Judah and all of Israel who were dwelling in Jerusalem. [22] In the eighteenth year of the reign of Josiah this passover was kept. [23] And the deeds of Josiah were upright in the sight of the Lord, for his heart was full of godliness. [24] The events of his reign have been recorded in the past, concerning those who sinned and acted wickedly toward the Lord beyond any other people or kingdom, and how they grieved the Lord deeply, so that the words of the Lord rose up against Israel. [25] After all these acts of Josiah, it happened that Pharaoh, king of Egypt, went to make war at Carchemish on the Euphrates, and Josiah went out against him.
[26] And the king of Egypt sent word to him saying, "What have we to do with each other, king of Judea? [27] I was not sent against you by the Lord God, for my war is at the Euphrates. And now the Lord is with me! The Lord is with me, urging me on! Stand aside, and do not oppose the Lord."
[28] But Josiah did not turn back to his chariot, but tried to fight with him, and did not heed the words of Jeremiah the prophet from the mouth of the Lord.
[29] He joined battle with him in the plain of Megiddo, and the commanders came down against King Josiah. [30] And the king said to his servants, "Take me away from the battle, for I am very weak." And immediately his servants took him out of the line of battle. [31] And he got into his second chariot; and after he was brought back to Jerusalem he died, and was buried in the tomb of his fathers. [32] And in all Judea they mourned for Josiah. Jeremiah the prophet lamented for Josiah, and the principal men, with the women, have made lamentation for him to this day; it was ordained that this should always be done throughout the whole nation of Israel. [33] These things are written in the book of the histories of the kings of Judea; and every one of the acts of Josiah, and his splendor, and his understanding of the law of the Lord, and the things that he had done before and these that are now told, are recorded in the book of the kings of Israel and Judah. [34] And the men of the nation took Jeconiah the son of Josiah, who was twenty-three years old, and made him king in succession to Josiah his father.
[35] And he reigned three months in Judah and Jerusalem. Then the king of Egypt deposed him from reigning in Jerusalem, [36] and fined the nation a

hundred talents of silver and a talent of gold. [37] And the king of Egypt made Jehoiakim his brother king of Judea and Jerusalem. [38] Jehoiakim put the nobles in prison, and seized his brother Zarius and brought him up out of Egypt. [39] Jehoiakim was twenty-five years old when he began to reign in Judea and Jerusalem, and he did what was evil in the sight of the Lord.

[40] And Nebuchadnezzar king of Babylon came up against him, and bound him with a chain of brass and took him away to Babylon. [41] Nebuchadnezzar also took some holy vessels of the Lord, and carried them away, and stored them in his temple in Babylon. [42] But the things that are reported about Jehoiakim and his uncleanness and impiety are written in the chronicles of the kings. [43] Jehoiachin his son became king in his stead; when he was made king he was eighteen years old,

[44] and he reigned three months and ten days in Jerusalem. He did what was evil in the sight of the Lord. [45] So after a year Nebuchadnezzar sent and removed him to Babylon, with the holy vessels of the Lord, [46] and made Zedekiah king of Judea and Jerusalem.

Zedekiah was twenty-one years old, and he reigned eleven years.

[47] He also did what was evil in the sight of the Lord, and did not heed the words that were spoken by Jeremiah the prophet from the mouth of the Lord. [48] And though King Nebuchadnezzar had made him swear by the name of the Lord, he broke his oath and rebelled; and he stiffened his neck and hardened his heart and transgressed the laws of the Lord, the God of Israel. [49] Even the leaders of the people and of the priests committed many acts of sacrilege and lawlessness beyond all the unclean deeds of all the nations, and polluted the temple of the Lord which had been hallowed in Jerusalem. [50] So the God of their fathers sent by his messenger to call them back, because he would have spared them and his dwelling place. [51] But they mocked his messengers, and whenever the Lord spoke, they scoffed at his prophets, [52] until in his anger against his people because of their ungodly acts he gave command to bring against them the kings of the Chaldeans. [53] These slew their young men with the sword around their holy temple, and did not spare young man or virgin, old man or child, for he gave them all into their hands. [54] And all the holy vessels of the Lord, great and small, and the treasure chests of the Lord, and the royal stores, they took and carried away to Babylon. [55] And they burned the house of the Lord and broke down the walls of Jerusalem and burned their towers with fire, [56] and utterly destroyed all its glorious things. The survivors he led away to Babylon with the sword, [57] and they were servants to him and to his sons until the Persians began to reign, in fulfillment of the word of the Lord by the mouth of Jeremiah: [58] "Until the land has enjoyed its sabbaths, it shall keep sabbath all the time of its desolation until the completion of seventy years."

2

[1] In the first year of Cyrus as king of the Persians, that the word of the Lord by the mouth of Jeremiah might be accomplished,

[2] the Lord stirred up the spirit of Cyrus king of the Persians, and he made a proclamation throughout all his kingdom and also put it in writing: [3] "Thus says Cyrus king of the Persians: The Lord of Israel, the Lord Most High, has made me king of the world,

[4] and he has commanded me to build him a house at Jerusalem, which is in Judea. [5] If any one of you, therefore, is of his people, may his Lord be with him, and let him go up to Jerusalem, which is in Judea, and build the house of the Lord of Israel -- he is the Lord who dwells in Jerusalem, [6] and let each man, wherever he may live, be helped by the men of his place with gold and silver, [7] with gifts and with horses and cattle, besides the other things added as votive offerings for the temple of the Lord which is in Jerusalem." [8] Then arose the heads of families of the tribes of Judah and Benjamin, and the priests and the Levites, and all whose spirit the Lord had stirred to go up to build the house in Jerusalem for the Lord;

[9] and their neighbors helped them with everything, with silver and gold, with horses and cattle, and with a very great number of votive offerings from many whose hearts were stirred. [10] Cyrus the king also brought out the holy vessels of the Lord which Nebuchadnezzar had carried away from Jerusalem and stored in his temple of idols.

[11] When Cyrus king of the Perians brought these out, he gave them to Mithridates his treasurer, [12] and by him they were given to Sheshbazzar the governor of Judea. [13] The number of these was: a thousand gold cups, a thousand silver cups, twenty-nine silver censers, thirty gold bowls, two thousand four hundred and ten silver bowls, and a thousand other vessels.

[14] All the vessels were handed over, gold and silver, five thousand four hundred and sixty-nine, [15] and they were carried back by Sheshbazzar with the returning exiles from Babylon to Jerusalem. [16] But in the time of Artaxerxes king of the Persians, Bishlam, Mithridates, Tabeel, Rehum, Beltethmus, Shimshai the scribe, and the rest of their associates, living in Samaria and other places, wrote him the following letter, against those who were living in Judea and Jerusalem:

[17] "To King Artaxerxes our lord, Your servants Rehum the recorder and Shimshai the scribe and the other judges of their council in Coelesyria and Phoenicia:

[18] Now be it known to our lord the king that the Jews who came up from you to us have gone to Jerusalem and are building that rebellious and wicked city, repairing its market places and walls and laying the foundations for a temple. [19] Now if this city is built and the walls finished, they will not only refuse to pay tribute but will even resist kings. [20] And since the building of the temple is now going on, we think it best

not to neglect such a matter, [21] but to speak to our lord the king, in order that, if it seems good to you, search may be made in the records of your fathers. [22] You will find in the chronicles what has been written about them, and will learn that this city was rebellious, troubling both kings and other cities, [23] and that the Jews were rebels and kept setting up blockades in it from of old. That is why this city was laid waste. [24] Therefore we now make known to you, O lord and king, that if this city is built and its walls finished, you will no longer have access to Coelesyria and Phoenicia." [25] Then the king, in reply to Rehum the recorder and Beltethmus and Shimshai the scribe and the others associated with them and living in Samaria and Syria and Phoenicia, wrote as follows:
[26] "I have read the letter which you sent me. So I ordered search to be made, and it has been found that this city from of old has fought against kings,
[27] and that the men in it were given to rebellion and war, and that mighty and cruel kings ruled in Jerusalem and exacted tribute from Coelesyria and Phoenicia. [28] Therefore I have now issued orders to prevent these men from building the city and to take care that nothing more be done [29] and that such wicked proceedings go no further to the annoyance of kings." [30] Then, when the letter from King Artaxerxes was read, Rehum and Shimshai the scribe and their associates went in haste to Jerusalem, with horsemen and a multitude in battle array, and began to hinder the builders. And the building of the temple in Jerusalem ceased until the second year of the reign of Darius king of the Persians.
3

[1] Now King Darius gave a great banquet for all that were under him and all that were born in his house and all the nobles of Media and Persia
[2] and all the satraps and generals and governors that were under him in the hundred and twenty-seven satrapies from India to Ethiopia. [3] They ate and drank, and when they were satisfied they departed; and Darius the king went to his bedroom, and went to sleep, and then awoke. [4] Then the three young men of the bodyguard, who kept guard over the person of the king, said to one another,
[5] "Let each of us state what one thing is strongest; and to him whose statement seems wisest, Darius the king will give rich gifts and great honors of victory. [6] He shall be clothed in purple, and drink from gold cups, and sleep on a gold bed, and have a chariot with gold bridles, and a turban of fine linen, and a necklace about his neck; [7] and because of his wisdom he shall sit next to Darius and shall be called kinsman of Darius." [8] Then each wrote his own statement, and they sealed them and put them under the pillow of Darius the king,

[9] and said, "When the king wakes, they will give him the writing; and to the one whose statement the king and the three nobles of Persia judge to be wisest the victory shall be given according to what is written." [10] The first wrote, "Wine is strongest." [11] The second wrote, "The king is strongest." [12] The third wrote, "Women are strongest, but truth is victor over all things." [13] When the king awoke, they took the writing and gave it to him, and he read it.
[14] Then he sent and summoned all the nobles of Persia and Media and the satraps and generals and governors and prefects, [15] and he took his seat in the council chamber, and the writing was read in their presence. [16] And he said, "Call the young men, and they shall explain their statements." So they were summoned, and came in. [17] And they said to them, "Explain to us what you have written."
Then the first, who had spoken of the strength of wine, began and said: [18] "Gentlemen, how is wine the strongest? It leads astray the minds of all who drink it. [19] It makes equal the mind of the king and the orphan, of the slave and the free, of the poor and the rich. [20] It turns every thought to feasting and mirth, and forgets all sorrow and debt. [21] It makes all hearts feel rich, forgets kings and satraps, and makes every one talk in millions. [22] When men drink they forget to be friendly with friends and brothers, and before long they draw their swords. [23] And when they recover from the wine, they do not remember what they have done. [24] Gentlemen, is not wine the strongest, since it forces men to do these things?" When he had said this, he stopped speaking.

4

[1] Then the second, who had spoken of the strength of the king, began to speak: [2] "Gentlemen, are not men strongest, who rule over land and sea and all that is in them? [3] But the king is stronger; he is their lord and master, and whatever he says to them they obey. [4] If he tells them to make war on one another, they do it; and if he sends them out against the enemy, they go, and conquer mountains, walls, and towers. [5] They kill and are killed, and do not disobey the king's command; if they win the victory, they bring everything to the king -- whatever spoil they take and everything else. [6] Likewise those who do not serve in the army or make war but till the soil, whenever they sow, reap the harvest and bring some to the king; and they compel one another to pay taxes to the king. [7] And yet he is only one man! If he tells them to kill, they kill; if he tells them to release, they release; [8] if he tells them to attack, they attack; if he tells them to lay waste, they lay waste; if he tells them to build, they build; [9] if he tells them to cut down, they cut down; if he tells them to plant, they plant. [10] All his

people and his armies obey him. Moreover, he reclines, he eats and drinks and sleeps, [11] but they keep watch around him and no one may go away to attend to his own affairs, nor do they disobey him. [12] Gentlemen, why is not the king the strongest, since he is to be obeyed in this fashion?" And he stopped speaking. [13] Then the third, that is Zerubbabel, who had spoken of women and truth, began to speak:

[14] Gentlemen, is not the king great, and are not men many, and is not wine strong? Who then is their master, or who is their lord? Is it not women? [15] Women gave birth to the king and to every people that rules over sea and land. [16] From women they came; and women brought up the very men who plant the vineyards from which comes wine. [17] Women make men's clothes; they bring men glory; men cannot exist without women. [18] If men gather gold and silver or any other beautiful thing, and then see a woman lovely in appearance and beauty, [19] they let all those things go, and gape at her, and with open mouths stare at her, and all prefer her to gold or silver or any other beautiful thing. [20] A man leaves his own father, who brought him up, and his own country, and cleaves to his wife. [21] With his wife he ends his days, with no thought of his father or his mother or his country. [22] Hence you must realize that women rule over you!
"Do you not labor and toil, and bring everything and give it to women? [23] A man takes his sword, and goes out to travel and rob and steal and to sail the sea and rivers; [24] he faces lions, and he walks in darkness, and when he steals and robs and plunders, he brings it back to the woman he loves. [25] A man loves his wife more than his father or his mother. [26] Many men have lost their minds because of women, and have become slaves because of them. [27] Many have perished, or stumbled, or sinned, because of women. [28] And now do you not believe me?
"Is not the king great in his power? Do not all lands fear to touch him? [29] Yet I have seen him with Apame, the king's concubine, the daughter of the illustrious Bartacus; she would sit at the king's right hand [30] and take the crown from the king's head and put it on her own, and slap the king with her left hand. [31] At this the king would gaze at her with mouth agape. If she smiles at him, he laughs; if she loses her temper with him, he flatters her, that she may be reconciled to him. [32] Gentlemen, why are not women strong, since they do such things?" [33] Then the king and the nobles looked at one another; and he began to speak about truth:
[34] "Gentlemen, are not women strong? The earth is vast, and heaven is high, and the sun is swift in its course, for it makes the circuit of the heavens and returns to its place in one day. [35] Is he not great who does these things? But truth is great, and stronger than all things. [36] The whole earth

18

calls upon truth, and heaven blesses her. All God's works quake and tremble, and with him there is nothing unrighteous. [37] Wine is unrighteous, the king is unrighteous, women are unrighteous, all the sons of men are unrighteous, all their works are unrighteous, and all such things. There is no truth in them and in their unrighteousness they will perish. [38] But truth endures and is strong for ever, and lives and prevails for ever and ever. [39] With her there is no partiality or preference, but she does what is righteous instead of anything that is unrighteous or wicked. All men approve her deeds, [40] and there is nothing unrighteous in her judgment. To her belongs the strength and the kingship and the power and the majesty of all the ages. Blessed be the God of truth!" [41] He ceased speaking; then all the people shouted, and said, "Great is truth, and strongest of all!" [42] Then the king said to him, "Ask what you wish, even beyond what is written, and we will give it to you, for you have been found to be the wisest. And you shall sit next to me, and be called my kinsman."

[43] Then he said to the king, "Remember the vow which you made to build Jerusalem, in the day when you became king, [44] and to send back all the vessels that were taken from Jerusalem, which Cyrus set apart when he began to destroy Babylon, and vowed to send them back there. [45] You also vowed to build the temple, which the Edomites burned when Judea was laid waste by the Chaldeans. [46] And now, O lord the king, this is what I ask and request of you, and this befits your greatness. I pray therefore that you fulfil the vow whose fulfilment you vowed to the King of heaven with your own lips." [47] Then Darius the king rose, and kissed him, and wrote letters for him to all the treasurers and governors and generals and satraps, that they should give escort to him and all who were going up with him to build Jerusalem.

[48] And he wrote letters to all the governors in Coelesyria and Phoenicia and to those in Lebanon, to bring cedar timber from Lebanon to Jerusalem, and to help him build the city. [49] And he wrote for all the Jews who were going up from his kingdom to Judea, in the interest of their freedom, that no officer or satrap or governor or treasurer should forcibly enter their doors; [50] that all the country which they would occupy should be theirs without tribute; that the Idumeans should give up the villages of the Jews which they held; [51] that twenty talents a year should be given for the building of the temple until it was completed, [52] and an additional ten talents a year for burnt offerings to be offered on the altar every day, in accordance with the commandment to make seventeen offerings; [53] and that all who came from Babylonia to build the city should have their freedom, they and their children and all the priests who came. [54] He wrote also concerning their support and the priests' garments in which they were to minister. [55] He wrote that the support for the Levites should be provided until the day when the temple should be finished and Jerusalem built. [56] He wrote that land and wages should be provided for all who guarded the city. [57] And

he sent back from Babylon all the vessels which Cyrus had set apart; everything that Cyrus had ordered to be done, he also commanded to be done and to be sent to Jerusalem. [58] When the young man went out, he lifted up his face to heaven toward Jerusalem, and praised the King of heaven, saying,
[59] "From thee is the victory; from thee is wisdom, and your is the glory. I am thy servant. [60] Blessed art thou, who hast given me wisdom; I give thee thanks, O Lord of our fathers." [61] So he took the letters, and went to Babylon and told this to all his brethren.
[62] And they praised the God of their fathers, because he had given them release and permission [63] to go up and build Jerusalem and the temple which is called by his name; and they feasted, with music and rejoicing, for seven days.
5

[1] After this the heads of fathers' houses were chosen to go up, according to their tribes, with their wives and sons and daughters, and their menservants and maidservants, and their cattle.
[2] And Darius sent with them a thousand horsemen to take them back to Jerusalem in safety, with the music of drums and flutes; [3] and all their brethren were making merry. And he made them go up with them. [4] These are the names of the men who went up, according to their fathers' houses in the tribes, over their groups:
[5] the priests, the sons of Phinehas, son of Aaron; Jeshua the son of Jozadak, son of Seraiah, and Joakim the son of Zerubbabel, son of Shealtiel, of the house of David, of the lineage of Phares, of the tribe of Judah, [6] who spoke wise words before Darius the king of the Persians, in the second year of his reign, in the month of Nisan, the first month. [7] These are the men of Judea who came up out of their sojourn in captivity, whom Nebuchadnezzar king of Babylon had carried away to Babylon
[8] and who returned to Jerusalem and the rest of Judea, each to his own town. They came with Zerubbabel and Jeshua, Nehemiah, Seraiah, Resaiah, Bigvai, Mordecai, Bilshan, Mispar, Reeliah, Rehum, and Baanah, their leaders. [9] The number of the men of the nation and their leaders: the sons of Parosh, two thousand one hundred and seventy-two. The sons of Shephatiah, four hundred and seventy-two.
[10] The sons of Arah, seven hundred and fifty-six. [11] The sons of Pahathmoab, of the sons of Jeshua and Joab, two thousand eight hundred and twelve. [12] The sons of Elam, one thousand two hundred and fifty-four. The sons of Zattu, nine hundred and forty-five. The sons of Chorbe, seven hundred and five. The sons of Bani, six hundred and forty-eight. [13] The sons of Bebai, six hundred and twenty-three. The sons of Azgad, one

thousand three hundred and twenty-two. [14] The sons of Adonikam, six hundred and sixty-seven. The sons of Bigvai, two thousand and sixty-six. The sons of Adin, four hundred and fifty-four. [15] The sons of Ater, namely of Hezekiah, ninety-two. The sons of Kilan and Azetas, sixty-seven. The sons of Azaru, four hundred and thirty-two. [16] The sons of Annias, one hundred and one. The sons of Arom. The sons of Bezai, three hundred and twenty-three. The sons of Jorah, one hundred and twelve. [17] The sons of Baiterus, three thousand and five. The sons of Bethlehem, one hundred and twenty-three. [18] The men of Netophah, fifty-five. The men of Anathoth, one hundred and fifty-eight. The men of Bethasmoth, forty-two. [19] The men of Kiriatharim, twenty-five. The men of Chephirah and Beeroth, seven hundred and forty-three. [20] The Chadiasans and Ammidians, four hundred and twenty-two. The men of Ramah and Geba, six hundred and twenty-one. [21] The men of Michmas, one hundred and twenty-two. The men of Bethel, fifty-two. The sons of Magbish, one hundred and fifty-six. [22] The sons of the other Elam and Ono, seven hundred and twenty-five. The sons of Jericho, three hundred and forty-five. [23] The sons of Senaah, three thousand three hundred and thirty. [24] The priests: the sons of Jedaiah the son of Jeshua, of the sons of Anasib, nine hundred and seventy-two. The sons of Immer, one thousand and fifty-two. [25] The sons of Pashhur, one thousand two hundred and forty-seven. The sons of Harim, one thousand and seventeen. [26] The Levites: the sons of Jeshua and Kadmiel and Bannas and Sudias, seventy-four.
[27] The temple singers: the sons of Asaph, one hundred and twenty-eight.
[28] The gatekeepers: the sons of Shallum, the sons of Ater, the sons of Talmon, the sons of Akkub, the sons of Hatita, the sons of Shobai, in all one hundred and thirty-nine. [29] The temple servants: the sons of Ziha, the sons of Hasupha, the sons of Tabbaoth, the sons of Keros, the sons of Siaha, the sons of Padon, the sons of Lebanah, the sons of Hagabah,
[30] the sons of Akkub, the sons of Uthai, the sons of Ketab, the sons of Hagab, the sons of Shamlai, the sons of Hana, the sons of Cathua, the sons of Gahar, [31] The sons of Reaiah, the sons of Rezin, the sons of Nekoda, the sons of Chezib, the sons of Gazzam, the sons of Uzza, the sons of Paseah, the sons of Hasrah, the sons of Besai, the sons of Asnah, the sons of the Meunites, the sons of Nephisim, the sons of Bakbuk, the sons of Hakupha, the sons of Asur, the sons of Pharakim, the sons of Bazluth, [32] the sons of Mehida, the sons of Cutha, the sons of Charea, the sons of Barkos, the sons of Sisera, the sons of Temah, the sons of Neziah, the sons of Hatipha. [33] The sons of Solomon's servants: the sons of Hassophereth, the sons of Peruda, the sons of Jaalah, the sons of Lozon, the sons of Giddel, the sons of Shephatiah,
[34] the sons of Hattil, the sons of Pochereth-hazzebaim, the sons of Sarothie, the sons of Masiah, the sons of Gas, the sons of Addus, the sons of Subas, the sons of Apherra, the sons of Barodis, the sons of Shaphat, the

sons of Ami. [35] All the temple servants and the sons of Solomon's servants were three hundred and seventy-two.

[36] The following are those who came up from Telmelah and Telharsha, under the leadership of Cherub, Addan, and Immer,

[37] though they could not prove by their fathers' houses or lineage that they belonged to Israel: the sons of Delaiah the son of Tobiah, the sons of Nekoda, six hundred and fifty-two. [38] Of the priests the following had assumed the priesthood but were not found registered: the sons of Habaiah, the sons of Hakkoz, the sons of Jaddus who had married Agia, one of the daughters of Barzillai, and was called by his name.

[39] And when the genealogy of these men was sought in the register and was not found, they were excluded from serving as priests. [40] And Nehemiah and Attharias told them not to share in the holy things until a high priest should appear wearing Urim and Thummim. [41] All those of Israel, twelve or more years of age, besides menservants and maidservants, were forty-two thousand three hundred and sixty;

[42] their menservants and maidservants were seven thousand three hundred and thirty-seven; there were two hundred and forty-five musicians and singers. [43] There were four hundred and thirty-five camels, and seven thousand and thirty-six horses, two hundred and forty-five mules, and five thousand five hundred and twenty-five asses. [44] Some of the heads of families, when they came to the temple of God which is in Jerusalem, vowed that they would erect the house on its site, to the best of their ability,

[45] and that they would give to the sacred treasury for the work a thousand minas of gold, five thousand minas of silver, and one hundred priests' garments. [46] The priests, the Levites, and some of the people settled in Jerusalem and its vicinity; and the temple singers, the gatekeepers, and all Israel in their towns.

[47] When the seventh month came, and the sons of Israel were each in his own home, they gathered as one man in the square before the first gate toward the east.

[48] Then Jeshua the son of Jozadak, with his fellow priests, and Zerubbabel the son of Shealtiel, with his kinsmen, took their places and prepared the altar of the God of Israel, [49] to offer burnt offerings upon it, in accordance with the directions in the book of Moses the man of God. [50] And some joined them from the other peoples of the land. And they erected the altar in its place, for all the peoples of the land were hostile to them and were stronger than they; and they offered sacrifices at the proper times and burnt offerings to the Lord morning and evening. [51] They kept the feast of booths, as it is commanded in the law, and offered the proper sacrifices every day, [52] and thereafter the continual offerings and sacrifices on sabbaths and at new moons and at all the consecrated feasts. [53] And all

who had made any vow to God began to offer sacrifices to God, from the new moon of the seventh month, though the temple of God was not yet built. [54] And they gave money to the masons and the carpenters, and food and drink [55] and carts to the Sidonians and the Tyrians, to bring cedar logs from Lebanon and convey them in rafts to the harbor of Joppa, according to the decree which they had in writing from Cyrus king of the Persians. [56] In the second year after their coming to the temple of God in Jerusalem, in the second month, Zerubbabel the son of Shealtiel and Jeshua the son of Jozadak made a beginning, together with their brethren and the Levitical priests and all who had come to Jerusalem from the captivity; [57] and they laid the foundation of the temple of God on the new moon of the second month in the second year after they came to Judea and Jerusalem. [58] And they appointed the Levites who were twenty or more years of age to have charge of the work of the Lord. And Jeshua arose, and his sons and brethren and Kadmiel his brother and the sons of Jeshua Emadabun and the sons of Joda son of Iliadun, with their sons and brethren, all the Levites, as one man pressing forward the work on the house of God. So the builders built the temple of the Lord.

[59] And the priests stood arrayed in their garments, with musical instruments and trumpets, and the Levites, the sons of Asaph, with cymbals, [60] praising the Lord and blessing him, according to the directions of David king of Israel; [61] and they sang hymns, giving thanks to the Lord, because his goodness and his glory are for ever upon all Israel.

[62] And all the people sounded trumpets and shouted with a great shout, praising the Lord for the erection of the house of the Lord. [63] Some of the Levitical priests and heads of fathers' houses, old men who had seen the former house, came to the building of this one with outcries and loud weeping, [64] while many came with trumpets and a joyful noise, [65] so that the people could not hear the trumpets because of the weeping of the people.

For the multitude sounded the trumpets loudly, so that the sound was heard afar;

[66] and when the enemies of the tribe of Judah and Benjamin heard it, they came to find out what the sound of the trumpets meant. [67] And they learned that those who had returned from captivity were building the temple for the Lord God of Israel. [68] So they approached Zerubbabel and Jeshua and the heads of the fathers' houses and said to them, "We will build with you. [69] For we obey your Lord just as you do and we have been sacrificing to him ever since the days of Esarhaddon king of the Assyrians, who brought us here." [70] But Zerubbabel and Jeshua and the heads of the fathers' houses in Israel said to them, "You have nothing to do with us in building the house for the Lord our God, [71] for we alone will build it for the Lord of Israel, as Cyrus the king of the Persians has commanded us."

[72] But the peoples of the land pressed hard upon those in Judea, cut off

their supplies, and hindered their building; [73] and by plots and demagoguery and uprisings they prevented the completion of the building as long as King Cyrus lived. And they were kept from building for two years, until the reign of Darius.

6

[1] Now in the second year of the reign of Darius, the prophets Haggai and Zechariah the son of Iddo prophesied to the Jews who were in Judea and Jerusalem, they prophesied to them in the name of the Lord God of Israel. [2] Then Zerubbabel the son of Shealtiel and Jeshua the son of Jozadak arose and began to build the house of the Lord which is in Jerusalem, with the help of the prophets of the Lord who were with them. [3] At the same time Sisinnes the governor of Syria and Phoenicia and Sathrabuzanes and their associates came to them and said,
[4] "By whose order are you building this house and this roof and finishing all the other things? And who are the builders that are finishing these things?" [5] Yet the elders of the Jews were dealt with kindly, for the providence of the Lord was over the captives; [6] and they were not prevented from building until word could be sent to Darius concerning them and a report made. [7] A copy of the letter which Sisinnes the governor of Syria and Phoenicia, and Sathrabuzanes, and their associates the local rulers in Syria and Phoenicia, wrote and sent to Darius:
[8] "To King Darius, greeting. Let it be fully known to our lord the king that, when we went to the country of Judea and entered the city of Jerusalem, we found the elders of the Jews, who had been in captivity,
[9] building in the city of Jerusalem a great new house for the Lord, of hewn stone, with costly timber laid in the walls. [10] These operations are going on rapidly, and the work is prospering in their hands and being completed with all splendor and care. [11] Then we asked these elders, `At whose command are you building this house and laying the foundations of this structure?' [12] And in order that we might inform you in writing who the leaders are, we questioned them and asked them for a list of the names of those who are at their head. [13] They answered us, `We are the servants of the Lord who created the heaven and the earth. [14] And the house was built many years ago by a king of Israel who was great and strong, and it was finished. [15] But when our fathers sinned against the Lord of Israel who is in heaven, and provoked him, he gave them over into the hands of Nebuchadnezzar king of Babylon, king of the Chaldeans; [16] and they pulled down the house, and burned it, and carried the people away captive to Babylon. [17] But in the first year that Cyrus reigned over the country of Babylonia, King Cyrus wrote that this house should be rebuilt. [18] And the holy vessels of gold and of silver, which Nebuchadnezzar had taken out of

the house in Jerusalem and stored in his own temple, these Cyrus the king took out again from the temple in Babylon, and they were delivered to Zerubbabel and Sheshbazzar the governor [19] with the command that he should take all these vessels back and put them in the temple at Jerusalem, and that this temple of the Lord should be rebuilt on its site. [20] Then this Sheshbazzar, after coming here, laid the foundations of the house of the Lord which is in Jerusalem, and although it has been in process of construction from that time until now, it has not yet reached completion.'

[21] Now therefore, if it seems wise, O king, let search be made in the royal archives of our lord the king that are in Babylon; [22] and if it is found that the building of the house of the Lord in Jerusalem was done with the consent of King Cyrus, and if it is approved by our lord the king, let him send us directions concerning these things." [23] Then Darius commanded that search be made in the royal archives that were deposited in Babylon. And in Ecbatana, the fortress which is in the country of Media, a scroll was found in which this was recorded:

[24] "In the first year of the reign of Cyrus, King Cyrus ordered the building of the house of the Lord in Jerusalem, where they sacrifice with perpetual fire; [25] its height to be sixty cubits and its breadth sixty cubits, with three courses of hewn stone and one course of new native timber; the cost to be paid from the treasury of Cyrus the king; [26] and that the holy vessels of the house of the Lord, both of gold and of silver, which Nebuchadnezzar took out of the house in Jerusalem and carried away to Babylon, should be restored to the house in Jerusalem, to be placed where they had been." [27] So Darius commanded Sisinnes the governor of Syria and Phoenicia, and Sathrabuzanes, and their associates, and those who were appointed as local rulers in Syria and Phoenicia, to keep away from the place, and to permit Zerubbabel, the servant of the Lord and governor of Judea, and the elders of the Jews to build this house of the Lord on its site.

[28] "And I command that it be built completely, and that full effort be made to help the men who have returned from the captivity of Judea, until the house of the Lord is finished; [29] and that out of the tribute of Coelesyria and Phoenicia a portion be scrupulously given to these men, that is, to Zerubbabel the governor, for sacrifices to the Lord, for bulls and rams and lambs, [30] and likewise wheat and salt and wine and oil, regularly every year, without quibbling, for daily use as the priests in Jerusalem may indicate, [31] in order that libations may be made to the Most High God for the king and his children, and prayers be offered for their life." [32] And he commanded that if any should transgress or nullify any of the things herein written, a beam should be taken out of his house and he should be hanged upon it, and his property should be forfeited to the king.

[33] "Therefore may the Lord, whose name is there called upon, destroy every king and nation that shall stretch out their hands to hinder or damage that house of the Lord in Jerusalem.

[34] "I, King Darius, have decreed that it be done with all diligence as here prescribed."

7

[1] Then Sisinnes the governor of Coelesyria and Phoenicia, and Sathrabuzanes, and their associates, following the orders of King Darius, [2] supervised the holy work with very great care, assisting the elders of the Jews and the chief officers of the temple. [3] And the holy work prospered, while the prophets Haggai and Zechariah prophesied; [4] and they completed it by the command of the Lord God of Israel. So with the consent of Cyrus and Darius and Artaxerxes, kings of the Persians, [5] the holy house was finished by the twenty-third day of the month of Adar, in the sixth year of King Darius. [6] And the people of Israel, the priests, the Levites, and the rest of those from the captivity who joined them, did according to what was written in the book of Moses. [7] They offered at the dedication of the temple of the Lord one hundred bulls, two hundred rams, four hundred lambs, [8] and twelve he-goats for the sin of all Israel, according to the number of the twelve leaders of the tribes of Israel; [9] and the priests and the Levites stood arrayed in their garments, according to kindred, for the services of the Lord God of Israel in accordance with the book of Moses; and the gatekeepers were at each gate. [10] The people of Israel who came from the captivity kept the passover on the fourteenth day of the first month, after the priests and the Levites were purified together. [11] Not all of the returned captives were purified, but the Levites were all purified together, [12] and they sacrificed the passover lamb for all the returned captives and for their brethren the priests and for themselves. [13] And the people of Israel who came from the captivity ate it, all those who had separated themselves from the abominations of the peoples of the land and sought the Lord. [14] And they kept the feast of unleavened bread seven days, rejoicing before the Lord, [15] Because he had changed the will of the king of the Assyrians concerning them, to strengthen their hands for the service of the Lord God of Israel.

8

[1] After these things, when Artaxerxes the king of the Persians was reigning, Ezra came, the son of Seraiah, son of Azariah, son of Hilkiah, son of Shallum,
[2] son of Zadok, son of Ahitub, son of Amariah, son of Uzzi, son of Bukki, son of Abishua, son of Phineas, son of Eleazar, son of Aaron the chief priest.
[3] This Ezra came up from Babylon as a scribe skilled in the law of Moses, which was given by the God of Israel; [4] and the king showed him honor, for he found favor before the king in all his requests. [5] There came up

with him to Jerusalem some of the people of Israel and some of the priests and Levites and temple singers and gatekeepers and temple servants, [6] in the seventh year of the reign of Artaxerxes, in the fifth month (this was the king's seventh year); for they left Babylon on the new moon of the first month and arrived in Jerusalem on the new moon of the fifth month, by the prosperous journey which the Lord gave them. [7] For Ezra possessed great knowledge, so that he omitted nothing from the law of the Lord or the commandments, but taught all Israel all the ordinances and judgments. [8] The following is a copy of the written commission from Artaxerxes the king which was delivered to Ezra the priest and reader of the law of the Lord: [9] "King Artaxerxes to Ezra the priest and reader of the law of the Lord, greeting.

[10] In accordance with my gracious decision, I have given orders that those of the Jewish nation and of the priests and Levites and others in our realm, who freely choose to do so, may go with you to Jerusalem. [11] Let as many as are so disposed, therefore, depart with you as I and the seven friends who are my counselors have decided, [12] in order to look into matters in Judea and Jerusalem, in accordance with what is in the law of the Lord, [13] and to carry to Jerusalem the gifts for the Lord of Israel which I and my friends have vowed, and to collect for the Lord in Jerusalem all the gold and silver that may be found in the country of Babylonia, [14] together with what is given by the nation for the temple of their Lord which is in Jerusalem, both gold and silver for bulls and rams and lambs and what goes with them, [15] so as to offer sacrifices upon the altar of their Lord which is in Jerusalem. [16] And whatever you and your brethren are minded to do with the gold and silver, perform it in accordance with the will of your God; [17] and deliver the holy vessels of the Lord which are given you for the use of the temple of your God which is in Jerusalem. [18] And whatever else occurs to you as necessary for the temple of your God, you may provide out of the royal treasury. [19] "And I, Artaxerxes the king, have commanded the treasurers of Syria and Phoenicia that whatever Ezra the priest and reader of the law of the Most High God sends for, they shall take care to give him, [20] up to a hundred talents of silver, and likewise up to a hundred cors of wheat, a hundred baths of wine, and salt in abundance. [21] Let all things prescribed in the law of God be scrupulously fulfilled for the Most High God, so that wrath may not come upon the kingdom of the king and his sons. [22] You are also informed that no tribute or any other tax is to be laid on any of the priests or Levites or temple singers or gatekeepers or temple servants or persons employed in this temple, and that no one has authority to impose any tax upon them. [23] "And you, Ezra, according to the wisdom of God, appoint judges and justices to judge all those who know the law of your God, throughout all Syria and Phoenicia; and those who do not know it you shall teach.

[24] And all who transgress the law of your God or the law of the kingdom

shall be strictly punished, whether by death or some other punishment, either fine or imprisonment." [25] Blessed be the Lord alone, who put this into the heart of the king, to glorify his house which is in Jerusalem, [26] and who honored me in the sight of the king and his counselors and all his friends and nobles. [27] I was encouraged by the help of the Lord my God, and I gathered men from Israel to go up with me. [28] These are the principal men, according to their fathers' houses and their groups, who went up with me from Babylon, in the reign of Artaxerxes the king: [29] Of the sons of Phineas, Gershom. Of the sons of Ithamar, Gamael. Of the sons of David, Hattush the son of Shecaniah. [30] Of the sons of Parosh, Zechariah, and with him a hundred and fifty men enrolled. [31] Of the sons of Pahathmoab, Eliehoenai the son of Zerahiah, and with him two hundred men. [32] Of the sons of Zattu, Shecaniah the son of Jahaziel, and with him three hundred men. Of the sons of Adin, Obed the son of Jonathan, and with him two hundred and fifty men. [33] Of the sons of Elam, Jeshaiah the son of Gotholiah, and with him seventy men. [34] Of the sons of Shephatiah, Zeraiah the son of Michael, and with him seventy men, [35] Of the sons of Joab, Obadiah the son of Jehiel, and with him two hundred and twelve men. [36] Of the sons of Bani, Shelomith the son of Josiphiah, and with him a hundred and sixty men. [37] Of the sons of Bebai, Zechariah the son of Bebai, and with him twenty-eight men. [38] Of the sons of Azgad, Johanan the son of Hakkatan, and with him a hundred and ten men. [39] Of the sons of Adonikam, the last ones, their names being Eliphelet, Jeuel, and Shemaiah, and with them seventy men. [40] Of the sons of Bigvai, Uthai the son of Istalcurus, and with him seventy men. [41] I assembled them at the river called Theras, and we encamped there three days, and I inspected them.

[42] When I found there none of the sons of the priests or of the Levites, [43] I sent word to Eliezar, Iduel, Maasmas, [44] Elnathan, Shemaiah, Jarib, Nathan, Elnathan, Zechariah, and Meshullam, who were leaders and men of understanding; [45] and I told them to go to Iddo, who was the leading man at the place of the treasury, [46] and ordered them to tell Iddo and his brethren and the treasurers at that place to send us men to serve as priests in the house of our Lord. [47] And by the mighty hand of our Lord they brought us competent men of the sons of Mahli the son of Levi, son of Israel, namely Sherebiah with his sons and kinsmen, eighteen; [48] also Hashabiah and Annunus and Jeshaiah his brother, of the sons of Hananiah, and their sons, twenty men; [49] and of the temple servants, whom David and the leaders had given for the service of the Levites, two hundred and twenty temple servants; the list of all their names was reported. [50] There I proclaimed a fast for the young men before our Lord, to seek from him a prosperous journey for ourselves and for our children and the cattle that were with us.

[51] For I was ashamed to ask the king for foot soldiers and horsemen and an escort to keep us safe from our adversaries; [52] for we had said to the king, "The power of our Lord will be with those who seek him, and will support them in every way." [53] And again we prayed to our Lord about these things, and we found him very merciful. [54] Then I set apart twelve of the leaders of the priests, Sherebiah and Hashabiah, and ten of their kinsmen with them;
[55] and I weighed out to them the silver and the gold and the holy vessels of the house of our Lord, which the king himself and his counselors and the nobles and all Israel had given. [56] I weighed and gave to them six hundred and fifty talents of silver, and silver vessels worth a hundred talents, and a hundred talents of gold, [57] and twenty golden bowls, and twelve bronze vessels of fine bronze that glittered like gold. [58] And I said to them, "You are holy to the Lord, and the vessels are holy, and the silver and the gold are vowed to the Lord, the Lord of our fathers. [59] Be watchful and on guard until you deliver them to the leaders of the priests and the Levites, and to the heads of the fathers' houses of Israel, in Jerusalem, in the chambers of the house of our Lord." [60] So the priests and the Levites who took the silver and the gold and the vessels which had been in Jerusalem carried them to the temple of the Lord. [61] We departed from the river Theras on the twelfth day of the first month; and we arrived in Jerusalem by the mighty hand of our Lord which was upon us; he delivered us from every enemy on the way, and so we came to Jerusalem.
[62] When we had been there three days, the silver and the gold were weighed and delivered in the house of our Lord to Meremoth the priest, son of Uriah; [63] and with him was Eleazar the son of Phinehas, and with them were Jozabad the son of Jeshua and Moeth the son of Binnui, the Levites.
[64] The whole was counted and weighed, and the weight of everything was recorded at that very time. [65] And those who had come back from captivity offered sacrifices to the Lord, the God of Israel, twelve bulls for all Israel, ninety-six rams, [66] seventy-two lambs, and as a thank offering twelve he-goats -- all as a sacrifice to the Lord. [67] And they delivered the king's orders to the royal stewards and to the governors of Coelesyria and Phoenicia; and these officials honored the people and the temple of the Lord. [68] After these things had been done, the principal men came to me and said,
[69] "The people of Israel and the leaders and the priests and the Levites have not put away from themselves the alien peoples of the land and their pollutions, the Canaanites, the Hittites, the Perizzites, the Jebusites, the Moabites, the Egyptians, and the Edomites. [70] For they and their sons have married the daughters of these people, and the holy race has been mixed with the alien peoples of the land; and from the beginning of this matter the leaders and the nobles have been sharing in this iniquity." [71] As soon as I heard these things I rent my garments and my holy mantle, and

pulled out hair from my head and beard, and sat down in anxiety and grief.
[72] And all who were ever moved at the word of the Lord of Israel
gathered round me, as I mourned over this iniquity, and I sat grief-stricken
until the evening sacrifice. [73] Then I rose from my fast, with my garments
and my holy mantle rent, and kneeling down and stretching forth my hands
to the Lord [74] I said, "O Lord, I am ashamed and confounded before thy
face.

[75] For our sins have risen higher than our heads, and our mistakes have
mounted up to heaven [76] from the times of our fathers, and we are in
great sin to this day. [77] And because of our sins and the sins of our fathers
we with our brethren and our kings and our priests were given over to the
kings of the earth, to the sword and captivity and plundering, in shame
until this day. [78] And now in some measure mercy has come to us from
thee, O Lord, to leave to us a root and a name in thy holy place, [79] and to
uncover a light for us in the house of the Lord our God, and to give us food
in the time of our servitude. [80] Even in our bondage we were not forsaken
by our Lord, but he brought us into favor with the kings of the Persians, so
that they have given us food [81] and glorified the temple of our Lord, and
raised Zion from desolation, to give us a stronghold in Judea and Jerusalem.
[82] "And now, O Lord, what shall we say, when we have these things? For
we have transgressed thy commandments, which thou didst give by thy
servants the prophets, saying,

[83] `The land which you are entering to take possession of it is a land
polluted with the pollution of the aliens of the land, and they have filled it
with their uncleanness. [84] Therefore do not give your daughters in
marriage to their sons, and do not take their daughters for your sons; [85]
and do not seek ever to have peace with them, in order that you may be
strong and eat the good things of the land and leave it for an inheritance to
your children for ever.' [86] And all that has happened to us has come
about because of our evil deeds and our great sins. For thou, O Lord, didst
lift the burden of our sins [87] and give us such a root as this; but we turned
back again to transgress thy law by mixing with the uncleanness of the
peoples of the land. [88] Wast thou not angry enough with us to destroy us
without leaving a root or seed or name? [89] O Lord of Israel, thou art true;
for we are left as a root to this day. [90] Behold, we are now before thee in
our iniquities; for we can no longer stand in thy presence because of these
things." [91] While Ezra was praying and making his confession, weeping
and lying upon the ground before the temple, there gathered about him a
very great throng from Jerusalem, men and women and youths; for there
was great weeping among the multitude.

[92] Then Shecaniah the son of Jehiel, one of the men of Israel, called out,
and said to Ezra, "We have sinned against the Lord, and have married
foreign women from the peoples of the land; but even now there is hope for

Israel. [93] Let us take an oath to the Lord about this, that we will put away all our foreign wives, with their children, [94] as seems good to you and to all who obey the law of the Lord. [95] Arise and take action, for it is your task, and we are with you to take strong measures." [96] Then Ezra arose and had the leaders of the priests and Levites of all Israel take oath that they would do this. And they took the oath.

9

[1] Then Ezra rose and went from the court of the temple to the chamber of Jehohanan the son of Eliashib,
[2] and spent the night there; and he did not eat bread or drink water, for he was mourning over the great iniquities of the multitude. [3] And a proclamation was made throughout Judea and Jerusalem to all who had returned from the captivity that they should assemble at Jerusalem, [4] and that if any did not meet there within two or three days, in accordance with the decision of the ruling elders, their cattle should be seized for sacrifice and the men themselves expelled from the multitude of those who had returned from the captivity. [5] Then the men of the tribe of Judah and Benjamin assembled at Jerusalem within three days; this was the ninth month, on the twentieth day of the month.
[6] And all the multitude sat in the open square before the temple, shivering because of the bad weather that prevailed. [7] Then Ezra rose and said to them, "You have broken the law and married foreign women, and so have increased the sin of Israel. [8] Now then make confession and give glory to the Lord the God of our fathers, [9] and do his will; separate yourselves from the peoples of the land and from your foreign wives." [10] Then all the multitude shouted and said with a loud voice, "We will do as you have said.
[11] But the multitude is great and it is winter, and we are not able to stand in the open air. This is not a work we can do in one day or two, for we have sinned too much in these things. [12] so let the leaders of the multitude stay, and let all those in our settlements who have foreign wives come at the time appointed, [13] with the elders and judges of each place, until we are freed from the wrath of the Lord over this matter." [14] Jonathan the son of Asahel and Jahzeiah the son of Tikvah undertook the matter on these terms, and Meshullam and Levi and Shabbethai served with them as judges. [15] And those who had returned from the captivity acted in accordance with all this. [16] Ezra the priest chose for himself the leading men of their fathers' houses, all of them by name; and on the new moon of the tenth month they began their sessions to investigate the matter.
[17] And the cases of the men who had foreign wives were brought to an end by the new moon of the first month. [18] Of the priests those who were brought in and found to have foreign wives were:
[19] of the sons of Jeshua the son of Jozadak and his brethren, Maaseiah, Eliezar, Jarib, and Jodan. [20] They pledged themselves to put away their

wives, and to give rams in expiation of their error. [21] Of the sons of
Immer: Hanani and Zebadiah and Maaseiah and Shemaiah and Jehiel and
Azariah. [22] Of the sons of Pashhur: Elioenai, Maaseiah, Ishmael, and
Nathanael, and Gedaliah, and Elasah. [23] And of the Levites: Jozabad and
Shimei and Kelaiah, who was Kelita, and Pethahiah and Judah and Jonah.
[24] Of the temple singers: Eliashib and Zaccur. [25] Of the gatekeepers:
Shallum and Telem. [26] Of Israel: of the sons of Parosh: Ramiah, Izziah,
Malchijah, Mijamin, and Eleazar, and Asibias, and Benaiah.
[27] Of the sons of Elam: Mattaniah and Zechariah, Jehiel and Abdi, and
Jeremoth and Elijah. [28] Of the sons of Zattu: Elioenai, Eliashib, Othoniah,
Jeremoth, and Zabad and Zerdaiah. [29] Of the sons of Bebai: Jehohanan
and Hananiah and Zabbai and Emathis. [30] Of the sons of Bani:
Meshullam, Malluch, Adaiah, Jashub, and Sheal and Jeremoth. [31] Of the
sons of Addi: Naathus and Moossias, Laccunus and Naidus, and
Bescaspasmys and Sesthel, and Belnuus and Manasseas. [32] Of the sons of
Annan, Elionas and Asaias and Melchias and Sabbaias and Simon
Chosamaeus. [33] Of the sons of Hashum: Mattenai and Mattattah and
Zabad and Eliphelet and Manasseh and Shimei. [34] Of the sons of Bani:
Jeremai, Maadai, Amram, Joel, Mamdai and Bedeiah and Vaniah,
Carabasion and Eliashib and Machnadebai, Eliasis, Binnui, Elialis, Shimei,
Shelemiah, Nethaniah. Of the sons of Ezora: Shashai, Azarel, Azael,
Shemaiah, Amariah, Joseph. [35] Of the sons of Nebo: Mattithiah, Zabad,
Iddo, Joel, Benaiah. [36] All these had married foreign women, and they put
them away with their children. [37] The priests and the Levites and the men
of Israel settled in Jerusalem and in the country. On the new moon of the
seventh month, when the sons of Israel were in their settlements,
[38] the whole multitude gathered with one accord into the open square
before the east gate of the temple; [39] and they told Ezra the chief priest
and reader to bring the law of Moses which had been given by the Lord God
of Israel. [40] So Ezra the chief priest brought the law, for all the multitude,
men and women, and all the priests to hear the law, on the new moon of the
seventh month. [41] And he read aloud in the open square before the gate
of the temple from early morning until midday, in the presence of both men
and women; and all the multitude gave attention to the law. [42] Ezra the
priest and reader of the law stood on the wooden platform which had been
prepared; [43] and beside him stood Mattathiah, Shema, Anaiah, Azariah,
Uriah, Hezekiah, and Baalsamus on his right hand, [44] and on his left
Pedaiah, Mishael, Malchijah, Lothasubus, Nabariah, and Zechariah. [45]
Then Ezra took up the book of the law in the sight of the multitude, for he
had the place of honor in the presence of all. [46] And when he opened the
law, they all stood erect. And Ezra blessed the Lord God Most High, the
God of hosts, the Almighty; [47] and all the multitude answered, "Amen."
And they lifted up their hands, and fell to the ground and worshiped the

Lord. [48] Jeshua and Anniuth and Sherebiah, Jamin, Akkub, Shabbethai, Hodiah, Maaseiah and Kelita, Azariah and Jozabad, Hanan, Pelaiah, the Levites, taught the law of the Lord, at the same time explaining what was read. [49] Then Attharates said to Ezra the chief priest and reader, and to the Levites who were teaching the multitude, and to all,

[50] "This day is holy to the Lord" -- now they were all weeping as they heard the law -- [51] "so go your way, eat the fat and drink the sweet, and send portions to those who have none; [52] for the day is holy to the Lord; and do not be sorrowful, for the Lord will exalt you." [53] And the Levites commanded all the people, saying, "This day is holy; do not be sorrowful."

[54] Then they all went their way, to eat and drink and enjoy themselves, and to give portions to those who had none, and to make great rejoicing;

[55] because they were inspired by the words which they had been taught. And they came together.

2 Esdras

4Ezra.1

[1] The second book of the prophet Ezra the son of Seraiah, son of Azariah, son of Hilkiah, son of Shallum, son of Zadok, son of Ahitub,
[2] son of Ahijah, son of Phinehas, son of Eli, son of Amariah, son of Azariah, son of Meraioth, son of Arna, son of Uzzi, son of Borith, son of Abishua, son of Phinehas, son of Eleazar,
[3] son of Aaron, of the tribe of Levi, who was a captive in the country of the Medes in the reign of Artaxerxes, king of the Persians.
[4] The word of the Lord came to me, saying,
[5] "Go and declare to my people their evil deeds, and to their children the iniquities which they have committed against me, so that they may tell their children's children [6] that the sins of their parents have increased in them, for they have forgotten me and have offered sacrifices to strange gods. [7] Was it not I who brought them out of the land of Egypt, out of the house of bondage? But they have angered me and despised my counsels. [8] Pull out the hair of your head and hurl all evils upon them, for they have not obeyed my law -- they are a rebellious people. [9] How long shall I endure them, on whom I have bestowed such great benefits? [10] For their sake I have overthrown many kings: I struck down Pharaoh with his servants, and all his army. [11] I have destroyed all nations before them, and scattered in the east the people of two provinces, Tyre and Sidon; I have slain all their enemies. [12] "But speak to them and say, Thus says the Lord:
[13] Surely it was I who brought you through the sea, and made safe highways for you where there was no road; I gave you Moses as leader and Aaron as priest; [14] I provided light for you from a pillar of fire, and did great wonders among you. Yet you have forgotten me, says the Lord. [15] "Thus says the Lord Almighty: The quails were a sign to you; I gave you camps for your protection, and in them you complained.
[16] You have not exulted in my name at the destruction of your enemies, but to this day you still complain. [17] Where are the benefits which I bestowed on you? When you were hungry and thirsty in the wilderness, did you not cry out to me, [18] saying, `Why hast thou led us into this wilderness to kill us? It would have been better for us to serve the Egyptians than to die in this wilderness.' [19] I pitied your groanings and gave you manna for food; you ate the bread of angels. [20] When you were thirsty, did I not cleave the rock so that waters flowed in abundance? Because of the heat I covered you with the leaves of trees. [21] I divided fertile lands

among you; I drove out the Canaanites, the Perizzites, and the Philistines before you. What more can I do for you? says the Lord. [22] Thus says the Lord Almighty: When you were in the wilderness, at the bitter stream, thirsty and blaspheming my name, [23] I did not send fire upon you for your blasphemies, but threw a tree into the water and made the stream sweet. [24] "What shall I do to you, O Jacob? You would not obey me, O Judah. I will turn to other nations and will give them my name, that they may keep my statutes.

[25] Because you have forsaken me, I also will forsake you. When you beg mercy of me, I will show you no mercy. [26] When you call upon me, I will not listen to you; for you have defiled your hands with blood, and your feet are swift to commit murder. [27] It is not as though you had forsaken me; you have forsaken yourselves, says the Lord. [28] "Thus says the Lord Almighty: Have I not entreated you as a father entreats his sons or a mother her daughters or a nurse her children,

[29] that you should be my people and I should be your God, and that you should be my sons and I should be your father? [30] I gathered you as a hen gathers her brood under her wings. But now, what shall I do to you? I will cast you out from my presence. [31] When you offer oblations to me, I will turn my face from you; for I have rejected your feast days, and new moons, and circumcisions of the flesh. [32] I sent to you my servants the prophets, but you have taken and slain them and torn their bodies in pieces; their blood I will require of you, says the Lord. [33] "Thus says the Lord Almighty: Your house is desolate; I will drive you out as the wind drives straw;

[34] and your sons will have no children, because with you they have neglected my commandment and have done what is evil in my sight. [35] I will give your houses to a people that will come, who without having heard me will believe. Those to whom I have shown no signs will do what I have commanded. [36] They have seen no prophets, yet will recall their former state. [37] I call to witness the gratitude of the people that is to come, whose children rejoice with gladness; though they do not see me with bodily eyes, yet with the spirit they will believe the things I have said. [38] "And now, father, look with pride and see the people coming from the east;

[39] to them I will give as leaders Abraham, Isaac, and Jacob and Hosea and Amos and Micah and Joel and Obadiah and Jonah [40] and Nahum and Habakkuk, Zephaniah, Haggai, Zechariah and Malachi, who is also called the messenger of the Lord.

2

[1] "Thus says the Lord: I brought this people out of bondage, and I gave them commandments through my servants the prophets; but they would not listen to them, and made my counsels void.

[2] The mother who bore them says to them, `Go, my children, because I am

a widow and forsaken. [3] I brought you up with gladness; but with mourning and sorrow I have lost you, because you have sinned before the Lord God and have done what is evil in my sight. [4] But now what can I do for you? For I am a widow and forsaken. Go, my children, and ask for mercy from the Lord.' [5] I call upon you, father, as a witness in addition to the mother of the children, because they would not keep my covenant, [6] that you may bring confusion upon them and bring their mother to ruin, so that they may have no offspring. [7] Let them be scattered among the nations, let their names be blotted out from the earth, because they have despised my covenant. [8] "Woe to you, Assyria, who conceal the unrighteous in your midst! O wicked nation, remember what I did to Sodom and Gomorrah,

[9] whose land lies in lumps of pitch and heaps of ashes. So will I do to those who have not listened to me, says the Lord Almighty." [10] Thus says the Lord to Ezra: "Tell my people that I will give them the kingdom of Jerusalem, which I was going to give to Israel.

[11] Moreover, I will take back to myself their glory, and will give to these others the everlasting habitations, which I had prepared for Israel. [12] The tree of life shall give them fragrant perfume, and they shall neither toil nor become weary. [13] Ask and you will receive; pray that your days may be few, that they may be shortened. The kingdom is already prepared for you; watch! [14] Call, O call heaven and earth to witness, for I left out evil and created good, because I live, says the Lord. [15] "Mother, embrace your sons; bring them up with gladness, as does the dove; establish their feet, because I have chosen you, says the Lord.

[16] And I will raise up the dead from their places, and will bring them out from their tombs, because I recognize my name in them. [17] Do not fear, mother of sons, for I have chosen you, says the Lord. [18] I will send you help, my servants Isaiah and Jeremiah. According to their counsel I have consecrated and prepared for you twelve trees loaded with various fruits,

[19] and the same number of springs flowing with milk and honey, and seven mighty mountains on which roses and lilies grow; by these I will fill your children with joy. [20] Guard the rights of the widow, secure justice for the fatherless, give to the needy, defend the orphan, clothe the naked, [21] care for the injured and the weak, do not ridicule a lame man, protect the maimed, and let the blind man have a vision of my splendor. [22] Protect the old and the young within your walls; [23] When you find any who are dead, commit them to the grave and mark it, and I will give you the first place in my resurrection. [24] Pause and be quiet, my people, because your rest will come. [25] Good nurse, nourish your sons, and strengthen their feet. [26] Not one of the servants whom I have given you will perish, for I will require them from among your number. [27] Do not be anxious, for when the day of tribulation and anguish comes, others shall weep and

be sorrowful, but you shall rejoice and have abundance. [28] The nations shall envy you but they shall not be able to do anything against you, says the Lord. [29] My hands will cover you, that your sons may not see Gehenna. [30] Rejoice, O mother, with your sons, because I will deliver you, says the Lord. [31] Remember your sons that sleep, because I will bring them out of the hiding places of the earth, and will show mercy to them; for I am merciful, says the Lord Almighty. [32] Embrace your children until I come, and proclaim mercy to them; because my springs run over, and my grace will not fail." [33] I, Ezra, received a command from the Lord on Mount Horeb to go to Israel. When I came to them they rejected me and refused the Lord's commandment.

[34] Therefore I say to you, O nations that hear and understand, "Await your shepherd; he will give you everlasting rest, because he who will come at the end of the age is close at hand. [35] Be ready for the rewards of the kingdom, because the eternal light will shine upon you for evermore. [36] Flee from the shadow of this age, receive the joy of your glory; I publicly call on my Savior to witness. [37] Receive what the Lord has entrusted to you and be joyful, giving thanks to him who has called you to heavenly kingdoms. [38] Rise and stand, and see at the feast of the Lord the number of those who have been sealed. [39] Those who have departed from the shadow of this age have received glorious garments from the Lord. [40] Take again your full number, O Zion, and conclude the list of your people who are clothed in white, who have fulfilled the law of the Lord. [41] The number of your children, whom you desired, is full; beseech the Lord's power that your people, who have been called from the beginning, may be made holy." [42] I, Ezra, saw on Mount Zion a great multitude, which I could not number, and they all were praising the Lord with songs.

[43] In their midst was a young man of great stature, taller than any of the others, and on the head of each of them he placed a crown, but he was more exalted than they. And I was held spellbound. [44] Then I asked an angel, "Who are these, my lord?" [45] He answered and said to me, "These are they who have put off mortal clothing and have put on the immortal, and they have confessed the name of God; now they are being crowned, and receive palms." [46] Then I said to the angel, "Who is that young man who places crowns on them and puts palms in their hands?" [47] He answered and said to me, "He is the Son of God, whom they confessed in the world." So I began to praise those who had stood valiantly for the name of the Lord. [48] Then the angel said to me, "Go, tell my people how great and many are the wonders of the Lord God which you have seen."

3

[1] In the thirtieth year after the destruction of our city, I Salathiel, who am also called Ezra, was in Babylon. I was troubled as I lay on my bed, and my thoughts welled up in my heart,

[2] because I saw the desolation of Zion and the wealth of those who lived in Babylon. [3] My spirit was greatly agitated, and I began to speak anxious words to the Most High, and said, [4] "O sovereign Lord, didst thou not speak at the beginning when thou didst form the earth -- and that without help -- and didst command the dust [5] and it gave thee Adam, a lifeless body? Yet he was the workmanship of thy hands, and thou didst breathe into him the breath of life, and he was made alive in thy presence. [6] And thou didst lead him into the garden which thy right hand had planted before the earth appeared. [7] And thou didst lay upon him one commandment of your; but he transgressed it, and immediately thou didst appoint death for him and for his descendants. From him there sprang nations and tribes, peoples and clans without number. [8] And every nation walked after its own will and did ungodly things before thee and scorned thee, and thou didst not hinder them. [9] But again, in its time thou didst bring the flood upon the inhabitants of the world and destroy them. [10] And the same fate befell them: as death came upon Adam, so the flood upon them. [11] But thou didst leave one of them, Noah with his household, and all the righteous who have descended from him. [12] "When those who dwelt on earth began to multiply, they produced children and peoples and many nations, and again they began to be more ungodly than were their ancestors.

[13] And when they were committing iniquity before thee, thou didst choose for thyself one of them, whose name was Abraham; [14] and thou didst love him, and to him only didst thou reveal the end of the times, secretly by night. [15] Thou didst make with him an everlasting covenant, and promise him that thou wouldst never forsake his descendants; and thou gavest to him Isaac, and to Isaac thou gavest Jacob and Esau. [16] And thou didst set apart Jacob for thyself, but Esau thou didst reject; and Jacob became a great multitude. [17] And when thou didst lead his descendants out of Egypt, thou didst bring them to Mount Sinai. [18] Thou didst bend down the heavens and shake the earth, and move the world, and make the depths to tremble, and trouble the times. [19] And thy glory passed through the four gates of fire and earthquake and wind and ice, to give the law to the descendants of Jacob, and thy commandment to the posterity of Israel. [20] "Yet thou didst not take away from them their evil heart, so that thy law might bring forth fruit in them.

[21] For the first Adam, burdened with an evil heart, transgressed and was overcome, as were also all who were descended from him. [22] Thus the disease became permanent; the law was in the people's heart along with the evil root, but what was good departed, and the evil remained. [23] So the times passed and the years were completed, and thou didst raise up for thyself a servant, named David. [24] And thou didst command him to build a city for thy name, and in it to offer thee oblations from what is your. [25]

This was done for many years; but the inhabitants of the city transgressed, [26] in everything doing as Adam and all his descendants had done, for they also had the evil heart. [27] So thou didst deliver the city into the hands of thy enemies. [28] "Then I said in my heart, Are the deeds of those who inhabit Babylon any better? Is that why she has gained dominion over Zion?

[29] For when I came here I saw ungodly deeds without number, and my soul has seen many sinners during these thirty years. And my heart failed me, [30] for I have seen how thou do endure those who sin, and hast spared those who act wickedly, and hast destroyed thy people, and hast preserved thy enemies, [31] and hast not shown to any one how thy way may be comprehended. Are the deeds of Babylon better than those of Zion? [32] Or has another nation known thee besides Israel? Or what tribes have so believed thy covenants as these tribes of Jacob? [33] Yet their reward has not appeared and their labor has borne no fruit. For I have traveled widely among the nations and have seen that they abound in wealth, though they are unmindful of thy commandments. [34] Now therefore weigh in a balance our iniquities and those of the inhabitants of the world; and so it will be found which way the turn of the scale will incline. [35] When have the inhabitants of the earth not sinned in thy sight? Or what nation has kept thy commandments so well? [36] Thou mayest indeed find individual men who have kept thy commandments, but nations thou wilt not find."

4

[1] Then the angel that had been sent to me, whose name was Uriel, answered

[2] and said to me, "Your understanding has utterly failed regarding this world, and do you think you can comprehend the way of the Most High?" [3] Then I said, "Yes, my lord." And he replied to me, "I have been sent to show you three ways, and to put before you three problems. [4] If you can solve one of them for me, I also will show you the way you desire to see, and will teach you why the heart is evil." [5] I said, "Speak on, my lord." And he said to me, "Go, weigh for me the weight of fire, or measure for me a measure of wind, or call back for me the day that is past."

[6] I answered and said, "Who of those that have been born can do this, that you ask me concerning these things?"

[7] And he said to me, "If I had asked you, `How many dwellings are in the heart of the sea, or how many streams are at the source of the deep, or how many streams are above the firmament, or which are the exits of hell, or which are the entrances of paradise?'

[8] Perhaps you would have said to me, `I never went down into the deep, nor as yet into hell, neither did I ever ascend into heaven.' [9] But now I have asked you only about fire and wind and the day, things through which you have passed and without which you cannot exist, and you have given

me no answer about them!" [10] And he said to me, "You cannot understand the things with which you have grown up; [11] how then can your mind comprehend the way of the Most High? And how can one who is already worn out by the corrupt world understand incorruption?" When I heard this, I fell on my face [12] and said to him, "It would be better for us not to be here than to come here and live in ungodliness, and to suffer and not understand why." [13] He answered me and said, "I went into a forest of trees of the plain, and they made a plan
[14] and said, `Come, let us go and make war against the sea, that it may recede before us, and that we may make for ourselves more forests.' [15] And in like manner the waves of the sea also made a plan and said, `Come, let us go up and subdue the forest of the plain so that there also we may gain more territory for ourselves.' [16] But the plan of the forest was in vain, for the fire came and consumed it; [17] likewise also the plan of the waves of the sea, for the sand stood firm and stopped them. [18] If now you were a judge between them, which would you undertake to justify, and which to condemn?" [19] I answered and said, "Each has made a foolish plan, for the land is assigned to the forest, and to the sea is assigned a place to carry its waves."
[20] He answered me and said, "You have judged rightly, but why have you not judged so in your own case?
[21] For as the land is assigned to the forest and the sea to its waves, so also those who dwell upon earth can understand only what is on the earth, and he who is above the heavens can understand what is above the height of the heavens." [22] Then I answered and said, "I beseech you, my lord, why have I been endowed with the power of understanding?
[23] For I did not wish to inquire about the ways above, but about those things which we daily experience: why Israel has been given over to the Gentiles as a reproach; why the people whom you loved has been given over to godless tribes, and the law of our fathers has been made of no effect and the written covenants no longer exist; [24] and why we pass from the world like locusts, and our life is like a mist, and we are not worthy to obtain mercy. [25] But what will he do for his name, by which we are called? It is about these things that I have asked." [26] He answered me and said, "If you are alive, you will see, and if you live long, you will often marvel, because the age is hastening swiftly to its end.
[27] For it will not be able to bring the things that have been promised to the righteous in their appointed times, because this age is full of sadness and infirmities. [28] For the evil about which you ask me has been sown, but the harvest of it has not yet come. [29] If therefore that which has been sown is not reaped, and if the place where the evil has been sown does not pass away, the field where the good has been sown will not come. [30] For a grain of evil seed was sown in Adam's heart from the beginning, and how

much ungodliness it has produced until now, and will produce until the time of threshing comes! [31] Consider now for yourself how much fruit of ungodliness a grain of evil seed has produced. [32] When heads of grain without number are sown, how great a threshing floor they will fill!" [33] Then I answered and said, "How long and when will these things be? Why are our years few and evil?"

[34] He answered me and said, "You do not hasten faster than the Most High, for your haste is for yourself, but the Highest hastens on behalf of many. [35] Did not the souls of the righteous in their chambers ask about these matters, saying, `How long are we to remain here? And when will come the harvest of our reward? [36] And Jeremiel the archangel answered them and said, `When the number of those like yourselves is completed; for he has weighed the age in the balance, [37] and measured the times by measure, and numbered the times by number; and he will not move or arouse them until that measure is fulfilled.'" [38] Then I answered and said, "O sovereign Lord, but all of us also are full of ungodliness.

[39] And it is perhaps on account of us that the time of threshing is delayed for the righteous -- on account of the sins of those who dwell on earth." [40] He answered me and said, "Go and ask a woman who is with child if, when her nine months have been completed, her womb can keep the child within her any longer."

[41] And I said, "No, lord, it cannot."

And he said to me, "In Hades the chambers of the souls are like the womb. [42] For just as a woman who is in travail makes haste to escape the pangs of birth, so also do these places hasten to give back those things that were committed to them from the beginning. [43] Then the things that you desire to see will be disclosed to you." [44] I answered and said, "If I have found favor in your sight, and if it is possible, and if I am worthy,

[45] show me this also: whether more time is to come than has passed, or whether for us the greater part has gone by. [46] For I know what has gone by, but I do not know what is to come." [47] And he said to me, "Stand at my right side, and I will show you the interpretation of a parable."

[48] So I stood and looked, and behold, a flaming furnace passed by before me, and when the flame had gone by I looked, and behold, the smoke remained.

[49] And after this a cloud full of water passed before me and poured down a heavy and violent rain, and when the rainstorm had passed, drops remained in the cloud. [50] And he said to me, "Consider it for yourself; for as the rain is more than the drops, and the fire is greater than the smoke, so the quantity that passed was far greater; but drops and smoke remained."

[51] Then I prayed and said, "Do you think that I shall live until those days? Or who will be alive in those days?"

[52] He answered me and said, "Concerning the signs about which you ask me, I can tell you in part; but I was not sent to tell you concerning your life,

for I do not know.
5

[1] "Now concerning the signs: behold, the days are coming when those who dwell on earth shall be seized with great terror, and the way of truth shall be hidden, and the land shall be barren of faith.
[2] And unrighteousness shall be increased beyond what you yourself see, and beyond what you heard of formerly. [3] And the land which you now see ruling shall be waste and untrodden, and men shall see it desolate. [4] But if the Most High grants that you live, you shall see it thrown into confusion after the third period; and the sun shall suddenly shine forth at night,and the moon during the day. [5] Blood shall drip from wood,and the stone shall utter its voice;the peoples shall be troubled, and the stars shall fall. [6] And one shall reign whom those who dwell on earth do not expect, and the birds shall fly away together; [7] and the sea of Sodom shall cast up fish; and one whom the many do not know shall make his voice heard by night, and all shall hear his voice. [8] There shall be chaos also in many places, and fire shall often break out, and the wild beasts shall roam beyond their haunts, and menstruous women shall bring forth monsters. [9] And salt waters shall be found in the sweet, and all friends shall conquer one another; then shall reason hide itself, and wisdom shall withdraw into its chamber, [10] and it shall be sought by many but shall not be found, and unrighteousness and unrestraint shall increase on earth. [11] And one country shall ask its neighbor, `Has righteousness, or any one who does right, passed through you?' And it will answer, `No.' [12] And at that time men shall hope but not obtain; they shall labor but their ways shall not prosper. [13] These are the signs which I am permitted to tell you, and if you pray again, and weep as you do now, and fast for seven days, you shall hear yet greater things than these." [14] Then I awoke, and my body shuddered violently, and my soul was so troubled that it fainted.
[15] But the angel who had come and talked with me held me and strengthened me and set me on my feet. [16] Now on the second night Phaltiel, a chief of the people, came to me and said, "Where have you been? And why is your face sad?
[17] Or do you not know that Israel has been entrusted to you in the land of their exile? [18] Rise therefore and eat some bread, so that you may not forsake us, like a shepherd who leaves his flock in the power of cruel wolves." [19] Then I said to him, "Depart from me and do not come near me for seven days, and then you may come to me." He heard what I said and left me.
[20] So I fasted seven days, mourning and weeping, as Uriel the angel had commanded me. [21] And after seven days the thoughts of my heart were

very grievous to me again.

[22] Then my soul recovered the spirit of understanding, and I began once more to speak words in the presence of the Most High. [23] And I said, "O sovereign Lord, from every forest of the earth and from all its trees thou hast chosen one vine, [24] and from all the lands of the world thou hast chosen for thyself one region, and from all the flowers of the world thou hast chosen for thyself one lily, [25] and from all the depths of the sea thou hast filled for thyself one river, and from all the cities that have been built thou hast consecrated Zion for thyself, [26] and from all the birds that have been created thou hast named for thyself one dove, and from all the flocks that have been made thou hast provided for thyself one sheep, [27] and from all the multitude of peoples thou hast gotten for thyself one people; and to this people, whom thou hast loved, thou hast given the law which is approved by all. [28] And now, O Lord, why hast thou given over the one to the many, and dishonored the one root beyond the others, and scattered your only one among the many? [29] And those who opposed thy promises have trodden down those who believed thy covenants. [30] If thou do really hate thy people, they should be punished at thy own hands." [31] When I had spoken these words, the angel who had come to me on a previous night was sent to me,

[32] and he said to me, "Listen to me, and I will instruct you; pay attention to me, and I will tell you more." [33] And I said, "Speak, my lord." And he said to me, "Are you greatly disturbed in mind over Israel? Or do you love him more than his Maker does?"

[34] And I said, "No, my lord, but because of my grief I have spoken; for every hour I suffer agonies of heart, while I strive to understand the way of the Most High and to search out part of his judgment."

[35] And he said to me, "You cannot." And I said, "Why not, my lord? Why then was I born? Or why did not my mother's womb become my grave, that I might not see the travail of Jacob and the exhaustion of the people of Israel?"

[36] He said to me, "Count up for me those who have not yet come, and gather for me the scattered raindrops, and make the withered flowers bloom again for me;

[37] open for me the closed chambers, and bring forth for me the winds shut up in them, or show me the picture of a voice; and then I will explain to you the travail that you ask to understand." [38] And I said, "O sovereign Lord, who is able to know these things except he whose dwelling is not with men? [39] As for me, I am without wisdom, and how can I speak concerning the things which thou hast asked me?" [40] He said to me, "Just as you cannot do one of the things that were mentioned, so you cannot discover my judgment, or the goal of the love that I have promised my people."

[41] And I said, "Yet behold, O Lord, thou do have charge of those who are alive at the end, but what will those do who were before us, or we, or those

who come after us?"

[42] He said to me, "I shall liken my judgment to a circle; just as for those who are last there is no slowness, so for those who are first there is no haste."

[43] Then I answered and said, "Couldst thou not have created at one time those who have been and those who are and those who will be, that thou mightest show thy judgment the sooner?"

[44] He replied to me and said, "The creation cannot make more haste than the Creator, neither can the world hold at one time those who have been created in it."

[45] And I said, "How hast thou said to thy servant that thou wilt certainly give life at one time to thy creation? If therefore all creatures will live at one time and the creation will sustain them, it might even now be able to support all of them present at one time."

[46] He said to me, "Ask a woman's womb, and say to it, `If you bear ten children, why one after another?' Request it therefore to produce ten at one time."

[47] I said, "Of course it cannot, but only each in its own time."

[48] He said to me, "Even so have I given the womb of the earth to those who from time to time are sown in it.

[49] For as an infant does not bring forth, and a woman who has become old does not bring forth any longer, so have I organized the world which I created." [50] Then I inquired and said, "Since thou hast now given me the opportunity, let me speak before thee. Is our mother, of whom thou hast told me, still young? Or is she now approaching old age?"

[51] He replied to me, "Ask a woman who bears children, and she will tell you.

[52] Say to her, "Why are those whom you have borne recently not like those whom you bore before, but smaller in stature?' [53] And she herself will answer you, `Those born in the strength of youth are different from those born during the time of old age, when the womb is failing.' [54] Therefore you also should consider that you and your contemporaries are smaller in stature than those who were before you, [55] and those who come after you will be smaller than you, as born of a creation which already is aging and passing the strength of youth." [56] And I said, "O Lord, I beseech thee, if I have found favor in thy sight, show thy servant through whom thou do visit thy creation."

6

[1] And he said to me, "At the beginning of the circle of the earth, before the portals of the world were in place, and before the assembled winds blew, [2] and before the rumblings of thunder sounded, and before the flashes of

lightning shone, and before the foundations of paradise were laid, [3] and before the beautiful flowers were seen, and before the powers of movement were established, and before the innumerable hosts of angels were gathered together, [4] and before the heights of the air were lifted up, and before the measures of the firmaments were named, and before the footstool of Zion was established, [5] and before the present years were reckoned; and before the imaginations of those who now sin were estranged, and before those who stored up treasures of faith were sealed -- [6] then I planned these things, and they were made through me and not through another, just as the end shall come through me and not through another." [7] And I answered and said, "What will be the dividing of the times? Or when will be the end of the first age and the beginning of the age that follows?"

[8] He said to me, "From Abraham to Isaac, because from him were born Jacob and Esau, for Jacob's hand held Esau's heel from the beginning.

[9] For Esau is the end of this age, and Jacob is the beginning of the age that follows. [10] For the beginning of a man is his hand, and the end of a man is his heel; between the heel and the hand seek for nothing else, Ezra!" [11] I answered and said, "O sovereign Lord, if I have found favor in thy sight, [12] show thy servant the end of thy signs which thou didst show me in part on a previous night." [13] He answered and said to me, "Rise to your feet and you will hear a full, resounding voice.

[14] And if the place where you are standing is greatly shaken [15] while the voice is speaking, do not be terrified; because the word concerns the end, and the foundations of the earth will understand [16] that the speech concerns them. They will tremble and be shaken, for they know that their end must be changed." [17] When I heard this, I rose to my feet and listened, and behold, a voice was speaking, and its sound was like the sound of many waters.

[18] And it said, "Behold, the days are coming, and it shall be that when I draw near to visit the inhabitants of the earth, [19] and when I require from the doers of iniquity the penalty of their iniquity, and when the humiliation of Zion is complete, [20] and when the seal is placed upon the age which is about to pass away, then I will show these signs: the books shall be opened before the firmament, and all shall see it together. [21] Infants a year old shall speak with their voices, and women with child shall give birth to premature children at three and four months, and these shall live and dance. [22] Sown places shall suddenly appear unsown, and full storehouses shall suddenly be found to be empty; [23] and the trumpet shall sound aloud, and when all hear it, they shall suddenly be terrified.

[24] At that time friends shall make war on friends like enemies, and the earth and those who inhabit it shall be terrified, and the springs of the fountains shall stand still, so that for three hours they shall not flow. [25] "And it shall be that whoever remains after all that I have foretold to you shall himself be saved and shall see my salvation and the end of my world.

[26] And they shall see the men who were taken up, who from their birth have not tasted death; and the heart of the earth's inhabitants shall be changed and converted to a different spirit. [27] For evil shall be blotted out, and deceit shall be quenched; [28] faithfulness shall flourish, and corruption shall be overcome, and the truth, which has been so long without fruit, shall be revealed." [29] While he spoke to me, behold, little by little the place where I was standing began to rock to and fro.

[30] And he said to me, "I have come to show you these things this night. [31] If therefore you will pray again and fast again for seven days, I will again declare to you greater things than these, [32] because your voice has surely been heard before the Most High; for the Mighty One has seen your uprightness and has also observed the purity which you have maintained from your youth. [33] Therefore he sent me to show you all these things, and to say to you: `Believe and do not be afraid! [34] Do not be quick to think vain thoughts concerning the former times, lest you be hasty concerning the last times.'" [35] Now after this I wept again and fasted seven days as before, in order to complete the three weeks as I had been told.

[36] And on the eighth night my heart was troubled within me again, and I began to speak in the presence of the Most High. [37] For my spirit was greatly aroused, and my soul was in distress. [38] I said, "O Lord, thou didst speak at the beginning of creation, and didst say on the first day, `Let heaven and earth be made,' and thy word accomplished the work.

[39] And then the Spirit was hovering, and darkness and silence embraced everything; the sound of man's voice was not yet there. [40] Then thou didst command that a ray of light be brought forth from thy treasuries, so that thy works might then appear. [41] "Again, on the second day, thou didst create the spirit of the firmament, and didst command him to divide and separate the waters, that one part might move upward and the other part remain beneath.

[42] "On the third day thou didst command the waters to be gathered together in the seventh part of the earth; six parts thou didst dry up and keep so that some of them might be planted and cultivated and be of service before thee.

[43] For thy word went forth, and at once the work was done. [44] For immediately fruit came forth in endless abundance and of varied appeal to the taste; and flowers of inimitable color; and odors of inexpressible fragrance. These were made on the third day. [45] "On the fourth day thou didst command the brightness of the sun, the light of the moon, and the arrangement of the stars to come into being;

[46] and thou didst command them to serve man, who was about to be formed. [47] "On the fifth day thou didst command the seventh part, where the water had been gathered together, to bring forth living creatures, birds,

46

and fishes; and so it was done.

[48] The dumb and lifeless water produced living creatures, as it was commanded, that therefore the nations might declare thy wondrous works.

[49] "Then thou didst keep in existence two living creatures; the name of one thou didst call Behemoth and the name of the other Leviathan.

[50] And thou didst separate one from the other, for the seventh part where the water had been gathered together could not hold them both. [51] And thou didst give Behemoth one of the parts which had been dried up on the third day, to live in it, where there are a thousand mountains; [52] but to Leviathan thou didst give the seventh part, the watery part; and thou hast kept them to be eaten by whom thou wilt, and when thou wilt. [53] "On the sixth day thou didst command the earth to bring forth before thee cattle, beasts, and creeping things;

[54] and over these thou didst place Adam, as ruler over all the works which thou hadst made; and from him we have all come, the people whom thou hast chosen. [55] "All this I have spoken before thee, O Lord, because thou hast said that it was for us that thou didst create this world.

[56] As for the other nations which have descended from Adam, thou hast said that they are nothing, and that they are like spittle, and thou hast compared their abundance to a drop from a bucket. [57] And now, O Lord, behold, these nations, which are reputed as nothing, domineer over us and devour us. [58] But we thy people, whom thou hast called thy first-born, only begotten, zealous for thee, and most dear, have been given into their hands. [59] If the world has indeed been created for us, why do we not possess our world as an inheritance? How long will this be so?"

7

[1] When I had finished speaking these words, the angel who had been sent to me on the former nights was sent to me again,

[2] and he said to me, "Rise, Ezra, and listen to the words that I have come to speak to you." [3] I said, "Speak, my lord." And he said to me, "There is a sea set in a wide expanse so that it is broad and vast,

[4] but it has an entrance set in a narrow place, so that it is like a river. [5] If any one, then, wishes to reach the sea, to look at it or to navigate it, how can he come to the broad part unless he passes through the narrow part? [6] Another example: There is a city built and set on a plain, and it is full of all good things; [7] but the entrance to it is narrow and set in a precipitous place, so that there is fire on the right hand and deep water on the left; [8] and there is only one path lying between them, that is, between the fire and the water, so that only one man can walk upon that path. [9] If now that city is given to a man for an inheritance, how will the heir receive his inheritance unless he passes through the danger set before him?" [10] I said, "He cannot, lord." And he said to me, "So also is Israel's portion.

[11] For I made the world for their sake, and when Adam transgressed my

statutes, what had been made was judged. [12] And so the entrances of this world were made narrow and sorrowful and toilsome; they are few and evil, full of dangers and involved in great hardships. [13] But the entrances of the greater world are broad and safe, and really yield the fruit of immortality. [14] Therefore unless the living pass through the difficult and vain experiences, they can never receive those things that have been reserved for them. [15] But now why are you disturbed, seeing that you are to perish? And why are you moved, seeing that you are mortal? [16] And why have you not considered in your mind what is to come, rather than what is now present?" [17] Then I answered and said, "O sovereign Lord, behold, thou hast ordained in thy law that the righteous shall inherit these things, but that the ungodly shall perish.

[18] The righteous therefore can endure difficult circumstances while hoping for easier ones; but those who have done wickedly have suffered the difficult circumstances and will not see the easier ones." [19] And he said to me, "You are not a better judge than God, or wiser than the Most High! [20] Let many perish who are now living, rather than that the law of God which is set before them be disregarded! [21] For God strictly commanded those who came into the world, when they came, what they should do to live, and what they should observe to avoid punishment. [22] Nevertheless they were not obedient, and spoke against him; they devised for themselves vain thoughts, [23] and proposed to themselves wicked frauds; they even declared that the Most High does not exist, and they ignored his ways! [24] They scorned his law, and denied his covenants; they have been unfaithful to his statutes, and have not performed his works. [25] "Therefore, Ezra, empty things are for the empty, and full things are for the full.

[26] For behold, the time will come, when the signs which I have foretold to you will come to pass, that the city which now is not seen shall appear, and the land which now is hidden shall be disclosed. [27] And every one who has been delivered from the evils that I have foretold shall see my wonders. [28] For my son the Messiah shall be revealed with those who are with him, and those who remain shall rejoice four hundred years. [29] And after these years my son the Messiah shall die, and all who draw human breath. [30] And the world shall be turned back to primeval silence for seven days, as it was at the first beginnings; so that no one shall be left. [31] And after seven days the world, which is not yet awake, shall be roused, and that which is corruptible shall perish. [32] And the earth shall give up those who are asleep in it, and the dust those who dwell silently in it; and the chambers shall give up the souls which have been committed to them. [33] And the Most High shall be revealed upon the seat of judgment, and compassion shall pass away, and patience shall be withdrawn; [34] but only judgment shall remain, truth shall stand, and faithfulness shall grow strong. [35] And recompense shall follow, and the reward shall be manifested; righteous

deeds shall awake, and unrighteous deeds shall not sleep. [36] Then the pit of torment shall appear, and opposite it shall be the place of rest; and the furnace of hell shall be disclosed, and opposite it the paradise of delight. [37] Then the Most High will say to the nations that have been raised from the dead, `Look now, and understand whom you have denied, whom you have not served, whose commandments you have despised! [38] Look on this side and on that; here are delight and rest, and there are fire and torments!' Thus he will speak to them on the day of judgment -- [39] a day that has no sun or moon or stars, [40] or cloud or thunder or lightning or wind or water or air, or darkness or evening or morning, [41] or summer or spring or heat or winter or frost or cold or hail or rain or dew, [42] or noon or night, or dawn or shining or brightness or light, but only the splendor of the glory of the Most High, by which all shall see what has been determined for them. [43] For it will last for about a week of years. [44] This is my judgment and its prescribed order; and to you alone have I shown these things." [45] I answered and said, "O sovereign Lord, I said then and I say now: Blessed are those who are alive and keep thy commandments!

[46] But what of those for whom I prayed? For who among the living is there that has not sinned, or who among men that has not transgressed thy covenant? [47] And now I see that the world to come will bring delight to few, but torments to many. [48] For an evil heart has grown up in us, which has alienated us from God, and has brought us into corruption and the ways of death, and has shown us the paths of perdition and removed us far from life -- and that not just a few of us but almost all who have been created!"

[49] He answered me and said, "Listen to me, Ezra, and I will instruct you, and will admonish you yet again.

[50] For this reason the Most High has made not one world but two. [51] For whereas you have said that the righteous are not many but few, while the ungodly abound, hear the explanation for this. [52] "If you have just a few precious stones, will you add to them lead and clay?"

[53] I said, "Lord, how could that be?"

[54] And he said to me, "Not only that, but ask the earth and she will tell you; defer to her, and she will declare it to you.

[55] Say to her, `You produce gold and silver and brass, and also iron and lead and clay; [56] but silver is more abundant than gold, and brass than silver, and iron than brass, and lead than iron, and clay than lead.' [57] Judge therefore which things are precious and desirable, those that are abundant or those that are rare?" [58] I said, "O sovereign Lord, what is plentiful is of less worth, for what is more rare is more precious."

[59] He answered me and said, "Weigh within yourself what you have thought, for he who has what is hard to get rejoices more than he who has what is plentiful.

[60] So also will be the judgment which I have promised; for I will rejoice over the few who shall be saved, because it is they who have made my glory

to prevail now, and through them my name has now been honored. [61] And I will not grieve over the multitude of those who perish; for it is they who are now like a mist, and are similar to a flame and smoke -- they are set on fire and burn hotly, and are extinguished." [62] I replied and said, "O earth, what have you brought forth, if the mind is made out of the dust like the other created things!

[63] For it would have been better if the dust itself had not been born, so that the mind might not have been made from it. [64] But now the mind grows with us, and therefore we are tormented, because we perish and know it.

[65] Let the human race lament, but let the beasts of the field be glad; let all who have been born lament, but let the four-footed beasts and the flocks rejoice! [66] For it is much better with them than with us; for they do not look for a judgment, nor do they know of any torment or salvation promised to them after death. [67] For what does it profit us that we shall be preserved alive but cruelly tormented? [68] For all who have been born are involved in iniquities, and are full of sins and burdened with transgressions. [69] And if we were not to come into judgment after death, perhaps it would have been better for us." [70] He answered me and said, "When the Most High made the world and Adam and all who have come from him, he first prepared the judgment and the things that pertain to the judgment.

[71] And now understand from your own words, for you have said that the mind grows with us. [72] For this reason, therefore, those who dwell on earth shall be tormented, because though they had understanding they committed iniquity, and though they received the commandments they did not keep them, and though they obtained the law they dealt unfaithfully with what they received. [73] What, then, will they have to say in the judgment, or how will they answer in the last times? [74] For how long the time is that the Most High has been patient with those who inhabit the world, and not for their sake, but because of the times which he has foreordained!" [75] I answered and said, "If I have found favor in thy sight, O Lord, show this also to thy servant: whether after death, as soon as every one of us yields up his soul, we shall be kept in rest until those times come when thou wilt renew the creation, or whether we shall be tormented at once?"

[76] He answered me and said, "I will show you that also, but do not be associated with those who have shown scorn, nor number yourself among those who are tormented.

[77] For you have a treasure of works laid up with the Most High; but it will not be shown to you until the last times. [78] Now, concerning death, the teaching is: When the decisive decree has gone forth from the Most High that a man shall die, as the spirit leaves the body to return again to him who gave it, first of all it adores the glory of the Most High. [79] And if it is one

of those who have shown scorn and have not kept the way of the Most High, and who have despised his law, and who have hated those who fear God -- [80] such spirits shall not enter into habitations, but shall immediately wander about in torments, ever grieving and sad, in seven ways. [81] The first way, because they have scorned the law of the Most High. [82] The second way, because they cannot now make a good repentance that they may live. [83] The third way, they shall see the reward laid up for those who have trusted the covenants of the Most High. [84] The fourth way, they shall consider the torment laid up for themselves in the last days. [85] The fifth way, they shall see how the habitations of the others are guarded by angels in profound quiet. [86] The sixth way, they shall see how some of them will pass over into torments. [87] The seventh way, which is worse than all the ways that have been mentioned, because they shall utterly waste away in confusion and be consumed with shame, and shall wither with fear at seeing the glory of the Most High before whom they sinned while they were alive, and before whom they are to be judged in the last times. [88] "Now this is the order of those who have kept the ways of the Most High, when they shall be separated from their mortal body. [89] During the time that they lived in it, they laboriously served the Most High, and withstood danger every hour, that they might keep the law of the Lawgiver perfectly. [90] Therefore this is the teaching concerning them: [91] First of all, they shall see with great joy the glory of him who receives them, for they shall have rest in seven orders. [92] The first order, because they have striven with great effort to overcome the evil thought which was formed with them, that it might not lead them astray from life into death. [93] The second order, because they see the perplexity in which the souls of the ungodly wander, and the punishment that awaits them. [94] The third order, they see the witness which he who formed them bears concerning them, that while they were alive they kept the law which was given them in trust. [95] The fourth order, they understand the rest which they now enjoy, being gathered into their chambers and guarded by angels in profound quiet, and the glory which awaits them in the last days. [96] The fifth order, they rejoice that they have now escaped what is corruptible, and shall inherit what is to come; and besides they see the straits and toil from which they have been delivered, and the spacious liberty which they are to receive and enjoy in immortality. [97] The sixth order, when it is shown to them how their face is to shine like the sun, and how they are to be made like the light of the stars, being incorruptible from then on. [98] The seventh order, which is greater than all that have been mentioned, because they shall rejoice with boldness, and shall be confident without confusion, and shall be glad without fear, for they hasten to behold the face of him whom they served in life and from whom they are to receive their reward when glorified. [99] This is the order of the souls of the righteous, as henceforth is announced; and the aforesaid are the ways of torment which those who would not give heed shall suffer hereafter." [100] I answered and said, "Will time therefore be given to the souls, after they have been separated from the bodies, to see what you have described to me?"

[101] He said to me, "They shall have freedom for seven days, so that during these seven days they may see the things of which you have been told, and afterwards they shall be gathered in their habitations."

[102] I answered and said, "If I have found favor in thy sight, show further to me, thy servant, whether on the day of judgment the righteous will be able to intercede for the ungodly or to entreat the Most High for them,

[103] fathers for sons or sons for parents, brothers for brothers, relatives for their kinsmen, or friends for those who are most dear." [104] He answered me and said, "Since you have found favor in my sight, I will show you this also. The day of judgment is decisive and displays to all the seal of truth. Just as now a father does not send his son, or a son his father, or a master his servant, or a friend his dearest friend, to be ill or sleep or eat or be healed in his stead,

[105] so no one shall ever pray for another on that day, neither shall any one lay a burden on another; for then every one shall bear his own righteousness and unrighteousness." [36(106)] I answered and said, "How then do we find that first Abraham prayed for the people of Sodom, and Moses for our fathers who sinned in the desert,

[37(107)] and Joshua after him for Israel in the days of Achan, [38(108)] and Samuel in the days of Saul, and David for the plague, and Solomon for those in the sanctuary, [39(109)] and Elijah for those who received the rain, and for the one who was dead, that he might live, [40(110)] and Hezekiah for the people in the days of Sennacherib, and many others prayed for many?

[41(111)] If therefore the righteous have prayed for the ungodly now, when corruption has increased and unrighteousness has multiplied, why will it not be so then as well?" [42(112)] He answered me and said, "This present world is not the end; the full glory does not abide in it; therefore those who were strong prayed for the weak.

[43(113)] But the day of judgment will be the end of this age and the beginning of the immortal age to come, in which corruption has passed away, [44(114)] sinful indulgence has come to an end, unbelief has been cut off, and righteousness has increased and truth has appeared. [45(115)] Therefore no one will then be able to have mercy on him who has been condemned in the judgment, or to harm him who is victorious." [46(116)] I answered and said, "This is my first and last word, that it would have been better if the earth had not produced Adam, or else, when it had produced him, had restrained him from sinning.

[47(117)] For what good is it to all that they live in sorrow now and expect punishment after death? [48(118)] O Adam, what have you done? For though it was you who sinned, the fall was not yours alone, but ours also

who are your descendants. [49(119)] For what good is it to us, if an eternal age has been promised to us, but we have done deeds that bring death? [50(120)] And what good is it that an everlasting hope has been promised to us, but we have miserably failed? [51(121)] Or that safe and healthful habitations have been reserved for us, but we have lived wickedly? [52(122)] Or that the glory of the Most High will defend those who have led a pure life, but we have walked in the most wicked ways? [53(123)] Or that a paradise shall be revealed, whose fruit remains unspoiled and in which are abundance and healing, but we shall not enter it, [54(124)] because we have lived in unseemly places? [55(125)] Or that the faces of those who practiced self-control shall shine more than the stars, but our faces shall be blacker than darkness? [56(126)] For while we lived and committed iniquity we did not consider what we should suffer after death." [57(127)] He answered and said, "This is the meaning of the contest which every man who is born on earth shall wage,
[58(128)] that if he is defeated he shall suffer what you have said, but if he is victorious he shall receive what I have said. [59(129)] For this is the way of which Moses, while he was alive, spoke to the people, saying, `Choose for yourself life, that you may live!' [60(130)] But they did not believe him, or the prophets after him, or even myself who have spoken to them. [61(131)] Therefore there shall not be grief at their destruction, so much as joy over those to whom salvation is assured." [62(132)] I answered and said, "I know, O Lord, that the Most High is now called merciful, because he has mercy on those who have not yet come into the world; [63(133)] and gracious, because he is gracious to those who turn in repentance to his law; [64(134)] and patient, because he shows patience toward those who have sinned, since they are his own works; [65(135)] and bountiful, because he would rather give than take away; [66(136)] and abundant in compassion, because he makes his compassions abound more and more to those now living and to those who are gone and to those yet to come, [67(137)] for if he did not make them abound, the world with those who inhabit it would not have life; [68(138)] and he is called giver, because if he did not give out of his goodness so that those who have committed iniquities might be relieved of them, not one ten-thousandth of mankind could have life; [69(139)] and judge, because if he did not pardon those who were created by his word and blot out the multitude of their sins, [70(140)] there would probably be left only very few of the innumerable multitude."
8

[1] He answered me and said, "The Most High made this world for the sake of many, but the world to come for the sake of few.
[2] But I tell you a parable, Ezra. Just as, when you ask the earth, it will tell you that it provides very much clay from which earthenware is made, but only a little dust from which gold comes; so is the course of the present

world.

[3] Many have been created, but few shall be saved."

[4] I answered and said, "Then drink your fill of understanding, O my soul, and drink wisdom, O my heart!

[5] For not of your own will did you come into the world, and against your will you depart, for you have been given only a short time to live.

[6] O Lord who are over us, grant to thy servant that we may pray before thee, and give us seed for our heart and cultivation of our understanding so that fruit may be produced, by which every mortal who bears the likeness of a human being may be able to live.

[7] For thou alone do exist, and we are a work of thy hands, as thou hast declared.

[8] And because thou do give life to the body which is now fashioned in the womb, and do furnish it with members, what thou hast created is preserved in fire and water, and for nine months the womb which thou has formed endures thy creation which has been created in it.

[9] But that which keeps and that which is kept shall both be kept by thy keeping. And when the womb gives up again what has been created in it,

[10] thou hast commanded that from the members themselves (that is, from the breasts) milk should be supplied which is the fruit of the breasts,

[11] so that what has been fashioned may be nourished for a time; and afterwards thou wilt guide him in thy mercy.

[12] Thou hast brought him up in thy righteousness, and instructed him in thy law, and reproved him in thy wisdom.

[13] Thou wilt take away his life, for he is thy creation; and thou wilt make him live, for he is thy work.

[14] If then thou wilt suddenly and quickly destroy him who with so great labor was fashioned by thy command, to what purpose was he made?

[15] And now I will speak out: About all mankind thou knowest best; but I will speak about thy people, for whom I am grieved,

[16] and about thy inheritance, for whom I lament, and about Israel, for whom I am sad, and about the seed of Jacob, for whom I am troubled.

[17] Therefore I will pray before thee for myself and for them, for I see the failings of us who dwell in the land,

[18] and I have heard of the swiftness of the judgment that is to come.

[19] Therefore hear my voice, and understand my words, and I will speak before thee." The beginning of the words of Ezra's prayer, before he was taken up. He said:

[20] "O Lord who inhabitest eternity, whose eyes are exalted and whose upper chambers are in the air,

[21] whose throne is beyond measure and whose glory is beyond comprehension, before whom the hosts of angels stand trembling

[22] and at whose command they are changed to wind and fire, whose word

is sure and whose utterances are certain, whose ordinance is strong and whose command is terrible,

[23] whose look dries up the depths and whose indignation makes the mountains melt away, and whose truth is established for ever --

[24] hear, O Lord, the prayer of thy servant, and give ear to the petition of thy creature; attend to my words.

[25] For as long as I live I will speak, and as long as I have understanding I will answer.

[26] O look not upon the sins of thy people, but at those who have served thee in truth.

[27] Regard not the endeavors of those who act wickedly, but the endeavors of those who have kept thy covenants amid afflictions.

[28] Think not on those who have lived wickedly in thy sight; but remember those who have willingly acknowledged that thou art to be feared.

[29] Let it not be thy will to destroy those who have had the ways of cattle; but regard those who have gloriously taught thy law.

[30] Be not angry with those who are deemed worse than beasts; but love those who have always put their trust in thy glory.

[31] For we and our fathers have passed our lives in ways that bring death, but thou, because of us sinners, are called merciful.

[32] For if thou hast desired to have pity on us, who have no works of righteousness, then thou wilt be called merciful.

[33] For the righteous, who have many works laid up with thee, shall receive their reward in consequence of their own deeds.

[34] But what is man, that thou art angry with him; or what is a corruptible race, that thou art so bitter against it?

[35] For in truth there is no one among those who have been born who has not acted wickedly, and among those who have existed there is no one who has not transgressed.

[36] For in this, O Lord, thy righteousness and goodness will be declared, when thou art merciful to those who have no store of good works."

[37] He answered me and said, "Some things you have spoken rightly, and it will come to pass according to your words.

[38] For indeed I will not concern myself about the fashioning of those who have sinned, or about their death, their judgment, or their destruction;

[39] but I will rejoice over the creation of the righteous, over their pilgrimage also, and their salvation, and their receiving their reward.

[40] As I have spoken, therefore, so it shall be.

[41] "For just as the farmer sows many seeds upon the ground and plants a multitude of seedlings, and yet not all that have been sown will come up in due season, and not all that were planted will take root; so also those who have been sown in the world will not all be saved."

[42] I answered and said, "If I have found favor before thee, let me speak.

[43] For if the farmer's seed does not come up, because it has not received

thy rain in due season, or if it has been ruined by too much rain, it perishes.
[44] But man, who has been formed by thy hands and is called thy own image because he is made like thee, and for whose sake thou hast formed all things -- hast thou also made him like the farmer's seed?
[45] No, O Lord who art over us! But spare thy people and have mercy on thy inheritance, for thou hast mercy on thy own creation."
[46] He answered me and said, "Things that are present are for those who live now, and things that are future are for those who will live hereafter.
[47] For you come far short of being able to love my creation more than I love it. But you have often compared yourself to the unrighteous. Never do so!
[48] But even in this respect you will be praiseworthy before the Most High,
[49] because you have humbled yourself, as is becoming for you, and have not deemed yourself to be among the righteous in order to receive the greatest glory.
[50] For many miseries will affect those who inhabit the world in the last times, because they have walked in great pride.
[51] But think of your own case, and inquire concerning the glory of those who are like yourself,
[52] because it is for you that paradise is opened, the tree of life is planted, the age to come is prepared, plenty is provided, a city is built, rest is appointed, goodness is established and wisdom perfected beforehand.
[53] The root of evil is sealed up from you, illness is banished from you, and death is hidden; hell has fled and corruption has been forgotten;
[54] sorrows have passed away, and in the end the treasure of immortality is made manifest.
[55] Therefore do not ask any more questions about the multitude of those who perish.
[56] For they also received freedom , but they despised the Most High, and were contemptuous of his law, and forsook his ways.
[57] Moreover they have even trampled upon his righteous ones,
[58] and said in their hearts that there is not God -- though knowing full well that they must die.
[59] For just as the things which I have predicted await you, so the thirst and torment which are prepared await them. For the Most High did not intend that men should be destroyed;
[60] but they themselves who were created have defiled the name of him who made them, and have been ungrateful to him who prepared life for them.
[61] Therefore my judgment is now drawing near;
[62] I have not shown this to all men, but only to you and a few like you."
Then I answered and said,
[63] "Behold, O Lord, thou hast now shown me a multitude of the signs

which thou wilt do in the last times, but thou hast not shown me when thou wilt do them."

9

[1] He answered me and said, "Measure carefully in your mind, and when you see that a certain part of the predicted signs are past,

[2] then you will know that it is the very time when the Most High is about to visit the world which he has made.

[3] So when there shall appear in the world earthquakes, tumult of peoples, intrigues of nations, wavering of leaders, confusion of princes,

[4] then you will know that it was of these that the Most High spoke from the days that were of old, from the beginning.

[5] For just as with everything that has occurred in the world, the beginning is evident, and the end manifest;

[6] so also are the times of the Most High: the beginnings are manifest in wonders and mighty works, and the end in requital and in signs.

[7] And it shall be that every one who will be saved and will be able to escape on account of his works, or on account of the faith by which he has believed,

[8] will survive the dangers that have been predicted, and will see my salvation in my land and within my borders, which I have sanctified for myself from the beginning.

[9] Then those who have now abused my ways shall be amazed, and those who have rejected them with contempt shall dwell in torments.

[10] For as many as did not acknowledge me in their lifetime, although they received my benefits,

[11] and as many as scorned my law while they still had freedom, and did not understand but despised it while an opportunity of repentance was still open to them,

[12] these must in torment acknowledge it after death.

[13] Therefore, do not continue to be curious as to how the ungodly will be punished; but inquire how the righteous will be saved, those to whom the age belongs and for whose sake the age was made."

[14] I answered and said,

[15] "I said before, and I say now, and will say it again: there are more who perish than those who will be saved,

[16] as a wave is greater than a drop of water."

[17] He answered me and said, "As is the field, so is the seed; and as are the flowers, so are the colors; and as is the work, so is the product; and as is the farmer, so is the threshing floor.

[18] For there was a time in this age when I was preparing for those who now exist, before the world was made for them to dwell in, and no one opposed me then, for no one existed;

[19] but now those who have been created in this world which is supplied both with an unfailing table and an inexhaustible pasture, have become

corrupt in their ways.

[20] So I considered my world, and behold, it was lost, and my earth, and behold, it was in peril because of the devices of those who had come into it.

[21] And I saw and spared some with great difficulty, and saved for myself one grape out of a cluster, and one plant out of a great forest.

[22] So let the multitude perish which has been born in vain, but let my grape and my plant be saved, because with much labor I have perfected them.

[23] But if you will let seven days more pass -- do not fast during them, however;

[24] but go into a field of flowers where no house has been built, and eat only of the flowers of the field, and taste no meat and drink no wine, but eat only flowers,

[25] and pray to the Most High continually -- then I will come and talk with you."

[26] So I went, as he directed me, into the field which is called Ardat; and there I sat among the flowers and ate of the plants of the field, and the nourishment they afforded satisfied me.

[27] And after seven days, as I lay on the grass, my heart was troubled again as it was before.

[28] And my mouth was opened, and I began to speak before the Most High, and said,

[29] "O Lord, thou didst show thyself among us, to our fathers in the wilderness when they came out from Egypt and when they came into the untrodden and unfruitful wilderness;

[30] and thou didst say, `Hear me, O Israel, and give heed to my words, O descendants of Jacob.

[31] For behold, I sow my law in you, and it shall bring forth fruit in you and you shall be glorified through it for ever.'

[32] But though our fathers received the law, they did not keep it, and did not observe the statutes; yet the fruit of the law did not perish -- for it could not, because it was your.

[33] Yet those who received it perished, because they did not keep what had been sown in them.

[34] And behold, it is the rule that, when the ground has received seed, or the sea a ship, or any dish food or drink, and when it happens that what was sown or what was launched or what was put in is destroyed,

[35] they are destroyed, but the things that held them remain; yet with us it has not been so.

[36] For we who have received the law and sinned will perish, as well as our heart which received it;

[37] the law, however, does not perish but remains in its glory."

[38] When I said these things in my heart, I lifted up my eyes and saw a

woman on my right, and behold, she was mourning and weeping with a loud voice, and was deeply grieved at heart, and her clothes were rent, and there were ashes on her head.

[39] Then I dismissed the thoughts with which I had been engaged, and turned to her

[40] and said to her, "Why are you weeping, and why are you grieved at heart?"

[41] And she said to me, "Let me alone, my lord, that I may weep for myself and continue to mourn, for I am greatly embittered in spirit and deeply afflicted."

[42] And I said to her, "What has happened to you? Tell me."

[43] And she said to me, "Your servant was barren and had no child, though I lived with my husband thirty years.

[44] And every hour and every day during those thirty years I besought the Most High, night and day.

[45] And after thirty years God heard your handmaid, and looked upon my low estate, and considered my distress, and gave me a son. And I rejoiced greatly over him, I and my husband and all my neighbors; and we gave great glory to the Mighty One.

[46] And I brought him up with much care.

[47] So when he grew up and I came to take a wife for him, I set a day for the marriage feast.

10

[1] "But it happened that when my son entered his wedding chamber, he fell down and died.

[2] Then we all put out the lamps, and all my neighbors attempted to console me; and I remained quiet until evening of the second day.

[3] But when they all had stopped consoling me, that I might be quiet, I got up in the night and fled, and came to this field, as you see.

[4] And now I intend not to return to the city, but to stay here, and I will neither eat nor drink, but without ceasing mourn and fast until I die."

[5] Then I broke off the reflections with which I was still engaged, and answered her in anger and said,

[6] "You most foolish of women, do you not see our mourning, and what has happened to us?

[7] For Zion, the mother of us all, is in deep grief and great affliction.

[8] It is most appropriate to mourn now, because we are all mourning, and to be sorrowful, because we are all sorrowing; you are sorrowing for one son, but we, the whole world, for our mother.

[9] Now ask the earth, and she will tell you that it is she who ought to mourn over so many who have come into being upon her.

[10] And from the beginning all have been born of her, and others will come; and behold, almost all go to perdition, and a multitude of them are destined for destruction.

[11] Who then ought to mourn the more, she who lost so great a multitude, or you who are grieving for one?

[12] But if you say to me, `My lamentation is not like the earth's, for I have lost the fruit of my womb, which I brought forth in pain and bore in sorrow;

[13] but it is with the earth according to the way of the earth -- the multitude that is now in it goes as it came';

[14] then I say to you, `As you brought forth in sorrow, so the earth also has from the beginning given her fruit, that is, man, to him who made her.'

[15] Now, therefore, keep your sorrow to yourself, and bear bravely the troubles that have come upon you.

[16] For if you acknowledge the decree of God to be just, you will receive your son back in due time, and will be praised among women.

[17] Therefore go into the city to your husband."

[18] She said to me, "I will not do so; I will not go into the city, but I will die here."

[19] So I spoke again to her, and said,

[20] "Do not say that, but let yourself be persuaded because of the troubles of Zion, and be consoled because of the sorrow of Jerusalem.

[21] For you see that our sanctuary has been laid waste, our altar thrown down, our temple destroyed;

[22] our harp has been laid low, our song has been silenced, and our rejoicing has been ended; the light of our lampstand has been put out, the ark of our covenant has been plundered, our holy things have been polluted, and the name by which we are called has been profaned; our free men have suffered abuse, our priests have been burned to death, our Levites have gone into captivity, our virgins have been defiled, and our wives have been ravished; our righteous men have been carried off, our little ones have been cast out, our young men have been enslaved and our strong men made powerless.

[23] And, what is more than all, the seal of Zion -- for she has now lost the seal of her glory, and has been given over into the hands of those that hate us.

[24] Therefore shake off your great sadness and lay aside your many sorrows, so that the Mighty One may be merciful to you again, and the Most High may give you rest, a relief from your troubles."

[25] While I was talking to her, behold, her face suddenly shone exceedingly, and her countenance flashed like lightning, so that I was too frightened to approach her, and my heart was terrified. While I was wondering what this meant,

[26] behold, she suddenly uttered a loud and fearful cry, so that the earth shook at the sound.

[27] And I looked, and behold, the woman was no longer visible to me, but there was an established city, and a place of huge foundations showed itself.

Then I was afraid, and cried with a loud voice and said,

[28] "Where is the angel Uriel, who came to me at first? For it was he who brought me into this overpowering bewilderment; my end has become corruption, and my prayer a reproach."

[29] As I was speaking these words, behold, the angel who had come to me at first came to me, and he looked upon me;

[30] and behold, I lay there like a corpse and I was deprived of my understanding. Then he grasped my right hand and strengthened me and set me on my feet, and said to me,

[31] "What is the matter with you? And why are you troubled? And why are your understanding and the thoughts of your mind troubled?"

[32] I said, "Because you have forsaken me! I did as you directed, and went out into the field, and behold, I saw, and still see, what I am unable to explain."

[33] He said to me, "Stand up like a man, and I will instruct you."

[34] I said, "Speak, my lord; only do not forsake me, lest I die before my time.

[35] For I have seen what I did not know, and I have heard what I do not understand.

[36] Or is my mind deceived, and my soul dreaming?

[37] Now therefore I entreat you to give your servant an explanation of this bewildering vision."

[38] He answered me and said, "Listen to me and I will inform you, and tell you about the things which you fear, for the Most High has revealed many secrets to you.

[39] For he has seen your righteous conduct, that you have sorrowed continually for your people, and mourned greatly over Zion.

[40] This therefore is the meaning of the vision.

[41] The woman who appeared to you a little while ago, whom you saw mourning and began to console --

[42] but you do not now see the form of a woman, but an established city has appeared to you --

[43] and as for her telling you about the misfortune of her son, this is the interpretation:

[44] This woman whom you saw, whom you now behold as an established city, is Zion.

[45] And as for her telling you that she was barren for thirty years, it is because there were three thousand years in the world before any offering was offered in it.

[46] And after three thousand years Solomon built the city, and offered offerings; then it was that the barren woman bore a son.

[47] And as for her telling you that she brought him up with much care, that was the period of residence in Jerusalem.

[48] And as for her saying to you , `When my son entered his wedding

chamber he died,' and that misfortune had overtaken her, that was the destruction which befell Jerusalem.

[49] And behold, you saw her likeness, how she mourned for her son, and you began to console her for what had happened.

[50] For now the Most High, seeing that you are sincerely grieved and profoundly distressed for her, has shown you the brilliance of her glory, and the loveliness of her beauty.

[51] Therefore I told you to remain in the field where no house had been built,

[52] for I knew that the Most High would reveal these things to you.

[53] Therefore I told you to go into the field where there was no foundation of any building,

[54] for no work of man's building could endure in a place where the city of the Most High was to be revealed.

[55] "Therefore do not be afraid, and do not let your heart be terrified; but go in and see the splendor and vastness of the building, as far as it is possible for your eyes to see it,

[56] and afterward you will hear as much as your ears can hear.

[57] For you are more blessed than many, and you have been called before the Most High, as but few have been.

[58] But tomorrow night you shall remain here,

[59] and the Most High will show you in those dream visions what the Most High will do to those who dwell on earth in the last days." So I slept that night and the following one, as he had commanded me.

11

[1] On the second night I had a dream, and behold, there came up from the sea an eagle that had twelve feathered wings and three heads.

[2] And I looked, and behold, he spread his wings over all the earth, and all the winds of heaven blew upon him, and the clouds were gathered about him.

[3] And I looked, and out of his wings there grew opposing wings; but they became little, puny wings.

[4] But his heads were at rest; the middle head was larger than the other heads, but it also was at rest with them.

[5] And I looked, and behold, the eagle flew with his wings, to reign over the earth and over those who dwell in it.

[6] And I saw how all things under heaven were subjected to him, and no one spoke against him, not even one creature that was on the earth.

[7] And I looked, and behold, the eagle rose upon his talons, and uttered a cry to his wings, saying,

[8] "Do not all watch at the same time; let each sleep in his own place, and watch in his turn;

[9] but let the heads be reserved for the last."

[10] And I looked, and behold, the voice did not come from his heads, but from the midst of his body.

[11] And I counted his opposing wings, and behold, there were eight of them.

[12] And I looked, and behold, on the right side one wing arose, and it reigned over all the earth.

[13] And while it was reigning it came to its end and disappeared, so that its place was not seen. Then the next wing arose and reigned, and it continued to reign a long time.

[14] And while it was reigning its end came also, so that it disappeared like the first.

[15] And behold, a voice sounded, saying to it.

[16] "Hear me, you who have ruled the earth all this time; I announce this to you before you disappear.

[17] After you no one shall rule as long as you, or even half as long."

[18] Then the third wing raised itself up, and held the rule like the former ones, and it also disappeared.

[19] And so it went with all the wings; they wielded power one after another and then were never seen again.

[20] And I looked, and behold, in due course the wings that followed also rose up on the right side, in order to rule. There were some of them that ruled, yet disappeared suddenly;

[21] and others of them rose up, but did not hold the rule.

[22] And after this I looked, and behold, the twelve wings and the two little wings disappeared;

[23] and nothing remained on the eagle's body except the three heads that were at rest and six little wings.

[24] And I looked, and behold, two little wings separated from the six and remained under the head that was on the right side; but four remained in their place.

[25] And I looked, and behold, these little wings planned to set themselves up and hold the rule.

[26] And I looked, and behold, one was set up, but suddenly disappeared;

[27] a second also, and this disappeared more quickly than the first.

[28] And I looked, and behold, the two that remained were planning between themselves to reign together;

[29] and while they were planning, behold, one of the heads that were at rest (the one which was in the middle) awoke; for it was greater than the other two heads.

[30] And I saw how it allied the two heads with itself,

[31] and behold, the head turned with those that were with it, and it devoured the two little wings which were planning to reign.

[32] Moreover this head gained control of the whole earth, and with much oppression dominated its inhabitants; and it had greater power over the

world than all the wings that had gone before.

[33] And after this I looked, and behold, the middle head also suddenly disappeared, just as the wings had done.

[34] But the two heads remained, which also ruled over the earth and its inhabitants.

[35] And I looked, and behold, the head on the right side devoured the one on the left.

[36] Then I heard a voice saying to me, "Look before you and consider what you see."

[37] And I looked, and behold, a creature like a lion was aroused out of the forest, roaring; and I heard how he uttered a man's voice to the eagle, and spoke, saying,

[38] "Listen and I will speak to you. The Most High says to you,

[39] `Are you not the one that remains of the four beasts which I had made to reign in my world, so that the end of my times might come through them?

[40] You, the fourth that has come, have conquered all the beasts that have gone before; and you have held sway over the world with much terror, and over all the earth with grievous oppression; and for so long you have dwelt on the earth with deceit.

[41] And you have judged the earth, but not with truth;

[42] for you have afflicted the meek and injured the peaceable; you have hated those who tell the truth, and have loved liars; you have destroyed the dwellings of those who brought forth fruit, and have laid low the walls of those who did you no harm.

[43] And so your insolence has come up before the Most High, and your pride to the Mighty One.

[44] And the Most High has looked upon his times, and behold, they are ended, and his ages are completed!

[45] Therefore you will surely disappear, you eagle, and your terrifying wings, and your most evil little wings, and your malicious heads, and your most evil talons, and your whole worthless body,

[46] so that the whole earth, freed from your violence, may be refreshed and relieved, and may hope for the judgment and mercy of him who made it.'"

12

[1] While the lion was saying these words to the eagle, I looked,

[2] and behold, the remaining head disappeared. And the two wings that had gone over to it arose and set themselves up to reign, and their reign was brief and full of tumult.

[3] And I looked, and behold, they also disappeared, and the whole body of the eagle was burned, and the earth was exceedingly terrified. Then I awoke in great perplexity of mind and great fear, and I said to my spirit,

[4] "Behold, you have brought this upon me, because you search out the

ways of the Most High.

[5] Behold, I am still weary in mind and very weak in my spirit, and not even a little strength is left in me, because of the great fear with which I have been terrified this night.

[6] Therefore I will now beseech the Most High that he may strengthen me to the end."

[7] And I said, "O sovereign Lord, if I have found favor in thy sight, and if I have been accounted righteous before thee beyond many others, and if my prayer has indeed come up before thy face,

[8] strengthen me and show me, thy servant, the interpretation and meaning of this terrifying vision, that thou mayest fully comfort my soul.

[9] For thou hast judged me worthy to be shown the end of the times and the last events of the times."

[10] He said to me, "This is the interpretation of this vision which you have seen:

[11] The eagle which you saw coming up from the sea is the fourth kingdom which appeared in a vision to your brother Daniel.

[12] But it was not explained to him as I now explain or have explained it to you.

[13] Behold, the days are coming when a kingdom shall arise on earth, and it shall be more terrifying than all the kingdoms that have been before it.

[14] And twelve kings shall reign in it, one after another.

[15] But the second that is to reign shall hold sway for a longer time than any other of the twelve.

[16] This is the interpretation of the twelve wings which you saw.

[17] As for your hearing a voice that spoke, coming not from the eagle's heads but from the midst of his body, this is the interpretation:

[18] In the midst of the time of that kingdom great struggles shall arise, and it shall be in danger of falling; nevertheless it shall not fall then, but shall regain its former power.

[19] As for your seeing eight little wings clinging to his wings, this is the interpretation:

[20] Eight kings shall arise in it, whose times shall be short and their years swift;

[21] and two of them shall perish when the middle of its time draws near; and four shall be kept for the time when its end approaches; but two shall be kept until the end.

[22] As for your seeing three heads at rest, this is the interpretation:

[23] In its last days the Most High will raise up three kings, and they shall renew many things in it, and shall rule the earth

[24] and its inhabitants more oppressively than all who were before them; therefore they are called the heads of the eagle.

[25] For it is they who shall sum up his wickedness and perform his last actions.

[26] As for your seeing that the large head disappeared, one of the kings shall die in his bed, but in agonies.

[27] But as for the two who remained, the sword shall devour them.

[28] For the sword of one shall devour him who was with him; but he also shall fall by the sword in the last days.

[29] As for your seeing two little wings passing over to the head which was on the right side,

[30] this is the interpretation: It is these whom the Most High has kept for the eagle's end; this was the reign which was brief and full of tumult, as you have seen.

[31] "And as for the lion whom you saw rousing up out of the forest and roaring and speaking to the eagle and reproving him for his unrighteousness, and as for all his words that you have heard,

[32] this is the Messiah whom the Most High has kept until the end of days, who will arise from the posterity of David, and will come and speak to them; he will denounce them for their ungodliness and for their wickedness, and will cast up before them their contemptuous dealings.

[33] For first he will set them living before his judgment seat, and when he has reproved them, then he will destroy them.

[34] But he will deliver in mercy the remnant of my people, those who have been saved throughout my borders, and he will make them joyful until the end comes, the day of judgment, of which I spoke to you at the beginning.

[35] This is the dream that you saw, and this is its interpretation.

[36] And you alone were worthy to learn this secret of the Most High.

[37] Therefore write all these things that you have seen in a book, and put it in a hidden place;

[38] and you shall teach them to the wise among your people, whose hearts you know are able to comprehend and keep these secrets.

[39] But wait here seven days more, so that you may be shown whatever it pleases the Most High to show you." Then he left me.

[40] When all the people heard that the seven days were past and I had not returned to the city, they all gathered together, from the least to the greatest, and came to me and spoke to me, saying,

[41] "How have we offended you, and what harm have we done you, that you have forsaken us and sit in this place?

[42] For of all the prophets you alone are left to us, like a cluster of grapes from the vintage, and like a lamp in a dark place, and like a haven for a ship saved from a storm.

[43] Are not the evils which have befallen us sufficient?

[44] Therefore if you forsake us, how much better it would have been for us if we also had been consumed in the burning of Zion!

[45] For we are no better than those who died there." And they wept with a loud voice. Then I answered them and said,

[46] "Take courage, O Israel; and do not be sorrowful, O house of Jacob;

[47] for the Most High has you in remembrance, and the Mighty One has not forgotten you in your struggle.

[48] As for me, I have neither forsaken you nor withdrawn from you; but I have come to this place to pray on account of the desolation of Zion, and to seek mercy on account of the humiliation of our sanctuary.

[49] Now go, every one of you to his house, and after these days I will come to you."

[50] So the people went into the city, as I told them to do.

[51] But I sat in the field seven days, as the angel had commanded me; and I ate only of the flowers of the field, and my food was of plants during those days.

13

[1] After seven days I dreamed a dream in the night;

[2] and behold, a wind arose from the sea and stirred up all its waves.

[3] And I looked, and behold, this wind made something like the figure of a man come up out of the heart of the sea. And I looked, and behold, that man flew with the clouds of heaven; and wherever he turned his face to look, everything under his gaze trembled,

[4] and whenever his voice issued from his mouth, all who heard his voice melted as wax melts when it feels the fire.

[5] After this I looked, and behold, an innumerable multitude of men were gathered together from the four winds of heaven to make war against the man who came up out of the sea.

[6] And I looked, and behold, he carved out for himself a great mountain, and flew up upon it. < br>[7] And I tried to see the region or place from which the mountain was carved, but I could not.

[8] After this I looked, and behold, all who had gathered together against him, to wage war with him, were much afraid, yet dared to fight.

[9] And behold, when he saw the onrush of the approaching multitude, he neither lifted his hand nor held a spear or any weapon of war;

[10] but I saw only how he sent forth from his mouth as it were a stream of fire, and from his lips a flaming breath, and from his tongue he shot forth a storm of sparks.

[11] All these were mingled together, the stream of fire and the flaming breath and the great storm, and fell on the onrushing multitude which was prepared to fight, and burned them all up, so that suddenly nothing was seen of the innumerable multitude but only the dust of ashes and the smell of smoke. When I saw it, I was amazed.

[12] After this I saw the same man come down from the mountain and call to him another multitude which was peaceable.

[13] Then many people came to him, some of whom were joyful and some sorrowful; some of them were bound, and some were bringing others as offerings. Then in great fear I awoke; and I besought the Most High, and

said,

[14] "From the beginning thou hast shown thy servant these wonders, and hast deemed me worthy to have my prayer heard by thee;

[15] now show me also the interpretation of this dream.

[16] For as I consider it in my mind, alas for those who will be left in those days! And still more, alas for those who are not left!

[17] For those who are not left will be sad,

[18] because they understand what is reserved for the last days, but cannot attain it.

[19] But alas for those also who are left, and for that very reason! For they shall see great dangers and much distress, as these dreams show.

[20] Yet it is better to come into these things, though incurring peril, than to pass from the world like a cloud, and not to see what shall happen in the last days." He answered me and said,

[21] "I will tell you the interpretation of the vision, and I will also explain to you the things which you have mentioned.

[22] As for what you said about those who are left, this is the interpretation:

[23] He who brings the peril at that time will himself protect those who fall into peril, who have works and have faith in the Almighty.

[24] Understand therefore that those who are left are more blessed than those who have died.

[25] This is the interpretation of the vision: As for your seeing a man come up from the heart of the sea,

[26] this is he whom the Most High has been keeping for many ages, who will himself deliver his creation; and he will direct those who are left.

[27] And as for your seeing wind and fire and a storm coming out of his mouth,

[28] and as for his not holding a spear or weapon of war, yet destroying the onrushing multitude which came to conquer him, this is the interpretation:

[29] Behold, the days are coming when the Most High will deliver those who are on the earth.

[30] And bewilderment of mind shall come over those who dwell on the earth.

[31] And they shall plan to make war against one another, city against city, place against place, people against people, and kingdom against kingdom.

[32] And when these things come to pass and the signs occur which I showed you before, then my Son will be revealed, whom you saw as a man coming up from the sea.

[33] And when all the nations hear his voice, every man shall leave his own land and the warfare that they have against one another;

[34] and an innumerable multitude shall be gathered together, as you saw, desiring to come and conquer him.

[35] But he shall stand on the top of Mount Zion.

[36] And Zion will come and be made manifest to all people, prepared and built, as you saw the mountain carved out without hands.

[37] And he, my Son, will reprove the assembled nations for their ungodliness (this was symbolized by the storm),

[38] and will reproach them to their face with their evil thoughts and the torments with which they are to be tortured (which were symbolized by the flames), and will destroy them without effort by the law (which was symbolized by the fire).

[39] And as for your seeing him gather to himself another multitude that was peaceable,

[40] these are the ten tribes which were led away from their own land into captivity in the days of King Hoshea, whom Shalmaneser the king of the Assyrians led captive; he took them across the river, and they were taken into another land.

[41] But they formed this plan for themselves, that they would leave the multitude of the nations and go to a more distant region, where mankind had never lived,

[42] that there at least they might keep their statutes which they had not kept in their own land.

[43] And they went in by the narrow passages of the Euphrates river.

[44] For at that time the Most High performed signs for them, and stopped the channels of the river until they had passed over.

[45] Through that region there was a long way to go, a journey of a year and a half; and that country is called Arzareth.

[46] "Then they dwelt there until the last times; and now, when they are about to come again,

[47] the Most High will stop the channels of the river again, so that they may be able to pass over. Therefore you saw the multitude gathered together in peace.

[48] But those who are left of your people, who are found within my holy borders, shall be saved.

[49] Therefore when he destroys the multitude of the nations that are gathered together, he will defend the people who remain.

[50] And then he will show them very many wonders."

[51] I said, "O sovereign Lord, explain this to me: Why did I see the man coming up from the heart of the sea?"

[52] He said to me, "Just as no one can explore or know what is in the depths of the sea, so no one on earth can see my Son or those who are with him, except in the time of his day.

[53] This is the interpretation of the dream which you saw. And you alone have been enlightened about this,

[54] because you have forsaken your own ways and have applied yourself to mine, and have searched out my law;

[55] for you have devoted your life to wisdom, and called understanding

your mother.

[56] Therefore I have shown you this, for there is a reward laid up with the Most High. And after three more days I will tell you other things, and explain weighty and wondrous matters to you."

[57] Then I arose and walked in the field, giving great glory and praise to the Most High because of his wonders, which he did from time to time,

[58] and because he governs the times and whatever things come to pass in their seasons. And I stayed there three days.

14

[1] On the third day, while I was sitting under an oak, behold, a voice came out of a bush opposite me and said, "Ezra, Ezra."

[2] And I said, "Here I am, Lord," and I rose to my feet.

[3] Then he said to me, "I revealed myself in a bush and spoke to Moses, when my people were in bondage in Egypt;

[4] and I sent him and led my people out of Egypt; and I led him up on Mount Sinai, where I kept him with me many days;

[5] and I told him many wondrous things, and showed him the secrets of the times and declared to him the end of the times. Then I commanded him, saying,

[6] `These words you shall publish openly, and these you shall keep secret.'

[7] And now I say to you;

[8] Lay up in your heart the signs that I have shown you, the dreams that you have seen, and the interpretations that you have heard;

[9] for you shall be taken up from among men, and henceforth you shall live with my Son and with those who are like you, until the times are ended.

[10] For the age has lost its youth, and the times begin to grow old.

[11] For the age is divided into twelve parts, and nine of its parts have already passed,

[12] as well as half of the tenth part; so two of its parts remain, besides half of the tenth part.

[13] Now therefore, set your house in order, and reprove your people; comfort the lowly among them, and instruct those that are wise. And now renounce the life that is corruptible,

[14] and put away from you mortal thoughts; cast away from you the burdens of man, and divest yourself now of your weak nature,

[15] and lay to one side the thoughts that are most grievous to you, and hasten to escape from these times.

[16] For evils worse than those which you have now seen happen shall be done hereafter.

[17] For the weaker the world becomes through old age, the more shall evils be multiplied among its inhabitants.

[18] For truth shall go farther away, and falsehood shall come near. For the eagle which you saw in the vision is already hastening to come."

[19] Then I answered and said, "Let me speak in thy presence, Lord.

[20] For behold, I will go, as thou hast commanded me, and I will reprove the people who are now living; but who will warn those who will be born hereafter? For the world lies in darkness, and its inhabitants are without light.

[21] For thy law has been burned, and so no one knows the things which have been done or will be done by thee.

[22] If then I have found favor before thee, send the Holy Spirit into me, and I will write everything that has happened in the world from the beginning, the things which were written in thy law, that men may be able to find the path, and that those who wish to live in the last days may live."

[23] He answered me and said, "Go and gather the people, and tell them not to seek you for forty days.

[24] But prepare for yourself many writing tablets, and take with you Sarea, Dabria, Selemia, Ethanus, and Asiel -- these five, because they are trained to write rapidly;

[25] and you shall come here, and I will light in your heart the lamp of understanding, which shall not be put out until what you are about to write is finished.

[26] And when you have finished, some things you shall make public, and some you shall deliver in secret to the wise; tomorrow at this hour you shall begin to write."

[27] Then I went as he commanded me, and I gathered all the people together, and said,

[28] "Hear these words, O Israel

[29] At first our fathers dwelt as aliens in Egypt, and they were delivered from there,

[30] and received the law of life, which they did not keep, which you also have transgressed after them.

[31] Then land was given to you for a possession in the land of Zion; but you and your fathers committed iniquity and did not keep the ways which the Most High commanded you.

[32] And because he is a righteous judge, in due time he took from you what he had given.

[33] And now you are here, and your brethren are farther in the interior.

[34] If you, then, will rule over your minds and discipline your hearts, you shall be kept alive, and after death you shall obtain mercy.

[35] For after death the judgment will come, when we shall live again; and then the names of the righteous will become manifest, and the deeds of the ungodly will be disclosed.

[36] But let no one come to me now, and let no one seek me for forty days."

[37] So I took the five men, as he commanded me, and we proceeded to the field, and remained there.

[38] And on the next day, behold, a voice called me, saying, "Ezra, open

your mouth and drink what I give you to drink."

[39] Then I opened my mouth, and behold, a full cup was offered to me; it was full of something like water, but its color was like fire.

[40] And I took it and drank; and when I had drunk it, my heart poured forth understanding, and wisdom increased in my breast, for my spirit retained its memory;

[41] and my mouth was opened, and was no longer closed.

[42] And the Most High gave understanding to the five men, and by turns they wrote what was dictated, in characters which they did not know. They sat forty days, and wrote during the daytime, and ate their bread at night.

[43] As for me, I spoke in the daytime and was not silent at night.

[44] So during the forty days ninety-four books were written.

[45] And when the forty days were ended, the Most High spoke to me, saying, "Make public the twenty-four books that you wrote first and let the worthy and the unworthy read them;

[46] but keep the seventy that were written last, in order to give them to the wise among your people.

[47] For in them is the spring of understanding, the fountain of wisdom, and the river of knowledge."

[48] And I did so.

15

[1] The Lord says, "Behold, speak in the ears of my people the words of the prophecy which I will put in your mouth,

[2] and cause them to be written on paper; for they are trustworthy and true.

[3] Do not fear the plots against you, and do not be troubled by the unbelief of those who oppose you.

[4] For every unbeliever shall die in his unbelief."

[5] "Behold," says the Lord, "I bring evils upon the world, the sword and famine and death and destruction.

[6] For iniquity has spread throughout every land, and their harmful deeds have reached their limit.

[7] Therefore," says the Lord,

[8] "I will be silent no longer concerning their ungodly deeds which they impiously commit, neither will I tolerate their wicked practices. Behold, innocent and righteous blood cries out to me, and the souls of the righteous cry out continually.

[9] I will surely avenge them," says the Lord, "and will receive to myself all the innocent blood from among them.

[10] Behold, my people is led like a flock to the slaughter; I will not allow them to live any longer in the land of Egypt,

[11] but I will bring them out with a mighty hand and with an uplifted arm, and will smite Egypt with plagues, as before, and will destroy all its land."

[12] Let Egypt mourn, and its foundations, for the plague of chastisement

and punishment that the Lord will bring upon it.

[13] Let the farmers that till the ground mourn, because their seed shall fail and their trees shall be ruined by blight and hail and by a terrible tempest.

[14] Alas for the world and for those who live in it!

[15] For the sword and misery draw near them, and nation shall rise up to fight against nation, with swords in their hands.

[16] For there shall be unrest among men; growing strong against one another, they shall in their might have no respect for their king or the chief of their leaders.

[17] For a man will desire to go into a city, and shall not be able.

[18] For because of their pride the cities shall be in confusion, the houses shall be destroyed, and people shall be afraid.

[19] A man shall have no pity upon his neighbors, but shall make an assault upon their houses with the sword, and plunder their goods, because of hunger for bread and because of great tribulation.

[20] "Behold," says God, "I call together all the kings of the earth to fear me, from the rising sun and from the south, from the east and from Lebanon; to turn and repay what they have given them.

[21] Just as they have done to my elect until this day, so I will do, and will repay into their bosom." Thus says the Lord God:

[22] "My right hand will not spare the sinners, and my sword will not cease from those who shed innocent blood on earth."

[23] And a fire will go forth from his wrath, and will consume the foundations of the earth, and the sinners, like straw that is kindled.

[24] "Woe to those who sin and do not observe my commandments," says the Lord;

[25] "I will not spare them. Depart, you faithless children! Do not pollute my sanctuary."

[26] For the Lord knows all who transgress against him; therefore he will hand them over to death and slaughter.

[27] For now calamities have come upon the whole earth, and you shall remain in them; for God will not deliver you, because you have sinned against him.

[28] Behold, a terrifying sight, appearing from the east!

[29] The nations of the dragons of Arabia shall come out with many chariots, and from the day that they set out, their hissing shall spread over the earth, so that all who hear them fear and tremble.

[30] Also the Carmonians, raging in wrath, shall go forth like wild boars of the forest, and with great power they shall come, and engage them in battle, and shall devastate a portion of the land of the Assyrians with their teeth.

[31] And then the dragons, remembering their origin, shall become still stronger; and if they combine in great power and turn to pursue them,

[32] then these shall be disorganized and silenced by their power, and shall turn and flee.

[33] And from the land of the Assyrians an enemy in ambush shall beset them and destroy one of them, and fear and trembling shall come upon their army, and indecision upon their kings.

[34] Behold, clouds from the east, and from the north to the south; and their appearance is very threatening, full of wrath and storm.

[35] They shall dash against one another and shall pour out a heavy tempest upon the earth, and their own tempest; and there shall be blood from the sword as high as a horse's belly

[36] and a man's thigh and a camel's hock.

[37] And there shall be fear and great trembling upon the earth; and those who see that wrath shall be horror-stricken, and they shall be seized with trembling.

[38] And, after that, heavy storm clouds shall be stirred up from the south, and from the north, and another part from the west.

[39] And the winds from the east shall prevail over the cloud that was raised in wrath, and shall dispel it; and the tempest that was to cause destruction by the east wind shall be driven violently toward the south and west.

[40] And great and mighty clouds, full of wrath and tempest, shall rise, to destroy all the earth and its inhabitants, and shall pour out upon every high and lofty place a terrible tempest,

[41] fire and hail and flying swords and floods of water, that all the fields and all the streams may be filled with the abundance of those waters.

[42] And they shall destroy cities and walls, mountains and hills, trees of the forests, and grass of the meadows, and their grain.

[43] And they shall go on steadily to Babylon, and shall destroy her.

[44] They shall come to her and surround her; they shall pour out the tempest and all its wrath upon her; then the dust and smoke shall go up to heaven, and all who are about her shall wail over her.

[45] And those who survive shall serve those who have destroyed her.

[46] And you, Asia, who share in the glamour of Babylon and the glory of her person --

[47] woe to you, miserable wretch! For you have made yourself like her; you have decked out your daughters in harlotry to please and glory in your lovers, who have always lusted after you.

[48] You have imitated that hateful harlot in all her deeds and devices; therefore God says,

[49] "I will send evils upon you, widowhood, poverty, famine, sword, and pestilence, to lay waste your houses and bring you to destruction and death.

[50] And the glory of your power shall wither like a flower, when the heat rises that is sent upon you.

[51] You shall be weakened like a wretched woman who is beaten and wounded, so that you cannot receive your mighty lovers.

[52] Would I have dealt with you so violently," says the Lord,

[53] "If you had not always killed my chosen people, exulting and clapping your hands and talking about their death when you were drunk?

[54] Trick out the beauty of your face!

[55] The reward of a harlot is in your bosom, therefore you shall receive your recompense.

[56] As you will do to my chosen people," says the Lord, "so God will do to you, and will hand you over to adversities.

[57] Your children shall die of hunger, and you shall fall by the sword, and your cities shall be wiped out, and all your people who are in the open country shall fall by the sword.

[58] And those who are in the mountains and highlands shall perish of hunger, and they shall eat their own flesh in hunger for bread and drink their own blood in thirst for water.

[59] Unhappy above all others, you shall come and suffer fresh afflictions.

[60] And as they pass they shall wreck the hateful city, and shall destroy a part of your land and abolish a portion of your glory, as they return from devastated Babylon.

[61] And you shall be broken down by them like stubble, and they shall be like fire to you.

[62] And they shall devour you and your cities, your land and your mountains; they shall burn with fire all your forests and your fruitful trees.

[63] They shall carry your children away captive, and shall plunder your wealth, and abolish the glory of your countenance."

16

[1] Woe to you, Babylon and Asia! Woe to you, Egypt and Syria!

[2] Gird yourselves with sackcloth and haircloth, and wail for your children, and lament for them; for your destruction is at hand.

[3] The sword has been sent upon you, and who is there to turn it back?

[4] A fire has been sent upon you, and who is there to quench it?

[5] Calamities have been sent upon you, and who is there to drive them away?

[6] Can one drive off a hungry lion in the forest, or quench a fire in the stubble, when once it has begun to burn?

[7] Can one turn back an arrow shot by a strong archer?

[8] The Lord God sends calamities, and who will drive them away?

[9] Fire will go forth from his wrath, and who is there to quench it?

[10] He will flash lightning, and who will not be afraid? He will thunder, and who will not be terrified?

[11] The Lord will threaten, and who will not be utterly shattered at his presence?

[12] The earth and its foundations quake, the sea is churned up from the depths, and its waves and the fish also shall be troubled at the presence of the Lord and before the glory of his power.

[13] For his right hand that bends the bow is strong, and his arrows that he

shoots are sharp and will not miss when they begin to be shot to the ends of the world.

[14] Behold, calamities are sent forth and shall not return until they come over the earth.

[15] The fire is kindled, and shall not be put out until it consumes the foundations of the earth.

[16] Just as an arrow shot by a mighty archer does not return, so the calamities that are sent upon the earth shall not return.

[17] Alas for me! Alas for me! Who will deliver me in those days?

[18] The beginning of sorrows, when there shall be much lamentation; the beginning of famine, when many shall perish; the beginning of wars, when the powers shall be terrified; the beginning of calamities, when all shall tremble. What shall they do in these circumstances, when the calamities come?

[19] Behold, famine and plague, tribulation and anguish are sent as scourges for the correction of men.

[20] Yet for all this they will not turn from their iniquities, nor be always mindful of the scourges.

[21] Behold, provision will be so cheap upon earth that men will imagine that peace is assured for them, and then the calamities shall spring up on the earth -- the sword, famine, and great confusion.

[22] For many of those who live on the earth shall perish by famine; and those who survive the famine shall die by the sword.

[23] And the dead shall be cast out like dung, and there shall be no one to console them; for the earth shall be left desolate, and its cities shall be demolished.

[24] No one shall be left to cultivate the earth or to sow it.

[25] The trees shall bear fruit, and who will gather it?

[26] The grapes shall ripen, and who will tread them? For in all places there shall be great solitude;

[27] one man will long to see another, or even to hear his voice.

[28] For out of a city, ten shall be left; and out of the field, two who have hidden themselves in thick groves and clefts in the rocks.

[29] As in an olive orchard three or four olives may be left on every tree,

[30] or as when a vineyard is gathered some clusters may be left by those who search carefully through the vineyard,

[31] so in those days three or four shall be left by those who search their houses with the sword.

[32] And the earth shall be left desolate, and its fields shall be for briers, and its roads and all its paths shall bring forth thorns, because no sheep will go along them.

[33] Virgins shall mourn because they have no bridegrooms; women shall mourn because they have no husbands; their daughters shall mourn,

because they have no helpers.

[34] Their bridegrooms shall be killed in war, and their husbands shall perish of famine.

[35] Listen now to these things, and understand them, O servants of the Lord.

[36] Behold the word of the Lord, receive it; do not disbelieve what the Lord says.

[37] Behold, the calamities draw near, and are not delayed.

[38] Just as a woman with child, in the ninth month, when the time of her delivery draws near, has great pains about her womb for two or three hours beforehand, and when the child comes forth from the womb, there will not be a moment's delay,

[39] so the calamities will not delay in coming forth upon the earth, and the world will groan, and pains will seize it on every side.

[40] "Hear my words, O my people; prepare for battle, and in the midst of the calamities be like strangers on the earth.

[41] Let him that sells be like one who will flee; let him that buys be like one who will lose;

[42] let him that does business be like one who will not make a profit; and let him that builds a house be like one who will not live in it;

[43] let him that sows be like one who will not reap; so also him that prunes the vines, like one who will not gather the grapes;

[44] them that marry, like those who will have no children; and them that do not marry, like those who are widowed.

[45] Because those who labor, labor in vain;

[46] for strangers shall gather their fruits, and plunder their goods, and overthrow their houses, and take their children captive; for in captivity and famine they will beget their children.

[47] Those who conduct business, do it only to be plundered; the more they adorn their cities, their houses and possessions, and their persons,

[48] the more angry I will be with them for their sins," says the Lord.

[49] Just as a respectable and virtuous woman abhors a harlot,

[50] so righteousness shall abhor iniquity, when she decks herself out, and shall accuse her to her face, when he comes who will defend him who searches out every sin on earth.

[51] Therefore do not be like her or her works.

[52] For behold, just a little while, and iniquity will be removed from the earth, and righteousness will reign over us.

[53] Let no sinner say that he has not sinned; for God will burn coals of fire on the head of him who says, "I have not sinned before God and his glory."

[54] Behold, the Lord knows all the works of men, their imaginations and their thoughts and their hearts.

[55] He said, "Let the earth be made," and it was made; "Let the heaven be made," and it was made.

[56] At his word the stars were fixed, and he knows the number of the stars.
[57] It is he who searches the deep and its treasures, who has measured the sea and its contents;
[58] who has enclosed the sea in the midst of the waters, and by his word has suspended the earth over the water;
[59] who has spread out the heaven like an arch, and founded it upon the waters;
[60] who has put springs of water in the desert, and pools on the tops of the mountains, to send rivers from the heights to water the earth;
[61] who formed man, and put a heart in the midst of his body, and gave him breath and life and understanding
[62] and the spirit of Almighty God; who made all things and searches out hidden things in hidden places.
[63] Surely he knows your imaginations and what you think in your hearts! Woe to those who sin and want to hide their sins!
[64] Because the Lord will strictly examine all their works, and will make a public spectacle of all of you.
[65] And when your sins come out before men, you shall be put to shame; and your own iniquities shall stand as your accusers in that day.
[66] What will you do? Or how will you hide your sins before God and his angels?
[67] Behold, God is the judge, fear him! Cease from your sins, and forget your iniquities, never to commit them again; so God will lead you forth and deliver you from all tribulation.
[68] For behold, the burning wrath of a great multitude is kindled over you, and they shall carry off some of you and shall feed you what was sacrificed to idols.
[69] And those who consent to eat shall be held in derision and contempt, and be trodden under foot.
[70] For in many places and in neighboring cities there shall be a great insurrection against those who fear the Lord.
[71] They shall be like mad men, sparing no one, but plundering and destroying those who continue to fear the Lord.
[72] For they shall destroy and plunder their goods, and drive them out of their houses.
[73] Then the tested quality of my elect shall be manifest, as gold that is tested by fire.
[74] "Hear, my elect," says the Lord. "Behold, the days of tribulation are at hand, and I will deliver you from them.
[75] Do not fear or doubt, for God is your guide.
[76] You who keep my commandments and precepts," says the Lord God, "do not let your sins pull you down, or your iniquities prevail over you."
[77] Woe to those who are choked by their sins and overwhelmed by their

iniquities, as a field is choked with underbrush and its path overwhelmed with thorns, so that no one can pass through!

[78] It is shut off and given up to be consumed by fire.

1 Maccabees

1Mac.1

[1] After Alexander son of Philip, the Macedonian, who came from the land of Kittim, had defeated Darius, king of the Persians and the Medes, he succeeded him as king. (He had previously become king of Greece.)
[2] He fought many battles, conquered strongholds, and put to death the kings of the earth.
[3] He advanced to the ends of the earth, and plundered many nations. When the earth became quiet before him, he was exalted, and his heart was lifted up.
[4] He gathered a very strong army and ruled over countries, nations, and princes, and they became tributary to him.
[5] After this he fell sick and perceived that he was dying.
[6] So he summoned his most honored officers, who had been brought up with him from youth, and divided his kingdom among them while he was still alive.
[7] And after Alexander had reigned twelve years, he died.
[8] Then his officers began to rule, each in his own place.
[9] They all put on crowns after his death, and so did their sons after them for many years; and they caused many evils on the earth.
[10] From them came forth a sinful root, Antiochus Epiphanes, son of Antiochus the king; he had been a hostage in Rome. He began to reign in the one hundred and thirty-seventh year of the kingdom of the Greeks.
[11] In those days lawless men came forth from Israel, and misled many, saying, "Let us go and make a covenant with the Gentiles round about us, for since we separated from them many evils have come upon us."
[12] This proposal pleased them,
[13] and some of the people eagerly went to the king. He authorized them to observe the ordinances of the Gentiles.
[14] So they built a gymnasium in Jerusalem, according to Gentile custom,
[15] and removed the marks of circumcision, and abandoned the holy covenant. They joined with the Gentiles and sold themselves to do evil.
[16] When Antiochus saw that his kingdom was established, he determined to become king of the land of Egypt, that he might reign over both kingdoms.
[17] So he invaded Egypt with a strong force, with chariots and elephants and cavalry and with a large fleet.
[18] He engaged Ptolemy king of Egypt in battle, and Ptolemy turned and

fled before him, and many were wounded and fell.

[19] And they captured the fortified cities in the land of Egypt, and he plundered the land of Egypt.

[20] After subduing Egypt, Antiochus returned in the one hundred and forty-third year. He went up against Israel and came to Jerusalem with a strong force.

[21] He arrogantly entered the sanctuary and took the golden altar, the lampstand for the light, and all its utensils.

[22] He took also the table for the bread of the Presence, the cups for drink offerings, the bowls, the golden censers, the curtain, the crowns, and the gold decoration on the front of the temple; he stripped it all off.

[23] He took the silver and the gold, and the costly vessels; he took also the hidden treasures which he found.

[24] Taking them all, he departed to his own land. He committed deeds of murder, and spoke with great arrogance.

[25] Israel mourned deeply in every community,

[26] rulers and elders groaned, maidens and young men became faint, the beauty of women faded.

[27] Every bridegroom took up the lament; she who sat in the bridal chamber was mourning.

[28] Even the land shook for its inhabitants, and all the house of Jacob was clothed with shame.

[29] Two years later the king sent to the cities of Judah a chief collector of tribute, and he came to Jerusalem with a large force.

[30] Deceitfully he spoke peaceable words to them, and they believed him; but he suddenly fell upon the city, dealt it a severe blow, and destroyed many people of Israel.

[31] He plundered the city, burned it with fire, and tore down its houses and its surrounding walls.

[32] And they took captive the women and children, and seized the cattle.

[33] Then they fortified the city of David with a great strong wall and strong towers, and it became their citadel.

[34] And they stationed there a sinful people, lawless men. These strengthened their position;

[35] they stored up arms and food, and collecting the spoils of Jerusalem they stored them there, and became a great snare.

[36] It became an ambush against the sanctuary, an evil adversary of Israel continually.

[37] On every side of the sanctuary they shed innocent blood; they even defiled the sanctuary.

[38] Because of them the residents of Jerusalem fled; she became a dwelling of strangers; she became strange to her offspring, and her children forsook her.

[39] Her sanctuary became desolate as a desert; her feasts were turned into

mourning, her sabbaths into a reproach,
her honor into contempt.

[40] Her dishonor now grew as great as her glory; her exaltation was turned into mourning.

[41] Then the king wrote to his whole kingdom that all should be one people,

[42] and that each should give up his customs.

[43] All the Gentiles accepted the command of the king. Many even from Israel gladly adopted his religion; they sacrificed to idols and profaned the sabbath.

[44] And the king sent letters by messengers to Jerusalem and the cities of Judah; he directed them to follow customs strange to the land,

[45] to forbid burnt offerings and sacrifices and drink offerings in the sanctuary, to profane sabbaths and feasts,

[46] to defile the sanctuary and the priests,

[47] to build altars and sacred precincts and shrines for idols, to sacrifice swine and unclean animals,

[48] and to leave their sons uncircumcised. They were to make themselves abominable by everything unclean and profane,

[49] so that they should forget the law and change all the ordinances.

[50] "And whoever does not obey the command of the king shall die."

[51] In such words he wrote to his whole kingdom. And he appointed inspectors over all the people and commanded the cities of Judah to offer sacrifice, city by city.

[52] Many of the people, every one who forsook the law, joined them, and they did evil in the land;

[53] they drove Israel into hiding in every place of refuge they had.

[54] Now on the fifteenth day of Chislev, in the one hundred and forty-fifth year, they erected a desolating sacrilege upon the altar of burnt offering. They also built altars in the surrounding cities of Judah,

[55] and burned incense at the doors of the houses and in the streets.

[56] The books of the law which they found they tore to pieces and burned with fire.

[57] Where the book of the covenant was found in the possession of any one, or if any one adhered to the law, the decree of the king condemned him to death.

[58] They kept using violence against Israel, against those found month after month in the cities.

[59] And on the twenty-fifth day of the month they offered sacrifice on the altar which was upon the altar of burnt offering.

[60] According to the decree, they put to death the women who had their children circumcised,

[61] and their families and those who circumcised them; and they hung the

infants from their mothers' necks.

[62] But many in Israel stood firm and were resolved in their hearts not to eat unclean food.

[63] They chose to die rather than to be defiled by food or to profane the holy covenant; and they did die.

[64] And very great wrath came upon Israel.

1Mac.2

[1] In those days Mattathias the son of John, son of Simeon, a priest of the sons of Joarib, moved from Jerusalem and settled in Modein.

[2] He had five sons, John surnamed Gaddi,

[3] Simon called Thassi,

[4] Judas called Maccabeus,

[5] Eleazar called Avaran, and Jonathan called Apphus.

[6] He saw the blasphemies being committed in Judah and Jerusalem,

[7] and said, "Alas! Why was I born to see this, the ruin of my people, the ruin of the holy city, and to dwell there when it was given over to the enemy, the sanctuary given over to aliens?

[8] Her temple has become like a man without honor;

[9] her glorious vessels have been carried into captivity. Her babes have been killed in her streets, her youths by the sword of the foe.

[10] What nation has not inherited her palaces and has not seized her spoils?

[11] All her adornment has been taken away; no longer free, she has become a slave.

[12] And behold, our holy place, our beauty, and our glory have been laid waste; the Gentiles have profaned it.

[13] Why should we live any longer?"

[14] And Mattathias and his sons rent their clothes, put on sackcloth, and mourned greatly.

[15] Then the king's officers who were enforcing the apostasy came to the city of Modein to make them offer sacrifice.

[16] Many from Israel came to them; and Mattathias and his sons were assembled.

[17] Then the king's officers spoke to Mattathias as follows: "You are a leader, honored and great in this city, and supported by sons and brothers.

[18] Now be the first to come and do what the king commands, as all the Gentiles and the men of Judah and those that are left in Jerusalem have done. Then you and your sons will be numbered among the friends of the king, and you and your sons will be honored with silver and gold and many gifts."

[19] But Mattathias answered and said in a loud voice: "Even if all the nations that live under the rule of the king obey him, and have chosen to do his commandments, departing each one from the religion of his fathers,

[20] yet I and my sons and my brothers will live by the covenant of our fathers.

[21] Far be it from us to desert the law and the ordinances.

[22] We will not obey the king's words by turning aside from our religion to the right hand or to the left."

[23] When he had finished speaking these words, a Jew came forward in the sight of all to offer sacrifice upon the altar in Modein, according to the king's command.

[24] When Mattathias saw it, be burned with zeal and his heart was stirred. He gave vent to righteous anger; he ran and killed him upon the altar.

[25] At the same time he killed the king's officer who was forcing them to sacrifice, and he tore down the altar.

[26] Thus he burned with zeal for the law, as Phinehas did against Zimri the son of Salu.

[27] Then Mattathias cried out in the city with a loud voice, saying: "Let every one who is zealous for the law and supports the covenant come out with me!"

[28] And he and his sons fled to the hills and left all that they had in the city.

[29] Then many who were seeking righteousness and justice went down to the wilderness to dwell there,

[30] they, their sons, their wives, and their cattle, because evils pressed heavily upon them.

[31] And it was reported to the king's officers, and to the troops in Jerusalem the city of David, that men who had rejected the king's command had gone down to the hiding places in the wilderness.

[32] Many pursued them, and overtook them; they encamped opposite them and prepared for battle against them on the sabbath day.

[33] And they said to them, "Enough of this! Come out and do what the king commands, and you will live."

[34] But they said, "We will not come out, nor will we do what the king commands and so profane the sabbath day."

[35] Then the enemy hastened to attack them.

[36] But they did not answer them or hurl a stone at them or block up their hiding places,

[37] for they said, "Let us all die in our innocence; heaven and earth testify for us that you are killing us unjustly."

[38] So they attacked them on the sabbath, and they died, with their wives and children and cattle, to the number of a thousand persons.

[39] When Mattathias and his friends learned of it, they mourned for them deeply.

[40] And each said to his neighbor: "If we all do as our brethren have done and refuse to fight with the Gentiles for our lives and for our ordinances, they will quickly destroy us from the earth."

[41] So they made this decision that day: "Let us fight against every man who comes to attack us on the sabbath day; let us not all die as our brethren

died in their hiding places."

[42] Then there united with them a company of Hasideans, mighty warriors of Israel, every one who offered himself willingly for the law.

[43] And all who became fugitives to escape their troubles joined them and reinforced them.

[44] They organized an army, and struck down sinners in their anger and lawless men in their wrath; the survivors fled to the Gentiles for safety.

[45] And Mattathias and his friends went about and tore down the altars;

[46] they forcibly circumcised all the uncircumcised boys that they found within the borders of Israel.

[47] They hunted down the arrogant men, and the work prospered in their hands.

[48] They rescued the law out of the hands of the Gentiles and kings, and they never let the sinner gain the upper hand.

[49] Now the days drew near for Mattathias to die, and he said to his sons: "Arrogance and reproach have now become strong; it is a time of ruin and furious anger.

[50] Now, my children, show zeal for the law, and give your lives for the covenant of our fathers.

[51] "Remember the deeds of the fathers, which they did in their generations; and receive great honor and an everlasting name.

[52] Was not Abraham found faithful when tested, and it was reckoned to him as righteousness?

[53] Joseph in the time of his distress kept the commandment, and became lord of Egypt.

[54] Phinehas our father, because he was deeply zealous, received the covenant of everlasting priesthood.

[55] Joshua, because he fulfilled the command, became a judge in Israel.

[56] Caleb, because he testified in the assembly, received an inheritance in the land.

[57] David, because he was merciful, inherited the throne of the kingdom for ever.

[58] Elijah because of great zeal for the law was taken up into heaven.

[59] Hannaniah, Azariah, and Mishael believed and were saved from the flame.

[60] Daniel because of his innocence was delivered from the mouth of the lions.

[61] "And so observe, from generation to generation, that none who put their trust in him will lack strength.

[62] Do not fear the words of a sinner, for his splendor will turn into dung and worms.

[63] Today he will be exalted, but tomorrow he will not be found, because he has returned to the dust, and his plans will perish.

[64] My children, be courageous and grow strong in the law, for by it you

will gain honor.

[65] "Now behold, I know that Simeon your brother is wise in counsel; always listen to him; he shall be your father.

[66] Judas Maccabeus has been a mighty warrior from his youth; he shall command the army for you and fight the battle against the peoples.

[67] You shall rally about you all who observe the law, and avenge the wrong done to your people.

[68] Pay back the Gentiles in full, and heed what the law commands."

[69] Then he blessed them, and was gathered to his fathers.

[70] He died in the one hundred and forty-sixth year and was buried in the tomb of his fathers at Modein. And all Israel mourned for him with great lamentation.

1Mac.3

[1] Then Judas his son, who was called Maccabeus, took command in his place.

[2] All his brothers and all who had joined his father helped him; they gladly fought for Israel.

[3] He extended the glory of his people. Like a giant he put on his breastplate; he girded on his armor of war and waged battles, protecting the host by his sword.

[4] He was like a lion in his deeds, like a lion's cub roaring for prey.

[5] He searched out and pursued the lawless; he burned those who troubled his people.

[6] Lawless men shrank back for fear of him; all the evildoers were confounded; and deliverance prospered by his hand.

[7] He embittered many kings, but he made Jacob glad by his deeds, and his memory is blessed for ever.

[8] He went through the cities of Judah; he destroyed the ungodly out of the land; thus he turned away wrath from Israel.

[9] He was renowned to the ends of the earth; he gathered in those who were perishing.

[10] But Apollonius gathered together Gentiles and a large force from Samaria to fight against Israel.

[11] When Judas learned of it, he went out to meet him, and he defeated and killed him. Many were wounded and fell, and the rest fled.

[12] Then they seized their spoils; and Judas took the sword of Apollonius, and used it in battle the rest of his life.

[13] Now when Seron, the commander of the Syrian army, heard that Judas had gathered a large company, including a body of faithful men who stayed with him and went out to battle,

[14] he said, "I will make a name for myself and win honor in the kingdom. I will make war on Judas and his companions, who scorn the king's command."

[15] And again a strong army of ungodly men went up with him to help him, to take vengeance on the sons of Israel.

[16] When he approached the ascent of Beth-horon, Judas went out to meet him with a small company.

[17] But when they saw the army coming to meet them, they said to Judas, "How can we, few as we are, fight against so great and strong a multitude? And we are faint, for we have eaten nothing today."

[18] Judas replied, "It is easy for many to be hemmed in by few, for in the sight of Heaven there is no difference between saving by many or by few.

[19] It is not on the size of the army that victory in battle depends, but strength comes from Heaven.

[20] They come against us in great pride and lawlessness to destroy us and our wives and our children, and to despoil us;

[21] but we fight for our lives and our laws.

[22] He himself will crush them before us; as for you, do not be afraid of them."

[23] When he finished speaking, he rushed suddenly against Seron and his army, and they were crushed before him.

[24] They pursued them down the descent of Beth-horon to the plain; eight hundred of them fell, and the rest fled into the land of the Philistines.

[25] Then Judas and his brothers began to be feared, and terror fell upon the Gentiles round about them.

[26] His fame reached the king, and the Gentiles talked of the battles of Judas.

[27] When king Antiochus heard these reports, he was greatly angered; and he sent and gathered all the forces of his kingdom, a very strong army.

[28] And he opened his coffers and gave a year's pay to his forces, and ordered them to be ready for any need.

[29] Then he saw that the money in the treasury was exhausted, and that the revenues from the country were small because of the dissension and disaster which he had caused in the land by abolishing the laws that had existed from the earliest days.

[30] He feared that he might not have such funds as he had before for his expenses and for the gifts which he used to give more lavishly than preceding kings.

[31] He was greatly perplexed in mind, and determined to go to Persia and collect the revenues from those regions and raise a large fund.

[32] He left Lysias, a distinguished man of royal lineage, in charge of the king's affairs from the river Euphrates to the borders of Egypt.

[33] Lysias was also to take care of Antiochus his son until he returned.

[34] And he turned over to Lysias half of his troops and the elephants, and gave him orders about all that he wanted done. As for the residents of Judea and Jerusalem,

[35] Lysias was to send a force against them to wipe out and destroy the

strength of Israel and the remnant of Jerusalem; he was to banish the memory of them from the place,

[36] settle aliens in all their territory, and distribute their land.

[37] Then the king took the remaining half of his troops and departed from Antioch his capital in the one hundred and forty-seventh year. He crossed the Euphrates river and went through the upper provinces.

[38] Lysias chose Ptolemy the son of Dorymenes, and Nicanor and Gorgias, mighty men among the friends of the king,

[39] and sent with them forty thousand infantry and seven thousand cavalry to go into the land of Judah and destroy it, as the king had commanded.

[40] so they departed with their entire force, and when they arrived they encamped near Emmaus in the plain.

[41] When the traders of the region heard what was said to them, they took silver and gold in immense amounts, and fetters, and went to the camp to get the sons of Israel for slaves. And forces from Syria and the land of the Philistines joined with them.

[42] Now Judas and his brothers saw that misfortunes had increased and that the forces were encamped in their territory. They also learned what the king had commanded to do to the people to cause their final destruction.

[43] But they said to one another, "Let us repair the destruction of our people, and fight for our people and the sanctuary."

[44] And the congregation assembled to be ready for battle, and to pray and ask for mercy and compassion.

[45] Jerusalem was uninhabited like a wilderness; not one of her children went in or out.The sanctuary was trampled own,
and the sons of aliens held the citadel; it was a lodging place for the Gentiles. Joy was taken from Jacob; the flute and the harp ceased to play.

[46] So they assembled and went to Mizpah, opposite Jerusalem, because Israel formerly had a place of prayer in Mizpah.

[47] They fasted that day, put on sackcloth and sprinkled ashes on their heads, and rent their clothes.

[48] And they opened the book of the law to inquire into those matters about which the Gentiles were consulting the images of their idols.

[49] They also brought the garments of the priesthood and the first fruits and the tithes, and they stirred up the Nazirites who had completed their days;

[50] and they cried aloud to Heaven, saying, "What shall we do with these? Where shall we take them?

[51] Your sanctuary is trampled down and profaned, and thy priests mourn in humiliation.

[52] And behold, the Gentiles are assembled against us to destroy us; thou knowest what they plot against us.

[53] How will we be able to withstand them, if thou do not help us?"

[54] Then they sounded the trumpets and gave a loud shout.

[55] After this Judas appointed leaders of the people, in charge of thousands and hundreds and fifties and tens.

[56] And he said to those who were building houses, or were betrothed, or were planting vineyards, or were fainthearted, that each should return to his home, according to the law.

[57] Then the army marched out and encamped to the south of Emmaus.

[58] And Judas said, "Gird yourselves and be valiant. Be ready early in the morning to fight with these Gentiles who have assembled against us to destroy us and our sanctuary.

[59] It is better for us to die in battle than to see the misfortunes of our nation and of the sanctuary.

[60] But as his will in heaven may be, so he will do."

1Mac.4

[1] Now Gorgias took five thousand infantry and a thousand picked cavalry, and this division moved out by night

[2] to fall upon the camp of the Jews and attack them suddenly. Men from the citadel were his guides.

[3] But Judas heard of it, and he and his mighty men moved out to attack the king's force in Emmaus

[4] while the division was still absent from the camp.

[5] When Gorgias entered the camp of Judas by night, he found no one there, so he looked for them in the hills, because he said, "These men are fleeing from us."

[6] At daybreak Judas appeared in the plain with three thousand men, but they did not have armor and swords such as they desired.

[7] And they saw the camp of the Gentiles, strong and fortified, with cavalry round about it; and these men were trained in war.

[8] But Judas said to the men who were with him, "Do not fear their numbers or be afraid when they charge.

[9] Remember how our fathers were saved at the Red Sea, when Pharaoh with his forces pursued them.

[10] And now let us cry to Heaven, to see whether he will favor us and remember his covenant with our fathers and crush this army before us today.

[11] Then all the Gentiles will know that there is one who redeems and saves Israel."

[12] When the foreigners looked up and saw them coming against them,

[13] they went forth from their camp to battle. Then the men with Judas blew their trumpets

[14] and engaged in battle. The Gentiles were crushed and fled into the plain,

[15] and all those in the rear fell by the sword. They pursued them to Gazara, and to the plains of Idumea, and to Azotus and Jamnia; and three

thousand of them fell.

[16] Then Judas and his force turned back from pursuing them,

[17] and he said to the people, "Do not be greedy for plunder, for there is a battle before us;

[18] Gorgias and his force are near us in the hills. But stand now against our enemies and fight them, and afterward seize the plunder boldly."

[19] Just as Judas was finishing this speech, a detachment appeared, coming out of the hills.

[20] They saw that their army had been put to flight, and that the Jews were burning the camp, for the smoke that was seen showed what had happened.

[21] When they perceived this they were greatly frightened, and when they also saw the army of Judas drawn up in the plain for battle,

[22] they all fled into the land of the Philistines.

[23] Then Judas returned to plunder the camp, and they seized much gold and silver, and cloth dyed blue and sea purple, and great riches.

[24] On their return they sang hymns and praises to Heaven, for he is good, for his mercy endures for ever.

[25] Thus Israel had a great deliverance that day.

[26] Those of the foreigners who escaped went and reported to Lysias all that had happened.

[27] When he heard it, he was perplexed and discouraged, for things had not happened to Israel as he had intended, nor had they turned out as the king had commanded him.

[28] But the next year he mustered sixty thousand picked infantrymen and five thousand cavalry to subdue them.

[29] They came into Idumea and encamped at Beth-zur, and Judas met them with ten thousand men.

[30] When he saw that the army was strong, he prayed, saying, "Blessed art thou, O Savior of Israel, who didst crush the attack of the mighty warrior by the hand of thy servant David, and didst give the camp of the Philistines into the hands of Jonathan, the son of Saul, and of the man who carried his armor.

[31] So do thou hem in this army by the hand of thy people Israel, and let them be ashamed of their troops and their cavalry.

[32] Fill them with cowardice; melt the boldness of their strength; let them tremble in their destruction.

[33] Strike them down with the sword of those who love thee, and let all who know thy name praise thee with hymns."

[34] Then both sides attacked, and there fell of the army of Lysias five thousand men; they fell in action.

[35] And when Lysias saw the rout of his troops and observed the boldness which inspired those of Judas, and how ready they were either to live or to die nobly, he departed to Antioch and enlisted mercenaries, to invade Judea

again with an even larger army.

[36] Then said Judas and his brothers, "Behold, our enemies are crushed; let us go up to cleanse the sanctuary and dedicate it."

[37] So all the army assembled and they went up to Mount Zion.

[38] And they saw the sanctuary desolate, the altar profaned, and the gates burned. In the courts they saw bushes sprung up as in a thicket, or as on one of the mountains. They saw also the chambers of the priests in ruins.

[39] Then they rent their clothes, and mourned with great lamentation, and sprinkled themselves with ashes.

[40] They fell face down on the ground, and sounded the signal on the trumpets, and cried out to Heaven.

[41] Then Judas detailed men to fight against those in the citadel until he had cleansed the sanctuary.

[42] He chose blameless priests devoted to the law,

[43] and they cleansed the sanctuary and removed the defiled stones to an unclean place.

[44] They deliberated what to do about the altar of burnt offering, which had been profaned.

[45] And they thought it best to tear it down, lest it bring reproach upon them, for the Gentiles had defiled it. So they tore down the altar,

[46] and stored the stones in a convenient place on the temple hill until there should come a prophet to tell what to do with them.

[47] Then they took unhewn stones, as the law directs, and built a new altar like the former one.

[48] They also rebuilt the sanctuary and the interior of the temple, and consecrated the courts.

[49] They made new holy vessels, and brought the lampstand, the altar of incense, and the table into the temple.

[50] Then they burned incense on the altar and lighted the lamps on the lampstand, and these gave light in the temple.

[51] They placed the bread on the table and hung up the curtains. Thus they finished all the work they had undertaken.

[52] Early in the morning on the twenty-fifth day of the ninth month, which is the month of Chislev, in the one hundred and forty-eighth year,

[53] they rose and offered sacrifice, as the law directs, on the new altar of burnt offering which they had built.

[54] At the very season and on the very day that the Gentiles had profaned it, it was dedicated with songs and harps and lutes and cymbals.

[55] All the people fell on their faces and worshiped and blessed Heaven, who had prospered them.

[56] So they celebrated the dedication of the altar for eight days, and offered burnt offerings with gladness; they offered a sacrifice of deliverance and praise.

[57] They decorated the front of the temple with golden crowns and small

shields; they restored the gates and the chambers for the priests, and furnished them with doors.

[58] There was very great gladness among the people, and the reproach of the Gentiles was removed.

[59] Then Judas and his brothers and all the assembly of Israel determined that every year at that season the days of dedication of the altar should be observed with gladness and joy for eight days, beginning with the twenty-fifth day of the month of Chislev.

[60] At that time they fortified Mount Zion with high walls and strong towers round about, to keep the Gentiles from coming and trampling them down as they had done before.

[61] And he stationed a garrison there to hold it. He also fortified Beth-zur, so that the people might have a stronghold that faced Idumea.

1Mac.5

[1] When the Gentiles round about heard that the altar had been built and the sanctuary dedicated as it was before, they became very angry,

[2] and they determined to destroy the descendants of Jacob who lived among them. So they began to kill and destroy among the people.

[3] But Judas made war on the sons of Esau in Idumea, at Akrabattene, because they kept lying in wait for Israel. He dealt them a heavy blow and humbled them and despoiled them.

[4] He also remembered the wickedness of the sons of Baean, who were a trap and a snare to the people and ambushed them on the highways.

[5] They were shut up by him in their towers; and he encamped against them, vowed their complete destruction, and burned with fire their towers and all who were in them.

[6] Then he crossed over to attack the Ammonites, where he found a strong band and many people with Timothy as their leader.

[7] He engaged in many battles with them and they were crushed before him; he struck them down.

[8] He also took Jazer and its villages; then he returned to Judea.

[9] Now the Gentiles in Gilead gathered together against the Israelites who lived in their territory, and planned to destroy them. But they fled to the stronghold of Dathema,

[10] and sent to Judas and his brothers a letter which said, "The Gentiles around us have gathered together against us to destroy us.

[11] They are preparing to come and capture the stronghold to which we have fled, and Timothy is leading their forces.

[12] Now then come and rescue us from their hands, for many of us have fallen,

[13] and all our brethren who were in the land of Tob have been killed; the enemy have captured their wives and children and goods, and have destroyed about a thousand men there."

[14] While the letter was still being read, behold, other messengers, with their garments rent, came from Galilee and made a similar report;

[15] they said that against them had gathered together men of Ptolemais and Tyre and Sidon, and all Galilee of the Gentiles, "to annihilate us."

[16] When Judas and the people heard these messages, a great assembly was called to determine what they should do for their brethren who were in distress and were being attacked by enemies.

[17] Then Judas said to Simon his brother, "Choose your men and go and rescue your brethren in Galilee; I and Jonathan my brother will go to Gilead."

[18] But he left Joseph, the son of Zechariah, and Azariah, a leader of the people, with the rest of the forces, in Judea to guard it;

[19] and he gave them this command, "Take charge of this people, but do not engage in battle with the Gentiles until we return."

[20] Then three thousand men were assigned to Simon to go to Galilee, and eight thousand to Judas for Gilead.

[21] so Simon went to Galilee and fought many battles against the Gentiles, and the Gentiles were crushed before him.

[22] He pursued them to the gate of Ptolemais, and as many as three thousand of the Gentiles fell, and he despoiled them.

[23] Then he took the Jews of Galilee and Arbatta, with their wives and children, and all they possessed, and led them to Judea with great rejoicing.

[24] Judas Maccabeus and Jonathan his brother crossed the Jordan and went three days' journey into the wilderness.

[25] They encountered the Nabateans, who met them peaceably and told them all that had happened to their brethren in Gilead:

[26] "Many of them have been shut up in Bozrah and Bosor, in Alema and Chaspho, Maked and Carnaim" -- all these cities were strong and large--

[27] "and some have been shut up in the other cities of Gilead; the enemy are getting ready to attack the strongholds tomorrow and take and destroy all these men in one day."

[28] Then Judas and his army quickly turned back by the wilderness road to Bozrah; and he took the city, and killed every male by the edge of the sword; then he seized all its spoils and burned it with fire.

[29] He departed from there at night, and they went all the way to the stronghold of Dathema.

[30] At dawn they looked up, and behold, a large company, that could not be counted, carrying ladders and engines of war to capture the stronghold, and attacking the Jews within.

[31] So Judas saw that the battle had begun and that the cry of the city went up to Heaven with trumpets and loud shouts,

[32] and he said to the men of his forces, "Fight today for your brethren!"

[33] Then he came up behind them in three companies, who sounded their trumpets and cried aloud in prayer.

[34] And when the army of Timothy realized that it was Maccabeus, they fled before him, and he dealt them a heavy blow. As many as eight thousand of them fell that day.

[35] Next he turned aside to Alema, and fought against it and took it; and he killed every male in it, plundered it, and burned it with fire.

[36] From there he marched on and took Chaspho, Maked, and Bosor, and the other cities of Gilead.

[37] After these things Timothy gathered another army and encamped opposite Raphon, on the other side of the stream.

[38] Judas sent men to spy out the camp, and they reported to him, "All the Gentiles around us have gathered to him; it is a very large force.

[39] They also have hired Arabs to help them, and they are encamped across the stream, ready to come and fight against you." And Judas went to meet them.

[40] Now as Judas and his army drew near to the stream of water, Timothy said to the officers of his forces, "If he crosses over to us first, we will not be able to resist him, for he will surely defeat us.

[41] But if he shows fear and camps on the other side of the river, we will cross over to him and defeat him."

[42] When Judas approached the stream of water, he stationed the scribes of the people at the stream and gave them this command, "Permit no man to encamp, but make them all enter the battle."

[43] Then he crossed over against them first, and the whole army followed him. All the Gentiles were defeated before him, and they threw away their arms and fled into the sacred precincts at Carnaim.

[44] But he took the city and burned the sacred precincts with fire, together with all who were in them. Thus Carnaim was conquered; they could stand before Judas no longer.

[45] Then Judas gathered together all the Israelites in Gilead, the small and the great, with their wives and children and goods, a very large company, to go to the land of Judah.

[46] So they came to Ephron. This was a large and very strong city on the road, and they could not go round it to the right or to the left; they had to go through it.

[47] But the men of the city shut them out and blocked up the gates with stones.

[48] And Judas sent them this friendly message, "Let us pass through your land to get to our land. No one will do you harm; we will simply pass by on foot." But they refused to open to him.

[49] Then Judas ordered proclamation to be made to the army that each should encamp where he was.

[50] So the men of the forces encamped, and he fought against the city all that day and all the night, and the city was delivered into his hands.

[51] He destroyed every male by the edge of the sword, and razed and plundered the city. Then he passed through the city over the slain.

[52] And they crossed the Jordan into the large plain before Beth-shan.

[53] And Judas kept rallying the laggards and encouraging the people all the way till he came to the land of Judah.

[54] So they went up to Mount Zion with gladness and joy, and offered burnt offerings, because not one of them had fallen before they returned in safety.

[55] Now while Judas and Jonathan were in Gilead and Simon his brother was in Galilee before Ptolemais,

[56] Joseph, the son of Zechariah, and Azariah, the commanders of the forces, heard of their brave deeds and of the heroic war they had fought.

[57] So they said, "Let us also make a name for ourselves; let us go and make war on the Gentiles around us."

[58] And they issued orders to the men of the forces that were with them, and they marched against Jamnia.

[59] And Gorgias and his men came out of the city to meet them in battle.

[60] Then Joseph and Azariah were routed, and were pursued to the borders of Judea; as many as two thousand of the people of Israel fell that day.

[61] Thus the people suffered a great rout because, thinking to do a brave deed, they did not listen to Judas and his brothers.

[62] But they did not belong to the family of those men through whom deliverance was given to Israel.

[63] The man Judas and his brothers were greatly honored in all Israel and among all the Gentiles, wherever their name was heard.

[64] Men gathered to them and praised them.

[65] Then Judas and his brothers went forth and fought the sons of Esau in the land to the south. He struck Hebron and its villages and tore down its strongholds and burned its towers round about.

[66] Then he marched off to go into the land of the Philistines, and passed through Marisa.

[67] On that day some priests, who wished to do a brave deed, fell in battle, for they went out to battle unwisely.

[68] But Judas turned aside to Azotus in the land of the Philistines; he tore down their altars, and the graven images of their gods he burned with fire; he plundered the cities and returned to the land of Judah.

1Mac.6

[1] King Antiochus was going through the upper provinces when he heard that Elymais in Persia was a city famed for its wealth in silver and gold.

[2] Its temple was very rich, containing golden shields, breastplates, and weapons left there by Alexander, the son of Philip, the Macedonian king who first reigned over the Greeks.

[3] So he came and tried to take the city and plunder it, but he could not,

because his plan became known to the men of the city

[4] and they withstood him in battle. So he fled and in great grief departed from there to return to Babylon.

[5] Then some one came to him in Persia and reported that the armies which had gone into the land of Judah had been routed;

[6] that Lysias had gone first with a strong force, but had turned and fled before the Jews; that the Jews had grown strong from the arms, supplies, and abundant spoils which they had taken from the armies they had cut down;

[7] that they had torn down the abomination which he had erected upon the altar in Jerusalem; and that they had surrounded the sanctuary with high walls as before, and also Beth-zur, his city.

[8] When the king heard this news, he was astounded and badly shaken. He took to his bed and became sick from grief, because things had not turned out for him as he had planned.

[9] He lay there for many days, because deep grief continually gripped him, and he concluded that he was dying.

[10] So he called all his friends and said to them, "Sleep departs from my eyes and I am downhearted with worry.

[11] I said to myself, `To what distress I have come! And into what a great flood I now am plunged! For I was kind and beloved in my power.'

[12] But now I remember the evils I did in Jerusalem. I seized all her vessels of silver and gold; and I sent to destroy the inhabitants of Judah without good reason.

[13] I know that it is because of this that these evils have come upon me; and behold, I am perishing of deep grief in a strange land."

[14] Then he called for Philip, one of his friends, and made him ruler over all his kingdom.

[15] He gave him the crown and his robe and the signet, that he might guide Antiochus his son and bring him up to be king.

[16] Thus Antiochus the king died there in the one hundred and forty-ninth year.

[17] And when Lysias learned that the king was dead, he set up Antiochus the king's son to reign. Lysias had brought him up as a boy, and he named him Eupator.

[18] Now the men in the citadel kept hemming Israel in around the sanctuary. They were trying in every way to harm them and strengthen the Gentiles.

[19] So Judas decided to destroy them, and assembled all the people to besiege them.

[20] They gathered together and besieged the citadel in the one hundred and fiftieth year; and he built siege towers and other engines of war.

[21] But some of the garrison escaped from the siege and some of the

ungodly Israelites joined them.

[22] They went to the king and said, "How long will you fail to do justice and to avenge our brethren?

[23] We were happy to serve your father, to live by what he said and to follow his commands.

[24] For this reason the sons of our people besieged the citadel and became hostile to us; moreover, they have put to death as many of us as they have caught, and they have seized our inheritances.

[25] And not against us alone have they stretched out their hands, but also against all the lands on their borders.

[26] And behold, today they have encamped against the citadel in Jerusalem to take it; they have fortified both the sanctuary and Beth-zur;

[27] and unless you quickly prevent them, they will do still greater things, and you will not be able to stop them."

[28] The king was enraged when he heard this. He assembled all his friends, the commanders of his forces and those in authority.

[29] And mercenary forces came to him from other kingdoms and from islands of the seas.

[30] The number of his forces was a hundred thousand foot soldiers, twenty thousand horsemen, and thirty-two elephants accustomed to war.

[31] They came through Idumea and encamped against Beth-zur, and for many days they fought and built engines of war; but the Jews sallied out and burned these with fire, and fought manfully.

[32] Then Judas marched away from the citadel and encamped at Beth-zechariah, opposite the camp of the king.

[33] Early in the morning the king rose and took his army by a forced march along the road to Beth-zechariah, and his troops made ready for battle and sounded their trumpets.

[34] They showed the elephants the juice of grapes and mulberries, to arouse them for battle.

[35] And they distributed the beasts among the phalanxes; with each elephant they stationed a thousand men armed with coats of mail, and with brass helmets on their heads; and five hundred picked horsemen were assigned to each beast.

[36] These took their position beforehand wherever the beast was; wherever it went they went with it, and they never left it.

[37] And upon the elephants were wooden towers, strong and covered; they were fastened upon each beast by special harness, and upon each were four armed men who fought from there, and also its Indian driver.

[38] The rest of the horsemen were stationed on either side, on the two flanks of the army, to harass the enemy while being themselves protected by the phalanxes.

[39] When the sun shone upon the shields of gold and brass, the hills were ablaze with them and gleamed like flaming torches.

[40] Now a part of the king's army was spread out on the high hills, and some troops were on the plain, and they advanced steadily and in good order.

[41] All who heard the noise made by their multitude, by the marching of the multitude and the clanking of their arms, trembled, for the army was very large and strong.

[42] But Judas and his army advanced to the battle, and six hundred men of the king's army fell.

[43] And Eleazar, called Avaran, saw that one of the beasts was equipped with royal armor. It was taller than all the others, and he supposed that the king was upon it.

[44] So he gave his life to save his people and to win for himself an everlasting name.

[45] He courageously ran into the midst of the phalanx to reach it; he killed men right and left, and they parted before him on both sides.

[46] He got under the elephant, stabbed it from beneath, and killed it; but it fell to the ground upon him and he died.

[47] And when the Jews saw the royal might and the fierce attack of the forces, they turned away in flight.

[48] The soldiers of the king's army went up to Jerusalem against them, and the king encamped in Judea and at Mount Zion.

[49] He made peace with the men of Beth-zur, and they evacuated the city, because they had no provisions there to withstand a siege, since it was a sabbatical year for the land.

[50] So the king took Beth-zur and stationed a guard there to hold it.

[51] Then he encamped before the sanctuary for many days. He set up siege towers, engines of war to throw fire and stones, machines to shoot arrows, and catapults.

[52] The Jews also made engines of war to match theirs, and fought for many days.

[53] But they had no food in storage, because it was the seventh year; those who found safety in Judea from the Gentiles had consumed the last of the stores.

[54] Few men were left in the sanctuary, because famine had prevailed over the rest and they had been scattered, each to his own place.

[55] Then Lysias heard that Philip, whom King Antiochus while still living had appointed to bring up Antiochus his son to be king,

[56] had returned from Persia and Media with the forces that had gone with the king, and that he was trying to seize control of the government.

[57] So he quickly gave orders to depart, and said to the king, to the commanders of the forces, and to the men, "We daily grow weaker, our food supply is scant, the place against which we are fighting is strong, and the affairs of the kingdom press urgently upon us.

[58] Now then let us come to terms with these men, and make peace with them and with all their nation,

[59] and agree to let them live by their laws as they did before; for it was on account of their laws which we abolished that they became angry and did all these things."

[60] The speech pleased the king and the commanders, and he sent to the Jews an offer of peace, and they accepted it.

[61] So the king and the commanders gave them their oath. On these conditions the Jews evacuated the stronghold.

[62] But when the king entered Mount Zion and saw what a strong fortress the place was, he broke the oath he had sworn and gave orders to tear down the wall all around.

[63] Then he departed with haste and returned to Antioch. He found Philip in control of the city, but he fought against him, and took the city by force.

1Mac.7

[1] In the one hundred and fifty-first year Demetrius the son of Seleucus set forth from Rome, sailed with a few men to a city by the sea, and there began to reign.

[2] As he was entering the royal palace of his fathers, the army seized Antiochus and Lysias to bring them to him.

[3] But when this act became known to him, he said, "Do not let me see their faces!"

[4] So the army killed them, and Demetrius took his seat upon the throne of his kingdom.

[5] Then there came to him all the lawless and ungodly men of Israel; they were led by Alcimus, who wanted to be high priest.

[6] And they brought to the king this accusation against the people: "Judas and his brothers have destroyed all your friends, and have driven us out of our land.

[7] Now then send a man whom you trust; let him go and see all the ruin which Judas has brought upon us and upon the land of the king, and let him punish them and all who help them."

[8] So the king chose Bacchides, one of the king's friends, governor of the province Beyond the River; he was a great man in the kingdom and was faithful to the king.

[9] And he sent him, and with him the ungodly Alcimus, whom he made high priest; and he commanded him to take vengeance on the sons of Israel.

[10] So they marched away and came with a large force into the land of Judah; and he sent messengers to Judas and his brothers with peaceable but treacherous words.

[11] But they paid no attention to their words, for they saw that they had come with a large force.

[12] Then a group of scribes appeared in a body before Alcimus and Bacchides to ask for just terms.

[13] The Hasideans were first among the sons of Israel to seek peace from them,

[14] for they said, "A priest of the line of Aaron has come with the army, and he will not harm us."

[15] And he spoke peaceable words to them and swore this oath to them, "We will not seek to injure you or your friends."

[16] So they trusted him; but he seized sixty of them and killed them in one day, in accordance with the word which was written,

[17] "The flesh of thy saints and their blood they poured out round about Jerusalem, and there was none to bury them."

[18] Then the fear and dread of them fell upon all the people, for they said, "There is no truth or justice in them, for they have violated the agreement and the oath which they swore."

[19] Then Bacchides departed from Jerusalem and encamped in Beth-zaith. And he sent and seized many of the men who had deserted to him, and some of the people, and killed them and threw them into a great pit.

[20] He placed Alcimus in charge of the country and left with him a force to help him; then Bacchides went back to the king.

[21] Alcimus strove for the high priesthood,

[22] and all who were troubling their people joined him. They gained control of the land of Judah and did great damage in Israel.

[23] And Judas saw all the evil that Alcimus and those with him had done among the sons of Israel; it was more than the Gentiles had done.

[24] So Judas went out into all the surrounding parts of Judea, and took vengeance on the men who had deserted, and he prevented those in the city from going out into the country.

[25] When Alcimus saw that Judas and those with him had grown strong, and realized that he could not withstand them, he returned to the king and brought wicked charges against them.

[26] Then the king sent Nicanor, one of his honored princes, who hated and detested Israel, and he commanded him to destroy the people.

[27] So Nicanor came to Jerusalem with a large force, and treacherously sent to Judas and his brothers this peaceable message,

[28] "Let there be no fighting between me and you; I shall come with a few men to see you face to face in peace."

[29] So he came to Judas, and they greeted one another peaceably. But the enemy were ready to seize Judas.

[30] It became known to Judas that Nicanor had come to him with treacherous intent, and he was afraid of him and would not meet him again.

[31] When Nicanor learned that his plan had been disclosed, he went out to meet Judas in battle near Caphar-salama.

[32] About five hundred men of the army of Nicanor fell, and the rest fled into the city of David.

[33] After these events Nicanor went up to Mount Zion. Some of the priests came out of the sanctuary, and some of the elders of the people, to greet him peaceably and to show him the burnt offering that was being offered for the king.

[34] But he mocked them and derided them and defiled them and spoke arrogantly,

[35] and in anger he swore this oath, "Unless Judas and his army are delivered into my hands this time, then if I return safely I will burn up this house." And he went out in great anger.

[36] Then the priests went in and stood before the altar and the temple, and they wept and said,

[37] "Thou didst choose this house to be called by thy name, and to be for thy people a house of prayer and supplication.

[38] Take vengeance on this man and on his army, and let them fall by the sword; remember their blasphemies, and let them live no longer."

[39] Now Nicanor went out from Jerusalem and encamped in Beth-horon, and the Syrian army joined him.

[40] And Judas encamped in Adasa with three thousand men. Then Judas prayed and said,

[41] "When the messengers from the king spoke blasphemy, thy angel went forth and struck down one hundred and eighty-five thousand of the Assyrians.

[42] So also crush this army before us today; let the rest learn that Nicanor has spoken wickedly against the sanctuary, and judge him according to this wickedness."

[43] So the armies met in battle on the thirteenth day of the month of Adar. The army of Nicanor was crushed, and he himself was the first to fall in the battle.

[44] When his army saw that Nicanor had fallen, they threw down their arms and fled.

[45] The Jews pursued them a day's journey, from Adasa as far as Gazara, and as they followed kept sounding the battle call on the trumpets.

[46] And men came out of all the villages of Judea round about, and they out-flanked the enemy and drove them back to their pursuers, so that they all fell by the sword; not even one of them was left.

[47] Then the Jews seized the spoils and the plunder, and they cut off Nicanor's head and the right hand which he so arrogantly stretched out, and brought them and displayed them just outside Jerusalem.

[48] The people rejoiced greatly and celebrated that day as a day of great gladness.

[49] And they decreed that this day should be celebrated each year on the thirteenth day of Adar.

[50] So the land of Judah had rest for a few days.

1Mac.8

[1] Now Judas heard of the fame of the Romans, that they were very strong and were well-disposed toward all who made an alliance with them, that they pledged friendship to those who came to them,

[2] and that they were very strong. Men told him of their wars and of the brave deeds which they were doing among the Gauls, how they had defeated them and forced them to pay tribute,

[3] and what they had done in the land of Spain to get control of the silver and gold mines there,

[4] and how they had gained control of the whole region by their planning and patience, even though the place was far distant from them. They also subdued the kings who came against them from the ends of the earth, until they crushed them and inflicted great disaster upon them; the rest paid them tribute every year.

[5] Philip, and Perseus king of the Macedonians, and the others who rose up against them, they crushed in battle and conquered.

[6] They also defeated Antiochus the Great, king of Asia, who went to fight against them with a hundred and twenty elephants and with cavalry and chariots and a very large army. He was crushed by them;

[7] they took him alive and decreed that he and those who should reign after him should pay a heavy tribute and give hostages and surrender some of their best provinces,

[8] the country of India and Media and Lydia. These they took from him and gave to Eumenes the king.

[9] The Greeks planned to come and destroy them,

[10] but this became known to them, and they sent a general against the Greeks and attacked them. Many of them were wounded and fell, and the Romans took captive their wives and children; they plundered them, conquered the land, tore down their strongholds, and enslaved them to this day.

[11] The remaining kingdoms and islands, as many as ever opposed them, they destroyed and enslaved;

[12] but with their friends and those who rely on them they have kept friendship. They have subdued kings far and near, and as many as have heard of their fame have feared them.

[13] Those whom they wish to help and to make kings, they make kings, and those whom they wish they depose; and they have been greatly exalted.

[14] Yet for all this not one of them has put on a crown or worn purple as a mark of pride,

[15] but they have built for themselves a senate chamber, and every day three hundred and twenty senators constantly deliberate concerning the people, to govern them well.

[16] They trust one man each year to rule over them and to control all their land; they all heed the one man, and there is no envy or jealousy among

them.

[17] So Judas chose Eupolemus the son of John, son of Accos, and Jason the son of Eleazar, and sent them to Rome to establish friendship and alliance,

[18] and to free themselves from the yoke; for they saw that the kingdom of the Greeks was completely enslaving Israel.

[19] They went to Rome, a very long journey; and they entered the senate chamber and spoke as follows:

[20] "Judas, who is also called Maccabeus, and his brothers and the people of the Jews have sent us to you to establish alliance and peace with you, that we may be enrolled as your allies and friends."

[21] The proposal pleased them,

[22] and this is a copy of the letter which they wrote in reply, on bronze tablets, and sent to Jerusalem to remain with them there as a memorial of peace and alliance:

[23] "May all go well with the Romans and with the nation of the Jews at sea and on land for ever, and may sword and enemy be far from them.

[24] If war comes first to Rome or to any of their allies in all their dominion,

[25] the nation of the Jews shall act as their allies wholeheartedly, as the occasion may indicate to them.

[26] And to the enemy who makes war they shall not give or supply grain, arms, money, or ships, as Rome has decided; and they shall keep their obligations without receiving any return.

[27] In the same way, if war comes first to the nation of the Jews, the Romans shall willingly act as their allies, as the occasion may indicate to them.

[28] And to the enemy allies shall be given no grain, arms, money, or ships, as Rome has decided; and they shall keep these obligations and do so without deceit.

[29] Thus on these terms the Romans make a treaty with the Jewish people.

[30] If after these terms are in effect both parties shall determine to add or delete anything, they shall do so at their discretion, and any addition or deletion that they may make shall be valid.

[31] "And concerning the wrongs which King Demetrius is doing to them we have written to him as follows, `Why have you made your yoke heavy upon our friends and allies the Jews?

[32] If now they appeal again for help against you, we will defend their rights and fight you on sea and on land.'"

1Mac.9

[1] When Demetrius heard that Nicanor and his army had fallen in battle, he sent Bacchides and Alcimus into the land of Judah a second time, and with them the right wing of the army.

[2] They went by the road which leads to Gilgal and encamped against Mesaloth in Arbela, and they took it and killed many people.

[3] In the first month of the one hundred and fifty-second year they

encamped against Jerusalem;

[4] then they marched off and went to Berea with twenty thousand foot soldiers and two thousand cavalry.

[5] Now Judas was encamped in Elasa, and with him were three thousand picked men.

[6] When they saw the huge number of the enemy forces, they were greatly frightened, and many slipped away from the camp, until no more than eight hundred of them were left.

[7] When Judas saw that his army had slipped away and the battle was imminent, he was crushed in spirit, for he had no time to assemble them.

[8] He became faint, but he said to those who were left, "Let us rise and go up against our enemies. We may be able to fight them."

[9] But they tried to dissuade him, saying, "We are not able. Let us rather save our own lives now, and let us come back with our brethren and fight them; we are too few."

[10] But Judas said, "Far be it from us to do such a thing as to flee from them. If our time has come, let us die bravely for our brethren, and leave no cause to question our honor."

[11] Then the army of Bacchides marched out from the camp and took its stand for the encounter. The cavalry was divided into two companies, and the slingers and the archers went ahead of the army, as did all the chief warriors.

[12] Bacchides was on the right wing. Flanked by the two companies, the phalanx advanced to the sound of the trumpets; and the men with Judas also blew their trumpets.

[13] The earth was shaken by the noise of the armies, and the battle raged from morning till evening.

[14] Judas saw that Bacchides and the strength of his army were on the right; then all the stouthearted men went with him,

[15] and they crushed the right wing, and he pursued them as far as Mount Azotus.

[16] When those on the left wing saw that the right wing was crushed, they turned and followed close behind Judas and his men.

[17] The battle became desperate, and many on both sides were wounded and fell.

[18] Judas also fell, and the rest fled.

[19] Then Jonathan and Simon took Judas their brother and buried him in the tomb of their fathers at Modein,

[20] and wept for him. And all Israel made great lamentation for him; they mourned many days and said,

[21] "How is the mighty fallen, the savior of Israel!"

[22] Now the rest of the acts of Judas, and his wars and the brave deeds that he did, and his greatness, have not been recorded, for they were very many.

[23] After the death of Judas, the lawless emerged in all parts of Israel; all the doers of injustice appeared.

[24] In those days a very great famine occurred, and the country deserted with them to the enemy.

[25] And Bacchides chose the ungodly and put them in charge of the country.

[26] They sought and searched for the friends of Judas, and brought them to Bacchides, and he took vengeance on them and made sport of them.

[27] Thus there was great distress in Israel, such as had not been since the time that prophets ceased to appear among them.

[28] Then all the friends of Judas assembled and said to Jonathan,

[29] "Since the death of your brother Judas there has been no one like him to go against our enemies and Bacchides, and to deal with those of our nation who hate us.

[30] So now we have chosen you today to take his place as our ruler and leader, to fight our battle."

[31] And Jonathan at that time accepted the leadership and took the place of Judas his brother.

[32] When Bacchides learned of this, he tried to kill him.

[33] But Jonathan and Simon his brother and all who were with him heard of it, and they fled into the wilderness of Tekoa and camped by the water of the pool of Asphar.

[34] Bacchides found this out on the sabbath day, and he with all his army crossed the Jordan.

[35] And Jonathan sent his brother as leader of the multitude and begged the Nabateans, who were his friends, for permission to store with them the great amount of baggage which they had.

[36] But the sons of Jambri from Medeba came out and seized John and all that he had, and departed with it.

[37] After these things it was reported to Jonathan and Simon his brother, "The sons of Jambri are celebrating a great wedding, and are conducting the bride, a daughter of one of the great nobles of Canaan, from Nadabath with a large escort."

[38] And they remembered the blood of John their brother, and went up and hid under cover of the mountain.

[39] They raised their eyes and looked, and saw a tumultuous procession with much baggage; and the bridegroom came out with his friends and his brothers to meet them with tambourines and musicians and many weapons.

[40] Then they rushed upon them from the ambush and began killing them. Many were wounded and fell, and the rest fled to the mountain; and they took all their goods.

[41] Thus the wedding was turned into mourning and the voice of their musicians into a funeral dirge.

[42] And when they had fully avenged the blood of their brother, they

returned to the marshes of the Jordan.

[43] When Bacchides heard of this, he came with a large force on the sabbath day to the banks of the Jordan.

[44] And Jonathan said to those with him, "Let us rise up now and fight for our lives, for today things are not as they were before.

[45] For look! the battle is in front of us and behind us; the water of the Jordan is on this side and on that, with marsh and thicket; there is no place to turn.

[46] Cry out now to Heaven that you may be delivered from the hands of our enemies."

[47] So the battle began, and Jonathan stretched out his hand to strike Bacchides, but he eluded him and went to the rear.

[48] Then Jonathan and the men with him leaped into the Jordan and swam across to the other side, and the enemy did not cross the Jordan to attack them.

[49] And about one thousand of Bacchides' men fell that day.

[50] Bacchides then returned to Jerusalem and built strong cities in Judea: the fortress in Jericho, and Emmaus, and Beth-horon, and Bethel, and Timnath, and Pharathon, and Tephon, with high walls and gates and bars.

[51] And he placed garrisons in them to harass Israel.

[52] He also fortified the city of Beth-zur, and Gazara, and the citadel, and in them he put troops and stores of food.

[53] And he took the sons of the leading men of the land as hostages and put them under guard in the citadel at Jerusalem.

[54] In the one hundred and fifty-third year, in the second month, Alcimus gave orders to tear down the wall of the inner court of the sanctuary. He tore down the work of the prophets!

[55] But he only began to tear it down, for at that time Alcimus was stricken and his work was hindered; his mouth was stopped and he was paralyzed, so that he could no longer say a word or give commands concerning his house.

[56] And Alcimus died at that time in great agony.

[57] When Bacchides saw that Alcimus was dead, he returned to the king, and the land of Judah had rest for two years.

[58] Then all the lawless plotted and said, "See! Jonathan and his men are living in quiet and confidence. So now let us bring Bacchides back, and he will capture them all in one night."

[59] And they went and consulted with him.

[60] He started to come with a large force, and secretly sent letters to all his allies in Judea, telling them to seize Jonathan and his men; but they were unable to do it, because their plan became known.

[61] And Jonathan's men seized about fifty of the men of the country who were leaders in this treachery, and killed them.

[62] Then Jonathan with his men, and Simon, withdrew to Bethbasi in the wilderness; he rebuilt the parts of it that had been demolished, and they fortified it.

[63] When Bacchides learned of this, he assembled all his forces, and sent orders to the men of Judea.

[64] Then he came and encamped against Bethbasi; he fought against it for many days and made machines of war.

[65] But Jonathan left Simon his brother in the city, while he went out into the country; and he went with only a few men.

[66] He struck down Odomera and his brothers and the sons of Phasiron in their tents.

[67] Then he began to attack and went into battle with his forces; and Simon and his men sallied out from the city and set fire to the machines of war.

[68] They fought with Bacchides, and he was crushed by them. They distressed him greatly, for his plan and his expedition had been in vain.

[69] So he was greatly enraged at the lawless men who had counseled him to come into the country, and he killed many of them. Then he decided to depart to his own land.

[70] When Jonathan learned of this, he sent ambassadors to him to make peace with him and obtain release of the captives.

[71] He agreed, and did as he said; and he swore to Jonathan that he would not try to harm him as long as he lived.

[72] He restored to him the captives whom he had formerly taken from the land of Judah; then he turned and departed to his own land, and came no more into their territory.

[73] Thus the sword ceased from Israel. And Jonathan dwelt in Michmash. And Jonathan began to judge the people, and he destroyed the ungodly out of Israel.

1Mac.10

[1] In the one hundred and sixtieth year Alexander Epiphanes, the son of Antiochus, landed and occupied Ptolemais. They welcomed him, and there he began to reign.

[2] When Demetrius the king heard of it, he assembled a very large army and marched out to meet him in battle.

[3] And Demetrius sent Jonathan a letter in peaceable words to honor him;

[4] for he said, "Let us act first to make peace with him before he makes peace with Alexander against us,

[5] for he will remember all the wrongs which we did to him and to his brothers and his nation."

[6] So Demetrius gave him authority to recruit troops, to equip them with arms, and to become his ally; and he commanded that the hostages in the citadel should be released to him.

[7] Then Jonathan came to Jerusalem and read the letter in the hearing of all the people and of the men in the citadel.

[8] They were greatly alarmed when they heard that the king had given him authority to recruit troops.

[9] But the men in the citadel released the hostages to Jonathan, and he returned them to their parents.

[10] And Jonathan dwelt in Jerusalem and began to rebuild and restore the city.

[11] He directed those who were doing the work to build the walls and encircle Mount Zion with squared stones, for better fortification; and they did so.

[12] Then the foreigners who were in the strongholds that Bacchides had built fled;

[13] each left his place and departed to his own land.

[14] Only in Beth-zur did some remain who had forsaken the law and the commandments, for it served as a place of refuge.

[15] Now Alexander the king heard of all the promises which Demetrius had sent to Jonathan, and men told him of the battles that Jonathan and his brothers had fought, of the brave deeds that they had done, and of the troubles that they had endured.

[16] So he said, "Shall we find another such man? Come now, we will make him our friend and ally."

[17] And he wrote a letter and sent it to him, in the following words:

[18] "King Alexander to his brother Jonathan, greeting.

[19] We have heard about you, that you are a mighty warrior and worthy to be our friend.

[20] And so we have appointed you today to be the high priest of your nation; you are to be called the king's friend" (and he sent him a purple robe and a golden crown) "and you are to take our side and keep friendship with us."

[21] So Jonathan put on the holy garments in the seventh month of the one hundred and sixtieth year, at the feast of tabernacles, and he recruited troops and equipped them with arms in abundance.

[22] When Demetrius heard of these things he was grieved and said,

[23] "What is this that we have done? Alexander has gotten ahead of us in forming a friendship with the Jews to strengthen himself.

[24] I also will write them words of encouragement and promise them honor and gifts, that I may have their help."

[25] So he sent a message to them in the following words: "King Demetrius to the nation of the Jews, greeting.

[26] Since you have kept your agreement with us and have continued your friendship with us, and have not sided with our enemies, we have heard of it and rejoiced.

[27] And now continue still to keep faith with us, and we will repay you with good for what you do for us.

[28] We will grant you many immunities and give you gifts.

[29] "And now I free you and exempt all the Jews from payment of tribute and salt tax and crown levies,

[30] and instead of collecting the third of the grain and the half of the fruit of the trees that I should receive, I release them from this day and henceforth. I will not collect them from the land of Judah or from the three districts added to it from Samaria and Galilee, from this day and for all time.

[31] And let Jerusalem and her environs, her tithes and her revenues, be holy and free from tax.

[32] I release also my control of the citadel in Jerusalem and give it to the high priest, that he may station in it men of his own choice to guard it.

[33] And every one of the Jews taken as a captive from the land of Judah into any part of my kingdom, I set free without payment; and let all officials cancel also the taxes on their cattle.

[34] "And all the feasts and sabbaths and new moons and appointed days, and the three days before a feast and the three after a feast -- let them all be days of immunity and release for all the Jews who are in my kingdom.

[35] No one shall have authority to exact anything from them or annoy any of them about any matter.

[36] "Let Jews be enrolled in the king's forces to the number of thirty thousand men, and let the maintenance be given them that is due to all the forces of the king.

[37] Let some of them be stationed in the great strongholds of the king, and let some of them be put in positions of trust in the kingdom. Let their officers and leaders be of their own number, and let them live by their own laws, just as the king has commanded in the land of Judah.

[38] "As for the three districts that have been added to Judea from the country of Samaria, let them be so annexed to Judea that they are considered to be under one ruler and obey no other authority but the high priest.

[39] Ptolemais and the land adjoining it I have given as a gift to the sanctuary in Jerusalem, to meet the necessary expenses of the sanctuary.

[40] I also grant fifteen thousand shekels of silver yearly out of the king's revenues from appropriate places.

[41] And all the additional funds which the government officials have not paid as they did in the first years, they shall give from now on for the service of the temple.

[42] Moreover, the five thousand shekels of silver which my officials have received every year from the income of the services of the temple, this too is canceled, because it belongs to the priests who minister there.

[43] And whoever takes refuge at the temple in Jerusalem, or in any of its precincts, because he owes money to the king or has any debt, let him be released and receive back all his property in my kingdom.

[44] "Let the cost of rebuilding and restoring the structures of the sanctuary

be paid from the revenues of the king.

[45] And let the cost of rebuilding the walls of Jerusalem and fortifying it round about, and the cost of rebuilding the walls in Judea, also be paid from the revenues of the king."

[46] When Jonathan and the people heard these words, they did not believe or accept them, because they remembered the great wrongs which Demetrius had done in Israel and how he had greatly oppressed them.

[47] They favored Alexander, because he had been the first to speak peaceable words to them, and they remained his allies all his days.

[48] Now Alexander the king assembled large forces and encamped opposite Demetrius.

[49] The two kings met in battle, and the army of Demetrius fled, and Alexander pursued him and defeated them.

[50] He pressed the battle strongly until the sun set, and Demetrius fell on that day.

[51] Then Alexander sent ambassadors to Ptolemy king of Egypt with the following message:

[52] "Since I have returned to my kingdom and have taken my seat on the throne of my fathers, and established my rule -- for I crushed Demetrius and gained control of our country;

[53] I met him in battle, and he and his army were crushed by us, and we have taken our seat on the throne of his kingdom --

[54] now therefore let us establish friendship with one another; give me now your daughter as my wife, and I will become your son-in-law, and will make gifts to you and to her in keeping with your position."

[55] Ptolemy the king replied and said, "Happy was the day on which you returned to the land of your fathers and took your seat on the throne of their kingdom.

[56] And now I will do for you as you wrote, but meet me at Ptolemais, so that we may see one another, and I will become your father-in-law, as you have said."

[57] So Ptolemy set out from Egypt, he and Cleopatra his daughter, and came to Ptolemais in the one hundred and sixty-second year.

[58] Alexander the king met him, and Ptolemy gave him Cleopatra his daughter in marriage, and celebrated her wedding at Ptolemais with great pomp, as kings do.

[59] Then Alexander the king wrote to Jonathan to come to meet him.

[60] So he went with pomp to Ptolemais and met the two kings; he gave them and their friends silver and gold and many gifts, and found favor with them.

[61] A group of pestilent men from Israel, lawless men, gathered together against him to accuse him; but the king paid no attention to them.

[62] The king gave orders to take off Jonathan's garments and to clothe him

in purple, and they did so.

[63] The king also seated him at his side; and he said to his officers, "Go forth with him into the middle of the city and proclaim that no one is to bring charges against him about any matter, and let no one annoy him for any reason."

[64] And when his accusers saw the honor that was paid him, in accordance with the proclamation, and saw him clothed in purple, they all fled.

[65] Thus the king honored him and enrolled him among his chief friends, and made him general and governor of the province.

[66] And Jonathan returned to Jerusalem in peace and gladness.

[67] In the one hundred and sixty-fifth year Demetrius the son of Demetrius came from Crete to the land of his fathers.

[68] When Alexander the king heard of it, he was greatly grieved and returned to Antioch.

[69] And Demetrius appointed Apollonius the governor of Coelesyria, and he assembled a large force and encamped against Jamnia. Then he sent the following message to Jonathan the high priest:

[70] "You are the only one to rise up against us, and I have become a laughingstock and reproach because of you. Why do you assume authority against us in the hill country?

[71] If you now have confidence in your forces, come down to the plain to meet us, and let us match strength with each other there, for I have with me the power of the cities.

[72] Ask and learn who I am and who the others are that are helping us. Men will tell you that you cannot stand before us, for your fathers were twice put to flight in their own land.

[73] And now you will not be able to withstand my cavalry and such an army in the plain, where there is no stone or pebble, or place to flee."

[74] When Jonathan heard the words of Apollonius, his spirit was aroused. He chose ten thousand men and set out from Jerusalem, and Simon his brother met him to help him.

[75] He encamped before Joppa, but the men of the city closed its gates, for Apollonius had a garrison in Joppa.

[76] So they fought against it, and the men of the city became afraid and opened the gates, and Jonathan gained possession of Joppa.

[77] When Apollonius heard of it, he mustered three thousand cavalry and a large army, and went to Azotus as though he were going farther. At the same time he advanced into the plain, for he had a large troop of cavalry and put confidence in it.

[78] Jonathan pursued him to Azotus, and the armies engaged in battle.

[79] Now Apollonius had secretly left a thousand cavalry behind them.

[80] Jonathan learned that there was an ambush behind him, for they surrounded his army and shot arrows at his men from early morning till late afternoon.

[81] But his men stood fast, as Jonathan commanded, and the enemy's horses grew tired.

[82] Then Simon brought forward his force and engaged the phalanx in battle (for the cavalry was exhausted); they were overwhelmed by him and fled,

[83] and the cavalry was dispersed in the plain. They fled to Azotus and entered Beth-dagon, the temple of their idol, for safety.

[84] But Jonathan burned Azotus and the surrounding towns and plundered them; and the temple of Dagon, and those who had taken refuge in it he burned with fire.

[85] The number of those who fell by the sword, with those burned alive, came to eight thousand men.

[86] Then Jonathan departed from there and encamped against Askalon, and the men of the city came out to meet him with great pomp.

[87] And Jonathan and those with him returned to Jerusalem with much booty.

[88] When Alexander the king heard of these things, he honored Jonathan still more;

[89] and he sent to him a golden buckle, such as it is the custom to give to the kinsmen of kings. He also gave him Ekron and all its environs as his possession.

1Mac.11

[1] Then the king of Egypt gathered great forces, like the sand by the seashore, and many ships; and he tried to get possession of Alexander's kingdom by trickery and add it to his own kingdom.

[2] He set out for Syria with peaceable words, and the people of the cities opened their gates to him and went to meet him, for Alexander the king had commanded them to meet him, since he was Alexander's father-in-law.

[3] But when Ptolemy entered the cities he stationed forces as a garrison in each city.

[4] When he approached Azotus, they showed him the temple of Dagon burned down, and Azotus and its suburbs destroyed, and the corpses lying about, and the charred bodies of those whom Jonathan had burned in the war, for they had piled them in heaps along his route.

[5] They also told the king what Jonathan had done, to throw blame on him; but the king kept silent.

[6] Jonathan met the king at Joppa with pomp, and they greeted one another and spent the night there.

[7] And Jonathan went with the king as far as the river called Eleutherus; then he returned to Jerusalem.

[8] So King Ptolemy gained control of the coastal cities as far as Seleucia by the sea, and he kept devising evil designs against Alexander.

[9] He sent envoys to Demetrius the king, saying, "Come, let us make a

covenant with each other, and I will give you in marriage my daughter who was Alexander's wife, and you shall reign over your father's kingdom.

[10] For I now regret that I gave him my daughter, for he has tried to kill me."

[11] He threw blame on Alexander because he coveted his kingdom.

[12] So he took his daughter away from him and gave her to Demetrius. He was estranged from Alexander, and their enmity became manifest.

[13] Then Ptolemy entered Antioch and put on the crown of Asia. Thus he put two crowns upon his head, the crown of Egypt and that of Asia.

[14] Now Alexander the king was in Cilicia at that time, because the people of that region were in revolt.

[15] And Alexander heard of it and came against him in battle. Ptolemy marched out and met him with a strong force, and put him to flight.

[16] So Alexander fled into Arabia to find protection there, and King Ptolemy was exalted.

[17] And Zabdiel the Arab cut off the head of Alexander and sent it to Ptolemy.

[18] But King Ptolemy died three days later, and his troops in the strongholds were killed by the inhabitants of the strongholds.

[19] So Demetrius became king in the one hundred and sixty-seventh year.

[20] In those days Jonathan assembled the men of Judea to attack the citadel in Jerusalem, and he built many engines of war to use against it.

[21] But certain lawless men who hated their nation went to the king and reported to him that Jonathan was besieging the citadel.

[22] When he heard this he was angry, and as soon as he heard it he set out and came to Ptolemais; and he wrote Jonathan not to continue the siege, but to meet him for a conference at Ptolemais as quickly as possible.

[23] When Jonathan heard this, he gave orders to continue the siege; and he chose some of the elders of Israel and some of the priests, and put himself in danger,

[24] for he went to the king at Ptolemais, taking silver and gold and clothing and numerous other gifts. And he won his favor.

[25] Although certain lawless men of his nation kept making complaints against him,

[26] the king treated him as his predecessors had treated him; he exalted him in the presence of all his friends.

[27] He confirmed him in the high priesthood and in as many other honors as he had formerly had, and made him to be regarded as one of his chief friends.

[28] Then Jonathan asked the king to free Judea and the three districts of Samaria from tribute, and promised him three hundred talents.

[29] The king consented, and wrote a letter to Jonathan about all these things; its contents were as follows:

[30] "King Demetrius to Jonathan his brother and to the nation of the Jews,

greeting.

[31] This copy of the letter which we wrote concerning you to Lasthenes our kinsman we have written to you also, so that you may know what it says.

[32] `King Demetrius to Lasthenes his father, greeting.

[33] To the nation of the Jews, who are our friends and fulfil their obligations to us, we have determined to do good, because of the good will they show toward us.

[34] We have confirmed as their possession both the territory of Judea and the three districts of Aphairema and Lydda and Rathamin; the latter, with all the region bordering them, were added to Judea from Samaria. To all those who offer sacrifice in Jerusalem, we have granted release from the royal taxes which the king formerly received from them each year, from the crops of the land and the fruit of the trees.

[35] And the other payments henceforth due to us of the tithes, and the taxes due to us, and the salt pits and the crown taxes due to us -- from all these we shall grant them release.

[36] And not one of these grants shall be canceled from this time forth for ever.

[37] Now therefore take care to make a copy of this, and let it be given to Jonathan and put up in a conspicuous place on the holy mountain.'"

[38] Now when Demetrius the king saw that the land was quiet before him and that there was no opposition to him, he dismissed all his troops, each man to his own place, except the foreign troops which he had recruited from the islands of the nations. So all the troops who had served his fathers hated him.

[39] Now Trypho had formerly been one of Alexander's supporters. He saw that all the troops were murmuring against Demetrius. So he went to Imalkue the Arab, who was bringing up Antiochus, the young son of Alexander,

[40] and insistently urged him to hand Antiochus over to him, to become king in place of his father. He also reported to Imalkue what Demetrius had done and told of the hatred which the troops of Demetrius had for him; and he stayed there many days.

[41] Now Jonathan sent to Demetrius the king the request that he remove the troops of the citadel from Jerusalem, and the troops in the strongholds; for they kept fighting against Israel.

[42] And Demetrius sent this message to Jonathan, "Not only will I do these things for you and your nation, but I will confer great honor on you and your nation, if I find an opportunity.

[43] Now then you will do well to send me men who will help me, for all my troops have revolted."

[44] So Jonathan sent three thousand stalwart men to him at Antioch, and when they came to the king, the king rejoiced at their arrival.

[45] Then the men of the city assembled within the city, to the number of a hundred and twenty thousand, and they wanted to kill the king.

[46] But the king fled into the palace. Then the men of the city seized the main streets of the city and began to fight.

[47] So the king called the Jews to his aid, and they all rallied about him and then spread out through the city; and they killed on that day as many as a hundred thousand men.

[48] They set fire to the city and seized much spoil on that day, and they saved the king.

[49] When the men of the city saw that the Jews had gained control of the city as they pleased, their courage failed and they cried out to the king with this entreaty,

[50] "Grant us peace, and make the Jews stop fighting against us and our city."

[51] And they threw down their arms and made peace. So the Jews gained glory in the eyes of the king and of all the people in his kingdom, and they returned to Jerusalem with much spoil.

[52] So Demetrius the king sat on the throne of his kingdom, and the land was quiet before him.

[53] But he broke his word about all that he had promised; and he became estranged from Jonathan and did not repay the favors which Jonathan had done him, but oppressed him greatly.

[54] After this Trypho returned, and with him the young boy Antiochus who began to reign and put on the crown.

[55] All the troops that Demetrius had cast off gathered around him, and they fought against Demetrius, and he fled and was routed.

[56] And Trypho captured the elephants and gained control of Antioch.

[57] Then the young Antiochus wrote to Jonathan, saying, "I confirm you in the high priesthood and set you over the four districts and make you one of the friends of the king."

[58] And he sent him gold plate and a table service, and granted him the right to drink from gold cups and dress in purple and wear a gold buckle.

[59] Simon his brother he made governor from the Ladder of Tyre to the borders of Egypt.

[60] Then Jonathan set forth and traveled beyond the river and among the cities, and all the army of Syria gathered to him as allies. When he came to Askalon, the people of the city met him and paid him honor.

[61] From there he departed to Gaza, but the men of Gaza shut him out. So he besieged it and burned its suburbs with fire and plundered them.

[62] Then the people of Gaza pleaded with Jonathan, and he made peace with them, and took the sons of their rulers as hostages and sent them to Jerusalem. And he passed through the country as far as Damascus.

[63] Then Jonathan heard that the officers of Demetrius had come to Kadesh in Galilee with a large army, intending to remove him from office.

[64] He went to meet them, but left his brother Simon in the country.

[65] Simon encamped before Beth-zur and fought against it for many days and hemmed it in.

[66] Then they asked him to grant them terms of peace, and he did so. He removed them from there, took possession of the city, and set a garrison over it.

[67] Jonathan and his army encamped by the waters of Gennesaret. Early in the morning they marched to the plain of Hazor,

[68] and behold, the army of the foreigners met him in the plain; they had set an ambush against him in the mountains, but they themselves met him face to face.

[69] Then the men in ambush emerged from their places and joined battle.

[70] All the men with Jonathan fled; not one of them was left except Mattathias the son of Absalom and Judas the son of Chalphi, commanders of the forces of the army.

[71] Jonathan rent his garments and put dust on his head, and prayed.

[72] Then he turned back to the battle against the enemy and routed them, and they fled.

[73] When his men who were fleeing saw this, they returned to him and joined him in the pursuit as far as Kadesh, to their camp, and there they encamped.

[74] As many as three thousand of the foreigners fell that day. And Jonathan returned to Jerusalem.

1Mac.12

[1] Now when Jonathan saw that the time was favorable for him, he chose men and sent them to Rome to confirm and renew the friendship with them.

[2] He also sent letters to the same effect to the Spartans and to other places.

[3] So they went to Rome and entered the senate chamber and said, "Jonathan the high priest and the Jewish nation have sent us to renew the former friendship and alliance with them."

[4] And the Romans gave them letters to the people in every place, asking them to provide for the envoys safe conduct to the land of Judah.

[5] This is a copy of the letter which Jonathan wrote to the Spartans:

[6] "Jonathan the high priest, the senate of the nation, the priests, and the rest of the Jewish people to their brethren the Spartans, greeting.

[7] Already in time past a letter was sent to Onias the high priest from Arius, who was king among you, stating that you are our brethren, as the appended copy shows.

[8] Onias welcomed the envoy with honor, and received the letter, which contained a clear declaration of alliance and friendship.

[9] Therefore, though we have no need of these things, since we have as encouragement the holy books which are in our hands,

[10] we have undertaken to send to renew our brotherhood and friendship

with you, so that we may not become estranged from you, for considerable time has passed since you sent your letter to us.

[11] We therefore remember you constantly on every occasion, both in our feasts and on other appropriate days, at the sacrifices which we offer and in our prayers, as it is right and proper to remember brethren.

[12] And we rejoice in your glory.

[13] But as for ourselves, many afflictions and many wars have encircled us; the kings round about us have waged war against us.

[14] We were unwilling to annoy you and our other allies and friends with these wars,

[15] for we have the help which comes from Heaven for our aid; and we were delivered from our enemies and our enemies were humbled.

[16] We therefore have chosen Numenius the son of Antiochus and Antipater the son of Jason, and have sent them to Rome to renew our former friendship and alli ance with them.

[17] We have commanded them to go also to you and greet you and deliver to you this letter from us concerning the renewal of our brotherhood.

[18] And now please send us a reply to this."

[19] This is a copy of the letter which they sent to Onias:

[20] "Arius, king of the Spartans, to Onias the high priest, greeting.

[21] It has been found in writing concerning the Spartans and the Jews that they are brethren and are of the family of Abraham.

[22] And now that we have learned this, please write us concerning your welfare;

[23] we on our part write to you that your cattle and your property belong to us, and ours belong to you. We therefore command that our envoys report to you accordingly."

[24] Now Jonathan heard that the commanders of Demetrius had returned, with a larger force than before, to wage war against him.

[25] So he marched away from Jerusalem and met them in the region of Hamath, for he gave them no opportunity to invade his own country.

[26] He sent spies to their camp, and they returned and reported to him that the enemy were being drawn up in formation to fall upon the Jews by night.

[27] So when the sun set, Jonathan commanded his men to be alert and to keep their arms at hand so as to be ready all night for battle, and he stationed outposts around the camp.

[28] When the enemy heard that Jonathan and his men were prepared for battle, they were afraid and were terrified at heart; so they kindled fires in their camp and withdrew.

[29] But Jonathan and his men did not know it until morning, for they saw the fires burning.

[30] Then Jonathan pursued them, but he did not overtake them, for they had crossed the Eleutherus river.

[31] So Jonathan turned aside against the Arabs who are called Zabadeans,

and he crushed them and plundered them.

[32] Then he broke camp and went to Damascus, and marched through all that region.

[33] Simon also went forth and marched through the country as far as Askalon and the neighboring strongholds. He turned aside to Joppa and took it by surprise,

[34] for he had heard that they were ready to hand over the stronghold to the men whom Demetrius had sent. And he stationed a garrison there to guard it.

[35] When Jonathan returned he convened the elders of the people and planned with them to build strongholds in Judea,

[36] to build the walls of Jerusalem still higher, and to erect a high barrier between the citadel and the city to separate it from the city, in order to isolate it so that its garrison could neither buy nor sell.

[37] So they gathered together to build up the city; part of the wall on the valley to the east had fallen, and he repaired the section called Chaphenatha.

[38] And Simon built Adida in the Shephelah; he fortified it and installed gates with bolts.

[39] Then Trypho attempted to become king in Asia and put on the crown, and to raise his hand against Antiochus the king.

[40] He feared that Jonathan might not permit him to do so, but might make war on him, so he kept seeking to seize and kill him, and he marched forth and came to Beth-shan.

[41] Jonathan went out to meet him with forty thousand picked fighting men, and he came to Beth-shan.

[42] When Trypho saw that he had come with a large army, he was afraid to raise his hand against him.

[43] So he received him with honor and commended him to all his friends, and he gave him gifts and commanded his friends and his troops to obey him as they would himself.

[44] Then he said to Jonathan, "Why have you wearied all these people when we are not at war?

[45] Dismiss them now to their homes and choose for yourself a few men to stay with you, and come with me to Ptolemais. I will hand it over to you as well as the other strongholds and the remaining troops and all the officials, and will turn round and go home. For that is why I am here."

[46] Jonathan trusted him and did as he said; he sent away the troops, and they returned to the land of Judah.

[47] He kept with himself three thousand men, two thousand of whom he left in Galilee, while a thousand accompanied him.

[48] But when Jonathan entered Ptolemais, the men of Ptolemais closed the gates and seized him, and all who had entered with him they killed with the

sword.

[49] Then Trypho sent troops and cavalry into Galilee and the Great Plain to destroy all Jonathan's soldiers.

[50] But they realized that Jonathan had been seized and had perished along with his men, and they encouraged one another and kept marching in close formation, ready for battle.

[51] When their pursuers saw that they would fight for their lives, they turned back.

[52] So they all reached the land of Judah safely, and they mourned for Jonathan and his companions and were in great fear; and all Israel mourned deeply.

[53] And all the nations round about them tried to destroy them, for they said, "They have no leader or helper. Now therefore let us make war on them and blot out the memory of them from among men."

1Mac.13

[1] Simon heard that Trypho had assembled a large army to invade the land of Judah and destroy it,

[2] and he saw that the people were trembling and fearful. So he went up to Jerusalem, and gathering the people together

[3] he encouraged them, saying to them, "You yourselves know what great things I and my brothers and the house of my father have done for the laws and the sanctuary; you know also the wars and the difficulties which we have seen.

[4] By reason of this all my brothers have perished for the sake of Israel, and I alone am left.

[5] And now, far be it from me to spare my life in any time of distress, for I am not better than my brothers.

[6] But I will avenge my nation and the sanctuary and your wives and children, for all the nations have gathered together out of hatred to destroy us."

[7] The spirit of the people was rekindled when they heard these words,

[8] and they answered in a loud voice, "You are our leader in place of Judas and Jonathan your brother.

[9] Fight our battles, and all that you say to us we will do."

[10] So he assembled all the warriors and hastened to complete the walls of Jerusalem, and he fortified it on every side.

[11] He sent Jonathan the son of Absalom to Joppa, and with him a considerable army; he drove out its occupants and remained there.

[12] Then Trypho departed from Ptolemais with a large army to invade the land of Judah, and Jonathan was with him under guard.

[13] And Simon encamped in Adida, facing the plain.

[14] Trypho learned that Simon had risen up in place of Jonathan his brother, and that he was about to join battle with him, so he sent envoys to him and said,

[15] "It is for the money that Jonathan your brother owed the royal treasury, in connection with the offices he held, that we are detaining him.
[16] Send now a hundred talents of silver and two of his sons as hostages, so that when released he will not revolt against us, and we will release him."
[17] Simon knew that they were speaking deceitfully to him, but he sent to get the money and the sons, lest he arouse great hostility among the people, who might say,
[18] "Because Simon did not send him the money and the sons, he perished."
[19] So he sent the sons and the hundred talents, but Trypho broke his word and did not release Jonathan.
[20] After this Trypho came to invade the country and destroy it, and he circled around by the way to Adora. But Simon and his army kept marching along opposite him to every place he went.
[21] Now the men in the citadel kept sending envoys to Trypho urging him to come to them by way of the wilderness and to send them food.
[22] So Trypho got all his cavalry ready to go, but that night a very heavy snow fell, and he did not go because of the snow. He marched off and went into the land of Gilead.
[23] When he approached Baskama, he killed Jonathan, and he was buried there.
[24] Then Trypho turned back and departed to his own land.
[25] And Simon sent and took the bones of Jonathan his brother, and buried him in Modein, the city of his fathers.
[26] All Israel bewailed him with great lamentation, and mourned for him many days.
[27] And Simon built a monument over the tomb of his father and his brothers; he made it high that it might be seen, with polished stone at the front and back.
[28] He also erected seven pyramids, opposite one another, for his father and mother and four brothers.
[29] And for the pyramids he devised an elaborate setting, erecting about them great columns, and upon the columns he put suits of armor for a permanent memorial, and beside the suits of armor carved ships, so that they could be seen by all who sail the sea.
[30] This is the tomb which he built in Modein; it remains to this day.
[31] Trypho dealt treacherously with the young king Antiochus; he killed him
[32] and became king in his place, putting on the crown of Asia; and he brought great calamity upon the land.
[33] But Simon built up the strongholds of Judea and walled them all around, with high towers and great walls and gates and bolts, and he stored food in the strongholds.
[34] Simon also chose men and sent them to Demetrius the king with a

request to grant relief to the country, for all that Trypho did was to plunder.

[35] Demetrius the king sent him a favorable reply to this request, and wrote him a letter as follows,

[36] "King Demetrius to Simon, the high priest and friend of kings, and to the elders and nation of the Jews, greeting.

[37] We have received the gold crown and the palm branch which you sent, and we are ready to make a general peace with you and to write to our officials to grant you release from tribute.

[38] All the grants that we have made to you remain valid, and let the strongholds that you have built be your possession.

[39] We pardon any errors and offenses committed to this day, and cancel the crown tax which you owe; and whatever other tax has been collected in Jerusalem shall be collected no longer.

[40] And if any of you are qualified to be enrolled in our bodyguard, let them be enrolled, and let there be peace between us."

[41] In the one hundred and seventieth year the yoke of the Gentiles was removed from Israel,

[42] and the people began to write in their documents and contracts, "In the first year of Simon the great high priest and commander and leader of the Jews."

[43] In those days Simon encamped against Gazara and surrounded it with troops. He made a siege engine, brought it up to the city, and battered and captured one tower.

[44] The men in the siege engine leaped out into the city, and a great tumult arose in the city.

[45] The men in the city, with their wives and children, went up on the wall with their clothes rent, and they cried out with a loud voice, asking Simon to make peace with them;

[46] they said, "Do not treat us according to our wicked acts but according to your mercy."

[47] So Simon reached an agreement with them and stopped fighting against them. But he expelled them from the city and cleansed the houses in which the idols were, and then entered it with hymns and praise.

[48] He cast out of it all uncleanness, and settled in it men who observed the law. He also strengthened its fortifications and built in it a house for himself.

[49] The men in the citadel at Jerusalem were prevented from going out to the country and back to buy and sell. So they were very hungry, and many of them perished from famine.

[50] Then they cried to Simon to make peace with them, and he did so. But he expelled them from there and cleansed the citadel from its pollutions.

[51] On the twenty-third day of the second month, in the one hundred and seventy-first year, the Jews entered it with praise and palm branches, and with harps and cymbals and stringed instruments, and with hymns and

songs, because a great enemy had been crushed and removed from Israel.
[52] And Simon decreed that every year they should celebrate this day with rejoicing. He strengthened the fortifications of the temple hill alongside the citadel, and he and his men dwelt there.
[53] And Simon saw that John his son had reached manhood, so he made him commander of all the forces, and he dwelt in Gazara.

1Mac.14

[1] In the one hundred and seventy-second year Demetrius the king assembled his forces and marched into Media to secure help, so that he could make war against Trypho.
[2] When Arsaces the king of Persia and Media heard that Demetrius had invaded his territory, he sent one of his commanders to take him alive.
[3] And he went and defeated the army of Demetrius, and seized him and took him to Arsaces, who put him under guard.
[4] The land had rest all the days of Simon. He sought the good of his nation; his rule was pleasing to them, as was the honor shown him, all his days.
[5] To crown all his honors he took Joppa for a harbor, and opened a way to the isles of the sea.
[6] He extended the borders of his nation, and gained full control of the country.
[7] He gathered a host of captives; he ruled over Gazara and Beth-zur and the citadel, and he removed its uncleanness from it; and there was none to oppose him.
[8] They tilled their land in peace; the ground gave its increase, and the trees of the plains their fruit.
[9] Old men sat in the streets; they all talked together of good things; and the youths donned the glories and garments of war.
[10] He supplied the cities with food, and furnished them with the means of defense, till his renown spread to the ends of the earth.
[11] He established peace in the land, and Israel rejoiced with great joy.
[12] Each man sat under his vine and his fig tree, and there was none to make them afraid.
[13] No one was left in the land to fight them, and the kings were crushed in those days.
[14] He strengthened all the humble of his people; he sought out the law, and did away with every lawless and wicked man.
[15] He made the sanctuary glorious, and added to the vessels of the sanctuary.
[16] It was heard in Rome, and as far away as Sparta, that Jonathan had died, and they were deeply grieved.
[17] When they heard that Simon his brother had become high priest in his place, and that he was ruling over the country and the cities in it,

[18] they wrote to him on bronze tablets to renew with him the friendship and alliance which they had established with Judas and Jonathan his brothers.

[19] And these were read before the assembly in Jerusalem.

[20] This is a copy of the letter which the Spartans sent: "The rulers and the city of the Spartans to Simon the high priest and to the elders and the priests and the rest of the Jewish people, our brethren, greeting.

[21] The envoys who were sent to our people have told us about your glory and honor, and we rejoiced at their coming.

[22] And what they said we have recorded in our public decrees, as follows, `Numenius the son of Antiochus and Antipater the son of Jason, envoys of the Jews, have come to us to renew their friendship with us.

[23] It has pleased our people to receive these men with honor and to put a copy of their words in the public archives, so that the people of the Spartans may have a record of them. And they have sent a copy of this to Simon the high priest.'"

[24] After this Simon sent Numenius to Rome with a large gold shield weighing a thousand minas, to confirm the alliance with the Romans.

[25] When the people heard these things they said, "How shall we thank Simon and his sons?

[26] For he and his brothers and the house of his father have stood firm; they have fought and repulsed Israel's enemies and established its freedom."

[27] So they made a record on bronze tablets and put it upon pillars on Mount Zion. This is a copy of what they wrote: "On the eighteenth day of Elul, in the one hundred and seventy-second year, which is the third year of Simon the great high priest,

[28] in Asaramel, in the great assembly of the priests and the people and the rulers of the nation and the elders of the country, the following was proclaimed to us:

[29] "Since wars often occurred in the country, Simon the son of Mattathias, a priest of the sons of Joarib, and his brothers, exposed themselves to danger and resisted the enemies of their nation, in order that their sanctuary and the law might be perserved; and they brought great glory to their nation.

[30] Jonathan rallied the nation, and became their high priest, and was gathered to his people.

[31] And when their enemies decided to invade their country and lay hands on their sanctuary,

[32] then Simon rose up and fought for his nation. He spent great sums of his own money; he armed the men of his nation's forces and paid them wages.

[33] He fortified the cities of Judea, and Beth-zur on the borders of Judea, where formerly the arms of the enemy had been stored, and he placed there a garrison of Jews.

[34] He also fortified Joppa, which is by the sea, and Gazara, which is on the

borders of Azotus, where the enemy formerly dwelt. He settled Jews there, and provided in those cities whatever was necessary for their restoration.
[35] "The people saw Simon's faithfulness and the glory which he had resolved to win for his nation, and they made him their leader and high priest, because he had done all these things and because of the justice and loyalty which he had maintained toward his nation. He sought in every way to exalt his people.
[36] And in his days things prospered in his hands, so that the Gentiles were put out of the country, as were also the men in the city of David in Jerusalem, who had built themselves a citadel from which they used to sally forth and defile the environs of the sanctuary and do great damage to its purity.
[37] He settled Jews in it, and fortified it for the safety of the country and of the city, and built the walls of Jerusalem higher.
[38] "In view of these things King Demetrius confirmed him in the high priesthood,
[39] and he made him one of the king's friends and paid him high honors.
[40] For he had heard that the Jews were addressed by the Romans as friends and allies and brethren, and that the Romans had received the envoys of Simon with honor.
[41] "And the Jews and their priests decided that Simon should be their leader and high priest for ever, until a trustworthy prophet should arise,
[42] and that he should be governor over them and that he should take charge of the sanctuary and appoint men over its tasks and over the country and the weapons and the strongholds, and that he should take charge of the sanctuary,
[43] and that he should be obeyed by all, and that all contracts in the country should be written in his name, and that he should be clothed in purple and wear gold.
[44] "And none of the people or priests shall be permitted to nullify any of these decisions or to oppose what he says, or to convene an assembly in the country without his permission, or to be clothed in purple or put on a gold buckle.
[45] Whoever acts contrary to these decisions or nullifies any of them shall be liable to punishment."
[46] And all the people agreed to grant Simon the right to act in accord with these decisions.
[47] So Simon accepted and agreed to be high priest, to be commander and ethnarch of the Jews and priests, and to be protector of them all.
[48] And they gave orders to inscribe this decree upon bronze tablets, to put them up in a conspicuous place in the precincts of the sanctuary,
[49] and to deposit copies of them in the treasury, so that Simon and his sons might have them.

1Mac.15

[1] Antiochus, the son of Demetrius the king, sent a letter from the islands of the sea to Simon, the priest and ethnarch of the Jews, and to all the nation;

[2] its contents were as follows: "King Antiochus to Simon the high priest and ethnarch and to the nation of the Jews, greeting.

[3] Whereas certain pestilent men have gained control of the kingdom of our fathers, and I intend to lay claim to the kingdom so that I may restore it as it formerly was, and have recruited a host of mercenary troops and have equipped warships,

[4] and intend to make a landing in the country so that I may proceed against those who have destroyed our country and those who have devastated many cities in my kingdom,

[5] now therefore I confirm to you all the tax remissions that the kings before me have granted you, and release from all the other payments from which they have released you.

[6] I permit you to mint your own coinage as money for your country,

[7] and I grant freedom to Jerusalem and the sanctuary. All the weapons which you have prepared and the strongholds which you have built and now hold shall remain yours.

[8] Every debt you owe to the royal treasury and any such future debts shall be canceled for you from henceforth and for all time.

[9] When we gain control of our kingdom, we will bestow great honor upon you and your nation and the temple, so that your glory will become manifest in all the earth."

[10] In the one hundred and seventy-fourth year Antiochus set out and invaded the land of his fathers. All the troops rallied to him, so that there were few with Trypho.

[11] Antiochus pursued him, and he came in his flight to Dor, which is by the sea;

[12] for he knew that troubles had converged upon him, and his troops had deserted him.

[13] So Antiochus encamped against Dor, and with him were a hundred and twenty thousand warriors and eight thousand cavalry.

[14] He surrounded the city, and the ships joined battle from the sea; he pressed the city hard from land and sea, and permitted no one to leave or enter it.

[15] Then Numenius and his companions arrived from Rome, with letters to the kings and countries, in which the following was written:

[16] "Lucius, consul of the Romans, to King Ptolemy, greeting.

[17] The envoys of the Jews have come to us as our friends and allies to renew our ancient friendship and alliance. They had been sent by Simon the high priest and by the people of the Jews,

[18] and have brought a gold shield weighing a thousand minas.

[19] We therefore have decided to write to the kings and countries that they

should not seek their harm or make war against them and their cities and their country, or make alliance with those who war against them.

[20] And it has seemed good to us to accept the shield from them.

[21] Therefore if any pestilent men have fled to you from their country, hand them over to Simon the high priest, that he may punish them according to their law."

[22] The consul wrote the same thing to Demetrius the king and to Attalus and Ariarathes and Arsaces,

[23] and to all the countries, and to Sampsames, and to the Spartans, and to Delos, and to Myndos, and to Sicyon, and to Caria, and to Samos, and to Pamphylia, and to Lycia, and to Halicarnassus, and to Rhodes, and to Phaselis, and to Cos, and to Side, and to Aradus and Gortyna and Cnidus and Cyprus and Cyrene.

[24] They also sent a copy of these things to Simon the high priest.

[25] Antiochus the king besieged Dor anew, continually throwing his forces against it and making engines of war; and he shut Trypho up and kept him from going out or in.

[26] And Simon sent to Antiochus two thousand picked men, to fight for him, and silver and gold and much military equipment.

[27] But he refused to receive them, and he broke all the agreements he formerly had made with Simon, and became estranged from him.

[28] He sent to him Athenobius, one of his friends, to confer with him, saying, "You hold control of Joppa and Gazara and the citadel in Jerusalem; they are cities of my kingdom.

[29] You have devastated their territory, you have done great damage in the land, and you have taken possession of many places in my kingdom.

[30] Now then, hand over the cities which you have seized and the tribute money of the places which you have conquered outside the borders of Judea;

[31] or else give me for them five hundred talents of silver, and for the destruction that you have caused and the tribute money of the cities, five hundred talents more. Otherwise we will come and conquer you."

[32] So Athenobius the friend of the king came to Jerusalem, and when he saw the splendor of Simon, and the sideboard with its gold and silver plate, and his great magnificence, he was amazed. He reported to him the words of the king,

[33] but Simon gave him this reply: "We have neither taken foreign land nor seized foreign property, but only the inheritance of our fathers, which at one time had been unjustly taken by our enemies.

[34] Now that we have the opportunity, we are firmly holding the inheritance of our fathers.

[35] As for Joppa and Gazara, which you demand, they were causing great damage among the people and to our land; for them we will give you a

hundred talents." Athenobius did not answer him a word,

[36] but returned in wrath to the king and reported to him these words and the splendor of Simon and all that he had seen. And the king was greatly angered.

[37] Now Trypho embarked on a ship and escaped to Orthosia.

[38] Then the king made Cendebeus commander-in-chief of the coastal country, and gave him troops of infantry and cavalry.

[39] He commanded him to encamp against Judea, and commanded him to build up Kedron and fortify its gates, and to make war on the people; but the king pursued Trypho.

[40] So Cendebeus came to Jamnia and began to provoke the people and invade Judea and take the people captive and kill them.

[41] He built up Kedron and stationed there horsemen and troops, so that they might go out and make raids along the highways of Judea, as the king had ordered him.

1Mac.16

[1] John went up from Gazara and reported to Simon his father what Cendebeus had done.

[2] And Simon called in his two older sons Judas and John, and said to them: "I and my brothers and the house of my father have fought the wars of Israel from our youth until this day, and things have prospered in our hands so that we have delivered Israel many times.

[3] But now I have grown old, and you by His mercy are mature in years. Take my place and my brother's, and go out and fight for our nation, and may the help which comes from Heaven be with you."

[4] So John chose out of the country twenty thousand warriors and horsemen, and they marched against Cendebeus and camped for the night in Modein.

[5] Early in the morning they arose and marched into the plain, and behold, a large force of infantry and horsemen was coming to meet them; and a stream lay between them.

[6] Then he and his army lined up against them. And he saw that the soldiers were afraid to cross the stream, so he crossed over first; and when his men saw him, they crossed over after him.

[7] Then he divided the army and placed the horsemen in the midst of the infantry, for the cavalry of the enemy were very numerous.

[8] And they sounded the trumpets, and Cendebeus and his army were put to flight, and many of them were wounded and fell; the rest fled into the stronghold.

[9] At that time Judas the brother of John was wounded, but John pursued them until Cendebeus reached Kedron, which he had built.

[10] They also fled into the towers that were in the fields of Azotus, and John burned it with fire, and about two thousand of them fell. And he returned to Judea safely.

[11] Now Ptolemy the son of Abubus had been appointed governor over the plain of Jericho, and he had much silver and gold,

[12] for he was son-in-law of the high priest.

[13] His heart was lifted up; he determined to get control of the country, and made treacherous plans against Simon and his sons, to do away with them.

[14] Now Simon was visiting the cities of the country and attending to their needs, and he went down to Jericho with Mattathias and Judas his sons, in the one hundred and seventy-seventh year, in the eleventh month, which is the month of Shebat.

[15] The son of Abubus received them treacherously in the little stronghold called Dok, which he had built; he gave them a great banquet, and hid men there.

[16] When Simon and his sons were drunk, Ptolemy and his men rose up, took their weapons, and rushed in against Simon in the banquet hall, and they killed him and his two sons and some of his servants.

[17] So he committed an act of great treachery and returned evil for good.

[18] Then Ptolemy wrote a report about these things and sent it to the king, asking him to send troops to aid him and to turn over to him the cities and the country.

[19] He sent other men to Gazara to do away with John; he sent letters to the captains asking them to come to him so that he might give them silver and gold and gifts;

[20] and he sent other men to take possession of Jerusalem and the temple hill.

[21] But some one ran ahead and reported to John at Gazara that his father and brothers had perished, and that "he has sent men to kill you also."

[22] When he heard this, he was greatly shocked; and he seized the men who came to destroy him and killed them, for he had found out that they were seeking to destroy him.

[23] The rest of the acts of John and his wars and the brave deeds which he did, and the building of the walls which he built, and his achievements,

[24] behold, they are written in the chronicles of his high priesthood, from the time that he became high priest after his father.

2 Maccabees

2Mac.1

[1] The Jewish brethren in Jerusalem and those in the land of Judea, To their Jewish brethren in Egypt, Greeting, and good peace.

[2] May God do good to you, and may he remember his covenant with Abraham and Isaac and Jacob, his faithful servants.

[3] May he give you all a heart to worship him and to do his will with a strong heart and a willing spirit.

[4] May he open your heart to his law and his commandments, and may he bring peace.

[5] May he hear your prayers and be reconciled to you, and may he not forsake you in time of evil.

[6] We are now praying for you here.

[7] In the reign of Demetrius, in the one hundred and sixty-ninth year, we Jews wrote to you, in the critical distress which came upon us in those years after Jason and his company revolted from the holy land and the kingdom

[8] and burned the gate and shed innocent blood. We besought the Lord and we were heard, and we offered sacrifice and cereal offering, and we lighted the lamps and we set out the loaves.

[9] And now see that you keep the feast of booths in the month of Chislev, in the one hundred and eighty-eighth year.

[10] Those in Jerusalem and those in Judea and the senate and Judas, To Aristobulus, who is of the family of the anointed priests, teacher of Ptolemy the king, and to the Jews in Egypt, Greeting, and good health.

[11] Having been saved by God out of grave dangers we thank him greatly for taking our side against the king.

[12] For he drove out those who fought against the holy city.

[13] For when the leader reached Persia with a force that seemed irresistible, they were cut to pieces in the temple of Nanea by a deception employed by the priests of Nanea.

[14] For under pretext of intending to marry her, Antiochus came to the place together with his friends, to secure most of its treasures as a dowry.

[15] When the priests of the temple of Nanea had set out the treasures and Antiochus had come with a few men inside the wall of the sacred precinct, they closed the temple as soon as he entered it.

[16] Opening the secret door in the ceiling, they threw stones and struck down the leader and his men, and dismembered them and cut off their heads and threw them to the people outside.

[17] Blessed in every way be our God, who has brought judgment upon those who have behaved impiously.

[18] Since on the twenty-fifth day of Chislev we shall celebrate the purification of the temple, we thought it necessary to notify you, in order that you also may celebrate the feast of booths and the feast of the fire given when Nehemiah, who built the temple and the altar, offered sacrifices.

[19] For when our fathers were being led captive to Persia, the pious priests of that time took some of the fire of the altar and secretly hid it in the hollow of a dry cistern, where they took such precautions that the place was unknown to any one.

[20] But after many years had passed, when it pleased God, Nehemiah, having been commissioned by the king of Persia, sent the descendants of the priests who had hidden the fire to get it. And when they reported to us that they had not found fire but thick liquid, he ordered them to dip it out and bring it.

[21] And when the materials for the sacrifices were presented, Nehemiah ordered the priests to sprinkle the liquid on the wood and what was laid upon it.

[22] When this was done and some time had passed and the sun, which had been clouded over, shone out, a great fire blazed up, so that all marveled.

[23] And while the sacrifice was being consumed, the priests offered prayer -- the priests and every one. Jonathan led, and the rest responded, as did Nehemiah.

[24] The prayer was to this effect:

"O Lord, Lord God, Creator of all things, who art awe-inspiring and strong and just and merciful, who alone art King and art kind, [25] who alone art bountiful, who alone art just and almighty and eternal, who do rescue Israel from every evil, who didst choose the fathers and consecrate them, [26] accept this sacrifice on behalf of all thy people Israel and preserve thy portion and make it holy. [27] Gather together our scattered people, set free those who are slaves among the Gentiles, look upon those who are rejected and despised, and let the Gentiles know that thou art our God. [28] Afflict those who oppress and are insolent with pride. [29] Plant thy people in thy holy place, as Moses said." [30] Then the priests sang the hymns. [31] And when the materials of the sacrifice were consumed, Nehemiah ordered that the liquid that was left should be poured upon large stones. [32] When this was done, a flame blazed up; but when the light from the altar shone back, it went out. [33] When this matter became known, and it was reported to the king of the Persians that, in the place where the exiled priests had hidden the fire, the liquid had appeared with which Nehemiah and his associates had burned the materials of the sacrifice, [34] the king investigated the matter, and enclosed the place and made it sacred. [35] And with those persons whom the king favored he exchanged many excellent gifts. [36]

Nehemiah and his associates called this "nephthar," which means
purification, but by most people it is called naphtha.
2Mac.2

[1] One finds in the records that Jeremiah the prophet ordered those who
were being deported to take some of the fire, as has been told,

[2] and that the prophet after giving them the law instructed those who
were being deported not to forget the commandments of the Lord, nor to be
led astray in their thoughts upon seeing the gold and silver statues and their
adornment.

[3] And with other similar words he exhorted them that the law should not
depart from their hearts.

[4] It was also in the writing that the prophet, having received an oracle,
ordered that the tent and the ark should follow with him, and that he went
out to the mountain where Moses had gone up and had seen the inheritance
of God.

[5] And Jeremiah came and found a cave, and he brought there the tent and
the ark and the altar of incense, and he sealed up the entrance.

[6] Some of those who followed him came up to mark the way, but could
not find it.

[7] When Jeremiah learned of it, he rebuked them and declared: "The place
shall be unknown until God gathers his people together again and shows
his mercy.

[8] And then the Lord will disclose these things, and the glory of the Lord
and the cloud will appear, as they were shown in the case of Moses, and as
Solomon asked that the place should be specially consecrated."

[9] It was also made clear that being possessed of wisdom Solomon offered
sacrifice for the dedication and completion of the temple.

[10] Just as Moses prayed to the Lord, and fire came down from heaven and
devoured the sacrifices, so also Solomon prayed, and the fire came down
and consumed the whole burnt offerings.

[11] And Moses said, "They were consumed because the sin offering had not
been eaten."

[12] Likewise Solomon also kept the eight days.

[13] The same things are reported in the records and in the memoirs of
Nehemiah, and also that he founded a library and collected the books about
the kings and prophets, and the writings of David, and letters of kings about
votive offerings.

[14] In the same way Judas also collected all the books that had been lost on
account of the war which had come upon us, and they are in our possession.

[15] So if you have need of them, send people to get them for you.

[16] Since, therefore, we are about to celebrate the purification, we write to
you. Will you therefore please keep the days?

[17] It is God who has saved all his people, and has returned the inheritance

to all, and the kingship and priesthood and consecration,

[18] as he promised through the law. For we have hope in God that he will soon have mercy upon us and will gather us from everywhere under heaven into his holy place, for he has rescued us from great evils and has purified the place.

[19] The story of Judas Maccabeus and his brothers, and the purification of the great temple, and the dedication of the altar,

[20] and further the wars against Antiochus Epiphanes and his son Eupator,

[21] and the appearances which came from heaven to those who strove zealously on behalf of Judaism, so that though few in number they seized the whole land and pursued the barbarian hordes,

[22] and recovered the temple famous throughout the world and freed the city and restored the laws that were about to be abolished, while the Lord with great kindness became gracious to them --

[23] all this, which has been set forth by Jason of Cyrene in five volumes, we shall attempt to condense into a single book.

[24] For considering the flood of numbers involved and the difficulty there is for those who wish to enter upon the narratives of history because of the mass of material,

[25] we have aimed to please those who wish to read, to make it easy for those who are inclined to memorize, and to profit all readers.

[26] For us who have undertaken the toil of abbreviating, it is no light matter but calls for sweat and loss of sleep,

[27] just as it is not easy for one who prepares a banquet and seeks the benefit of others. However, to secure the gratitude of many we will gladly endure the uncomfortable toil,

[28] leaving the responsibility for exact details to the compiler, while devoting our effort to arriving at the outlines of the condensation.

[29] For as the master builder of a new house must be concerned with the whole construction, while the one who undertakes its painting and decoration has to consider only what is suitable for its adornment, such in my judgment is the case with us.

[30] It is the duty of the original historian to occupy the ground and to discuss matters from every side and to take trouble with details,

[31] but the one who recasts the narrative should be allowed to strive for brevity of expression and to forego exhaustive treatment.

[32] At this point therefore let us begin our narrative, adding only so much to what has already been said; for it is foolish to lengthen the preface while cutting short the history itself.

2Mac.3

[1] While the holy city was inhabited in unbroken peace and the laws were very well observed because of the piety of the high priest Onias and his hatred of wickedness,

[2] it came about that the kings themselves honored the place and glorified the temple with the finest presents,

[3] so that even Seleucus, the king of Asia, defrayed from his own revenues all the expenses connected with the service of the sacrifices.

[4] But a man named Simon, of the tribe of Benjamin, who had been made captain of the temple, had a disagreement with the high priest about the administration of the city market;

[5] and when he could not prevail over Onias he went to Apollonius of Tarsus, who at that time was governor of Coelesyria and Phoenicia.

[6] He reported to him that the treasury in Jerusalem was full of untold sums of money, so that the amount of the funds could not be reckoned, and that they did not belong to the account of the sacrifices, but that it was possible for them to fall under the control of the king.

[7] When Apollonius met the king, he told him of the money about which he had been informed. The king chose Heliodorus, who was in charge of his affairs, and sent him with commands to effect the removal of the aforesaid money.

[8] Heliodorus at once set out on his journey, ostensibly to make a tour of inspection of the cities of Coelesyria and Phoenicia, but in fact to carry out the king's purpose.

[9] When he had arrived at Jerusalem and had been kindly welcomed by the high priest of the city, he told about the disclosure that had been made and stated why he had come, and he inquired whether this really was the situation.

[10] The high priest explained that there were some deposits belonging to widows and orphans,

[11] and also some money of Hyrcanus, son of Tobias, a man of very prominent position, and that it totaled in all four hundred talents of silver and two hundred of gold. To such an extent the impious Simon had misrepresented the facts.

[12] And he said that it was utterly impossible that wrong should be done to those people who had trusted in the holiness of the place and in the sanctity and inviolability of the temple which is honored throughout the whole world.

[13] But Heliodorus, because of the king's commands which he had, said that this money must in any case be confiscated for the king's treasury.

[14] So he set a day and went in to direct the inspection of these funds. There was no little distress throughout the whole city.

[15] The priests prostrated themselves before the altar in their priestly garments and called toward heaven upon him who had given the law about deposits, that he should keep them safe for those who had deposited them.

[16] To see the appearance of the high priest was to be wounded at heart, for his face and the change in his color disclosed the anguish of his soul.

[17] For terror and bodily trembling had come over the man, which plainly

showed to those who looked at him the pain lodged in his heart.

[18] People also hurried out of their houses in crowds to make a general supplication because the holy place was about to be brought into contempt.

[19] Women, girded with sackcloth under their breasts, thronged the streets. Some of the maidens who were kept indoors ran together to the gates, and some to the walls, while others peered out of the windows.

[20] And holding up their hands to heaven, they all made entreaty.

[21] There was something pitiable in the prostration of the whole populace and the anxiety of the high priest in his great anguish.

[22] While they were calling upon the Almighty Lord that he would keep what had been entrusted safe and secure for those who had entrusted it,

[23] Heliodorus went on with what had been decided.

[24] But when he arrived at the treasury with his bodyguard, then and there the Sovereign of spirits and of all authority caused so great a manifestation that all who had been so bold as to accompany him were astounded by the power of God, and became faint with terror.

[25] For there appeared to them a magnificently caparisoned horse, with a rider of frightening mien, and it rushed furiously at Heliodorus and struck at him with its front hoofs. Its rider was seen to have armor and weapons of gold.

[26] Two young men also appeared to him, remarkably strong, gloriously beautiful and splendidly dressed, who stood on each side of him and scourged him continuously, inflicting many blows on him.

[27] When he suddenly fell to the ground and deep darkness came over him, his men took him up and put him on a stretcher

[28] and carried him away, this man who had just entered the aforesaid treasury with a great retinue and all his bodyguard but was now unable to help himself; and they recognized clearly the sovereign power of God.

[29] While he lay prostrate, speechless because of the divine intervention and deprived of any hope of recovery,

[30] they praised the Lord who had acted marvelously for his own place. And the temple, which a little while before was full of fear and disturbance, was filled with joy and gladness, now that the Almighty Lord had appeared.

[31] Quickly some of Heliodorus' friends asked Onias to call upon the Most High and to grant life to one who was lying quite at his last breath.

[32] And the high priest, fearing that the king might get the notion that some foul play had been perpetrated by the Jews with regard to Heliodorus, offered sacrifice for the man's recovery.

[33] While the high priest was making the offering of atonement, the same young men appeared again to Heliodorus dressed in the same clothing, and they stood and said, "Be very grateful to Onias the high priest, since for his sake the Lord has granted you your life.

[34] And see that you, who have been scourged by heaven, report to all men the majestic power of God." Having said this they vanished.

[35] Then Heliodorus offered sacrifice to the Lord and made very great vows to the Savior of his life, and having bidden Onias farewell, he marched off with his forces to the king.

[36] And he bore testimony to all men of the deeds of the supreme God, which he had seen with his own eyes.

[37] When the king asked Heliodorus what sort of person would be suitable to send on another mission to Jerusalem, he replied,

[38] "If you have any enemy or plotter against your government, send him there, for you will get him back thoroughly scourged, if he escapes at all, for there certainly is about the place some power of God.

[39] For he who has his dwelling in heaven watches over that place himself and brings it aid, and he strikes and destroys those who come to do it injury."

[40] This was the outcome of the episode of Heliodorus and the protection of the treasury.

2Mac.4

[1] The previously mentioned Simon, who had informed about the money against his own country, slandered Onias, saying that it was he who had incited Heliodorus and had been the real cause of the misfortune.

[2] He dared to designate as a plotter against the government the man who was the benefactor of the city, the protector of his fellow countrymen, and a zealot for the laws.

[3] When his hatred progressed to such a degree that even murders were committed by one of Simon's approved agents,

[4] Onias recognized that the rivalry was serious and that Apollonius, the son of Menestheus and governor of Coelesyria and Phoenicia, was intensifying the malice of Simon.

[5] So he betook himself to the king, not accusing his fellow citizens but having in view the welfare, both public and private, of all the people.

[6] For he saw that without the king's attention public affairs could not again reach a peaceful settlement, and that Simon would not stop his folly.

[7] When Seleucus died and Antiochus who was called Epiphanes succeeded to the kingdom, Jason the brother of Onias obtained the high priesthood by corruption,

[8] promising the king at an interview three hundred and sixty talents of silver and, from another source of revenue, eighty talents.

[9] In addition to this he promised to pay one hundred and fifty more if permission were given to establish by his authority a gymnasium and a body of youth for it, and to enrol the men of Jerusalem as citizens of Antioch.

[10] When the king assented and Jason came to office, he at once shifted his countrymen over to the Greek way of life.

[11] He set aside the existing royal concessions to the Jews, secured through John the father of Eupolemus, who went on the mission to establish friendship and alliance with the Romans; and he destroyed the lawful ways of living and introduced new customs contrary to the law.

[12] For with alacrity he founded a gymnasium right under the citadel, and he induced the noblest of the young men to wear the Greek hat.

[13] There was such an extreme of Hellenization and increase in the adoption of foreign ways because of the surpassing wickedness of Jason, who was ungodly and no high priest,

[14] that the priests were no longer intent upon their service at the altar. Despising the sanctuary and neglecting the sacrifices, they hastened to take part in the unlawful proceedings in the wrestling arena after the call to the discus,

[15] disdaining the honors prized by their fathers and putting the highest value upon Greek forms of prestige.

[16] For this reason heavy disaster overtook them, and those whose ways of living they admired and wished to imitate completely became their enemies and punished them.

[17] For it is no light thing to show irreverence to the divine laws -- a fact which later events will make clear.

[18] When the quadrennial games were being held at Tyre and the king was present,

[19] the vile Jason sent envoys, chosen as being Antiochian citizens from Jerusalem, to carry three hundred silver drachmas for the sacrifice to Hercules. Those who carried the money, however, thought best not to use it for sacrifice, because that was inappropriate, but to expend it for another purpose.

[20] So this money was intended by the sender for the sacrifice to Hercules, but by the decision of its carriers it was applied to the construction of triremes.

[21] When Apollonius the son of Menestheus was sent to Egypt for the coronation of Philometor as king, Antiochus learned that Philometor had become hostile to his government, and he took measures for his own security. Therefore upon arriving at Joppa he proceeded to Jerusalem.

[22] He was welcomed magnificently by Jason and the city, and ushered in with a blaze of torches and with shouts. Then he marched into Phoenicia.

[23] After a period of three years Jason sent Menelaus, the brother of the previously mentioned Simon, to carry the money to the king and to complete the records of essential business.

[24] But he, when presented to the king, extolled him with an air of authority, and secured the high priesthood for himself, outbidding Jason by three hundred talents of silver.

[25] After receiving the king's orders he returned, possessing no

qualification for the high priesthood, but having the hot temper of a cruel tyrant and the rage of a savage wild beast.

[26] So Jason, who after supplanting his own brother was supplanted by another man, was driven as a fugitive into the land of Ammon.

[27] And Menelaus held the office, but he did not pay regularly any of the money promised to the king.

[28] When Sostratus the captain of the citadel kept requesting payment, for the collection of the revenue was his responsibility, the two of them were summoned by the king on account of this issue.

[29] Menelaus left his own brother Lysimachus as deputy in the high priesthood, while Sostratus left Crates, the commander of the Cyprian troops.

[30] While such was the state of affairs, it happened that the people of Tarsus and of Mallus revolted because their cities had been given as a present to Antiochis, the king's concubine.

[31] So the king went hastily to settle the trouble, leaving Andronicus, a man of high rank, to act as his deputy.

[32] But Menelaus, thinking he had obtained a suitable opportunity, stole some of the gold vessels of the temple and gave them to Andronicus; other vessels, as it happened, he had sold to Tyre and the neighboring cities.

[33] When Onias became fully aware of these acts he publicly exposed them, having first withdrawn to a place of sanctuary at Daphne near Antioch.

[34] Therefore Menelaus, taking Andronicus aside, urged him to kill Onias. Andronicus came to Onias, and resorting to treachery offered him sworn pledges and gave him his right hand, and in spite of his suspicion persuaded Onias to come out from the place of sanctuary; then, with no regard for justice, he immediately put him out of the way.

[35] For this reason not only Jews, but many also of other nations, were grieved and displeased at the unjust murder of the man.

[36] When the king returned from the region of Cilicia, the Jews in the city appealed to him with regard to the unreasonable murder of Onias, and the Greeks shared their hatred of the crime.

[37] Therefore Antiochus was grieved at heart and filled with pity, and wept because of the moderation and good conduct of the deceased;

[38] and inflamed with anger, he immediately stripped off the purple robe from Andronicus, tore off his garments, and led him about the whole city to that very place where he had committed the outrage against Onias, and there he dispatched the bloodthirsty fellow. The Lord thus repaid him with the punishment he deserved.

[39] When many acts of sacrilege had been committed in the city by Lysimachus with the connivance of Menelaus, and when report of them had spread abroad, the populace gathered against Lysimachus, because many of the gold vessels had already been stolen.

[40] And since the crowds were becoming aroused and filled with anger,

Lysimachus armed about three thousand men and launched an unjust attack, under the leadership of a certain Auranus, a man advanced in years and no less advanced in folly.

[41] But when the Jews became aware of Lysimachus' attack, some picked up stones, some blocks of wood, and others took handfuls of the ashes that were lying about, and threw them in wild confusion at Lysimachus and his men.

[42] As a result, they wounded many of them, and killed some, and put them all to flight; and the temple robber himself they killed close by the treasury.

[43] Charges were brought against Menelaus about this incident.

[44] When the king came to Tyre, three men sent by the senate presented the case before him.

[45] But Menelaus, already as good as beaten, promised a substantial bribe to Ptolemy son of Dorymenes to win over the king.

[46] Therefore Ptolemy, taking the king aside into a colonnade as if for refreshment, induced the king to change his mind.

[47] Menelaus, the cause of all the evil, he acquitted of the charges against him, while he sentenced to death those unfortunate men, who would have been freed uncondemned if they had pleaded even before Scythians.

[48] And so those who had spoken for the city and the villages and the holy vessels quickly suffered the unjust penalty.

[49] Therefore even the Tyrians, showing their hatred of the crime, provided magnificently for their funeral.

[50] But Menelaus, because of the cupidity of those in power, remained in office, growing in wickedness, having become the chief plotter against his fellow citizens.

2Mac.5

[1] About this time Antiochus made his second invasion of Egypt.

[2] And it happened that over all the city, for almost forty days, there appeared golden-clad horsemen charging through the air, in companies fully armed with lances and drawn swords --

[3] troops of horsemen drawn up, attacks and counterattacks made on this side and on that, brandishing of shields, massing of spears, hurling of missiles, the flash of golden trappings, and armor of all sorts.

[4] Therefore all men prayed that the apparition might prove to have been a good omen.

[5] When a false rumor arose that Antiochus was dead, Jason took no less than a thousand men and suddenly made an assault upon the city. When the troops upon the wall had been forced back and at last the city was being taken, Menelaus took refuge in the citadel.

[6] But Jason kept relentlessly slaughtering his fellow citizens, not realizing that success at the cost of one's kindred is the greatest misfortune, but

imagining that he was setting up trophies of victory over enemies and not over fellow countrymen.

[7] He did not gain control of the government, however; and in the end got only disgrace from his conspiracy, and fled again into the country of the Ammonites.

[8] Finally he met a miserable end. Accused before Aretas the ruler of the Arabs, fleeing from city to city, pursued by all men, hated as a rebel against the laws, and abhorred as the executioner of his country and his fellow citizens, he was cast ashore in Egypt;

[9] and he who had driven many from their own country into exile died in exile, having embarked to go to the Lacedaemonians in hope of finding protection because of their kinship.

[10] He who had cast out many to lie unburied had no one to mourn for him; he had no funeral of any sort and no place in the tomb of his fathers.

[11] When news of what had happened reached the king, he took it to mean that Judea was in revolt. So, raging inwardly, he left Egypt and took the city by storm.

[12] And he commanded his soldiers to cut down relentlessly every one they met and to slay those who went into the houses.

[13] Then there was killing of young and old, destruction of boys, women, and children, and slaughter of virgins and infants.

[14] Within the total of three days eighty thousand were destroyed, forty thousand in hand-to-hand fighting; and as many were sold into slavery as were slain.

[15] Not content with this, Antiochus dared to enter the most holy temple in all the world, guided by Menelaus, who had become a traitor both to the laws and to his country.

[16] He took the holy vessels with his polluted hands, and swept away with profane hands the votive offerings which other kings had made to enhance the glory and honor of the place.

[17] Antiochus was elated in spirit, and did not perceive that the Lord was angered for a little while because of the sins of those who dwelt in the city, and that therefore he was disregarding the holy place.

[18] But if it had not happened that they were involved in many sins, this man would have been scourged and turned back from his rash act as soon as he came forward, just as Heliodorus was, whom Seleucus the king sent to inspect the treasury.

[19] But the Lord did not choose the nation for the sake of the holy place, but the place for the sake of the nation.

[20] Therefore the place itself shared in the misfortunes that befell the nation and afterward participated in its benefits; and what was forsaken in the wrath of the Almighty was restored again in all its glory when the great Lord became reconciled.

[21] So Antiochus carried off eighteen hundred talents from the temple, and

hurried away to Antioch, thinking in his arrogance that he could sail on the land and walk on the sea, because his mind was elated.

[22] And he left governors to afflict the people: at Jerusalem, Philip, by birth a Phrygian and in character more barbarous than the man who appointed him;

[23] and at Gerizim, Andronicus; and besides these Menelaus, who lorded it over his fellow citizens worse than the others did. In his malice toward the Jewish citizens,

[24] Antiochus sent Apollonius, the captain of the Mysians, with an army of twenty-two thousand, and commanded him to slay all the grown men and to sell the women and boys as slaves.

[25] When this man arrived in Jerusalem, he pretended to be peaceably disposed and waited until the holy sabbath day; then, finding the Jews not at work, he ordered his men to parade under arms.

[26] He put to the sword all those who came out to see them, then rushed into the city with his armed men and killed great numbers of people.

[27] But Judas Maccabeus, with about nine others, got away to the wilderness, and kept himself and his companions alive in the mountains as wild animals do; they continued to live on what grew wild, so that they might not share in the defilement.

2Mac.6

[1] Not long after this, the king sent an Athenian senator to compel the Jews to forsake the laws of their fathers and cease to live by the laws of God,

[2] and also to pollute the temple in Jerusalem and call it the temple of Olympian Zeus, and to call the one in Gerizim the temple of Zeus the Friend of Strangers, as did the people who dwelt in that place.

[3] Harsh and utterly grievous was the onslaught of evil.

[4] For the temple was filled with debauchery and reveling by the Gentiles, who dallied with harlots and had intercourse with women within the sacred precincts, and besides brought in things for sacrifice that were unfit.

[5] The altar was covered with abominable offerings which were forbidden by the laws.

[6] A man could neither keep the sabbath, nor observe the feasts of his fathers, nor so much as confess himself to be a Jew.

[7] On the monthly celebration of the king's birthday, the Jews were taken, under bitter constraint, to partake of the sacrifices; and when the feast of Dionysus came, they were compelled to walk in the procession in honor of Dionysus, wearing wreaths of ivy.

[8] At the suggestion of Ptolemy a decree was issued to the neighboring Greek cities, that they should adopt the same policy toward the Jews and make them partake of the sacrifices,

[9] and should slay those who did not choose to change over to Greek customs. One could see, therefore, the misery that had come upon them.

[10] For example, two women were brought in for having circumcised their children. These women they publicly paraded about the city, with their babies hung at their breasts, then hurled them down headlong from the wall.

[11] Others who had assembled in the caves near by, to observe the seventh day secretly, were betrayed to Philip and were all burned together, because their piety kept them from defending themselves, in view of their regard for that most holy day.

[12] Now I urge those who read this book not to be depressed by such calamities, but to recognize that these punishments were designed not to destroy but to discipline our people.

[13] In fact, not to let the impious alone for long, but to punish them immediately, is a sign of great kindness.

[14] For in the case of the other nations the Lord waits patiently to punish them until they have reached the full measure of their sins; but he does not deal in this way with us,

[15] in order that he may not take vengeance on us afterward when our sins have reached their height.

[16] Therefore he never withdraws his mercy from us. Though he disciplines us with calamities, he does not forsake his own people.

[17] Let what we have said serve as a reminder; we must go on briefly with the story.

[18] Eleazar, one of the scribes in high position, a man now advanced in age and of noble presence, was being forced to open his mouth to eat swine's flesh.

[19] But he, welcoming death with honor rather than life with pollution, went up to the the rack of his own accord, spitting out the flesh,

[20] as men ought to go who have the courage to refuse things that it is not right to taste, even for the natural love of life.

[21] Those who were in charge of that unlawful sacrifice took the man aside, because of their long acquaintance with him, and privately urged him to bring meat of his own providing, proper for him to use, and pretend that he was eating the flesh of the sacrificial meal which had been commanded by the king,

[22] so that by doing this he might be saved from death, and be treated kindly on account of his old friendship with them.

[23] But making a high resolve, worthy of his years and the dignity of his old age and the gray hairs which he had reached with distinction and his excellent life even from childhood, and moreover according to the holy God-given law, he declared himself quickly, telling them to send him to Hades.

[24] "Such pretense is not worthy of our time of life," he said, "lest many of the young should suppose that Eleazar in his ninetieth year has gone over to an alien religion,

[25] and through my pretense, for the sake of living a brief moment longer, they should be led astray because of me, while I defile and disgrace my old age.

[26] For even if for the present I should avoid the punishment of men, yet whether I live or die I shall not escape the hands of the Almighty.

[27] Therefore, by manfully giving up my life now, I will show myself worthy of my old age

[28] and leave to the young a noble example of how to die a good death willingly and nobly for the revered and holy laws." When he had said this, he went at once to the rack.

[29] And those who a little before had acted toward him with good will now changed to ill will, because the words he had uttered were in their opinion sheer madness.

[30] When he was about to die under the blows, he groaned aloud and said: "It is clear to the Lord in his holy knowledge that, though I might have been saved from death, I am enduring terrible sufferings in my body under this beating, but in my soul I am glad to suffer these things because I fear him."

[31] So in this way he died, leaving in his death an example of nobility and a memorial of courage, not only to the young but to the great body of his nation.

2Mac.7

[1] It happened also that seven brothers and their mother were arrested and were being compelled by the king, under torture with whips and cords, to partake of unlawful swine's flesh.

[2] One of them, acting as their spokesman, said, "What do you intend to ask and learn from us? For we are ready to die rather than transgress the laws of our fathers."

[3] The king fell into a rage, and gave orders that pans and caldrons be heated.

[4] These were heated immediately, and he commanded that the tongue of their spokesman be cut out and that they scalp him and cut off his hands and feet, while the rest of the brothers and the mother looked on.

[5] When he was utterly helpless, the king ordered them to take him to the fire, still breathing, and to fry him in a pan. The smoke from the pan spread widely, but the brothers and their mother encouraged one another to die nobly, saying,

[6] "The Lord God is watching over us and in truth has compassion on us, as Moses declared in his song which bore witness against the people to their faces, when he said, `And he will have compassion on his servants.'"

[7] After the first brother had died in this way, they brought forward the second for their sport. They tore off the skin of his head with the hair, and asked him, "Will you eat rather than have your body punished limb by limb?"

[8] He replied in the language of his fathers, and said to them, "No."
Therefore he in turn underwent tortures as the first brother had done.
[9] And when he was at his last breath, he said, "You accursed wretch, you dismiss us from this present life, but the King of the universe will raise us up to an everlasting renewal of life, because we have died for his laws."
[10] After him, the third was the victim of their sport. When it was demanded, he quickly put out his tongue and courageously stretched forth his hands,
[11] and said nobly, "I got these from Heaven, and because of his laws I disdain them, and from him I hope to get them back again."
[12] As a result the king himself and those with him were astonished at the young man's spirit, for he regarded his sufferings as nothing.
[13] When he too had died, they maltreated and tortured the fourth in the same way.
[14] And when he was near death, he said, "One cannot but choose to die at the hands of men and to cherish the hope that God gives of being raised again by him. But for you there will be no resurrection to life!"
[15] Next they brought forward the fifth and maltreated him.
[16] But he looked at the king, and said, "Because you have authority among men, mortal though you are, you do what you please. But do not think that God has forsaken our people.
[17] Keep on, and see how his mighty power will torture you and your descendants!"
[18] After him they brought forward the sixth. And when he was about to die, he said, "Do not deceive yourself in vain. For we are suffering these things on our own account, because of our sins against our own God. Therefore astounding things have happened.
[19] But do not think that you will go unpunished for having tried to fight against God!"
[20] The mother was especially admirable and worthy of honorable memory. Though she saw her seven sons perish within a single day, she bore it with good courage because of her hope in the Lord.
[21] She encouraged each of them in the language of their fathers. Filled with a noble spirit, she fired her woman's reasoning with a man's courage, and said to them,
[22] "I do not know how you came into being in my womb. It was not I who gave you life and breath, nor I who set in order the elements within each of you.
[23] Therefore the Creator of the world, who shaped the beginning of man and devised the origin of all things, will in his mercy give life and breath back to you again, since you now forget yourselves for the sake of his laws."
[24] Antiochus felt that he was being treated with contempt, and he was suspicious of her reproachful tone. The youngest brother being still alive, Antiochus not only appealed to him in words, but promised with oaths that

he would make him rich and enviable if he would turn from the ways of his fathers, and that he would take him for his friend and entrust him with public affairs.

[25] Since the young man would not listen to him at all, the king called the mother to him and urged her to advise the youth to save himself.

[26] After much urging on his part, she undertook to persuade her son.

[27] But, leaning close to him, she spoke in their native tongue as follows, deriding the cruel tyrant: "My son, have pity on me. I carried you nine months in my womb, and nursed you for three years, and have reared you and brought you up to this point in your life, and have taken care of you.

[28] I beseech you, my child, to look at the heaven and the earth and see everything that is in them, and recognize that God did not make them out of things that existed. Thus also mankind comes into being.

[29] Do not fear this butcher, but prove worthy of your brothers. Accept death, so that in God's mercy I may get you back again with your brothers."

[30] While she was still speaking, the young man said, "What are you waiting for? I will not obey the king's command, but I obey the command of the law that was given to our fathers through Moses.

[31] But you, who have contrived all sorts of evil against the Hebrews, will certainly not escape the hands of God.

[32] For we are suffering because of our own sins.

[33] And if our living Lord is angry for a little while, to rebuke and discipline us, he will again be reconciled with his own servants.

[34] But you, unholy wretch, you most defiled of all men, do not be elated in vain and puffed up by uncertain hopes, when you raise your hand against the children of heaven.

[35] You have not yet escaped the judgment of the almighty, all-seeing God.

[36] For our brothers after enduring a brief suffering have drunk of everflowing life under God's covenant; but you, by the judgment of God, will receive just punishment for your arrogance.

[37] I, like my brothers, give up body and life for the laws of our fathers, appealing to God to show mercy soon to our nation and by afflictions and plagues to make you confess that he alone is God,

[38] and through me and my brothers to bring to an end the wrath of the Almighty which has justly fallen on our whole nation."

[39] The king fell into a rage, and handled him worse than the others, being exasperated at his scorn.

[40] So he died in his integrity, putting his whole trust in the Lord.

[41] Last of all, the mother died, after her sons.

[42] Let this be enough, then, about the eating of sacrifices and the extreme tortures.

2Mac.8

[1] But Judas, who was also called Maccabeus, and his companions secretly

entered the villages and summoned their kinsmen and enlisted those who had continued in the Jewish faith, and so they gathered about six thousand men.

[2] They besought the Lord to look upon the people who were oppressed by all, and to have pity on the temple which had been profaned by ungodly men,

[3] and to have mercy on the city which was being destroyed and about to be leveled to the ground, and to hearken to the blood that cried out to him,

[4] and to remember also the lawless destruction of the innocent babies and the blasphemies committed against his name, and to show his hatred of evil.

[5] As soon as Maccabeus got his army organized, the Gentiles could not withstand him, for the wrath of the Lord had turned to mercy.

[6] Coming without warning, he would set fire to towns and villages. He captured strategic positions and put to flight not a few of the enemy.

[7] He found the nights most advantageous for such attacks. And talk of his valor spread everywhere.

[8] When Philip saw that the man was gaining ground little by little, and that he was pushing ahead with more frequent successes, he wrote to Ptolemy, the governor of Coelesyria and Phoenicia, for aid to the king's government.

[9] And Ptolemy promptly appointed Nicanor the son of Patroclus, one of the king's chief friends, and sent him, in command of no fewer than twenty thousand Gentiles of all nations, to wipe out the whole race of Judea. He associated with him Gorgias, a general and a man of experience in military service.

[10] Nicanor determined to make up for the king the tribute due to the Romans, two thousand talents, by selling the captured Jews into slavery.

[11] And he immediately sent to the cities on the seacoast, inviting them to buy Jewish slaves and promising to hand over ninety slaves for a talent, not expecting the judgment from the Almighty that was about to overtake him.

[12] Word came to Judas concerning Nicanor's invasion; and when he told his companions of the arrival of the army,

[13] those who were cowardly and distrustful of God's justice ran off and got away.

[14] Others sold all their remaining property, and at the same time besought the Lord to rescue those who had been sold by the ungodly Nicanor before he ever met them,

[15] if not for their own sake, yet for the sake of the covenants made with their fathers, and because he had called them by his holy and glorious name.

[16] But Maccabeus gathered his men together, to the number six thousand, and exhorted them not to be frightened by the enemy and not to fear the great multitude of Gentiles who were wickedly coming against them, but to fight nobly,

[17] keeping before their eyes the lawless outrage which the Gentiles had committed against the holy place, and the torture of the derided city, and besides, the overthrow of their ancestral way of life.

[18] "For they trust to arms and acts of daring," he said, "but we trust in the Almighty God, who is able with a single nod to strike down those who are coming against us and even the whole world."

[19] Moreover, he told them of the times when help came to their ancestors; both the time of Sennacherib, when one hundred and eighty-five thousand perished,

[20] and the time of the battle with the Galatians that took place in Babylonia, when eight thousand in all went into the affair, with four thousand Macedonians; and when the Macedonians were hard pressed, the eight thousand, by the help that came to them from heaven, destroyed one hundred and twenty thousand and took much booty.

[21] With these words he filled them with good courage and made them ready to die for their laws and their country; then he divided his army into four parts.

[22] He appointed his brothers also, Simon and Joseph and Jonathan, each to command a division, putting fifteen hundred men under each.

[23] Besides, he appointed Eleazar to read aloud from the holy book, and gave the watchword, "God's help"; then, leading the first division himself, he joined battle with Nicanor.

[24] With the Almighty as their ally, they slew more than nine thousand of the enemy, and wounded and disabled most of Nicanor's army, and forced them all to flee.

[25] They captured the money of those who had come to buy them as slaves. After pursuing them for some distance, they were obliged to return because the hour was late.

[26] For it was the day before the sabbath, and for that reason they did not continue their pursuit.

[27] And when they had collected the arms of the enemy and stripped them of their spoils, they kept the sabbath, giving great praise and thanks to the Lord, who had preserved them for that day and allotted it to them as the beginning of mercy.

[28] After the sabbath they gave some of the spoils to those who had been tortured and to the widows and orphans, and distributed the rest among themselves and their children.

[29] When they had done this, they made common supplication and besought the merciful Lord to be wholly reconciled with his servants.

[30] In encounters with the forces of Timothy and Bacchides they killed more than twenty thousand of them and got possession of some exceedingly high strongholds, and they divided very much plunder, giving to those who had been tortured and to the orphans and widows, and also to the aged,

shares equal to their own.

[31] Collecting the arms of the enemy, they stored them all carefully in strategic places, and carried the rest of the spoils to Jerusalem.

[32] They killed the commander of Timothy's forces, a most unholy man, and one who had greatly troubled the Jews.

[33] While they were celebrating the victory in the city of their fathers, they burned those who had set fire to the sacred gates, Callisthenes and some others, who had fled into one little house; so these received the proper recompense for their impiety.

[34] The thrice-accursed Nicanor, who had brought the thousand merchants to buy the Jews,

[35] having been humbled with the help of the Lord by opponents whom he regarded as of the least account, took off his splendid uniform and made his way alone like a runaway slave across the country till he reached Antioch, having succeeded chiefly in the destruction of his own army!

[36] Thus he who had undertaken to secure tribute for the Romans by the capture of the people of Jerusalem proclaimed that the Jews had a Defender, and that therefore the Jews were invulnerable, because they followed the laws ordained by him.

2Mac.9

[1] About that time, as it happened, Antiochus had retreated in disorder from the region of Persia.

[2] For he had entered the city called Persepolis, and attempted to rob the temples and control the city. Therefore the people rushed to the rescue with arms, and Antiochus and his men were defeated, with the result that Antiochus was put to flight by the inhabitants and beat a shameful retreat.

[3] While he was in Ecbatana, news came to him of what had happened to Nicanor and the forces of Timothy.

[4] Transported with rage, he conceived the idea of turning upon the Jews the injury done by those who had put him to flight; so he ordered his charioteer to drive without stopping until he completed the journey. But the judgment of heaven rode with him! For in his arrogance he said, "When I get there I will make Jerusalem a cemetery of Jews."

[5] But the all-seeing Lord, the God of Israel, struck him an incurable and unseen blow. As soon as he ceased speaking he was seized with a pain in his bowels for which there was no relief and with sharp internal tortures --

[6] and that very justly, for he had tortured the bowels of others with many and strange inflictions.

[7] Yet he did not in any way stop his insolence, but was even more filled with arrogance, breathing fire in his rage against the Jews, and giving orders to hasten the journey. And so it came about that he fell out of his chariot as it was rushing along, and the fall was so hard as to torture every limb of his body.

[8] Thus he who had just been thinking that he could command the waves

of the sea, in his superhuman arrogance, and imagining that he could weigh the high mountains in a balance, was brought down to earth and carried in a litter, making the power of God manifest to all.

[9] And so the ungodly man's body swarmed with worms, and while he was still living in anguish and pain, his flesh rotted away, and because of his stench the whole army felt revulsion at his decay.

[10] Because of his intolerable stench no one was able to carry the man who a little while before had thought that he could touch the stars of heaven.

[11] Then it was that, broken in spirit, he began to lose much of his arrogance and to come to his senses under the scourge of God, for he was tortured with pain every moment.

[12] And when he could not endure his own stench, he uttered these words: "It is right to be subject to God, and no mortal should think that he is equal to God."

[13] Then the abominable fellow made a vow to the Lord, who would no longer have mercy on him, stating

[14] that the holy city, which he was hastening to level to the ground and to make a cemetery, he was now declaring to be free;

[15] and the Jews, whom he had not considered worth burying but had planned to throw out with their children to the beasts, for the birds to pick, he would make, all of them, equal to citizens of Athens;

[16] and the holy sanctuary, which he had formerly plundered, he would adorn with the finest offerings; and the holy vessels he would give back, all of them, many times over; and the expenses incurred for the sacrifices he would provide from his own revenues;

[17] and in addition to all this he also would become a Jew and would visit every inhabited place to proclaim the power of God.

[18] But when his sufferings did not in any way abate, for the judgment of God had justly come upon him, he gave up all hope for himself and wrote to the Jews the following letter, in the form of a supplication. This was its content:

[19] "To his worthy Jewish citizens, Antiochus their king and general sends hearty greetings and good wishes for their health and prosperity.

[20] If you and your children are well and your affairs are as you wish, I am glad. As my hope is in heaven,

[21] I remember with affection your esteem and good will. On my way back from the region of Persia I suffered an annoying illness, and I have deemed it necessary to take thought for the general security of all.

[22] I do not despair of my condition, for I have good hope of recovering from my illness,

[23] but I observed that my father, on the occasions when he made expeditions into the upper country, appointed his successor,

[24] so that, if anything unexpected happened or any unwelcome news

came, the people throughout the realm would not be troubled, for they would know to whom the government was left.

[25] Moreover, I understand how the princes along the borders and the neighbors to my kingdom keep watching for opportunities and waiting to see what will happen. So I have appointed my son Antiochus to be king, whom I have often entrusted and commended to most of you when I hastened off to the upper provinces; and I have written to him what is written here.

[26] I therefore urge and beseech you to remember the public and private services rendered to you and to maintain your present good will, each of you, toward me and my son.

[27] For I am sure that he will follow my policy and will treat you with moderation and kindness."

[28] So the murderer and blasphemer, having endured the more intense suffering, such as he had inflicted on others, came to the end of his life by a most pitiable fate, among the mountains in a strange land.

[29] And Philip, one of his courtiers, took his body home; then, fearing the son of Antiochus, he betook himself to Ptolemy Philometor in Egypt.

2Mac.10

[1] Now Maccabeus and his followers, the Lord leading them on, recovered the temple and the city;

[2] and they tore down the altars which had been built in the public square by the foreigners, and also destroyed the sacred precincts.

[3] They purified the sanctuary, and made another altar of sacrifice; then, striking fire out of flint, they offered sacrifices, after a lapse of two years, and they burned incense and lighted lamps and set out the bread of the Presence.

[4] And when they had done this, they fell prostrate and besought the Lord that they might never again fall into such misfortunes, but that, if they should ever sin, they might be disciplined by him with forbearance and not be handed over to blasphemous and barbarous nations.

[5] It happened that on the same day on which the sanctuary had been profaned by the foreigners, the purification of the sanctuary took place, that is, on the twenty-fifth day of the same month, which was Chislev.

[6] And they celebrated it for eight days with rejoicing, in the manner of the feast of booths, remembering how not long before, during the feast of booths, they had been wandering in the mountains and caves like wild animals.

[7] Therefore bearing ivy-wreathed wands and beautiful branches and also fronds of palm, they offered hymns of thanksgiving to him who had given success to the purifying of his own holy place.

[8] They decreed by public ordinance and vote that the whole nation of the Jews should observe these days every year.

[9] Such then was the end of Antiochus, who was called Epiphanes.

[10] Now we will tell what took place under Antiochus Eupator, who was the son of that ungodly man, and will give a brief summary of the principal calamities of the wars.

[11] This man, when he succeeded to the kingdom, appointed one Lysias to have charge of the government and to be chief governor of Coelesyria and Phoenicia.

[12] Ptolemy, who was called Macron, took the lead in showing justice to the Jews because of the wrong that had been done to them, and attempted to maintain peaceful relations with them.

[13] As a result he was accused before Eupator by the king's friends. He heard himself called a traitor at every turn, because he had abandoned Cyprus, which Philometor had entrusted to him, and had gone over to Antiochus Epiphanes. Unable to command the respect due his office, he took poison and ended his life.

[14] When Gorgias became governor of the region, he maintained a force of mercenaries, and at every turn kept on warring against the Jews.

[15] Besides this, the Idumeans, who had control of important strongholds, were harassing the Jews; they received those who were banished from Jerusalem, and endeavored to keep up the war.

[16] But Maccabeus and his men, after making solemn supplication and beseeching God to fight on their side, rushed to the strongholds of the Idumeans.

[17] Attacking them vigorously, they gained possession of the places, and beat off all who fought upon the wall, and slew those whom they encountered, killing no fewer than twenty thousand.

[18] When no less than nine thousand took refuge in two very strong towers well equipped to withstand a siege,

[19] Maccabeus left Simon and Joseph, and also Zacchaeus and his men, a force sufficient to besiege them; and he himself set off for places where he was more urgently needed.

[20] But the men with Simon, who were money-hungry, were bribed by some of those who were in the towers, and on receiving seventy thousand drachmas let some of them slip away.

[21] When word of what had happened came to Maccabeus, he gathered the leaders of the people, and accused these men of having sold their brethren for money by setting their enemies free to fight against them.

[22] Then he slew these men who had turned traitor, and immediately captured the two towers.

[23] Having success at arms in everything he undertook, he destroyed more than twenty thousand in the two strongholds.

[24] Now Timothy, who had been defeated by the Jews before, gathered a tremendous force of mercenaries and collected the cavalry from Asia in no small number. He came on, intending to take Judea by storm.

[25] As he drew near, Maccabeus and his men sprinkled dust upon their heads and girded their loins with sackcloth, in supplication to God.

[26] Falling upon the steps before the altar, they besought him to be gracious to them and to be an enemy to their enemies and an adversary to their adversaries, as the law declares.

[27] And rising from their prayer they took up their arms and advanced a considerable distance from the city; and when they came near to the enemy they halted.

[28] Just as dawn was breaking, the two armies joined battle, the one having as pledge of success and victory not only their valor but their reliance upon the Lord, while the other made rage their leader in the fight.

[29] When the battle became fierce, there appeared to the enemy from heaven five resplendent men on horses with golden bridles, and they were leading the Jews.

[30] Surrounding Maccabeus and protecting him with their own armor and weapons, they kept him from being wounded. And they showered arrows and thunderbolts upon the enemy, so that, confused and blinded, they were thrown into disorder and cut to pieces.

[31] Twenty thousand five hundred were slaughtered, besides six hundred horsemen.

[32] Timothy himself fled to a stronghold called Gazara, especially well garrisoned, where Chaereas was commander.

[33] Then Maccabeus and his men were glad, and they besieged the fort for four days.

[34] The men within, relying on the strength of the place, blasphemed terribly and hurled out wicked words.

[35] But at dawn of the fifth day, twenty young men in the army of Maccabeus, fired with anger because of the blasphemies, bravely stormed the wall and with savage fury cut down every one they met.

[36] Others who came up in the same way wheeled around against the defenders and set fire to the towers; they kindled fires and burned the blasphemers alive. Others broke open the gates and let in the rest of the force, and they occupied the city.

[37] They killed Timothy, who was hidden in a cistern, and his brother Chaereas, and Apollophanes.

[38] When they had accomplished these things, with hymns and thanksgivings they blessed the Lord who shows great kindness to Israel and gives them the victory.

2Mac.11

[1] Very soon after this, Lysias, the king's guardian and kinsman, who was in charge of the government, being vexed at what had happened,

[2] gathered about eighty thousand men and all his cavalry and came against the Jews. He intended to make the city a home for Greeks,

[3] and to levy tribute on the temple as he did on the sacred places of the

other nations, and to put up the high priesthood for sale every year.

[4] He took no account whatever of the power of God, but was elated with his ten thousands of infantry, and his thousands of cavalry, and his eighty elephants.

[5] Invading Judea, he approached Beth-zur, which was a fortified place about five leagues from Jerusalem, and pressed it hard.

[6] When Maccabeus and his men got word that Lysias was besieging the strongholds, they and all the people, with lamentations and tears, besought the Lord to send a good angel to save Israel.

[7] Maccabeus himself was the first to take up arms, and he urged the others to risk their lives with him to aid their brethren. Then they eagerly rushed off together.

[8] And there, while they were still near Jerusalem, a horseman appeared at their head, clothed in white and brandishing weapons of gold.

[9] And they all together praised the merciful God, and were strengthened in heart, ready to assail not only men but the wildest beasts or walls of iron.

[10] They advanced in battle order, having their heavenly ally, for the Lord had mercy on them.

[11] They hurled themselves like lions against the enemy, and slew eleven thousand of them and sixteen hundred horsemen, and forced all the rest to flee.

[12] Most of them got away stripped and wounded, and Lysias himself escaped by disgraceful flight.

[13] And as he was not without intelligence, he pondered over the defeat which had befallen him, and realized that the Hebrews were invincible because the mighty God fought on their side. So he sent to them

[14] and persuaded them to settle everything on just terms, promising that he would persuade the king, constraining him to be their friend.

[15] Maccabeus, having regard for the common good, agreed to all that Lysias urged. For the king granted every request in behalf of the Jews which Maccabeus delivered to Lysias in writing.

[16] The letter written to the Jews by Lysias was to this effect: "Lysias to the people of the Jews, greeting.

[17] John and Absalom, who were sent by you, have delivered your signed communication and have asked about the matters indicated therein.

[18] I have informed the king of everything that needed to be brought before him, and he has agreed to what was possible.

[19] If you will maintain your good will toward the government, I will endeavor for the future to help promote your welfare.

[20] And concerning these matters and their details, I have ordered these men and my representatives to confer with you.

[21] Farewell. The one hundred and forty-eighth year, Dioscorinthius twenty-fourth."

[22] The king's letter ran thus: "King Antiochus to his brother Lysias, greeting.

[23] Now that our father has gone on to the gods, we desire that the subjects of the kingdom be undisturbed in caring for their own affairs.

[24] We have heard that the Jews do not consent to our father's change to Greek customs but prefer their own way of living and ask that their own customs be allowed them.

[25] Accordingly, since we choose that this nation also be free from disturbance, our decision is that their temple be restored to them and that they live according to the customs of their ancestors.

[26] You will do well, therefore, to send word to them and give them pledges of friendship, so that they may know our policy and be of good cheer and go on happily in the conduct of their own affairs."

[27] To the nation the king's letter was as follows: "King Antiochus to the senate of the Jews and to the other Jews, greeting.

[28] If you are well, it is as we desire. We also are in good health.

[29] Menelaus has informed us that you wish to return home and look after your own affairs.

[30] Therefore those who go home by the thirtieth day of Xanthicus will have our pledge of friendship and full permission

[31] for the Jews to enjoy their own food and laws, just as formerly, and none of them shall be molested in any way for what he may have done in ignorance.

[32] And I have also sent Menelaus to encourage you.

[33] Farewell. The one hundred and forty-eighth year, Xanthicus fifteenth."

[34] The Romans also sent them a letter, which read thus: "Quintus Memmius and Titus Manius, envoys of the Romans, to the people of the Jews, greeting.

[35] With regard to what Lysias the kinsman of the king has granted you, we also give consent.

[36] But as to the matters which he decided are to be referred to the king, as soon as you have considered them, send some one promptly, so that we may make proposals appropriate for you. For we are on our way to Antioch.

[37] Therefore make haste and send some men, so that we may have your judgment.

[38] Farewell. The one hundred and forty-eighth year, Xanthicus fifteenth."

2Mac.12

[1] When this agreement had been reached, Lysias returned to the king, and the Jews went about their farming.

[2] But some of the governors in various places, Timothy and Apollonius the son of Gennaeus, as well as Hieronymus and Demophon, and in addition to these Nicanor the governor of Cyprus, would not let them live quietly and in peace.

[3] And some men of Joppa did so ungodly a deed as this: they invited the

Jews who lived among them to embark, with their wives and children, on boats which they had provided, as though there were no ill will to the Jews; [4] and this was done by public vote of the city. And when they accepted, because they wished to live peaceably and suspected nothing, the men of Joppa took them out to sea and drowned them, not less than two hundred.

[5] When Judas heard of the cruelty visited on his countrymen, he gave orders to his men

[6] and, calling upon God the righteous Judge, attacked the murderers of his brethren. He set fire to the harbor by night, and burned the boats, and massacred those who had taken refuge there.

[7] Then, because the city's gates were closed, he withdrew, intending to come again and root out the whole community of Joppa.

[8] But learning that the men in Jamnia meant in the same way to wipe out the Jews who were living among them,

[9] he attacked the people of Jamnia by night and set fire to the harbor and the fleet, so that the glow of the light was seen in Jerusalem, thirty miles distant.

[10] When they had gone more than a mile from there, on their march against Timothy, not less than five thousand Arabs with five hundred horsemen attacked them.

[11] After a hard fight Judas and his men won the victory, by the help of God. The defeated nomads besought Judas to grant them pledges of friendship, promising to give him cattle and to help his people in all other ways.

[12] Judas, thinking that they might really be useful in many ways, agreed to make peace with them; and after receiving his pledges they departed to their tents.

[13] He also attacked a certain city which was strongly fortified with earthworks and walls, and inhabited by all sorts of Gentiles. Its name was Caspin.

[14] And those who were within, relying on the strength of the walls and on their supply of provisions, behaved most insolently toward Judas and his men, railing at them and even blaspheming and saying unholy things.

[15] But Judas and his men, calling upon the great Sovereign of the world, who without battering-rams or engines of war overthrew Jericho in the days of Joshua, rushed furiously upon the walls.

[16] They took the city by the will of God, and slaughtered untold numbers, so that the adjoining lake, a quarter of a mile wide, appeared to be running over with blood.

[17] When they had gone ninety-five miles from there, they came to Charax, to the Jews who are called Toubiani.

[18] They did not find Timothy in that region, for he had by then departed from the region without accomplishing anything, though in one place he

had left a very strong garrison.

[19] Dositheus and Sosipater, who were captains under Maccabeus, marched out and destroyed those whom Timothy had left in the stronghold, more than ten thousand men.

[20] But Maccabeus arranged his army in divisions, set men in command of the divisions, and hastened after Timothy, who had with him a hundred and twenty thousand infantry and two thousand five hundred cavalry.

[21] When Timothy learned of the approach of Judas, he sent off the women and the children and also the baggage to a place called Carnaim; for that place was hard to besiege and difficult of access because of the narrowness of all the approaches.

[22] But when Judas' first division appeared, terror and fear came over the enemy at the manifestation to them of him who sees all things; and they rushed off in flight and were swept on, this way and that, so that often they were injured by their own men and pierced by the points of their swords.

[23] And Judas pressed the pursuit with the utmost vigor, putting the sinners to the sword, and destroyed as many as thirty thousand men.

[24] Timothy himself fell into the hands of Dositheus and Sosipater and their men. With great guile he besought them to let him go in safety, because he held the parents of most of them and the brothers of some and no consideration would be shown them.

[25] And when with many words he had confirmed his solemn promise to restore them unharmed, they let him go, for the sake of saving their brethren.

[26] Then Judas marched against Carnaim and the temple of Atargatis, and slaughtered twenty-five thousand people.

[27] After the rout and destruction of these, he marched also against Ephron, a fortified city where Lysias dwelt with multitudes of people of all nationalities. Stalwart young men took their stand before the walls and made a vigorous defense; and great stores of war engines and missiles were there.

[28] But the Jews called upon the Sovereign who with power shatters the might of his enemies, and they got the city into their hands, and killed as many as twenty-five thousand of those who were within it.

[29] Setting out from there, they hastened to Scythopolis, which is seventy-five miles from Jerusalem.

[30] But when the Jews who dwelt there bore witness to the good will which the people of Scythopolis had shown them and their kind treatment of them in times of misfortune,

[31] they thanked them and exhorted them to be well disposed to their race in the future also. Then they went up to Jerusalem, as the feast of weeks was close at hand.

[32] After the feast called Pentecost, they hastened against Gorgias, the governor of Idumea.

[33] And he came out with three thousand infantry and four hundred cavalry.

[34] When they joined battle, it happened that a few of the Jews fell.

[35] But a certain Dositheus, one of Bacenor's men, who was on horseback and was a strong man, caught hold of Gorgias, and grasping his cloak was dragging him off by main strength, wishing to take the accursed man alive, when one of the Thracian horsemen bore down upon him and cut off his arm; so Gorgias escaped and reached Marisa.

[36] As Esdris and his men had been fighting for a long time and were weary, Judas called upon the Lord to show himself their ally and leader in the battle.

[37] In the language of their fathers he raised the battle cry, with hymns; then he charged against Gorgias' men when they were not expecting it, and put them to flight.

[38] Then Judas assembled his army and went to the city of Adullam. As the seventh day was coming on, they purified themselves according to the custom, and they kept the sabbath there.

[39] On the next day, as by that time it had become necessary, Judas and his men went to take up the bodies of the fallen and to bring them back to lie with their kinsmen in the sepulchres of their fathers.

[40] Then under the tunic of every one of the dead they found sacred tokens of the idols of Jamnia, which the law forbids the Jews to wear. And it became clear to all that this was why these men had fallen.

[41] So they all blessed the ways of the Lord, the righteous Judge, who reveals the things that are hidden;

[42] and they turned to prayer, beseeching that the sin which had been committed might be wholly blotted out. And the noble Judas exhorted the people to keep themselves free from sin, for they had seen with their own eyes what had happened because of the sin of those who had fallen.

[43] He also took up a collection, man by man, to the amount of two thousand drachmas of silver, and sent it to Jerusalem to provide for a sin offering. In doing this he acted very well and honorably, taking account of the resurrection.

[44] For if he were not expecting that those who had fallen would rise again, it would have been superfluous and foolish to pray for the dead.

[45] But if he was looking to the splendid reward that is laid up for those who fall asleep in godliness, it was a holy and pious thought. Therefore he made atonement for the dead, that they might be delivered from their sin.

2Mac.13

[1] In the one hundred and forty-ninth year word came to Judas and his men that Antiochus Eupator was coming with a great army against Judea,

[2] and with him Lysias, his guardian, who had charge of the government. Each of them had a Greek force of one hundred and ten thousand infantry,

five thousand three hundred cavalry, twenty-two elephants, and three hundred chariots armed with scythes.

[3] Menelaus also joined them and with utter hypocrisy urged Antiochus on, not for the sake of his country's welfare, but because he thought that he would be established in office.

[4] But the King of kings aroused the anger of Antiochus against the scoundrel; and when Lysias informed him that this man was to blame for all the trouble, he ordered them to take him to Beroea and to put him to death by the method which is the custom in that place.

[5] For there is a tower in that place, fifty cubits high, full of ashes, and it has a rim running around it which on all sides inclines precipitously into the ashes.

[6] There they all push to destruction any man guilty of sacrilege or notorious for other crimes.

[7] By such a fate it came about that Menelaus the lawbreaker died, without even burial in the earth.

[8] And this was eminently just; because he had committed many sins against the altar whose fire and ashes were holy, he met his death in ashes.

[9] The king with barbarous arrogance was coming to show the Jews things far worse than those that had been done in his father's time.

[10] But when Judas heard of this, he ordered the people to call upon the Lord day and night, now if ever to help those who were on the point of being deprived of the law and their country and the holy temple,

[11] and not to let the people who had just begun to revive fall into the hands of the blasphemous Gentiles.

[12] When they had all joined in the same petition and had besought the merciful Lord with weeping and fasting and lying prostrate for three days without ceasing, Judas exhorted them and ordered them to stand ready.

[13] After consulting privately with the elders, he determined to march out and decide the matter by the help of God before the king's army could enter Judea and get possession of the city.

[14] So, committing the decision to the Creator of the world and exhorting his men to fight nobly to the death for the laws, temple, city, country, and commonwealth, he pitched his camp near Modein.

[15] He gave his men the watchword, "God's victory," and with a picked force of the bravest young men, he attacked the king's pavilion at night and slew as many as two thousand men in the camp. He stabbed the leading elephant and its rider.

[16] In the end they filled the camp with terror and confusion and withdrew in triumph.

[17] This happened, just as day was dawning, because the Lord's help protected him.

[18] The king, having had a taste of the daring of the Jews, tried strategy in attacking their positions.

[19] He advanced against Beth-zur, a strong fortress of the Jews, was turned back, attacked again, and was defeated.

[20] Judas sent in to the garrison whatever was necessary.

[21] But Rhodocus, a man from the ranks of the Jews, gave secret information to the enemy; he was sought for, caught, and put in prison.

[22] The king negotiated a second time with the people in Beth-zur, gave pledges, received theirs, withdrew, attacked Judas and his men, was defeated;

[23] he got word that Philip, who had been left in charge of the government, had revolted in Antioch; he was dismayed, called in the Jews, yielded and swore to observe all their rights, settled with them and offered sacrifice, honored the sanctuary and showed generosity to the holy place.

[24] He received Maccabeus, left Hegemonides as governor from Ptolemais to Gerar,

[25] and went to Ptolemais. The people of Ptolemais were indignant over the treaty; in fact they were so angry that they wanted to annul its terms.

[26] Lysias took the public platform, made the best possible defense, convinced them, appeased them, gained their good will, and set out for Antioch. This is how the king's attack and withdrawal turned out.

2Mac.14

[1] Three years later, word came to Judas and his men that Demetrius, the son of Seleucus, had sailed into the harbor of Tripolis with a strong army and a fleet,

[2] and had taken possession of the country, having made away with Antiochus and his guardian Lysias.

[3] Now a certain Alcimus, who had formerly been high priest but had wilfully defiled himself in the times of separation, realized that there was no way for him to be safe or to have access again to the holy altar,

[4] and went to King Demetrius in about the one hundred and fifty-first year, presenting to him a crown of gold and a palm, and besides these some of the customary olive branches from the temple. During that day he kept quiet.

[5] But he found an opportunity that furthered his mad purpose when he was invited by Demetrius to a meeting of the council and was asked about the disposition and intentions of the Jews. He answered:

[6] "Those of the Jews who are called Hasideans, whose leader is Judas Maccabeus, are keeping up war and stirring up sedition, and will not let the kingdom attain tranquillity.

[7] Therefore I have laid aside my ancestral glory -- I mean the high priesthood -- and have now come here,

[8] first because I am genuinely concerned for the interests of the king, and second because I have regard also for my fellow citizens. For through the folly of those whom I have mentioned our whole nation is now in no small

misfortune.

[9] Since you are acquainted, O king, with the details of this matter, deign to take thought for our country and our hard-pressed nation with the gracious kindness which you show to all.

[10] For as long as Judas lives, it is impossible for the government to find peace."

[11] When he had said this, the rest of the king's friends, who were hostile to Judas, quickly inflamed Demetrius still more.

[12] And he immediately chose Nicanor, who had been in command of the elephants, appointed him governor of Judea, and sent him off

[13] with orders to kill Judas and scatter his men, and to set up Alcimus as high priest of the greatest temple.

[14] And the Gentiles throughout Judea, who had fled before Judas, flocked to join Nicanor, thinking that the misfortunes and calamities of the Jews would mean prosperity for themselves.

[15] When the Jews heard of Nicanor's coming and the gathering of the Gentiles, they sprinkled dust upon their heads and prayed to him who established his own people for ever and always upholds his own heritage by manifesting himself.

[16] At the command of the leader, they set out from there immediately and engaged them in battle at a village called Dessau.

[17] Simon, the brother of Judas, had encountered Nicanor, but had been temporarily checked because of the sudden consternation created by the enemy.

[18] Nevertheless Nicanor, hearing of the valor of Judas and his men and their courage in battle for their country, shrank from deciding the issue by bloodshed.

[19] Therefore he sent Posidonius and Theodotus and Mattathias to give and receive pledges of friendship.

[20] When the terms had been fully considered, and the leader had informed the people, and it had appeared that they were of one mind, they agreed to the covenant.

[21] And the leaders set a day on which to meet by themselves. A chariot came forward from each army; seats of honor were set in place;

[22] Judas posted armed men in readiness at key places to prevent sudden treachery on the part of the enemy; they held the proper conference.

[23] Nicanor stayed on in Jerusalem and did nothing out of the way, but dismissed the flocks of people that had gathered.

[24] And he kept Judas always in his presence; he was warmly attached to the man.

[25] And he urged him to marry and have children; so he married, settled down, and shared the common life.

[26] But when Alcimus noticed their good will for one another, he took the covenant that had been made and went to Demetrius. He told him that

Nicanor was disloyal to the government, for he had appointed that conspirator against the kingdom, Judas, to be his successor.

[27] The king became excited and, provoked by the false accusations of that depraved man, wrote to Nicanor, stating that he was displeased with the covenant and commanding him to send Maccabeus to Antioch as a prisoner without delay.

[28] When this message came to Nicanor, he was troubled and grieved that he had to annul their agreement when the man had done no wrong.

[29] Since it was not possible to oppose the king, he watched for an opportunity to accomplish this by a stratagem.

[30] But Maccabeus, noticing that Nicanor was more austere in his dealings with him and was meeting him more rudely than had been his custom, concluded that this austerity did not spring from the best motives. So he gathered not a few of his men, and went into hiding from Nicanor.

[31] When the latter became aware that he had been cleverly outwitted by the man, he went to the great and holy temple while the priests were offering the customary sacrifices, and commanded them to hand the man over.

[32] And when they declared on oath that they did not know where the man was whom he sought,

[33] he stretched out his right hand toward the sanctuary, and swore this oath: "If you do not hand Judas over to me as a prisoner, I will level this precinct of God to the ground and tear down the altar, and I will build here a splendid temple to Dionysus."

[34] Having said this, he went away. Then the priests stretched forth their hands toward heaven and called upon the constant Defender of our nation, in these words:

[35] "O Lord of all, who hast need of nothing, thou wast pleased that there be a temple for thy habitation among us;

[36] so now, O holy One, Lord of all holiness, keep undefiled for ever this house that has been so recently purified."

[37] A certain Razis, one of the elders of Jerusalem, was denounced to Nicanor as a man who loved his fellow citizens and was very well thought of and for his good will was called father of the Jews.

[38] For in former times, when there was no mingling with the Gentiles, he had been accused of Judaism, and for Judaism he had with all zeal risked body and life.

[39] Nicanor, wishing to exhibit the enmity which he had for the Jews, sent more than five hundred soldiers to arrest him;

[40] for he thought that by arresting him he would do them an injury.

[41] When the troops were about to capture the tower and were forcing the door of the courtyard, they ordered that fire be brought and the doors burned. Being surrounded, Razis fell upon his own sword,

[42] preferring to die nobly rather than to fall into the hands of sinners and suffer outrages unworthy of his noble birth.

[43] But in the heat of the struggle he did not hit exactly, and the crowd was now rushing in through the doors. He bravely ran up on the wall, and manfully threw himself down into the crowd.

[44] But as they quickly drew back, a space opened and he fell in the middle of the empty space.

[45] Still alive and aflame with anger, he rose, and though his blood gushed forth and his wounds were severe he ran through the crowd; and standing upon a steep rock,

[46] with his blood now completely drained from him, he tore out his entrails, took them with both hands and hurled them at the crowd, calling upon the Lord of life and spirit to give them back to him again. This was the manner of his death.

2Mac.15

[1] When Nicanor heard that Judas and his men were in the region of Samaria, he made plans to attack them with complete safety on the day of rest.

[2] And when the Jews who were compelled to follow him said, "Do not destroy so savagely and barbarously, but show respect for the day which he who sees all things has honored and hallowed above other days,"

[3] the thrice-accursed wretch asked if there were a sovereign in heaven who had commanded the keeping of the sabbath day.

[4] And when they declared, "It is the living Lord himself, the Sovereign in heaven, who ordered us to observe the seventh day,"

[5] he replied, "And I am a sovereign also, on earth, and I command you to take up arms and finish the king's business." Nevertheless, he did not succeed in carrying out his abominable design.

[6] This Nicanor in his utter boastfulness and arrogance had determined to erect a public monument of victory over Judas and his men.

[7] But Maccabeus did not cease to trust with all confidence that he would get help from the Lord.

[8] And he exhorted his men not to fear the attack of the Gentiles, but to keep in mind the former times when help had come to them from heaven, and now to look for the victory which the Almighty would give them.

[9] Encouraging them from the law and the prophets, and reminding them also of the struggles they had won, he made them the more eager.

[10] And when he had aroused their courage, he gave his orders, at the same time pointing out the perfidy of the Gentiles and their violation of oaths.

[11] He armed each of them not so much with confidence in shields and spears as with the inspiration of brave words, and he cheered them all by relating a dream, a sort of vision, which was worthy of belief.

[12] What he saw was this: Onias, who had been high priest, a noble and good man, of modest bearing and gentle manner, one who spoke fittingly

and had been trained from childhood in all that belongs to excellence, was praying with outstretched hands for the whole body of the Jews.

[13] Then likewise a man appeared, distinguished by his gray hair and dignity, and of marvelous majesty and authority.

[14] And Onias spoke, saying, "This is a man who loves the brethren and prays much for the people and the holy city, Jeremiah, the prophet of God."

[15] Jeremiah stretched out his right hand and gave to Judas a golden sword, and as he gave it he addressed him thus:

[16] "Take this holy sword, a gift from God, with which you will strike down your adversaries."

[17] Encouraged by the words of Judas, so noble and so effective in arousing valor and awaking manliness in the souls of the young, they determined not to carry on a campaign but to attack bravely, and to decide the matter, by fighting hand to hand with all courage, because the city and the sanctuary and the temple were in danger.

[18] Their concern for wives and children, and also for brethren and relatives, lay upon them less heavily; their greatest and first fear was for the consecrated sanctuary.

[19] And those who had to remain in the city were in no little distress, being anxious over the encounter in the open country.

[20] When all were now looking forward to the coming decision, and the enemy was already close at hand with their army drawn up for battle, the elephants strategically stationed and the cavalry deployed on the flanks,

[21] Maccabeus, perceiving the hosts that were before him and the varied supply of arms and the savagery of the elephants, stretched out his hands toward heaven and called upon the Lord who works wonders; for he knew that it is not by arms, but as the Lord decides, that he gains the victory for those who deserve it.

[22] And he called upon him in these words: "O Lord, thou didst send thy angel in the time of Hezekiah king of Judea, and he slew fully a hundred and eighty-five thousand in the camp of Sennacherib.

[23] So now, O Sovereign of the heavens, send a good angel to carry terror and trembling before us.

[24] By the might of thy arm may these blasphemers who come against thy holy people be struck down." With these words he ended his prayer.

[25] Nicanor and his men advanced with trumpets and battle songs;

[26] and Judas and his men met the enemy in battle with invocation to God and prayers.

[27] So, fighting with their hands and praying to God in their hearts, they laid low no less than thirty-five thousand men, and were greatly gladdened by God's manifestation.

[28] When the action was over and they were returning with joy, they recognized Nicanor, lying dead, in full armor.

[29] Then there was shouting and tumult, and they blessed the Sovereign Lord in the language of their fathers.

[30] And the man who was ever in body and soul the defender of his fellow citizens, the man who maintained his youthful good will toward his countrymen, ordered them to cut off Nicanor's head and arm and carry them to Jerusalem.

[31] And when he arrived there and had called his countrymen together and stationed the priests before the altar, he sent for those who were in the citadel.

[32] He showed them the vile Nicanor's head and that profane man's arm, which had been boastfully stretched out against the holy house of the Almighty;

[33] and he cut out the tongue of the ungodly Nicanor and said that he would give it piecemeal to the birds and hang up these rewards of his folly opposite the sanctuary.

[34] And they all, looking to heaven, blessed the Lord who had manifested himself, saying, "Blessed is he who has kept his own place undefiled."

[35] And he hung Nicanor's head from the citadel, a clear and conspicuous sign to every one of the help of the Lord.

[36] And they all decreed by public vote never to let this day go unobserved, but to celebrate the thirteenth day of the twelfth month -- which is called Adar in the Syrian language -- the day before Mordecai's day.

[37] This, then, is how matters turned out with Nicanor. And from that time the city has been in the possession of the Hebrews. So I too will here end my story.

[38] If it is well told and to the point, that is what I myself desired; if it is poorly done and mediocre, that was the best I could do.

[39] For just as it is harmful to drink wine alone, or, again, to drink water alone, while wine mixed with water is sweet and delicious and enhances one's enjoyment, so also the style of the story delights the ears of those who read the work. And here will be the end.

3 Maccabees

3Mac.1

[1] When Philopator learned from those who returned that the regions which he had controlled had been seized by Antiochus, he gave orders to all his forces, both infantry and cavalry, took with him his sister Arsinoe, and marched out to the region near Raphia, where Antiochus's supporters were encamped.

[2] But a certain Theodotus, determined to carry out the plot he had devised, took with him the best of the Ptolemaic arms that had been previously issued to him, and crossed over by night to the tent of Ptolemy, intending single-handed to kill him and thereby end the war.

[3] But Dositheus, known as the son of Drimylus, a Jew by birth who later changed his religion and apostatized from the ancestral traditions, had led the king away and arranged that a certain insignificant man should sleep in the tent; and so it turned out that this man incurred the vengeance meant for the king.

[4] When a bitter fight resulted, and matters were turning out rather in favor of Antiochus, Arsinoe went to the troops with wailing and tears, her locks all disheveled, and exhorted them to defend themselves and their children and wives bravely, promising to give them each two minas of gold if they won the battle.

[5] And so it came about that the enemy was routed in the action, and many captives also were taken.

[6] Now that he had foiled the plot, Ptolemy decided to visit the neighboring cities and encourage them.

[7] By doing this, and by endowing their sacred enclosures with gifts, he strengthened the morale of his subjects.

[8] Since the Jews had sent some of their council and elders to greet him, to bring him gifts of welcome, and to congratulate him on what had happened, he was all the more eager to visit them as soon as possible.

[9] After he had arrived in Jerusalem, he offered sacrifice to the supreme God and made thank-offerings and did what was fitting for the holy place. Then, upon entering the place and being impressed by its excellence and its beauty,

[10] he marveled at the good order of the temple, and conceived a desire to enter the holy of holies.

[11] When they said that this was not permitted, because not even members

of their own nation were allowed to enter, nor even all of the priests, but only the high priest who was pre-eminent over all, and he only once a year, the king was by no means persuaded.

[12] Even after the law had been read to him, he did not cease to maintain that he ought to enter, saying, "Even if those men are deprived of this honor, I ought not to be."

[13] And he inquired why, when he entered every other temple, no one there had stopped him.

[14] And someone heedlessly said that it was wrong to take this as a sign in itself.

[15] "But since this has happened," the king said, "why should not I at least enter, whether they wish it or not?"

[16] Then the priests in all their vestments prostrated themselves and entreated the supreme God to aid in the present situation and to avert the violence of this evil design, and they filled the temple with cries and tears;

[17] and those who remained behind in the city were agitated and hurried out, supposing that something mysterious was occurring.

[18] The virgins who had been enclosed in their chambers rushed out with their mothers, sprinkled their hair with dust, and filled the streets with groans and lamentations.

[19] Those women who had recently been arrayed for marriage abandoned the bridal chambers prepared for wedded union, and, neglecting proper modesty, in a disorderly rush flocked together in the city.

[20] Mothers and nurses abandoned even newborn children here and there, some in houses and some in the streets, and without a backward look they crowded together at the most high temple.

[21] Various were the supplications of those gathered there because of what the king was profanely plotting.

[22] In addition, the bolder of the citizens would not tolerate the completion of his plans or the fulfillment of his intended purpose.

[23] They shouted to their fellows to take arms and die courageously for the ancestral law, and created a considerable disturbance in the holy place; and being barely restrained by the old men and the elders, they resorted to the same posture of supplication as the others.

[24] Meanwhile the crowd, as before, was engaged in prayer,

[25] while the elders near the king tried in various ways to change his arrogant mind from the plan that he had conceived.

[26] But he, in his arrogance, took heed of nothing, and began now to approach, determined to bring the aforesaid plan to a conclusion.

[27] When those who were around him observed this, they turned, together with our people, to call upon him who has all power to defend them in the present trouble and not to overlook this unlawful and haughty deed.

[28] The continuous, vehement, and concerted cry of the crowds resulted in an immense uproar;

[29] for it seemed that not only the men but also the walls and the whole earth around echoed, because indeed all at that time preferred death to the profanation of the place.

3Mac.2

[1] Then the high priest Simon, facing the sanctuary, bending his knees and extending his hands with calm dignity, prayed as follows:

[2] "Lord, Lord, king of the heavens, and sovereign of all creation, holy among the holy ones, the only ruler, almighty, give attention to us who are suffering grievously from an impious and profane man, puffed up in his audacity and power.

[3] For you, the creator of all things and the governor of all, are a just Ruler, and you judge those who have done anything in insolence and arrogance.

[4] You destroyed those who in the past committed injustice, among whom were even giants who trusted in their strength and boldness, whom you destroyed by bringing upon them a boundless flood.

[5] You consumed with fire and sulphur the men of Sodom who acted arrogantly, who were notorious for their vices; and you made them an example to those who should come afterward.

[6] You made known your mighty power by inflicting many and varied punishments on the audacious Pharaoh who had enslaved your holy people Israel.

[7] And when he pursued them with chariots and a mass of troops, you overwhelmed him in the depths of the sea, but carried through safely those who had put their confidence in you, the Ruler over the whole creation.

[8] And when they had seen works of your hands, they praised you, the Almighty.

[9] You, O King, when you had created the boundless and immeasurable earth, chose this city and sanctified this place for your name, though you have no need of anything; and when you had glorified it by your magnificent manifestation, you made it a firm foundation for the glory of your great and honored name.

[10] And because you love the house of Israel, you promised that if we should have reverses, and tribulation should overtake us, you would listen to our petition when we come to this place and pray.

[11] And indeed you are faithful and true.

[12] And because oftentimes when our fathers were oppressed you helped them in their humiliation, and rescued them from great evils,

[13] see now, O holy King, that because of our many and great sins we are crushed with suffering, subjected to our enemies, and overtaken by helplessness.

[14] In our downfall this audacious and profane man undertakes to violate the holy place on earth dedicated to your glorious name.

[15] For your dwelling, the heaven of heavens, is unapproachable by man.

[16] But because you graciously bestowed your glory upon your people Israel, you sanctified this place.

[17] Do not punish us for the defilement committed by these men, or call us to account for this profanation, lest the transgressors boast in their wrath or exult in the arrogance of their tongue, saying,

[18] `We have trampled down the house of the sanctuary as offensive houses are trampled down.'

[19] Wipe away our sins and disperse our errors, and reveal your mercy at this hour.

[20] Speedily let your mercies overtake us, and put praises in the mouth of those who are downcast and broken in spirit, and give us peace."

[21] Thereupon God, who oversees all things, the first Father of all, holy among the holy ones, having heard the lawful supplication, scourged him who had exalted himself in insolence and audacity.

[22] He shook him on this side and that as a reed is shaken by the wind, so that he lay helpless on the ground and, besides being paralyzed in his limbs, was unable even to speak, since he was smitten by a righteous judgment.

[23] Then both friends and bodyguards, seeing the severe punishment that had overtaken him, and fearing lest he should lose his life, quickly dragged him out, panic-stricken in their exceedingly great fear.

[24] After a while he recovered, and though he had been punished, he by no means repented, but went away uttering bitter threats.

[25] When he arrived in Egypt, he increased in his deeds of malice, abetted by the previously mentioned drinking companions and comrades, who were strangers to everything just.

[26] He was not content with his uncounted licentious deeds, but he also continued with such audacity that he framed evil reports in the various localities; and many of his friends, intently observing the king's purpose, themselves also followed his will.

[27] He proposed to inflict public disgrace upon the Jewish community, and he set up a stone on the tower in the courtyard with this inscription:

[28] "None of those who do not sacrifice shall enter their sanctuaries, and all Jews shall be subjected to a registration involving poll tax and to the status of slaves. Those who object to this are to be taken by force and put to death;

[29] those who are registered are also to be branded on their bodies by fire with the ivy-leaf symbol of Dionysus, and they shall also be reduced to their former limited status."

[30] In order that he might not appear to be an enemy to all, he inscribed below: "But if any of them prefer to join those who have been initiated into the mysteries, they shall have equal citizenship with the Alexandrians."

[31] Now some, however, with an obvious abhorrence of the price to be exacted for maintaining the religion of their city, readily gave themselves up, since they expected to enhance their reputation by their future association with the king.

[32] But the majority acted firmly with a courageous spirit and did not depart from their religion; and by paying money in exchange for life they confidently attempted to save themselves from the registration.

[33] They remained resolutely hopeful of obtaining help, and they abhorred those who separated themselves from them, considering them to be enemies of the Jewish nation, and depriving them of common fellowship and mutual help.

3Mac.3

[1] When the impious king comprehended this situation, he became so infuriated that not only was he enraged against those Jews who lived in Alexandria, but was still more bitterly hostile toward those in the countryside; and he ordered that all should promptly be gathered into one place, and put to death by the most cruel means.

[2] While these matters were being arranged, a hostile rumor was circulated against the Jewish nation by men who conspired to do them ill, a pretext being given by a report that they hindered others from the observance of their customs.

[3] The Jews, however, continued to maintain good will and unswerving loyalty toward the dynasty;

[4] but because they worshiped God and conducted themselves by his law, they kept their separateness with respect to foods. For this reason they appeared hateful to some;

[5] but since they adorned their style of life with the good deeds of upright people, they were established in good repute among all men.

[6] Nevertheless those of other races paid no heed to their good service to their nation, which was common talk among all;

[7] instead they gossiped about the differences in worship and foods, alleging that these people were loyal neither to the king nor to his authorities, but were hostile and greatly opposed to his government. So they attached no ordinary reproach to them.

[8] The Greeks in the city, though wronged in no way, when they saw an unexpected tumult around these people and the crowds that suddenly were forming, were not strong enough to help them, for they lived under tyranny. They did try to console them, being grieved at the situation, and expected that matters would change;

[9] for such a great community ought not be left to its fate when it had committed no offense.

[10] And already some of their neighbors and friends and business associates had taken some of them aside privately and were pledging to protect them and to exert more earnest efforts for their assistance.

[11] Then the king, boastful of his present good fortune, and not considering the might of the supreme God, but assuming that he would persevere constantly in his same purpose, wrote this letter against them:

[12] "King Ptolemy Philopator to his generals and soldiers in Egypt and all its districts, greetings and good health.

[13] I myself and our government are faring well.

[14] When our expedition took place in Asia, as you yourselves know, it was brought to conclusion, according to plan, by the gods' deliberate alliance with us in battle,

[15] and we considered that we should not rule the nations inhabiting Coele-Syria and Phoenicia by the power of the spear but should cherish them with clemency and great benevolence, gladly treating them well.

[16] And when we had granted very great revenues to the temples in the cities, we came on to Jerusalem also, and went up to honor the temple of those wicked people, who never cease from their folly.

[17] They accepted our presence by word, but insincerely by deed, because when we proposed to enter their inner temple and honor it with magnificent and most beautiful offerings,

[18] they were carried away by their traditional conceit, and excluded us from entering; but they were spared the exercise of our power because of the benevolence which we have toward all.

[19] By maintaining their manifest ill-will toward us, they become the only people among all nations who hold their heads high in defiance of kings and their own benefactors, and are unwilling to regard any action as sincere.

[20] "But we, when we arrived in Egypt victorious, accommodated ourselves to their folly and did as was proper, since we treat all nations with benevolence.

[21] Among other things, we made known to all our amnesty toward their compatriots here, both because of their alliance with us and the myriad affairs liberally entrusted to them from the beginning; and we ventured to make a change, by deciding both to deem them worthy of Alexandrian citizenship and to make them participants in our regular religious rites.

[22] But in their innate malice they took this in a contrary spirit, and disdained what is good. Since they incline constantly to evil,

[23] they not only spurn the priceless citizenship, but also both by speech and by silence they abominate those few among them who are sincerely disposed toward us; in every situation, in accordance with their infamous way of life, they secretly suspect that we may soon alter our policy.

[24] Therefore, fully convinced by these indications that they are ill-disposed toward us in every way, we have taken precautions lest, if a sudden disorder should later arise against us, we should have these impious people behind our backs as traitors and barbarous enemies.

[25] Therefore we have given orders that, as soon as this letter shall arrive, you are to send to us those who live among you, together with their wives and children, with insulting and harsh treatment, and bound securely with iron fetters, to suffer the sure and shameful death that befits enemies.

[26] For when these all have been punished, we are sure that for the

remaining time the government will be established for ourselves in good order and in the best state.

[27] But whoever shelters any of the Jews, old people or children or even infants, will be tortured to death with the most hateful torments, together with his family.

[28] Any one willing to give information will receive the property of the one who incurs the punishment, and also two thousand drachmas from the royal treasury, and will be awarded his freedom.

[29] Every place detected sheltering a Jew is to be made unapproachable and burned with fire, and shall become useless for all time to any mortal creature."

[30] The letter was written in the above form.

3Mac.4

[1] In every place, then, where this decree arrived, a feast at public expense was arranged for the Gentiles with shouts and gladness, for the inveterate enmity which had long ago been in their minds was now made evident and outspoken.

[2] But among the Jews there was incessant mourning, lamentation, and tearful cries; everywhere their hearts were burning, and they groaned because of the unexpected destruction that had suddenly been decreed for them.

[3] What district or city, or what habitable place at all, or what streets were not filled with mourning and wailing for them?

[4] For with such a harsh and ruthless spirit were they being sent off, all together, by the generals in the several cities, that at the sight of their unusual punishments, even some of their enemies, perceiving the common object of pity before their eyes, reflected upon the uncertainty of life and shed tears at the most miserable expulsion of these people.

[5] For a multitude of gray-headed old men, sluggish and bent with age, was being led away, forced to march at a swift pace by the violence with which they were driven in such a shameful manner.

[6] And young women who had just entered the bridal chamber to share married life exchanged joy for wailing, their myrrh-perfumed hair sprinkled with ashes, and were carried away unveiled, all together raising a lament instead of a wedding song, as they were torn by the harsh treatment of the heathen.

[7] In bonds and in public view they were violently dragged along as far as the place of embarkation.

[8] Their husbands, in the prime of youth, their necks encircled with ropes instead of garlands, spent the remaining days of their marriage festival in lamentations instead of good cheer and youthful revelry, seeing death immediately before them.

[9] They were brought on board like wild animals, driven under the

constraint of iron bonds; some were fastened by the neck to the benches of the boats, others had their feet secured by unbreakable fetters,

[10] and in addition they were confined under a solid deck, so that with their eyes in total darkness, they should undergo treatment befitting traitors during the whole voyage.

[11] When these men had been brought to the place called Schedia, and the voyage was concluded as the king had decreed, he commanded that they should be enclosed in the hippodrome which had been built with a monstrous perimeter wall in front of the city, and which was well suited to make them an obvious spectacle to all coming back into the city and to those from the city going out into the country, so that they could neither communicate with the king's forces nor in any way claim to be inside the circuit of the city.

[12] And when this had happened, the king, hearing that the Jews' compatriots from the city frequently went out in secret to lament bitterly the ignoble misfortune of their brothers,

[13] ordered in his rage that these men be dealt with in precisely the same fashion as the others, not omitting any detail of their punishment.

[14] The entire race was to be registered individually, not for the hard labor that has been briefly mentioned before, but to be tortured with the outrages that he had ordered, and at the end to be destroyed in the space of a single day.

[15] The registration of these people was therefore conducted with bitter haste and zealous intentness from the rising of the sun till its setting, and though uncompleted it stopped after forty days.

[16] The king was greatly and continually filled with joy, organizing feasts in honor of all his idols, with a mind alienated from truth and with a profane mouth, praising speechless things that are not able even to communicate or to come to one's help, and uttering improper words against the supreme God.

[17] But after the previously mentioned interval of time the scribes declared to the king that they were no longer able to take the census of the Jews because of their innumerable multitude,

[18] although most of them were still in the country, some still residing in their homes, and some at the place; the task was impossible for all the generals in Egypt.

[19] After he had threatened them severely, charging that they had been bribed to contrive a means of escape, he was clearly convinced about the matter

[20] when they said and proved that both the paper and the pens they used for writing had already given out.

[21] But this was an act of the invincible providence of him who was aiding the Jews from heaven.

3Mac.5

[1] Then the king, completely inflexible, was filled with overpowering anger and wrath; so he summoned Hermon, keeper of the elephants,

[2] and ordered him on the following day to drug all the elephants -- five hundred in number -- with large handfuls of frankincense and plenty of unmixed wine, and to drive them in, maddened by the lavish abundance of liquor, so that the Jews might meet their doom.

[3] When he had given these orders he returned to his feasting, together with those of his friends and of the army who were especially hostile toward the Jews.

[4] And Hermon, keeper of the elephants, proceeded faithfully to carry out the orders.

[5] The servants in charge of the Jews went out in the evening and bound the hands of the wretched people and arranged for their continued custody through the night, convinced that the whole nation would experience its final destruction.

[6] For to the Gentiles it appeared that the Jews were left without any aid,

[7] because in their bonds they were forcibly confined on every side. But with tears and a voice hard to silence they all called upon the Almighty Lord and Ruler of all power, their merciful God and Father, praying

[8] that he avert with vengeance the evil plot against them and in a glorious manifestation rescue them from the fate now prepared for them.

[9] So their entreaty ascended fervently to heaven.

[10] Hermon, however, when he had drugged the pitiless elephants until they had been filled with a great abundance of wine and satiated with frankincense, presented himself at the courtyard early in the morning to report to the king about these preparations.

[11] But the Lord sent upon the king a portion of sleep, that beneficence which from the beginning, night and day, is bestowed by him who grants it to whomever he wishes.

[12] And by the action of the Lord he was overcome by so pleasant and deep a sleep that he quite failed in his lawless purpose and was completely frustrated in his inflexible plan.

[13] Then the Jews, since they had escaped the appointed hour, praised their holy God and again begged him who is easily reconciled to show the might of his all-powerful hand to the arrogant Gentiles.

[14] But now, since it was nearly the middle of the tenth hour, the person who was in charge of the invitations, seeing that the guests were assembled, approached the king and nudged him.

[15] And when he had with difficulty roused him, he pointed out that the hour of the banquet was already slipping by, and he gave him an account of the situation.

[16] The king, after considering this, returned to his drinking, and ordered those present for the banquet to recline opposite him.

[17] When this was done he urged them to give themselves over to revelry and to make the present portion of the banquet joyful by celebrating all the more.

[18] After the party had been going on for some time, the king summoned Hermon and with sharp threats demanded to know why the Jews had been allowed to remain alive through the present day.

[19] But when he, with the corroboration of his friends, pointed out that while it was still night he had carried out completely the order given him,

[20] the king, possessed by a savagery worse than that of Phalaris, said that the Jews were benefited by today's sleep, "but," he added, "tomorrow without delay prepare the elephants in the same way for the destruction of the lawless Jews!"

[21] When the king had spoken, all those present readily and joyfully with one accord gave their approval, and each departed to his own home.

[22] But they did not so much employ the duration of the night in sleep as in devising all sorts of insults for those they thought to be doomed.

[23] Then, as soon as the cock had crowed in the early morning, Hermon, having equipped the beasts, began to move them along in the great colonnade.

[24] The crowds of the city had been assembled for this most pitiful spectacle and they were eagerly waiting for daybreak.

[25] But the Jews, at their last gasp, since the time had run out, stretched their hands toward heaven and with most tearful supplication and mournful dirges implored the supreme God to help them again at once.

[26] The rays of the sun were not yet shed abroad, and while the king was receiving his friends, Hermon arrived and invited him to come out, indicating that what the king desired was ready for action.

[27] But he, upon receiving the report and being struck by the unusual invitation to come out -- since he had been completely overcome by incomprehension -- inquired what the matter was for which this had been so zealously completed for him.

[28] This was the act of God who rules over all things, for he had implanted in the king's mind a forgetfulness of the things he had previously devised.

[29] Then Hermon and all the king's friends pointed out that the beasts and the armed forces were ready, "O king, according to your eager purpose."

[30] But at these words he was filled with an overpowering wrath, because by the providence of God his whole mind had been deranged in regard to these matters; and with a threatening look he said,

[31] "Were your parents or children present, I would have prepared them to be a rich feast for the savage beasts instead of the Jews, who give me no ground for complaint and have exhibited to an extraordinary degree a full and firm loyalty to my ancestors.

[32] In fact you would have been deprived of life instead of these, were it not for an affection arising from our nurture in common and your

usefulness."

[33] So Hermon suffered an unexpected and dangerous threat, and his eyes wavered and his face fell.

[34] The king's friends one by one sullenly slipped away and dismissed the assembled people, each to his own occupation.

[35] Then the Jews, upon hearing what the king had said, praised the manifest Lord God, King of kings, since this also was his aid which they had received.

[36] The king, however, reconvened the party in the same manner and urged the guests to return to their celebrating.

[37] After summoning Hermon he said in a threatening tone, "How many times, you poor wretch, must I give you orders about these things?

[38] Equip the elephants now once more for the destruction of the Jews tomorrow!"

[39] But the officials who were at table with him, wondering at his instability of mind, remonstrated as follows:

[40] "O king, how long will you try us, as though we are idiots, ordering now for a third time that they be destroyed, and again revoking your decree in the matter?

[41] As a result the city is in a tumult because of its expectation; it is crowded with masses of people, and also in constant danger of being plundered."

[42] Upon this the king, a Phalaris in everything and filled with madness, took no account of the changes of mind which had come about within him for the protection of the Jews, and he firmly swore an irrevocable oath that he would send them to death without delay, mangled by the knees and feet of the beasts,

[43] and would also march against Judea and rapidly level it to the ground with fire and spear, and by burning to the ground the temple inaccessible to him would quickly render it forever empty of those who offered sacrifices there.

[44] Then the friends and officers departed with great joy, and they confidently posted the armed forces at the places in the city most favorable for keeping guard.

[45] Now when the beasts had been brought virtually to a state of madness, so to speak, by the very fragrant draughts of wine mixed with frankincense and had been equipped with frightful devices, the elephant keeper

[46] entered at about dawn into the courtyard -- the city now being filled with countless masses of people crowding their way into the hippodrome -- and urged the king on to the matter at hand.

[47] So he, when he had filled his impious mind with a deep rage, rushed out in full force along with the beasts, wishing to witness, with invulnerable heart and with his own eyes, the grievous and pitiful destruction of the

aforementioned people.

[48] And when the Jews saw the dust raised by the elephants going out at the gate and by the following armed forces, as well as by the trampling of the crowd, and heard the loud and tumultuous noise,

[49] they thought that this was their last moment of life, the end of their most miserable suspense, and giving way to lamentation and groans they kissed each other, embracing relatives and falling into one another's arms -- parents and children, mothers and daughters, and others with babies at their breasts who were drawing their last milk.

[50] Not only this, but when they considered the help which they had received before from heaven they prostrated themselves with one accord on the ground, removing the babies from their breasts,

[51] and cried out in a very loud voice, imploring the Ruler over every power to manifest himself and be merciful to them, as they stood now at the gates of death.

3Mac.6

[1] Then a certain Eleazar, famous among the priests of the country, who had attained a ripe old age and throughout his life had been adorned with every virtue, directed the elders around him to cease calling upon the holy God and prayed as follows:

[2] "King of great power, Almighty God Most High, governing all creation with mercy,

[3] look upon the descendants of Abraham, O Father, upon the children of the sainted Jacob, a people of your consecrated portion who are perishing as foreigners in a foreign land.

[4] Pharaoh with his abundance of chariots, the former ruler of this Egypt, exalted with lawless insolence and boastful tongue, you destroyed together with his arrogant army by drowning them in the sea, manifesting the light of your mercy upon the nation of Israel.

[5] Sennacherib exulting in his countless forces, oppressive king of the Assyrians, who had already gained control of the whole world by the spear and was lifted up against your holy city, speaking grievous words with boasting and insolence, you, O Lord, broke in pieces, showing your power to many nations.

[6] The three companions in Babylon who had voluntarily surrendered their lives to the flames so as not to serve vain things, you rescued unharmed, even to a hair, moistening the fiery furnace with dew and turning the flame against all their enemies.

[7] Daniel, who through envious slanders was cast down into the ground to lions as food for wild beasts, you brought up to the light unharmed.

[8] And Jonah, wasting away in the belly of a huge, sea-born monster, you, Father, watched over and restored unharmed to all his family.

[9] And now, you who hate insolence, all-merciful and protector of all, reveal yourself quickly to those of the nation of Israel -- who are being

175

outrageously treated by the abominable and lawless Gentiles.

[10] Even if our lives have become entangled in impieties in our exile, rescue us from the hand of the enemy, and destroy us, Lord, by whatever fate you choose.

[11] Let not the vain-minded praise their vanities at the destruction of your beloved people, saying, `Not even their god has rescued them.'

[12] But you, O Eternal One, who have all might and all power, watch over us now and have mercy upon us who by the senseless insolence of the lawless are being deprived of life in the manner of traitors.

[13] And let the Gentiles cower today in fear of your invincible might, O honored One, who have power to save the nation of Jacob.

[14] The whole throng of infants and their parents entreat you with tears.

[15] Let it be shown to all the Gentiles that you are with us, O Lord, and have not turned your face from us; but just as you have said, `Not even when they were in the land of their enemies did I neglect them,' so accomplish it, O Lord."

[16] Just as Eleazar was ending his prayer, the king arrived at the hippodrome with the beasts and all the arrogance of his forces.

[17] And when the Jews observed this they raised great cries to heaven so that even the nearby valleys resounded with them and brought an uncontrollable terror upon the army.

[18] Then the most glorious, almighty, and true God revealed his holy face and opened the heavenly gates, from which two glorious angels of fearful aspect descended, visible to all but the Jews.

[19] They opposed the forces of the enemy and filled them with confusion and terror, binding them with immovable shackles.

[20] Even the king began to shudder bodily, and he forgot his sullen insolence.

[21] The beasts turned back upon the armed forces following them and began trampling and destroying them.

[22] Then the king's anger was turned to pity and tears because of the things that he had devised beforehand.

[23] For when he heard the shouting and saw them all fallen headlong to destruction, he wept and angrily threatened his friends, saying,

[24] "You are committing treason and surpassing tyrants in cruelty; and even me, your benefactor, you are now attempting to deprive of dominion and life by secretly devising acts of no advantage to the kingdom.

[25] Who is it that has taken each man from his home and senselessly gathered here those who faithfully have held the fortresses of our country?

[26] Who is it that has so lawlessly encompassed with outrageous treatment those who from the beginning differed from all nations in their goodwill toward us and often have accepted willingly the worst of human dangers?

[27] Loose and untie their unjust bonds! Send them back to their homes in

peace, begging pardon for your former actions!

[28] Release the sons of the almighty and living God of heaven, who from the time of our ancestors until now has granted an unimpeded and notable stability to our government."

[29] These then were the things he said; and the Jews, immediately released, praised their holy God and Savior, since they now had escaped death.

[30] Then the king, when he had returned to the city, summoned the official in charge of the revenues and ordered him to provide to the Jews both wines and everything else needed for a festival of seven days, deciding that they should celebrate their rescue with all joyfulness in that same place in which they had expected to meet their destruction.

[31] Accordingly those disgracefully treated and near to death, or rather, who stood at its gates, arranged for a banquet of deliverance instead of a bitter and lamentable death, and full of joy they apportioned to celebrants the place which had been prepared for their destruction and burial.

[32] They ceased their chanting of dirges and took up the song of their fathers, praising God, their Savior and worker of wonders. Putting an end to all mourning and wailing, they formed choruses as a sign of peaceful joy.

[33] Likewise also the king, after convening a great banquet to celebrate these events, gave thanks to heaven unceasingly and lavishly for the unexpected rescue which he had experienced.

[34] And those who had previously believed that the Jews would be destroyed and become food for birds, and had joyfully registered them, groaned as they themselves were overcome by disgrace, and their fire-breathing boldness was ignominiously quenched.

[35] But the Jews, when they had arranged the aforementioned choral group, as we have said before, passed the time in feasting to the accompaniment of joyous thanksgiving and psalms.

[36] And when they had ordained a public rite for these things in their whole community and for their descendants, they instituted the observance of the aforesaid days as a festival, not for drinking and gluttony, but because of the deliverance that had come to them through God.

[37] Then they petitioned the king, asking for dismissal to their homes.

[38] So their registration was carried out from the twenty-fifth of Pachon to the fourth of Epeiph, for forty days; and their destruction was set for the fifth to the seventh of Epeiph, the three days

[39] on which the Lord of all most gloriously revealed his mercy and rescued them all together and unharmed.

[40] Then they feasted, provided with everything by the king, until the fourteenth day, on which also they made the petition for their dismissal.

[41] The king granted their request at once and wrote the following letter for them to the generals in the cities, magnanimously expressing his concern:

3Mac.7

[1] "King Ptolemy Philopator to the generals in Egypt and all in authority in

his government, greetings and good health.

[2] We ourselves and our children are faring well, the great God guiding our affairs according to our desire.

[3] Certain of our friends, frequently urging us with malicious intent, persuaded us to gather together the Jews of the kingdom in a body and to punish them with barbarous penalties as traitors;

[4] for they declared that our government would never be firmly established until this was accomplished, because of the ill-will which these people had toward all nations.

[5] They also led them out with harsh treatment as slaves, or rather as traitors, and, girding themselves with a cruelty more savage than that of Scythian custom, they tried without any inquiry or examination to put them to death.

[6] But we very severely threatened them for these acts, and in accordance with the clemency which we have toward all men we barely spared their lives. Since we have come to realize that the God of heaven surely defends the Jews, always taking their part as a father does for his children,

[7] and since we have taken into account the friendly and firm goodwill which they had toward us and our ancestors, we justly have acquitted them of every charge of whatever kind.

[8] We also have ordered each and every one to return to his own home, with no one in any place doing them harm at all or reproaching them for the irrational things that have happened.

[9] For you should know that if we devise any evil against them or cause them any grief at all, we always shall have not man but the Ruler over every power, the Most High God, in everything and inescapably as an antagonist to avenge such acts. Farewell."

[10] Upon receiving this letter the Jews did not immediately hurry to make their departure, but they requested of the king that at their own hands those of the Jewish nation who had willfully transgressed against the holy God and the law of God should receive the punishment they deserved.

[11] For they declared that those who for the belly's sake had transgressed the divine commandments would never be favorably disposed toward the king's government.

[12] The king then, admitting and approving the truth of what they said, granted them a general license so that freely and without royal authority or supervision they might destroy those everywhere in his kingdom who had transgressed the law of God.

[13] When they had applauded him in fitting manner, their priests and the whole multitude shouted the Hallelujah and joyfully departed.

[14] And so on their way they punished and put to a public and shameful death any whom they met of their fellow-countrymen who had become defiled.

[15] In that day they put to death more than three hundred men; and they kept the day as a joyful festival, since they had destroyed the profaners.

[16] But those who had held fast to God even to death and had received the full enjoyment of deliverance began their departure from the city, crowned with all sorts of very fragrant flowers, joyfully and loudly giving thanks to the one God of their fathers, the eternal Savior of Israel, in words of praise and all kinds of melodious songs.

[17] When they had arrived at Ptolemais, called "rose-bearing" because of a characteristic of the place, the fleet waited for them, in accord with the common desire, for seven days.

[18] There they celebrated their deliverance, for the king had generously provided all things to them for their journey, to each as far as his own house.

[19] And when they had landed in peace with appropriate thanksgiving, there too in like manner they decided to observe these days as a joyous festival during the time of their stay.

[20] Then, after inscribing them as holy on a pillar and dedicating a place of prayer at the site of the festival, they departed unharmed, free, and overjoyed, since at the king's command they had been brought safely by land and sea and river each to his own place.

[21] They also possessed greater prestige among their enemies, being held in honor and awe; and they were not subject at all to confiscation of their belongings by any one.

[22] Besides they all recovered all of their property, in accordance with the registration, so that those who held any restored it to them with extreme fear. So the supreme God perfectly performed great deeds for their deliverance.

[23] Blessed be the Deliverer of Israel through all times! Amen.

4 Maccabees

4Mac.1

[1] The subject that I am about to discuss is most philosophical, that is, whether devout reason is sovereign over the emotions. So it is right for me to advise you to pay earnest attention to philosophy.

[2] For the subject is essential to everyone who is seeking knowledge, and in addition it includes the praise of the highest virtue -- I mean, of course, rational judgment.

[3] If, then, it is evident that reason rules over those emotions that hinder self-control, namely, gluttony and lust,

[4] it is also clear that it masters the emotions that hinder one from justice, such as malice, and those that stand in the way of courage, namely anger, fear, and pain.

[5] Some might perhaps ask, "If reason rules the emotions, why is it not sovereign over forgetfulness and ignorance?" Their attempt at argument is ridiculous!

[6] For reason does not rule its own emotions, but those that are opposed to justice, courage, and self-control; and it is not for the purpose of destroying them, but so that one may not give way to them.

[7] I could prove to you from many and various examples that reason is dominant over the emotions,

[8] but I can demonstrate it best from the noble bravery of those who died for the sake of virtue, Eleazar and the seven brothers and their mother.

[9] All of these, by despising sufferings that bring death, demonstrated that reason controls the emotions.

[10] On this anniversary it is fitting for me to praise for their virtues those who, with their mother, died for the sake of nobility and goodness, but I would also call them blessed for the honor in which they are held.

[11] For all people, even their torturers, marveled at their courage and endurance, and they became the cause of the downfall of tyranny over their nation. By their endurance they conquered the tyrant, and thus their native land was purified through them.

[12] I shall shortly have an opportunity to speak of this; but, as my custom is, I shall begin by stating my main principle, and then I shall turn to their story, giving glory to the all-wise God.

[13] Our inquiry, accordingly, is whether reason is sovereign over the

emotions.

[14] We shall decide just what reason is and what emotion is, how many kinds of emotions there are, and whether reason rules over all these.

[15] Now reason is the mind that with sound logic prefers the life of wisdom.

[16] Wisdom, next, is the knowledge of divine and human matters and the causes of these.

[17] This, in turn, is education in the law, by which we learn divine matters reverently and human affairs to our advantage.

[18] Now the kinds of wisdom are rational judgment, justice, courage, and self-control.

[19] Rational judgment is supreme over all of these, since by means of it reason rules over the emotions.

[20] The two most comprehensive types of the emotions are pleasure and pain; and each of these is by nature concerned with both body and soul.

[21] The emotions of both pleasure and pain have many consequences.

[22] Thus desire precedes pleasure and delight follows it.

[23] Fear precedes pain and sorrow comes after.

[24] Anger, as a man will see if he reflects on this experience, is an emotion embracing pleasure and pain.

[25] In pleasure there exists even a malevolent tendency, which is the most complex of all the emotions.

[26] In the soul it is boastfulness, covetousness, thirst for honor, rivalry, and malice;

[27] in the body, indiscriminate eating, gluttony, and solitary gormandizing.

[28] Just as pleasure and pain are two plants growing from the body and the soul, so there are many offshoots of these plants,

[29] each of which the master cultivator, reason, weeds and prunes and ties up and waters and thoroughly irrigates, and so tames the jungle of habits and emotions.

[30] For reason is the guide of the virtues, but over the emotions it is sovereign. Observe now first of all that rational judgment is sovereign over the emotions by virtue of the restraining power of self-control.

[31] Self-control, then, is dominance over the desires.

[32] Some desires are mental, others are physical, and reason obviously rules over both.

[33] Otherwise how is it that when we are attracted to forbidden foods we abstain from the pleasure to be had from them? Is it not because reason is able to rule over appetites? I for one think so.

[34] Therefore when we crave seafood and fowl and animals and all sorts of foods that are forbidden to us by the law, we abstain because of domination by reason.

[35] For the emotions of the appetites are restrained, checked by the temperate mind, and all the impulses of the body are bridled by reason.

4Mac.2

[1] And why is it amazing that the desires of the mind for the enjoyment of beauty are rendered powerless?

[2] It is for this reason, certainly, that the temperate Joseph is praised, because by mental effort he overcame sexual desire.

[3] For when he was young and in his prime for intercourse, by his reason he nullified the frenzy of the passions.

[4] Not only is reason proved to rule over the frenzied urge of sexual desire, but also over every desire.

[5] Thus the law says, "You shall not covet your neighbor's wife...or anything that is your neighbor's."

[6] In fact, since the law has told us not to covet, I could prove to you all the more that reason is able to control desires. Just so it is with the emotions that hinder one from justice.

[7] Otherwise how could it be that someone who is habitually a solitary gormandizer, a glutton, or even a drunkard can learn a better way, unless reason is clearly lord of the emotions?

[8] Thus, as soon as a man adopts a way of life in accordance with the law, even though he is a lover of money, he is forced to act contrary to his natural ways and to lend without interest to the needy and to cancel the debt when the seventh year arrives.

[9] If one is greedy, he is ruled by the law through his reason so that he neither gleans his harvest nor gathers the last grapes from the vineyard. In all other matters we can recognize that reason rules the emotions.

[10] For the law prevails even over affection for parents, so that virtue is not abandoned for their sakes.

[11] It is superior to love for one's wife, so that one rebukes her when she breaks the law.

[12] It takes precedence over love for children, so that one punishes them for misdeeds.

[13] It is sovereign over the relationship of friends, so that one rebukes friends when they act wickedly.

[14] Do not consider it paradoxical when reason, through the law, can prevail even over enmity. The fruit trees of the enemy are not cut down, but one preserves the property of enemies from the destroyers and helps raise up what has fallen.

[15] It is evident that reason rules even the more violent emotions: lust for power, vainglory, boasting, arrogance, and malice.

[16] For the temperate mind repels all these malicious emotions, just as it repels anger -- for it is sovereign over even this.

[17] When Moses was angry with Dathan and Abiram he did nothing against them in anger, but controlled his anger by reason.

[18] For, as I have said, the temperate mind is able to get the better of the

emotions, to correct some, and to render others powerless.

[19] Why else did Jacob, our most wise father, censure the households of Simeon and Levi for their irrational slaughter of the entire tribe of the Shechemites, saying, "Cursed be their anger"?

[20] For if reason could not control anger, he would not have spoken thus.

[21] Now when God fashioned man, he planted in him emotions and inclinations,

[22] but at the same time he enthroned the mind among the senses as a sacred governor over them all.

[23] To the mind he gave the law; and one who lives subject to this will rule a kingdom that is temperate, just, good, and courageous.

[24] How is it then, one might say, that if reason is master of the emotions, it does not control forgetfulness and ignorance?

4Mac.3

[1] This notion is entirely ridiculous; for it is evident that reason rules not over its own emotions, but over those of the body.

[2] No one of us can eradicate that kind of desire, but reason can provide a way for us not to be enslaved by desire.

[3] No one of us can eradicate anger from the mind, but reason can help to deal with anger.

[4] No one of us can eradicate malice, but reason can fight at our side so that we are not overcome by malice.

[5] For reason does not uproot the emotions but is their antagonist.

[6] Now this can be explained more clearly by the story of King David's thirst.

[7] David had been attacking the Philistines all day long, and together with the soldiers of his nation had slain many of them.

[8] Then when evening fell, he came, sweating and quite exhausted, to the royal tent, around which the whole army of our ancestors had encamped.

[9] Now all the rest were at supper,

[10] but the king was extremely thirsty, and although springs were plentiful there, he could not satisfy his thirst from them.

[11] But a certain irrational desire for the water in the enemy's territory tormented and inflamed him, undid and consumed him.

[12] When his guards complained bitterly because of the king's craving, two staunch young soldiers, respecting the king's desire, armed themselves fully, and taking a pitcher climbed over the enemy's ramparts.

[13] Eluding the sentinels at the gates, they went searching throughout the enemy camp

[14] and found the spring, and from it boldly brought the king a drink.

[15] But David, although he was burning with thirst, considered it an altogether fearful danger to his soul to drink what was regarded as equivalent to blood.

[16] Therefore, opposing reason to desire, he poured out the drink as an

offering to God.

[17] For the temperate mind can conquer the drives of the emotions and quench the flames of frenzied desires;

[18] it can overthrow bodily agonies even when they are extreme, and by nobility of reason spurn all domination by the emotions.

[19] The present occasion now invites us to a narrative demonstration of temperate reason.

[20] At a time when our fathers were enjoying profound peace because of their observance of the law and were prospering, so that even Seleucus Nicanor, king of Asia, had both appropriated money to them for the temple service and recognized their commonwealth --

[21] just at that time certain men attempted a revolution against the public harmony and caused many and various disasters.

4Mac.4

[1] Now there was a certain Simon, a political opponent of the noble and good man, Onias, who then held the high priesthood for life. When despite all manner of slander he was unable to injure Onias in the eyes of the nation, he fled the country with the purpose of betraying it.

[2] So he came to Apollonius, governor of Syria, Phoenicia, and Cilicia, and said,

[3] "I have come here because I am loyal to the king's government, to report that in the Jerusalem treasuries there are deposited tens of thousands in private funds, which are not the property of the temple but belong to King Seleucus."

[4] When Apollonius learned the details of these things, he praised Simon for his service to the king and went up to Seleucus to inform him of the rich treasure.

[5] On receiving authority to deal with this matter, he proceeded quickly to our country accompanied by the accursed Simon and a very strong military force.

[6] He said that he had come with the king's authority to seize the private funds in the treasury.

[7] The people indignantly protested his words, considering it outrageous that those who had committed deposits to the sacred treasury should be deprived of them, and did all that they could to prevent it.

[8] But, uttering threats, Apollonius went on to the temple.

[9] While the priests together with women and children were imploring God in the temple to shield the holy place that was being treated so contemptuously,

[10] and while Apollonius was going up with his armed forces to seize the money, angels on horseback with lightning flashing from their weapons appeared from heaven, instilling in them great fear and trembling.

[11] Then Apollonius fell down half dead in the temple area that was open

to all, stretched out his hands toward heaven, and with tears besought the Hebrews to pray for him and propitiate the wrath of the heavenly army.

[12] For he said that he had committed a sin deserving of death, and that if he were delivered he would praise the blessedness of the holy place before all people.

[13] Moved by these words, Onias the high priest, although otherwise he had scruples about doing so, prayed for him lest King Seleucus suppose that Apollonius had been overcome by human treachery and not by divine justice.

[14] So Apollonius, having been preserved beyond all expectations, went away to report to the king what had happened to him.

[15] When King Seleucus died, his son Antiochus Epiphanes succeeded to the throne, an arrogant and terrible man,

[16] who removed Onias from the priesthood and appointed Onias's brother Jason as high priest.

[17] Jason agreed that if the office were conferred upon him he would pay the king three thousand six hundred and sixty talents annually.

[18] So the king appointed him high priest and ruler of the nation.

[19] Jason changed the nation's way of life and altered its form of government in complete violation of the law,

[20] so that not only was a gymnasium constructed at the very citadel of our native land, but also the temple service was abolished.

[21] The divine justice was angered by these acts and caused Antiochus himself to make war on them.

[22] For when he was warring against Ptolemy in Egypt, he heard that a rumor of his death had spread and that the people of Jerusalem had rejoiced greatly. He speedily marched against them,

[23] and after he had plundered them he issued a decree that if any of them should be found observing the ancestral law they should die.

[24] When, by means of his decrees, he had not been able in any way to put an end to the people's observance of the law, but saw that all his threats and punishments were being disregarded,

[25] even to the point that women, because they had circumcised their sons, were thrown headlong from heights along with their infants, though they had known beforehand that they would suffer this --

[26] when, then, his decrees were despised by the people, he himself, through torture, tried to compel everyone in the nation to eat defiling foods and to renounce Judaism.

4Mac.5

[1] The tyrant Antiochus, sitting in state with his counselors on a certain high place, and with his armed soldiers standing about him,

[2] ordered the guards to seize each and every Hebrew and to compel them to eat pork and food sacrificed to idols.

[3] If any were not willing to eat defiling food, they were to be broken on the

wheel and killed.

[4] And when many persons had been rounded up, one man, Eleazar by name, leader of the flock, was brought before the king. He was a man of priestly family, learned in the law, advanced in age, and known to many in the tyrant's court because of his philosophy.

[5] When Antiochus saw him he said,

[6] "Before I begin to torture you, old man, I would advise you to save yourself by eating pork,

[7] for I respect your age and your gray hairs. Although you have had them for so long a time, it does not seem to me that you are a philosopher when you observe the religion of the Jews.

[8] Why, when nature has granted it to us, should you abhor eating the very excellent meat of this animal?

[9] It is senseless not to enjoy delicious things that are not shameful, and wrong to spurn the gifts of nature.

[10] It seems to me that you will do something even more senseless if, by holding a vain opinion concerning the truth, you continue to despise me to your own hurt.

[11] Will you not awaken from your foolish philosophy, dispel your futile reasonings, adopt a mind appropriate to your years, philosophize according to the truth of what is beneficial,

[12] and have compassion on your old age by honoring my humane advice?

[13] For consider this, that if there is some power watching over this religion of yours, it will excuse you from any transgression that arises out of compulsion."

[14] When the tyrant urged him in this fashion to eat meat unlawfully, Eleazar asked to have a word.

[15] When he had received permission to speak, he began to address the people as follows:

[16] "We, O Antiochus, who have been persuaded to govern our lives by the divine law, think that there is no compulsion more powerful than our obedience to the law.

[17] Therefore we consider that we should not transgress it in any respect.

[18] Even if, as you suppose, our law were not truly divine and we had wrongly held it to be divine, not even so would it be right for us to invalidate our reputation for piety.

[19] Therefore do not suppose that it would be a petty sin if we were to eat defiling food;

[20] to transgress the law in matters either small or great is of equal seriousness,

[21] for in either case the law is equally despised.

[22] You scoff at our philosophy as though living by it were irrational,

[23] but it teaches us self-control, so that we master all pleasures and

186

desires, and it also trains us in courage, so that we endure any suffering willingly;

[24] it instructs us in justice, so that in all our dealings we act impartially, and it teaches us piety, so that with proper reverence we worship the only real God.

[25] "Therefore we do not eat defiling food; for since we believe that the law was established by God, we know that in the nature of things the Creator of the world in giving us the law has shown sympathy toward us.

[26] He has permitted us to eat what will be most suitable for our lives, but he has forbidden us to eat meats that would be contrary to this.

[27] It would be tyrannical for you to compel us not only to transgress the law, but also to eat in such a way that you may deride us for eating defiling foods, which are most hateful to us.

[28] But you shall have no such occasion to laugh at me,

[29] nor will I transgress the sacred oaths of my ancestors concerning the keeping of the law,

[30] not even if you gouge out my eyes and burn my entrails.

[31] I am not so old and cowardly as not to be young in reason on behalf of piety.

[32] Therefore get your torture wheels ready and fan the fire more vehemently!

[33] I do not so pity my old age as to break the ancestral law by my own act.

[34] I will not play false to you, O law that trained me, nor will I renounce you, beloved self-control.

[35] I will not put you to shame, philosophical reason, nor will I reject you, honored priesthood and knowledge of the law.

[36] You, O king, shall not stain the honorable mouth of my old age, nor my long life lived lawfully.

[37] The fathers will receive me as pure, as one who does not fear your violence even to death.

[38] You may tyrannize the ungodly, but you shall not dominate my religious principles either by word or by deed."

4Mac.6

[1] When Eleazar in this manner had made eloquent response to the exhortations of the tyrant, the guards who were standing by dragged him violently to the instruments of torture.

[2] First they stripped the old man, who remained adorned with the gracefulness of his piety.

[3] And after they had tied his arms on each side they scourged him,

[4] while a herald opposite him cried out, "Obey the king's commands!"

[5] But the courageous and noble man, as a true Eleazar, was unmoved, as though being tortured in a dream;

[6] yet while the old man's eyes were raised to heaven, his flesh was being torn by scourges, his blood flowing, and his sides were being cut to pieces.

[7] And though he fell to the ground because his body could not endure the agonies, he kept his reason upright and unswerving.

[8] One of the cruel guards rushed at him and began to kick him in the side to make him get up again after he fell.

[9] But he bore the pains and scorned the punishment and endured the tortures.

[10] And like a noble athlete the old man, while being beaten, was victorious over his torturers;

[11] in fact, with his face bathed in sweat, and gasping heavily for breath, he amazed even his torturers by his courageous spirit.

[12] At that point, partly out of pity for his old age,

[13] partly out of sympathy from their acquaintance with him, partly out of admiration for his endurance, some of the king's retinue came to him and said,

[14] "Eleazar, why are you so irrationally destroying yourself through these evil things?

[15] We will set before you some cooked meat; save yourself by pretending to eat pork."

[16] But Eleazar, as though more bitterly tormented by this counsel, cried out:

[17] "May we, the children of Abraham, never think so basely that out of cowardice we feign a role unbecoming to us!

[18] For it would be irrational if we, who have lived in accordance with truth to old age and have maintained in accordance with law the reputation of such a life, should now change our course

[19] become a pattern of impiety to the young, in becoming an example of the eating of defiling food.

[20] It would be shameful if we should survive for a little while and during that time be a laughing stock to all for our cowardice,

[21] and if we should be despised by the tyrant as unmanly, and not protect our divine law even to death.

[22] Therefore, O children of Abraham, die nobly for your religion!

[23] And you, guards of the tyrant, why do you delay?"

[24] When they saw that he was so courageous in the face of the afflictions, and that he had not been changed by their compassion, the guards brought him to the fire.

[25] There they burned him with maliciously contrived instruments, threw him down, and poured stinking liquids into his nostrils.

[26] When he was now burned to his very bones and about to expire, he lifted up his eyes to God and said,

[27] "You know, O God, that though I might have saved myself, I am dying in burning torments for the sake of the law.

[28] Be merciful to your people, and let our punishment suffice for them.

[29] Make my blood their purification, and take my life in exchange for theirs."

[30] And after he said this, the holy man died nobly in his tortures, and by reason he resisted even to the very tortures of death for the sake of the law.

[31] Admittedly, then, devout reason is sovereign over the emotions.

[32] For if the emotions had prevailed over reason, we would have testified to their domination.

[33] But now that reason has conquered the emotions, we properly attribute to it the power to govern.

[34] And it is right for us to acknowledge the dominance of reason when it masters even external agonies. It would be ridiculous to deny it.

[35] And I have proved not only that reason has mastered agonies, but also that it masters pleasures and in no respect yields to them.

4Mac.7

[1] For like a most skilful pilot, the reason of our father Eleazar steered the ship of religion over the sea of the emotions,

[2] and though buffeted by the stormings of the tyrant and overwhelmed by the mighty waves of tortures,

[3] in no way did he turn the rudder of religion until he sailed into the haven of immortal victory.

[4] No city besieged with many ingenious war machines has ever held out as did that most holy man. Although his sacred life was consumed by tortures and racks, he conquered the besiegers with the shield of his devout reason.

[5] For in setting his mind firm like a jutting cliff, our father Eleazar broke the maddening waves of the emotions.

[6] O priest, worthy of the priesthood, you neither defiled your sacred teeth nor profaned your stomach, which had room only for reverence and purity, by eating defiling foods.

[7] O man in harmony with the law and philosopher of divine life!

[8] Such should be those who are administrators of the law, shielding it with their own blood and noble sweat in sufferings even to death.

[9] You, father, strengthened our loyalty to the law through your glorious endurance, and you did not abandon the holiness which you praised, but by your deeds you made your words of divine philosophy credible.

[10] O aged man, more powerful than tortures; O elder, fiercer than fire; O supreme king over the passions, Eleazar!

[11] For just as our father Aaron, armed with the censer, ran through the multitude of the people and conquered the fiery angel,

[12] so the descendant of Aaron, Eleazar, though being consumed by the fire, remained unmoved in his reason.

[13] Most amazing, indeed, though he was an old man, his body no longer tense and firm, his muscles flabby, his sinews feeble, he became young again

[14] in spirit through reason; and by reason like that of Isaac he rendered the many-headed rack ineffective.

[15] O man of blessed age and of venerable gray hair and of law-abiding life, whom the faithful seal of death has perfected!

[16] If, therefore, because of piety an aged man despised tortures even to death, most certainly devout reason is governor of the emotions.

[17] Some perhaps might say, "Not every one has full command of his emotions, because not every one has prudent reason."

[18] But as many as attend to religion with a whole heart, these alone are able to control the passions of the flesh,

[19] since they believe that they, like our patriarchs Abraham and Isaac and Jacob, do not die to God, but live in God.

[20] No contradiction therefore arises when some persons appear to be dominated by their emotions because of the weakness of their reason.

[21] What person who lives as a philosopher by the whole rule of philosophy, and trusts in God,

[22] and knows that it is blessed to endure any suffering for the sake of virtue, would not be able to overcome the emotions through godliness?

[23] For only the wise and courageous man is lord of his emotions.

4Mac.8

[1] For this is why even the very young, by following a philosophy in accordance with devout reason, have prevailed over the most painful instruments of torture.

[2] For when the tyrant was conspicuously defeated in his first attempt, being unable to compel an aged man to eat defiling foods, then in violent rage he commanded that others of the Hebrew captives be brought, and that any who ate defiling food should be freed after eating, but if any were to refuse, these should be tortured even more cruelly.

[3] When the tyrant had given these orders, seven brothers -- handsome, modest, noble, and accomplished in every way -- were brought before him along with their aged mother.

[4] When the tyrant saw them, grouped about their mother as if in a chorus, he was pleased with them. And struck by their appearance and nobility, he smiled at them, and summoned them nearer and said,

[5] "Young men, I admire each and every one of you in a kindly manner, and greatly respect the beauty and the number of such brothers. Not only do I advise you not to display the same madness as that of the old man who has just been tortured, but I also exhort you to yield to me and enjoy my friendship.

[6] Just as I am able to punish those who disobey my orders, so I can be a benefactor to those who obey me.

[7] Trust me, then, and you will have positions of authority in my government if you will renounce the ancestral tradition of your national life.

[8] And enjoy your youth by adopting the Greek way of life and by changing your manner of living.

[9] But if by disobedience you rouse my anger, you will compel me to destroy each and every one of you with dreadful punishments through tortures.

[10] Therefore take pity on yourselves. Even I, your enemy, have compassion for your youth and handsome appearance.

[11] Will you not consider this, that if you disobey, nothing remains for you but to die on the rack?"

[12] When he had said these things, he ordered the instruments of torture to be brought forward so as to persuade them out of fear to eat the defiling food.

[13] And when the guards had placed before them wheels and joint-dislocators, rack and hooks and catapults and caldrons, braziers and thumbscrews and iron claws and wedges and bellows, the tyrant resumed speaking:

[14] "Be afraid, young fellows, and whatever justice you revere will be merciful to you when you transgress under compulsion."

[15] But when they had heard the inducements and saw the dreadful devices, not only were they not afraid, but they also opposed the tyrant with their own philosophy, and by their right reasoning nullified his tyranny.

[16] Let us consider, on the other hand, what arguments might have been used if some of them had been cowardly and unmanly. Would they not have been these?

[17] "O wretches that we are and so senseless! Since the king has summoned and exhorted us to accept kind treatment if we obey him,

[18] why do we take pleasure in vain resolves and venture upon a disobedience that brings death?

[19] O men and brothers, should we not fear the instruments of torture and consider the threats of torments, and give up this vain opinion and this arrogance that threatens to destroy us?

[20] Let us take pity on our youth and have compassion on our mother's age;

[21] and let us seriously consider that if we disobey we are dead!

[22] Also, divine justice will excuse us for fearing the king when we are under compulsion.

[23] Why do we banish ourselves from this most pleasant life and deprive ourselves of this delightful world?

[24] Let us not struggle against compulsion nor take hollow pride in being put to the rack.

[25] Not even the law itself would arbitrarily slay us for fearing the instruments of torture.

[26] Why does such contentiousness excite us and such a fatal stubbornness please us, when we can live in peace if we obey the king?"

[27] But the youths, though about to be tortured, neither said any of these things nor even seriously considered them.

[28] For they were contemptuous of the emotions and sovereign over agonies,

[29] so that as soon as the tyrant had ceased counseling them to eat defiling food, all with one voice together, as from one mind, said:

4Mac.9

[1] "Why do you delay, O tyrant? For we are ready to die rather than transgress our ancestral commandments;

[2] we are obviously putting our forefathers to shame unless we should practice ready obedience to the law and to Moses our counselor.

[3] Tyrant and counselor of lawlessness, in your hatred for us do not pity us more than we pity ourselves.

[4] For we consider this pity of yours which insures our safety through transgression of the law to be more grievous than death itself.

[5] You are trying to terrify us by threatening us with death by torture, as though a short time ago you learned nothing from Eleazar.

[6] And if the aged men of the Hebrews because of their religion lived piously while enduring torture, it would be even more fitting that we young men should die despising your coercive tortures, which our aged instructor also overcame.

[7] Therefore, tyrant, put us to the test; and if you take our lives because of our religion, do not suppose that you can injure us by torturing us.

[8] For we, through this severe suffering and endurance, shall have the prize of virtue and shall be with God, for whom we suffer;

[9] but you, because of your bloodthirstiness toward us, will deservedly undergo from the divine justice eternal torment by fire."

[10] When they had said these things the tyrant not only was angry, as at those who are disobedient, but also was enraged, as at those who are ungrateful.

[11] Then at his command the guards brought forward the eldest, and having torn off his tunic, they bound his hands and arms with thongs on each side.

[12] When they had worn themselves out beating him with scourges, without accomplishing anything, they placed him upon the wheel.

[13] When the noble youth was stretched out around this, his limbs were dislocated,

[14] and though broken in every member he denounced the tyrant, saying,

[15] "Most abominable tyrant, enemy of heavenly justice, savage of mind, you are mangling me in this manner, not because I am a murderer, or as one who acts impiously, but because I protect the divine law."

[16] And when the guards said, "Agree to eat so that you may be released from the tortures,"

[17] he replied, "You abominable lackeys, your wheel is not so powerful as to strangle my reason. Cut my limbs, burn my flesh, and twist my joints.
[18] Through all these tortures I will convince you that sons of the Hebrews alone are invincible where virtue is concerned."
[19] While he was saying these things, they spread fire under him, and while fanning the flames they tightened the wheel further.
[20] The wheel was completely smeared with blood, and the heap of coals was being quenched by the drippings of gore, and pieces of flesh were falling off the axles of the machine.
[21] Although the ligaments joining his bones were already severed, the courageous youth, worthy of Abraham, did not groan,
[22] but as though transformed by fire into immortality he nobly endured the rackings.
[23] "Imitate me, brothers," he said. "Do not leave your post in my struggle or renounce our courageous brotherhood.
[24] Fight the sacred and noble battle for religion. Thereby the just Providence of our ancestors may become merciful to our nation and take vengeance on the accursed tyrant."
[25] When he had said this, the saintly youth broke the thread of life.
[26] While all were marveling at his courageous spirit, the guards brought in the next eldest, and after fitting themselves with iron gauntlets having sharp hooks, they bound him to the torture machine and catapult.
[27] Before torturing him, they inquired if he were willing to eat, and they heard this noble decision.
[28] These leopard-like beasts tore out his sinews with the iron hands, flayed all his flesh up to his chin, and tore away his scalp. But he steadfastly endured this agony and said,
[29] "How sweet is any kind of death for the religion of our fathers!"
[30] To the tyrant he said, "Do you not think, you most savage tyrant, that you are being tortured more than I, as you see the arrogant design of your tyranny being defeated by our endurance for the sake of religion?
[31] I lighten my pain by the joys that come from virtue,
[32] but you suffer torture by the threats that come from impiety. You will not escape, most abominable tyrant, the judgments of the divine wrath."
4Mac.10
[1] When he too had endured a glorious death, the third was led in, and many repeatedly urged him to save himself by tasting the meat.
[2] But he shouted, "Do you not know that the same father begot me and those who died, and the same mother bore me, and that I was brought up on the same teachings?
[3] I do not renounce the noble kinship that binds me to my brothers."
[4]
[5] Enraged by the man's boldness, they disjointed his hands and feet with their instruments, dismembering him by prying his limbs from their sockets,

193

[6] and breaking his fingers and arms and legs and elbows.

[7] Since they were not able in any way to break his spirit, they abandoned the instruments and scalped him with their fingernails in a Scythian fashion.

[8] They immediately brought him to the wheel, and while his vertebrae were being dislocated upon it he saw his own flesh torn all around and drops of blood flowing from his entrails.

[9] When he was about to die, he said,

[10] "We, most abominable tyrant, are suffering because of our godly training and virtue,

[11] but you, because of your impiety and bloodthirstiness, will undergo unceasing torments."

[12] When he also had died in a manner worthy of his brothers, they dragged in the fourth, saying,

[13] "As for you, do not give way to the same insanity as your brothers, but obey the king and save yourself."

[14] But he said to them, "You do not have a fire hot enough to make me play the coward.

[15] No, by the blessed death of my brothers, by the eternal destruction of the tyrant, and by the everlasting life of the pious, I will not renounce our noble brotherhood.

[16] Contrive tortures, tyrant, so that you may learn from them that I am a brother to those who have just been tortured."

[17] When he heard this, the bloodthirsty, murderous, and utterly abominable Antiochus gave orders to cut out his tongue.

[18] But he said, "Even if you remove my organ of speech, God hears also those who are mute.

[19] See, here is my tongue; cut it off, for in spite of this you will not make our reason speechless.

[20] Gladly, for the sake of God, we let our bodily members be mutilated.

[21] God will visit you swiftly, for you are cutting out a tongue that has been melodious with divine hymns."

4Mac.11

[1] When this one died also, after being cruelly tortured, the fifth leaped up, saying,

[2] "I will not refuse, tyrant, to be tortured for the sake of virtue.

[3] I have come of my own accord, so that by murdering me you will incur punishment from the heavenly justice for even more crimes.

[4] Hater of virtue, hater of mankind, for what act of ours are you destroying us in this way?

[5] Is it because we revere the Creator of all things and live according to his virtuous law?

[6] But these deeds deserve honors, not tortures."

[7]

[9] While he was saying these things, the guards bound him and dragged him to the catapult;

[10] they tied him to it on his knees, and fitting iron clamps on them, they twisted his back around the wedge on the wheel, so that he was completely curled back like a scorpion, and all his members were disjointed.

[11] In this condition, gasping for breath and in anguish of body,

[12] he said, "Tyrant, they are splendid favors that you grant us against your will, because through these noble sufferings you give us an opportunity to show our endurance for the law."

[13] After he too had died, the sixth, a mere boy, was led in. When the tyrant inquired whether he was willing to eat and be released, he said,

[14] "I am younger in age than my brothers, but I am their equal in mind.

[15] Since to this end we were born and bred, we ought likewise to die for the same principles.

[16] So if you intend to torture me for not eating defiling foods, go on torturing!"

[17] When he had said this, they led him to the wheel.

[18] He was carefully stretched tight upon it, his back was broken, and he was roasted from underneath.

[19] To his back they applied sharp spits that had been heated in the fire, and pierced his ribs so that his entrails were burned through.

[20] While being tortured he said, "O contest befitting holiness, in which so many of us brothers have been summoned to an arena of sufferings for religion, and in which we have not been defeated!

[21] For religious knowledge, O tyrant, is invincible.

[22] I also, equipped with nobility, will die with my brothers,

[23] and I myself will bring a great avenger upon you, you inventor of tortures and enemy of those who are truly devout.

[24] We six boys have paralyzed your tyranny!

[25] Since you have not been able to persuade us to change our mind or to force us to eat defiling foods, is not this your downfall?

[26] Your fire is cold to us, and the catapults painless, and your violence powerless.

[27] For it is not the guards of the tyrant but those of the divine law that are set over us; therefore, unconquered, we hold fast to reason."

4Mac.12

[1] When he also, thrown into the caldron, had died a blessed death, the seventh and youngest of all came forward.

[2] Even though the tyrant had been fearfully reproached by the brothers, he felt strong compassion for this child when he saw that he was already in fetters. He summoned him to come nearer and tried to console him, saying,

[3] "You see the result of your brothers' stupidity, for they died in torments because of their disobedience.

[4] You too, if you do not obey, will be miserably tortured and die before

your time,

[5] but if you yield to persuasion you will be my friend and a leader in the government of the kingdom."

[6] When he had so pleaded, he sent for the boy's mother to show compassion on her who had been bereaved of so many sons and to influence her to persuade the surviving son to obey and save himself.

[7] But when his mother had exhorted him in the Hebrew language, as we shall tell a little later,

[8] he said, "Let me loose, let me speak to the king and to all his friends that are with him."

[9] Extremely pleased by the boy's declaration, they freed him at once.

[10] Running to the nearest of the braziers,

[11] he said, "You profane tyrant, most impious of all the wicked, since you have received good things and also your kingdom from God, were you not ashamed to murder his servants and torture on the wheel those who practice religion?

[12] Because of this, justice has laid up for you intense and eternal fire and tortures, and these throughout all time will never let you go.

[13] As a man, were you not ashamed, you most savage beast, to cut out the tongues of men who have feelings like yours and are made of the same elements as you, and to maltreat and torture them in this way?

[14] Surely they by dying nobly fulfilled their service to God, but you will wail bitterly for having slain without cause the contestants for virtue."

[15] Then because he too was about to die, he said,

[16] "I do not desert the excellent example of my brothers,

[17] and I call on the God of our fathers to be merciful to our nation;

[18] but on you he will take vengeance both in this present life and when you are dead."

[19] After he had uttered these imprecations, he flung himself into the braziers and so ended his life.

4Mac.13

[1] Since, then, the seven brothers despised sufferings even unto death, everyone must concede that devout reason is sovereign over the emotions.

[2] For if they had been slaves to their emotions and had eaten defiling food, we would say that they had been conquered by these emotions.

[3] But in fact it was not so. Instead, by reason, which is praised before God, they prevailed over their emotions.

[4] The supremacy of the mind over these cannot be overlooked, for the brothers mastered both emotions and pains.

[5] How then can one fail to confess the sovereignty of right reason over emotion in those who were not turned back by fiery agonies?

[6] For just as towers jutting out over harbors hold back the threatening waves and make it calm for those who sail into the inner basin,

[7] so the seven-towered right reason of the youths, by fortifying the harbor of religion, conquered the tempest of the emotions.

[8] For they constituted a holy chorus of religion and encouraged one another, saying,

[9] "Brothers, let us die like brothers for the sake of the law; let us imitate the three youths in Assyria who despised the same ordeal of the furnace.

[10] Let us not be cowardly in the demonstration of our piety."

[11] While one said, "Courage, brother," another said, "Bear up nobly,"

[12] and another reminded them, "Remember whence you came, and the father by whose hand Isaac would have submitted to being slain for the sake of religion."

[13] Each of them and all of them together looking at one another, cheerful and undaunted, said, "Let us with all our hearts consecrate ourselves to God, who gave us our lives, and let us use our bodies as a bulwark for the law.

[14] Let us not fear him who thinks he is killing us,

[15] for great is the struggle of the soul and the danger of eternal torment lying before those who transgress the commandment of God.

[16] Therefore let us put on the full armor of self-control, which is divine reason.

[17] For if we so die, Abraham and Isaac and Jacob will welcome us, and all the fathers will praise us."

[18] Those who were left behind said to each of the brothers who were being dragged away, "Do not put us to shame, brother, or betray the brothers who have died before us."

[19] You are not ignorant of the affection of brotherhood, which the divine and all-wise Providence has bequeathed through the fathers to their descendants and which was implanted in the mother's womb.

[20] There each of the brothers dwelt the same length of time and was shaped during the same period of time; and growing from the same blood and through the same life, they were brought to the light of day.

[21] When they were born after an equal time of gestation, they drank milk from the same fountains. For such embraces brotherly-loving souls are nourished;

[22] and they grow stronger from this common nurture and daily companionship, and from both general education and our discipline in the law of God.

[23] Therefore, when sympathy and brotherly affection had been so established, the brothers were the more sympathetic to one another.

[24] Since they had been educated by the same law and trained in the same virtues and brought up in right living, they loved one another all the more.

[25] A common zeal for nobility expanded their goodwill and harmony toward one another,

[26] because, with the aid of their religion, they rendered their brotherly

love more fervent.

[27] But although nature and companionship and virtuous habits had augmented the affection of brotherhood, those who were left endured for the sake of religion, while watching their brothers being maltreated and tortured to death.

4Mac.14

[1] Furthermore, they encouraged them to face the torture, so that they not only despised their agonies, but also mastered the emotions of brotherly love.

[2] O reason, more royal than kings and freer than the free!

[3] O sacred and harmonious concord of the seven brothers on behalf of religion!

[4] None of the seven youths proved coward or shrank from death,

[5] but all of them, as though running the course toward immortality, hastened to death by torture.

[6] Just as the hands and feet are moved in harmony with the guidance of the mind, so those holy youths, as though moved by an immortal spirit of devotion, agreed to go to death for its sake.

[7] O most holy seven, brothers in harmony! For just as the seven days of creation move in choral dance around religion,

[8] so these youths, forming a chorus, encircled the sevenfold fear of tortures and dissolved it.

[9] Even now, we ourselves shudder as we hear of the tribulations of these young men; they not only saw what was happening, yes, not only heard the direct word of threat, but also bore the sufferings patiently, and in agonies of fire at that.

[10] What could be more excruciatingly painful than this? For the power of fire is intense and swift, and it consumed their bodies quickly.

[11] Do not consider it amazing that reason had full command over these men in their tortures, since the mind of woman despised even more diverse agonies,

[12] for the mother of the seven young men bore up under the rackings of each one of her children.

[13] Observe how complex is a mother's love for her children, which draws everything toward an emotion felt in her inmost parts.

[14] Even unreasoning animals, like mankind, have a sympathy and parental love for their offspring.

[15] For example, among birds, the ones that are tame protect their young by building on the housetops,

[16] and the others, by building in precipitous chasms and in holes and tops of trees, hatch the nestlings and ward off the intruder.

[17] If they are not able to keep him away, they do what they can to help their young by flying in circles around them in the anguish of love, warning

them with their own calls.

[18] And why is it necessary to demonstrate sympathy for children by the example of unreasoning animals,

[19] since even bees at the time for making honeycombs defend themselves against intruders as though with an iron dart sting those who approach their hive and defend it even to the death?

[20] But sympathy for her children did not sway the mother of the young men; she was of the same mind as Abraham.

4Mac.15

[1] O reason of the children, tyrant over the emotions! O religion, more desirable to the mother than her children!

[2] Two courses were open to this mother, that of religion, and that of preserving her seven sons for a time, as the tyrant had promised.

[3] She loved religion more, religion that preserves them for eternal life according to God's promise.

[4] In what manner might I express the emotions of parents who love their children? We impress upon the character of a small child a wondrous likeness both of mind and of form. Especially is this true of mothers, who because of their birthpangs have a deeper sympathy toward their offspring than do the fathers.

[5] Considering that mothers are the weaker sex and give birth to many, they are more devoted to their children.

[6] The mother of the seven boys, more than any other mother, loved her children. In seven pregnancies she had implanted in herself tender love toward them,

[7] and because of the many pains she suffered with each of them she had sympathy for them;

[8] yet because of the fear of God she disdained the temporary safety of her children.

[9] Not only so, but also because of the nobility of her sons and their ready obedience to the law she felt a greater tenderness toward them.

[10] For they were righteous and self-controlled and brave and magnanimous, and loved their brothers and their mother, so that they obeyed her even to death in keeping the ordinances.

[11] Nevertheless, though so many factors influenced the mother to suffer with them out of love for her children, in the case of none of them were the various tortures strong enough to pervert her reason.

[12] Instead, the mother urged them on, each child singly and all together, to death for the sake of religion.

[13] O sacred nature and affection of parental love, yearning of parents toward offspring, nurture and indomitable suffering by mothers!

[14] This mother, who saw them tortured and burned one by one, because of religion did not change her attitude.

[15] She watched the flesh of her children consumed by fire, their toes and

fingers scattered on the ground, and the flesh of the head to the chin exposed like masks.

[16] O mother, tried now by more bitter pains than even the birth-pangs you suffered for them!

[17] O woman, who alone gave birth to such complete devotion!

[18] When the first-born breathed his last it did not turn you aside, nor when the second in torments looked at you piteously nor when the third expired;

[19] nor did you weep when you looked at the eyes of each one in his tortures gazing boldly at the same agonies, and saw in their nostrils the signs of the approach of death.

[20] When you saw the flesh of children burned upon the flesh of other children, severed hands upon hands, scalped heads upon heads, and corpses fallen on other corpses and when you saw the place filled with many spectators of the torturings, you did not shed tears.

[21] Neither the melodies of sirens nor the songs of swans attract the attention of their hearers as did the voices of the children in torture calling to their mother.

[22] How great and how many torments the mother then suffered as her sons were tortured on the wheel and with the hot irons!

[23] But devout reason, giving her heart a man's courage in the very midst of her emotions, strengthened her to disregard her temporal love for her children.

[24] Although she witnessed the destruction of seven children and the ingenious and various rackings, this noble mother disregarded all these because of faith in God.

[25] For as in the council chamber of her own soul she saw mighty advocates -- nature, family, parental love, and the rackings of her children --

[26] this mother held two ballots, one bearing death and the other deliverance for her children.

[27] She did not approve the deliverance which would preserve the seven sons for a short time,

[28] but as the daughter of God-fearing Abraham she remembered his fortitude.

[29] O mother of the nation, vindicator of the law and champion of religion, who carried away the prize of the contest in your heart!

[30] O more noble than males in steadfastness, and more manly than men in endurance!

[31] Just as Noah's ark, carrying the world in the universal flood, stoutly endured the waves,

[32] so you, O guardian of the law, overwhelmed from every side by the flood of your emotions and the violent winds, the torture of your sons, endured nobly and withstood the wintry storms that assail religion.

4Mac.16

[1] If, then, a woman, advanced in years and mother of seven sons, endured seeing her children tortured to death, it must be admitted that devout reason is sovereign over the emotions.

[2] Thus I have demonstrated not only that men have ruled over the emotions, but also that a woman has despised the fiercest tortures.

[3] The lions surrounding Daniel were not so savage, nor was the raging fiery furnace of Mishael so intensely hot, as was her innate parental love, inflamed as she saw her seven sons tortured in such varied ways.

[4] But the mother quenched so many and such great emotions by devout reason.

[5] Consider this also. If this woman, though a mother, had been fainthearted, she would have mourned over them and perhaps spoken as follows:

[6] "O how wretched am I and many times unhappy! After bearing seven children, I am now the mother of none!

[7] O seven childbirths all in vain, seven profitless pregnancies, fruitless nurturings and wretched nursings!

[8] In vain, my sons, I endured many birth-pangs for you, and the more grievous anxieties of your upbringing.

[9] Alas for my children, some unmarried, others married and without offspring. I shall not see your children or have the happiness of being called grandmother.

[10] Alas, I who had so many and beautiful children am a widow and alone, with many sorrows.

[11] Nor when I die, shall I have any of my sons to bury me."

[12] Yet the sacred and God-fearing mother did not wail with such a lament for any of them, nor did she dissuade any of them from dying, nor did she grieve as they were dying,

[13] but, as though having a mind like adamant and giving rebirth for immortality to the whole number of her sons, she implored them and urged them on to death for the sake of religion.

[14] O mother, soldier of God in the cause of religion, elder and woman! By steadfastness you have conquered even a tyrant, and in word and deed you have proved more powerful than a man.

[15] For when you and your sons were arrested together, you stood and watched Eleazar being tortured, and said to your sons in the Hebrew language,

[16] "My sons, noble is the contest to which you are called to bear witness for the nation. Fight zealously for our ancestral law.

[17] For it would be shameful if, while an aged man endures such agonies for the sake of religion, you young men were to be terrified by tortures.

[18] Remember that it is through God that you have had a share in the world and have enjoyed life,

[19] and therefore you ought to endure any suffering for the sake of God.

[20] For his sake also our father Abraham was zealous to sacrifice his son Isaac, the ancestor of our nation; and when Isaac saw his father's hand wielding a sword and descending upon him, he did not cower.

[21] And Daniel the righteous was thrown to the lions, and Hananiah, Azariah, and Mishael were hurled into the fiery furnace and endured it for the sake of God.

[22] You too must have the same faith in God and not be grieved.

[23] It is unreasonable for people who have religious knowledge not to withstand pain."

[24] By these words the mother of the seven encouraged and persuaded each of her sons to die rather than violate God's commandment.

[25] They knew also that those who die for the sake of God live in God, as do Abraham and Isaac and Jacob and all the patriarchs.

4Mac.17

[1] Some of the guards said that when she also was about to be seized and put to death she threw herself into the flames so that no one might touch her body.

[2] O mother, who with your seven sons nullified the violence of the tyrant, frustrated his evil designs, and showed the courage of your faith!

[3] Nobly set like a roof on the pillars of your sons, you held firm and unswerving against the earthquake of the tortures.

[4] Take courage, therefore, O holy-minded mother, maintaining firm an enduring hope in God.

[5] The moon in heaven, with the stars, does not stand so august as you, who, after lighting the way of your star-like seven sons to piety, stand in honor before God and are firmly set in heaven with them.

[6] For your children were true descendants of father Abraham.

[7] If it were possible for us to paint the history of your piety as an artist might, would not those who first beheld it have shuddered as they saw the mother of the seven children enduring their varied tortures to death for the sake of religion?

[8] Indeed it would be proper to inscribe upon their tomb these words as a reminder to the people of our nation:

[9] "Here lie buried an aged priest and an aged woman and seven sons, because of the violence of the tyrant who wished to destroy the way of life of the Hebrews.

[10] They vindicated their nation, looking to God and enduring torture even to death."

[11] Truly the contest in which they were engaged was divine,

[12] for on that day virtue gave the awards and tested them for their endurance. The prize was immortality in endless life.

[13] Eleazar was the first contestant, the mother of the seven sons entered

the competition, and the brothers contended.

[14] The tyrant was the antagonist, and the world and the human race were the spectators.

[15] Reverence for God was victor and gave the crown to its own athletes.

[16] Who did not admire the athletes of the divine legislation? Who were not amazed?

[17] The tyrant himself and all his council marveled at their endurance,

[18] because of which they now stand before the divine throne and live through blessed eternity.

[19] For Moses says, "All who are consecrated are under your hands."

[20] These, then, who have been consecrated for the sake of God, are honored, not only with this honor, but also by the fact that because of them our enemies did not rule over our nation,

[21] the tyrant was punished, and the homeland purified -- they having become, as it were, a ransom for the sin of our nation.

[22] And through the blood of those devout ones and their death as an expiation, divine Providence preserved Israel that previously had been afflicted.

[23] For the tyrant Antiochus, when he saw the courage of their virtue and their endurance under the tortures, proclaimed them to his soldiers as an example for their own endurance,

[24] and this made them brave and courageous for infantry battle and siege, and he ravaged and conquered all his enemies.

4Mac.18

[1] O Israelite children, offspring of the seed of Abraham, obey this law and exercise piety in every way,

[2] knowing that devout reason is master of all emotions, not only of sufferings from within, but also of those from without.

[3] Therefore those who gave over their bodies in suffering for the sake of religion were not only admired by men, but also were deemed worthy to share in a divine inheritance.

[4] Because of them the nation gained peace, and by reviving observance of the law in the homeland they ravaged the enemy.

[5] The tyrant Antiochus was both punished on earth and is being chastised after his death. Since in no way whatever was he able to compel the Israelites to become pagans and to abandon their ancestral customs, he left Jerusalem and marched against the Persians.

[6] The mother of seven sons expressed also these principles to her children:

[7] "I was a pure virgin and did not go outside my father's house; but I guarded the rib from which woman was made.

[8] No seducer corrupted me on a desert plain, nor did the destroyer, the deceitful serpent, defile the purity of my virginity.

[9] In the time of my maturity I remained with my husband, and when these sons had grown up their father died. A happy man was he, who lived out

his life with good children, and did not have the grief of bereavement.

[10] While he was still with you, he taught you the law and the prophets.

[11] He read to you about Abel slain by Cain, and Isaac who was offered as a burnt offering, and of Joseph in prison.

[12] He told you of the zeal of Phineas, and he taught you about Hananiah, Azariah, and Mishael in the fire.

[13] He praised Daniel in the den of the lions and blessed him.

[14] He reminded you of the scripture of Isaiah, which says, `Even though you go through the fire, the flame shall not consume you.'

[15] He sang to you songs of the psalmist David, who said, `Many are the afflictions of the righteous.'

[16] He recounted to you Solomon's proverb, `There is a tree of life for those who do his will.'

[17] He confirmed the saying of Ezekiel, `Shall these dry bones live?'

[18] For he did not forget to teach you the song that Moses taught, which says,

[19] `I kill and I make alive: this is your life and the length of your days.'"

[20] O bitter was that day -- and yet not bitter -- when that bitter tyrant of the Greeks quenched fire with fire in his cruel caldrons, and in his burning rage brought those seven sons of the daughter of Abraham to the catapult and back again to more tortures,

[21] pierced the pupils of their eyes and cut out their tongues, and put them to death with various tortures.

[22] For these crimes divine justice pursued and will pursue the accursed tyrant.

[23] But the sons of Abraham with their victorious mother are gathered together into the chorus of the fathers, and have received pure and immortal souls from God,

[24] to whom be glory for ever and ever. Amen.

Letter (Epistle) of Jeremiah

EpJer.6

[1] A copy of a letter which Jeremiah sent to those who were to be taken to Babylon as captives by the king of the Babylonians, to give them the message which God had commanded him.

[2] Because of the sins which you have committed before God, you will be taken to Babylon as captives by Nebuchadnezzar, king of the Babylonians.

[3] Therefore when you have come to Babylon you will remain there for many years, for a long time, up to seven generations; after that I will bring you away from there in peace.

[4] Now in Babylon you will see gods made of silver and gold and wood, which are carried on men's shoulders and inspire fear in the heathen.

[5] So take care not to become at all like the foreigners or to let fear for these gods possess you, when you see the multitude before and behind them worshiping them.

[6] But say in your heart, "It is thou, O Lord, whom we must worship."

[7] For my angel is with you, and he is watching your lives.

[8] Their tongues are smoothed by the craftsman, and they themselves are overlaid with gold and silver; but they are false and cannot speak.

[9] People take gold and make crowns for the heads of their gods, as they would for a girl who loves ornaments;

[10] and sometimes the priests secretly take gold and silver from their gods and spend it upon themselves,

[11] and even give some of it to the harlots in the brothel. They deck their gods out with garments like men -- these gods of silver and gold and wood,

[12] which cannot save themselves from rust and corrosion. When they have been dressed in purple robes,

[13] their faces are wiped because of the dust from the temple, which is thick upon them.

[14] Like a local ruler the god holds a scepter, though unable to destroy any one who offends it.

[15] It has a dagger in its right hand, and has an axe; but it cannot save itself from war and robbers.

[16] Therefore they evidently are not gods; so do not fear them.

[17] For just as one's dish is useless when it is broken, so are the gods of the heathen, when they have been set up in the temples. Their eyes are full of the dust raised by the feet of those who enter.

[18] And just as the gates are shut on every side upon a man who has offended a king, as though he were sentenced to death, so the priests make their temples secure with doors and locks and bars, in order that they may

not be plundered by robbers.

[19] They light lamps, even more than they light for themselves, though their gods can see none of them.

[20] They are just like a beam of the temple, but men say their hearts have melted, when worms from the earth devour them and their robes. They do not notice

[21] when their faces have been blackened by the smoke of the temple.

[22] Bats, swallows, and birds light on their bodies and heads; and so do cats.

[23] From this you will know that they are not gods; so do not fear them.

[24] As for the gold which they wear for beauty -- they will not shine unless some one wipes off the rust; for even when they were being cast, they had no feeling.

[25] They are bought at any cost, but there is no breath in them.

[26] Having no feet, they are carried on men's shoulders, revealing to mankind their worthlessness.

[27] And those who serve them are ashamed because through them these gods are made to stand, lest they fall to the ground. If any one sets one of them upright, it cannot move itself; and if it is tipped over, it cannot straighten itself; but gifts are placed before them just as before the dead.

[28] The priests sell the sacrifices that are offered to these gods and use the money; and likewise their wives preserve some with salt, but give none to the poor or helpless.

[29] Sacrifices to them may be touched by women in menstruation or at childbirth. Since you know by these things that they are not gods, do not fear them.

[30] For why should they be called gods? Women serve meals for gods of silver and gold and wood;

[31] and in their temples the priests sit with their clothes rent, their heads and beards shaved, and their heads uncovered.

[32] They howl and shout before their gods as some do at a funeral feast for a man who has died.

[33] The priests take some of the clothing of their gods to clothe their wives and children.

[34] Whether one does evil to them or good, they will not be able to repay it. They cannot set up a king or depose one.

[35] Likewise they are not able to give either wealth or money; if one makes a vow to them and does not keep it, they will not require it.

[36] They cannot save a man from death or rescue the weak from the strong.

[37] They cannot restore sight to a blind man; they cannot rescue a man who is in distress.

[38] They cannot take pity on a widow or do good to an orphan.

[39] These things that are made of wood and overlaid with gold and silver

are like stones from the mountain, and those who serve them will be put to shame.

[40] Why then must any one think that they are gods, or call them gods? Besides, even the Chaldeans themselves dishonor them;

[41] for when they see a dumb man, who cannot speak, they bring him and pray Bel that the man may speak, as though Bel were able to understand.

[42] Yet they themselves cannot perceive this and abandon them, for they have no sense.

[43] And the women, with cords about them, sit along the passageways, burning bran for incense; and when one of them is led off by one of the passers-by and is lain with, she derides the woman next to her, because she was not as attractive as herself and her cord was not broken.

[44] Whatever is done for them is false. Why then must any one think that they are gods, or call them gods?

[45] They are made by carpenters and goldsmiths; they can be nothing but what the craftsmen wish them to be.

[46] The men that make them will certainly not live very long themselves; how then can the things that are made by them be gods?

[47] They have left only lies and reproach for those who come after.

[48] For when war or calamity comes upon them, the priests consult together as to where they can hide themselves and their gods.

[49] How then can one fail to see that these are not gods, for they cannot save themselves from war or calamity?

[50] Since they are made of wood and overlaid with gold and silver, it will afterward be known that they are false.

[51] It will be manifest to all the nations and kings that they are not gods but the work of men's hands, and that there is no work of God in them.

[52] Who then can fail to know that they are not gods?

[53] For they cannot set up a king over a country or give rain to men.

[54] They cannot judge their own cause or deliver one who is wronged, for they have no power; they are like crows between heaven and earth.

[55] When fire breaks out in a temple of wooden gods overlaid with gold or silver, their priests will flee and escape, but the gods will be burnt in two like beams.

[56] Besides, they can offer no resistance to a king or any enemies. Why then must any one admit or think that they are gods?

[57] Gods made of wood and overlaid with silver and gold are not able to save themselves from thieves and robbers.

[58] Strong men will strip them of their gold and silver and of the robes they wear, and go off with this booty, and they will not be able to help themselves.

[59] So it is better to be a king who shows his courage, or a household utensil that serves its owner's need, than to be these false gods; better even the door of a house that protects its contents, than these false gods; better

also a wooden pillar in a palace, than these false gods.

[60] For sun and moon and stars, shining and sent forth for service, are obedient.

[61] So also the lightning, when it flashes, is widely seen; and the wind likewise blows in every land.

[62] When God commands the clouds to go over the whole world, they carry out his command.

[63] And the fire sent from above to consume mountains and woods does what it is ordered. But these idols are not to be compared with them in appearance or power.

[64] Therefore one must not think that they are gods nor call them gods, for they are not able either to decide a case or to do good to men.

[65] Since you know then that they are not gods, do not fear them.

[66] For they can neither curse nor bless kings;

[67] they cannot show signs in the heavens and among the nations, or shine like the sun or give light like the moon.

[68] The wild beasts are better than they are, for they can flee to cover and help themselves.

[69] So we have no evidence whatever that they are gods; therefore do not fear them.

[70] Like a scarecrow in a cucumber bed, that guards nothing, so are their gods of wood, overlaid with gold and silver.

[71] In the same way, their gods of wood, overlaid with gold and silver, and like a thorn bush in a garden, on which every bird sits; or like a dead body cast out in the darkness.

[72] By the purple and linen that rot upon them you will know that they are not gods; and they will finally themselves be consumed, and be a reproach in the land.

[73] Better therefore is a just man who has no idols, for he will be far from reproach.

Prayer of Azariah

1

[1] And they walked in the midst of the fire, praising God and blessing the Lord

[2] Then Azariah stood and offered this prayer; in the midst of the fire he opened his mouth and said:

[3] "Blessed art thou, O Lord, God of our fathers, and worthy of praise; and thy name is glorified for ever.

[4] For thou art just in all that thou hast done to us, and all thy works are true and thy ways right, and all thy judgments are truth.

[5] Thou hast executed true judgments in all that thou hast brought upon us and upon Jerusalem, the holy city of our fathers, for in truth and justice thou hast brought all this upon us because of our sins.

[6] For we have sinfully and lawlessly departed from thee, and have sinned in all things and have not obeyed thy commandments;

[7] we have not observed them or done them, as thou hast commanded us that it might go well with us.

[8] So all that thou hast brought upon us, and all that thou hast done to us, thou hast done in true judgment.

[9] Thou hast given us into the hands of lawless enemies, most hateful rebels, and to an unjust king, the most wicked in all the world.

[10] And now we cannot open our mouths; shame and disgrace have befallen thy servants and worshipers.

[11] For thy name's sake do not give us up utterly, and do not break thy covenant,

[12] and do not withdraw thy mercy from us,

for the sake of Abraham thy beloved and for the sake of Isaac thy servant and Israel thy holy one,

[13] to whom thou didst promise to make their descendants as many as the stars of heaven and as the sand on the shore of the sea.

[14] For we, O Lord, have become fewer than any nation, and are brought low this day in all the world because of our sins.

[15] And at this time there is no prince, or prophet, or leader, no burnt offering, or sacrifice, or oblation, or incense, no place to make an offering before thee or to find mercy.

[16] Yet with a contrite heart and a humble spirit may we be accepted, as though it were with burnt offerings of rams and bulls, and with tens of thousands of fat lambs;

[17] such may our sacrifice be in thy sight this day, and may we wholly follow thee, for there will be no shame for those who trust in thee.

[18] And now with all our heart we follow thee, we fear thee and seek thy

face.
[19] Do not put us to shame, but deal with us in thy forbearance and in thy abundant mercy.
[20] Deliver us in accordance with thy marvelous works, and give glory to thy name, O Lord! Let all who do harm to thy servants be put to shame;
[21] let them be disgraced and deprived of all power and dominion, and let their strength be broken.
[22] Let them know that thou art the Lord, the only God, glorious over the whole world."
[23] Now the king's servants who threw them in did not cease feeding the furnace fires with naphtha, pitch, tow, and brush.
[24] And the flame streamed out above the furnace forty-nine cubits,
[25] and it broke through and burned those of the Chaldeans whom it caught about the furnace.
[26] But the angel of the Lord came down into the furnace to be with Azariah and his companions, and drove the fiery flame out of the furnace,
[27] and made the midst of the furnace like a moist whistling wind, so that the fire did not touch them at all or hurt or trouble them.
[28] Then the three, as with one mouth, praised and glorified and blessed God in the furnace, saying: [29] "Blessed art thou, O Lord, God of our fathers, and to be praised and highly exalted for ever; [30] And blessed is thy glorious, holy name and to be highly praised and highly exalted for ever; [31] Blessed art thou in the temple of thy holy glory and to be extolled and highly glorified for ever. [32] Blessed art thou, who sittest upon cherubim and lookest upon the deeps, and to be praised and highly exalted for ever. [33] Blessed art thou upon the throne of thy kingdom and to be extolled and highly exalted for ever. [34] Blessed art thou in the firmament of heavenand to be sung and glorified for ever. [35] "Bless the Lord, all works of the Lord, sing praise to him and highly exalt him for ever. [36] Bless the Lord, you heavens, sing praise to him and highly exalt him for ever. [37] Bless the Lord, you angels of the Lord, sing praise to him and highly exalt him for ever. [38] Bless the Lord, all waters above the heaven, sing praise to him and highly exalt him for ever. [39] Bless the Lord, all powers, sing praise to him and highly exalt him for ever. [40] Bless the Lord, sun and moon, sing praise to him and highly exalt him for ever. [41] Bless the Lord, stars of heaven, sing praise to him and highly exalt him for ever. [42] Bless the Lord, all rain and dew, sing praise to him and highly exalt him for ever. [43] Bless the Lord, all winds, sing praise to him and highly exalt him for ever. [44] Bless the Lord, fire and heat, sing praise to him and highly exalt him for ever. [45] Bless the Lord, winter cold and summer heat, sing praise to him and highly exalt him for ever. [46] Bless the Lord, dews and snows, sing praise to him and highly exalt him for ever. [47] Bless the Lord, nights and days, sing praise to him and highly exalt him

for ever. [48] Bless the Lord, light and darkness, sing praise to him and highly exalt him for ever. [49] Bless the Lord, ice and cold, sing praise to him and highly exalt him for ever. [50] Bless the Lord, frosts and snows, sing praise to him and highly exalt him for ever. [51] Bless the Lord, lightnings and clouds, sing praise to him and highly exalt him for ever. [52] Let the earth bless the Lord; let it sing praise to him and highly exalt him for ever. [53] Bless the Lord, mountains and hills, sing praise to him and highly exalt him for ever. [54] Bless the Lord, all things that grow on the earth, sing praise to him and highly exalt him for ever. [55] Bless the Lord, you springs, sing praise to him and highly exalt him for ever. [56] Bless the Lord, seas and rivers, sing praise to him and highly exalt him for ever. [57] Bless the Lord, you whales and all creatures that move in the waters, sing praise to him and highly exalt him for ever. [58] Bless the Lord, all birds of the air, sing praise to him and highly exalt him for ever. [59] Bless the Lord, all beasts and cattle, sing praise to him and highly exalt him for ever. [60] Bless the Lord, you sons of men, sing praise to him and highly exalt him for ever. [61] Bless the Lord, O Israel, sing praise to him and highly exalt him for ever. [62] Bless the Lord, you priests of the Lord, sing praise to him and highly exalt him for ever. [63] Bless the Lord, you servants of the Lord sing praise to him and highly exalt him for ever. [64] Bless the Lord, spirits and souls of the righteous, sing praise to him and highly exalt him for ever. [65] Bless the Lord, you who are holy and humble in heart, sing praise to him and highly exalt him for ever. [66] Bless the Lord, Hananiah, Azariah, and Mishael, sing praise to him and highly exalt him for ever; for he has rescued us from Hades and saved us from the hand of death, and delivered us from the midst of the burning fiery furnace; from the midst of the fire he has delivered us. [67] Give thanks to the Lord, for he is good, for his mercy endures for ever. [68] Bless him, all who worship the Lord, the God of gods, sing praise to him and give thanks to him, for his mercy endures for ever."

Baruch

Bar.1

[1] These are the words of the book which Baruch the son of Neraiah, son of Mahseiah, son of Zedekiah, son of Hasadiah, son of Hilkiah, wrote in Babylon,

[2] in the fifth year, on the seventh day of the month, at the time when the Chaldeans took Jerusalem and burned it with fire.

[3] And Baruch read the words of this book in the hearing of Jeconiah the son of Jehoiakim, king of Judah, and in the hearing of all the people who came to hear the book,

[4] and in the hearing of the mighty men and the princes, and in the hearing of the elders, and in the hearing of all the people, small and great, all who dwelt in Babylon by the river Sud.

[5] Then they wept, and fasted, and prayed before the Lord;

[6] and they collected money, each giving what he could;

[7] and they sent it to Jerusalem to Jehoiakim the high priest, the son of Hilkiah, son of Shallum, and to the priests, and to all the people who were present with him in Jerusalem.

[8] At the same time, on the tenth day of Sivan, Baruch took the vessels of the house of the Lord, which had been carried away from the temple, to return them to the land of Judah -- the silver vessels which Zedekiah the son of Josiah, king of Judah, had made,

[9] after Nebuchadnezzar king of Babylon had carried away from Jerusalem Jeconiah and the princes and the prisoners and the mighty men and the people of the land, and brought them to Babylon.

[10] And they said: "Herewith we send you money; so buy with the money burnt offerings and sin offerings and incense, and prepare a cereal offering, and offer them upon the altar of the Lord our God;

[11] and pray for the life of Nebuchadnezzar king of Babylon, and for the life of Belshazzar his son, that their days on earth may be like the days of heaven.

[12] And the Lord will give us strength, and he will give light to our eyes, and we shall live under the protection of Nebuchadnezzar king of Babylon, and under the protection of Belshazzar his son, and we shall serve them many days and find favor in their sight.

[13] And pray for us to the Lord our God, for we have sinned against the Lord our God, and to this day the anger of the Lord and his wrath have not

turned away from us.

[14] And you shall read this book which we are sending you, to make your confession in the house of the Lord on the days of the feasts and at appointed seasons.

[15] "And you shall say: `Righteousness belongs to the Lord our God, but confusion of face, as at this day, to us, to the men of Judah, to the inhabitants of Jerusalem,

[16] and to our kings and our princes and our priests and our prophets and our fathers,

[17] because we have sinned before the Lord,

[18] and have disobeyed him, and have not heeded the voice of the Lord our God, to walk in the statutes of the Lord which he set before us.

[19] From the day when the Lord brought our fathers out of the land of Egypt until today, we have been disobedient to the Lord our God, and we have been negligent, in not heeding his voice.

[20] So to this day there have clung to us the calamities and the curse which the Lord declared through Moses his servant at the time when he brought our fathers out of the land of Egypt to give to us a land flowing with milk and honey.

[21] We did not heed the voice of the Lord our God in all the words of the prophets whom he sent to us, but we each followed the intent of his own wicked heart by serving other gods and doing what is evil in the sight of the Lord our God.

Bar.2

[1] "`So the Lord confirmed his word, which he spoke against us, and against our judges who judged Israel, and against our kings and against our princes and against the men of Israel and Judah.

[2] Under the whole heaven there has not been done the like of what he has done in Jerusalem, in accordance with what is written in the law of Moses,

[3] that we should eat, one the flesh of his son and another the flesh of his daughter.

[4] And he gave them into subjection to all the kingdoms around us, to be a reproach and a desolation among all the surrounding peoples, where the Lord has scattered them.

[5] They were brought low and not raised up, because we sinned against the Lord our God, in not heeding his voice.

[6] "`Righteousness belongs to the Lord our God, but confusion of face to us and our fathers, as at this day.

[7] All those calamities with which the Lord threatened us have come upon us.

[8] Yet we have not entreated the favor of the Lord by turning away, each of us, from the thoughts of his wicked heart.

[9] And the Lord has kept the calamities ready, and the Lord has brought them upon us, for the Lord is righteous in all his works which he has commanded us to do.

[10] Yet we have not obeyed his voice, to walk in the statutes of the Lord which he set before us.

[11] "`And now, O Lord God of Israel, who didst bring thy people out of the land of Egypt with a mighty hand and with signs and wonders and with great power and outstretched arm, and hast made thee a name, as at this day,

[12] we have sinned, we have been ungodly, we have done wrong, O Lord our God, against all thy ordinances.

[13] Let thy anger turn away from us, for we are left, few in number, among the nations where thou hast scattered us.

[14] Hear, O Lord, our prayer and our supplication, and for thy own sake deliver us, and grant us favor in the sight of those who have carried us into exile;

[15] that all the earth may know that thou art the Lord our God, for Israel and his descendants are called by thy name.

[16] O Lord, look down from thy holy habitation, and consider us. Incline thy ear, O Lord, and hear;

[17] open thy eyes, O Lord, and see; for the dead who are in Hades, whose spirit has been taken from their bodies, will not ascribe glory or justice to the Lord,

[18] but the person that is greatly distressed, that goes about bent over and feeble, and the eyes that are failing, and the person that hungers, will ascribe to thee glory and righteousness, O Lord.

[19] For it is not because of any righteous deeds of our fathers or our kings that we bring before thee our prayer for mercy, O Lord our God.

[20] For thou hast sent thy anger and thy wrath upon us, as thou didst declare by thy servants the prophets, saying:

[21] "Thus says the Lord: Bend your shoulders and serve the king of Babylon, and you will remain in the land which I gave to your fathers.

[22] But if you will not obey the voice of the Lord and will not serve the king of Babylon,

[23] I will make to cease from the cities of Judah and from the region about Jerusalem the voice of mirth and the voice of gladness, the voice of the bridegroom and the voice of the bride, and the whole land will be a desolation without inhabitants."

[24] "`But we did not obey thy voice, to serve the king of Babylon; and thou hast confirmed thy words, which thou didst speak by thy servants the prophets, that the bones of our kings and the bones of our fathers would be

brought out of their graves;

[25] and behold, they have been cast out to the heat of day and the frost of night. They perished in great misery, by famine and sword and pestilence.

[26] And the house which is called by thy name thou hast made as it is today, because of the wickedness of the house of Israel and the house of Judah.

[27] "Yet thou hast dealt with us, O Lord our God, in all thy kindness and in all thy great compassion,

[28] as thou didst speak by thy servant Moses on the day when thou didst command him to write thy law in the presence of the people of Israel, saying,

[29] "If you will not obey my voice, this very great multitude will surely turn into a small number among the nations, where I will scatter them.

[30] For I know that they will not obey me, for they are a stiff-necked people. But in the land of their exile they will come to themselves,

[31] and they will know that I am the Lord their God. I will give them a heart that obeys and ears that hear;

[32] and they will praise me in the land of their exile, and will remember my name,

[33] and will turn from their stubbornness and their wicked deeds; for they will remember the ways of their fathers, who sinned before the Lord.

[34] I will bring them again into the land which I swore to give to their fathers, to Abraham and to Isaac and to Jacob, and they will rule over it; and I will increase them, and they will not be diminished.

[35] I will make an everlasting covenant with them to be their God and they shall be my people; and I will never again remove my people Israel from the land which I have given them."

Bar.3

[1] "O Lord Almighty, God of Israel, the soul in anguish and the wearied spirit cry out to thee.

[2] Hear, O Lord, and have mercy, for we have sinned before thee.

[3] For thou art enthroned for ever, and we are perishing for ever.

[4] O Lord Almighty, God of Israel, hear now the prayer of the dead of Israel and of the sons of those who sinned before thee, who did not heed the voice of the Lord their God, so that calamities have clung to us.

[5] Remember not the iniquities of our fathers, but in this crisis remember thy power and thy name.

[6] For thou art the Lord our God, and thee, O Lord, will we praise.

[7] For thou hast put the fear of thee in our hearts in order that we should call upon thy name; and we will praise thee in our exile, for we have put

away from our hearts all the iniquity of our fathers who sinned before thee. [8] Behold, we are today in our exile where thou hast scattered us, to be reproached and cursed and punished for all the iniquities of our fathers who forsook the Lord our God.'"

[9] Hear the commandments of life, O Israel; give ear, and learn wisdom! [10] Why is it, O Israel, why is it that you are in the land of your enemies, that you are growing old in a foreign country, that you are defiled with the dead,

[11] that you are counted among those in Hades?

[12] You have forsaken the fountain of wisdom. [13] If you had walked in the way of God, you would be dwelling in peace for ever. [14] Learn where there is wisdom, where there is strength, where there is understanding, that you may at the same time discern where there is length of days, and life, where there is light for the eyes, and peace. [15] Who has found her place? And who has entered her storehouses? [16] Where are the princes of the nations, and those who rule over the beasts on earth; [17] those who have sport with the birds of the air, and who hoard up silver and gold, in which men trust, and there is no end to their getting; [18] those who scheme to get silver, and are anxious, whose labors are beyond measure? [19] They have vanished and gone down to Hades, and others have arisen in their place.

[20] Young men have seen the light of day, and have dwelt upon the earth; but they have not learned the way to knowledge, nor understood her paths, nor laid hold of her. [21] Their sons have strayed far from her way. [22] She has not been heard of in Canaan, nor seen in Teman; [23] the sons of Hagar, who seek for understanding on the earth, the merchants of Merran and Teman, the story-tellers and the seekers for understanding, have not learned the way to wisdom, nor given thought to her paths. [24] O Israel, how great is the house of God! And how vast the territory that he possesses! [25] It is great and has no bounds; it is high and immeasurable. [26] The giants were born there, who were famous of old, great in stature, expert in war. [27] God did not choose them, nor give them the way to knowledge; [28] so they perished because they had no wisdom, they perished through their folly.

[29] Who has gone up into heaven, and taken her, and brought her down from the clouds? [30] Who has gone over the sea, and found her, and will buy her for pure gold? [31] No one knows the way to her, or is concerned about the path to her. [32] But he who knows all things knows her, he found her by his understanding. He who prepared the earth for all time filled it with four-footed creatures; [33] he who sends forth the light, and it goes, called it, and it obeyed him in fear; [34] the stars shone in their watches, and were glad; he called them, and they said, "Here we are!" They shone with gladness for him who made them. [35] This is our God; no other can be compared to him! [36] He found the whole way to knowledge, and gave her to Jacob his servant and to Israel whom he loved. [37] Afterward

she appeared upon earth and lived among men.

Bar.4

[1] She is the book of the commandments of God, and the law that endures for ever. All who hold her fast will live, and those who forsake her will die.
[2] Turn, O Jacob, and take her; walk toward the shining of her light.
[3] Do not give your glory to another, or your advantages to an alien people.
[4] Happy are we, O Israel, for we know what is pleasing to God.
[5] Take courage, my people, O memorial of Israel!
[6] It was not for destruction that you were sold to the nations, but you were handed over to your enemies because you angered God.
[7] For you provoked him who made you, by sacrificing to demons and not to God.
[8] You forgot the everlasting God, who brought you up, and you grieved Jerusalem, who reared you.
[9] For she saw the wrath that came upon you from God, and she said:
"Hearken, you neighbors of Zion, God has brought great sorrow upon me;
[10] for I have seen the captivity of my sons and daughters, which the Everlasting brought upon them.
[11] With joy I nurtured them, but I sent them away with weeping and sorrow.
[12] Let no one rejoice over me, a widow and bereaved of many; I was left desolate because of the sins of my children, because they turned away from the law of God.
[13] They had no regard for his statutes; they did not walk in the ways of God's commandments, nor tread the paths of discipline in his righteousness.
[14] Let the neighbors of Zion come; remember the capture of my sons and daughters, which the Everlasting brought upon them.
[15] For he brought against them a nation from afar, a shameless nation, of a strange language, who had no respect for an old man, and had no pity for a child.
[16] They led away the widow's beloved sons, and bereaved the lonely woman of her daughters.
[17] "But I, how can I help you?
[18] For he who brought these calamities upon you will deliver you from the hand of your enemies.
[19] Go, my children, go; for I have been left desolate.
[20] I have taken off the robe of peace and put on the sackcloth of my supplication; I will cry to the Everlasting all my days.
[21] "Take courage, my children, cry to God, and he will deliver you from the power and hand of the enemy.

[22] For I have put my hope in the Everlasting to save you, and joy has come to me from the Holy One, because of the mercy which soon will come to you from your everlasting Savior.

[23] For I sent you out with sorrow and weeping, but God will give you back to me with joy and gladness for ever.

[24] For as the neighbors of Zion have now seen your capture, so they soon will see your salvation by God, which will come to you with great glory and with the splendor of the Everlasting.

[25] My children, endure with patience the wrath that has come upon you from God. Your enemy has overtaken you, but you will soon see their destruction and will tread upon their necks.

[26] My tender sons have traveled rough roads; they were taken away like a flock carried off by the enemy.

[27] "Take courage, my children, and cry to God, for you will be remembered by him who brought this upon you.

[28] For just as you purposed to go astray from God, return with tenfold zeal to seek him.

[29] For he who brought these calamities upon you will bring you everlasting joy with your salvation."

[30] Take courage, O Jerusalem, for he who named you will comfort you.

[31] Wretched will be those who afflicted you and rejoiced at your fall.

[32] Wretched will be the cities which your children served as slaves; wretched will be the city which received your sons.

[33] For just as she rejoiced at your fall and was glad for your ruin, so she will be grieved at her own desolation.

[34] And I will take away her pride in her great population, and her insolence will be turned to grief.

[35] For fire will come upon her from the Everlasting for many days, and for a long time she will be inhabited by demons.

[36] Look toward the east, O Jerusalem, and see the joy that is coming to you from God!

[37] Behold, your sons are coming, whom you sent away; they are coming, gathered from east and west, at the word of the Holy One, rejoicing in the glory of God.

Bar.5

[1] Take off the garment of your sorrow and affliction, O Jerusalem, and put on for ever the beauty of the glory from God.

[2] Put on the robe of the righteousness from God; put on your head the

diadem of the glory of the Everlasting.

[3] For God will show your splendor everywhere under heaven.

[4] For your name will for ever be called by God, "Peace of righteousness and glory of godliness."

[5] Arise, O Jerusalem, stand upon the height and look toward the east, and see your children gathered from west and east, at the word of the Holy One, rejoicing that God has remembered them.

[6] For they went forth from you on foot, led away by their enemies; but God will bring them back to you, carried in glory, as on a royal throne.

[7] For God has ordered that every high mountain and the everlasting hills be made low and the valleys filled up, to make level ground, so that Israel may walk safely in the glory of God.

[8] The woods and every fragrant tree have shaded Israel at God's command.

[9] For God will lead Israel with joy, in the light of his glory, with the mercy and righteousness that come from him.

Prayer of Manasseh

PrMan.1

[1] Lord, Almighty God of Abraham, Isaac, Jacob, and their righteous seed
[2] thou who hast made heaven and earth with all their order;
[3] who hast shackled the sea by thy word of command, who hast confined the deep and sealed it with thy terrible and glorious name;
[4] at whom all things shudder, and tremble before thy power,
[5] for thy glorious splendor cannot be borne, and the wrath of thy threat to sinners is irresistible;
[6] yet immeasurable and unsearchable is thy promised mercy,
[7] for thou art the Lord Most High, of great compassion, long-suffering, and very merciful, and repentest over the evils of men. Thou, O Lord, according to thy great goodness hast promised repentance and forgiveness to those who have sinned against thee; and in the multitude of thy mercies thou hast appointed repentance for sinners, that they may be saved.
[8] Therefore thou, O Lord, God of the righteous, hast not appointed repentance for the righteous, for Abraham and Isaac and Jacob, who did not sin against thee, but thou hast appointed repentance for me, who am a sinner.
[9] For the sins I have committed are more in number than the sand of the sea; my transgressions are multiplied, O Lord, they are multiplied! I am unworthy to look up and see the height of heaven because of the multitude of my iniquities.
[10] I am weighted down with many an iron fetter, so that I am rejected because of my sins, and I have no relief; for I have provoked thy wrath and have done what is evil in thy sight, setting up abominations and multiplying offenses.
[11] And now I bend the knee of my heart, beseeching thee for thy kindness.
[12] I have sinned, O Lord, I have sinned, and I know my transgressions.
[13] I earnestly beseech thee, forgive me, O Lord, forgive me! Do not destroy me with my transgressions! Do not be angry with me for ever or lay up evil for me; do not condemn me to the depths of the earth. For thou, O Lord, art the God of those who repent,
[14] and in me thou wilt manifest thy goodness; for, unworthy as I am, thou wilt save me in thy great mercy,
[15] and I will praise thee continually all the days of my life. For all the host of heaven sings thy praise, and your is the glory for ever. Amen.

Bel and the Dragon

Bel.1

[1] When King Astyages was laid with his fathers, Cyrus the Persian received his kingdom.

[2] And Daniel was a companion of the king, and was the most honored of his friends.

[3] Now the Babylonians had an idol called Bel, and every day they spent on it twelve bushels of fine flour and forty sheep and fifty gallons of wine.

[4] The king revered it and went every day to worship it. But Daniel worshiped his own God.

[5] And the king said to him, "Why do you not worship Bel?" He answered, "Because I do not revere man-made idols, but the living God, who created heaven and earth and has dominion over all flesh."

[6] The king said to him, "Do you not think that Bel is a living God? Do you not see how much he eats and drinks every day?"

[7] Then Daniel laughed, and said, "Do not be deceived, O king; for this is but clay inside and brass outside, and it never ate or drank anything."

[8] Then the king was angry, and he called his priests and said to them, "If you do not tell me who is eating these provisions, you shall die.

[9] But if you prove that Bel is eating them, Daniel shall die, because he blasphemed against Bel." And Daniel said to the king, "Let it be done as you have said."

[10] Now there were seventy priests of Bel, besides their wives and children. And the king went with Daniel into the temple of Bel.

[11] And the priests of Bel said, "Behold, we are going outside; you yourself, O king, shall set forth the food and mix and place the wine, and shut the door and seal it with your signet.

[12] And when you return in the morning, if you do not find that Bel has eaten it all, we will die; or else Daniel will, who is telling lies about us."

[13] They were unconcerned, for beneath the table they had made a hidden entrance, through which they used to go in regularly and consume the provisions.

[14] When they had gone out, the king set forth the food for Bel. Then Daniel ordered his servants to bring ashes and they sifted them throughout the whole temple in the presence of the king alone. Then they went out, shut the door and sealed it with the king's signet, and departed.

[15] In the night the priests came with their wives and children, as they were accustomed to do, and ate and drank everything.

[16] Early in the morning the king rose and came, and Daniel with him.

[17] And the king said, "Are the seals unbroken, Daniel?" He answered,

"They are unbroken, O king."

[18] As soon as the doors were opened, the king looked at the table, and shouted in a loud voice, "You are great, O Bel; and with you there is no deceit, none at all."

[19] Then Daniel laughed, and restrained the king from going in, and said, "Look at the floor, and notice whose footsteps these are."

[20] The king said, "I see the footsteps of men and women and children."

[21] Then the king was enraged, and he seized the priests and their wives and children; and they showed him the secret doors through which they were accustomed to enter and devour what was on the table.

[22] Therefore the king put them to death, and gave Bel over to Daniel, who destroyed it and its temple.

[23] There was also a great dragon, which the Babylonians revered.

[24] And the king said to Daniel, "You cannot deny that this is a living god; so worship him."

[25] Daniel said, "I will worship the Lord my God, for he is the living God.

[26] But if you, O king, will give me permission, I will slay the dragon without sword or club." The king said, "I give you permission."

[27] Then Daniel took pitch, fat, and hair, and boiled them together and made cakes, which he fed to the dragon. The dragon ate them, and burst open. And Daniel said, "See what you have been worshiping!"

[28] When the Babylonians heard it, they were very indignant and conspired against the king, saying, "The king has become a Jew; he has destroyed Bel, and slain the dragon, and slaughtered the priests."

[29] Going to the king, they said, "Hand Daniel over to us, or else we will kill you and your household."

[30] The king saw that they were pressing him hard, and under compulsion he handed Daniel over to them.

[31] They threw Daniel into the lions' den, and he was there for six days.

[32] There were seven lions in the den, and every day they had been given two human bodies and two sheep; but these were not given to them now, so that they might devour Daniel.

[33] Now the prophet Habakkuk was in Judea. He had boiled pottage and had broken bread into a bowl, and was going into the field to take it to the reapers.

[34] But the angel of the Lord said to Habakkuk, "Take the dinner which you have to Babylon, to Daniel, in the lions' den."

[35] Habakkuk said, "Sir, I have never seen Babylon, and I know nothing about the den."

[36] Then the angel of the Lord took him by the crown of his head, and lifted him by his hair and set him down in Babylon, right over the den, with the rushing sound of the wind itself.

[37] Then Habakkuk shouted, "Daniel, Daniel! Take the dinner which God

has sent you."

[38] And Daniel said, "Thou hast remembered me, O God, and hast not forsaken those who love thee."

[39] So Daniel arose and ate. And the angel of God immediately returned Habakkuk to his own place.

[40] On the seventh day the king came to mourn for Daniel. When he came to the den he looked in, and there sat Daniel.

[41] And the king shouted with a loud voice, "Thou art great, O Lord God of Daniel, and there is no other besides thee."

[42] And he pulled Daniel out, and threw into the den the men who had attempted his destruction, and they were devoured immediately before his eyes.

Wisdom of Jesus Son of Sirach

Sir.0

[1-14] Whereas many great teachings have been given to us through the law and the prophets and the others that followed them, on account of which we should praise Israel for instruction and wisdom; and since it is necessary not only that the readers themselves should acquire understanding but also that those who love learning should be able to help the outsiders by both speaking and writing, my grandfather Jesus, after devoting himself especially to the reading of the law and the prophets and the other books of our fathers, and after acquiring considerable proficiency in them, was himself also led to write something pertaining to instruction and wisdom, in order that, by becoming conversant with this also, those who love learning should make even greater progress in living according to the law.
[15-26]
You are urged therefore to read with good will and attention, and to be indulgent in cases where, despite out diligent labor in translating, we may seem to have rendered some phrases imperfectly. For what was originally expressed in Hebrew does not have exactly the same sense when translated into another language. Not only this work, but even the law itself, the prophecies, and the rest of the books differ not a little as originally expressed.
[27-36]
When I came to Egypt in the thirty-eighth year of the reign of Euergetes and stayed for some time, I found opportunity for no little instruction. It seemed highly necessary that I should myself devote some pains and labor to the translation of the following book, using in that period of time great watchfulness and skill in order to complete and publish the book for those living abroad who wished to gain learning, being prepared in character to live according to the law.

Sir.1

[1] All wisdom comes from the Lord and is with him for ever.
[2] The sand of the sea, the drops of rain, and the days of eternity -- who can count them?

[3] The height of heaven, the breadth of the earth, the abyss, and wisdom -- who can search them out?

[4] Wisdom was created before all things, and prudent understanding from eternity.

[5] The root of wisdom -- to whom has it been revealed? Her clever devices -- who knows them?

[6] There is One who is wise, greatly to be feared, sitting upon his throne.

[7] The Lord himself created wisdom; he saw her and apportioned her, he poured her out upon all his works.

[8] She dwells with all flesh according to his gift, and he supplied her to those who love him.

[9] The fear of the Lord is glory and exultation, and gladness and a crown of rejoicing.

[10] The fear of the Lord delights the heart, and gives gladness and joy and long life.

[11] With him who fears the Lord it will go well at the end; on the day of his death he will be blessed.

[12] To fear the Lord is the beginning of wisdom; she is created with the faithful in the womb.

[13] She made among men an eternal foundation, and among their descendants she will be trusted.

[14] To fear the Lord is wisdom's full measure; she satisfies men with her fruits;

[15] she fills their whole house with desirable goods, and their storehouses with her produce.

[16] The fear of the Lord is the crown of wisdom, making peace and perfect health to flourish.

[17] He saw her and apportioned her; he rained down knowledge and discerning comprehension, and he exalted the glory of those who held her fast.

[18] To fear the Lord is the root of wisdom, and her branches are long life.

[22] Unrighteous anger cannot be justified, for a man's anger tips the scale to his ruin.

[23] A patient man will endure until the right moment, and then joy will burst forth for him.

[24] He will hide his words until the right moment, and the lips of many will tell of his good sense.

[25] In the treasuries of wisdom are wise sayings, but godliness is an abomination to a sinner.

[26] If you desire wisdom, keep the commandments, and the Lord will supply it for you.

[27] For the fear of the Lord is wisdom and instruction, and he delights in fidelity and meekness.

[28] Do not disobey the fear of the Lord; do not approach him with a

divided mind.

[29] Be not a hypocrite in men's sight, and keep watch over your lips.

[30] Do not exalt yourself lest you fall, and thus bring dishonor upon yourself. The Lord will reveal your secrets

and cast you down in the midst of the congregation, because you did not come in the fear of the Lord, and your heart was full of deceit.

Sir.2

[1] My son, if you come forward to serve the Lord, prepare yourself for temptation.

[2] Set your heart right and be steadfast, and do not be hasty in time of calamity.

[3] Hold fast to him and do not depart, that you may be honored at the end of your life.

[4] Accept whatever is brought upon you, and in changes that humble you be patient.

[5] For gold is tested in the fire, and acceptable men in the furnace of humiliation.

[6] Trust in him, and he will help you; make your ways straight, and hope in him.

[7] You who fear the Lord, wait for his mercy; and turn not aside, lest you fall.

[8] You who fear the Lord, trust in him, and your reward will not fail;

[9] you who fear the Lord, hope for good things, for everlasting joy and mercy.

[10] Consider the ancient generations and see: who ever trusted in the Lord and was put to shame? Or who ever persevered in the fear of the Lord and was forsaken? Or who ever called upon him and was overlooked?

[11] For the Lord is compassionate and merciful; he forgives sins and saves in time of affliction.

[12] Woe to timid hearts and to slack hands, and to the sinner who walks along two ways!

[13] Woe to the faint heart, for it has no trust! Therefore it will not be sheltered.

[14] Woe to you who have lost your endurance! What will you do when the Lord punishes you?

[15] Those who fear the Lord will not disobey his words, and those who love him will keep his ways.

[16] Those who fear the Lord will seek his approval, and those who love him will be filled with the law.

[17] Those who fear the Lord will prepare their hearts, and will humble themselves before him.

[18] Let us fall into the hands of the Lord, but not into the hands of men; for as his majesty is, so also is his mercy.

Sir.3

[1] Listen to me your father, O children; and act accordingly, that you may be kept in safety.

[2] For the Lord honored the father above the children, and he confirmed the right of the mother over her sons.

[3] Whoever honors his father atones for sins,

[4] and whoever glorifies his mother is like one who lays up treasure.

[5] Whoever honors his father will be gladdened by his own children, and when he prays he will be heard.

[6] Whoever glorifies his father will have long life, and whoever obeys the Lord will refresh his mother;

[7] he will serve his parents as his masters.

[8] Honor your father by word and deed, that a blessing from him may come upon you.

[9] For a father's blessing strengthens the houses of the children, but a mother's curse uproots their foundations.

[10] Do not glorify yourself by dishonoring your father, for your father's dishonor is no glory to you.

[11] For a man's glory comes from honoring his father, and it is a disgrace for children not to respect their mother.

[12] O son, help your father in his old age, and do not grieve him as long as he lives;

[13] even if he is lacking in understanding, show forbearance; in all your strength do not despise him.

[14] For kindness to a father will not be forgotten, and against your sins it will be credited to you;

[15] in the day of your affliction it will be remembered in your favor; as frost in fair weather, your sins will melt away.

[16] Whoever forsakes his father is like a blasphemer, and whoever angers his mother is cursed by the Lord.

[17] My son, perform your tasks in meekness; then you will be loved by those whom God accepts.

[18] The greater you are, the more you must humble yourself; so you will find favor in the sight of the Lord.

[20] For great is the might of the Lord; he is glorified by the humble.

[21] Seek not what is too difficult for you, nor investigate what is beyond

your power.

[22] Reflect upon what has been assigned to you, for you do not need what is hidden.

[23] Do not meddle in what is beyond your tasks, for matters too great for human understanding have been shown you.

[24] For their hasty judgment has led many astray, and wrong opinion has caused their thoughts to slip.

[26] A stubborn mind will be afflicted at the end, and whoever loves danger will perish by it.

[27] A stubborn mind will be burdened by troubles, and the sinner will heap sin upon sin.

[28] The affliction of the proud has no healing, for a plant of wickedness has taken root in him.

[29] The mind of the intelligent man will ponder a parable, and an attentive ear is the wise man's desire.

[30] Water extinguishes a blazing fire: so almsgiving atones for sin.

[31] Whoever requites favors gives thought to the future; at the moment of his falling he will find support.

Sir.4

[1] My son, deprive not the poor of his living, and do not keep needy eyes waiting.

[2] Do not grieve the one who is hungry, nor anger a man in want.

[3] Do not add to the troubles of an angry mind, nor delay your gift to a beggar.

[4] Do not reject an afflicted suppliant, nor turn your face away from the poor.

[5] Do not avert your eye from the needy, nor give a man occasion to curse you;

[6] for if in bitterness of soul he calls down a curse upon you, his Creator will hear his prayer.

[7] Make yourself beloved in the congregation; bow your head low to a great man.

[8] Incline your ear to the poor, and answer him peaceably and gently.

[9] Deliver him who is wronged from the hand of the wrongdoer; and do not be fainthearted in judging a case.

[10] Be like a father to orphans, and instead of a husband to their mother; you will then be like a son of the Most High,

and he will love you more than does your mother.

[11] Wisdom exalts her sons and gives help to those who seek her.

[12] Whoever loves her loves life, and those who seek her early will be filled with joy.

[13] Whoever holds her fast will obtain glory, and the Lord will bless the place she enters.

[14] Those who serve her will minister to the Holy One; the Lord loves those who love her.

[15] He who obeys her will judge the nations, and whoever gives heed to her will dwell secure.

[16] If he has faith in her he will obtain her; and his descendants will remain in possession of her.

[17] For at first she will walk with him on tortuous paths, she will bring fear and cowardice upon him, and will torment him by her discipline until she trusts him, and she will test him with her ordinances.

[18] Then she will come straight back to him and gladden him, and will reveal her secrets to him.

[19] If he goes astray she will forsake him, and hand him over to his ruin.

[20] Observe the right time, and beware of evil; and do not bring shame on yourself.

[21] For there is a shame which brings sin, and there is a shame which is glory and favor.

[22] Do not show partiality, to your own harm, or deference, to your downfall.

[23] Do not refrain from speaking at the crucial time, and do not hide your wisdom.

[24] For wisdom is known through speech, and education through the words of the tongue.

[25] Never speak against the truth, but be mindful of your ignorance.

[26] Do not be ashamed to confess your sins, and do not try to stop the current of a river.

[27] Do not subject yourself to a foolish fellow, nor show partiality to a ruler.

[28] Strive even to death for the truth and the Lord God will fight for you.

[29] Do not be reckless in your speech, or sluggish and remiss in your deeds.

[30] Do not be like a lion in your home, nor be a faultfinder with your servants.

[31] Let not your hand be extended to receive, but withdrawn when it is time to repay.

Sir.5

[1] Do not set your heart on your wealth, nor say, "I have enough."

[2] Do not follow your inclination and strength, walking according to the desires of your heart.

[3] Do not say, "Who will have power over me?" for the Lord will surely punish you.

[4] Do not say, "I sinned, and what happened to me?" for the Lord is slow to anger.

[5] Do not be so confident of atonement that you add sin to sin.

[6] Do not say, "His mercy is great, he will forgive the multitude of my sins," for both mercy and wrath are with him,

and his anger rests on sinners.

[7] Do not delay to turn to the Lord, nor postpone it from day to day; for suddenly the wrath of the Lord will go forth,

and at the time of punishment you will perish.

[8] Do not depend on dishonest wealth, for it will not benefit you in the day of calamity.

[9] Do not winnow with every wind, nor follow every path: the double-tongued sinner does that.

[10] Be steadfast in your understanding, and let your speech be consistent.

[11] Be quick to hear, and be deliberate in answering.

[12] If you have understanding, answer your neighbor; but if not, put your hand on your mouth.

[13] Glory and dishonor come from speaking, and a man's tongue is his downfall.

[14] Do not be called a slanderer, and do not lie in ambush with your tongue; for shame comes to the thief, and severe condemnation to the double-tongued.

[15] In great and small matters do not act amiss,

Sir.6

[1] and do not become an enemy instead of a friend; for a bad name incurs shame and reproach: so fares the double-tongued sinner.

[2] Do not exalt yourself through your soul's counsel, lest your soul be torn in pieces like a bull.

[3] You will devour your leaves and destroy your fruit, and will be left like a withered tree.

[4] An evil soul will destroy him who has it, and make him the laughingstock of his enemies.

[5] A pleasant voice multiplies friends, and a gracious tongue multiplies courtesies.

[6] Let those that are at peace with you be many, but let your advisers be one in a thousand.

[7] When you gain a friend, gain him through testing, and do not trust him

hastily.

[8] For there is a friend who is such at his own convenience, but will not stand by you in your day of trouble.

[9] And there is a friend who changes into an enemy, and will disclose a quarrel to your disgrace.

[10] And there is a friend who is a table companion, but will not stand by you in your day of trouble.

[11] In prosperity he will make himself your equal, and be bold with your servants;

[12] but if you are brought low he will turn against you, and will hide himself from your presence.

[13] Keep yourself far from your enemies, and be on guard toward your friends.

[14] A faithful friend is a sturdy shelter: he that has found one has found a treasure.

[15] There is nothing so precious as a faithful friend, and no scales can measure his excellence.

[16] A faithful friend is an elixir of life; and those who fear the Lord will find him.

[17] Whoever fears the Lord directs his friendship aright, for as he is, so is his neighbor also.

[18] My son, from your youth up choose instruction, and until you are old you will keep finding wisdom.

[19] Come to her like one who plows and sows, and wait for her good harvest. For in her service you will toil a little while, and soon you will eat of her produce.

[20] She seems very harsh to the uninstructed; a weakling will not remain with her.

[21] She will weigh him down like a heavy testing stone, and he will not be slow to cast her off.

[22] For wisdom is like her name, and is not manifest to many.

[23] Listen, my son, and accept my judgment; do not reject my counsel.

[24] Put your feet into her fetters, and your neck into her collar.

[25] Put your shoulder under her and carry her, and do not fret under her bonds.

[26] Come to her with all your soul, and keep her ways with all your might.

[27] Search out and seek, and she will become known to you; and when you get hold of her, do not let her go.

[28] For at last you will find the rest she gives, and she will be changed into joy for you.

[29] Then her fetters will become for you a strong protection, and her collar a glorious robe.

[30] Her yoke is a golden ornament, and her bonds are a cord of blue.

[31] You will wear her like a glorious robe, and put her on like a crown of

gladness.

[32] If you are willing, my son, you will be taught, and if you apply yourself you will become clever.

[33] If you love to listen you will gain knowledge, and if you incline your ear you will become wise.

[34] Stand in the assembly of the elders. Who is wise? Hold fast to him.

[35] Be ready to listen to every narrative, and do not let wise proverbs escape you.

[36] If you see an intelligent man, visit him early; let your foot wear out his doorstep.

[37] Reflect on the statutes of the Lord, and meditate at all times on his commandments. It is he who will give insight to your mind, and your desire for wisdom will be granted.

Sir.7

[1] Do no evil, and evil will never befall you.

[2] Stay away from wrong, and it will turn away from you.

[3] My son, do not sow the furrows of injustice, and you will not reap a sevenfold crop.

[4] Do not seek from the Lord the highest office, nor the seat of honor from the king.

[5] Do not assert your righteousness before the Lord, nor display your wisdom before the king.

[6] Do not seek to become a judge, lest you be unable to remove iniquity, lest you be partial to a powerful man, and thus put a blot on your integrity.

[7] Do not offend against the public, and do not disgrace yourself among the people.

[8] Do not commit a sin twice; even for one you will not go unpunished.

[9] Do not say, "He will consider the multitude of my gifts, and when I make an offering to the Most High God he will accept it."

[10] Do not be fainthearted in your prayer, nor neglect to give alms.

[11] Do not ridicule a man who is bitter in soul, for there is One who abases and exalts.

[12] Do not devise a lie against your brother, nor do the like to a friend.

[13] Refuse to utter any lie, for the habit of lying serves no good.

[14] Do not prattle in the assembly of the elders, nor repeat yourself in your prayer.

[15] Do not hate toilsome labor, or farm work, which were created by the Most High.

[16] Do not count yourself among the crowd of sinners; remember that

wrath does not delay.

[17] Humble yourself greatly, for the punishment of the ungodly is fire and worms.

[18] Do not exchange a friend for money, or a real brother for the gold of Ophir.

[19] Do not deprive yourself of a wise and good wife, for her charm is worth more than gold.

[20] Do not abuse a servant who performs his work faithfully, or a hired laborer who devotes himself to you.

[21] Let your soul love an intelligent servant; do not withhold from him his freedom.

[22] Do you have cattle? Look after them; if they are profitable to you, keep them.

[23] Do you have children? Discipline them, and make them obedient from their youth.

[24] Do you have daughters? Be concerned for their chastity, and do not show yourself too indulgent with them.

[25] Give a daughter in marriage; you will have finished a great task. But give her to a man of understanding.

[26] If you have a wife who pleases you, do not cast her out; but do not trust yourself to one whom you detest.

[27] With all your heart honor your father, and do not forget the birth pangs of your mother.

[28] Remember that through your parents you were born; and what can you give back to them that equals their gift to you?

[29] With all your soul fear the Lord, and honor his priests.

[30] With all your might love your Maker, and do not forsake his ministers.

[31] Fear the Lord and honor the priest, and give him his portion, as is commanded you: the first fruits, the guilt offering, the gift of the shoulders, the sacrifice of sanctification, and the first fruits of the holy things.

[32] Stretch forth your hand to the poor, so that your blessing may be complete.

[33] Give graciously to all the living, and withhold not kindness from the dead.

[34] Do not fail those who weep, but mourn with those who mourn.

[35] Do not shrink from visiting a sick man, because for such deeds you will be loved.

[36] In all you do, remember the end of your life, and then you will never sin.

Sir.8

[1] Do not contend with a powerful man, lest you fall into his hands.

[2] Do not quarrel with a rich man, lest his resources outweigh yours; for gold has ruined many, and has perverted the minds of kings.

[3] Do not argue with a chatterer, nor heap wood on his fire.

[4] Do not jest with an ill-bred person, lest your ancestors be disgraced.

[5] Do not reproach a man who is turning away from sin; remember that we all deserve punishment.

[6] Do not disdain a man when he is old, for some of us are growing old.

[7] Do not rejoice over any one's death; remember that we all must die.

[8] Do not slight the discourse of the sages, but busy yourself with their maxims; because from them you will gain instruction and learn how to serve great men.

[9] Do not disregard the discourse of the aged, for they themselves learned from their fathers; because from them you will gain understanding and learn how to give an answer in time of need.

[10] Do not kindle the coals of a sinner, lest you be burned in his flaming fire.

[11] Do not get up and leave an insolent fellow, lest he lie in ambush against your words.

[12] Do not lend to a man who is stronger than you; but if you do lend anything, be as one who has lost it.

[13] Do not give surety beyond your means, but if you give surety, be concerned as one who must pay.

[14] Do not go to law against a judge, for the decision will favor him because of his standing.

[15] Do not travel on the road with a foolhardy fellow, lest he be burdensome to you; for he will act as he pleases, and through his folly you will perish with him.

[16] Do not fight with a wrathful man, and do not cross the wilderness with him; because blood is as nothing in his sight,
and where no help is at hand, he will strike you down.

[17] Do not consult with a fool, for he will not be able to keep a secret.

[18] In the presence of a stranger do nothing that is to be kept secret, for you do not know what he will divulge.

[19] Do not reveal your thoughts to every one, lest you drive away your good luck.

Sir.9

[1] Do not be jealous of the wife of your bosom, and do not teach her an evil lesson to your own hurt.

[2] Do not give yourself to a woman so that she gains mastery over your

strength.

[3] Do not go to meet a loose woman, lest you fall into her snares.

[4] Do not associate with a woman singer, lest you be caught in her intrigues.

[5] Do not look intently at a virgin, lest you stumble and incur penalties for her.

[6] Do not give yourself to harlots lest you lose your inheritance.

[7] Do not look around in the streets of a city, nor wander about in its deserted sections.

[8] Turn away your eyes from a shapely woman, and do not look intently at beauty belonging to another; many have been misled by a woman's beauty, and by it passion is kindled like a fire.

[9] Never dine with another man's wife, nor revel with her at wine; lest your heart turn aside to her, and in blood you be plunged into destruction.

[10] Forsake not an old friend, for a new one does not compare with him. A new friend is like new wine; when it has aged you will drink it with pleasure.

[11] Do not envy the honors of a sinner, for you do not know what his end will be.

[12] Do not delight in what pleases the ungodly; remember that they will not be held guiltless as long as they live.

[13] Keep far from a man who has the power to kill, and you will not be worried by the fear of death. But if you approach him, make no misstep, lest he rob you of your life. Know that you are walking in the midst of snares, and that you are going about on the city battlements.

[14] As much as you can, aim to know your neighbors, and consult with the wise.

[15] Let your conversation be with men of understanding, and let all your discussion be about the law of the Most High.

[16] Let righteous men be your dinner companions, and let your glorying be in the fear of the Lord.

[17] A work will be praised for the skill of the craftsmen; so a people's leader is proved wise by his words.

[18] A babbler is feared in his city, and the man who is reckless in speech will be hated.

Sir.10

[1] A wise magistrate will educate his people, and the rule of an understanding man will be well ordered.

[2] Like the magistrate of the people, so are his officials; and like the ruler of the city, so are all its inhabitants.

[3] An undisciplined king will ruin his people, but a city will grow through the understanding of its rulers.

[4] The government of the earth is in the hands of the Lord, and over it he will raise up the right man for the time.

[5] The success of a man is in the hands of the Lord, and he confers his honor upon the person of the scribe.

[6] Do not be angry with your neighbor for any injury, and do not attempt anything by acts of insolence.

[7] Arrogance is hateful before the Lord and before men, and injustice is outrageous to both.

[8] Sovereignty passes from nation to nation on account of injustice and insolence and wealth.

[9] How can he who is dust and ashes be proud? for even in life his bowels decay.

[10] A long illness baffles the physician; the king of today will die tomorrow.

[11] For when a man is dead, he will inherit creeping things, and wild beasts, and worms.

[12] The beginning of man's pride is to depart from the Lord; his heart has forsaken his Maker.

[13] For the beginning of pride is sin, and the man who clings to it pours out abominations. Therefore the Lord brought upon them extraordinary afflictions, and destroyed them utterly.

[14] The Lord has cast down the thrones of rulers, and has seated the lowly in their place.

[15] The Lord has plucked up the roots of the nations, and has planted the humble in their place.

[16] The Lord has overthrown the lands of the nations, and has destroyed them to the foundations of the earth.

[17] He has removed some of them and destroyed them, and has extinguished the memory of them from the earth.

[18] Pride was not created for men, nor fierce anger for those born of women.

[19] What race is worthy of honor? The human race. What race is worthy of honor? Those who fear the Lord. What race is unworthy of honor? The human race. What race is unworthy of honor? Those who transgress the commandments.

[20] Among brothers their leader is worthy of honor, and those who fear the Lord are worthy of honor in his eyes.

[22] The rich, and the eminent, and the poor -- their glory is the fear of the Lord.

[23] It is not right to despise an intelligent poor man, nor is it proper to honor a sinful man.

[24] The nobleman, and the judge, and the ruler will be honored, but none of them is greater than the man who fears the Lord.

[25] Free men will be at the service of a wise servant, and a man of understanding will not grumble.

[26] Do not make a display of your wisdom when you do your work, nor glorify yourself at a time when you are in want.

[27] Better is a man who works and has an abundance of everything, than one who goes about boasting, but lacks bread.

[28] My son, glorify yourself with humility, and ascribe to yourself honor according to your worth.

[29] Who will justify the man that sins against himself? And who will honor the man that dishonors his own life?

[30] A poor man is honored for his knowledge, while a rich man is honored for his wealth.

[31] A man honored in poverty, how much more in wealth! And a man dishonored in wealth, how much more in poverty!

Sir.11

[1] The wisdom of a humble man will lift up his head, and will seat him among the great.

[2] Do not praise a man for his good looks, nor loathe a man because of his appearance.

[3] The bee is small among flying creatures, but her product is the best of sweet things.

[4] Do not boast about wearing fine clothes, nor exalt yourself in the day that you are honored; for the works of the Lord are wonderful, and his works are concealed from men.

[5] Many kings have had to sit on the ground, but one who was never thought of has worn a crown.

[6] Many rulers have been greatly disgraced, and illustrious men have been handed over to others.

[7] Do not find fault before you investigate; first consider, and then reprove.

[8] Do not answer before you have heard, nor interrupt a speaker in the midst of his words.

[9] Do not argue about a matter which does not concern you, nor sit with sinners when they judge a case.

[10] My son, do not busy yourself with many matters; if you multiply activities you will not go unpunished, and if you pursue you will not overtake, and by fleeing you will not escape.

[11] There is a man who works, and toils, and presses on, but is so much the more in want.

[12] There is another who is slow and needs help, who lacks strength and abounds in poverty; but the eyes of the Lord look upon him for his good; he lifts him out of his low estate

[13] and raises up his head, so that many are amazed at him.

[14] Good things and bad, life and death, poverty and wealth, come from the Lord.

[17] The gift of the Lord endures for those who are godly, and what he approves will have lasting success.

[18] There is a man who is rich through his diligence and self-denial, and this is the reward allotted to him:

[19] when he says, "I have found rest, and now I shall enjoy my goods!" he does not know how much time will pass
until he leaves them to others and dies.

[20] Stand by your covenant and attend to it, and grow old in your work.

[21] Do not wonder at the works of a sinner, but trust in the Lord and keep at your toil; for it is easy in the sight of the Lord to enrich a poor man quickly and suddenly.

[22] The blessing of the Lord is the reward of the godly, and quickly God causes his blessing to flourish.

[23] Do not say, "What do I need, and what prosperity could be mine in the future?"

[24] Do not say, "I have enough, and what calamity could happen to me in the future?"

[25] In the day of prosperity, adversity is forgotten, and in the day of adversity, prosperity is not remembered.

[26] For it is easy in the sight of the Lord to reward a man on the day of death according to his conduct.

[27] The misery of an hour makes one forget luxury, and at the close of a man's life his deeds will be revealed.

[28] Call no one happy before his death; a man will be known through his children.

[29] Do not bring every man into your home, for many are the wiles of the crafty.

[30] Like a decoy partridge in a cage, so is the mind of a proud man, and like a spy he observes your weakness;

[31] for he lies in wait, turning good into evil, and to worthy actions he will attach blame.

[32] From a spark of fire come many burning coals, and a sinner lies in wait to shed blood.

[33] Beware of a scoundrel, for he devises evil, lest he give you a lasting blemish.

[34] Receive a stranger into your home and he will upset you with commotion, and will estrange you from your family.

Sir.12

[1] If you do a kindness, know to whom you do it, and you will be thanked for your good deeds.

[2] Do good to a godly man, and you will be repaid --if not by him, certainly by the Most High.

[3] No good will come to the man who persists in evil or to him who does not give alms.

[4] Give to the godly man, but do not help the sinner.

[5] Do good to the humble, but do not give to the ungodly; hold back his bread, and do not give it to him, lest by means of it he subdue you; for you will receive twice as much evil for all the good which you do to him.

[6] For the Most High also hates sinners and will inflict punishment on the ungodly.

[7] Give to the good man, but do not help the sinner.

[8] A friend will not be known in prosperity, nor will an enemy be hidden in adversity.

[9] A man's enemies are grieved when he prospers, and in his adversity even his friend will separate from him.

[10] Never trust your enemy, for like the rusting of copper, so is his wickedness.

[11] Even if he humbles himself and goes about cringing, watch yourself, and be on your guard against him; and you will be to him like one who has polished a mirror, and you will know that it was not hopelessly tarnished.

[12] Do not put him next to you, lest he overthrow you and take your place; do not have him sit at your right, lest he try to take your seat of honor, and at last you will realize the truth of my words, and be stung by what I have said.

[13] Who will pity a snake charmer bitten by a serpent, or any who go near wild beasts?

[14] So no one will pity a man who associates with a sinner and becomes involved in his sins.

[15] He will stay with you for a time, but if you falter, he will not stand by you.

[16] An enemy will speak sweetly with his lips, but in his mind he will plan to throw you into a pit; an enemy will weep with his eyes, but if he finds an opportunity his thirst for blood will be insatiable.

[17] If calamity befalls you, you will find him there ahead of you; and while pretending to help you, he will trip you by the heel;

[18] he will shake his head, and clap his hands, and whisper much, and change his expression.

Sir.13

[1] Whoever touches pitch will be defiled, and whoever associates with a proud man will become like him.
[2] Do not lift a weight beyond your strength, nor associate with a man mightier and richer than you. How can the clay pot associate with the iron kettle? The pot will strike against it, and will itself be broken.
[3] A rich man does wrong, and he even adds reproaches; a poor man suffers wrong, and he must add apologies.
[4] A rich man will exploit you if you can be of use to him, but if you are in need he will forsake you.
[5] If you own something, he will live with you; he will drain your resources and he will not care.
[6] When he needs you he will deceive you, he will smile at you and give you hope. He will speak to you kindly and say, "What do you need?"
[7] He will shame you with his foods, until he has drained you two or three times; and finally he will deride you. Should he see you afterwards, he will forsake you, and shake his head at you.
[8] Take care not to be led astray, and not to be humiliated in your feasting.
[9] When a powerful man invites you, be reserved; and he will invite you the more often.
[10] Do not push forward, lest you be repulsed; and do not remain at a distance, lest you be forgotten.
[11] Do not try to treat him as an equal, nor trust his abundance of words; for he will test you through much talk, and while he smiles he will be examining you.
[12] Cruel is he who does not keep words to himself; he will not hesitate to injure or to imprison.
[13] Keep words to yourself and be very watchful, for you are walking about with your own downfall.
[15] Every creature loves its like, and every person his neighbor;
[16] all living beings associate by species, and a man clings to one like himself.
[17] What fellowship has a wolf with a lamb? No more has a sinner with a godly man.
[18] What peace is there between a hyena and a dog? And what peace between a rich man and a poor man?
[19] Wild asses in the wilderness are the prey of lions; likewise the poor are pastures for the rich.
[20] Humility is an abomination to a proud man; likewise a poor man is an

abomination to a rich one.

[21] When a rich man totters, he is steadied by friends, but when a humble man falls, he is even pushed away by friends.

[22] If a rich man slips, his helpers are many; he speaks unseemly words, and they justify him. If a humble man slips, they even reproach him; he speaks sensibly, and receives no attention.

[23] When the rich man speaks all are silent, and they extol to the clouds what he says. When the poor man speaks they say, "Who is this fellow?" And should he stumble, they even push him down.

[24] Riches are good if they are free from sin, and poverty is evil in the opinion of the ungodly.

[25] A man's heart changes his countenance, either for good or for evil.

[26] The mark of a happy heart is a cheerful face, but to devise proverbs requires painful thinking.

Sir.14

[1] Blessed is the man who does not blunder with his lips and need not suffer grief for sin.

[2] Blessed is he whose heart does not condemn him, and who has not given up his hope.

[3] Riches are not seemly for a stingy man; and of what use is property to an envious man?

[4] Whoever accumulates by depriving himself, accumulates for others; and others will live in luxury on his goods.

[5] If a man is mean to himself, to whom will he be generous? He will not enjoy his own riches.

[6] No one is meaner than the man who is grudging to himself, and this is the retribution for his baseness;

[7] even if he does good, he does it unintentionally, and betrays his baseness in the end.

[8] Evil is the man with a grudging eye; he averts his face and disregards people.

[9] A greedy man's eye is not satisfied with a portion, and mean injustice withers the soul.

[10] A stingy man's eye begrudges bread, and it is lacking at his table.

[11] My son, treat yourself well, according to your means, and present worthy offerings to the Lord.

[12] Remember that death will not delay, and the decree of Hades has not been shown to you.

[13] Do good to a friend before you die, and reach out and give to him as much as you can.

[14] Do not deprive yourself of a happy day; let not your share of desired good pass by you.

[15] Will you not leave the fruit of your labors to another, and what you acquired by toil to be divided by lot?

[16] Give, and take, and beguile yourself, because in Hades one cannot look for luxury.

[17] All living beings become old like a garment, for the decree from of old is, "You must surely die!"

[18] Like flourishing leaves on a spreading tree which sheds some and puts forth others, so are the generations of flesh and blood: one dies and another is born.

[19] Every product decays and ceases to exist, and the man who made it will pass away with it.

[20] Blessed is the man who meditates on wisdom and who reasons intelligently.

[21] He who reflects in his mind on her ways will also ponder her secrets.

[22] Pursue wisdom like a hunter, and lie in wait on her paths.

[23] He who peers through her windows will also listen at her doors;

[24] he who encamps near her house will also fasten his tent peg to her walls;

[25] he will pitch his tent near her, and will lodge in an excellent lodging place;

[26] he will place his children under her shelter, and will camp under her boughs;

[27] he will be sheltered by her from the heat, and will dwell in the midst of her glory.

Sir.15

[1] The man who fears the Lord will do this, and he who holds to the law will obtain wisdom.

[2] She will come to meet him like a mother, and like the wife of his youth she will welcome him.

[3] She will feed him with the bread of understanding, and give him the water of wisdom to drink.

[4] He will lean on her and will not fall, and he will rely on her and will not be put to shame.

[5] She will exalt him above his neighbors, and will open his mouth in the midst of the assembly.

[6] He will find gladness and a crown of rejoicing, and will acquire an everlasting name.

[7] Foolish men will not obtain her, and sinful men will not see her.

[8] She is far from men of pride, and liars will never think of her.

[9] A hymn of praise is not fitting on the lips of a sinner, for it has not been sent from the Lord.

[10] For a hymn of praise should be uttered in wisdom, and the Lord will prosper it.

[11] Do not say, "Because of the Lord I left the right way"; for he will not do what he hates.

[12] Do not say, "It was he who led me astray"; for he had no need of a sinful man.

[13] The Lord hates all abominations, and they are not loved by those who fear him.

[14] It was he who created man in the beginning, and he left him in the power of his own inclination.

[15] If you will, you can keep the commandments, and to act faithfully is a matter of your own choice.

[16] He has placed before you fire and water: stretch out your hand for whichever you wish.

[17] Before a man are life and death, and whichever he chooses will be given to him.

[18] For great is the wisdom of the Lord; he is mighty in power and sees everything;

[19] his eyes are on those who fear him, and he knows every deed of man.

[20] He has not commanded any one to be ungodly, and he has not given any one permission to sin.

Sir.16

[1] Do not desire a multitude of useless children, nor rejoice in ungodly sons.

[2] If they multiply , do not rejoice in them, unless the fear of the Lord is in them.

[3] Do not trust in their survival, and do not rely on their multitude; for one is better than a thousand, and to die childless is better than to have ungodly children.

[4] For through one man of understanding a city will be filled with people, but through a tribe of lawless men it will be made desolate.

[5] Many such things my eye has seen, and my ear has heard things more striking than these.

[6] In an assembly of sinners a fire will be kindled, and in a disobedient nation wrath was kindled.

[7] He was not propitiated for the ancient giants who revolted in their

might.

[8] He did not spare the neighbors of Lot, whom he loathed on account of their insolence.

[9] He showed no pity for a nation devoted to destruction, for those destroyed in their sins;

[10] nor for the six hundred thousand men on foot, who rebelliously assembled in their stubbornness.

[11] Even if there is only one stiff-necked person, it will be a wonder if he remains unpunished. For mercy and wrath are with the Lord; he is mighty to forgive, and he pours out wrath.

[12] As great as his mercy, so great is also his reproof; he judges a man according to his deeds.

[13] The sinner will not escape with his plunder, and the patience of the godly will not be frustrated.

[14] He will make room for every act of mercy; every one will receive in accordance with his deeds.

[17] Do not say, "I shall be hidden from the Lord, and who from on high will remember me? Among so many people I shall not be known, for what is my soul in the boundless creation?

[18] Behold, heaven and the highest heaven, the abyss and the earth, will tremble at his visitation.

[19] The mountains also and the foundations of the earth shake with trembling when he looks upon them.

[20] And no mind will reflect on this. Who will ponder his ways?

[21] Like a tempest which no man can see, so most of his works are concealed.

[22] Who will announce his acts of justice? Or who will await them? For the covenant is far off."

[23] This is what one devoid of understanding thinks; a senseless and misguided man thinks foolishly.

[24] Listen to me, my son, and acquire knowledge, and pay close attention to my words.

[25] I will impart instruction by weight, and declare knowledge accurately.

[26] The works of the Lord have existed from the beginning by his creation, and when he made them, he determined their divisions.

[27] He arranged his works in an eternal order, and their dominion for all generations; they neither hunger nor grow weary, and they do not cease from their labors.

[28] They do not crowd one another aside, and they will never disobey his word.

[29] After this the Lord looked upon the earth, and filled it with his good things;

[30] with all kinds of living beings he covered its surface, and to it they

return.

Sir.17

[1] The Lord created man out of earth, and turned him back to it again.
[2] He gave to men few days, a limited time, but granted them authority over the things upon the earth.
[3] He endowed them with strength like his own, and made them in his own image.
[4] He placed the fear of them in all living beings, and granted them dominion over beasts and birds.
[6] He made for them tongue and eyes; he gave them ears and a mind for thinking.
[7] He filled them with knowledge and understanding, and showed them good and evil.
[8] He set his eye upon their hearts to show them the majesty of his works.
[10] And they will praise his holy name, to proclaim the grandeur of his works.
[11] He bestowed knowledge upon them, and allotted to them the law of life.
[12] He established with them an eternal covenant, and showed them his judgments.
[13] Their eyes saw his glorious majesty, and their ears heard the glory of his voice.
[14] And he said to them, "Beware of all unrighteousness." And he gave commandment to each of them concerning
his neighbor.
[15] Their ways are always before him, they will not be hid from his eyes.
[17] He appointed a ruler for every nation, but Israel is the Lord's own portion.
[19] All their works are as the sun before him, and his eyes are continually upon their ways.
[20] Their iniquities are not hidden from him, and all their sins are before the Lord.
[22] A man's almsgiving is like a signet with the Lord and he will keep a person's kindness like the apple of his eye.
[23] Afterward he will arise and requite them, and he will bring their recompense on their heads.
[24] Yet to those who repent he grants a return, and he encourages those whose endurance is failing.
[25] Turn to the Lord and forsake your sins; pray in his presence and lessen your offenses.

[26] Return to the Most High and turn away from iniquity, and hate abominations intensely.

[27] Who will sing praises to the Most High in Hades, as do those who are alive and give thanks?

[28] From the dead, as from one who does not exist, thanksgiving has ceased; he who is alive and well sings the Lord's praises.

[29] How great is the mercy of the Lord, and his forgiveness for those who turn to him!

[30] For all things cannot be in men, since a son of man is not immortal.

[31] What is brighter than the sun? Yet its light fails. So flesh and blood devise evil.

[32] He marshals the host of the height of heaven; but all men are dust and ashes.

Sir.18

[1] He who lives for ever created the whole universe;

[2] the Lord alone will be declared righteous.

[4] To none has he given power to proclaim his works; and who can search out his mighty deeds?

[5] Who can measure his majestic power? And who can fully recount his mercies?

[6] It is not possible to diminish or increase them, nor is it possible to trace the wonders of the Lord.

[7] When a man has finished, he is just beginning, and when he stops, he will be at a loss.

[8] What is man, and of what use is he? What is his good and what is his evil?

[9] The number of a man's days is great if he reaches a hundred years.

[10] Like a drop of water from the sea and a grain of sand so are a few years in the day of eternity.

[11] Therefore the Lord is patient with them and pours out his mercy upon them.

[12] He sees and recognizes that their end will be evil; therefore he grants them forgiveness in abundance.

[13] The compassion of man is for his neighbor, but the compassion of the Lord is for all living beings. He rebukes and trains and teaches them, and turns them back, as a shepherd his flock.

[14] He has compassion on those who accept his discipline and who are eager for his judgments.

[15] My son, do not mix reproach with your good deeds, nor cause grief by

your words when you present a gift.

[16] Does not the dew assuage the scorching heat? So a word is better than a gift.

[17] Indeed, does not a word surpass a good gift? Both are to be found in a gracious man.

[18] A fool is ungracious and abusive, and the gift of a grudging man makes the eyes dim.

[19] Before you speak, learn, and before you fall ill, take care of your health.

[20] Before judgment, examine yourself, and in the hour of visitation you will find forgiveness.

[21] Before falling ill, humble yourself, and when you are on the point of sinning, turn back.

[22] Let nothing hinder you from paying a vow promptly, and do not wait until death to be released from it.

[23] Before making a vow, prepare yourself; and do not be like a man who tempts the Lord.

[24] Think of his wrath on the day of death, and of the moment of vengeance when he turns away his face.

[25] In the time of plenty think of the time of hunger; in the days of wealth think of poverty and need.

[26] From morning to evening conditions change, and all things move swiftly before the Lord.

[27] A wise man is cautious in everything, and in days of sin he guards against wrongdoing.

[28] Every intelligent man knows wisdom, and he praises the one who finds her.

[29] Those who understand sayings become skilled themselves, and pour forth apt proverbs.

[30] Do not follow your base desires, but restrain your appetites.

[31] If you allow your soul to take pleasure in base desire, it will make you the laughingstock of your enemies.

[32] Do not revel in great luxury, lest you become impoverished by its expense.

[33] Do not become a beggar by feasting with borrowed money, when you have nothing in your purse.

Sir.19

[1] A workman who is a drunkard will not become rich; he who despises small things will fail little by little.

[2] Wine and women lead intelligent men astray, and the man who consorts with harlots is very reckless.

[3] Decay and worms will inherit him, and the reckless soul will be snatched away.

[4] One who trusts others too quickly is lightminded, and one who sins does wrong to himself.

[5] One who rejoices in wickedness will be condemned,

[6] and for one who hates gossip evil is lessened.

[7] Never repeat a conversation, and you will lose nothing at all.

[8] With friend or foe do not report it, and unless it would be a sin for you, do not disclose it;

[9] for some one has heard you and watched you, and when the time comes he will hate you.

[10] Have you heard a word? Let it die with you. Be brave! It will not make you burst!

[11] With such a word a fool will suffer pangs like a woman in labor with a child.

[12] Like an arrow stuck in the flesh of the thigh, so is a word inside a fool.

[13] Question a friend, perhaps he did not do it; but if he did anything, so that he may do it no more.

[14] Question a neighbor, perhaps he did not say it; but if he said it, so that he may not say it again.

[15] Question a friend, for often it is slander; so do not believe everything you hear.

[16] A person may make a slip without intending it. Who has never sinned with his tongue?

[17] Question your neighbor before you threaten him; and let the law of the Most High take its course.

[20] All wisdom is the fear of the Lord, and in all wisdom there is the fulfilment of the law.

[22] But the knowledge of wickedness is not wisdom, nor is there prudence where sinners take counsel.

[23] There is a cleverness which is abominable, but there is a fool who merely lacks wisdom.

[24] Better is the God-fearing man who lacks intelligence, than the highly prudent man who transgresses the law.

[25] There is a cleverness which is scrupulous but unjust, and there are people who distort kindness to gain a verdict.

[26] There is a rascal bowed down in mourning, but inwardly he is full of deceit.

[27] He hides his face and pretends not to hear; but where no one notices, he will forestall you.

[28] And if by lack of strength he is prevented from sinning, he will do evil when he finds an opportunity.

[29] A man is known by his appearance, and a sensible man is known by his

face, when you meet him.

[30] A man's attire and open-mouthed laughter, and a man's manner of walking, show what he is.

Sir.20

[1] There is a reproof which is not timely; and there is a man who keeps silent but is wise.

[2] How much better it is to reprove than to stay angry! And the one who confesses his fault will be kept from loss.

[4] Like a eunuch's desire to violate a maiden is a man who executes judgments by violence.

[5] There is one who by keeping silent is found wise, while another is detested for being too talkative.

[6] There is one who keeps silent because he has no answer, while another keeps silent because he knows when to speak.

[7] A wise man will be silent until the right moment, but a braggart and fool goes beyond the right moment.

[8] Whoever uses too many words will be loathed, and whoever usurps the right to speak will be hated.

[9] There may be good fortune for a man in adversity, and a windfall may result in a loss.

[10] There is a gift that profits you nothing, and there is a gift that brings a double return.

[11] There are losses because of glory, and there are men who have raised their heads from humble circumstances.

[12] There is a man who buys much for a little, but pays for it seven times over.

[13] The wise man makes himself beloved through his words, but the courtesies of fools are wasted.

[14] A fool's gift will profit you nothing, for he has many eyes instead of one.

[15] He gives little and upbraids much, he opens his mouth like a herald; today he lends and tomorrow he asks it back;
such a one is a hateful man.

[16] A fool will say, "I have no friend, and there is no gratitude for my good deeds; those who eat my bread speak unkindly."

[17] How many will ridicule him, and how often!

[18] A slip on the pavement is better than a slip of the tongue; so the downfall of the wicked will occur speedily.

[19] An ungracious man is like a story told at the wrong time, which is continually on the lips of the ignorant.

[20] A proverb from a fool's lips will be rejected, for he does not tell it at its proper time.

[21] A man may be prevented from sinning by his poverty, so when he rests he feels no remorse.

[22] A man may lose his life through shame, or lose it because of his foolish look.

[23] A man may for shame make promises to a friend, and needlessly make him an enemy.

[24] A lie is an ugly blot on a man; it is continually on the lips of the ignorant.

[25] A thief is preferable to a habitual liar, but the lot of both is ruin.

[26] The disposition of a liar brings disgrace, and his shame is ever with him.

[27] He who speaks wisely will advance himself, and a sensible man will please great men.

[28] Whoever cultivates the soil will heap up his harvest, and whoever pleases great men will atone for injustice.

[29] Presents and gifts blind the eyes of the wise; like a muzzle on the mouth they avert reproofs.

[30] Hidden wisdom and unseen treasure, what advantage is there in either of them?

[31] Better is the man who hides his folly than the man who hides his wisdom.

Sir.21

[1] Have you sinned, my son? Do so no more, but pray about your former sins.

[2] Flee from sin as from a snake; for if you approach sin, it will bite you. Its teeth are lion's teeth, and destroy the souls of men.

[3] All lawlessness is like a two-edged sword; there is no healing for its wound.

[4] Terror and violence will lay waste riches; thus the house of the proud will be laid waste.

[5] The prayer of a poor man goes from his lips to the ears of God, and his judgment comes speedily.

[6] Whoever hates reproof walks in the steps of the sinner, but he that fears the Lord will repent in his heart.

[7] He who is mighty in speech is known from afar; but the sensible man, when he slips, is aware of it.

[8] A man who builds his house with other people's money is like one who

gathers stones for his burial mound.

[9] An assembly of the wicked is like tow gathered together, and their end is a flame of fire.

[10] The way of sinners is smoothly paved with stones, but at its end is the pit of Hades.

[11] Whoever keeps the law controls his thoughts, and wisdom is the fulfilment of the fear of the Lord.

[12] He who is not clever cannot be taught, but there is a cleverness which increases bitterness.

[13] The knowledge of a wise man will increase like a flood, and his counsel like a flowing spring.

[14] The mind of a fool is like a broken jar; it will hold no knowledge.

[15] When a man of understanding hears a wise saying, he will praise it and add to it; when a reveler hears it, he dislikes it
and casts it behind his back.

[16] A fool's narration is like a burden on a journey, but delight will be found in the speech of the intelligent.

[17] The utterance of a sensible man will be sought in the assembly, and they will ponder his words in their minds.

[18] Like a house that has vanished, so is wisdom to a fool; and the knowledge of the ignorant is unexamined talk.

[19] To a senseless man education is fetters on his feet, and like manacles on his right hand.

[20] A fool raises his voice when he laughs, but a clever man smiles quietly.

[21] To a sensible man education is like a golden ornament, and like a bracelet on the right arm.

[22] The foot of a fool rushes into a house, but a man of experience stands respectfully before it.

[23] A boor peers into the house from the door, but a cultivated man remains outside.

[24] It is ill-mannered for a man to listen at a door, and a discreet man is grieved by the disgrace.

[25] The lips of strangers will speak of these things, but the words of the prudent will be weighed in the balance.

[26] The mind of fools is in their mouth, but the mouth of wise men is in their mind.

[27] When an ungodly man curses his adversary, he curses his own soul.

[28] A whisperer defiles his own soul and is hated in his neighborhood.

Sir.22

[1] The indolent may be compared to a filthy stone, and every one hisses at

his disgrace.

[2] The indolent may be compared to the filth of dunghills; any one that picks it up will shake it off his hand.

[3] It is a disgrace to be the father of an undisciplined son, and the birth of a daughter is a loss.

[4] A sensible daughter obtains her husband, but one who acts shamefully brings grief to her father.

[5] An impudent daughter disgraces father and husband, and will be despised by both.

[6] Like music in mourning is a tale told at the wrong time, but chastising and discipline are wisdom at all times.

[7] He who teaches a fool is like one who glues potsherds together, or who rouses a sleeper from deep slumber.

[8] He who tells a story to a fool tells it to a drowsy man; and at the end he will say, "What is it?"

[11] Weep for the dead, for he lacks the light; and weep for the fool, for he lacks intelligence; weep less bitterly for the dead, for he has attained rest; but the life of the fool is worse than death.

[12] Mourning for the dead lasts seven days, but for a fool or an ungodly man it lasts all his life.

[13] Do not talk much with a foolish man, and do not visit an unintelligent man; guard yourself from him to escape trouble,
and you will not be soiled when he shakes himself off; avoid him and you will find rest, and you will never be wearied by his madness.

[14] What is heavier than lead? And what is its name except "Fool"?

[15] Sand, salt, and a piece of iron are easier to bear than a stupid man.

[16] A wooden beam firmly bonded into a building will not be torn loose by an earthquake; so the mind firmly fixed on a reasonable counsel will not be afraid in a crisis.

[17] A mind settled on an intelligent thought is like the stucco decoration on the wall of a colonnade.

[18] Fences set on a high place will not stand firm against the wind; so a timid heart with a fool's purpose will not stand firm against any fear.

[19] A man who pricks an eye will make tears fall, and one who pricks the heart makes it show feeling.

[20] One who throws a stone at birds scares them away, and one who reviles a friend will break off the friendship.

[21] Even if you have drawn your sword against a friend, do not despair, for a renewal of friendship is possible.

[22] If you have opened your mouth against your friend, do not worry, for reconciliation is possible; but as for reviling, arrogance, disclosure of secrets, or a treacherous blow -- in these cases any friend will flee.

[23] Gain the trust of your neighbor in his poverty, that you may rejoice

with him in his prosperity; stand by him in time of affliction, that you may share with him in his inheritance.

[24] The vapor and smoke of the furnace precede the fire; so insults precede bloodshed.

[25] I will not be ashamed to protect a friend, and I will not hide from him;

[26] but if some harm should happen to me because of him, whoever hears of it will beware of him.

[27] O that a guard were set over my mouth, and a seal of prudence upon my lips, that it may keep me from falling, so that my tongue may not destroy me!

Sir.23

[1] O Lord, Father and Ruler of my life, do not abandon me to their counsel, and let me not fall because of them!

[2] O that whips were set over my thoughts, and the discipline of wisdom over my mind! That they may not spare me in my errors, and that it may not pass by my sins;

[3] in order that my mistakes may not be multiplied, and my sins may not abound; then I will not fall before my adversaries, and my enemy will not rejoice over me.

[4] O Lord, Father and God of my life, do not give me haughty eyes,

[5] and remove from me evil desire.

[6] Let neither gluttony nor lust overcome me, and do not surrender me to a shameless soul.

[7] Listen, my children, to instruction concerning speech; the one who observes it will never be caught.

[8] The sinner is overtaken through his lips, the reviler and the arrogant are tripped by them.

[9] Do not accustom your mouth to oaths, and do not habitually utter the name of the Holy One;

[10] for as a servant who is continually examined under torture will not lack bruises, so also the man who always swears and utters the Name will not be cleansed from sin.

[11] A man who swears many oaths will be filled with iniquity, and the scourge will not leave his house; if he offends, his sin remains on him, and if he disregards it, he sins doubly; if he has sworn needlessly, he will not be justified, for his house will be filled with calamities.

[12] There is an utterance which is comparable to death; may it never be found in the inheritance of Jacob! For all these errors will be far from the godly, and they will not wallow in sins.

[13] Do not accustom your mouth to lewd vulgarity, for it involves sinful

speech.

[14] Remember your father and mother when you sit among great men; lest you be forgetful in their presence, and be deemed a fool on account of your habits; then you will wish that you had never been born, and you will curse the day of your birth.

[15] A man accustomed to use insulting words will never become disciplined all his days.

[16] Two sorts of men multiply sins, and a third incurs wrath. The soul heated like a burning fire will not be quenched until it is consumed; a man who commits fornication with his near of kin will never cease until the fire burns him up.

[17] To a fornicator all bread tastes sweet; he will never cease until he dies.

[18] A man who breaks his marriage vows says to himself, "Who sees me? Darkness surrounds me, and the walls hide me, and no one sees me. Why should I fear? The Most High will not take notice of my sins."

[19] His fear is confined to the eyes of men, and he does not realize that the eyes of the Lord are ten thousand times brighter than the sun; they look upon all the ways of men, and perceive even the hidden places.

[20] Before the universe was created, it was known to him; so it was also after it was finished.

[21] This man will be punished in the streets of the city, and where he least suspects it, he will be seized.

[22] So it is with a woman who leaves her husband and provides an heir by a stranger.

[23] For first of all, she has disobeyed the law of the Most High; second, she has committed an offense against her husband; and third, she has committed adultery through harlotry and brought forth children by another man.

[24] She herself will be brought before the assembly, and punishment will fall on her children.

[25] Her children will not take root, and her branches will not bear fruit.

[26] She will leave her memory for a curse, and her disgrace will not be blotted out.

[27] Those who survive her will recognize that nothing is better than the fear of the Lord, and nothing sweeter than to heed the commandments of the Lord.

Sir.24

[1] Wisdom will praise herself, and will glory in the midst of her people.

[2] In the assembly of the Most High she will open her mouth, and in the

presence of his host she will glory:

[3] "I came forth from the mouth of the Most High, and covered the earth like a mist.

[4] I dwelt in high places, and my throne was in a pillar of cloud.

[5] Alone I have made the circuit of the vault of heaven and have walked in the depths of the abyss.

[6] In the waves of the sea, in the whole earth, and in every people and nation I have gotten a possession.

[7] Among all these I sought a resting place; I sought in whose territory I might lodge.

[8] "Then the Creator of all things gave me a commandment, and the one who created me assigned a place for my tent.

And he said, `Make your dwelling in Jacob, and in Israel receive your inheritance.'

[9] From eternity, in the beginning, he created me, and for eternity I shall not cease to exist.

[10] In the holy tabernacle I ministered before him, and so I was established in Zion.

[11] In the beloved city likewise he gave me a resting place, and in Jerusalem was my dominion.

[12] So I took root in an honored people, in the portion of the Lord, who is their inheritance.

[13] "I grew tall like a cedar in Lebanon, and like a cypress on the heights of Hermon.

[14] I grew tall like a palm tree in En-ge'di, and like rose plants in Jericho; like a beautiful olive tree in the field, and like a plane tree I grew tall.

[15] Like cassia and camel's thorn I gave forth the aroma of spices, and like choice myrrh I spread a pleasant odor, like galbanum, onycha, and stacte, and like the fragrance of frankincense in the tabernacle.

[16] Like a terebinth I spread out my branches, and my branches are glorious and graceful.

[17] Like a vine I caused loveliness to bud, and my blossoms became glorious and abundant fruit.

[19] "Come to me, you who desire me, and eat your fill of my produce.

[20] For the remembrance of me is sweeter than honey, and my inheritance sweeter than the honeycomb.

[21] Those who eat me will hunger for more, and those who drink me will thirst for more.

[22] Whoever obeys me will not be put to shame, and those who work with my help will not sin."

[23] All this is the book of the covenant of the Most High God, the law which Moses commanded us as an inheritance for the congregations of Jacob.

[25] It fills men with wisdom, like the Pishon, and like the Tigris at the time

of the first fruits.

[26] It makes them full of understanding, like the Euphrates, and like the Jordan at harvest time.

[27] It makes instruction shine forth like light, like the Gihon at the time of vintage.

[28] Just as the first man did not know her perfectly, the last one has not fathomed her;

[29] for her thought is more abundant than the sea, and her counsel deeper than the great abyss.

[30] I went forth like a canal from a river and like a water channel into a garden.

[31] I said, "I will water my orchard and drench my garden plot"; and lo, my canal became a river, and my river became a sea.

[32] I will again make instruction shine forth like the dawn, and I will make it shine afar;

[33] I will again pour out teaching like prophecy, and leave it to all future generations.

[34] Observe that I have not labored for myself alone, but for all who seek instruction.

Sir.25

[1] My soul takes pleasure in three things, and they are beautiful in the sight of the Lord and of men; agreement between brothers, friendship between neighbors, and a wife and a husband who live in harmony.

[2] My soul hates three kinds of men, and I am greatly offended at their life: a beggar who is proud, a rich man who is a liar, and an adulterous old man who lacks good sense.

[3] You have gathered nothing in your youth; how then can you find anything in your old age?

[4] What an attractive thing is judgment in gray-haired men, and for the aged to possess good counsel!

[5] How attractive is wisdom in the aged, and understanding and counsel in honorable men!

[6] Rich experience is the crown of the aged, and their boast is the fear of the Lord.

[7] With nine thoughts I have gladdened my heart, and a tenth I shall tell with my tongue: a man rejoicing in his children;
a man who lives to see the downfall of his foes;

[8] happy is he who lives with an intelligent wife, and he who has not made a slip with his tongue, and he who has not served a man inferior to himself;

[9] happy is he who has gained good sense, and he who speaks to attentive listeners.

[10] How great is he who has gained wisdom! But there is no one superior to him who fears the Lord.

[11] The fear of the Lord surpasses everything; to whom shall be likened the one who holds it fast?

[13] Any wound, but not a wound of the heart! Any wickedness, but not the wickedness of a wife!

[14] Any attack, but not an attack from those who hate! And any vengeance, but not the vengeance of enemies!

[15] There is no venom worse than a snake's venom, and no wrath worse than an enemy's wrath.

[16] I would rather dwell with a lion and a dragon than dwell with an evil wife.

[17] The wickedness of a wife changes her appearance, and darkens her face like that of a bear.

[18] Her husband takes his meals among the neighbors, and he cannot help sighing bitterly.

[19] Any iniquity is insignificant compared to a wife's iniquity; may a sinner's lot befall her!

[20] A sandy ascent for the feet of the aged -- such is a garrulous wife for a quiet husband.

[21] Do not be ensnared by a woman's beauty, and do not desire a woman for her possessions.

[22] There is wrath and impudence and great disgrace when a wife supports her husband.

[23] A dejected mind, a gloomy face, and a wounded heart are caused by an evil wife. Drooping hands and weak knees
are caused by the wife who does not make her husband happy.

[24] From a woman sin had its beginning, and because of her we all die.

[25] Allow no outlet to water, and no boldness of speech in an evil wife.

[26] If she does not go as you direct, separate her from yourself.

Sir.26

[1] Happy is the husband of a good wife; the number of his days will be doubled.

[2] A loyal wife rejoices her husband, and he will complete his years in peace.

[3] A good wife is a great blessing; she will be granted among the blessings of the man who fears the Lord.

[4] Whether rich or poor, his heart is glad, and at all times his face is

cheerful.

[5] Of three things my heart is afraid, and of a fourth I am frightened: The slander of a city, the gathering of a mob, and false accusation -- all these are worse than death.

[6] There is grief of heart and sorrow when a wife is envious of a rival, and a tongue-lashing makes it known to all.

[7] An evil wife is an ox yoke which chafes; taking hold of her is like grasping a scorpion.

[8] There is great anger when a wife is drunken; she will not hide her shame.

[9] A wife's harlotry shows in her lustful eyes, and she is known by her eyelids.

[10] Keep strict watch over a headstrong daughter, lest, when she finds liberty, she use it to her hurt.

[11] Be on guard against her impudent eye, and do not wonder if she sins against you.

[12] As a thirsty wayfarer opens his mouth and drinks from any water near him, so will she sit in front of every post and open her quiver to the arrow.

[13] A wife's charm delights her husband, and her skill puts fat on his bones.

[14] A silent wife is a gift of the Lord, and there is nothing so precious as a disciplined soul.

[15] A modest wife adds charm to charm, and no balance can weigh the value of a chaste soul.

[16] Like the sun rising in the heights of the Lord, so is the beauty of a good wife in her well-ordered home.

[17] Like the shining lamp on the holy lampstand, so is a beautiful face on a stately figure.

[18] Like pillars of gold on a base of silver, so are beautiful feet with a steadfast heart.

[28] At two things my heart is grieved, and because of a third anger comes over me: a warrior in want through poverty,

and intelligent men who are treated contemptuously; a man who turns back from righteousness to sin -- the Lord will prepare him for the sword!

[29] A merchant can hardly keep from wrongdoing, and a tradesman will not be declared innocent of sin.

Sir.27

[1] Many have committed sin for a trifle, and whoever seeks to get rich will avert his eyes.

[2] As a stake is driven firmly into a fissure between stones, so sin is wedged in between selling and buying.

[3] If a man is not steadfast and zealous in the fear of the Lord, his house will be quickly overthrown.

[4] When a sieve is shaken, the refuse remains; so a man's filth remains in his thoughts.

[5] The kiln tests the potter's vessels; so the test of a man is in his reasoning.

[6] The fruit discloses the cultivation of a tree; so the expression of a thought discloses the cultivation of a man's mind.

[7] Do not praise a man before you hear him reason, for this is the test of men.

[8] If you pursue justice, you will attain it and wear it as a glorious robe.

[9] Birds flock with their kind; so truth returns to those who practice it.

[10] A lion lies in wait for prey; so does sin for the workers of iniquity.

[11] The talk of the godly man is always wise, but the fool changes like the moon.

[12] Among stupid people watch for a chance to leave, but among thoughtful people stay on.

[13] The talk of fools is offensive, and their laughter is wantonly sinful.

[14] The talk of men given to swearing makes one's hair stand on end, and their quarrels make a man stop his ears.

[15] The strife of the proud leads to bloodshed, and their abuse is grievous to hear.

[16] Whoever betrays secrets destroys confidence, and he will never find a congenial friend.

[17] Love your friend and keep faith with him; but if you betray his secrets, do not run after him.

[18] For as a man destroys his enemy, so you have destroyed the friendship of your neighbor.

[19] And as you allow a bird to escape from your hand, so you have let your neighbor go, and will not catch him again.

[20] Do not go after him, for he is too far off, and has escaped like a gazelle from a snare.

[21] For a wound may be bandaged, and there is reconciliation after abuse, but whoever has betrayed secrets is without hope.

[22] Whoever winks his eye plans evil deeds, and no one can keep him from them.

[23] In your presence his mouth is all sweetness, and he admires your words; but later he will twist his speech and with your own words he will give offense.

[24] I have hated many things, but none to be compared to him; even the Lord will hate him.

[25] Whoever throws a stone straight up throws it on his own head; and a treacherous blow opens up wounds.

[26] He who digs a pit will fall into it, and he who sets a snare will be caught in it.

[27] If a man does evil, it will roll back upon him, and he will not know where it came from.

[28] Mockery and abuse issue from the proud man, but vengeance lies in wait for him like a lion.

[29] Those who rejoice in the fall of the godly will be caught in a snare, and pain will consume them before their death.

[30] Anger and wrath, these also are abominations, and the sinful man will possess them.

Sir.28

[1] He that takes vengeance will suffer vengeance from the Lord, and he will firmly establish his sins.

[2] Forgive your neighbor the wrong he has done, and then your sins will be pardoned when you pray.

[3] Does a man harbor anger against another, and yet seek for healing from the Lord?

[4] Does he have no mercy toward a man like himself, and yet pray for his own sins?

[5] If he himself, being flesh, maintains wrath, who will make expiation for his sins?

[6] Remember the end of your life, and cease from enmity, remember destruction and death, and be true to the commandments.

[7] Remember the commandments, and do not be angry with your neighbor; remember the covenant of the Most High, and overlook ignorance.

[8] Refrain from strife, and you will lessen sins; for a man given to anger will kindle strife,

[9] and a sinful man will disturb friends and inject enmity among those who are at peace.

[10] In proportion to the fuel for the fire, so will be the burning, and in proportion to the obstinacy of strife will be the burning; in proportion to the strength of the man will be his anger, and in proportion to his wealth he will heighten his wrath.

[11] A hasty quarrel kindles fire, and urgent strife sheds blood.

[12] If you blow on a spark, it will glow; if you spit on it, it will be put out; and both come out of your mouth.

[13] Curse the whisperer and deceiver, for he has destroyed many who were at peace.

[14] Slander has shaken many, and scattered them from nation to nation, and destroyed strong cities, and overturned the houses of great men.

[15] Slander has driven away courageous women, and deprived them of the

fruit of their toil.

[16] Whoever pays heed to slander will not find rest, nor will he settle down in peace.

[17] The blow of a whip raises a welt, but a blow of the tongue crushes the bones.

[18] Many have fallen by the edge of the sword, but not so many as have fallen because of the tongue.

[19] Happy is the man who is protected from it, who has not been exposed to its anger, who has not borne its yoke,

and has not been bound with its fetters;

[20] for its yoke is a yoke of iron, and its fetters are fetters of bronze;

[21] its death is an evil death, and Hades is preferable to it.

[22] It will not be master over the godly, and they will not be burned in its flame.

[23] Those who forsake the Lord will fall into its power; it will burn among them and will not be put out. It will be sent out against them like a lion; like a leopard it will mangle them.

[24] See that you fence in your property with thorns, lock up your silver and gold,

[25] make balances and scales for your words, and make a door and a bolt for your mouth.

[26] Beware lest you err with your tongue, lest you fall before him who lies in wait.

Sir.29

[1] He that shows mercy will lend to his neighbor, and he that strengthens him with his hand keeps the commandments.

[2] Lend to your neighbor in the time of his need; and in turn, repay your neighbor promptly.

[3] Confirm your word and keep faith with him, and on every occasion you will find what you need.

[4] Many persons regard a loan as a windfall, and cause trouble to those who help them.

[5] A man will kiss another's hands until he gets a loan, and will lower his voice in speaking of his neighbor's money;

but at the time for repayment he will delay, and will pay in words of unconcern, and will find fault with the time.

[6] If the lender exert pressure, he will hardly get back half, and will regard that as a windfall. If he does not, the borrower has robbed him of his money, and he has needlessly made him his enemy; he will repay him with curses and reproaches,

and instead of glory will repay him with dishonor.

[7] Because of such wickedness, therefore, many have refused to lend; they have been afraid of being defrauded needlessly.

[8] Nevertheless, be patient with a man in humble circumstances, and do not make him wait for your alms.

[9] Help a poor man for the commandment's sake, and because of his need do not send him away empty.

[10] Lose your silver for the sake of a brother or a friend, and do not let it rust under a stone and be lost.

[11] Lay up your treasure according to the commandments of the Most High, and it will profit you more than gold.

[12] Store up almsgiving in your treasury, and it will rescue you from all affliction;

[13] more than a mighty shield and more than a heavy spear, it will fight on your behalf against your enemy.

[14] A good man will be surety for his neighbor, but a man who has lost his sense of shame will fail him.

[15] Do not forget all the kindness of your surety, for he has given his life for you.

[16] A sinner will overthrow the prosperity of his surety,

[17] and one who does not feel grateful will abandon his rescuer.

[18] Being surety has ruined many men who were prosperous, and has shaken them like a wave of the sea; it has driven men of power into exile, and they have wandered among foreign nations.

[19] The sinner who has fallen into suretyship and pursues gain will fall into lawsuits.

[20] Assist your neighbor according to your ability, but take heed to yourself lest you fall.

[21] The essentials for life are water and bread and clothing and a house to cover one's nakedness.

[22] Better is the life of a poor man under the shelter of his roof than sumptuous food in another man's house.

[23] Be content with little or much.

[24] It is a miserable life to go from house to house, and where you are a stranger you may not open your mouth;

[25] you will play the host and provide drink without being thanked, and besides this you will hear bitter words:

[26] "Come here, stranger, prepare the table, and if you have anything at hand, let me have it to eat."

[27] "Give place, stranger, to an honored person; my brother has come to stay with me; I need my house."

[28] These things are hard to bear for a man who has feeling: scolding about lodging and the reproach of the moneylender.

Sir.30

[1] He who loves his son will whip him often, in order that he may rejoice at the way he turns out.

[2] He who disciplines his son will profit by him, and will boast of him among acquaintances.

[3] He who teaches his son will make his enemies envious, and will glory in him in the presence of friends.

[4] The father may die, and yet he is not dead, for he has left behind him one like himself;

[5] while alive he saw and rejoiced, and when he died he was not grieved;

[6] he has left behind him an avenger against his enemies, and one to repay the kindness of his friends.

[7] He who spoils his son will bind up his wounds, and his feelings will be troubled at every cry.

[8] A horse that is untamed turns out to be stubborn, and a son unrestrained turns out to be wilful.

[9] Pamper a child, and he will frighten you; play with him, and he will give you grief.

[10] Do not laugh with him, lest you have sorrow with him, and in the end you will gnash your teeth.

[11] Give him no authority in his youth, and do not ignore his errors.

[12] Bow down his neck in his youth, and beat his sides while he is young, lest he become stubborn and disobey you,
and you have sorrow of soul from him.

[13] Discipline your son and take pains with him, that you may not be offended by his shamelessness.

[14] Better off is a poor man who is well and strong in constitution than a rich man who is severely afflicted in body.

[15] Health and soundness are better than all gold, and a robust body than countless riches.

[16] There is no wealth better than health of body, and there is no gladness above joy of heart.

[17] Death is better than a miserable life, and eternal rest than chronic sickness.

[18] Good things poured out upon a mouth that is closed are like offerings of food placed upon a grave.

[19] Of what use to an idol is an offering of fruit? For it can neither eat nor smell. So is he who is afflicted by the Lord;

[20] he sees with his eyes and groans, like a eunuch who embraces a maiden and groans.

[21] Do not give yourself over to sorrow, and do not afflict yourself deliberately.

[22] Gladness of heart is the life of man, and the rejoicing of a man is length of days.

[23] Delight your soul and comfort your heart, and remove sorrow far from you, for sorrow has destroyed many, and there is no profit in it.

[24] Jealousy and anger shorten life, and anxiety brings on old age too soon.

[25] A man of cheerful and good heart will give heed to the food he eats.

Sir.31

[1] Wakefulness over wealth wastes away one's flesh, and anxiety about it removes sleep.

[2] Wakeful anxiety prevents slumber, and a severe illness carries off sleep.

[3] The rich man toils as his wealth accumulates, and when he rests he fills himself with his dainties.

[4] The poor man toils as his livelihood diminishes, and when he rests he becomes needy.

[5] He who loves gold will not be justified, and he who pursues money will be led astray by it.

[6] Many have come to ruin because of gold, and their destruction has met them face to face.

[7] It is a stumbling block to those who are devoted to it, and every fool will be taken captive by it.

[8] Blessed is the rich man who is found blameless, and who does not go after gold.

[9] Who is he? And we will call him blessed, for he has done wonderful things among his people.

[10] Who has been tested by it and been found perfect? Let it be for him a ground for boasting. Who has had the power to transgress and did not transgress, and to do evil and did not do it?

[11] His prosperity will be established, and the assembly will relate his acts of charity.

[12] Are you seated at the table of a great man? Do not be greedy at it, and do not say, "There is certainly much upon it!"

[13] Remember that a greedy eye is a bad thing. What has been created more greedy than the eye? Therefore it sheds tears from every face.

[14] Do not reach out your hand for everything you see, and do not crowd your neighbor at the dish.

[15] Judge your neighbor's feelings by your own, and in every matter be thoughtful.

[16] Eat like a human being what is set before you, and do not chew greedily, lest you be hated.

[17] Be the first to stop eating, for the sake of good manners, and do not be insatiable, lest you give offense.

[18] If you are seated among many persons, do not reach out your hand before they do.

[19] How ample a little is for a well-disciplined man! He does not breathe heavily upon his bed.

[20] Healthy sleep depends on moderate eating; he rises early, and feels fit. The distress of sleeplessness and of nausea
and colic are with the glutton.

[21] If you are overstuffed with food, get up in the middle of the meal, and you will have relief.

[22] Listen to me, my son, and do not disregard me, and in the end you will appreciate my words. In all your work be industrious, and no sickness will overtake you.

[23] Men will praise the one who is liberal with food, and their testimony to his excellence is trustworthy.

[24] The city will complain of the one who is niggardly with food, and their testimony to his niggardliness is accurate.

[25] Do not aim to be valiant over wine, for wine has destroyed many.

[26] Fire and water prove the temper of steel, so wine tests hearts in the strife of the proud.

[27] Wine is like life to men, if you drink it in moderation. What is life to a man who is without wine? It has been created to make men glad.

[28] Wine drunk in season and temperately is rejoicing of heart and gladness of soul.

[29] Wine drunk to excess is bitterness of soul, with provocation and stumbling.

[30] Drunkenness increases the anger of a fool to his injury, reducing his strength and adding wounds.

[31] Do not reprove your neighbor at a banquet of wine, and do not despise him in his merrymaking; speak no word of reproach to him, and do not afflict him by making demands of him.

Sir.32

[1] If they make you master of the feast, do not exalt yourself; be among them as one of them; take good care of them and then be seated;

[2] when you have fulfilled your duties, take your place, that you may be merry on their account and receive a wreath for your excellent leadership.

[3] Speak, you who are older, for it is fitting that you should, but with

accurate knowledge, and do not interrupt the music.

[4] Where there is entertainment, do not pour out talk; do not display your cleverness out of season.

[5] A ruby seal in a setting of gold is a concert of music at a banquet of wine.

[6] A seal of emerald in a rich setting of gold is the melody of music with good wine.

[7] Speak, young man, if there is need of you, but no more than twice, and only if asked.

[8] Speak concisely, say much in few words; be as one who knows and yet holds his tongue.

[9] Among the great do not act as their equal; and when another is speaking, do not babble.

[10] Lightning speeds before the thunder, and approval precedes a modest man.

[11] Leave in good time and do not be the last; go home quickly and do not linger.

[12] Amuse yourself there, and do what you have in mind, but do not sin through proud speech.

[13] And for these things bless him who made you and satisfies you with his good gifts.

[14] He who fears the Lord will accept his discipline, and those who rise early to seek him will find favor.

[15] He who seeks the law will be filled with it, but the hypocrite will stumble at it.

[16] Those who fear the Lord will form true judgments, and like a light they will kindle righteous deeds.

[17] A sinful man will shun reproof, and will find a decision according to his liking.

[18] A man of judgment will not overlook an idea, and an insolent and proud man will not cower in fear.

[19] Do nothing without deliberation; and when you have acted, do not regret it.

[20] Do not go on a path full of hazards, and do not stumble over stony ground.

[21] Do not be overconfident on a smooth way,

[22] and give good heed to your paths.

[23] Guard yourself in every act, for this is the keeping of the commandments.

[24] He who believes the law gives heed to the commandments, and he who trusts the Lord will not suffer loss.

Sir.33

[1] No evil will befall the man who fears the Lord, but in trial he will deliver him again and again.

[2] A wise man will not hate the law, but he who is hypocritical about it is like a boat in a storm.

[3] A man of understanding will trust in the law; for him the law is as dependable as an inquiry by means of Urim.

[4] Prepare what to say, and thus you will be heard; bind together your instruction, and make your answer.

[5] The heart of a fool is like a cart wheel, and his thoughts like a turning axle.

[6] A stallion is like a mocking friend; he neighs under every one who sits on him.

[7] Why is any day better than another, when all the daylight in the year is from the sun?

[8] By the Lord's decision they were distinguished, and he appointed the different seasons and feasts;

[9] some of them he exalted and hallowed, and some of them he made ordinary days.

[10] All men are from the ground, and Adam was created of the dust.

[11] In the fullness of his knowledge the Lord distinguished them and appointed their different ways;

[12] some of them he blessed and exalted, and some of them he made holy and brought near to himself; but some of them he cursed and brought low, and he turned them out of their place.

[13] As clay in the hand of the potter -- for all his ways are as he pleases -- so men are in the hand of him who made them, to give them as he decides.

[14] Good is the opposite of evil, and life the opposite of death; so the sinner is the opposite of the godly.

[15] Look upon all the works of the Most High; they likewise are in pairs, one the opposite of the other.

[16] I was the last on watch; I was like one who gleans after the grape-gatherers; by the blessing of the Lord I excelled,

and like a grape-gatherer I filled my wine press.

[17] Consider that I have not labored for myself alone, but for all who seek instruction.

[18] Hear me, you who are great among the people, and you leaders of the congregation, hearken.

[19] To son or wife, to brother or friend, do not give power over yourself, as long as you live; and do not give your property to another, lest you change your mind and must ask for it.

[20] While you are still alive and have breath in you, do not let any one take your place.

[21] For it is better that your children should ask from you than that you should look to the hand of you sons.
[22] Excel in all that you do; bring no stain upon your honor.
[23] At the time when you end the days of your life, in the hour of death, distribute your inheritance.
[24] Fodder and a stick and burdens for an ass; bread and discipline and work for a servant.
[25] Set your slave to work, and you will find rest; leave his hands idle, and he will seek liberty.
[26] Yoke and thong will bow the neck, and for a wicked servant there are racks and tortures.
[27] Put him to work, that he may not be idle, for idleness teaches much evil.
[28] Set him to work, as is fitting for him, and if he does not obey, make his fetters heavy.
[29] Do not act immoderately toward anybody, and do nothing without discretion.
[30] If you have a servant, let him be as yourself, because you have bought him with blood.
[31] If you have a servant, treat him as a brother, for as your own soul you will need him. If you ill-treat him, and he leaves and runs away, which way will you go to seek him?

Sir.34

[1] A man of no understanding has vain and false hopes, and dreams give wings to fools.
[2] As one who catches at a shadow and pursues the wind, so is he who gives heed to dreams.
[3] The vision of dreams is this against that, the likeness of a face confronting a face.
[4] From an unclean thing what will be made clean? And from something false what will be true?
[5] Divinations and omens and dreams are folly, and like a woman in travail the mind has fancies.
[6] Unless they are sent from the Most High as a visitation, do not give your mind to them.
[7] For dreams have deceived many, and those who put their hope in them have failed.
[8] Without such deceptions the law will be fulfilled, and wisdom is made perfect in truthful lips.
[9] An educated man knows many things, and one with much experience

will speak with understanding.

[10] He that is inexperienced knows few things, but he that has traveled acquires much cleverness.

[11] I have seen many things in my travels, and I understand more than I can express.

[12] I have often been in danger of death, but have escaped because of these experiences.

[13] The spirit of those who fear the Lord will live, for their hope is in him who saves them.

[14] He who fears the Lord will not be timid, nor play the coward, for he is his hope.

[15] Blessed is the soul of the man who fears the Lord! To whom does he look? And who is his support?

[16] The eyes of the Lord are upon those who love him, a mighty protection and strong support, a shelter from the hot wind and a shade from noonday sun, a guard against stumbling and a defense against falling.

[17] He lifts up the soul and gives light to the eyes; he grants healing, life, and blessing.

[18] If one sacrifices from what has been wrongfully obtained, the offering is blemished; the gifts of the lawless are not acceptable.

[19] The Most High is not pleased with the offerings of the ungodly; and he is not propitiated for sins by a multitude of sacrifices.

[20] Like one who kills a son before his father's eyes is the man who offers a sacrifice from the property of the poor.

[21] The bread of the needy is the life of the poor; whoever deprives them of it is a man of blood.

[22] To take away a neighbor's living is to murder him; to deprive an employee of his wages is to shed blood.

[23] When one builds and another tears down, what do they gain but toil?

[24] When one prays and another curses, to whose voice will the Lord listen?

[25] If a man washes after touching a dead body, and touches it again, what has he gained by his washing?

[26] So if a man fasts for his sins, and goes again and does the same things, who will listen to his prayer? And what has he gained by humbling himself?

Sir.35

[1] He who keeps the law makes many offerings; he who heeds the commandments sacrifices a peace offering.

[2] He who returns a kindness offers fine flour, and he who gives alms sacrifices a thank offering.

[3] To keep from wickedness is pleasing to the Lord, and to forsake unrighteousness is atonement.

[4] Do not appear before the Lord empty-handed,

[5] for all these things are to be done because of the commandment.

[6] The offering of a righteous man anoints the altar, and its pleasing odor rises before the Most High.

[7] The sacrifice of a righteous man is acceptable, and the memory of it will not be forgotten.

[8] Glorify the Lord generously, and do not stint the first fruits of your hands.

[9] With every gift show a cheerful face, and dedicate your tithe with gladness.

[10] Give to the Most High as he has given, and as generously as your hand has found.

[11] For the Lord is the one who repays, and he will repay you sevenfold.

[12] Do not offer him a bribe, for he will not accept it; and do not trust to an unrighteous sacrifice; for the Lord is the judge, and with him is no partiality.

[13] He will not show partiality in the case of a poor man; and he will listen to the prayer of one who is wronged.

[14] He will not ignore the supplication of the fatherless, nor the widow when she pours out her story.

[15] Do not the tears of the widow run down her cheek as she cries out against him who has caused them to fall?

[16] He whose service is pleasing to the Lord will be accepted, and his prayer will reach to the clouds.

[17] The prayer of the humble pierces the clouds, and he will not be consoled until it reaches the Lord; he will not desist until the Most High visits him, and does justice for the righteous, and executes judgment.

[18] And the Lord will not delay, neither will he be patient with them, till he crushes the loins of the unmerciful and repays vengeance on the nations; till he takes away the multitude of the insolent, and breaks the scepters of the unrighteous;

[19] till he repays the man according to his deeds, and the works of men according to their devices; till he judges the case of his people and makes them rejoice in his mercy.

[20] Mercy is as welcome when he afflicts them as clouds of rain in the time of drought.

Sir.36

[1] Have mercy upon us, O Lord, the God of all, and look upon us,

[2] and cause the fear of thee to fall upon all the nations.

[3] Lift up thy hand against foreign nations and let them see thy might.

[4] As in us thou hast been sanctified before them, so in them be thou magnified before us;

[5] and let them know thee, as we have known that there is not God but thee, O Lord.

[6] Show signs anew, and work further wonders; make thy hand and thy right arm glorious.

[7] Rouse thy anger and pour out thy wrath; destroy the adversary and wipe out the enemy.

[8] Hasten the day, and remember the appointed time, and let people recount thy mighty deeds.

[9] Let him who survives be consumed in the fiery wrath, and may those who harm thy people meet destruction.

[10] Crush the heads of the rulers of the enemy, who say, "There is no one but ourselves."

[11] Gather all the tribes of Jacob, and give them their inheritance, as at the beginning.

[12] Have mercy, O Lord, upon the people called by thy name, upon Israel, whom thou hast likened to a first-born son.

[13] Have pity on the city of thy sanctuary, Jerusalem, the place of thy rest.

[14] Fill Zion with the celebration of thy wondrous deeds, and thy temple with thy glory.

[15] Bear witness to those whom thou didst create in the beginning, and fulfil the prophecies spoken in thy name.

[16] Reward those who wait for thee, and let thy prophets be found trustworthy.

[17] Hearken, O Lord, to the prayer of thy servants, according to the blessing of Aaron for thy people, and all who are on the earth will know that thou art the Lord, the God of the ages.

[18] The stomach will take any food, yet one food is better than another.

[19] As the palate tastes the kinds of game, so an intelligent mind detects false words.

[20] A perverse mind will cause grief, but a man of experience will pay him back.

[21] A woman will accept any man, but one daughter is better than another.

[22] A woman's beauty gladdens the countenance, and surpasses every human desire.

[23] If kindness and humility mark her speech, her husband is not like other men.

[24] He who acquires a wife gets his best possession, a helper fit for him and a pillar of support.

[25] Where there is no fence, the property will be plundered; and where there is no wife, a man will wander about and sigh.

[26] For who will trust a nimble robber that skips from city to city? So who will trust a man that has no home,
and lodges wherever night finds him?

Sir.37

[1] Every friend will say, "I too am a friend"; but some friends are friends only in name.
[2] Is it not a grief to the death when a companion and friend turns to enmity?
[3] O evil imagination, why were you formed to cover the land with deceit?
[4] Some companions rejoice in the happiness of a friend, but in time of trouble are against him.
[5] Some companions help a friend for their stomach's sake, and in the face of battle take up the shield.
[6] Do not forget a friend in your heart, and be not unmindful of him in your wealth.
[7] Every counselor praises counsel, but some give counsel in their own interest.
[8] Be wary of a counselor, and learn first what is his interest -- for he will take thought for himself -- lest he cast the lot against you
[9] and tell you, "Your way is good," and then stand aloof to see what will happen to you.
[10] Do not consult the one who looks at you suspiciously; hide your counsel from those who are jealous of you.
[11] Do not consult with a woman about her rival or with a coward about war, with a merchant about barter or with a buyer about selling, with a grudging man about gratitude or with a merciless man about kindness, with an idler about any work or with a man hired for a year about completing his work, with a lazy servant about a big task -- pay no attention to these in any matter of counsel.
[12] But stay constantly with a godly man whom you know to be a keeper of the commandments, whose soul is in accord with your soul, and who will sorrow with you if you fail.
[13] And establish the counsel of your own heart, for no one is more faithful to you than it is.
[14] For a man's soul sometimes keeps him better informed than seven watchmen sitting high on a watchtower.
[15] And besides all this pray to the Most High that he may direct your way in truth.
[16] Reason is the beginning of every work, and counsel precedes every

undertaking.

[17] As a clue to changes of heart

[18] four turns of fortune appear, good and evil, life and death; and it is the tongue that continually rules them.

[19] A man may be shrewd and the teacher of many, and yet be unprofitable to himself.

[20] A man skilled in words may be hated; he will be destitute of all food,

[21] for grace was not given him by the Lord, since he is lacking in all wisdom.

[22] A man may be wise to his own advantage, and the fruits of his understanding may be trustworthy on his lips.

[23] A wise man will instruct his own people, and the fruits of his understanding will be trustworthy.

[24] A wise man will have praise heaped upon him, and all who see him will call him happy.

[25] The life of a man is numbered by days, but the days of Israel are without number.

[26] He who is wise among his people will inherit confidence, and his name will live for ever.

[27] My son, test your soul while you live; see what is bad for it and do not give it that.

[28] For not everything is good for every one, and not every person enjoys everything.

[29] Do not have an insatiable appetite for any luxury, and do not give yourself up to food;

[30] for overeating brings sickness, and gluttony leads to nausea.

[31] Many have died of gluttony, but he who is careful to avoid it prolongs his life.

Sir.38

[1] Honor the physician with the honor due him, according to your need of him, for the Lord created him;

[2] for healing comes from the Most High, and he will receive a gift from the king.

[3] The skill of the physician lifts up his head, and in the presence of great men he is admired.

[4] The Lord created medicines from the earth, and a sensible man will not despise them.

[5] Was not water made sweet with a tree in order that his power might be known?

[6] And he gave skill to men that he might be glorified in his marvelous

works.

[7] By them he heals and takes away pain;

[8] the pharmacist makes of them a compound. His works will never be finished; and from him health is upon the face of the earth.

[9] My son, when you are sick do not be negligent, but pray to the Lord, and he will heal you.

[10] Give up your faults and direct your hands aright, and cleanse your heart from all sin.

[11] Offer a sweet-smelling sacrifice, and a memorial portion of fine flour, and pour oil on your offering, as much as you can afford.

[12] And give the physician his place, for the Lord created him; let him not leave you, for there is need of him.

[13] There is a time when success lies in the hands of physicians,

[14] for they too will pray to the Lord that he should grant them success in diagnosis and in healing, for the sake of preserving life.

[15] He who sins before his Maker, may he fall into the care of a physician.

[16] My son, let your tears fall for the dead, and as one who is suffering grievously begin the lament. Lay out his body with the honor due him, and do not neglect his burial.

[17] Let your weeping be bitter and your wailing fervent; observe the mourning according to his merit, for one day, or two, to avoid criticism; then be comforted for your sorrow.

[18] For sorrow results in death, and sorrow of heart saps one's strength.

[19] In calamity sorrow continues, and the life of the poor man weighs down his heart.

[20] Do not give your heart to sorrow; drive it away, remembering the end of life.

[21] Do not forget, there is no coming back; you do the dead no good, and you injure yourself.

[22] "Remember my doom, for yours is like it: yesterday it was mine, and today it is yours."

[23] When the dead is at rest, let his remembrance cease, and be comforted for him when his spirit is departed.

[24] The wisdom of the scribe depends on the opportunity of leisure; and he who has little business may become wise.

[25] How can he become wise who handles the plow, and who glories in the shaft of a goad, who drives oxen and is occupied with their work, and whose talk is about bulls?

[26] He sets his heart on plowing furrows, and he is careful about fodder for the heifers.

[27] So too is every craftsman and master workman who labors by night as well as by day; those who cut the signets of seals, each is diligent in making a great variety; he sets his heart on painting a lifelike image, and he is

careful to finish his work.

[28] So too is the smith sitting by the anvil, intent upon his handiwork in iron; the breath of the fire melts his flesh, and he wastes away in the heat of the furnace; he inclines his ear to the sound of the hammer, and his eyes are on the pattern of the object. He sets his heart on finishing his handiwork, and he is careful to complete its decoration.

[29] So too is the potter sitting at his work and turning the wheel with his feet; he is always deeply concerned over his work, and all his output is by number.

[30] He moulds the clay with his arm and makes it pliable with his feet; he sets his heart to finish the glazing, and he is careful to clean the furnace.

[31] All these rely upon their hands, and each is skilful in his own work.

[32] Without them a city cannot be established, and men can neither sojourn nor live there.

[33] Yet they are not sought out for the council of the people, nor do they attain eminence in the public assembly.

They do not sit in the judge's seat, nor do they understand the sentence of judgment; they cannot expound discipline or judgment, and they are not found using proverbs.

[34] But they keep stable the fabric of the world, and their prayer is in the practice of their trade.

Sir.39

[1] On the other hand he who devotes himself to the study of the law of the Most High will seek out the wisdom of all the ancients, and will be concerned with prophecies;

[2] he will preserve the discourse of notable men and penetrate the subtleties of parables;

[3] he will seek out the hidden meanings of proverbs and be at home with the obscurities of parables.

[4] He will serve among great men and appear before rulers; he will travel through the lands of foreign nations, for he tests the good and the evil among men.

[5] He will set his heart to rise early to seek the Lord who made him, and will make supplication before the Most High; he will open his mouth in prayer and make supplication for his sins.

[6] If the great Lord is willing, he will be filled with the spirit of understanding; he will pour forth words of wisdom and give thanks to the Lord in prayer.

[7] He will direct his counsel and knowledge aright, and meditate on his secrets.

[8] He will reveal instruction in his teaching, and will glory in the law of the Lord's covenant.

[9] Many will praise his understanding, and it will never be blotted out; his memory will not disappear, and his name will live through all generations.

[10] Nations will declare his wisdom, and the congregation will proclaim his praise;

[11] if he lives long, he will leave a name greater than a thousand, and if he goes to rest, it is enough for him.

[12] I have yet more to say, which I have thought upon, and I am filled, like the moon at the full.

[13] Listen to me, O you holy sons, and bud like a rose growing by a stream of water;

[14] send forth fragrance like frankincense, and put forth blossoms like a lily. Scatter the fragrance, and sing a hymn of praise; bless the Lord for all his works;

[15] ascribe majesty to his name and give thanks to him with praise, with songs on your lips, and with lyres; and this you shall say in thanksgiving:

[16] "All things are the works of the Lord, for they are very good, and whatever he commands will be done in his time."

[17] No one can say, "What is this?" "Why is that?" for in God's time all things will be sought after. At his word the waters stood in a heap, and the reservoirs of water at the word of his mouth.

[18] At his command whatever pleases him is done, and none can limit his saving power.

[19] The works of all flesh are before him, and nothing can be hid from his eyes.

[20] From everlasting to everlasting he beholds them, and nothing is marvelous to him.

[21] No one can say, "What is this?" "Why is that?" for everything has been created for its use.

[22] His blessing covers the dry land like a river, and drenches it like a flood.

[23] The nations will incur his wrath, just as he turns fresh water into salt.

[24] To the holy his ways are straight, just as they are obstacles to the wicked.

[25] From the beginning good things were created for good people, just as evil things for sinners.

[26] Basic to all the needs of man's life are water and fire and iron and salt and wheat flour and milk and honey, the blood of the grape, and oil and clothing.

[27] All these are for good to the godly, just as they turn into evils for sinners.

[28] There are winds that have been created for vengeance, and in their

anger they scourge heavily; in the time of consummation they will pour out their strength and calm the anger of their Maker.

[29] Fire and hail and famine and pestilence, all these have been created for vengeance;

[30] the teeth of wild beasts, and scorpions and vipers, and the sword that punishes the ungodly with destruction;

[31] they will rejoice in his commands, and be made ready on earth for their service, and when their times come they will not transgress his word.

[32] Therefore from the beginning I have been convinced, and have thought this out and left it in writing:

[33] The works of the Lord are all good, and he will supply every need in its hour.

[34] And no one can say, "This is worse than that," for all things will prove good in their season.

[35] So now sing praise with all your heart and voice, and bless the name of the Lord.

Sir.40

[1] Much labor was created for every man, and a heavy yoke is upon the sons of Adam, from the day they come forth from their mother's womb till the day they return to the mother of all.

[2] Their perplexities and fear of heart -- their anxious thought is the day of death,

[3] from the man who sits on a splendid throne to the one who is humbled in dust and ashes,

[4] from the man who wears purple and a crown to the one who is clothed in burlap;

[5] there is anger and envy and trouble and unrest, and fear of death, and fury and strife. And when one rests upon his bed, his sleep at night confuses his mind.

[6] He gets little or no rest, and afterward in his sleep, as though he were on watch, he is troubled by the visions of his mind like one who has escaped from the battle-front;

[7] at the moment of his rescue he wakes up, and wonders that his fear came to nothing.

[8] With all flesh, both man and beast, and upon sinners seven times more,

[9] are death and bloodshed and strife and sword, calamities, famine and affliction and plague.

[10] All these were created for the wicked, and on their account the flood came.

[11] All things that are from the earth turn back to the earth, and what is

from the waters returns to the sea.

[12] All bribery and injustice will be blotted out, but good faith will stand for ever.

[13] The wealth of the unjust will dry up like a torrent, and crash like a loud clap of thunder in a rain.

[14] A generous man will be made glad; likewise transgressors will utterly fail.

[15] The children of the ungodly will not put forth many branches; they are unhealthy roots upon sheer rock.

[16] The reeds by any water or river bank will be plucked up before any grass.

[17] Kindness is like a garden of blessings, and almsgiving endures for ever.

[18] Life is sweet for the self-reliant and the worker, but he who finds treasure is better off than both.

[19] Children and the building of a city establish a man's name, but a blameless wife is accounted better than both.

[20] Wine and music gladden the heart, but the love of wisdom is better than both.

[21] The flute and the harp make pleasant melody, but a pleasant voice is better than both.

[22] The eye desires grace and beauty, but the green shoots of grain more than both.

[23] A friend or a companion never meets one amiss, but a wife with her husband is better than both.

[24] Brothers and help are for a time of trouble, but almsgiving rescues better than both.

[25] Gold and silver make the foot stand sure, but good counsel is esteemed more than both.

[26] Riches and strength lift up the heart, but the fear of the Lord is better than both. There is no loss in the fear of the Lord, and with it there is no need to seek for help.

[27] The fear of the Lord is like a garden of blessing, and covers a man better than any glory.

[28] My son, do not lead the life of a beggar; it is better to die than to beg.

[29] When a man looks to the table of another, his existence cannot be considered as life. He pollutes himself with another man's food, but a man who is intelligent and well instructed guards against that.

[30] In the mouth of the shameless begging is sweet, but in his stomach a fire is kindled.

Sir.41

[1] O death, how bitter is the reminder of you to one who lives at peace among his possessions, to a man without distractions, who is prosperous in everything, and who still has the vigor to enjoy his food!

[2] O death, how welcome is your sentence to one who is in need and is failing in strength, very old and distracted over everything; to one who is contrary, and has lost his patience!

[3] Do not fear the sentence of death; remember your former days and the end of life; this is the decree from the Lord for all flesh,

[4] and how can you reject the good pleasure of the Most High? Whether life is for ten or a hundred or a thousand years,
there is no inquiry about it in Hades.

[5] The children of sinners are abominable children, and they frequent the haunts of the ungodly.

[6] The inheritance of the children of sinners will perish, and on their posterity will be a perpetual reproach.

[7] Children will blame an ungodly father, for they suffer reproach because of him.

[8] Woe to you, ungodly men, who have forsaken the law of the Most High God!

[9] When you are born, you are born to a curse; and when you die, a curse is your lot.

[10] Whatever is from the dust returns to dust; so the ungodly go from curse to destruction.

[11] The mourning of men is about their bodies, but the evil name of sinners will be blotted out.

[12] Have regard for your name, since it will remain for you longer than a thousand great stores of gold.

[13] The days of a good life are numbered, but a good name endures for ever.

[14] My children, observe instruction and be at peace; hidden wisdom and unseen treasure, what advantage is there in either of them?

[15] Better is the man who hides his folly than the man who hides his wisdom.

[16] Therefore show respect for my words: For it is good to retain every kind of shame, and not everything is confidently esteemed by every one.

[17] Be ashamed of immorality, before your father or mother; and of a lie, before a prince or a ruler;

[18] of a transgression, before a judge or magistrate; and of iniquity, before a congregation or the people; of unjust dealing, before your partner or friend;

[19] and of theft, in the place where you live. Be ashamed before the truth of God and his covenant. Be ashamed of selfish behavior at meals, of surliness in receiving and giving,

[20] and of silence, before those who greet you; of looking at a woman who is a harlot,

[21] and of rejecting the appeal of a kinsman; of taking away some one's portion or gift, and of gazing at another man's wife;
[22] of meddling with his maidservant -- and do not approach her bed; of abusive words, before friends -- and do not upbraid after making a gift;
[23] of repeating and telling what you hear, and of revealing secrets. Then you will show proper shame, and will find favor with every man.

Sir.42

[1] Of the following things do not be ashamed, and do not let partiality lead you to sin:
[2] of the law of the Most High and his covenant, and of rendering judgment to acquit the ungodly;
[3] of keeping accounts with a partner or with traveling companions, and of dividing the inheritance of friends;
[4] of accuracy with scales and weights, and of acquiring much or little;
[5] of profit from dealing with merchants, and of much discipline of children, and of whipping a wicked servant severely.
[6] Where there is an evil wife, a seal is a good thing; and where there are many hands, lock things up.
[7] Whatever you deal out, let it be by number and weight, and make a record of all that you give out or take in.
[8] Do not be ashamed to instruct the stupid or foolish or the aged man who quarrels with the young. Then you will be truly instructed, and will be approved before all men.
[9] A daughter keeps her father secretly wakeful, and worry over her robs him of sleep; when she is young, lest she do not marry, or if married, lest she be hated;
[10] while a virgin, lest she be defiled or become pregnant in her father's house; or having a husband, lest she prove unfaithful, or, though married, lest she be barren.
[11] Keep strict watch over a headstrong daughter, lest she make you a laughingstock to your enemies, a byword in the city and notorious among the people, and put you to shame before the great multitude.
[12] Do not look upon any one for beauty, and do not sit in the midst of women;
[13] for from garments comes the moth, and from a woman comes woman's wickedness.
[14] Better is the wickedness of a man than a woman who does good; and it is a woman who brings shame and disgrace.
[15] I will now call to mind the works of the Lord, and will declare what I

have seen. By the words of the Lord his works are done.

[16] The sun looks down on everything with its light, and the work of the Lord is full of his glory.

[17] The Lord has not enabled his holy ones to recount all his marvelous works, which the Lord the Almighty has established that the universe may stand firm in his glory.

[18] He searches out the abyss, and the hearts of men, and considers their crafty devices. For the Most High knows all that may be known, and he looks into the signs of the age.

[19] He declares what has been and what is to be, and he reveals the tracks of hidden things.

[20] No thought escapes him, and not one word is hidden from him.

[21] He has ordained the splendors of his wisdom, and he is from everlasting and to everlasting. Nothing can be added or taken away, and he needs no one to be his counselor.

[22] How greatly to be desired are all his works, and how sparkling they are to see!

[23] All these things live and remain for ever for every need, and are all obedient.

[24] All things are twofold, one opposite the other, and he has made nothing incomplete.

[25] One confirms the good things of the other, and who can have enough of beholding his glory?

Sir.43

[1] The pride of the heavenly heights is the clear firmament, the appearance of heaven in a spectacle of glory.

[2] The sun, when it appears, making proclamation as it goes forth, is a marvelous instrument, the work of the Most High.

[3] At noon it parches the land; and who can withstand its burning heat?

[4] A man tending a furnace works in burning heat, but the sun burns the mountains three times as much; it breathes out fiery vapors, and with bright beams it blinds the eyes.

[5] Great is the Lord who made it; and at his command it hastens on its course.

[6] He made the moon also, to serve in its season to mark the times and to be an everlasting sign.

[7] From the moon comes the sign for feast days, a light that wanes when it has reached the full.

[8] The month is named for the moon, increasing marvelously in its phases, an instrument of the hosts on high shining forth in the firmament of heaven.

[9] The glory of the stars is the beauty of heaven, a gleaming array in the heights of the Lord.

[10] At the command of the Holy One they stand as ordered, they never relax in their watches.

[11] Look upon the rainbow, and praise him who made it, exceedingly beautiful in its brightness.

[12] It encircles the heaven with its glorious arc; the hands of the Most High have stretched it out.

[13] By his command he sends the driving snow and speeds the lightnings of his judgment.

[14] Therefore the storehouses are opened, and the clouds fly forth like birds.

[15] In his majesty he amasses the clouds, and the hailstones are broken in pieces.

[16] At his appearing the mountains are shaken; at his will the south wind blows.

[17] The voice of his thunder rebukes the earth; so do the tempest from the north and the whirlwind. He scatters the snow like birds flying down, and its descent is like locusts alighting.

[18] The eye marvels at the beauty of its whiteness, and the mind is amazed at its falling.

[19] He pours the hoarfrost upon the earth like salt, and when it freezes, it becomes pointed thorns.

[20] The cold north wind blows, and ice freezes over the water; it rests upon every pool of water, and the water puts it on like a breastplate.

[21] He consumes the mountains and burns up the wilderness, and withers the tender grass like fire.

[22] A mist quickly heals all things; when the dew appears, it refreshes from the heat.

[23] By his counsel he stilled the great deep and planted islands in it.

[24] Those who sail the sea tell of its dangers, and we marvel at what we hear.

[25] for in it are strange and marvelous works, all kinds of living things, and huge creatures of the sea.

[26] Because of him his messenger finds the way, and by his word all things hold together.

[27] Though we speak much we cannot reach the end, and the sum of our words is: "He is the all."

[28] Where shall we find strength to praise him? For he is greater than all his works.

[29] Terrible is the Lord and very great, and marvelous is his power.

[30] When you praise the Lord, exalt him as much as you can; for he will surpass even that. When you exalt him, put forth all your strength, and do

not grow weary, for you cannot praise him enough.

[31] Who has seen him and can describe him? Or who can extol him as he is?

[32] Many things greater than these lie hidden, for we have seen but few of his works.

[33] For the Lord has made all things, and to the godly he has granted wisdom.

Sir.44

[1] Let us now praise famous men, and our fathers in their generations.

[2] The Lord apportioned to them great glory, his majesty from the beginning.

[3] There were those who ruled in their kingdoms, and were men renowned for their power, giving counsel by their understanding, and proclaiming prophecies;

[4] leaders of the people in their deliberations and in understanding of learning for the people, wise in their words of instruction;

[5] those who composed musical tunes, and set forth verses in writing;

[6] rich men furnished with resources, living peaceably in their habitations - -

[7] all these were honored in their generations, and were the glory of their times.

[8] There are some of them who have left a name, so that men declare their praise.

[9] And there are some who have no memorial, who have perished as though they had not lived; they have become as though they had not been born, and so have their children after them.

[10] But these were men of mercy, whose righteous deeds have not been forgotten;

[11] their prosperity will remain with their descendants, and their inheritance to their children's children.

[12] Their descendants stand by the covenants; their children also, for their sake.

[13] Their posterity will continue for ever, and their glory will not be blotted out.

[14] Their bodies were buried in peace, and their name lives to all generations.

[15] Peoples will declare their wisdom, and the congregation proclaims their praise.

[16] Enoch pleased the Lord, and was taken up; he was an example of repentance to all generations.

[17] Noah was found perfect and righteous; in the time of wrath he was taken in exchange; therefore a remnant was left to the earth when the flood came.

[18] Everlasting covenants were made with him that all flesh should not be blotted out by a flood.

[19] Abraham was the great father of a multitude of nations, and no one has been found like him in glory;

[20] he kept the law of the Most High, and was taken into covenant with him; he established the covenant in his flesh, and when he was tested he was found faithful.

[21] Therefore the Lord assured him by an oath that the nations would be blessed through his posterity; that he would multiply him like the dust of the earth, and exalt his posterity like the stars, and cause them to inherit from sea to sea and from the River to the ends of the earth.

[22] To Isaac also he gave the same assurance for the sake of Abraham his father.

[23] The blessing of all men and the covenant he made to rest upon the head of Jacob; he acknowledged him with his blessings, and gave him his inheritance; he determined his portions, and distributed them among twelve tribes.

Sir.45

[1] From his descendants the Lord brought forth a man of mercy, who found favor in the sight of all flesh and was beloved by God and man, Moses, whose memory is blessed.

[2] He made him equal in glory to the holy ones, and made him great in the fears of his enemies.

[3] By his words he caused signs to cease; the Lord glorified him in the presence of kings. He gave him commands for his people, and showed him part of his glory.

[4] He sanctified him through faithfulness and meekness; he chose him out of all mankind.

[5] He made him hear his voice, and led him into the thick darkness, and gave him the commandments face to face, the law of life and knowledge, to teach Jacob the covenant, and Israel his judgments.

[6] He exalted Aaron, the brother of Moses, a holy man like him, of the tribe of Levi.

[7] He made an everlasting covenant with him, and gave him the priesthood of the people. He blessed him with splendid vestments, and put a glorious robe upon him.

[8] He clothed him with superb perfection, and strengthened him with the symbols of authority, the linen breeches, the long robe, and the ephod.

[9] And he encircled him with pomegranates, with very many golden bells round about, to send forth a sound as he walked, to make their ringing heard in the temple as a reminder to the sons of his people;

[10] with a holy garment, of gold and blue and purple, the work of an embroiderer; with the oracle of judgment, Urim and Thummim;

[11] with twisted scarlet, the work of a craftsman; with precious stones engraved like signets, in a setting of gold, the work of a jeweler, for a reminder, in engraved letters, according to the number of the tribes of Israel;

[12] with a gold crown upon his turban, inscribed like a signet with "Holiness," a distinction to be prized, the work of an expert, the delight of the eyes, richly adorned.

[13] Before his time there never were such beautiful things. No outsider ever put them on, but only his sons and his descendants perpetually.

[14] His sacrifices shall be wholly burned twice every day continually.

[15] Moses ordained him, and anointed him with holy oil; it was an everlasting covenant for him and for his descendants all the days of heaven, to minister to the Lord and serve as priest and bless his people in his name.

[16] He chose him out of all the living to offer sacrifice to the Lord, incense and a pleasing odor as a memorial portion, to make atonement for the people.

[17] In his commandments he gave him authority and statutes and judgments, to teach Jacob the testimonies, and to enlighten Israel with his law.

[18] Outsiders conspired against him, and envied him in the wilderness, Dathan and Abiram and their men and the company of Korah, in wrath and anger.

[19] The Lord saw it and was not pleased, and in the wrath of his anger they were destroyed; he wrought wonders against them to consume them in flaming fire.

[20] He added glory to Aaron and gave him a heritage; he allotted to him the first of the first fruits, he prepared bread of first fruits in abundance;

[21] for they eat the sacrifices to the Lord, which he gave to him and his descendants.

[22] But in the land of the people he has no inheritance, and he has no portion among the people; for the Lord himself is his portion and inheritance.

[23] Phinehas the son of Eleazar is the third in glory, for he was zealous in the fear of the Lord, and stood fast, when the people turned away, in the ready goodness of his soul, and made atonement for Israel.

[24] Therefore a covenant of peace was established with him, that he should be leader of the sanctuary and of his people,

that he and his descendants should have the dignity of the priesthood for ever.

[25] A covenant was also established with David, the son of Jesse, of the tribe of Judah: the heritage of the king is from son to son only; so the heritage of Aaron is for his descendants.

[26] May the Lord grant you wisdom in your heart to judge his people in righteousness, so that their prosperity may not vanish, and that their glory may endure throughout their generations.

Sir.46

[1] Joshua the son of Nun was mighty in war, and was the successor of Moses in prophesying. He became, in accordance with his name, a great savior of God's elect, to take vengeance on the enemies that rose against them, so that he might give Israel its inheritance.

[2] How glorious he was when he lifted his hands and stretched out his sword against the cities!

[3] Who before him ever stood so firm? For he waged the wars of the Lord.

[4] Was not the sun held back by his hand? And did not one day become as long as two?

[5] He called upon the Most High, the Mighty One, when enemies pressed him on every side,

[6] and the great Lord answered him with hailstones of mighty power. He hurled down war upon that nation, and at the descent of Beth-horon he destroyed those who resisted, so that the nations might know his armament, that he was fighting in the sight of the Lord; for he wholly followed the Mighty One.

[7] And in the days of Moses he did a loyal deed, he and Caleb the son of Jephunneh: they withstood the congregation,

restrained the people from sin, and stilled their wicked murmuring.

[8] And these two alone were preserved out of six hundred thousand people on foot, to bring them into their inheritance,

into a land flowing with milk and honey.

[9] And the Lord gave Caleb strength, which remained with him to old age, so that he went up to the hill country, and his children obtained it for an inheritance;

[10] so that all the sons of Israel might see that it is good to follow the Lord.

[11] The judges also, with their respective names, those whose hearts did not fall into idolatry and who did not turn away from the Lord -- may their memory be blessed!

[12] May their bones revive from where they lie, and may the name of those who have been honored live again in their sons!

[13] Samuel, beloved by his Lord, a prophet of the Lord, established the kingdom and anointed rulers over his people.

[14] By the law of the Lord he judged the congregation, and the Lord watched over Jacob.

[15] By his faithfulness he was proved to be a prophet, and by his words he became known as a trustworthy seer.

[16] He called upon the Lord, the Mighty One, when his enemies pressed him on every side, and he offered in sacrifice a sucking lamb.

[17] Then the Lord thundered from heaven, and made his voice heard with a mighty sound;

[18] and he wiped out the leaders of the people of Tyre and all the rulers of the Philistines.

[19] Before the time of his eternal sleep, Samuel called men to witness before the Lord and his anointed: "I have not taken any one's property, not so much as a pair of shoes." And no man accused him.

[20] Even after he had fallen asleep he prophesied and revealed to the king his death, and lifted up his voice out of the earth in prophecy, to blot out the wickedness of the people.

Sir.47

[1] And after him Nathan rose up to prophesy in the days of David.

[2] As the fat is selected from the peace offering, so David was selected from the sons of Israel.

[3] He played with lions as with young goats, and with bears as with lambs of the flock.

[4] In his youth did he not kill a giant, and take away reproach from the people, when he lifted his hand with a stone in the sling and struck down the boasting of Goliath?

[5] For he appealed to the Lord, the Most High, and he gave him strength in his right hand to slay a man mighty in war, to exalt the power of his people.

[6] So they glorified him for his ten thousands, and praised him for the blessings of the Lord, when the glorious diadem was bestowed upon him.

[7] For he wiped out his enemies on every side, and annihilated his adversaries the Philistines; he crushed their power even to this day.

[8] In all that he did he gave thanks to the Holy One, the Most High, with ascriptions of glory; he sang praise with all his heart, and he loved his Maker.

[9] He placed singers before the altar, to make sweet melody with their voices.

[10] He gave beauty to the feasts, and arranged their times throughout the year, while they praised God's holy name, and the sanctuary resounded

from early morning.

[11] The Lord took away his sins, and exalted his power for ever; he gave him the covenant of kings and a throne of glory in Israel.

[12] After him rose up a wise son who fared amply because of him;

[13] Solomon reigned in days of peace, and God gave him rest on every side, that he might build a house for his name and prepare a sanctuary to stand for ever.

[14] How wise you became in your youth! You overflowed like a river with understanding.

[15] Your soul covered the earth, and you filled it with parables and riddles.

[16] Your name reached to far-off islands, and you were loved for your peace.

[17] For your songs and proverbs and parables, and for your interpretations, the countries marveled at you.

[18] In the name of the Lord God, who is called the God of Israel, you gathered gold like tin and amassed silver like lead.

[19] But you laid your loins beside women, and through your body you were brought into subjection.

[20] You put stain upon your honor, and defiled your posterity, so that you brought wrath upon your children and they were grieved at your folly,

[21] so that the sovereignty was divided and a disobedient kingdom arose out of Ephraim.

[22] But the Lord will never give up his mercy, nor cause any of his works to perish; he will never blot out the descendants of his chosen one, nor destroy the posterity of him who loved him; so he gave a remnant to Jacob, and to David a root of his stock.

[23] Solomon rested with his fathers, and left behind him one of his sons, ample in folly and lacking in understanding,
Rehoboam, whose policy caused the people to revolt. Also Jeroboam the son of Nebat, who caused Israel to sin and gave to Ephraim a sinful way.

[24] Their sins became exceedingly many, so as to remove them from their land.

[25] For they sought out every sort of wickedness, till vengeance came upon them.

Sir.48

[1] Then the prophet Elijah arose like a fire, and his word burned like a torch.

[2] He brought a famine upon them, and by his zeal he made them few in number.

[3] By the word of the Lord he shut up the heavens, and also three times brought down fire.

[4] How glorious you were, O Elijah, in your wondrous deeds! And who has the right to boast which you have?

[5] You who raised a corpse from death and from Hades, by the word of the Most High;

[6] who brought kings down to destruction, and famous men from their beds;

[7] who heard rebuke at Sinai and judgments of vengeance at Horeb;

[8] who anointed kings to inflict retribution, and prophets to succeed you.

[9] You who were taken up by a whirlwind of fire, in a chariot with horses of fire;

[10] you who are ready at the appointed time, it is written, to calm the wrath of God before it breaks out in fury, to turn the heart of the father to the son, and to restore the tribes of Jacob.

[11] Blessed are those who saw you, and those who have been adorned in love; for we also shall surely live.

[12] It was Elijah who was covered by the whirlwind, and Elisha was filled with his spirit; in all his days he did not tremble before any ruler, and no one brought him into subjection.

[13] Nothing was too hard for him, and when he was dead his body prophesied.

[14] As in his life he did wonders, so in death his deeds were marvelous.

[15] For all this the people did not repent, and they did not forsake their sins, till they were carried away captive from their land and were scattered over all the earth; the people were left very few in number, but with rulers from the house of David.

[16] Some of them did what was pleasing to God, but others multiplied sins.

[17] Hezekiah fortified his city, and brought water into the midst of it; he tunneled the sheer rock with iron and built pools for water.

[18] In his days Sennacherib came up, and sent the Rabshakeh; he lifted up his hand against Zion and made great boasts in his arrogance.

[19] Then their hearts were shaken and their hands trembled, and they were in anguish, like women in travail.

[20] But they called upon the Lord who is merciful, spreading forth their hands toward him; and the Holy One quickly heard them from heaven, and delivered them by the hand of Isaiah.

[21] The Lord smote the camp of the Assyrians, and his angel wiped them out.

[22] For Hezekiah did what was pleasing to the Lord, and he held strongly to the ways of David his father, which Isaiah the prophet commanded, who was great and faithful in his vision.

[23] In his days the sun went backward, and he lengthened the life of the king.

[24] By the spirit of might he saw the last things, and comforted those who mourned in Zion.

[25] He revealed what was to occur to the end of time, and the hidden things before they came to pass.

Sir.49

[1] The memory of Josiah is like a blending of incense prepared by the art of the perfumer; it is sweet as honey to every mouth, and like music at a banquet of wine.

[2] He was led aright in converting the people, and took away the abominations of iniquity.

[3] He set his heart upon the Lord; in the days of wicked men he strengthened godliness.

[4] Except David and Hezekiah and Josiah they all sinned greatly, for they forsook the law of the Most High; the kings of Judah came to an end;

[5] for they gave their power to others, and their glory to a foreign nation,

[6] who set fire to the chosen city of the sanctuary, and made her streets desolate, according to the word of Jeremiah.

[7] For they had afflicted him; yet he had been consecrated in the womb as prophet, to pluck up and afflict and destroy,
and likewise to build and to plant.

[8] It was Ezekiel who saw the vision of glory which God showed him above the chariot of the cherubim.

[9] For God remembered his enemies with storm, and did good to those who directed their ways aright.

[10] May the bones of the twelve prophets revive from where they lie, for they comforted the people of Jacob and delivered them with confident hope.

[11] How shall we magnify Zerubbabel? He was like a signet on the right hand,

[12] and so was Jeshua the son of Jozadak; in their days they built the house and raised a temple holy to the Lord,
prepared for everlasting glory.

[13] The memory of Nehemiah also is lasting; he raised for us the walls that had fallen, and set up the gates and bars and rebuilt our ruined houses.

[14] No one like Enoch has been created on earth, for he was taken up from the earth.

[15] And no man like Joseph has been born, and his bones are cared for.

[16] Shem and Seth were honored among men, and Adam above every living being in the creation.

Sir.50

[1] The leader of his brethren and the pride of his people was Simon the high priest, son of Onias, who in his life repaired the house, and in his time fortified the temple.

[2] He laid the foundations for the high double walls, the high retaining walls for the temple enclosure.

[3] In his days a cistern for water was quarried out, a reservoir like the sea in circumference.

[4] He considered how to save his people from ruin, and fortified the city to withstand a seige.

[5] How glorious he was when the people gathered round him as he came out of the inner sanctuary!

[6] Like the morning star among the clouds, like the moon when it is full;

[7] like the sun shining upon the temple of the Most High, and like the rainbow gleaming in glorious clouds;

[8] like roses in the days of the first fruits, like lilies by a spring of water, like a green shoot on Lebanon on a summer day;

[9] like fire and incense in the censer, like a vessel of hammered gold adorned with all kinds of precious stones;

[10] like an olive tree putting forth its fruit, and like a cypress towering in the clouds.

[11] When he put on his glorious robe and clothed himself with superb perfection and went up to the holy altar, he made the court of the sanctuary glorious.

[12] And when he received the portions from the hands of the priests, as he stood by the hearth of the altar with a garland of brethren around him, he was like a young cedar on Lebanon; and they surrounded him like the trunks of palm trees,

[13] all the sons of Aaron in their splendor with the Lord's offering in their hands, before the whole congregation of Israel.

[14] Finishing the service at the altars, and arranging the offering to the Most High, the Almighty,

[15] he reached out his hand to the cup and poured a libation of the blood of the grape; he poured it out at the foot of the altar, a pleasing odor to the Most High, the King of all.

[16] Then the sons of Aaron shouted, they sounded the trumpets of hammered work, they made a great noise to be heard for remembrance before the Most High.

[17] Then all the people together made haste and fell to the ground upon their faces to worship their Lord, the Almighty, God Most High.

[18] And the singers praised him with their voices in sweet and full-toned

melody.

[19] And the people besought the Lord Most High in prayer before him who is merciful, till the order of worship of the Lord was ended; so they completed his service.

[20] Then Simon came down, and lifted up his hands over the whole congregation of the sons of Israel, to pronounce the blessing of the Lord with his lips, and to glory in his name;

[21] and they bowed down in worship a second time, to receive the blessing from the Most High.

[22] And now bless the God of all, who in every way does great things; who exalts our days from birth, and deals with us according to his mercy.

[23] May he give us gladness of heart, and grant that peace may be in our days in Israel, as in the days of old.

[24] May he entrust to us his mercy! And let him deliver us in our days!

[25] With two nations my soul is vexed, and the third is no nation:

[26] Those who live on Mount Seir, and the Philistines, and the foolish people that dwell in Shechem.

[27] Instruction in understanding and knowledge I have written in this book, Jesus the son of Sirach, son of Eleazar, of Jerusalem, who out of his heart poured forth wisdom.

[28] Blessed is he who concerns himself with these things, and he who lays them to heart will become wise.

[29] For if he does them, he will be strong for all things, for the light of the Lord is his path.

Sir.51

[1] I will give thanks to thee, O Lord and King, and will praise thee as God my Savior. I give thanks to thy name,

[2] for thou hast been my protector and helper and hast delivered my body from destruction and from the snare of a slanderous tongue, from lips that utter lies. Before those who stood by thou wast my helper,

[3] and didst deliver me, in the greatness of thy mercy and of thy name, from the gnashings of teeth about to devour me,
from the hand of those who sought my life, from the many afflictions that I endured,

[4] from choking fire on every side and from the midst of fire which I did not kindle,

[5] from the depths of the belly of Hades, from an unclean tongue and lying words --

[6] the slander of an unrighteous tongue to the king. My soul drew near to

death, and my life was very near to Hades beneath.

[7] They surrounded me on every side, and there was no one to help me; I looked for the assistance of men, and there was none.

[8] Then I remembered thy mercy, O Lord, and thy work from of old, that thou do deliver those who wait for thee and do save them from the hand of their enemies.

[9] And I sent up my supplication from the earth, and prayed for deliverance from death.

[10] I appealed to the Lord, the Father of my lord, not to forsake me in the days of affliction, at the time when there is no help against the proud.

[11] I will praise thy name continually, and will sing praise with thanksgiving. My prayer was heard,

[12] for thou didst save me from destruction and rescue me from an evil plight. Therefore I will give thanks to thee and praise thee, and I will bless the name of the Lord.

[13] While I was still young, before I went on my travels, I sought wisdom openly in my prayer.

[14] Before the temple I asked for her, and I will search for her to the last.

[15] From blossom to ripening grape my heart delighted in her; my foot entered upon the straight path; from my youth I followed her steps.

[16] I inclined my ear a little and received her, and I found for myself much instruction.

[17] I made progress therein; to him who gives wisdom I will give glory.

[18] For I resolved to live according to wisdom, and I was zealous for the good; and I shall never be put to shame.

[19] My soul grappled with wisdom, and in my conduct I was strict; I spread out my hands to the heavens, and lamented my ignorance of her.

[20] I directed my soul to her, and through purification I found her. I gained understanding with her from the first,

therefore I will not be forsaken.

[21] My heart was stirred to seek her, therefore I have gained a good possession.

[22] The Lord gave me a tongue as my reward, and I will praise him with it.

[23] Draw near to me, you who are untaught, and lodge in my school.

[24] Why do you say you are lacking in these things, and why are your souls very thirsty?

[25] I opened my mouth and said, Get these things for yourselves without money.

[26] Put your neck under the yoke, and let your souls receive instruction; it is to be found close by.

[27] See with your eyes that I have labored little and found myself much rest.

[28] Get instruction with a large sum of silver, and you will gain by it much gold.

[29] May your soul rejoice in his mercy, and may you not be put to shame when you praise him.

[30] Do your work before the appointed time, and in God's time he will give you your reward.

Wisdom of Solomon

Wis.1

[1] Love righteousness, you rulers of the earth, think of the Lord with uprightness, and seek him with sincerity of heart;

[2] because he is found by those who do not put him to the test, and manifests himself to those who do not distrust him.

[3] For perverse thoughts separate men from God, and when his power is tested, it convicts the foolish;

[4] because wisdom will not enter a deceitful soul, nor dwell in a body enslaved to sin.

[5] For a holy and disciplined spirit will flee from deceit, and will rise and depart from foolish thoughts, and will be ashamed at the approach of unrighteousness.

[6] For wisdom is a kindly spirit and will not free a blasphemer from the guilt of his words; because God is witness of his inmost feelings, and a true observer of his heart, and a hearer of his tongue.

[7] Because the Spirit of the Lord has filled the world, and that which holds all things together knows what is said;

[8] therefore no one who utters unrighteous things will escape notice, and justice, when it punishes, will not pass him by.

[9] For inquiry will be made into the counsels of an ungodly man, and a report of his words will come to the Lord, to convict him of his lawless deeds;

[10] because a jealous ear hears all things, and the sound of murmurings does not go unheard.

[11] Beware then of useless murmuring, and keep your tongue from slander; because no secret word is without result, and a lying mouth destroys the soul.

[12] Do not invite death by the error of your life, nor bring on destruction by the works of your hands;

[13] because God did not make death, and he does not delight in the death of the living.

[14] For he created all things that they might exist, and the generative forces of the world are wholesome, and there is no destructive poison in them; and the dominion of Hades is not on earth.

[15] For righteousness is immortal.

[16] But ungodly men by their words and deeds summoned death; considering him a friend, they pined away, and they made a covenant with him, because they are fit to belong to his party.

Wis.2

[1] For they reasoned unsoundly, saying to themselves, Short and sorrowful is our life, and there is no remedy when a man comes to his end, and no one has been known to return from Hades.

[2] Because we were born by mere chance, and hereafter we shall be as though we had never been; because the breath in our nostrils is smoke, and reason is a spark kindled by the beating of our hearts.

[3] When it is extinguished, the body will turn to ashes, and the spirit will dissolve like empty air.

[4] Our name will be forgotten in time and no one will remember our works; our life will pass away like the traces of a cloud, and be scattered like mist that is chased by the rays of the sun and overcome by its heat.

[5] For our allotted time is the passing of a shadow, and there is no return from our death, because it is sealed up and no one turns back.

[6] "Come, therefore, let us enjoy the good things that exist, and make use of the creation to the full as in youth.

[7] Let us take our fill of costly wine and perfumes, and let no flower of spring pass by us.

[8] Let us crown ourselves with rosebuds before they wither.

[9] Let none of us fail to share in our revelry, everywhere let us leave signs of enjoyment, because this is our portion, and this our lot.

[10] Let us oppress the righteous poor man; let us not spare the widow nor regard the gray hairs of the aged.

[11] But let our might be our law of right, for what is weak proves itself to be useless.

[12] "Let us lie in wait for the righteous man, because he is inconvenient to us and opposes our actions; he reproaches us for sins against the law, and accuses us of sins against our training.

[13] He professes to have knowledge of God, and calls himself a child of the Lord.

[14] He became to us a reproof of our thoughts;

[15] the very sight of him is a burden to us, because his manner of life is unlike that of others, and his ways are strange.

[16] We are considered by him as something base, and he avoids our ways as unclean; he calls the last end of the righteous happy, and boasts that God is his father.

[17] Let us see if his words are true, and let us test what will happen at the end of his life;

[18] for if the righteous man is God's son, he will help him, and will deliver him from the hand of his adversaries.

[19] Let us test him with insult and torture, that we may find out how gentle he is, and make trial of his forbearance.

[20] Let us condemn him to a shameful death, for, according to what he says, he will be protected."

[21] Thus they reasoned, but they were led astray, for their wickedness blinded them,

[22] and they did not know the secret purposes of God, nor hope for the wages of holiness, nor discern the prize for blameless souls;

[23] for God created man for incorruption, and made him in the image of his own eternity,

[24] but through the devil's envy death entered the world, and those who belong to his party experience it.

Wis.3

[1] But the souls of the righteous are in the hand of God, and no torment will ever touch them.

[2] In the eyes of the foolish they seemed to have died, and their departure was thought to be an affliction,

[3] and their going from us to be their destruction; but they are at peace.

[4] For though in the sight of men they were punished, their hope is full of immortality.

[5] Having been disciplined a little, they will receive great good, because God tested them and found them worthy of himself;

[6] like gold in the furnace he tried them, and like a sacrificial burnt offering he accepted them.

[7] In the time of their visitation they will shine forth, and will run like sparks through the stubble.

[8] They will govern nations and rule over peoples, and the Lord will reign over them for ever.

[9] Those who trust in him will understand truth, and the faithful will abide with him in love, because grace and mercy are upon his elect, and he watches over his holy ones.

[10] But the ungodly will be punished as their reasoning deserves, who disregarded the righteous man and rebelled against the Lord;

[11] for whoever despises wisdom and instruction is miserable. Their hope is vain, their labors are unprofitable, and their works are useless.

[12] Their wives are foolish, and their children evil;

[13] their offspring are accursed. For blessed is the barren woman who is undefiled, who has not entered into a sinful union; she will have fruit when God examines souls.

[14] Blessed also is the eunuch whose hands have done no lawless deed, and

who has not devised wicked things against the Lord; for special favor will be shown him for his faithfulness, and a place of great delight in the temple of the Lord.

[15] For the fruit of good labors is renowned, and the root of understanding does not fail.

[16] But children of adulterers will not come to maturity, and the offspring of an unlawful union will perish.

[17] Even if they live long they will be held of no account, and finally their old age will be without honor.

[18] If they die young, they will have no hope and no consolation in the day of decision.

[19] For the end of an unrighteous generation is grievous.

Wis.4

[1] Better than this is childlessness with virtue, for in the memory of virtue is immortality, because it is known both by God and by men.

[2] When it is present, men imitate it, and they long for it when it has gone; and throughout all time it marches crowned in triumph, victor in the contest for prizes that are undefiled.

[3] But the prolific brood of the ungodly will be of no use, and none of their illegitimate seedlings will strike a deep root or take a firm hold.

[4] For even if they put forth boughs for a while, standing insecurely they will be shaken by the wind, and by the violence of the winds they will be uprooted.

[5] The branches will be broken off before they come to maturity, and their fruit will be useless, not ripe enough to eat, and good for nothing.

[6] For children born of unlawful unions are witnesses of evil against their parents when God examines them.

[7] But the righteous man, though he die early, will be at rest.

[8] For old age is not honored for length of time, nor measured by number of years;

[9] but understanding is gray hair for men, and a blameless life is ripe old age.

[10] There was one who pleased God and was loved by him, and while living among sinners he was taken up.

[11] He was caught up lest evil change his understanding or guile deceive his soul.

[12] For the fascination of wickedness obscures what is good, and roving desire perverts the innocent mind.

[13] Being perfected in a short time, he fulfilled long years;

[14] for his soul was pleasing to the Lord, therefore he took him quickly from the midst of wickedness.

[15] Yet the peoples saw and did not understand, nor take such a thing to heart, that God's grace and mercy are with his elect, and he watches over his holy ones.

[16] The righteous man who had died will condemn the ungodly who are living, and youth that is quickly perfected will condemn the prolonged old age of the unrighteous man.

[17] For they will see the end of the wise man, and will not understand what the Lord purposed for him, and for what he kept him safe.

[18] They will see, and will have contempt for him, but the Lord will laugh them to scorn. After this they will become dishonored corpses, and an outrage among the dead for ever;

[19] because he will dash them speechless to the ground, and shake them from the foundations; they will be left utterly dry and barren, and they will suffer anguish, and the memory of them will perish.

[20] They will come with dread when their sins are reckoned up, and their lawless deeds will convict them to their face.

Wis.5

[1] Then the righteous man will stand with great confidence in the presence of those who have afflicted him, and those who make light of his labors.

[2] When they see him, they will be shaken with dreadful fear, and they will be amazed at his unexpected salvation.

[3] They will speak to one another in repentance, and in anguish of spirit they will groan, and say,

[4] "This is the man whom we once held in derision and made a byword of reproach -- we fools! We thought that his life was madness and that his end was without honor.

[5] Why has he been numbered among the sons of God? And why is his lot among the saints?

[6] So it was we who strayed from the way of truth, and the light of righteousness did not shine on us, and the sun did not rise upon us.

[7] We took our fill of the paths of lawlessness and destruction, and we journeyed through trackless deserts, but the way of the Lord we have not known.

[8] What has our arrogance profited us? And what good has our boasted wealth brought us?

[9] "All those things have vanished like a shadow, and like a rumor that passes by;

[10] like a ship that sails through the billowy water, and when it has passed

no trace can be found, nor track of its keel in the waves;

[11] or as, when a bird flies through the air, no evidence of its passage is found; the light air, lashed by the beat of its pinions and pierced by the force of its rushing flight, is traversed by the movement of its wings, and afterward no sign of its coming is found there;

[12] or as, when an arrow is shot at a target, the air, thus divided, comes together at once, so that no one knows its pathway.

[13] So we also, as soon as we were born, ceased to be, and we had no sign of virtue to show, but were consumed in our wickedness."

[14] Because the hope of the ungodly man is like chaff carried by the wind, and like a light hoarfrost driven away by a storm; it is dispersed like smoke before the wind, and it passes like the remembrance of a guest who stays but a day.

[15] But the righteous live for ever, and their reward is with the Lord; the Most High takes care of them.

[16] Therefore they will receive a glorious crown and a beautiful diadem from the hand of the Lord, because with his right hand he will cover them, and with his arm he will shield them.

[17] The Lord will take his zeal as his whole armor, and will arm all creation to repel his enemies;

[18] he will put on righteousness as a breastplate, and wear impartial justice as a helmet;

[19] he will take holiness as an invincible shield,

[20] and sharpen stern wrath for a sword, and creation will join with him to fight against the madmen.

[21] Shafts of lightning will fly with true aim, and will leap to the target as from a well-drawn bow of clouds,

[22] and hailstones full of wrath will be hurled as from a catapult; the water of the sea will rage against them, and rivers will relentlessly overwhelm them;

[23] a mighty wind will rise against them , and like a tempest it will winnow them away. Lawlessness will lay waste the whole earth, and evil-doing will overturn the thrones of rulers.

Wis.6

[1] Listen therefore, O kings, and understand; learn, O judges of the ends of the earth.

[2] Give ear, you that rule over multitudes, and boast of many nations.

[3] For your dominion was given you from the Lord, and your sovereignty from the Most High, who will search out your works and inquire into your

plans.

[4] Because as servants of his kingdom you did not rule rightly, nor keep the law, nor walk according to the purpose of God,

[5] he will come upon you terribly and swiftly, because severe judgment falls on those in high places.

[6] For the lowliest man may be pardoned in mercy, but mighty men will be mightily tested.

[7] For the Lord of all will not stand in awe of any one, nor show deference to greatness; because he himself made both small and great, and he takes thought for all alike.

[8] But a strict inquiry is in store for the mighty.

[9] To you then, O monarchs, my words are directed, that you may learn wisdom and not transgress.

[10] For they will be made holy who observe holy things in holiness, and those who have been taught them will find a defense.

[11] Therefore set your desire on my words; long for them, and you will be instructed.

[12] Wisdom is radiant and unfading, and she is easily discerned by those who love her, and is found by those who seek her.

[13] She hastens to make herself known to those who desire her.

[14] He who rises early to seek her will have no difficulty, for he will find her sitting at his gates.

[15] To fix one's thought on her is perfect understanding, and he who is vigilant on her account will soon be free from care,

[16] because she goes about seeking those worthy of her, and she graciously appears to them in their paths, and meets them in every thought.

[17] The beginning of wisdom is the most sincere desire for instruction, and concern for instruction is love of her,

[18] and love of her is the keeping of her laws, and giving heed to her laws is assurance of immortality,

[19] and immortality brings one near to God;

[20] so the desire for wisdom leads to a kingdom.

[21] Therefore if you delight in thrones and scepters, O monarchs over the peoples, honor wisdom, that you may reign for ever.

[22] I will tell you what wisdom is and how she came to be, and I will hide no secrets from you, but I will trace her course from the beginning of creation, and make knowledge of her clear, and I will not pass by the truth;

[23] neither will I travel in the company of sickly envy, for envy does not associate with wisdom.

[24] A multitude of wise men is the salvation of the world, and a sensible king is the stability of his people.

[25] Therefore be instructed by my words, and you will profit.

Wis.7

[1] I also am mortal, like all men, a descendant of the first-formed child of earth; and in the womb of a mother I was molded into flesh,

[2] within the period of ten months, compacted with blood, from the seed of a man and the pleasure of marriage.

[3] And when I was born, I began to breathe the common air, and fell upon the kindred earth, and my first sound was a cry, like that of all.

[4] I was nursed with care in swaddling cloths.

[5] For no king has had a different beginning of existence;

[6] there is for all mankind one entrance into life, and a common departure.

[7] Therefore I prayed, and understanding was given me; I called upon God, and the spirit of wisdom came to me.

[8] I preferred her to scepters and thrones, and I accounted wealth as nothing in comparison with her.

[9] Neither did I liken to her any priceless gem, because all gold is but a little sand in her sight, and silver will be accounted as clay before her.

[10] I loved her more than health and beauty, and I chose to have her rather than light, because her radiance never ceases.

[11] All good things came to me along with her, and in her hands uncounted wealth.

[12] I rejoiced in them all, because wisdom leads them; but I did not know that she was their mother.

[13] I learned without guile and I impart without grudging; I do not hide her wealth,

[14] for it is an unfailing treasure for men; those who get it obtain friendship with God, commended for the gifts that come from instruction.

[15] May God grant that I speak with judgment and have thought worthy of what I have received, for he is the guide even of wisdom and the corrector of the wise.

[16] For both we and our words are in his hand, as are all understanding and skill in crafts.

[17] For it is he who gave me unerring knowledge of what exists, to know the structure of the world and the activity of the elements;

[18] the beginning and end and middle of times, the alternations of the solstices and the changes of the seasons,

[19] the cycles of the year and the constellations of the stars,

[20] the natures of animals and the tempers of wild beasts, the powers of spirits and the reasonings of men, the varieties of plants and the virtues of roots;

[21] I learned both what is secret and what is manifest,

[22] for wisdom, the fashioner of all things, taught me. For in her there is a

spirit that is intelligent, holy, unique, manifold, subtle, mobile, clear, unpolluted, distinct, invulnerable, loving the good, keen, irresistible,
[23] beneficent, humane, steadfast, sure, free from anxiety, all-powerful, overseeing all, and penetrating through all spirits
that are intelligent and pure and most subtle.
[24] For wisdom is more mobile than any motion; because of her pureness she pervades and penetrates all things.
[25] For she is a breath of the power of God, and a pure emanation of the glory of the Almighty; therefore nothing defiled gains entrance into her.
[26] For she is a reflection of eternal light, a spotless mirror of the working of God, and an image of his goodness.
[27] Though she is but one, she can do all things, and while remaining in herself, she renews all things; in every generation she passes into holy souls and makes them friends of God, and prophets;
[28] for God loves nothing so much as the man who lives with wisdom.
[29] For she is more beautiful than the sun, and excels every constellation of the stars. Compared with the light she is found to be superior,
[30] for it is succeeded by the night, but against wisdom evil does not prevail.

Wis.8

[1] She reaches mightily from one end of the earth to the other, and she orders all things well.
[2] I loved her and sought her from my youth, and I desired to take her for my bride, and I became enamored of her beauty.
[3] She glorifies her noble birth by living with God, and the Lord of all loves her.
[4] For she is an initiate in the knowledge of God, and an associate in his works.
[5] If riches are a desirable possession in life, what is richer than wisdom who effects all things?
[6] And if understanding is effective, who more than she is fashioner of what exists?
[7] And if any one loves righteousness, her labors are virtues; for she teaches self-control and prudence, justice and courage; nothing in life is more profitable for men than these.
[8] And if any one longs for wide experience, she knows the things of old, and infers the things to come; she understands turns of speech and the solutions of riddles; she has foreknowledge of signs and wonders and of the outcome of seasons and times.
[9] Therefore I determined to take her to live with me, knowing that she

would give me good counsel and encouragement in cares and grief.

[10] Because of her I shall have glory among the multitudes and honor in the presence of the elders, though I am young.

[11] I shall be found keen in judgment, and in the sight of rulers I shall be admired.

[12] When I am silent they will wait for me, and when I speak they will give heed; and when I speak at greater length
they will put their hands on their mouths.

[13] Because of her I shall have immortality, and leave an everlasting remembrance to those who come after me.

[14] I shall govern peoples, and nations will be subject to me;

[15] dread monarchs will be afraid of me when they hear of me; among the people I shall show myself capable, and courageous in war.

[16] When I enter my house, I shall find rest with her, for companionship with her has no bitterness, and life with her has no pain, but gladness and joy.

[17] When I considered these things inwardly, and thought upon them in my mind, that in kinship with wisdom there is immortality,

[18] and in friendship with her, pure delight, and in the labors of her hands, unfailing wealth, and in the experience of her company, understanding, and renown in sharing her words, I went about seeking how to get her for myself.

[19] As a child I was by nature well endowed, and a good soul fell to my lot;

[20] or rather, being good, I entered an undefiled body.

[21] But I perceived that I would not possess wisdom unless God gave her to me -- and it was a mark of insight to know whose gift she was -- so I appealed to the Lord and besought him, and with my whole heart I said:

Wis.9

[1] "O God of my fathers and Lord of mercy, who hast made all things by thy word,

[2] and by thy wisdom hast formed man, to have dominion over the creatures thou hast made,

[3] and rule the world in holiness and righteousness, and pronounce judgment in uprightness of soul,

[4] give me the wisdom that sits by thy throne, and do not reject me from among thy servants.

[5] For I am thy slave and the son of thy maidservant, a man who is weak and short-lived, with little understanding of judgment and laws;

[6] for even if one is perfect among the sons of men, yet without the wisdom

that comes from thee he will be regarded as nothing.

[7] Thou hast chosen me to be king of thy people and to be judge over thy sons and daughters.

[8] Thou hast given command to build a temple on thy holy mountain, and an altar in the city of thy habitation, a copy of the holy tent which thou didst prepare from the beginning.

[9] With thee is wisdom, who knows thy works and was present when thou didst make the world, and who understand what is pleasing in thy sight and what is right according to thy commandments.

[10] Send her forth from the holy heavens, and from the throne of thy glory send her, that she may be with me and toil,

and that I may learn what is pleasing to thee.

[11] For she knows and understands all things, and she will guide me wisely in my actions and guard me with her glory.

[12] Then my works will be acceptable, and I shall judge thy people justly, and shall be worthy of the throne of my father.

[13] For what man can learn the counsel of God? Or who can discern what the Lord wills?

[14] For the reasoning of mortals is worthless, and our designs are likely to fail,

[15] for a perishable body weighs down the soul, and this earthy tent burdens the thoughtful mind.

[16] We can hardly guess at what is on earth, and what is at hand we find with labor; but who has traced out what is in the heavens?

[17] Who has learned thy counsel, unless thou hast given wisdom and sent thy holy Spirit from on high?

[18] And thus the paths of those on earth were set right, and men were taught what pleases thee, and were saved by wisdom."

Wis.10

[1] Wisdom protected the first-formed father of the world, when he alone had been created; she delivered him from his transgression,

[2] and gave him strength to rule all things.

[3] But when an unrighteous man departed from her in his anger, he perished because in rage he slew his brother.

[4] When the earth was flooded because of him, wisdom again saved it, steering the righteous man by a paltry piece of wood.

[5] Wisdom also, when the nations in wicked agreement had been confounded, recognized the righteous man and preserved him blameless before God, and kept him strong in the face of his compassion for his child.

[6] Wisdom rescued a righteous man when the ungodly were perishing; he

escaped the fire that descended on the Five Cities.

[7] Evidence of their wickedness still remains: a continually smoking wasteland, plants bearing fruit that does not ripen,
and a pillar of salt standing as a monument to an unbelieving soul.

[8] For because they passed wisdom by, they not only were hindered from recognizing the good, but also left for mankind a reminder of their folly, so that their failures could never go unnoticed.

[9] Wisdom rescued from troubles those who served her.

[10] When a righteous man fled from his brother's wrath, she guided him on straight paths; she showed him the kingdom of God, and gave him knowledge of angels; she prospered him in his labors, and increased the fruit of his toil.

[11] When his oppressors were covetous, she stood by him and made him rich.

[12] She protected him from his enemies, and kept him safe from those who lay in wait for him; in his arduous contest she gave him the victory, so that he might learn that godliness is more powerful than anything.

[13] When a righteous man was sold, wisdom did not desert him, but delivered him from sin. She descended with him into the dungeon,

[14] and when he was in prison she did not leave him, until she brought him the scepter of a kingdom and authority over his masters. Those who accused him she showed to be false, and she gave him everlasting honor.

[15] A holy people and blameless race wisdom delivered from a nation of oppressors.

[16] She entered the soul of a servant of the Lord, and withstood dread kings with wonders and signs.

[17] She gave holy men the reward of their labors; she guided them along a marvelous way, and became a shelter to them by day, and a starry flame through the night.

[18] She brought them over the Red Sea, and led them through deep waters;

[19] but she drowned their enemies, and cast them up from the depth of the sea.

[20] Therefore the righteous plundered the ungodly; they sang hymns, O Lord, to thy holy name, and praised with one accord thy defending hand,

[21] because wisdom opened the mouth of the dumb, and made the tongues of babes speak clearly.

Wis.11

[1] Wisdom prospered their works by the hand of a holy prophet.

[2] They journeyed through an uninhabited wilderness, and pitched their

tents in untrodden places.

[3] They withstood their enemies and fought off their foes.

[4] When they thirsted they called upon thee, and water was given them out of flinty rock, and slaking of thirst from hard stone.

[5] For through the very things by which their enemies were punished, they themselves received benefit in their need.

[6] Instead of the fountain of an ever-flowing river, stirred up and defiled with blood

[7] in rebuke for the decree to slay the infants, thou gavest them abundant water unexpectedly,

[8] showing by their thirst at that time how thou didst punish their enemies.

[9] For when they were tried, though they were being disciplined in mercy, they learned how the ungodly were tormented
when judged in wrath.

[10] For thou didst test them as a father does in warning, but thou didst examine the ungodly as a stern
king does in condemnation.

[11] Whether absent or present, they were equally distressed,

[12] for a twofold grief possessed them, and a groaning at the memory of what had occurred.

[13] For when they heard that through their own punishments the righteous had received benefit, they perceived it was the Lord's doing.

[14] For though they had mockingly rejected him who long before had been cast out and exposed, at the end of the events they marveled at him, for their thirst was not like that of the righteous.

[15] In return for their foolish and wicked thoughts, which led them astray to worship irrational serpents and worthless animals, thou didst send upon them a multitude of irrational creatures to punish them,

[16] that they might learn that one is punished by the very things by which he sins.

[17] For thy all-powerful hand, which created the world out of formless matter, did not lack the means to send upon them a multitude of bears, or bold lions,

[18] or newly created unknown beasts full of rage, or such as breathe out fiery breath, or belch forth a thick pall of smoke, or flash terrible sparks from their eyes;

[19] not only could their damage exterminate men, but the mere sight of them could kill by fright.

[20] Even apart from these, men could fall at a single breath when pursued by justice and scattered by the breath of thy power. But thou hast arranged all things by measure and number and weight.

[21] For it is always in thy power to show great strength, and who can withstand the might of thy arm?

[22] Because the whole world before thee is like a speck that tips the scales,

and like a drop of morning dew that falls upon the ground.

[23] But thou art merciful to all, for thou canst do all things, and thou do overlook men's sins, that they may repent.

[24] For thou lovest all things that exist, and hast loathing for none of the things which thou hast made, for thou wouldst not have made anything if thou hadst hated it.

[25] How would anything have endured if thou hadst not willed it? Or how would anything not called forth by thee
have been preserved?

[26] Thou sparest all things, for they are your, O Lord who lovest the living.

Wis.12

[1] For thy immortal spirit is in all things.

[2] Therefore thou do correct little by little those who trespass, and do remind and warn them of the things wherein they sin, that they may be freed from wickedness and put their trust in thee, O Lord.

[3] Those who dwelt of old in thy holy land

[4] thou didst hate for their detestable practices, their works of sorcery and unholy rites,

[5] their merciless slaughter of children, and their sacrificial feasting on human flesh and blood. These initiates from the midst of a heathen cult,

[6] these parents who murder helpless lives, thou didst will to destroy by the hands of our fathers,

[7] that the land most precious of all to thee might receive a worthy colony of the servants of God.

[8] But even these thou didst spare, since they were but men, and didst send wasps as forerunners of thy army, to destroy them little by little,

[9] though thou wast not unable to give the ungodly into the hands of the righteous in battle, or to destroy them at one blow by dread wild beasts or thy stern word.

[10] But judging them little by little thou gavest them a chance to repent, though thou wast not unaware that their origin was evil and their wickedness inborn, and that their way of thinking would never change.

[11] For they were an accursed race from the beginning, and it was not through fear of any one that thou didst leave them unpunished for their sins.

[12] For who will say, "What hast thou done?" Or will resist thy judgment? Who will accuse thee for the destruction of
nations which thou didst make? Or who will come before thee to plead as an advocate for unrighteous men?

[13] For neither is there any god besides thee, whose care is for all men, to whom thou shouldst prove that thou hast not judged unjustly;

[14] nor can any king or monarch confront thee about those whom thou hast punished.

[15] Thou art righteous and rulest all things righteously, deeming it alien to thy power to condemn him who does not deserve to be punished.

[16] For thy strength is the source of righteousness, and thy sovereignty over all causes thee to spare all.

[17] For thou do show thy strength when men doubt the completeness of thy power, and do rebuke any insolence among those who know it.

[18] Thou who art sovereign in strength do judge with mildness, and with great forbearance thou do govern us; for thou hast power to act whenever thou do choose.

[19] Through such works thou has taught thy people that the righteous man must be kind, and thou hast filled thy sons with good hope, because thou givest repentance for sins.

[20] For if thou didst punish with such great care and indulgence the enemies of thy servants and those deserving of death,
granting them time and opportunity to give up their wickedness,

[21] with what strictness thou hast judged thy sons, to whose fathers thou gavest oaths and covenants full of good promises!

[22] So while chastening us thou scourgest our enemies ten thousand times more, so that we may meditate upon thy goodness when we judge, and when we are judged we may expect mercy.

[23] Therefore those who in folly of life lived unrighteously thou didst torment through their own abominations.

[24] For they went far astray on the paths of error, accepting as gods those animals which even their enemies despised;
they were deceived like foolish babes.

[25] Therefore, as to thoughtless children, thou didst send thy judgment to mock them.

[26] But those who have not heeded the warning of light rebukes will experience the deserved judgment of God.

[27] For when in their suffering they became incensed at those creatures which they had thought to be gods, being punished by means of them, they saw and recognized as the true God him whom they had before refused to know.
Therefore the utmost condemnation came upon them.

Wis.13

[1] For all men who were ignorant of God were foolish by nature; and they

were unable from the good things that
are seen to know him who exists, nor did they recognize the craftsman
while paying heed to his works;
[2] but they supposed that either fire or wind or swift air, or the circle of the
stars, or turbulent water, or the luminaries of heaven were the gods that rule
the world.
[3] If through delight in the beauty of these things men assumed them to be
gods, let them know how much better than these is their Lord, for the
author of beauty created them.
[4] And if men were amazed at their power and working, let them perceive
from them how much more powerful is he who formed them.
[5] For from the greatness and beauty of created things comes a
corresponding perception of their Creator.
[6] Yet these men are little to be blamed, for perhaps they go astray while
seeking God and desiring to find him.
[7] For as they live among his works they keep searching, and they trust in
what they see, because the things that are seen are beautiful.
[8] Yet again, not even they are to be excused;
[9] for if they had the power to know so much that they could investigate
the world, how did they fail to find sooner the Lord of these things?
[10] But miserable, with their hopes set on dead things, are the men who
give the name "gods" to the works of men's hands, gold and silver fashioned
with skill, and likenesses of animals, or a useless stone, the work of an
ancient hand.
[11] A skilled woodcutter may saw down a tree easy to handle and skilfully
strip off all its bark, and then with pleasing workmanship make a useful
vessel that serves life's needs,
[12] and burn the castoff pieces of his work to prepare his food, and eat his
fill.
[13] But a castoff piece from among them, useful for nothing, a stick crooked
and full of knots, he takes and carves with care in his leisure, and shapes it
with skill gained in idleness; he forms it like the image of a man,
[14] or makes it like some worthless animal, giving it a coat of red paint and
coloring its surface red and covering every blemish in it with paint;
[15] then he makes for it a niche that befits it, and sets it in the wall, and
fastens it there with iron.
[16] So he takes thought for it, that it may not fall, because he knows that it
cannot help itself, for it is only an image and has need of help.
[17] When he prays about possessions and his marriage and children, he is
not ashamed to address a lifeless thing.
[18] For health he appeals to a thing that is weak; for life he prays to a thing
that is dead; for aid he entreats a thing that is utterly inexperienced; for a
prosperous journey, a thing that cannot take a step;

[19] for money-making and work and success with his hands he asks strength of a thing whose hands have no strength.

Wis.14

[1] Again, one preparing to sail and about to voyage over raging waves calls upon a piece of wood more fragile than the ship which carries him.

[2] For it was desire for gain that planned that vessel, and wisdom was the craftsman who built it;

[3] but it is thy providence, O Father, that steers its course, because thou hast given it a path in the sea, and a safe way through the waves,

[4] showing that thou canst save from every danger, so that even if a man lacks skill, he may put to sea.

[5] It is thy will that works of thy wisdom should not be without effect; therefore men trust their lives even to the smallest piece of wood, and passing through the billows on a raft they come safely to land.

[6] For even in the beginning, when arrogant giants were perishing, the hope of the world took refuge on a raft, and guided by thy hand left to the world the seed of a new generation.

[7] For blessed is the wood by which righteousness comes.

[8] But the idol made with hands is accursed, and so is he who made it; because he did the work, and the perishable thing was named a god.

[9] For equally hateful to God are the ungodly man and his ungodliness,

[10] for what was done will be punished together with him who did it.

[11] Therefore there will be a visitation also upon the heathen idols, because, though part of what God created, they became an abomination, and became traps for the souls of men and a snare to the feet of the foolish.

[12] For the idea of making idols was the beginning of fornication, and the invention of them was the corruption of life,

[13] for neither have they existed from the beginning nor will they exist for ever.

[14] For through the vanity of men they entered the world, and therefore their speedy end has been planned.

[15] For a father, consumed with grief at an untimely bereavement, made an image of his child, who had been suddenly
taken from him; and he now honored as a god what was once a dead human being, and handed on to his dependents secret rites and initiations.

[16] Then the ungodly custom, grown strong with time, was kept as a law, and at the command of monarchs graven images were worshiped.

[17] When men could not honor monarchs in their presence, since they lived at a distance, they imagined their appearance far away, and made a visible image of the king whom they honored, so that by their zeal they might

flatter the absent one as though present.

[18] Then the ambition of the craftsman impelled even those who did not know the king to intensify their worship.

[19] For he, perhaps wishing to please his ruler, skilfully forced the likeness to take more beautiful form,

[20] and the multitude, attracted by the charm of his work, now regarded as an object of worship the one whom shortly before they had honored as a man.

[21] And this became a hidden trap for mankind, because men, in bondage to misfortune or to royal authority, bestowed on objects of stone or wood the name that ought not to be shared.

[22] Afterward it was not enough for them to err about the knowledge of God, but they live in great strife due to ignorance, and they call such great evils peace.

[23] For whether they kill children in their initiations, or celebrate secret mysteries, or hold frenzied revels with strange customs,

[24] they no longer keep either their lives or their marriages pure, but they either treacherously kill one another, or grieve one another by adultery,

[25] and all is a raging riot of blood and murder, theft and deceit, corruption, faithlessness, tumult, perjury,

[26] confusion over what is good, forgetfulness of favors, pollution of souls, sex perversion, disorder in marriage, adultery, and debauchery.

[27] For the worship of idols not to be named is the beginning and cause and end of every evil.

[28] For their worshipers either rave in exultation, or prophesy lies, or live unrighteously, or readily commit perjury;

[29] for because they trust in lifeless idols they swear wicked oaths and expect to suffer no harm.

[30] But just penalties will overtake them on two counts: because they thought wickedly of God in devoting themselves to idols, and because in deceit they swore unrighteously through contempt for holiness.

[31] For it is not the power of the things by which men swear, but the just penalty for those who sin, that always pursues the transgression of the unrighteous.

Wis.15

[1] But thou, our God, art kind and true, patient, and ruling all things in mercy.

[2] For even if we sin we are your, knowing thy power; but we will not sin, because we know that we are accounted your.

[3] For to know thee is complete righteousness, and to know thy power is the root of immortality.

[4] For neither has the evil intent of human art misled us, nor the fruitless toil of painters, a figure stained with varied colors,

[5] whose appearance arouses yearning in fools, so that they desire the lifeless form of a dead image.

[6] Lovers of evil things and fit for such objects of hope are those who either make or desire or worship them.

[7] For when a potter kneads the soft earth and laboriously molds each vessel for our service, he fashions out of the same clay both the vessels that serve clean uses and those for contrary uses, making all in like manner; but which shall be the use of each of these the worker in clay decides.

[8] With misspent toil, he forms a futile god from the same clay -- this man who was made of earth a short time before
and after a little while goes to the earth from which he was taken, when he is required to return the soul that was lent him.

[9] But he is not concerned that he is destined to die or that his life is brief, but he competes with workers in gold and silver, and imitates workers in copper; and he counts it his glory that he molds counterfeit gods.

[10] His heart is ashes, his hope is cheaper than dirt, and his life is of less worth than clay,

[11] because he failed to know the one who formed him and inspired him with an active soul and breathed into him a living spirit.

[12] But he considered our existence an idle game, and life a festival held for profit, for he says one must get money however one can, even by base means.

[13] For this man, more than all others, knows that he sins when he makes from earthy matter fragile vessels and graven images.

[14] But most foolish, and more miserable than an infant, are all the enemies who oppressed thy people.

[15] For they thought that all their heathen idols were gods, though these have neither the use of their eyes to see with, nor nostrils with which to draw breath, nor ears with which to hear, nor fingers to feel with, and their feet are of no use for walking.

[16] For a man made them, and one whose spirit is borrowed formed them; for no man can form a god which is like himself.

[17] He is mortal, and what he makes with lawless hands is dead, for he is better than the objects he worships, since he has life, but they never have.

[18] The enemies of thy people worship even the most hateful animals, which are worse than all others, when judged by their lack of intelligence;

[19] and even as animals they are not so beautiful in appearance that one would desire them, but they have escaped both the praise of God and his blessing.

Wis.16

[1] Therefore those men were deservedly punished through such creatures, and were tormented by a multitude of animals.

[2] Instead of this punishment thou didst show kindness to thy people, and thou didst prepare quails to eat, a delicacy to satisfy the desire of appetite;

[3] in order that those men, when they desired food, might lose the least remnant of appetite because of the odious creatures sent to them, while thy people, after suffering want a short time, might partake of delicacies.

[4] For it was necessary that upon those oppressors inexorable want should come, while to these it was merely shown how their enemies were being tormented.

[5] For when the terrible rage of wild beasts came upon thy people and they were being destroyed by the bites of writhing serpents, thy wrath did not continue to the end;

[6] they were troubled for a little while as a warning, and received a token of deliverance to remind them of thy law's command.

[7] For he who turned toward it was saved, not by what he saw, but by thee, the Savior of all.

[8] And by this also thou didst convince our enemies that it is thou who deliverest from every evil.

[9] For they were killed by the bites of locusts and flies, and no healing was found for them, because they deserved to be punished by such things;

[10] but thy sons were not conquered even by the teeth of venomous serpents, for thy mercy came to their help and healed them.

[11] To remind them of thy oracles they were bitten, and then were quickly delivered, lest they should fall into deep forgetfulness and become unresponsive to thy kindness.

[12] For neither herb nor poultice cured them, but it was thy word, O Lord, which heals all men.

[13] For thou hast power over life and death; thou do lead men down to the gates of Hades and back again.

[14] A man in his wickedness kills another, but he cannot bring back the departed spirit, nor set free the imprisoned soul.

[15] To escape from thy hand is impossible;

[16] for the ungodly, refusing to know thee, were scourged by the strength of thy arm, pursued by unusual rains and hail and relentless storms, and utterly consumed by fire.

[17] For -- most incredible of all -- in the water, which quenches all things, the fire had still greater effect, for the universe defends the righteous.

[18] At one time the flame was restrained, so that it might not consume the

creatures sent against the ungodly, but that seeing this they might know that they were being pursued by the judgment of God;

[19] and at another time even in the midst of water it burned more intensely than fire, to destroy the crops of the unrighteous land.

[20] Instead of these things thou didst give thy people food of angels, and without their toil thou didst supply them
from heaven with bread ready to eat, providing every pleasure and suited to every taste.

[21] For thy sustenance manifested thy sweetness toward thy children; and the bread, ministering to the desire of the one who took it, was changed to suit every one's liking.

[22] Snow and ice withstood fire without melting, so that they might know that the crops of their enemies were being destroyed by the fire that blazed in the hail and flashed in the showers of rain;

[23] whereas the fire, in order that the righteous might be fed, even forgot its native power.

[24] For creation, serving thee who hast made it, exerts itself to punish the unrighteous, and in kindness relaxes on behalf of those who trust in thee.

[25] Therefore at that time also, changed into all forms, it served thy all-nourishing bounty, according to the desire of those who had need,

[26] so that thy sons, whom thou didst love, O Lord, might learn that it is not the production of crops that feeds man, but that thy word preserves those who trust in thee.

[27] For what was not destroyed by fire was melted when simply warmed by a fleeting ray of the sun,

[28] to make it known that one must rise before the sun to give thee thanks, and must pray to thee at the dawning of the light;

[29] for the hope of an ungrateful man will melt like wintry frost, and flow away like waste water.

Wis.17

[1] Great are thy judgments and hard to describe; therefore unintructed souls have gone astray.

[2] For when lawless men supposed that they held the holy nation in their power, they themselves lay as captives of darkness and prisoners of long night, shut in under their roofs, exiles from eternal providence.

[3] For thinking that in their secret sins they were unobserved behind a dark curtain of forgetfulness, they were scattered, terribly alarmed, and appalled by specters.

[4] For not even the inner chamber that held them protected them from fear, but terrifying sounds rang out around them,

and dismal phantoms with gloomy faces appeared.

[5] And no power of fire was able to give light, nor did the brilliant flames of the stars avail to illumine that hateful night.

[6] Nothing was shining through to them except a dreadful, self-kindled fire, and in terror they deemed the things which they saw to be worse than that unseen appearance.

[7] The delusions of their magic art lay humbled, and their boasted wisdom was scornfully rebuked.

[8] For those who promised to drive off the fears and disorders of a sick soul were sick themselves with ridiculous fear.

[9] For even if nothing disturbing frightened them, yet, scared by the passing of beasts and the hissing of serpents,

[10] they perished in trembling fear, refusing to look even at the air, though it nowhere could be avoided.

[11] For wickedness is a cowardly thing, condemned by its own testimony; distressed by conscience, it has always exaggerated the difficulties.

[12] For fear is nothing but surrender of the helps that come from reason;

[13] and the inner expectation of help, being weak, prefers ignorance of what causes the torment.

[14] But throughout the night, which was really powerless, and which beset them from the recesses of powerless Hades,
they all slept the same sleep,

[15] and now were driven by monstrous specters, and now were paralyzed by their souls' surrender, for sudden and unexpected fear overwhelmed them.

[16] And whoever was there fell down, and thus was kept shut up in a prison not made of iron;

[17] for whether he was a farmer or a shepherd or a workman who toiled in the wilderness, he was seized, and endured the inescapable fate; for with one chain of darkness they all were bound.

[18] Whether there came a whistling wind, or a melodious sound of birds in wide-spreading branches, or the rhythm of violently rushing water,

[19] or the harsh crash of rocks hurled down, or the unseen running of leaping animals, or the sound of the most savage roaring beasts, or an echo thrown back from a hollow of the mountains, it paralyzed them with terror.

[20] For the whole world was illumined with brilliant light, and was engaged in unhindered work,

[21] while over those men alone heavy night was spread, an image of the darkness that was destined to receive them;
but still heavier than darkness were they to themselves.

Wis.18

[1] But for thy holy ones there was very great light. Their enemies heard their voices but did not see their forms, and counted them happy for not having suffered,

[2] and were thankful that thy holy ones, though previously wronged, were doing them no injury; and they begged their pardon for having been at variance with them.

[3] Therefore thou didst provide a flaming pillar of fire as a guide for thy people's unknown journey, and a harmless sun for their glorious wandering.

[4] For their enemies deserved to be deprived of light and imprisoned in darkness, those who had kept thy sons imprisoned, through whom the imperishable light of the law was to be given to the world.

[5] When they had resolved to kill the babes of thy holy ones, and one child had been exposed and rescued, thou didst in punishment take away a multitude of their children; and thou didst destroy them all together by a mighty flood.

[6] That night was made known beforehand to our fathers, so that they might rejoice in sure knowledge of the oaths in which they trusted.

[7] The deliverance of the righteous and the destruction of their enemies were expected by thy people.

[8] For by the same means by which thou didst punish our enemies thou didst call us to thyself and glorify us.

[9] For in secret the holy children of good men offered sacrifices, and with one accord agreed to the divine law, that the saints would share alike the same things, both blessings and dangers; and already they were singing the praises of the fathers.

[10] But the discordant cry of their enemies echoed back, and their piteous lament for their children was spread abroad.

[11] The slave was punished with the same penalty as the master, and the common man suffered the same loss as the king;

[12] and they all together, by the one form of death, had corpses too many to count. For the living were not sufficient even to bury them, since in one instant their most valued children had been destroyed.

[13] For though they had disbelieved everything because of their magic arts, yet, when their first-born were destroyed,
they acknowledged thy people to be God's son.

[14] For while gentle silence enveloped all things, and night in its swift course was now half gone,

[15] thy all-powerful word leaped from heaven, from the royal throne, into the midst of the land that was doomed,
a stern warrior

[16] carrying the sharp sword of thy authentic command, and stood and

317

filled all things with death, and touched heaven while standing on the earth.
[17] Then at once apparitions in dreadful dreams greatly troubled them, and
unexpected fears assailed them;
[18] and one here and another there, hurled down half dead, made known
why they were dying;
[19] for the dreams which disturbed them forewarned them of this, so that
they might not perish without knowing
why they suffered.
[20] The experience of death touched also the righteous, and a plague came
upon the multitude in the desert, but the wrath did not long continue.
[21] For a blameless man was quick to act as their champion; he brought
forward the shield of his ministry, prayer and propitiation by incense; he
withstood the anger and put an end to the disaster, showing that he was thy
servant.
[22] He conquered the wrath not by strength of body, and not by force of
arms, but by his word he subdued the punisher,
appealing to the oaths and covenants given to our fathers.
[23] For when the dead had already fallen on one another in heaps, he
intervened and held back the wrath, and cut off its way to the living.
[24] For upon his long robe the whole world was depicted, and the glories of
the fathers were engraved on the four rows of stones, and thy majesty on
the diadem upon his head.
[25] To these the destroyer yielded, these he feared; for merely to test the
wrath was enough.

Wis.19

[1] But the ungodly were assailed to the end by pitiless anger, for God knew
in advance even their future actions,
[2] that, though they themselves had permitted thy people to depart and
hastily sent them forth, they would change their minds and pursue them.
[3] For while they were still busy at mourning, and were lamenting at the
graves of their dead, they reached another foolish decision, and pursued as
fugitives those whom they had begged and compelled to depart.
[4] For the fate they deserved drew them on to this end, and made them
forget what had happened, in order that they might fill up the punishment
which their torments still lacked,
[5] and that thy people might experience an incredible journey, but they
themselves might meet a strange death.
[6] For the whole creation in its nature was fashioned anew, complying with
thy commands, that thy children might be kept unharmed.

[7] The cloud was seen overshadowing the camp, and dry land emerging where water had stood before, an unhindered way out of the Red Sea, and a grassy plain out of the raging waves,

[8] where those protected by thy hand passed through as one nation, after gazing on marvelous wonders.

[9] For they ranged like horses, and leaped like lambs, praising thee, O Lord, who didst deliver them.

[10] For they still recalled the events of their sojourn, how instead of producing animals the earth brought forth gnats,

and instead of fish the river spewed out vast numbers of frogs.

[11] Afterward they saw also a new kind of birds, when desire led them to ask for luxurious food;

[12] for, to give them relief, quails came up from the sea.

[13] The punishments did not come upon the sinners without prior signs in the violence of thunder, for they justly suffered because of their wicked acts; for they practiced a more bitter hatred of strangers.

[14] Others had refused to receive strangers when they came to them, but these made slaves of guests who were their benefactors.

[15] And not only so, but punishment of some sort will come upon the former for their hostile reception of the aliens;

[16] but the latter, after receiving them with festal celebrations, afflicted with terrible sufferings those who had already shared the same rights.

[17] They were stricken also with loss of sight -- just as were those at the door of the righteous man --when, surrounded by yawning darkness, each tried to find the way through his own door.

[18] For the elements changed places with one another, as on a harp the notes vary the nature of the rhythm, while each note remains the same. This may be clearly inferred from the sight of what took place.

[19] For land animals were transformed into water creatures, and creatures that swim moved over to the land.

[20] Fire even in water retained its normal power, and water forgot its fire-quenching nature.

[21] Flames, on the contrary, failed to consume the flesh of perishable creatures that walked among them, nor did they melt the crystalline, easily melted kind of heavenly food.

[22] For in everything, O Lord, thou hast exalted and glorified thy people; and thou hast not neglected to help them at all times and in all places.

Additions to the Book of Esther

AddEsth.11
[1] In the fourth year of Ptolomeus and Cleopatra, Dositheus and Leuite, who claimed to be a priest brought the Epistle of Phurim that was in Jerusalem and had it interpreted.
[2] In the second year of the reign of Artaxerxes the Great, on the first day of Nisan, Mordecai the son of Jair, son of Shimei, son of Kish, of the tribe of Benjamin, had a dream.
[3] He was a Jew, dwelling in the city of Susa, a great man, serving in the court of the king.
[4] He was one of the captives whom Nebuchadnezzar king of Babylon had brought from Jerusalem with Jeconiah king of Judea. And this was his dream:
[5] Behold, noise and confusion, thunders and earthquake, tumult upon the earth!
[6] And behold, two great dragons came forward, both ready to fight, and they roared terribly.
[7] And at their roaring every nation prepared for war, to fight against the nation of the righteous.
[8] And behold, a day of darkness and gloom, tribulation and distress, affliction and great tumult upon the earth!
[9] And the whole righteous nation was troubled; they feared the evils that threatened them, and were ready to perish.
[10] Then they cried to God; and from their cry, as though from a tiny spring, there came a great river, with abundant water; [11] light came, and the sun rose, and the lowly were exalted and consumed those held in honor.
[12] Mordecai saw in this dream what God had determined to do, and after he awoke he had it on his mind and sought all day to understand it in every detail.

AddEsth.12

[1] Now Mordecai took his rest in the courtyard with Gabatha and Tharra, the two eunuchs of the king who kept watch in the courtyard.
[2] He overheard their conversation and inquired into their purposes, and learned that they were preparing to lay hands upon Artaxerxes the king; and he informed the king concerning them.
[3] Then the king examined the two eunuchs, and when they confessed they

were led to execution.

[4] The king made a permanent record of these things, and Mordecai wrote an account of them.

[5] And the king ordered Mordecai to serve in the court and rewarded him for these things.

[6] But Haman, the son of Hammedatha, a Bougaean, was in great honor with the king, and he sought to injure Mordecai and his people because of the two eunuchs of the king.

AddEsth.13

[1] This is a copy of the letter: "The Great King, Artaxerxes, to the rulers of the hundred and twenty-seven provinces from India to Ethiopia and to the governors under them, writes thus:

[2] "Having become ruler of many nations and master of the whole world, not elated with presumption of authority but always acting reasonably and with kindness, I have determined to settle the lives of my subjects in lasting tranquillity and, in order to make my kingdom peaceable and open to travel throughout all its extent, to re-establish the peace which all men desire.

[3] "When I asked my counselors how this might be accomplished, Haman, who excels among us in sound judgment, and is distinguished for his unchanging good will and steadfast fidelity, and has attained the second place in the kingdom,

[4] pointed out to us that among all the nations in the world there is scattered a certain hostile people, who have laws contrary to those of every nation and continually disregard the ordinances of the kings, so that the unifying of the kingdom which we honorably intend cannot be brought about.

[5] We understand that this people, and it alone, stands constantly in opposition to all men, perversely following a strange manner of life and laws, and is ill-disposed to our government, doing all the harm they can so that our kingdom may not attain stability.

[6] "Therefore we have decreed that those indicated to you in the letters of Haman, who is in charge of affairs and is our second father, shall all, with their wives and children, be utterly destroyed by the sword of their enemies, without pity or mercy, on the fourteenth day of the twelfth month, Adar, of this present year,

[7] so that those who have long been and are now hostile may in one day go down in violence to Hades, and leave our government completely secure and untroubled hereafter."

[8] Then Mordecai prayed to the Lord, calling to remembrance all the works of the Lord. He said:

[9] "O Lord, Lord, King who rulest over all things, for the universe is in thy

power and there is no one who can oppose thee if it is thy will to save Israel.
[10] For thou hast made heaven and earth and every wonderful thing under heaven,
[11] and thou art Lord of all, and there is no one who can resist thee, who art the Lord.
[12] Thou knowest all things; thou knowest, O Lord, that it was not in insolence or pride or for any love of glory that I did this, and refused to bow down to this proud Haman.
[13] For I would have been willing to kiss the soles of his feet, to save Israel!
[14] But I did this, that I might not set the glory of man above the glory of God, and I will not bow down to any one but to thee, who art my Lord; and I will not do these things in pride.
[15] And now, O Lord God and King, God of Abraham, spare thy people; for the eyes of our foes are upon us to annihilate us, and they desire to destroy the inheritance that has been your from the beginning.
[16] Do not neglect thy portion, which thou didst redeem for thyself out of the land of Egypt.
[17] Hear my prayer, and have mercy upon thy inheritance turn our mourning into feasting, that we may live and sing praise to thy name, O Lord; do not destroy the mouth of those who praise thee."
[18] And all Israel cried out mightily, for their death was before their eyes.

AddEsth.14

[1] And Esther the queen, seized with deathly anxiety, fled to the Lord;
[2] she took off her splendid apparel and put on the garments of distress and mourning, and instead of costly perfumes she covered her head with ashes and dung, and she utterly humbled her body, and every part that she loved to adorn she covered with her tangled hair.
[3] And she prayed to the Lord God of Israel, and said: Lord, thou only art our King; help me, who am alone and have no helper but thee,
[4] for my danger is in my hand.
[5] Ever since I was born I have heard in the tribe of my family that thou, O Lord, didst take Israel out of all the nations, and our fathers from among all their ancestors, for an everlasting inheritance, and that thou didst do for them all that thou didst promise.
[6] And now we have sinned before thee, and thou hast given us into the hands of our enemies,
[7] because we glorified their gods. Thou art righteous, O Lord!
[8] And now they are not satisfied that we are in bitter slavery, but they have covenanted with their idols
[9] to abolish what thy mouth has ordained and to destroy thy inheritance,

to stop the mouths of those who praise thee and to quench thy altar and the glory of thy house,

[10] to open the mouths of the nations for the praise of vain idols, and to magnify for ever a mortal king.

[11] O Lord, do not surrender thy scepter to what has no being; and do not let them mock at our downfall; but turn their plan against themselves, and make an example of the man who began this against us.

[12] Remember, O Lord; make thyself known in this time of our affliction, and give me courage, O King of the gods and Master of all dominion!

[13] Put eloquent speech in my mouth before the lion, and turn his heart to hate the man who is fighting against us, so that there may be an end of him and those who agree with him.

[14] But save us by thy hand, and help me, who am alone and have no helper but thee, O Lord.

[15] Thou hast knowledge of all things; and thou knowest that I hate the splendor of the wicked and abhor the bed of the uncircumcised and of any alien.

[16] Thou knowest my necessity -- that I abhor the sign of my proud position, which is upon my head on the days when I appear in public. I abhor it like a menstruous rag, and I do not wear it on the days when I am at leisure.

[17] And thy servant has not eaten at Haman's table, and I have not honored the king's feast or drunk the wine of the libations.

[18] Your servant has had no joy since the day that I was brought here until now, except in thee, O Lord God of Abraham.

[19] O God, whose might is over all, hear the voice of the despairing, and save us from the hands of evildoers. And save me from my fear!"

AddEsth.15

[1] On the third day, when she ended her prayer, she took off the garments in which she had worshiped, and arrayed herself in splendid attire.

[2] Then, majestically adorned, after invoking the aid of the all-seeing God and Savior, she took her two maids with her,

[3] leaning daintily on one,

[4] while the other followed carrying her train.

[5] She was radiant with perfect beauty, and she looked happy, as if beloved, but her heart was frozen with fear.

[6] When she had gone through all the doors, she stood before the king. He was seated on his royal throne, clothed in the full array of his majesty, all covered with gold and precious stones. And he was most terrifying.

[7] Lifting his face, flushed with splendor, he looked at her in fierce anger.

And the queen faltered, and turned pale and faint, and collapsed upon the head of the maid who went before her.

[8] Then God changed the spirit of the king to gentleness, and in alarm he sprang from his throne and took her in his arms until she came to herself. And he comforted her with soothing words, and said to her,

[9] "What is it, Esther? I am your brother. Take courage;

[10] you shall not die, for our law applies only to the people. Come near."

[11] Then he raised the golden scepter and touched it to her neck;

[12] and he embraced her, and said, "Speak to me."

[13] And she said to him, "I saw you, my lord, like an angel of God and my heart was shaken with fear at your glory.

[14] For you are wonderful, my lord, and your countenance is full of grace."

[15] But as she was speaking, she fell fainting.

[16] And the king was agitated, and all his servants sought to comfort her.

AddEsth.16

[1] The following is a copy of this letter: "The Great King, Artaxerxes, to the rulers of the provinces from India to Ethiopia, one hundred and twenty-seven satrapies, and to those who are loyal to our government, greeting.

[2] "The more often they are honored by the too great kindness of their benefactors, the more proud do many men become.

[3] They not only seek to injure our subjects, but in their inability to stand prosperity they even undertake to scheme against their own benefactors.

[4] They not only take away thankfulness from among men, but, carried away by the boasts of those who know nothing of goodness, they suppose that they will escape the evil-hating justice of God, who always sees everything.

[5] And often many of those who are set in places of authority have been made in part responsible for the shedding of innocent blood, and have been involved in irremediable calamities, by the persuasion of friends who have been entrusted with the administration of public affairs,

[6] when these men by the false trickery of their evil natures beguile the sincere good will of their sovereigns.

[7] "What has been wickedly accomplished through the pestilent behavior of those who exercise authority unworthily, can be seen not so much from the more ancient records which we hand on as from investigation of matters close at hand.

[8] For the future we will take care to render our kingdom quiet and peaceable for all men,

[9] by changing our methods and always judging what comes before our

eyes with more equitable consideration.

[10] For Haman, the son of Hammedatha, a Macedonian (really an alien to the Persian blood, and quite devoid of our kindliness), having become our guest,

[11] so far enjoyed the good will that we have for every nation that he was called our father and was continually bowed down to by all as the person second to the royal throne.

[12] But, unable to restrain his arrogance, he undertook to deprive us of our kingdom and our life,

[13] and with intricate craft and deceit asked for the destruction of Mordecai, our savior and perpetual benefactor, and of Esther, the blameless partner of our kingdom, together with their whole nation.

[14] He thought that in this way he would find us undefended and would transfer the kingdom of the Persians to the Macedonians.

[15] "But we find that the Jews, who were consigned to annihilation by this thrice accursed man, are not evildoers but are governed by most righteous laws

[16] and are sons of the Most High, the most mighty living God, who has directed the kingdom both for us and for our fathers in the most excellent order.

[17] "You will therefore do well not to put in execution the letters sent by Haman the son of Hammedatha,

[18] because the man himself who did these things has been hanged at the gate of Susa, with all his household. For God, who rules over all things, has speedily inflicted on him the punishment he deserved.

[19] "Therefore post a copy of this letter publicly in every place, and permit the Jews to live under their own laws.

[20] And give them reinforcements, so that on the thirteenth day of the twelfth month, Adar, on that very day they may defend themselves against those who attack them at the time of their affliction.

[21] For God, who rules over all things, has made this day to be a joy to his chosen people instead of a day of destruction for them.

[22] "Therefore you shall observe this with all good cheer as a notable day among your commemorative festivals,

[23] so that both now and hereafter it may mean salvation for us and the loyal Persians, but that for those who plot against us it may be a reminder of destruction.

[24] "Every city and country, without exception, which does not act accordingly, shall be destroyed in wrath with spear and fire. It shall be made not only impassable for men, but also most hateful for all time to beasts and birds."

AddEsth.10

[1] And Mordecai said, "These things have come from God.

[2] For I remember the dream that I had concerning these matters, and none of them has failed to be fulfilled.

[3] The tiny spring which became a river, and there was light and the sun and abundant water -- the river is Esther, whom the king married and made queen.

[4] The two dragons are Haman and myself.

[5] The nations are those that gathered to destroy the name of the Jews.

[6] And my nation, this is Israel, who cried out to God and were saved. The Lord has saved his people; the Lord has delivered us from all these evils; God has done great signs and wonders, which have not occurred among the nations.

[7] For this purpose he made two lots, one for the people of God and one for all the nations.

[8] And these two lots came to the hour and moment and day of decision before God and among all the nations.

[9] And God remembered his people and vindicated his inheritance.

[10] So they will observe these days in the month of Adar, on the fourteenth and fifteenth of that month, with an assembly and joy and gladness before God, from generation to generation for ever among his people Israel."

AddEsth.11

[1] In the fourth year of the reign of Ptolemy and Cleopatra, Dositheus, who said that he was a priest and a Levite, and Ptolemy his son brought to Egypt the preceeding Letter of Purim, which they said was genuine and had been translated by Lysimachus the son of Ptolemy, one of the residents of Jerusalem.

Tobit

Tob.1

[1] The book of the acts of Tobit the son of Tobiel, son of Ananiel, son of Aduel, son of Gabael, of the descendants of Asiel and the tribe of Naphtali,
[2] who in the days of Shalmaneser, king of the Assyrians, was taken into captivity from Thisbe, which is to the south of Kedesh Naphtali in Galilee above Asher.
[3] I, Tobit, walked in the ways of truth and righteousness all the days of my life, and I performed many acts of charity to my brethren and countrymen who went with me into the land of the Assyrians, to Nineveh.
[4] Now when I was in my own country, in the land of Israel, while I was still a young man, the whole tribe of Naphtali my forefather deserted the house of Jerusalem. This was the place which had been chosen from among all the tribes of Israel, where all the tribes should sacrifice and where the temple of the dwelling of the Most High was consecrated and established for all generations for ever.
[5] All the tribes that joined in apostasy used to sacrifice to the calf Baal, and so did the house of Naphtali my forefather.
[6] But I alone went often to Jerusalem for the feasts, as it is ordained for all Israel by an everlasting decree. Taking the first fruits and the tithes of my produce and the first shearings, I would give these to the priests, the sons of Aaron, at the altar.
[7] Of all my produce I would give a tenth to the sons of Levi who ministered at Jerusalem; a second tenth I would sell, and I would go and spend the proceeds each year at Jerusalem;
[8] the third tenth I would give to those to whom it was my duty, as Deborah my father's mother had commanded me, for I was left an orphan by my father.
[9] When I became a man I married Anna, a member of our family, and by her I became the father of Tobias.
[10] Now when I was carried away captive to Nineveh, all my brethren and my relatives ate the food of the Gentiles;
[11] but I kept myself from eating it,
[12] because I remembered God with all my heart.
[13] Then the Most High gave me favor and good appearance in the sight of Shalmaneser, and I was his buyer of provisions.
[14] So I used to go into Media, and once at Rages in Media I left ten talents of silver in trust with Gabael, the brother of Gabrias.
[15] But when Shalmaneser died, Sennacherib his son reigned in his place; and under him the highways were unsafe, so that I could no longer go into

Media.

[16] In the days of Shalmaneser I performed many acts of charity to my brethren.

[17] I would give my bread to the hungry and my clothing to the naked; and if I saw any one of my people dead and thrown out behind the wall of Nineveh, I would bury him.

[18] And if Sennacherib the king put to death any who came fleeing from Judea, I buried them secretly. For in his anger he put many to death. When the bodies were sought by the king, they were not found.

[19] Then one of the men of Nineveh went and informed the king about me, that I was burying them; so I hid myself. When I learned that I was being searched for, to be put to death, I left home in fear.

[20] Then all my property was confiscated and nothing was left to me except my wife Anna and my son Tobias.

[21] But not fifty days passed before two of Sennacherib's sons killed him, and they fled to the mountains of Ararat. Then Esarhaddon, his son, reigned in his place; and he appointed Ahikar, the son of my brother Anael, over all the accounts of his kingdom and over the entire administration.

[22] Ahikar interceded for me, and I returned to Nineveh. Now Ahikar was cupbearer, keeper of the signet, and in charge of administration of the accounts, for Esarhaddon had appointed him second to himself. He was my nephew.

Tob.2

[1] When I arrived home and my wife Anna and my son Tobias were restored to me, at the feast of Pentecost, which is the sacred festival of the seven weeks, a good dinner was prepared for me and I sat down to eat.

[2] Upon seeing the abundance of food I said to my son, "Go and bring whatever poor man of our brethren you may find who is mindful of the Lord, and I will wait for you."

[3] But he came back and said, "Father, one of our people has been strangled and thrown into the market place."

[4] So before I tasted anything I sprang up and removed the body to a place of shelter until sunset.

[5] And when I returned I washed myself and ate my food in sorrow.

[6] Then I remembered the prophecy of Amos, how he said, "Your feasts shall be turned into mourning, and all your festivities into lamentation." And I wept.

[7] When the sun had set I went and dug a grave and buried the body.

[8] And my neighbors laughed at me and said, "He is no longer afraid that

he will be put to death for doing this; he once ran away, and here he is burying the dead again!"

[9] On the same night I returned from burying him, and because I was defiled I slept by the wall of the courtyard, and my face was uncovered.

[10] I did not know that there were sparrows on the wall and their fresh droppings fell into my open eyes and white films formed on my eyes. I went to physicians, but they did not help me. Ahikar, however, took care of me until he went to Elymais.

[11] Then my wife Anna earned money at women's work.

[12] She used to send the product to the owners. Once when they paid her wages, they also gave her a kid;

[13] and when she returned to me it began to bleat. So I said to her, "Where did you get the kid? It is not stolen, is it? Return it to the owners; for it is not right to eat what is stolen."

[14] And she said, "It was given to me as a gift in addition to my wages." But I did not believe her, and told her to return it to the owners; and I blushed for her. Then she replied to me, "Where are your charities and your righteous deeds? You seem to know everything!"

Tob.3

[1] Then in my grief I wept, and I prayed in anguish, saying,

[2] "Righteous art thou, O Lord; all thy deeds and all they ways are mercy and truth, and thou do render true and righteous judgment for ever.

[3] Remember me and look favorably upon me; do not punish me for my sins and for my unwitting offences and those which my fathers committed before thee.

[4] For they disobeyed thy commandments, and thou gavest us over to plunder, captivity, and death; thou madest us a byword of reproach in all the nations among which we have been dispersed.

[5] And now thy many judgments are true in exacting penalty from me for my sins and those of my fathers, because we did not keep thy commandments. For we did not walk in truth before thee.

[6] And now deal with me according to thy pleasure; command my spirit to be taken up, that I may depart and become dust. For it is better for me to die than to live, because I have heard false reproaches, and great is the sorrow within me. Command that I now be released from my distress to go to the eternal abode; do not turn thy face away from me."

[7] On the same day, at Ecbatana in Media, it also happened that Sarah, the daughter of Raguel, was reproached by her father's maids,

[8] because she had been given to seven husbands, and the evil demon Asmodeus had slain each of them before he had been with her as his wife.

So the maids said to her, "Do you not know that you strangle your husbands? You already have had seven and have had no benefit from any of them.

[9] Why do you beat us? If they are dead, go with them! May we never see a son or daughter of yours!"

[10] When she heard these things she was deeply grieved, even to the thought of hanging herself. But she said, "I am the only child of my father; if I do this, it will be a disgrace to him, and I shall bring his old age down in sorrow to the grave.

[11] So she prayed by her window and said, "Blessed art thou, O Lord my God, and blessed is thy holy and honored name for ever. May all thy works praise thee for ever.

[12] And now, O Lord, I have turned my eyes and my face toward thee.

[13] Command that I be released from the earth and that I hear reproach no more.

[14] Thou knowest, O Lord, that I am innocent of any sin with man,

[15] and that I did not stain my name or the name of my father in the land of my captivity. I am my father's only child, and he has no child to be his heir, no near kinsman or kinsman's son for whom I should keep myself as wife. Already seven husbands of mine are dead. Why should I live? But if it be not pleasing to thee to take my life, command that respect be shown to me and pity be taken upon me, and that I hear reproach no more."

[16] The prayer of both was heard in the presence of the glory of the great God.

[17] And Raphael was sent to heal the two of them: to scale away the white films of Tobit's eyes; to give Sarah the daughter of Raguel in marriage to Tobias the son of Tobit, and to bind Asmodeus the evil demon, because Tobias was entitled to possess her. At that very moment Tobit returned and entered his house and Sarah the daughter of Raguel came down from her upper room.

Tob.4

[1] On that day Tobit remembered the money which he had left in trust with Gabael at Rages in Media, and he said to himself;

[2] "I have asked for death. Why do I not call my son Tobias so that I may explain to him about the money before I die?"

[3] So he called him and said, "My son, when I die, bury me, and do not neglect your mother. Honor her all the days of your life; do what is pleasing to her, and do not grieve her.

[4] Remember, my son, that she faced many dangers for you while you were

yet unborn. When she dies bury her beside me in the same grave.

[5] "Remember the Lord our God all your days, my son, and refuse to sin or to transgress his commandments. Live uprightly all the days of your life, and do not walk in the ways of wrongdoing.

[6] For if you do what is true, your ways will prosper through your deeds.

[7] Give alms from your possessions to all who live uprightly, and do not let your eye begrudge the gift when you make it. Do not turn your face away from any poor man, and the face of God will not be turned away from you.

[8] If you have many possessions, make your gift from them in proportion; if few, do not be afraid to give according to the little you have.

[9] So you will be laying up a good treasure for yourself against the day of necessity.

[10] For charity delivers from death and keeps you from entering the darkness;

[11] and for all who practice it charity is an excellent offering in the presence of the Most High.

[12] "Beware, my son, of all immorality. First of all take a wife from among the descendants of your fathers and do not marry a foreign woman, who is not of your father's tribe; for we are the sons of the prophets. Remember, my son, that Noah, Abraham, Isaac, and Jacob, our fathers of old, all took wives from among their brethren. They were blessed in their children, and their posterity will inherit the land.

[13] So now, my son, love your brethren, and in your heart do not disdain your brethren and the sons and daughters of your people by refusing to take a wife for yourself from among them. For in pride there is ruin and great confusion; and in shiftlessness there is loss and great want, because shiftlessness is the mother of famine.

[14] Do not hold over till the next day the wages of any man who works for you, but pay him at once; and if you serve God you will receive payment. "Watch yourself, my son, in everything you do, and be disciplined in all your conduct.

[15] And what you hate, do not do to any one. Do not drink wine to excess or let drunkenness go with you on your way.

[16] Give of your bread to the hungry, and of your clothing to the naked. Give all your surplus to charity, and do not let your eye begrudge the gift when you made it.

[17] Place your bread on the grave of the righteous, but give none to sinners.

[18] Seek advice from every wise man, and do not despise any useful counsel.

[19] Bless the Lord God on every occasion; ask him that your ways may be made straight and that all your paths and plans may prosper. For none of the nations has understanding; but the Lord himself gives all good things, and according to his will he humbles whomever he wishes. "So, my son, remember my commands, and do not let them be blotted out of your mind.

[20] And now let me explain to you about the ten talents of silver which I left in trust with Gabael the son of Gabrias at Rages in Media.
[21] Do not be afraid, my son, because we have become poor. You have great wealth if you fear God and refrain from every sin and do what is pleasing in his sight."

Tob.5

[1] Then Tobias answered him, "Father, I will do everything that you have commanded me;
[2] but how can I obtain the money when I do not know the man?"
[3] Then Tobit gave him the receipt, and said to him, "Find a man to go with you and I will pay him wages as long as I live; and go and get the money."
[4] So he went to look for a man; and he found Raphael, who was an angel,
[5] but Tobias did not know it. Tobias said to him, "Can you go with me to Rages in Media? Are you acquainted with that region?"
[6] The angel replied, "I will go with you; I am familiar with the way, and I have stayed with our brother Gabael."
[7] Then Tobias said to him, "Wait for me, and I shall tell my father."
[8] And he said to him, "Go, and do not delay." So he went in and said to his father, "I have found some one to go with me." He said, "Call him to me, so that I may learn to what tribe he belongs, and whether he is a reliable man to go with you."
[9] So Tobias invited him in; he entered and they greeted each other.
[10] Then Tobit said to him, "My brother, to what tribe and family do you belong? Tell me. "
[11] But he answered, "Are you looking for a tribe and a family or for a man whom you will pay to go with your son?" And Tobit said to him, "I should like to know, my brother, your people and your name."
[12] He replied, "I am Azarias the son of the great Ananias, one of your relatives."
[13] Then Tobit said to him, "You are welcome, my brother. Do not be angry with me because I tried to learn your tribe and family. You are a relative of mine, of a good and noble lineage. For I used to know Ananias and Jathan, the sons of the great Shemaiah, when we went together to Jerusalem to worship and offered the first-born of our flocks and the tithes of our produce. They did not go astray in the error of our brethren. My brother, you come of good stock.
[14] But tell me, what wages am I to pay you -- a drachma a day, and expenses for yourself as for my son?
[15] And besides, I will add to your wages if you both return safe and

sound." So they agreed to these terms.

[16] Then he said to Tobias, "Get ready for the journey, and good success to you both." So his son made the preparations for the journey. And his father said to him, "Go with this man; God who dwells in heaven will prosper your way, and may his angel attend you." So they both went out and departed, and the young man's dog was with them.

[17] But Anna, his mother, began to weep, and said to Tobit, "Why have you sent our child away? Is he not the staff of our hands as he goes in and out before us?

[18] Do not add money to money, but consider it as rubbish as compared to our child.

[19] For the life that is given to us by the Lord is enough for us."

[20] And Tobit said to her, "Do not worry, my sister; he will return safe and sound, and your eyes will see him.

[21] For a good angel will go with him; his journey will be successful, and he will come back safe and sound." Tob 5:[22] So she stopped weeping.

Tob.6

[1] Now as they proceeded on their way they came at evening to the Tigris river and camped there.

[2] Then the young man went down to wash himself. A fish leaped up from the river and would have swallowed the young man;

[3] and the angel said to him, "Catch the fish." So the young man seized the fish and threw it up on the land.

[4] Then the angel said to him, "Cut open the fish and take the heart and liver and gall and put them away safely."

[5] So the young man did as the angel told him; and they roasted and ate the fish. And they both continued on their way until they came near to Ecbatana.

[6] Then the young man said to the angel, "Brother Azarias, of what use is the liver and heart and gall of the fish?"

[7] He replied, "As for the heart and liver, if a demon or evil spirit gives trouble to any one, you make a smoke from these before the man or woman, and that person will never be troubled again.

[8] And as for the gall, anoint with it a man who has white films in his eyes, and he will be cured."

[9] When they approached Ecbatana,

[10] the angel said to the young man, "Brother, today we shall stay with Raguel. He is your relative, and he has an only daughter named Sarah. I will suggest that she be given to you in marriage,

[11] because you are entitled to her and to her inheritance, for you are her

only eligible kinsman.

[12] The girl is also beautiful and sensible. Now listen to my plan. I will speak to her father, and as soon as we return from Rages we will celebrate the marriage. For I know that Raguel, according to the law of Moses, cannot give her to another man without incurring the penalty of death, because you rather than any other man are entitled to the inheritance."

[13] Then the young man said to the angel, "Brother Azarias, I have heard that the girl has been given to seven husbands and that each died in the bridal chamber.

[14] Now I am the only son my father has, and I am afraid that if I go in I will die as those before me did, for a demon is in love with her, and he harms no one except those who approach her. So now I fear that I may die and bring the lives of my father and mother to the grave in sorrow on my account. And they have no other son to bury them."

[15] But the angel said to him, "Do you not remember the words with which your father commanded you to take a wife from among your own people? Now listen to me, brother, for she will become your wife; and do not worry about the demon, for this very night she will be given to you in marriage.

[16] When you enter the bridal chamber, you shall take live ashes of incense and lay upon them some of the heart and liver of the fish so as to make a smoke.

[17] Then the demon will smell it and flee away, and will never again return. And when you approach her, rise up, both of you, and cry out to the merciful God, and he will save you and have mercy on you. Do not be afraid, for she was destined for you from eternity. You will save her, and she will go with you, and I suppose that you will have children by her." When Tobias heard these things, he fell in love with her and yearned deeply for her.

Tob.7

[1] When they reached Ecbatana and arrived at the house of Raguel, Sarah met them and greeted them. They returned her greeting, and she brought them into the house.

[2] Then Raguel said to his wife Edna, "How much the young man resembles my cousin Tobit!"

[3] And Raguel asked them, "Where are you from, brethren?" They answered him, "We belong to the sons of Naphtali, who are captives in Nineveh."

[4] So he said to them, "Do you know our brother Tobit?" And they said, "Yes, we do." And he asked them, "Is he in good health?"

[5] They replied, "He is alive and in good health." And Tobias said, "He is my father."

[6] Then Raguel sprang up and kissed him and wept.

[7] And he blessed him and exclaimed, "Son of that good and noble man!" When he heard that Tobit had lost his sight, he was stricken with grief and wept.

[8] And his wife Edna and his daughter Sarah wept. They received them very warmly; and they killed a ram from the flock and set large servings of food before them. Then Tobias said to Raphael, "Brother Azarias, speak of those things which you talked about on the journey, and let the matter be settled."

[9] So he communicated the proposal to Raguel. And Raguel said to Tobias, "Eat, drink, and be merry;

[10] for it is your right to take my child. But let me explain the true situation to you.

[11] I have given my daughter to seven husbands, and when each came to her he died in the night. But for the present be merry." And Tobias said, "I will eat nothing here until you make a binding agreement with me."

[12] So Raguel said, "Take her right now, in accordance with the law. You are her relative, and she is yours. The merciful God will guide you both for the best."

[13] Then he called his daughter Sarah, and taking her by the hand he gave her to Tobias to be his wife, saying, "Here she is; take her according to the law of Moses, and take her with you to your father." And he blessed them.

[14] Next he called his wife Edna, and took a scroll and wrote out the contract; and they set their seals to it.

[15] Then they began to eat.

[16] And Raguel called his wife Edna and said to her, "Sister, make up the other room, and take her into it."

[17] so she did as he said, and took her there; and the girl began to weep. But the mother comforted her daughter in her tears, and said to her,

[18] "Be brave, my child; the Lord of heaven and earth grant you joy in place of this sorrow of yours. Be brave, my daughter."

Tob.8

[1] When they had finished eating, they escorted Tobias in to her.

[2] As he went he remembered the words of Raphael, and he took the live ashes of incense and put the heart and liver of the fish upon them and made a smoke.

[3] And when the demon smelled the odor he fled to the remotest parts of Egypt, and the angel bound him.

[4] When the door was shut and the two were alone, Tobias got up from the bed and said, "Sister, get up, and let us pray that the Lord may have mercy upon us."

[5] And Tobias began to pray, "Blessed art thou, O God of our fathers, and blessed be thy holy and glorious name for ever. Let the heavens and all thy creatures bless thee.

[6] Thou madest Adam and gavest him Eve his wife as a helper and support. From them the race of mankind has sprung. Thou didst say, `It is not good that the man should be alone; let us make a helper for him like himself.'

[7] And now, O Lord, I am not taking this sister of mine because of lust, but with sincerity. Grant that I may find mercy and may grow old together with her."

[8] And she said with him, "Amen."

[9] Then they both went to sleep for the night. But Raguel arose and went and dug a grave,

[10] with the thought, "Perhaps he too will die."

[11] Then Raguel went into his house

[12] and said to his wife Edna, "Send one of the maids to see whether he is alive; and if he is not, let us bury him without any one knowing about it."

[13] So the maid opened the door and went in, and found them both asleep.

[14] And she came out and told them that he was alive.

[15] Then Raguel blessed God and said, "Blessed art thou, O God, with every pure and holy blessing. Let thy saints and all thy creatures bless thee; let all thy angels and thy chosen people bless thee for ever.

[16] Blessed art thou, because thou hast made me glad. It has not happened to me as I expected; but thou hast treated us according to thy great mercy.

[17] Blessed art thou, because thou hast had compassion on two only children. Show them mercy, O Lord; and bring their lives to fulfilment in health and happiness and mercy."

[18] Then he ordered his servants to fill in the grave.

[19] After this he gave a wedding feast for them which lasted fourteen days.

[20] And before the days of the feast were over, Raguel declared by oath to Tobias that he should not leave until the fourteen days of the wedding feast were ended,

[21] that then he should take half of Raguel's property and return in safety to his father, and that the rest would be his "when my wife and I die."

Tob.9

[1] Then Tobias called Raphael and said to him,

[2] "Brother Azarias, take a servant and two camels with you and go to Gabael at Rages in Media and get the money for me; and bring him to the wedding feast.

[3] For Raguel has sworn that I should not leave;

[4] but my father is counting the days, and if I delay long he will be greatly distressed."

[5] So Raphael made the journey and stayed over night with Gabael. He gave him the receipt, and Gabael brought out the money bags with their seals intact and gave them to him.

[6] In the morning they both got up early and came to the wedding feast. And Gabael blessed Tobias and his wife.

Tob.10

[1] Now his father Tobit was counting each day, and when the days for the journey had expired and they did not arrive,

[2] he said, "Is it possible that he has been detained? Or is it possible that Gabael has died and there is no one to give him the money?"

[3] And he was greatly distressed.

[4] And his wife said to him, "The lad has perished; his long delay proves it." Then she began to mourn for him, and said,

[5] "Am I not distressed, my child, that I let you go, you who are the light of my eyes?"

[6] But Tobit said to her, "Be still and stop worrying; he is well."

[7] And she answered him, "Be still and stop deceiving me; my child has perished." And she went out every day to the road by which they had left; she ate nothing in the daytime, and throughout the nights she never stopped mourning for her son Tobias, until the fourteen days of the wedding feast had expired which Raguel had sworn that he should spend there. At that time Tobias said to Raguel, "Send me back, for my father and mother have given up hope of ever seeing me again."

[8] But his father-in-law said to him, "Stay with me, and I will send messengers to your father, and they will inform him how things are with you."

[9] Tobias replied, "No, send me back to my father."

[10] So Raguel arose and gave him his wife Sarah and half of his property in slaves, cattle, and money.

[11] And when he had blessed them he sent them away, saying, "The God of heaven will prosper you, my children, before I die."

[12] He said also to his daughter, "Honor your father-in-law and your mother-in-law; they are now your parents. Let me hear a good report of you. " And he kissed her. And Edna said to Tobias, "The Lord of heaven

bring you back safely, dear brother, and grant me to see your children by my daughter Sarah, that I may rejoice before the Lord. See, I am entrusting my daughter to you; do nothing to grieve her."

Tob.11

[1] After this Tobias went on his way, praising God because he had made his journey a success. And he blessed Raguel and his wife Edna. So he continued on his way until they came near to Nineveh.
[2] Then Raphael said to Tobias, "Are you not aware, brother, of how you left your father?
[3] Let us run ahead of your wife and prepare the house.
[4] And take the gall of the fish with you." So they went their way, and the dog went along behind them.
[5] Now Anna sat looking intently down the road for her son.
[6] And she caught sight of him coming, and said to his father, "Behold, your son is coming, and so is the man who went with him!"
[7] Raphael said, "I know, Tobias, that your father will open his eyes.
[8] You therefore must anoint his eyes with the gall; and when they smart he will rub them, and will cause the white films to fall away, and he will see you."
[9] Then Anna ran to meet them, and embraced her son, and said to him, "I have seen you, my child; now I am ready to die." And they both wept.
[10] Tobit started toward the door, and stumbled. But his son ran to him
[11] and took hold of his father, and he sprinkled the gall upon his father's eyes, saying, "Be of good cheer, father."
[12] And when his eyes began to smart he rubbed them,
[13] and the white films scaled off from the corners of his eyes.
[14] Then he saw his son and embraced him, and he wept and said, "Blessed art thou, O God, and blessed is thy name for ever, and blessed are all thy holy angels.
[15] For thou hast afflicted me, but thou hast had mercy upon me; here I see my son Tobias!" And his son went in rejoicing, and he reported to his father the great things that had happened to him in Media.
[16] Then Tobit went out to meet his daughter-in-law at the gate of Nineveh, rejoicing and praising God. Those who saw him as he went were amazed because he could see.
[17] And Tobit gave thanks before them that God had been merciful to him. When Tobit came near to Sarah his daughter-in-law, he blessed her, saying, "Welcome, daughter! Blessed is God who has brought you to us, and blessed are your father and your mother." So there was rejoicing among all

his brethren in Nineveh.

[18] Ahikar and his nephew Nadab came,

[19] and Tobias' marriage was celebrated for seven days with great festivity.

Tob.12

[1] Tobit then called his son Tobias and said to him, "My son, see to the wages of the man who went with you; and he must also be given more."

[2] He replied, "Father, it would do me no harm to give him half of what I have brought back.

[3] For he has led me back to you safely, he cured my wife, he obtained the money for me, and he also healed you."

[4] The old man said, "He deserves it."

[5] So he called the angel and said to him, "Take half of all that you two have brought back."

[6] Then the angel called the two of them privately and said to them: "Praise God and give thanks to him; exalt him and give thanks to him in the presence of all the living for what he has done for you. It is good to praise God and to exalt his name, worthily declaring the works of God. Do not be slow to give him thanks.

[7] It is good to guard the secret of a king, but gloriously to reveal the works of God. Do good, and evil will not overtake you.

[8] Prayer is good when accompanied by fasting, almsgiving, and righteousness. A little with righteousness is better than much with wrongdoing. It is better to give alms than to treasure up gold.

[9] For almsgiving delivers from death, and it will purge away every sin. Those who perform deeds of charity and of righteousness will have fulness of life;

[10] but those who commit sin are the enemies of their own lives.

[11] "I will not conceal anything from you. I have said, `It is good to guard the secret of a king, but gloriously to reveal the works of God.'

[12] And so, when you and your daughter-in-law Sarah prayed, I brought a reminder of your prayer before the Holy One; and when you buried the dead, I was likewise present with you.

[13] When you did not hesitate to rise and leave your dinner in order to go and lay out the dead, your good deed was not hidden from me, but I was with you.

[14] So now God sent me to heal you and your daughter-in-law Sarah.

[15] I am Raphael, one of the seven holy angels who present the prayers of the saints and enter into the presence of the glory of the Holy One."

[16] They were both alarmed; and they fell upon their faces, for they were afraid.

[17] But he said to them, "Do not be afraid; you will be safe. But praise God for ever.

[18] For I did not come as a favor on my part, but by the will of our God. Therefore praise him for ever.

[19] All these days I merely appeared to you and did not eat or drink, but you were seeing a vision.

[20] And now give thanks to God, for I am ascending to him who sent me. Write in a book everything that has happened."

[21] Then they stood up; but they saw him no more.

[22] So they confessed the great and wonderful works of God, and acknowledged that the angel of the Lord had appeared to them.

Tob.13

[1] Then Tobit wrote a prayer of rejoicing, and said:
"Blessed is God who lives for ever, and blessed is his kingdom. [2] For he afflicts, and he shows mercy; he leads down to Hades, and brings up again, and there is no one who can escape his hand. [3] Acknowledge him before the nations, O sons of Israel; for he has scattered us among them. [4] Make his greatness known there, and exalt him in the presence of all the living; because he is our Lord and God, he is our Father for ever. [5] He will afflict us for our iniquities; and again he will show mercy, and will gather us from all the nations among whom you have been scattered. [6] If you turn to him with all your heart and with all your soul, to do what is true before him, then he will turn to you and will not hide his face from you. But see what he will do with you; give thanks to him with your full voice. Praise the Lord of righteousness, and exalt the King of the ages. I give him thanks in the land of my captivity, and I show his power and majesty to a nation of sinners. Turn back, you sinners, and do right before him; who knows if he will accept you and have mercy on you? [7] I exalt my God; my soul exalts the King of heaven, and will rejoice in his majesty. [8] Let all men speak, and give him thanks in Jerusalem. [9] O Jerusalem, the holy city, he will afflict you for the deeds of your sons, but again he will show mercy to the sons of the righteous. [10] Give thanks worthily to the Lord, and praise the King of the ages, that his tent may be raised for you again with joy. May he cheer those within you who are captives, and love those within you who are distressed, to all generations for ever. [11] Many nations will come from afar to the name of the Lord God, bearing gifts in their hands, gifts for the King of heaven. Generations of generations will give you joyful praise. [12] Cursed are all who hate you; blessed for ever will be all who love you. [13] Rejoice and be glad for the sons of the righteous; for they will be gathered

together, and will praise the Lord of the righteous. [14] How blessed are those who love you! They will rejoice in your peace. Blessed are those who grieved over all your afflictions; for they will rejoice for you upon seeing all your glory, and they will be made glad for ever. [15] Let my soul praise God the great King. [16] For Jerusalem will be built with sapphires and emeralds, her walls with precious stones, and her towers and battlements with pure gold. [17] The streets of Jerusalem will be paved with beryl and ruby and stones of Ophir; [18] all her lanes will cry `Hallelujah!' and will give praise, saying, `Blessed is God, who has exalted you for ever.'"

Tob.14

[1] Here Tobit ended his words of praise.

[2] He was fifty-eight years old when he lost his sight, and after eight years he regained it. He gave alms, and he continued to fear the Lord God and to praise him.

[3] When he had grown very old he called his son and grandsons, and said to him, "My son, take your sons; behold, I have grown old and am about to depart this life.

[4] Go to Media, my son, for I fully believe what Jonah the prophet said about Nineveh, that it will be overthrown. But in Media there will be peace for a time. Our brethren will be scattered over the earth from the good land, and Jerusalem will be desolate. The house of God in it will be burned down and will be in ruins for a time.

[5] But God will again have mercy on them, and bring them back into their land; and they will rebuild the house of God, though it will not be like the former one until the times of the age are completed. After this they will return from the places of their captivity, and will rebuild Jerusalem in splendor. And the house of God will be rebuilt there with a glorious building for all generations for ever, just as the prophets said of it.

[6] Then all the Gentiles will turn to fear the Lord God in truth, and will bury their idols.

[7] All the Gentiles will praise the Lord, and his people will give thanks to God, and the Lord will exalt his people. And all who love the Lord God in truth and righteousness will rejoice, showing mercy to our brethren.

[8] "So now, my son, leave Nineveh, because what the prophet Jonah said will surely happen.

[9] But keep the law and the commandments, and be merciful and just, so that it may be well with you.

[10] Bury me properly, and your mother with me. And do not live in Nineveh any longer. See, my son, what Nadab did to Ahikar who had reared him, how he brought him from light into darkness, and with what he

repaid him. But Ahikar was saved, and the other received repayment as he himself went down into the darkness. Ahikar gave alms and escaped the deathtrap which Nadab had set for him; but Nadab fell into the trap and perished.

[11] So now, my children, consider what almsgiving accomplishes and how righteousness delivers." As he said this he died in his bed. He was a hundred and fifty-eight years old; and Tobias gave him a magnificent funeral.

[12] And when Anna died he buried her with his father. Then Tobias returned with his wife and his sons to Ecbatana, to Raguel his father-in-law.

[13] He grew old with honor, and he gave his father-in-law and mother-in-law magnificent funerals. He inherited their property and that of his father Tobit.

[14] He died in Ecbatana of Media at the age of a hundred and twenty-seven years.

[15] But before he died he heard of the destruction of Nineveh, which Nebuchadnezzar and Ahasuerus had captured. Before his death he rejoiced over Nineveh.

Judith

Jdt.1

[1] In the twelfth year of the reign of Nebuchadnezzar, who ruled over the Assyrians in the great city of Nineveh, in the days of Arphaxad, who ruled over the Medes in Ecbatana --
[2] he is the king who built walls about Ecbatana with hewn stones three cubits thick and six cubits long; he made the walls seventy cubits high and fifty cubits wide;
[3] at the gates he built towers a hundred cubits high and sixty cubits wide at the foundations;
[4] and he made its gates, which were seventy cubits high and forty cubits wide, so that his armies could march out in force and his infantry form their ranks --
[5] it was in those days that King Nebuchadnezzar made war against King Arphaxad in the great plain which is on the borders of Ragae.
[6] He was joined by all the people of the hill country and all those who lived along the Euphrates and the Tigris and the Hydaspes and in the plain where Arioch ruled the Elymaeans. Many nations joined the forces of the Chaldeans.
[7] Then Nebuchadnezzar king of the Assyrians sent to all who lived in Persia and to all who lived in the west, those who lived in Cilicia and Damascus and Lebanon and Antilebanon and all who lived along the seacoast,
[8] and those among the nations of Carmel and Gilead, and Upper Galilee and the great Plain of Esdraelon,
[9] and all who were in Samaria and its surrounding towns, and beyond the Jordan as far as Jerusalem and Bethany and Chelous and Kadesh and the river of Egypt, and Tahpanhes and Raamses and the whole land of Goshen,
[10] even beyond Tanis and Memphis, and all who lived in Egypt as far as the borders of Ethiopia.
[11] But all who lived in the whole region disregarded the orders of Nebuchadnezzar king of the Assyrians, and refused to join him in the war; for they were not afraid of him, but looked upon him as only one man, and they sent back his messengers empty-handed and shamefaced.
[12] Then Nebuchadnezzar was very angry with this whole region, and swore by his throne and kingdom that he would surely take revenge on the whole territory of Cilicia and Damascus and Syria, that he would kill them by the sword, and also all the inhabitants of the land of Moab, and the people of Ammon, and all Judea, and every one in Egypt, as far as the coasts of the two seas.

[13] In the seventeenth year he led his forces against King Arphaxad, and defeated him in battle, and overthrew the whole army of Arphaxad, and all his cavalry and all his chariots.

[14] Thus he took possession of his cities, and came to Ecbatana, captured its towers, plundered its markets, and turned its beauty into shame.

[15] He captured Arphaxad in the mountains of Ragae and struck him down with hunting spears; and he utterly destroyed him, to this day.

[16] Then he returned with them to Nineveh, he and all his combined forces, a vast body of troops; and there he and his forces rested and feasted for one hundred and twenty days.

Jdt.2

[1] In the eighteenth year, on the twenty-second day of the first month, there was talk in the palace of Nebuchadnezzar king of the Assyrians about carrying out his revenge on the whole region, just as he said.

[2] He called together all his officers and all his nobles and set forth to them his secret plan and recounted fully, with his own lips, all the wickedness of the region;

[3] and it was decided that every one who had not obeyed his command should be destroyed.

[4] When he had finished setting forth his plan, Nebuchadnezzar king of the Assyrians called Holofernes, the chief general of his army, second only to himself, and said to him,

[5] "Thus says the Great King, the lord of the whole earth: When you leave my presence, take with you men confident in their strength, to the number of one hundred and twenty thousand foot soldiers and twelve thousand cavalry.

[6] Go and attack the whole west country, because they disobeyed my orders.

[7] Tell them to prepare earth and water, for I am coming against them in my anger, and will cover the whole face of the earth with the feet of my armies, and will hand them over to be plundered by my troops,

[8] till their wounded shall fill their valleys, and every brook and river shall be filled with their dead, and overflow;

[9] and I will lead them away captive to the ends of the whole earth.

[10] You shall go and seize all their territory for me in advance. They will yield themselves to you, and you shall hold them for me till the day of their punishment.

[11] But if they refuse, your eye shall not spare and you shall hand them over to slaughter and plunder throughout your whole region.

[12] For as I live, and by the power of my kingdom, what I have spoken my hand will execute.

[13] And you -- take care not to transgress any of your sovereign's commands, but be sure to carry them out just as I have ordered you; and do not delay about it."

[14] So Holofernes left the presence of his master, and called together all the commanders, generals, and officers of the Assyrian army,

[15] and mustered the picked troops by divisions as his lord had ordered him to do, one hundred and twenty thousand of them, together with twelve thousand archers on horseback,

[16] and he organized them as a great army is marshaled for a campaign.

[17] He collected a vast number of camels and asses and mules for transport, and innumerable sheep and oxen and goats for provision;

[18] also plenty of food for every man, and a huge amount of gold and silver from the royal palace.

[19] So he set out with his whole army, to go ahead of King Nebuchadnezzar and to cover the whole face of the earth to the west with their chariots and horsemen and picked troops of infantry.

[20] Along with them went a mixed crowd like a swarm of locusts, like the dust of the earth -- a multitude that could not be counted.

[21] They marched for three days from Nineveh to the plain of Bectileth, and camped opposite Bectileth near the mountain which is to the north of Upper Cilicia.

[22] From there Holofernes took his whole army, his infantry, cavalry, and chariots, and went up into the hill country

[23] and ravaged Put and Lud, and plundered all the people of Rassis and the Ishmaelites who lived along the desert, south of the country of the Chelleans.

[24] Then he followed the Euphrates and passed through Mesopotamia and destroyed all the hilltop cities along the brook Abron, as far as the sea.

[25] He also seized the territory of Cilicia, and killed every one who resisted him, and came to the southern borders of Japheth, fronting toward Arabia.

[26] He surrounded all the Midianites, and burned their tents and plundered their sheepfolds.

[27] Then he went down into the plain of Damascus during the wheat harvest, and burned all their fields and destroyed their flocks and herds and sacked their cities and ravaged their lands and put to death all their young men with the edge of the sword.

[28] So fear and terror of him fell upon all the people who lived along the seacoast, at Sidon and Tyre, and those who lived in Sur and Ocina and all who lived in Jamnia. Those who lived in Azotus and Ascalon feared him exceedingly.

Jdt.3

[1] So they sent messengers to sue for peace, and said,
[2] "Behold, we the servants of Nebuchadnezzar, the Great King, lie prostrate before you. Do with us whatever you will.
[3] Behold, our buildings, and all our land, and all our wheat fields, and our flocks and herds, and all our sheepfolds with their tents, lie before you; do with them whatever you please.
[4] Our cities also and their inhabitants are your slaves; come and deal with them in any way that seems good to you."
[5] The men came to Holofernes and told him all this.
[6] Then he went down to the seacoast with his army and stationed garrisons in the hilltop cities and took picked men from them as his allies.
[7] And these people and all in the country round about welcomed him with garlands and dances and tambourines.
[8] And he demolished all their shrines and cut down their sacred groves; for it had been given to him to destroy all the gods of the land, so that all nations should worship Nebuchadnezzar only, and all their tongues and tribes should call upon him as god.
[9] Then he came to the edge of Esdraelon, near Dothan, fronting the great ridge of Judea;
[10] here he camped between Geba and Scythopolis, and remained for a whole month in order to assemble all the supplies for his army.

Jdt.4

[1] By this time the people of Israel living in Judea heard of everything that Holofernes, the general of Nebuchadnezzar the king of the Assyrians, had done to the nations, and how he had plundered and destroyed all their temples;
[2] they were therefore very greatly terrified at his approach, and were alarmed both for Jerusalem and for the temple of the Lord their God.
[3] For they had only recently returned from the captivity, and all the people of Judea were newly gathered together, and the sacred vessels and the altar and the temple had been consecrated after their profanation.
[4] So they sent to every district of Samaria, and to Kona and Beth-horon and Belmain and Jericho and to Choba and Aesora and the valley of Salem,
[5] and immediately seized all the high hilltops and fortified the villages on them and stored up food in preparation for war -- since their fields had recently been harvested.

[6] And Joakim, the high priest, who was in Jerusalem at the time, wrote to the people of Bethulia and Betomesthaim, which faces Esdraelon opposite the plain near Dothan,

[7] ordering them to seize the passes up into the hills, since by them Judea could be invaded, and it was easy to stop any who tried to enter, for the approach was narrow, only wide enough for two men at the most.

[8] So the Israelites did as Joakim the high priest and the senate of the whole people of Israel, in session at Jerusalem, had given order.

[9] And every man of Israel cried out to God with great fervor, and they humbled themselves with much fasting.

[10] They and their wives and their children and their cattle and every resident alien and hired laborer and purchased slave -- they all girded themselves with sackcloth.

[11] And all the men and women of Israel, and their children, living at Jerusalem, prostrated themselves before the temple and put ashes on their heads and spread out their sackcloth before the Lord.

[12] They even surrounded the altar with sackcloth and cried out in unison, praying earnestly to the God of Israel not to give up their infants as prey and their wives as booty, and the cities they had inherited to be destroyed, and the sanctuary to be profaned and desecrated to the malicious joy of the Gentiles.

[13] So the Lord heard their prayers and looked upon their affliction; for the people fasted many days throughout Judea and in Jerusalem before the sanctuary of the Lord Almighty.

[14] And Joakim the high priest and all the priests who stood before the Lord and ministered to the Lord, with their loins girded with sackcloth, offered the continual burnt offerings and the vows and freewill offerings of the people.

[15] With ashes upon their turbans, they cried out to the Lord with all their might to look with favor upon the whole house of Israel.

Jdt.5

[1] When Holofernes, the general of the Assyrian army, heard that the people of Israel had prepared for war and had closed the passes in the hills and fortified all the high hilltops and set up barricades in the plains,

[2] he was very angry. So he called together all the princes of Moab and the commanders of Ammon and all the governors of the coastland,

[3] and said to them, "Tell me, you Canaanites, what people is this that lives in the hill country? What cities do they inhabit? How large is their army, and in what does their power or strength consist? Who rules over them as king, leading their army?

[4] And why have they alone, of all who live in the west, refused to come out and meet me?"

[5] Then Achior, the leader of all the Ammonites, said to him, "Let my lord now hear a word from the mouth of your servant, and I will tell you the truth about this people that dwells in the nearby mountain district. No falsehood shall come from your servant's mouth.

[6] This people is descended from the Chaldeans.

[7] At one time they lived in Mesopotamia, because they would not follow the gods of their fathers who were in Chaldea.

[8] For they had left the ways of their ancestors, and they worshiped the God of heaven, the God they had come to know; hence they drove them out from the presence of their gods; and they fled to Mesopotamia, and lived there for a long time.

[9] Then their God commanded them to leave the place where they were living and go to the land of Canaan. There they settled, and prospered, with much gold and silver and very many cattle.

[10] When a famine spread over Canaan they went down to Egypt and lived there as long as they had food; and there they became a great multitude -- so great that they could not be counted.

[11] So the king of Egypt became hostile to them; he took advantage of them and set them to making bricks, and humbled them and made slaves of them.

[12] Then they cried out to their God, and he afflicted the whole land of Egypt with incurable plagues; and so the Egyptians drove them out of their sight.

[13] Then God dried up the Red Sea before them,

[14] and he led them by the way of Sinai and Kadesh-barnea, and drove out all the people of the wilderness.

[15] So they lived in the land of the Amorites, and by their might destroyed all the inhabitants of Heshbon; and crossing over the Jordan they took possession of all the hill country.

[16] And they drove out before them the Canaanites and the Perizzites and the Jebusites and the Shechemites and all the Gergesites, and lived there a long time.

[17] As long as they did not sin against their God they prospered, for the God who hates iniquity is with them.

[18] But when they departed from the way which he had appointed for them, they were utterly defeated in many battles and were led away captive to a foreign country; the temple of their God was razed to the ground, and their cities were captured by their enemies.

[19] But now they have returned to their God, and have come back from the places to which they were scattered, and have occupied Jerusalem, where their sanctuary is, and have settled in the hill country, because it was uninhabited.

[20] Now therefore, my master and lord, if there is any unwitting error in this people and they sin against their God and we find out their offense, then we will go up and defeat them.

[21] But if there is no transgression in their nation, then let my lord pass them by; for their Lord will defend them, and their God will protect them, and we shall be put to shame before the whole world."

[22] When Achior had finished saying this, all the men standing around the tent began to complain; Holofernes' officers and all the men from the seacoast and from Moab insisted that he must be put to death.

[23] "For," they said, "we will not be afraid of the Israelites; they are a people with no strength or power for making war.

[24] Therefore let us go up, Lord Holofernes, and they will be devoured by your vast army."

Jdt.6

[1] When the disturbance made by the men outside the council died down, Holofernes, the commander of the Assyrian army, said to Achior and all the Moabites in the presence of all the foreign contingents:

[2] "And who are you, Achior, and you hirelings of Ephraim, to prophesy among us as you have done today and tell us not to make war against the people of Israel because their God will defend them? Who is God except Nebuchadnezzar?

[3] He will send his forces and will destroy them from the face of the earth, and their God will not deliver them -- we the king's servants will destroy them as one man. They cannot resist the might of our cavalry.

[4] We will burn them up, and their mountains will be drunk with their blood, and their fields will be full of their dead. They cannot withstand us, but will utterly perish. So says King Nebuchadnezzar, the lord of the whole earth. For he has spoken; none of his words shall be in vain.

[5] "But you, Achior, you Ammonite hireling, who have said these words on the day of your iniquity, you shall not see my face again from this day until I take revenge on this race that came out of Egypt.

[6] Then the sword of my army and the spear of my servants shall pierce your sides, and you shall fall among their wounded, when I return.

[7] Now my slaves are going to take you back into the hill country and put you in one of the cities beside the passes,

[8] and you will not die until you perish along with them.

[9] If you really hope in your heart that they will not be taken, do not look downcast! I have spoken and none of my words shall fail."

[10] Then Holofernes ordered his slaves, who waited on him in his tent, to seize Achior and take him to Bethulia and hand him over to the men of

Israel.

[11] So the slaves took him and led him out of the camp into the plain, and from the plain they went up into the hill country and came to the springs below Bethulia.

[12] When the men of the city saw them, they caught up their weapons and ran out of the city to the top of the hill, and all the slingers kept them from coming up by casting stones at them.

[13] However, they got under the shelter of the hill and they bound Achior and left him lying at the foot of the hill, and returned to their master.

[14] Then the men of Israel came down from their city and found him; and they untied him and brought him into Bethulia and placed him before the magistrates of their city,

[15] who in those days were Uzziah the son of Micah, of the tribe of Simeon, and Chabris the son of Gothoniel, and Charmis the son of Melchiel.

[16] They called together all the elders of the city, and all their young men and their women ran to the assembly; and they set Achior in the midst of all their people, and Uzziah asked him what had happened.

[17] He answered and told them what had taken place at the council of Holofernes, and all that he had said in the presence of the Assyrian leaders, and all that Holofernes had said so boastfully against the house of Israel.

[18] Then the people fell down and worshiped God, and cried out to him, and said,

[19] "O Lord God of heaven, behold their arrogance, and have pity on the humiliation of our people, and look this day upon the faces of those who are consecrated to thee."

[20] Then they consoled Achior, and praised him greatly.

[21] And Uzziah took him from the assembly to his own house and gave a banquet for the elders; and all that night they called on the God of Israel for help.

Jdt.7

[1] The next day Holofernes ordered his whole army, and all the allies who had joined him, to break camp and move against Bethulia, and to seize the passes up into the hill country and make war on the Israelites.

[2] So all their warriors moved their camp that day; their force of men of war was one hundred and seventy thousand infantry and twelve thousand cavalry, together with the baggage and the foot soldiers handling it, a very great multitude.

[3] They encamped in the valley near Bethulia, beside the spring, and they spread out in breadth over Dothan as far as Balbaim and in length from

Bethulia to Cyamon, which faces Esdraelon.

[4] When the Israelites saw their vast numbers they were greatly terrified, and every one said to his neighbor, "These men will now lick up the face of the whole land; neither the high mountains nor the valleys nor the hills will bear their weight."

[5] Then each man took up his weapons, and when they had kindled fires on their towers they remained on guard all that night.

[6] On the second day Holofernes led out all his cavalry in full view of the Israelites in Bethulia,

[7] and examined the approaches to the city, and visited the springs that supplied their water, and seized them and set guards of soldiers over them, and then returned to his army.

[8] Then all the chieftains of the people of Esau and all the leaders of the Moabites and the commanders of the coastland came to him and said,

[9] "Let our lord hear a word, lest his army be defeated.

[10] For these people, the Israelites, do not rely on their spears but on the height of the mountains where they live, for it is not easy to reach the tops of their mountains.

[11] Therefore, my lord, do not fight against them in battle array, and not a man of your army will fall.

[12] Remain in your camp, and keep all the men in your forces with you; only let your servants take possession of the spring of water that flows from the foot of the mountain --

[13] for this is where all the people of Bethulia get their water. So thirst will destroy them, and they will give up their city. We and our people will go up to the tops of the nearby mountains and camp there to keep watch that not a man gets out of the city.

[14] They and their wives and children will waste away with famine, and before the sword reaches them they will be strewn about in the streets where they live.

[15] So you will pay them back with evil, because they rebelled and did not receive you peaceably."

[16] These words pleased Holofernes and all his servants, and he gave orders to do as they had said.

[17] So the army of the Ammonites moved forward, together with five thousand Assyrians, and they encamped in the valley and seized the water supply and the springs of the Israelites.

[18] And the sons of Esau and the sons of Ammon went up and encamped in the hill country opposite Dothan; and they sent some of their men toward the south and the east, toward Acraba, which is near Chusi beside the brook Mochmur. The rest of the Assyrian army encamped in the plain, and covered the whole face of the land, and their tents and supply trains spread out in great number, and they formed a vast multitude.

[19] The people of Israel cried out to the Lord their God, for their courage

failed, because all their enemies had surrounded them and there was no way of escape from them.

[20] The whole Assyrian army, their infantry, chariots, and cavalry, surrounded them for thirty-four days, until all the vessels of water belonging to every inhabitant of Bethulia were empty;

[21] their cisterns were going dry, and they did not have enough water to drink their fill for a single day, because it was measured out to them to drink.

[22] Their children lost heart, and the women and young men fainted from thirst and fell down in the streets of the city and in the passages through the gates; there was no strength left in them any longer.

[23] Then all the people, the young men, the women, and the children, gathered about Uzziah and the rulers of the city and cried out with a loud voice, and said before all the elders,

[24] "God be judge between you and us! For you have done us a great injury in not making peace with the Assyrians.

[25] For now we have no one to help us; God has sold us into their hands, to strew us on the ground before them with thirst and utter destruction.

[26] Now call them in and surrender the whole city to the army of Holofernes and to all his forces, to be plundered.

[27] For it would be better for us to be captured by them; for we will be slaves, but our lives will be spared, and we shall not witness the death of our babes before our eyes, or see our wives and children draw their last breath.

[28] We call to witness against you heaven and earth and our God, the Lord of our fathers, who punishes us according to our sins and the sins of our fathers. Let him not do this day the things which we have described!"

[29] Then great and general lamentation arose throughout the assembly, and they cried out to the Lord God with a loud voice.

[30] And Uzziah said to them, "Have courage, my brothers! Let us hold out for five more days; by that time the Lord our God will restore to us his mercy, for he will not forsake us utterly.

[31] But if these days pass by, and no help comes for us, I will do what you say."

[32] Then he dismissed the people to their various posts, and they went up on the walls and towers of their city. The women and children he sent home. And they were greatly depressed in the city.

Jdt.8

[1] At that time Judith heard about these things: she was the daughter of

Merari the son of Ox, son of Joseph, son of Oziel, son of Elkiah, son of Ananias, son of Gideon, son of Raphaim, son of Ahitub, son of Elijah, son of Hilkiah, son of Eliab, son of Nathanael, son of Salamiel, son of Sarasadai, son of Israel.

[2] Her husband Manasseh, who belonged to her tribe and family, had died during the barley harvest.

[3] For as he stood overseeing the men who were binding sheaves in the field, he was overcome by the burning heat, and took to his bed and died in Bethulia his city. So they buried him with his fathers in the field between Dothan and Balamon.

[4] Judith had lived at home as a widow for three years and four months.

[5] She set up a tent for herself on the roof of her house, and girded sackcloth about her loins and wore the garments of her widowhood.

[6] She fasted all the days of her widowhood, except the day before the sabbath and the sabbath itself, the day before the new moon and the day of the new moon, and the feasts and days of rejoicing of the house of Israel.

[7] She was beautiful in appearance, and had a very lovely face; and her husband Manasseh had left her gold and silver, and men and women slaves, and cattle, and fields; and she maintained this estate.

[8] No one spoke ill of her, for she feared God with great devotion.

[9] When Judith heard the wicked words spoken by the people against the ruler, because they were faint for lack of water, and when she heard all that Uzziah said to them, and how he promised them under oath to surrender the city to the Assyrians after five days,

[10] she sent her maid, who was in charge of all she possessed, to summon Chabris and Charmis, the elders of her city.

[11] They came to her, and she said to them, "Listen to me, rulers of the people of Bethulia! What you have said to the people today is not right; you have even sworn and pronounced this oath between God and you, promising to surrender the city to our enemies unless the Lord turns and helps us within so many days.

[12] Who are you, that have put God to the test this day, and are setting yourselves up in the place of God among the sons of men?

[13] You are putting the Lord Almighty to the test -- but you will never know anything!

[14] You cannot plumb the depths of the human heart, nor find out what a man is thinking; how do you expect to search out God, who made all these things, and find out his mind or comprehend his thought? No, my brethren, do not provoke the Lord our God to anger.

[15] For if he does not choose to help us within these five days, he has power to protect us within any time he pleases, or even to destroy us in the presence of our enemies.

[16] Do not try to bind the purposes of the Lord our God; for God is not like man, to be threatened, nor like a human being, to be won over by pleading.

[17] Therefore, while we wait for his deliverance, let us call upon him to help us, and he will hear our voice, if it pleases him.

[18] "For never in our generation, nor in these present days, has there been any tribe or family or people or city of ours which worshiped gods made with hands, as was done in days gone by --

[19] and that was why our fathers were handed over to the sword, and to be plundered, and so they suffered a great catastrophe before our enemies.

[20] But we know no other god but him, and therefore we hope that he will not disdain us or any of our nation.

[21] For if we are captured all Judea will be captured and our sanctuary will be plundered; and he will exact of us the penalty for its desecration.

[22] And the slaughter of our brethren and the captivity of the land and the desolation of our inheritance -- all this he will bring upon our heads among the Gentiles, wherever we serve as slaves; and we shall be an offense and a reproach in the eyes of those who acquire us.

[23] For our slavery will not bring us into favor, but the Lord our God will turn it to dishonor.

[24] "Now therefore, brethren, let us set an example to our brethren, for their lives depend upon us, and the sanctuary and the temple and the altar rest upon us.

[25] In spite of everything let us give thanks to the Lord our God, who is putting us to the test as he did our forefathers.

[26] Remember what he did with Abraham, and how he tested Isaac, and what happened to Jacob in Mesopotamia in Syria, while he was keeping the sheep of Laban, his mother's brother.

[27] For he has not tried us with fire, as he did them, to search their hearts, nor has he taken revenge upon us; but the Lord scourges those who draw near to him, in order to admonish them."

[28] Then Uzziah said to her, "All that you have said has been spoken out of a true heart, and there is no one who can deny your words.

[29] Today is not the first time your wisdom has been shown, but from the beginning of your life all the people have recognized your understanding, for your heart's disposition is right.

[30] But the people were very thirsty, and they compelled us to do for them what we have promised, and made us take an oath which we cannot break.

[31] So pray for us, since you are a devout woman, and the Lord will send us rain to fill our cisterns and we will no longer be faint."

[32] Judith said to them, "Listen to me. I am about to do a thing which will go down through all generations of our descendants.

[33] Stand at the city gate tonight, and I will go out with my maid; and within the days after which you have promised to surrender the city to our enemies, the Lord will deliver Israel by my hand.

[34] Only, do not try to find out what I plan; for I will not tell you until I

have finished what I am about to do."

[35] Uzziah and the rulers said to her, "Go in peace, and may the Lord God go before you, to take revenge upon our enemies."

[36] So they returned from the tent and went to their posts.

Jdt.9

[1] Then Judith fell upon her face, and put ashes on her head, and uncovered the sackcloth she was wearing; and at the very time when that evening's incense was being offered in the house of God in Jerusalem, Judith cried out to the Lord with a loud voice, and said,

[2] "O Lord God of my father Simeon, to whom thou gavest a sword to take revenge on the strangers who had loosed the girdle of a virgin to defile her, and uncovered her thigh to put her to shame, and polluted her womb to disgrace her; for thou hast said, `It shall not be done' -- yet they did it.

[3] So thou gavest up their rulers to be slain, and their bed, which was ashamed of the deceit they had practiced, to be stained with blood, and thou didst strike down slaves along with princes, and princes on their thrones;

[4] and thou gavest their wives for a prey and their daughters to captivity, and all their booty to be divided among thy beloved sons, who were zealous for thee, and abhorred the pollution of their blood, and called on thee for help -- O God, my God, hear me also, a widow.

[5] "For thou hast done these things and those that went before and those that followed; thou hast designed the things that are now, and those that are to come. Yea, the things thou didst intend came to pass,

[6] and the things thou didst will presented themselves and said, `Lo, we are here'; for all they ways are prepared in advance, and thy judgment is with foreknowledge.

[7] "Behold now, the Assyrians are increased in their might; they are exalted, with their horses and riders; they glory in the strength of their foot soldiers; they trust in shield and spear, in bow and sling, and know not that thou art the Lord who crushest wars; the Lord is thy name.

[8] Break their strength by thy might, and bring down their power in thy anger; for they intend to defile thy sanctuary, and to pollute the tabernacle where thy glorious name rests, and to cast down the horn of thy altar with the sword.

[9] Behold their pride, and send thy wrath upon their heads; give to me, a widow, the strength to do what I plan.

[10] By the deceit of my lips strike down the slave with the prince and the prince with his servant; crush their arrogance by the hand of a woman.

[11] "For thy power depends not upon numbers, nor thy might upon men of strength; for thou art God of the lowly, helper of the oppressed, upholder of

the weak, protector of the forlorn, savior of those without hope.

[12] Hear, O hear me, God of my father, God of the inheritance of Israel, Lord of heaven and earth, Creator of the waters, King of all thy creation, hear my prayer!

[13] Make my deceitful words to be their wound and stripe, for they have planned cruel things against thy covenant, and against thy consecrated house, and against the top of Zion, and against the house possessed by thy children.

[14] And cause thy whole nation and every tribe to know and understand that thou art God, the God of all power and might, and that there is no other who protects the people of Israel but thou alone!"

Jdt.10

[1] When Judith had ceased crying out to the God of Israel, and had ended all these words,

[2] she rose from where she lay prostrate and called her maid and went down into the house where she lived on sabbaths and on her feast days;

[3] and she removed the sackcloth which she had been wearing, and took off her widow's garments, and bathed her body with water, and anointed herself with precious ointment, and combed her hair and put on a tiara, and arrayed herself in her gayest apparel, which she used to wear while her husband Manasseh was living.

[4] And she put sandals on her feet, and put on her anklets and bracelets and rings, and her earrings and all her ornaments, and made herself very beautiful, to entice the eyes of all men who might see her.

[5] And she gave her maid a bottle of wine and a flask of oil, and filled a bag with parched grain and a cake of dried fruit and fine bread; and she wrapped up all her vessels and gave them to her to carry.

[6] Then they went out to the city gate of Bethulia, and found Uzziah standing there with the elders of the city, Chabris and Charmis.

[7] When they saw her, and noted how her face was altered and her clothing changed, they greatly admired her beauty, and said to her,

[8] "May the God of our fathers grant you favor and fulfil your plans, that the people of Israel may glory and Jerusalem may be exalted." And she worshiped God.

[9] Then she said to them, "Order the gate of the city to be opened for me, and I will go out and accomplish the things about which you spoke with me." So they ordered the young men to open the gate for her, as she had said.

[10] When they had done this, Judith went out, she and her maid with her;

and the men of the city watched her until she had gone down the mountain and passed through the valley and they could no longer see her.

[11] The women went straight on through the valley; and an Assyrian patrol met her

[12] and took her into custody, and asked her, "To what people do you belong, and where are you coming from, and where are you going?" She replied, "I am a daughter of the Hebrews, but I am fleeing from them, for they are about to be handed over to you to be devoured.

[13] I am on my way to the presence of Holofernes the commander of your army, to give him a true report; and I will show him a way by which he can go and capture all the hill country without losing one of his men, captured or slain."

[14] When the men heard her words, and observed her face -- she was in their eyes marvelously beautiful -- they said to her,

[15] "You have saved your life by hurrying down to the presence of our lord. Go at once to his tent; some of us will escort you and hand you over to him.

[16] And when you stand before him, do not be afraid in your heart, but tell him just what you have said, and he will treat you well."

[17] They chose from their number a hundred men to accompany her and her maid, and they brought them to the tent of Holofernes.

[18] There was great excitement in the whole camp, for her arrival was reported from tent to tent, and they came and stood around her as she waited outside the tent of Holofernes while they told him about her.

[19] And they marveled at her beauty, and admired the Israelites, judging them by her, and every one said to his neighbor, "Who can despise these people, who have women like this among them? Surely not a man of them had better be left alive, for if we let them go they will be able to ensnare the whole world!"

[20] Then Holofernes' companions and all his servants came out and led her into the tent.

[21] Holofernes was resting on his bed, under a canopy which was woven with purple and gold and emeralds and precious stones.

[22] When they told him of her he came forward to the front of the tent, with silver lamps carried before him.

[23] And when Judith came into the presence of Holofernes and his servants, they all marveled at the beauty of her face; and she prostrated herself and made obeisance to him, and his slaves raised her up.

Jdt.11

[1] Then Holofernes said to her, "Take courage, woman, and do not be afraid

in your heart, for I have never hurt any one who chose to serve Nebuchadnezzar, the king of all the earth.

[2] And even now, if your people who live in the hill country had not slighted me, I would never have lifted my spear against them; but they have brought all this on themselves.

[3] And now tell me why you have fled from them and have come over to us -- since you have come to safety.

[4] Have courage; you will live, tonight and from now on. No one will hurt you, but all will treat you well, as they do the servants of my lord King Nebuchadnezzar."

[5] Judith replied to him, "Accept the words of your servant, and let your maidservant speak in your presence, and I will tell nothing false to my lord this night.

[6] And if you follow out the words of your maidservant, God will accomplish something through you, and my lord will not fail to achieve his purposes.

[7] Nebuchadnezzar the king of the whole earth lives, and as his power endures, who had sent you to direct every living soul, not only do men serve him because of you, but also the beasts of the field and the cattle and the birds of the air will live by your power under Nebuchadnezzar and all his house.

[8] For we have heard of your wisdom and skill, and it is reported throughout the whole world that you are the one good man in the whole kingdom, thoroughly informed and marvelous in military strategy.

[9] "Now as for the things Achior said in your council, we have heard his words, for the men of Bethulia spared him and he told them all he had said to you.

[10] Therefore, my lord and master, do not disregard what he said, but keep it in your mind, for it is true: our nation cannot be punished, nor can the sword prevail against them, unless they sin against their God.

[11] "And now, in order that my lord may not be defeated and his purpose frustrated, death will fall upon them, for a sin has overtaken them by which they are about to provoke their God to anger when they do what is wrong.

[12] Since their food supply is exhausted and their water has almost given out, they have planned to kill their cattle and have determined to use all that God by his laws has forbidden them to eat.

[13] They have decided to consume the first fruits of the grain and the tithes of the wine and oil, which they had consecrated and set aside for the priests who minister in the presence of our God at Jerusalem -- although it is not lawful for any of the people so much as to touch these things with their hands.

[14] They have sent men to Jerusalem, because even the people living there have been doing this, to bring back to them permission from the senate.

[15] When the word reaches them and they proceed to do this, on that very day they will be handed over to you to be destroyed.

[16] "Therefore, when I, your servant, learned all this, I fled from them; and God has sent me to accomplish with you things that will astonish the whole world, as many as shall hear about them.

[17] For your servant is religious, and serves the God of heaven day and night; therefore, my lord, I will remain with you, and every night your servant will go out into the valley, and I will pray to God and he will tell me when they have committed their sins.

[18] And I will come and tell you, and then you shall go out with your whole army, and not one of them will withstand you.

[19] Then I will lead you through the middle of Judea, till you come to Jerusalem; and I will set your throne in the midst of it; and you will lead them like sheep that have no shepherd, and not a dog will so much as open its mouth to growl at you. For this has been told me, by my foreknowledge; it was announced to me, and I was sent to tell you."

[20] Her words pleased Holofernes and all his servants, and they marveled at her wisdom and said,

[21] "There is not such a woman from one end of the earth to the other, either for beauty of face or wisdom of speech!"

[22] And Holofernes said to her, "God has done well to send you before the people, to lend strength to our hands and to bring destruction upon those who have slighted my lord.

[23] You are not only beautiful in appearance, but wise in speech; and if you do as you have said, your God shall be my God, and you shall live in the house of King Nebuchadnezzar and be renowned throughout the whole world."

Jdt.12

[1] Then he commanded them to bring her in where his silver dishes were kept, and ordered them to set a table for her with some of his own food and to serve her with his own wine.

[2] But Judith said, "I cannot eat it, lest it be an offense; but I will be provided from the things I have brought with me."

[3] Holofernes said to her, "If your supply runs out, where can we get more like it for you? For none of your people is here with us."

[4] Judith replied, "As your soul lives, my lord, your servant will not use up the things I have with me before the Lord carries out by my hand what he has determined to do."

[5] Then the servants of Holofernes brought her into the tent, and she slept until midnight. Along toward the morning watch she arose

[6] and sent to Holofernes and said, "Let my lord now command that your servant be permitted to go out and pray."

[7] So Holofernes commanded his guards not to hinder her. And she remained in the camp for three days, and went out each night to the valley of Bethulia, and bathed at the spring in the camp.

[8] When she came up from the spring she prayed the Lord God of Israel to direct her way for the raising up of her people.

[9] So she returned clean and stayed in the tent until she ate her food toward evening.

[10] On the fourth day Holofernes held a banquet for his slave only, and did not invite any of his officers.

[11] And he said to Bagoas, the eunuch who had charge of his personal affairs, "Go now and persuade the Hebrew woman who is in your care to join us and eat and drink with us.

[12] For it will be a disgrace if we let such a woman go without enjoying her company, for if we do not embrace her she will laugh at us."

[13] So Bagoas went out from the presence of Holofernes, and approached her and said, "This beautiful maidservant will please come to my lord and be honored in his presence, and drink wine and be merry with us, and become today like one of the daughters of the Assyrians who serve in the house of Nebuchadnezzar."

[14] And Judith said, "Who am I, to refuse my lord? Surely whatever pleases him I will do at once, and it will be a joy to me until the day of my death!"

[15] So she got up and arrayed herself in all her woman's finery, and her maid went and spread on the ground for her before Holofernes the soft fleeces which she had received from Bagoas for her daily use, so that she might recline on them when she ate.

[16] Then Judith came in and lay down, and Holofernes' heart was ravished with her and he was moved with great desire to possess her; for he had been waiting for an opportunity to deceive her, ever since the day he first saw her.

[17] So Holofernes said to her. "Drink now, and be merry with us!"

[18] Judith said, "I will drink now, my lord, because my life means more to me today than in all the days since I was born."

[19] Then she took and ate and drank before him what her maid had prepared.

[20] And Holofernes was greatly pleased with her, and drank a great quantity of wine, much more than he had ever drunk in any one day since he was born.

Jdt.13

[1] When evening came, his slaves quickly withdrew, and Bagoas closed the tent from outside and shut out the attendants from his master's presence; and they went to bed, for they all were weary because the banquet had lasted long.

[2] So Judith was left alone in the tent , with Holofernes stretched out on his bed, for he was overcome with wine.

[3] Now Judith had told her maid to stand outside the bedchamber and to wait for her to come out, as she did every day; for she said she would be going out for her prayers. And she had said the same thing to Bagoas.

[4] So every one went out, and no one, either small or great, was left in the bedchamber. Then Judith, standing beside his bed, said in her heart, "O Lord God of all might, look in this hour upon the work of my hands for the exaltation of Jerusalem.

[5] For now is the time to help thy inheritance, and to carry out my undertaking for the destruction of the enemies who have risen up against us."

[6] She went up to the post at the end of the bed, above Holofernes' head, and took down his sword that hung there.

[7] She came close to his bed and took hold of the hair of his head, and said, "Give me strength this day, O Lord God of Israel!"

[8] And she struck his neck twice with all her might, and severed it from his body.

[9] Then she tumbled his body off the bed and pulled down the canopy from the posts; after a moment she went out, and gave Holofernes' head to her maid,

[10] who placed it in her food bag. Then the two of them went out together, as they were accustomed to go for prayer; and they passed through the camp and circled around the valley and went up the mountain to Bethulia and came to its gates.

[11] Judith called out from afar to the watchmen at the gates, "Open, open the gate! God, our God, is still with us, to show his power in Israel, and his strength against our enemies, even as he has done this day!"

[12] When the men of her city heard her voice, they hurried down to the city gate and called together the elders of the city.

[13] They all ran together, both small and great, for it was unbelievable that she had returned; they opened the gate and admitted them, and they kindled a fire for light, and gathered around them.

[14] Then she said to them with a loud voice, "Praise God, O praise him! Praise God, who has not withdrawn his mercy from the house of Israel, but has destroyed our enemies by my hand this very night!"

[15] Then she took the head out of the bag and showed it to them, and said, "See, here is the head of Holofernes, the commander of the Assyrian army, and here is the canopy beneath which he lay in his drunken stupor. The Lord has struck him down by the hand of a woman.
[16] As the Lord lives, who has protected me in the way I went, it was my face that tricked him to his destruction, and yet he committed no act of sin with me, to defile and shame me."
[17] All the people were greatly astonished, and bowed down and worshiped God, and said with one accord, "Blessed art thou, our God, who hast brought into contempt this day the enemies of thy people."
[18] And Uzziah said to her, "O daughter, you are blessed by the Most High God above all women on earth; and blessed be the Lord God, who created the heavens and the earth, who has guided you to strike the head of the leader of our enemies.
[19] Your hope will never depart from the hearts of men, as they remember the power of God.
[20] May God grant this to be a perpetual honor to you, and may he visit you with blessings, because you did not spare your own life when our nation was brought low, but have avenged our ruin, walking in the straight path before our God." And all the people said, "So be it, so be it!"

Jdt.14

[1] Then Judith said to them, "Listen to me, my brethren, and take this head and hang it upon the parapet of your wall.
[2] And as soon as morning comes and the sun rises, let every valiant man take his weapons and go out of the city, and set a captain over them, as if you were going down to the plain against the Assyrian outpost; only do not go down.
[3] Then they will seize their arms and go into the camp and rouse the officers of the Assyrian army; and they will rush into the tent of Holofernes, and will not find him. Then fear will come over them, and they will flee before you,
[4] and you and all who live within the borders of Israel shall pursue them and cut them down as they flee.
[5] But before you do all this, bring Achior the Ammonite to me, and let him see and recognize the man who despised the house of Israel and sent him to us as if to his death."
[6] So they summoned Achior from the house of Uzziah. And when he came and saw the head of Holofernes in the hand of one of the men at the gathering of the people, he fell down on his face and his spirit failed him.
[7] And when they raised him up he fell at Judith's feet, and knelt before

her, and said, "Blessed are you in every tent of Judah! In every nation those who hear your name will be alarmed.

[8] Now tell me what you have done during these days." Then Judith described to him in the presence of the people all that she had done, from the day she left until the moment of her speaking to them.

[9] And when she had finished, the people raised a great shout and made a joyful noise in their city.

[10] And when Achior saw all that the God of Israel had done, he believed firmly in God, and was circumcised, and joined the house of Israel, remaining so to this day.

[11] As soon as it was dawn they hung the head of Holofernes on the wall, and every man took his weapons, and they went out in companies to the passes in the mountains.

[12] And when the Assyrians saw them they sent word to their commanders, and they went to the generals and the captains and to all their officers.

[13] So they came to Holofernes' tent and said to the steward in charge of all his personal affairs, "Wake up our lord, for the slaves have been so bold as to come down against us to give battle, in order to be destroyed completely."

[14] So Bagoas went in and knocked at the door of the tent, for he supposed that he was sleeping with Judith.

[15] But when no one answered, he opened it and went into the bedchamber and found him thrown down on the platform dead, with his head cut off and missing.

[16] And he cried out with a loud voice and wept and groaned and shouted, and rent his garments.

[17] Then he went to the tent where Judith had stayed, and when he did not find her he rushed out to the people and shouted,

[18] "The slaves have tricked us! One Hebrew woman has brought disgrace upon the house of King Nebuchadnezzar! For look, here is Holofernes lying on the ground, and his head is not on him!"

[19] When the leaders of the Assyrian army heard this, they rent their tunics and were greatly dismayed, and their loud cries and shouts arose in the midst of the camp.

Jdt.15

[1] When the men in the tents heard it, they were amazed at what had happened.

[2] Fear and trembling came over them, so that they did not wait for one another, but with one impulse all rushed out and fled by every path across

the plain and through the hill country.

[3] Those who had camped in the hills around Bethulia also took to flight. Then the men of Israel, every one that was a soldier, rushed out upon them.

[4] And Uzziah sent men to Betomasthaim and Bebai and Choba and Kola, and to all the frontiers of Israel, to tell what had taken place and to urge all to rush out upon their enemies to destroy them.

[5] And when the Israelites heard it, with one accord they fell upon the enemy, and cut them down as far as Choba. Those in Jerusalem and all the hill country also came, for they were told what had happened in the camp of the enemy; and those in Gilead and in Galilee outflanked them with great slaughter, even beyond Damascus and its borders.

[6] The rest of the people of Bethulia fell upon the Assyrian camp and plundered it, and were greatly enriched.

[7] And the Israelites, when they returned from the slaughter, took possession of what remained, and the villages and towns in the hill country and in the plain got a great amount of booty, for there was a vast quantity of it.

[8] Then Joakim the high priest, and the senate of the people of Israel who lived at Jerusalem, came to witness the good things which the Lord had done for Israel, and to see Judith and to greet her.

[9] And when they met her they all blessed her with one accord and said to her, "You are the exaltation of Jerusalem, you are the great glory of Israel, you are the great pride of our nation!

[10] You have done all this singlehanded; you have done great good to Israel, and God is well pleased with it. May the Almighty Lord bless you for ever!" And all the people said, "So be it!"

[11] So all the people plundered the camp for thirty days. They gave Judith the tent of Holofernes and all his silver dishes and his beds and his bowls and all his furniture; and she took them and loaded her mule and hitched up her carts and piled the things on them.

[12] Then all the women of Israel gathered to see her, and blessed her, and some of them performed a dance for her; and she took branches in her hands and gave them to the women who were with her;

[13] and they crowned themselves with olive wreaths, she and those who were with her; and she went before all the people in the dance, leading all the women, while all the men of Israel followed, bearing their arms and wearing garlands and with songs on their lips.

Jdt.16

[1] Then Judith began this thanksgiving before all Israel, and all the people

loudly sang this song of praise.

[2] And Judith said, Begin a song to my God with tambourines, sing to my Lord with cymbals. Raise to him a new psalm; exalt him, and call upon his name.

[3] For God is the Lord who crushes wars; for he has delivered me out of the hands of my pursuers, and brought me to his camp, in the midst of the people.

[4] The Assyrian came down from the mountains of the north; he came with myriads of his warriors; their multitude blocked up the valleys, their cavalry covered the hills.

[5] He boasted that he would burn up my territory, and kill my young men with the sword, and dash my infants to the ground and seize my children as prey, and take my virgins as booty.

[6] But the Lord Almighty has foiled them by the hand of a woman.

[7] For their mighty one did not fall by the hands of the young men, nor did the sons of the Titans smite him, nor did tall giants set upon him; but Judith the daughter of Merari undid him with the beauty of her countenance.

[8] For she took off her widow's mourning to exalt the oppressed in Israel. She anointed her face with ointment and fastened her hair with a tiara and put on a linen gown to deceive him.

[9] Her sandal ravished his eyes, her beauty captivated his mind, and the sword severed his neck.

[10] The Persians trembled at her boldness, the Medes were daunted at her daring.

[11] Then my oppressed people shouted for joy; my weak people shouted and the enemy trembled; they lifted up their voices, and the enemy were turned back.

[12] The sons of maidservants have pierced them through; they were wounded like the children of fugitives, they perished before the army of my Lord.

[13] I will sing to my God a new song: O Lord, thou are great and glorious, wonderful in strength, invincible.

[14] Let all thy creatures serve thee, for thou didst speak, and they were made. Thou didst send forth thy Spirit, and it formed them; there is none that can resist thy voice.

[15] For the mountains shall be shaken to their foundations with the waters; at thy presence the rocks shall melt like wax, but to those who fear thee thou wilt continue to show mercy.

[16] For every sacrifice as a fragrant offering is a small thing, and all fat for burnt offerings to thee is a very little thing, but he who fears the Lord shall be great for ever.

[17] Woe to the nations that rise up against my people! The Lord Almighty will take vengeance on them in the day of judgment; fire and worms he will give to their flesh; they shall weep in pain for ever.

[18] When they arrived at Jerusalem they worshiped God. As soon as the people were purified, they offered their burnt offerings, their freewill offerings, and their gifts.

[19] Judith also dedicated to God all the vessels of Holofernes, which the people had given her; and the canopy which she took for herself from his bedchamber she gave as a votive offering to the Lord.

[20] So the people continued feasting in Jerusalem before the sanctuary for three months, and Judith remained with them.

[21] After this every one returned home to his own inheritance, and Judith went to Bethulia, and remained on her estate, and was honored in her time throughout the whole country.

[22] Many desired to marry her, but she remained a widow all the days of her life after Manasseh her husband died and was gathered to his people.

[23] She became more and more famous, and grew old in her husband's house, until she was one hundred and five years old. She set her maid free. She died in Bethulia, and they buried her in the cave of her husband Manasseh,

[24] and the house of Israel mourned for her seven days. Before she died she distributed her property to all those who were next of kin to her husband Manasseh, and to her own nearest kindred.

[25] And no one ever again spread terror among the people of Israel in the days of Judith, or for a long time after her death.

Susanna

Sus.1

[1] There lived a man in Babylon named Joacim:

[2] And he took a wife named Susanna, the daughter of Hilkiah, a very beautiful woman and one who feared the Lord.

[3] Her parents were righteous, and had taught their daughter according to the law of Moses.

[4] Joakim was very rich, and had a spacious garden adjoining his house; and the Jews used to come to him because he was the most honored of them all.

[5] In that year two elders from the people were appointed as judges. Concerning them the Lord had said: "Iniquity came forth from Babylon, from elders who were judges, who were supposed to govern the people."

[6] These men were frequently at Joakim's house, and all who had suits at law came to them.

[7] When the people departed at noon, Susanna would go into her husband's garden to walk.

[8] The two elders used to see her every day, going in and walking about, and they began to desire her.

[9] And they perverted their minds and turned away their eyes from looking to Heaven or remembering righteous judgments.

[10] Both were overwhelmed with passion for her, but they did not tell each other of their distress,

[11] for they were ashamed to disclose their lustful desire to possess her.

[12] And they watched eagerly, day after day, to see her.

[13] They said to each other, "Let us go home, for it is mealtime."

[14] And when they went out, they parted from each other. But turning back, they met again; and when each pressed the other for the reason, they confessed their lust. And then together they arranged for a time when they could find her alone.

[15] Once, while they were watching for an opportune day, she went in as before with only two maids, and wished to bathe in the garden, for it was very hot.

[16] And no one was there except the two elders, who had hid themselves and were watching her.

[17] She said to her maids, "Bring me oil and ointments, and shut the garden doors so that I may bathe."

[18] They did as she said, shut the garden doors, and went out by the side doors to bring what they had been commanded; and they did not see the elders, because they were hidden.

[19] When the maids had gone out, the two elders rose and ran to her, and

said:

[20] "Look, the garden doors are shut, no one sees us, and we are in love with you; so give your consent, and lie with us.

[21] If you refuse, we will testify against you that a young man was with you, and this was why you sent your maids away."

[22] Susanna sighed deeply, and said, "I am hemmed in on every side. For if I do this thing, it is death for me; and if I do not, I shall not escape your hands.

[23] I choose not to do it and to fall into your hands, rather than to sin in the sight of the Lord."

[24] Then Susanna cried out with a loud voice, and the two elders shouted against her.

[25] And one of them ran and opened the garden doors.

[26] When the household servants heard the shouting in the garden, they rushed in at the side door to see what had happened to her.

[27] And when the elders told their tale, the servants were greatly ashamed, for nothing like this had ever been said about Susanna.

[28] The next day, when the people gathered at the house of her husband Joakim, the two elders came, full of their wicked plot to have Susanna put to death.

[29] They said before the people, "Send for Susanna, the daughter of Hilkiah, who is the wife of Joakim."

[30] So they sent for her. And she came, with her parents, her children, and all her kindred.

[31] Now Susanna was a woman of great refinement, and beautiful in appearance.

[32] As she was veiled, the wicked men ordered her to be unveiled, that they might feed upon her beauty.

[33] But her family and friends and all who saw her wept.

[34] Then the two elders stood up in the midst of the people, and laid their hands upon her head.

[35] And she, weeping, looked up toward heaven, for her heart trusted in the Lord.

[36] The elders said, "As we were walking in the garden alone, this woman came in with two maids, shut the garden doors, and dismissed the maids.

[37] Then a young man, who had been hidden, came to her and lay with her.

[38] We were in a corner of the garden, and when we saw this wickedness we ran to them.

[39] We saw them embracing, but we could not hold the man, for he was too strong for us, and he opened the doors and dashed out.

[40] So we seized this woman and asked her who the young man was, but she would not tell us. These things we testify."

[41] The assembly believed them, because they were elders of the people

and judges; and they condemned her to death.

[42] Then Susanna cried out with a loud voice, and said, "O eternal God, who do discern what is secret, who art aware of all things before they come to be,

[43] thou knowest that these men have borne false witness against me. And now I am to die! Yet I have done none of the things that they have wickedly invented against me!"

[44] The Lord heard her cry.

[45] And as she was being led away to be put to death, God aroused the holy spirit of a young lad named Daniel;

[46] and he cried with a loud voice, "I am innocent of the blood of this woman."

[47] All the people turned to him, and said, "What is this that you have said?"

[48] Taking his stand in the midst of them, he said, "Are you such fools, you sons of Israel? Have you condemned a daughter of Israel without examination and without learning the facts?

[49] Return to the place of judgment. For these men have borne false witness against her."

[50] Then all the people returned in haste. And the elders said to him, "Come, sit among us and inform us, for God has given you that right."

[51] And Daniel said to them, "Separate them far from each other, and I will examine them."

[52] When they were separated from each other, he summoned one of them and said to him, "You old relic of wicked days, your sins have now come home, which you have committed in the past,

[53] pronouncing unjust judgments, condemning the innocent and letting the guilty go free, though the Lord said, `Do not put to death an innocent and righteous person.'

[54] Now then, if you really saw her, tell me this: Under what tree did you see them being intimate with each other?" He answered, "Under a mastic tree."

[55] And Daniel said, "Very well! You have lied against your own head, for the angel of God has received the sentence from God and will immediately cut you in two."

[56] Then he put him aside, and commanded them to bring the other. And he said to him, "You offspring of Canaan and not of Judah, beauty has deceived you and lust has perverted your heart.

[57] This is how you both have been dealing with the daughters of Israel, and they were intimate with you through fear; but a daughter of Judah would not endure your wickedness.

[58] Now then, tell me: Under what tree did you catch them being intimate with each other?" He answered, "Under an evergreen oak."

[59] And Daniel said to him, "Very well! You also have lied against your

own head, for the angel of God is waiting with his sword to saw you in two, that he may destroy you both."

[60] Then all the assembly shouted loudly and blessed God, who saves those who hope in him.

[61] And they rose against the two elders, for out of their own mouths Daniel had convicted them of bearing false witness;

[62] and they did to them as they had wickedly planned to do to their neighbor; acting in accordance with the law of Moses, they put them to death. Thus innocent blood was saved that day.

[63] And Hilkiah and his wife praised God for their daughter Susanna, and so did Joakim her husband and all her kindred, because nothing shameful was found in her.

[64] And from that day onward Daniel had a great reputation among the people.

Psalm 151

Ps151.1

[1] I was the smallest in my father's house and the youngest of my brothers. I took care of my father's sheep.

[2] My hands made a harp, my fingers fashioned a lyre.

[3] And who will declare it to my Lord? The Lord himself; it is he who hears.

[4] It was he who sent his messenger and took me from my father's sheep, and anointed me with his anointing oil.

[5] My brothers were handsome and tall, but the Lord was not pleased with them.

[6] I went out to meet the Philistine, and he cursed me by his idols.

[7] But I drew his own sword; I beheaded him, and removed reproach from the people of Israel.

THE BOOK OF ENOCH

[Chapter 1]

1 The words of the blessing of Enoch, with which he blessed the elect and righteous, who will be living in the day of tribulation, when all the wicked and godless are to be removed.

2 And he began his story saying: Enoch a righteous man, whose eyes were opened by God, saw the vision of the Holy One in heaven, which the angels showed me, and I heard everything from them, and I saw and understood, but it was not for this generation, but for a remote one which is to come.

3 Concerning the elect I said, as I began my story concerning them: The Holy Great One will come out from His dwelling,

4 And the eternal God will tread on the earth, (even) on Mount Sinai, and appear in the strength of His might from heaven.

5 And all shall be very afraid, And the Watchers shall shake, And great fear and trembling shall seize them to the ends of the earth.

6 And the high mountains shall be shaken, and the high hills shall be laid low, and shall melt like wax in the flame.

7 And the earth shall be wholly torn apart, and all that is on the earth shall be destroyed, And there shall be a judgment on all.

8 But with the righteous He will make peace; and will protect the elect and mercy shall be on them. And they shall all belong to God, and they shall prosper, and they shall be blessed. And the light of God shall shine on them.

9 And behold! He comes with ten thousand of His holy ones (saints) to execute judgment on all, and to destroy all the ungodly (wicked); and to convict all flesh of all the works of their ungodliness which they have ungodly committed, and of all the hard things which ungodly sinners have spoken against Him.

[Chapter 2]

1 Observe everything that takes place in the sky, how the lights do not change their orbits, and the luminaries which are in heaven, how they all rise and set in order each in its season (proper time), and do not transgress against their appointed order.

2 Consider the earth, and give understanding to the things which take place on it from start to finish, how steadfast they are, how none of the things on the earth change, but all the works of God appear to you.

3 Behold the summer and the winter, how the whole earth is filled with water, and clouds and dew and rain lie on it.

[Chapter 3]

1 Observe and see how (in the winter) all the trees seem as though they had withered and shed all their leaves, except fourteen trees, which do not lose their foliage but retain the old foliage from two to three years until the new comes.

[Chapter 4]

1 And again, observe the days of summer how the sun is above the earth. And you seek shade and shelter because of the heat of the sun, and the earth also burns with growing heat, and so you cannot walk on the earth, or on a rock because of its heat.

[Chapter 5]

1 Observe how the trees are covered with green leaves and how they bear fruit. Understand, know, and recognize that He that lives for ever made them this way for you.

2 And all His works go on before Him from year to year for ever, and all the work and the tasks which they accomplish for Him do not change, and so is it done.

3 Consider how the sea and the rivers in like manner accomplish their course do not change because of His commandments.

4 But you, you have neither held to nor have you done the commandments of the Lord, But you have turned away and spoken proud and hard words with your unclean mouths against His greatness. Oh, you hard-hearted, you shall find no peace.

5 Therefore shall you curse your days, and the years of your life shall perish, and the years of your destruction shall be multiplied and in an eternal curse you shall find no mercy.

6 In those days you shall make your names an eternal curse to all the righteous, and by you shall all who curse, curse, and all the sinners and godless shall curse you forever. And for you the godless there shall be a curse.

7 And all the elect shall rejoice, and there shall be forgiveness of sins, and mercy and peace and forbearance and joy. There shall be salvation for them, (like/and) a good light. And for all of you sinners there shall be no salvation, but on you all shall abide a curse.

8 But for the elect there shall be light and joy and peace, and they shall inherit the earth.

9 And then wisdom shall be given to the elect, and they shall all live and never again sin, either through forgetfulness or through pride: But those who are given wisdom shall be humble.

10 And they shall not again transgress, Nor shall they sin all the days of their life, Nor shall they die of the anger or wrath of God, But they shall complete the number of the days of their lives. And their lives shall be increased in peace, and their years will grow in joy and eternal gladness and peace, all the days of their lives.

[Chapter 6]

1 And it came to pass when the children of men had multiplied that in those days were born to them beautiful and fair daughters.

2 And the angels, the sons of heaven, saw and lusted after them, and said to one another: 'Come, let us choose us wives from among the children of men

3 And have children with them.' And Semjaza, who was their leader, said to them: 'I fear you will not agree to do this deed,

4 And I alone shall have to pay the penalty of this great sin.'

5 And they all answered him and said: 'Let us all swear an oath, and all bind ourselves by mutual curses so we will not abandon this plan but to do this

thing.' Then they all swore together and bound themselves by mutual curses.

6 And they were in all two hundred who descended in the days of Jared in the summit of Mount Hermon, and they called it Mount Hermon, because they had sworn and bound themselves by mutual curses on the act.

7 And these are the names of their leaders: Samlazaz, their leader, Araklba, Rameel, Kokablel, Tamlel, Ramlel, Danel, Ezeqeel, Baraqijal,

(Author's note: Samlazaz could be another spelling of Semjaza, and possibly be the same entity.)

8 Asael, Armaros, Batarel, Ananel, Zaqiel, Samsapeel, Satarel, Turel, Jomjael, Sariel. These are their chiefs of tens.

[Chapter 7]

1 And all of them together went and took wives for themselves, each choosing one for himself, and they began to go in to them and to defile themselves with sex with them,

2 And the angels taught them charms and spells, and the cutting of roots, and made them acquainted with plants.

3 And the women became pregnant, and they bare large giants, whose height was three thousand cubits (ells).

4 The giants consumed all the work and toil of men. And when men could no longer sustain them, the giants turned against them and devoured mankind.

5 And they began to sin against birds, and beasts, and reptiles, and fish, and to devour one another's flesh, and drank the blood.

6 Then the earth laid accusation against the lawless ones.
[Chapter 8]

1 And Azazel taught men to make swords, and knives, and shields, and breastplates, and taught them about metals of the earth and the art of working them, and bracelets, and ornaments, and the use of antimony, and the beautifying of the eyelids, and all kinds of precious stones, and all coloring and dyes.

2 And there was great impiety, they turned away from God, and committed fornication, and they were led astray, and became corrupt in all their ways.

3 Semjaza taught the casting of spells, and root-cuttings, Armaros taught counter-spells (release from spells), Baraqijal taught astrology, Kokabel taught the constellations (portents), Ezeqeel the knowledge of the clouds, Araqiel the signs of the earth, Shamsiel the signs of the sun, and Sariel the course of the moon. And as men perished, they cried, and their cry went up to heaven.

[Chapter 9]

1 And then Michael, Uriel, Raphael, and Gabriel looked down from heaven and saw much blood being shed on the earth, and all lawlessness being done on the earth.

2 And they said to each other: 'Let the cries from the destruction of Earth ascend up to the gates of heaven.

3 And now to you, the holy ones of heaven, the souls of men make their petition, saying, "Bring our cause before the Most High."'

4 And they said to the Lord of the ages: 'Lord of lords, God of gods, King of kings, and God of the ages, the throne of your glory endures through all the generations of the ages, and your name holy and glorious and blessed to all the ages!

5 You have made all things, and you have power over all things: and all things are revealed and open in your sight, and you see all things, and nothing can hide itself from you.

6 Look at what Azazel has done, who has taught all unrighteousness on earth and revealed the eternal secrets which were made and kept in heaven, which men were striving to learn:

7 And Semjaza, who taught spells, to whom you gave authority to rule over his associates.

8 And they have gone to the daughters of men on the earth, and have had sex with the women, and have defiled themselves, and revealed to them all kinds of sins.

9 And the women have borne giants, and the whole earth has thereby been filled with blood and unrighteousness.

10 And now, behold, the souls of those who have died are crying out and making their petition to the gates of heaven, and their lament has ascended and cannot cease because of the lawless deeds which are done on the earth.

11 And you know all things before they come to pass, and you see these things and you have permitted them, and say nothing to us about these things. What are we to do with them about these things?'

[Chapter 10]

1 Then said the Most High, the Great and Holy One, "Uriel, go to the son of Lamech.

2 Say to him: 'Go to Noah and tell him in my name "Hide yourself!" and reveal to him the end that is approaching: that the whole earth will be destroyed, and a flood is about to come on the whole earth, and will destroy everything on it.'

3 'And now instruct him as to what he must do to escape that his offspring may be preserved for all the generations of the world.'

.

4 And again the Lord said to Raphael: 'Bind Azazel hand and foot, and cast him into the darkness and split open the desert, which is in Dudael, and cast him in.

5 And fill the hole by covering him rough and jagged rocks, and cover him with darkness, and let him live there for ever, and cover his face that he may not see the light.

6 And on the day of the great judgment he shall be hurled into the fire.

7 And heal the earth which the angels have ruined, and proclaim the healing of the earth, for I will restore the earth and heal the plague, that not all of the children of men may perish through all the secret things that the Watchers have disclosed and have taught their sons.

8 The whole earth has been corrupted through the works that were taught by Azazel: to him ascribe ALL SIN.'

9 To Gabriel said the Lord: 'Proceed against the bastards and the reprobates, and against the children of fornication and destroy the children of fornication and the children of the Watchers. Cause them to go against one another that they may destroy each other in battle: Shorten their days.

10 No request that (the Watchers) their fathers make of you shall be granted them on their behalf; for they hope to live an eternal life, and that each one of them will live five hundred years.'

11 And the Lord said to Michael: 'Go, bind Semjaza and his team who have associated with women and have defiled themselves in all their uncleanness.

12 When their sons have slain one another, and they have seen the destruction of their beloved ones, bind them fast for seventy generations under the hills of the earth, until the day of the consummation of their judgment and until the eternal judgment is accomplished.

(Author's note: 70 generations of 500 years = 3500 years.)

13 In those days they shall be led off to the abyss of fire and to the torment and the prison in which they shall be confined for ever.'

14 Then Semjaza shall be burnt up with the condemned and they will be destroyed, having been bound together with them to the end of all generations.

15 Destroy all the spirits of lust and the children of the Watchers, because they have wronged mankind.

16 Destroy all wrong from the face of the earth and let every evil work come to an end and let (the earth be planted with righteousness) the plant of righteousness and truth appear; and it shall prove a blessing, the works of righteousness and truth shall be planted in truth and joy for evermore.

17 And then shall all the righteous survive, and shall live until they beget thousands of children, and all the days of their youth and their old age shall they complete in peace.

18 And then shall the whole earth be untilled in righteousness and shall be planted with trees and be full of blessing. And all desirable trees shall be planted on it, and they shall plant vines on it.

19 And the vine which they plant shall yield fruit in abundance, and as for all the seed which is sown, each measurement (of it) shall bear a thousand, and each measurement of olives shall yield ten presses of oil.

20 You shall cleanse the earth from all oppression, and from all unrighteousness, and from all sin, and from all godlessness, and all the uncleanness that is brought on the earth you shall destroy from off the earth.

21 All the children of men shall become righteous, and all nations shall offer adoration and shall praise Me,

22 And all shall worship Me. And the earth shall be cleansed from all defilement, and from all sin, and from all punishment, and from all torment, and I will never again send another flood from this generation to all generations and for ever.

[Chapter 11]

1 And in those days I will open the storehouse of blessings in heaven, and rain down blessings on the earth and over the work and labor of the children of men.

2 Truth and peace shall be united throughout all the days of the world and throughout all the generations of men.'

[Chapter 12]

1 Then Enoch disappeared and no one of the children of men knew where he was hidden, and where he abode;

2 And what had become of him. And his activities were with the Holy Ones and the Watchers.

3 And I, Enoch, was blessing the Lord of majesty and the King of the ages, and lo! the Watchers called me, Enoch the scribe, and said to me:

4 'Enoch, you scribe of righteousness, go, tell the Watchers of heaven who have left the high heaven, the holy eternal place, and have defiled

themselves with women, and have done as the children of earth do, and have taken to themselves wives:

5 "You have done great destruction on the earth: And you shall have no peace nor forgiveness of sin:

6 Since they delight themselves in their children, They shall see the murder of their beloved ones, and the destruction of their children shall and they shall lament, and shall make supplication forever, you will receive neither mercy or peace."

[Chapter 13]

1 And Enoch went and said: 'Azazel, you shall have no peace: a severe sentence has been passed against you that you should be bound:

2 And you shall not have rest or mercy (toleration nor request granted), because of the unrighteousness which you have taught, and because of all the works of godlessness,

3 And unrighteousness and sin which you have shown to men.

4 Then I went and spoke to them all together, and they were all afraid, and fear and trembling seized them.

5 And they asked me to write a petition for them that they might find forgiveness, and to read their petition in the presence of the Lord of heaven. They had been forbidden to speak (with Him) nor were they to lift up their eyes to heaven for shame of their sins because they had been condemned.

6 Then I wrote out their petition, and the prayer in regard to their spirits and their deeds individually and in regard to their requests that they should obtain forgiveness and forbearance.

7 And I went off and sat down at the waters of Dan, in the land of Dan, to the southwest of Hermon: I read their petition until I fell asleep.

8 And I had a dream, and I saw a vision of their chastisement, and a voice came to me that I would reprimand (reprove) them.

9 And when I awoke, I came to them, and they were all sitting gathered together, weeping in Abelsjail, which is between Lebanon and Seneser, with their faces covered.

10 And I recounted to them all the visions which I had seen when I was asleep, and I began to speak the words of righteousness, and to reprimand heavenly Watchers.

[Chapter 14]

1 This is the book of the words of righteousness, and of the reprimand of the eternal Watchers in accordance with the command of the Holy Great One in that vision I saw in my sleep.

2 What I will now say with a tongue of flesh and with the breath of my mouth: which the Great One has given to men to speak with it and to understand with the heart.

3 As He has created and given to man the power of understanding the word of wisdom, so has He created me also and given me the power of reprimanding the Watchers, the children of heaven.

4 I wrote out your petition, and in my vision it appeared that your petition will not be granted to you throughout all the days of eternity, and that judgment has been finally passed on you:

5 Your petition will not be granted. From here on you shall not ascend into heaven again for all eternity, and you will be bound on earth for all eternity.

6 Before this you will see the destruction of your beloved sons and you shall have no pleasure in them, but they shall fall before you by the sword.
7 Your petition shall not be granted on their behalf or on yours, even though you weep and pray and speak all the words contained in my writings.

8 In the vision I saw clouds that invited me and summoned me into a mist, and the course of the stars and the flashes of lightning and hurried me and drove me,

9 And the winds in the vision caused me to fly and lifted me up, and bore me into heaven. And I went in until I drew near to a wall which was built out of crystals and surrounded by tongues of fire, and it began to frighten me.

10 I went into the tongues of fire and drew near a large house which was built of crystals: and the walls of the house were like a mosaic of hailstones and the floor was made of crystals like snow.

11 Its ceiling was like the path of the stars and lightning flashes, and between them were fiery cherubim,

12 Their sky was clear as water. A flaming fire surrounded the walls, and its doors blazed with fire.

13 I entered that house, and it was hot as fire and cold as ice; there were no pleasures or life therein: fear covered me, and trembling got hold of me.

14 As I shook and trembled, I fell on my face.

15 And I saw a vision, And lo! there was a second house, greater than the first,

16 And the all the doors stood open before me, and it was built of flames of fire. And in every respect it was splendid and magnificent to the extent that I cannot describe it to you.

17 Its floor was of fire, and above it was lightning and the path of the stars, and its ceiling also was flaming fire.

18 And I looked and saw a throne set on high, its appearance was like crystal, and its wheels were like a shining sun, and there was the vision of cherubim.

19 And from underneath the throne came rivers of fire so that I could not look at it.

20 And He who is Great in Glory sat on the throne, and His raiment shone more brightly than the sun and was whiter than any snow.

21 None of the angels could enter or could behold His face because of the magnificence and glory and no flesh could behold Him.

22 The sea of fire surrounded Him, and a great fire stood in front of Him, and no one could draw close to Him: ten thousand times ten thousand stood before Him, but He needed no Holy council.

23 The most Holy Ones who were near to Him did not leave night or day.

24 And until then I had been prostrate on my face, trembling, and the Lord called me with His own mouth, and said to me:

25 'Come here, Enoch, and hear my word.' And one of the Holy Ones came to me picked me up and brought me to the door: and I bowed down my face.

[Chapter 15]

1 And He answered and said to me, and I heard His voice: 'Do not be afraid, Enoch, you righteous man and scribe of righteousness.

2 Approach and hear my voice. Go and say to the Watchers of heaven, for whom you have come to intercede: "You should intercede for men, and not men for you."

3 Why and for what cause have you left the high, holy, and eternal heaven, and had sex with women, and defiled yourselves with the daughters of men and taken to yourselves wives, and done like the children of earth, and begotten giants (as your) sons?

4 Though you were holy, spiritual, living the eternal life, you have defiled yourselves with the blood of women, and have begotten children with the blood of flesh, and, as the children of men, you have lusted after flesh and blood like those who die and are killed.

5 This is why I have given men wives, that they might impregnate them, and have children by them, that deeds might continue on the earth.

6 But you were formerly spiritual, living the eternal life, and immortal for all generations of the world.

7 Therefore I have not appointed wives for you; you are spiritual beings of heaven, and in heaven was your dwelling place.

8 And now, the giants, who are produced from the spirits and flesh, shall be called evil spirits on the earth,

9 And shall live on the earth. Evil spirits have come out from their bodies because they are born from men and from the holy Watchers, their beginning is of primal origin;

10 They shall be evil spirits on earth, and evil spirits shall they be called spirits of the evil ones. [As for the spirits of heaven, in heaven shall be their dwelling, but as for the spirits of the earth which were born on the earth, on the earth shall be their dwelling.] And the spirits of the giants afflict, oppress, destroy, attack, war, destroy, and cause trouble on the earth.

11 They take no food, but do not hunger or thirst. They cause offences but are not observed.

12 And these spirits shall rise up against the children of men and against the women, because they have proceeded from them in the days of the slaughter and destruction.'

[Chapter 16]

1 'And at the death of the giants, spirits will go out and shall destroy without incurring judgment, coming from their bodies their flesh shall be destroy until the day of the consummation, the great judgment in which the age shall be consummated, over the Watchers and the godless, and shall be wholly consummated.'

2 And now as to the Watchers who have sent you to intercede for them, who had been in heaven before,

3 (Say to them): "You were in heaven, but all the mysteries of heaven had not been revealed to you, and you knew worthless ones, and these in the hardness of your hearts you have made known to the women, and through these mysteries women and men work much evil on earth."

4 Say to them therefore: " You have no peace."'

[Chapter 17]

1 And they took me to a place in which those who were there were like flaming fire,

2 And, when they wished, they made themselves appear as men. They brought me to the place of darkness, and to a mountain the point of whose summit reached to heaven.

3 And I saw the lighted places and the treasuries of the stars and of the thunder and in the uttermost depths, where were

4 A fiery bow and arrows and their quiver, and a fiery sword and all the lightning. And they took me to the waters of life, and to the fire of the west, which receives every setting of the sun.

5 And I came to a river of fire in which the fire flows like water into the great sea towards the west.

6 I saw the great rivers and came to the great darkness, and went to the place where no flesh walks.

7 I saw the mountains of the darkness of winter and the place from where all the waters of the deep flow.

8 I saw the mouths of all the rivers of the earth and the mouth of the deep.

[Chapter 18]

1 I saw the storehouse of all the winds: I saw how He had adorned the whole creation with them and the firm foundations of the earth.

2 And I saw the corner-stone of the earth: I saw the four winds which support the earth and the firmament of the heaven.

3 I saw how the winds stretch out the height of heaven, and have their station between heaven and earth; these are the pillars of heaven.

4 I saw the winds of heaven which turn and bring the sky and the sun and all the stars to their setting place.

5 I saw the winds on the earth carrying the clouds: I saw the paths of the angels. I saw at the end of the earth the firmament of heaven above.

6 And I continued south and saw a place which burns day and night, where there are seven mountains of magnificent stones, three towards the east, and three towards the south.

7 And as for those towards the east, they were of colored stone, and one of pearl, and one of jacinth (a stone of healing), and those towards the south of red stone.

8 But the middle one reached to heaven like the throne of God, and was made of alabaster.

9 And the summit of the throne was of sapphire.

10 And I saw a great abyss of the earth, with pillars of heavenly fire, and I saw among them fiery pillars of Heaven, which were falling,

11 And as regards both height and depth, they were immeasurable.

12 And beyond that abyss I saw a place which had no firmament of heaven above, and no firmly founded earth beneath it: there was no water on it, and no birds,

13 But it was a desert and a horrible place. I saw there seven stars like great burning mountains,

14 And an angel questioned me regarding them. The angel said: 'This place is the end of heaven and earth.

15 This has become a prison for the stars and the host of heaven. And the stars which roll over the fire are they which have transgressed the commandment of the Lord in the beginning of their rising, because they did not come out at their proper times.

16 And He was angry with them, and bound them until the time when their guilt should be consummated even for ten thousand years.'

[Chapter 19]

1 And Uriel said to me: 'The angels who have had sex with women shall stand here, and their spirits, having assumed many different forms, are defiling mankind and shall lead them astray into sacrificing to demons as gods, here shall they stand, until the day of the great judgment in which they shall be judged and are made an end of.

2 And the women also of the angels who went astray shall become sirens (other versions read 'shall become peaceful' also, another version reads, 'shall salute them').'

3 And I, Enoch, alone saw the vision, the ends of all things: and no man shall see as I have seen.

[Chapter 20]

1 These are the names of the holy angels who watch.

2 Uriel, one of the holy angels, who is over the world, turmoil and terror.

3 Raphael, one of the holy angels, who is over the spirits of men.

4 Raguel, one of the holy angels who takes vengeance on the world of the luminaries.

5 Michael, one of the holy angels, set over the virtues of mankind and over chaos.

6 Saraqael, one of the holy angels, who is set over the spirits, who sin in the spirit.

7 Gabriel, one of the holy angels, who is over Paradise and the serpents and the Cherubim.

8 Remiel, one of the holy angels, whom God set over those who rise.

[Chapter 21]

1 Then, I proceeded to where things were chaotic and void.

2 And I saw there something horrible: I saw neither a heaven above nor a firmly founded earth, but a place chaotic and horrible.

3 And there I saw seven stars of heaven bound together in it, like great mountains and burning with fire.

4 Then I said: 'For what sin are they bound, and on why have they been cast in here?'

5 Then said Uriel, one of the holy angels, who was with me, and was chief over them: 'Enoch, why do you ask, and why art you eager for the truth?

6 These are some of the stars of heaven, which have transgressed the commandment of the Lord, and are bound here until ten thousand years, the time entailed by their sins, are consummated.'

7 And I went out from there to another place, which was still more horrible than the former, and I saw a terrible thing: a great fire there which burnt and blazed, and the place was cleft as far as the abyss, full of great falling columns of fire:

8 Neither its width or breadth could I see, nor could I see its source.

9 Then I said: 'I am afraid of this place and cannot stand to look at it.!' Then Uriel, one of the holy angels who was with me, answered and said to me: 'Enoch, why are you so afraid?'

10 And I answered: 'Because of this fearful place, and because of the spectacle of the pain.' And he said to me: 'This place is the prison of the angels, and here they will be imprisoned for ever.'

[Chapter 22]

1 And I went out to another place west where there was a mountain and hard rock.

2 And there was in it four hollow places, deep and wide and very smooth. How smooth are the hollow places and looked deep and dark.

3 Then Raphael answered, one of the holy angels who was with me, and said to me: 'These hollow places have been created for this very purpose, that the spirits of the souls of the dead should be gathered here, that all the souls of the children of men should brought together here. And these places have been made to receive them until the day of their judgment and until the period appointed, until the great judgment comes on them.'

4 I saw the spirit of a dead man, and his voice went out to heaven and made petitions.

5 And I asked Raphael the angel who was with me, and I said to him: 'This spirit which petitions,

6 Whose is it, whose voice goes up and petitions heaven?'

7 And he answered me saying: 'This is the spirit which went out from Abel, whom his brother Cain slew, and he makes his suit against him until his offspring is destroyed from the face of the earth, and his offspring are annihilated from among the children of men.'

8 Then I asked, regarding all the hollow places: 'Why is one separated from the other?'

9 And he answered me and said to me: 'These three have been made that the spirits of the dead might be separated. Divisions have been made for the spirits of the righteous, in which there is the bright spring of water.

10 And one for sinners when they die and are buried in the earth and judgment has not been executed on them in their lifetime.

11 Here their spirits shall be set apart in this great pain until the great day of judgment and punishment and torment of those who curse for ever and retribution for their spirits.

12 There He shall bind them for ever. And such a division has been made for the spirits of those who make their petitions, who make disclosures concerning their destruction, when they were slain in the days of the sinners.

13 Such has been made for the spirits of men who were not righteous but sinners, who were complete in transgression, and of the transgressors they shall be companions, but their spirits shall not be destroyed in the day of judgment nor shall they be raised from here.'

14 Then I blessed the Lord of glory and said: 'Blessed be my Lord, the Lord of righteousness, who rules for ever.'

[Chapter 23]

1 From here I went to another place to the west of the ends of the earth.

2 And I saw a burning fire which ran without resting, and never stopped from its course day or night but flowed always in the same way.

3 And I asked saying: 'What is this which never stops?'

4 Then Raguel, one of the holy angels who was with me, answered me and said to me: 'This course of fire which you have seen is the fire in the west and is the fire of all the lights of heaven.'

[Chapter 24]

1 And from here I went to another place on the earth, and he showed me a mountain range of fire which burned day and night.

2 And I went beyond it and saw seven magnificent mountains, all differing from each other, and their stones were magnificent and beautiful, and their form was glorious: three towards the east, one founded on the other, and three towards the south, one on the other, and deep rough ravines, no one of which joined with any other.

3 And the seventh mountain was in the midst of these, and it was higher than them, resembling the seat of a throne.

4 And fragrant trees encircled the throne. And among them was a tree such as I had never smelled, nor was any among them or were others like it; it had a fragrance beyond all fragrance, and its leaves and blooms and wood would not ever wither:

5 And its fruit is beautiful, and its fruit resembles the dates of a palm. Then I said: 'How beautiful is this tree, and fragrant, and its leaves are fair, and its blooms very delightful in appearance.'

6 Then Michael, one of the holy and honored angels who was with me, and was their leader, spoke.

[Chapter 25]

1 And he said to me: 'Enoch, why do you ask me about the fragrance of the tree, and why do you wish to learn the truth?'

2 Then I answered him saying: 'I wish to know about everything, but especially about this tree.'

3 And he answered saying: 'This high mountain which you have seen, whose summit is like the throne of God, is His throne, where the Holy Great One, the Lord of Glory, the Eternal King, will sit, when He shall come down to visit the earth with goodness.

4 And as for this fragrant tree, no mortal is permitted to touch it until the great judgment, when He shall take vengeance on all and bring everything to its completion for ever.

5 It shall then be given to the righteous and holy. Its fruit shall be for food to the Elect: it shall be transplanted to the holy place, to the temple of the Lord, the Eternal King.

6 Then they shall rejoice and be glad, and enter into the holy place; And its fragrance shall enter into their bones, And they shall live a long life on earth, as your fathers lived. And in their days there will be no sorrow or pain or torment or toil.'

7 Then I blessed the God of Glory, the Eternal King, who has prepared such things for the righteous, and has created them and promised to give to them.

[Chapter 26]

1 And I went from there to the middle of the earth, and I saw a blessed place in which there were trees with branches alive and blooming on a tree that had been cut down.

2 And there I saw a holy mountain,

3 And underneath the mountain to the east there was a stream and it flowed towards the south. And I saw towards the east another mountain higher than this, and between them a deep and narrow valley.

4 In it ran a stream underneath the mountain. And to the west of it there was another mountain, lower than the former and of small elevation, and a dry, deep valley between them; and another deep and dry valley was at the edge of the three mountains.

5 And all the valleys were deep and narrow, being formed from hard rock, and there were no trees planted on them.

6 And I was very amazed at the rocks in the valleys.

[Chapter 27]

1 Then I said: 'What is the purpose of this blessed land, which is entirely filled with trees, and what is the purpose of this accursed valley between them?'

2 Then Uriel, one of the holy angels who was with me, answered and said: 'This accursed valley is for those who are cursed for ever: Here shall all the accursed be gathered together who utter with their lips words against the Lord not befitting His glory or say hard things against Him. Here shall they be gathered together, and here shall be their place of judgment.

3 In the last days there shall be the spectacle of righteous judgment on them in the presence of the righteous for ever: here shall the merciful bless the Lord of glory, the Eternal King.

4 In the days of judgment they shall bless Him for the mercy in that He has shown them.'

5 Then I blessed the Lord of Glory and set out His glory and praised Him gloriously.

[Chapter 28]

1 Then, I went towards the east, into the midst of the mountain range in the desert, and I saw a wilderness.

2 And it was solitary, full of trees and plants. And water gushed out from above.

3 Rushing like a torrent which flowed towards the north-west it caused clouds and dew to fall on every side.

[Chapter 29]

1 Then I went to another place in the desert, and approached to the east of this mountain range.

2 And there I saw aromatic trees exuding the fragrance of frankincense and myrrh, and the trees also were similar to the almond tree.

[Chapter 30]

1 Beyond these, I went far to the east,

2 And I saw another place, a valley full of water like one that would not run dry.

3 And there was a tree, the color of fragrant trees was that of mastic. And on the sides of those valleys I saw fragrant cinnamon. And beyond these I proceeded to the east.

[Chapter 31]

1 And I saw other mountains, and among them were groves of trees, and there was nectar that flowed from them, which is named Sarara and Galbanum.

2 And beyond these mountains I saw another mountain to the east of the ends of the earth, on which there were aloe trees, and all the trees were full of fruit, being like almond trees.

3 And when it was burned it smelled sweeter than any fragrant odor.

[Chapter 32]

1 And after I had smelled these fragrant odors, I looked towards the north over the mountains I saw seven mountains full of fine nard and fragrant trees of cinnamon and pepper.

2 And then I went over the summits of all these mountains, far towards the east of the earth, and passed over the Red Sea and went far from it, and passed over the angel Zotiel.

3 And I came to the Garden of Righteousness. I saw far beyond those trees more trees and they were numerous and large. There were two trees there, very large, beautiful, glorious, and magnificent. The tree of knowledge, whose holy fruit they ate and acquired great wisdom.

4 That tree is in height like the fir, and its leaves are like those of the Carob tree,

5 And its fruit is like the clusters of the grapes, very beautiful: and the fragrance of the tree carries far.

6 Then I said: 'How beautiful is the tree, and how attractive is its look!' Then Raphael the holy angel, who was with me, answered me and said: 'This is the tree of wisdom, of which your father of old and your mother of old, who were your progenitors, have eaten, and they learned wisdom and their eyes were opened, and they knew that they were naked and they were driven out of the garden.'

[Chapter 33]

1 And from there I went to the ends of the earth and saw there large beasts, and each differed from the other; and I saw birds also differing in appearance and beauty and voice, the one differing from the other.

2 And to the east of those beasts I saw the ends of the earth where heaven rests on it, and the doors of heaven open. And I saw how the stars of heaven come out, and I counted the gates from which they came out,
3 And wrote down all their outlets, of each individual star by their number and their names, their courses and their positions, and their times and their months, as Uriel the holy angel who was with me showed me.

4 He showed me all things and wrote them down for me; also their names he wrote for me, and their laws and their functions.

[Chapter 34]

1 From there I went towards the north to the ends of the earth, and there I saw a great and glorious device at the ends of the whole earth.

2 And here I saw three gates of heaven open : through each of them proceed north winds: when they blow there is cold, hail, frost, snow, dew, and rain.

3 And out of one gate they blow for good: but when they blow through the other two gates, it is for violence and torment on the earth, and they blow with force.

[Chapter 35]

1 Then I went towards the west to the ends of the earth, and saw there three gates of heaven open such as I had seen in the east, the same number of gates, and the same number of outlets.

[Chapter 36]

1 And from there I went to the south to the ends of the earth, and saw there three open gates of heaven.

2 And from them come dew, rain, and wind. And from there I went to the east to the ends of heaven, and saw here the three eastern gates of heaven open and small gates above them.

3 Through each of these small gates pass the stars of heaven and they run their course to the west on the path which is shown to them.

4 And as often as I saw I blessed always the Lord of Glory, and I continued to bless the Lord of Glory who has done great and glorious wonders, who has shown the greatness of His work to the angels and to spirits and to men, that they might praise His work and all His creation: that they might see the power of His might and praise the great work of His hands and bless Him for ever.

[Chapter 37]

1 The second vision which he saw, the vision of wisdom which Enoch the son of Jared, the son of Mahalalel,

2 The son of Cainan, the son of Enos, the son of Seth, the son of Adam, saw. And this is the beginning of the words of wisdom which I lifted up my voice

to speak and say to those which dwell on earth: Hear, you men of old time, and see, you that come after, the words of the Holy One which I will speak before the Lord of spirits.

3 The words are for the men of old time, and to those that come after. We will not withhold the beginning of wisdom from this present day. Such wisdom has never been given by the Lord of spirits as I have received according to my insight, according to the good pleasure of the Lord of spirits by whom the lot of eternal life has been given to me.

4 Now three Parables were imparted to me, and I lifted up my voice and recounted them to those that dwell on the earth.

[Chapter 38]

1 The first Parable: When the congregation of the righteous shall appear, and sinners shall be judged for their sins, and shall be driven from the face of the earth;

2 And when the Righteous One shall appear before the eyes of the elect righteous ones, whose works are weighed by the Lord of spirits, light shall appear to the righteous and the elect who dwell on the earth. Where will there be the dwelling for sinners, and where the will there be a resting-place for those who have denied the Lord of spirits? It had been good for them if they had not been born.

3 When the secrets of the righteous shall be revealed and the sinners judged, and the godless driven from the presence of the righteous and elect,

4 From that time those that possess the earth shall no longer be powerful and mighty: And they shall not be able to look at the face of the holy ones, because the Lord of spirits has caused His light to appear on the face of the holy, righteous, and elect.

5 Then the kings and the mighty shall be destroyed and be turned over into the hands of the righteous and holy.

6 And from then on none shall seek mercy from the Lord of spirits for themselves for their life is at an end.

[Chapter 39]

1 And it shall come to pass in those days that elect and holy children will descend from the high heaven, and their offspring will become one with the children of men.

2 And in those days Enoch received books of indignation and wrath, and books of turmoil and confusion. There will be no mercy for them, says the Lord of spirits.

3 And in those days a whirlwind carried me off from the earth, And set me down at the end of heaven.

4 There I saw another vision, the dwelling-places of the holy, and the resting-places of the righteous.

5 Here my eyes saw the dwelling places of His righteous angels, and the resting-places of the Holy Ones. And they petitioned and interceded and prayed for the children of men, and righteousness flowed before them like water, and mercy fell like dew on the earth: Thus it is among them for ever and ever.

6 And in that place my eyes saw the Elect One of righteousness and of faith,

7 And I saw his dwelling-place under the wings of the Lord of spirits.

8 And righteousness shall prevail in his days, and the righteous and elect shall be innumerable and will be before Him for ever and ever.

9 And all the righteous and elect ones before Him shall be as bright as fiery lights, and their mouth shall be full of blessing, and their lips shall praise the name of the Lord of spirits. Righteousness and truth before Him shall never fail.

10 There I wished to dwell, and my spirit longed for that dwelling-place; and thus it was decided and my portion was assigned and established by the Lord of spirits.

11 In those days I praised and exalted the name of the Lord of spirits with blessings and praises, because He had destined me for blessing and glory according to the good pleasure of the Lord of spirits.

12 For a long time my eyes looked at that place, and I blessed Him and praised Him, saying: 'Blessed is He, and may He be blessed from the beginning and for evermore. And in His presence there is no end.

13 He knows before the world was created what is for ever and what will be from generation to generation.

14 Those who do not sleep bless you, they stand before your glory and bless, praise, and exalt you, saying: "Holy, holy, holy, is the Lord of spirits: He fills the earth with spirits."'

15 And here my eyes saw all those who do not sleep: they stand before Him and bless Him saying: 'Blessed be you, and blessed be the name of the Lord for ever and ever.'

16 And my face was changed; for I could no longer see.

[Chapter 40]

1 And after that I saw thousands of thousands and ten thousand times ten thousand,

2 I saw a multitude beyond number and reckoning, who stood before the Lord of spirits. And on the four sides of the Lord of spirits I saw four figures, different from those that did not sleep, and I learned their names; for the angel that went with me told me their names, and showed me all the hidden things.

3 And I heard the voices of those four presences as they uttered praises before the Lord of glory.

4 The first voice blessed the Lord of spirits for ever and ever.

5 The second voice I heard blessing the Elect One and the elect ones who depend on the Lord of spirits.

6 And the third voice I heard pray and intercede for those who live on the earth and pray earnestly in the name of the Lord of spirits.

7 And I heard the fourth voice fending off the Satans (advisories or accusers) and forbidding them to come before the Lord of spirits to accuse them who dwell on the earth.

8 After that I asked the angel of peace who went with me, who showed me everything that is hidden: 'Who are these four figures which I have seen and whose words I have heard and written down?'

9 And he said to me: 'This first is Michael, the merciful and long-suffering; and the second, who is set over all the diseases and all the wounds of the children of men, is Raphael; and the third, who is set over all the powers, is Gabriel' and the fourth, who is set over the repentance and those who hope to inherit eternal life, is named Phanuel.'

10 And these are the four angels of the Lord of spirits and the four voices I heard in those days.

[Chapter 41]

1 And after that I saw all the secrets of heavens, and how the kingdom is divided, and how the actions of men are weighed in the balance.

2 And there I saw the mansions of the elect and the mansions of the holy, and my eyes saw all the sinners being driven from there which deny the name of the Lord of spirits, and they were being dragged off; and they could not live because of the punishment which proceeds from the Lord of spirits.

3 And there my eyes saw the secrets of the lightning and of the thunder, and the secrets of the winds, how they are divided to blow over the earth, and the secrets of the clouds and dew,

4 And there I saw where they came from and how they saturate the dusty earth.

5 And there I saw closed storehouses out of which the winds are divided, the storehouse of the hail and winds, the storehouse of the mist, and of the clouds, and the cloud thereof hovers over the earth from the beginning of the world.

6 And I saw the storehouses of the sun and moon, where they go and where they come, and their glorious return, and how one is superior to the other, and their stately orbit, and how they do not leave their orbit, and they add nothing to their orbit and they take nothing from it, and they keep faith with each other, in accordance with the oath by which they are bound together.

7 And first the sun goes out and traverses his path according to the commandment of the Lord of spirits, and mighty is His name for ever and

ever. And after that I saw the invisible and the visible path of the moon, and she accomplishes the course of her path in that place by day and by night-the one holding a position opposite to the other before the Lord of spirits. And they give thanks and praise and rest not; but their thanksgiving is for ever and ever.

8 For the sun makes many revolutions for a blessing or a curse, and the course of the path of the moon is light to the righteous and darkness to the sinners in the name of the Lord, who made a separation between the light and the darkness, and divided the spirits of men and strengthened the spirits of the righteous, in the name of His righteousness.

9 For no angel hinders and no power is able to hinder; for He appoints a judge for them all and He judges them all Himself.

[Chapter 42]

1 Wisdom found no place where she might dwell; then a dwelling-place was assigned her in heavens.

2 Wisdom went out to make her dwelling among the children of men, and found no dwelling-place. Wisdom returned to her place, and took her seat among the angels.

3 And unrighteousness went out from her storehouses. She found those she did not seek, and dwelt with them, (she sought no one in particular but found a place...); as rain in a desert and dew on a thirsty land.

[Chapter 43]

1 And I saw other lightning and the stars of heaven, and I saw how He called them all by their names and they obeyed Him.

2 And I saw how they are weighed in a righteous balance according to their proportions of light: I saw the width of their spaces and the day of their appearing, and how their revolution produces lightning:

3 And I saw their revolution according to the number of the angels, and how they keep faith with each other. And I asked the angel who went with me who showed me what was hidden:

4 'What are these?' And he said to me: 'The Lord of spirits has shown you their parable: these are the names of the holy who dwell on the earth and believe in the name of the Lord of spirits for ever and ever.'

[Chapter 44]

1 Also another phenomenon I saw in regard to the lightning: how some of the stars arise and become lightning and cannot part with their new form.

[Chapter 45]

1 And this is the second Parable: concerning those who deny the name of the dwelling of the holy ones and the Lord of spirits.

2 They shall not ascend to heaven, and they shall not come on the earth: Such shall be the lot of the sinners who have denied the name of the Lord of spirits, who are preserved for the day of suffering and tribulation.

3 On that day My Elect One shall sit on the throne of glory and shall try the works of the righteous, and their places of rest shall be innumerable. And their souls shall grow strong within them when they see My Elect One, And those who have called on My glorious name:

4 Then will I cause My Elect One to dwell among them. I will transform heaven and make it an eternal blessing and light,

5 And I will transform the earth and make it a blessing, and I will cause My elect ones to dwell on it. But the sinners and evil-doers shall not set foot on it.

6 For I have seen and satisfied My righteous ones with peace and have caused them to dwell before Me, but for the sinners there is judgment impending with Me, so that I shall destroy them from the face of the earth.

[Chapter 46]

1 And there I saw One whose face looked ancient. His head was white like wool, and with Him was another being whose countenance had the appearance of a man, and his face was full of graciousness, like one of the holy angels.

2 And I asked the angel who went with me and showed me all the hidden things, concerning that Son of Man, who he was, and where came from, and why he went with the Ancient One? And he answered and said to me:

3 "This is the son of Man who has righteousness, with whom dwells righteousness, and who reveals all the treasures of that which is hidden, because the Lord of spirits has chosen him, and whose lot has preeminence before the Lord of spirits in righteousness and is for ever.

4 And this Son of Man whom you have seen shall raise up the kings and the mighty from their seats, and the strong from their thrones and shall loosen the reins of the strong, and break the teeth of the sinners.

5 And he shall put down the kings from their thrones and kingdoms because they do not exalt and praise Him, nor humbly acknowledge who bestowed their kingdom on them.

6 And he shall make the strong hang their heads, and shall fill them with shame. And darkness shall be their dwelling, and worms shall be their bed, and they shall have no hope of rising from their beds, because they do not exalt the name of the Lord of spirits."

7 They raise their hands against the Most High and tread on the earth and dwell on it and all their deeds manifest unrighteousness. Their power rests on their riches, and their faith is in the gods which they have made with their hands. They deny the name of the Lord of spirits,

8 And they persecute the houses of His congregations, and the faithful who depend on the name of the Lord of Spirits.

[Chapter 47]

1 In those days the prayer of the righteous shall have ascended, and the blood of the righteous from the earth shall be before the Lord of spirits.

2 In those days the holy ones who dwell above in heavens shall unite with one voice and supplicate and pray and praise, and give thanks and bless the name of the Lord of spirits on behalf of the blood of the righteous which has been shed, that the prayer of the righteous may not be in vain before the Lord of spirits, that they may have justice, and that they may not have to wait for ever.

3 In those days I saw the "Head of Days" when He seated himself on the throne of His glory, and the books of the living were opened before Him; and all His host which is in heaven above and His counselors stood before Him,

4 And the hearts of the holy were filled with joy because the number of the righteous had been offered, and the prayer of the righteous had been heard, and the blood of the righteous not been required before the Lord of spirits.

[Chapter 48]

1 And in that place I saw the spring of righteousness which was inexhaustible. And around it were many springs of wisdom. And all the thirsty drank of them, and were filled with wisdom, and their dwellings were with the righteous and holy and elect.

2 And at that hour that Son of Man was named in the presence of the Lord of spirits, And his name was brought before the Head of Days.

3 Even before the sun and the signs were created, before the stars of heaven were made, His name was named before the Lord of spirits.

4 He shall be a staff to the righteous and they shall steady themselves and not fall. And he shall be the light of the Gentiles, and the hope of those who are troubled of heart.

5 All who dwell on earth shall fall down and worship before him, and will praise and bless and sing and celebrate the Lord of spirits.

6 And for this reason he has been chosen and hidden in front of (kept safe by) Him, before the creation of the world and for evermore.

7 And the wisdom of the Lord of spirits has revealed him to the holy and righteous; For he has preserved the lot of the righteous, because they have hated and rejected this world of unrighteousness, and have hated all its works and ways in the name of the Lord of spirits. For in his name they are saved, and according to his good pleasure and it is He who has regard to their life.

8 In these days the kings of the earth and the strong who possess the land because of the works of their hands will be shamed, because on the day of their anguish and affliction they shall not be able to save themselves. And I will give them over into the hands of My elect.

9 As straw in the fire so shall they burn before the face of the holy; as lead in the water shall they sink before the face of the righteous, and no trace of them shall be found anymore.

10 And on the day of their affliction there shall be rest on the earth (because the evil ones will be destroyed), and before Him they shall fall down and not rise again, and there shall be no one to take them with his hands and raise them up; for they have denied the Lord of spirits and His Anointed. The name of the Lord of spirits be blessed.

[Chapter 49]

1 For wisdom is poured out like water, and glory will not fail before him ever.

2 For he is mighty in all the secrets of righteousness, and unrighteousness shall disappear like a shadow, and will no longer exist; because the Elect One stands before the Lord of spirits, and his glory is for ever and ever, and his might for all generations.

3 In him dwells the spirit of wisdom, and the spirit which gives insight, and the spirit of understanding and of might, and the spirit of those who have fallen asleep in righteousness.

4 And he shall judge the secret things, and no one shall be able to utter a lying or idle word before him, for he is the Elect One before the Lord of spirits according to His good pleasure.

[Chapter 50]

1 And in those days a change shall take place for the holy and elect, and the light of days shall abide on them, and glory and honor shall turn to the Holy.

2 On the day of trouble, affliction will be heaped on the evil. And the righteous shall be victorious in the name of the Lord of spirits. For He will this to others that they may repent and turn away from the works of their hands.

3 They shall have no honor through the name of the Lord of spirits, but through His name they shall be saved, and the Lord of spirits will have compassion on them, for His mercy is great.

4 He is righteous also in His judgment, and in the presence of His glory unrighteousness also shall not stand: At His judgment the unrepentant shall perish before Him.

5 And from now on I will have no mercy on them, says the Lord of spirits.

[Chapter 51]

1 And in those days shall the earth also give back that which has been entrusted to it, and Sheol (the grave) also shall give back that which it has received, and hell shall give back that which it owes. For in those days the Elect One shall arise,

2 And he shall choose the righteous and holy from among them. For the day has drawn near that they should be saved.

3 And in those days the Elect One shall sit on His throne, and all the secrets of wisdom and counsel shall pour from His mouth, for the Lord of spirits has given them to Him and has glorified Him.

4 In those days shall the mountains leap like rams, and the hills shall skip like lambs satisfied with milk, and the faces of all the angels in heaven shall be lighted up with joy.

5 And the earth shall rejoice, and the righteous shall dwell on it, and the elect shall walk on it.

[Chapter 52]

1 And after those days in that place where I had seen all the visions of that which is hidden, for I had been carried off in a whirlwind and they had borne me towards the west.

2 There my eyes saw all the secret things of heaven that shall be, a mountain of iron, and a mountain of copper, and a mountain of silver, and a mountain of gold, and a mountain of soft metal, and a mountain of lead.

3 And I asked the angel who went with me, saying, 'What things are these which I have seen in secret?'

4 And he said to me: 'All these things which you have seen shall serve the authority of His Messiah that he may be powerful and mighty on the earth.'

5 The angel of peace answered me saying: 'Wait a little while, and all secret things shall be revealed to you, things which surround the Lord of spirits.

6 And these mountains which your eyes have seen, the mountain of iron, and the mountain of copper, and the mountain of silver, and the mountain of gold, and the mountain of soft metal, and the mountain of lead, all of these shall be like wax before a fire in the presence of the Elect One. Like the water which streams down from above on those mountains, and they shall be weak under his feet.

7 And it shall come to pass in those days that none shall be saved, either by gold or by silver, and none will be able to save themselves or escape.

8 And there shall be no iron for war, nor materials for breastplates. Bronze shall be of no use, tin shall be worthless, and lead shall not be desired.

9 All these things shall be destroyed from the face of the earth, when the Elect One appears before the Lord of spirits.'

[Chapter 53]

1 There my eyes saw a deep valley with its mouth open, and all who dwell on the earth and sea and islands shall bring gifts and presents and tokens of homage to Him, but that deep valley shall not become full.

2 And their hands commit lawless deeds, and everything the righteous work at the sinners devour. The sinners shall be destroyed in front of the face of the Lord of spirits, and they shall be banished from off the face of His earth, and they shall perish for ever and ever.

3 For I saw all the angels of punishment abiding there and preparing all the instruments of Satan.

4 And I asked the angel of peace who went with me: 'For whom are they preparing these instruments?'

5 And he said to me: 'They prepare these for the kings and the powerful of this earth, that they may with them they be destroyed.

6 After this the Righteous and Elect One shall cause the house of His congregation to appear and from then on they shall hinder no more, in the name of the Lord of spirits.

7 And these mountains shall not stand as solid ground before His righteousness, but the hills shall be like springs of water, and the righteous shall have rest from the oppression of sinners.'

[Chapter 54]

1 And I looked and turned to another part of the earth, and saw there a deep valley with burning fire.

2 And they brought the kings and the powerful, and began to cast them into this deep valley.

3 And there my eyes saw how they made their instruments for them, iron chains of immeasurable weight.

4 And I asked the angel of peace who was with me, saying: 'For whom are these chains being prepared ?'

5 And he said to me: 'These are being prepared for the hosts of Azazel, so that they may take them and throw them into the bottom of the pit of hell, and they shall cover their jaws with rough stones as the Lord of spirits commanded.

6 And Michael, and Gabriel, and Raphael, and Phanuel shall take hold of them on that great day, and throw them into the burning furnace on that day, that the Lord of spirits may take vengeance on them for their unrighteousness in becoming servants to Satan and for leading astray those who live on the earth.'

7 And in those days punishment will come from the Lord of spirits, and he will open all the storehouses of waters above heavens, and of the fountains which are under the surface of the earth.

8 And all the waters shall be come together (flow into or be joined) with the waters of heaven (above the sky), that which is above heavens is the masculine, and the water which is beneath the earth is the feminine.

9 And they shall destroy all who live on the dry land and those who live under the ends of heaven.

(Author's note: The previous verse refers to Noah's flood).

10 And when they have acknowledged the unrighteousness which they have done on the earth, by these they shall perish.

[Chapter 55]

1 And after that the Head of Days repented and said: 'I have destroyed all who dwell on the earth to no avail.'

2 And He swore by His great name: 'From now on I will not do this to all who dwell on the earth again, and I will set a sign in heaven: and this shall be a covenant of good faith between Me and them for ever, so long as heaven is above the earth. And this is in accordance with My command.

(Author's note: The previous verse refers to the rainbow).

3 When I have desired to take hold of them by the hand of the angels on the day of tribulation, anger, and pain because of this, I will cause My punishment and anger to abide on them, says God, the Lord of spirits.

4 You mighty kings who live on the earth, you shall have to watch My Elect One, sit on the throne of glory and judge Azazel, and all his associates, and all his hosts in the name of the Lord of spirits.'

[Chapter 56]

1 And I saw there the hosts of the angels of punishment going, and they held scourges and chains of iron and bronze.

2 And I asked the angel of peace who went with me, saying: 'To whom are these who hold the scourges going?'
3 And he said to me: 'Each one to the ones they have chosen and to their loved ones, that they may be cast into the chasm of the abyss in the valley.

4 And then that valley shall be filled with ones they chose and their loved ones, and the days of their lives shall be at an end, and the days of their leading astray shall no longer be remembered (counted).

5 In those days the angels shall return and gather together and throw themselves to the east on the Parthians and Medes. They shall stir up the kings, so that a spirit of unrest and disturbance will come on them, and they shall drive them from their thrones, that they may rush out like lions from their lairs, and as hungry wolves among their flocks.

(Author's note: The names of certain countries help set the date of the manuscript. Scholars believe, based on the names of the countries mentioned in Enoch that the book could not have been written prior to 250 B.C. since some countries did not exist before that date. One could add that the particular part of Enoch is the only thing dated, since the book consists of several disjointed parts.)

6 And they shall go up and trample the lands of My elect ones, and the land of His elect ones shall be before them a threshing-floor (trampled, barren ground and a highway).

7 But the city of my righteous ones shall be a hindrance to their horses, and they shall begin to fight among themselves, and their own right hand shall be strong against themselves, and a man shall not know his brother, nor a son his father or his mother, until there will be innumerable corpses because of their slaughter, and their punishment shall be not in vain.

8 In those days hell (Sheol) shall open its jaws, and they shall be swallowed up. Their destruction shall be final. Hell (Sheol) shall devour the sinners in the presence of the elect.'

[Chapter 57]

1 And it came to pass after this that I saw another host of chariots, and men riding on them. They were coming on the winds from the east, and from the west to the south.

2 The noise of their chariots was heard, and when this turmoil took place the holy ones from heaven watched it, and the pillars of the earth were shaken and moved, and the sound of it was heard from the one end of heaven to the other, in one day.

3 And all shall fall down and worship the Lord of spirits. This is the end of the second Parable.

[Chapter 58]

1 And I began to speak the third Parable concerning the righteous and elect.

2 Blessed are you, you righteous and elect, for glorious shall be your lot.

3 And the righteous shall be in the light of the sun, and the elect will be in the light of eternal life. The days of their life shall be unending, and the days of the holy will be without number.

4 And they shall seek the light and find righteousness with the Lord of spirits. Peace to the righteous in the name of the Eternal Lord!

5 And after this it shall be said to the holy in heaven that they should seek secrets of righteousness, and the destiny of faith. For it has become bright as the sun on earth, and the darkness is passed away.

6 And there shall be a light that never ends, and to a number of days they shall not come, for the darkness shall first have been destroyed, [And the light established before the Lord of spirits] and the light of righteousness established for ever before the Lord of spirits.

[Chapter 59]

1 In those days my eyes saw the secrets of the lightning, and of the lights, and they judge and execute their judgment, and they illuminate for a blessing or a curse as the Lord of spirits wills.

2 And there I saw the secrets of the thunder, and how when it resounds above in heaven, the sound thereof is heard, and he caused me to see the judgments executed on the earth, whether they are for well-being and blessing, or for a curse according to the word of the Lord of spirits.

3 And after that all the secrets of the lights and lightning were shown to me, and they lighten for blessing and for satisfying.

[Chapter 60] - Noah's Vision

1 In the year 500, in the seventh month, on the fourteenth day of the month in the life of Enoch, in that parable I saw how a mighty quaking made the heaven of heavens to quake, and the host of the Most High, and the angels, a thousand thousands and ten thousand times ten thousand, were disquieted with great foreboding.

2 And the Head of Days sat on the throne of His glory, and the angels and the righteous stood around Him.

3 And a great trembling seized me, and fear took hold of me, and my legs gave way, and I melted with weakness and fell on my face.

4 And Michael sent another angel from among the holy ones and he raised me up, and when he had raised me up my spirit returned; for I had not been

able to endure the look of this host, and the disturbance and the shaking of heaven.

5 And Michael said to me: 'Why are you upset with such a vision? Until this day, His mercy and long-suffering has lasted toward those who dwell on the earth.'

6 And when the day, and the power, and the punishment, and the judgment come, which the Lord of spirits has prepared for those who worship not the righteous law, and for those who deny the righteous judgment, and for those who take His name in vain, that day is prepared. It will be a covenant for the elect, but for sinners an inquisition. When the punishment of the Lord of spirits shall rest on them, it will not come in vain, and it shall slay the children with their mothers and the children with their fathers.

7 And on that day two monsters were separated from one another, a female monster named Leviathan, to dwell in the abyss of the ocean over the fountains of the waters;

8 And the male is named Behemoth, who occupied with his breast a wasted wilderness named Duidain, on the east of the garden where the elect and righteous dwell, where my (great) grandfather was taken up, the seventh from Adam, the first man whom the Lord of spirits created.

9 And I asked the other angel to show me the might of those monsters, how they were separated on one day and thrown, the one into the abyss of the sea, and the other to the earth's desert.

10 And he said to me: ' Son of man, you wish to know what is kept secret.'

11 And the other angel who went with me and showed me what was kept secret; told me what is first and last in heaven in the sky, and beneath the earth in the depth, and at the ends of heaven, and on the foundation of heaven.

12 And the storehouse of the winds, and how the winds are divided, and how they are weighed, and how the doors of the winds are calculated for each according to the power of the wind, and the power of the lights of the moon according to the power that is fitting; and the divisions of the stars according to their names, and how all the divisions are divided.

13 And the thunder according to the places where they fall, and all the divisions that are made among the lightning that it may light, and their host that they may at once obey.

14 For the thunder has places of rest which are assigned while it is waiting for its peal; and the thunder and lightning are inseparable, and although not one and undivided, they both go together in spirit and are not separate.

15 For when the lightning flashes, the thunder utters its voice, and the spirit enforces a pause during the peal, and divides equally between them; for the treasury of their peals is like the sand (of an hourglass), and each one of them as it peals is held in with a bridle, and turned back by the power of the spirit, and pushed forward according to the many parts of the earth.

16 And the spirit of the sea is masculine and strong, and according to the might of His strength He draws it back with a rein, and in like manner it is driven forward and disperses in the midst of all the mountains of the earth.

17 And the spirit of the hoar-frost is his own angel, and the spirit of the hail is a good angel. And the spirit of the snow has forsaken his storehouse because of his strength.

18 There is a special spirit there, and that which ascends from it is like smoke, and its name is frost. And the spirit of the mist is not united with them in their storehouse, but it has a special storehouse; for its course is glorious both in light and in darkness, and in winter and in summer, and in its storehouse is an angel.

19 And the spirit of the dew has its dwelling at the ends of heaven, and is connected with the storehouse of the rain, and its course is in winter and summer; and its clouds and the clouds of the mist are connected, and the one gives to the other.

20 And when the spirit of the rain goes out from its storehouse, the angels come and open the storehouse and lead it out, and when it is diffused over the whole earth it unites with the water on the earth.

21 And whenever it unites with the water on the earth, (for the waters are for those who live on the earth), they are (become) nourishment for the earth from the Most High who is in heaven.

22 Therefore there is a measurement for the rain, and the angels are in charge of it. And these things I saw towards the Garden of the Righteous.

23 And the Angel of Peace who was with me, said to me:

24 "These two monsters, prepared in accordance with the greatness of the Lord, will feed them the punishment of the Lord. And children will be killed with their mothers, and sons with their fathers.

[Chapter 61]

1 And I saw in those days that long cords were given to those angels, and they took to themselves wings and flew, and they went towards the north.

2 I asked the angel, saying to him: 'Why have those angels who have cords taken flight?' And he said to me: 'They have gone to take measurements.'

3 And the angel who went with me said to me: 'These shall bring the measurements of the righteous, and the cords of the righteous to the righteous, that they may rely on the name of the Lord of spirits for ever and ever.

4 The elect shall begin to dwell with the elect, and those are the measurements which shall be given to faith and which shall strengthen righteousness.

5 And these measurements shall reveal all the secrets of the depths of the earth, and those who have been destroyed by the desert, and those who have been devoured by the beasts, and those who have been devoured by the fish of the sea, that they may return and rely on the day of the Elect One. For none shall be destroyed before the Lord of spirits, and none can be destroyed.

6 And all who dwell in heaven received a command and power and one voice and one light like to fire.

7 And they blessed Him with their first words and exalted and praised Him in their wisdom. And they were wise in utterance and in the spirit of life.

8 And the Lord of spirits placed the Elect One on the throne of glory. And he shall judge all the works of the holy above in heaven, and in the balance their deeds shall be weighed.

9 And when he shall lift up his face to judge their secret ways according to the word of the name of the Lord of spirits, and their path according to the

way of the righteous judgment of the Lord of spirits; then they shall all speak with one voice and bless and glorify and exalt the name of the Lord of spirits.

10 And He will summon all the host of heavens, and all the holy ones above, and the host of God, the cherubim, seraphim and ophannim, and all the angels of power, and all the angels of principalities (angels that rule over other angels), and the Elect One, and the other powers on the earth and over the water. On that day shall raise one voice, and bless and glorify and exalt in the spirit of faith, and in the spirit of wisdom, and in the spirit of patience, and in the spirit of mercy, and in the spirit of judgment and of peace, and in the spirit of goodness, and shall all say with one voice: "Blessed is He, and may the name of the Lord of spirits be blessed for ever and ever."

11 All who do not sleep above in heaven shall bless Him. All the holy ones who are in heaven shall bless Him; and all the elect who dwell in the garden of life, and every spirit who is able to bless, and glorify, and exalt, and praise Your blessed name, and to the extent of its ability all flesh shall glorify and bless Your name for ever and ever.

12 For great is the mercy of the Lord of spirits. He is long-suffering, and all His works and all that He has created He has revealed to the righteous and elect, in the name of the Lord of spirits.

[Chapter 62]

1 Thus the Lord commanded the kings and the mighty and the exalted, and those who dwell on the earth, and said: 'Open your eyes and lift up your horns if you are able to recognize the Elect One.'

2 And the Lord of spirits seated Him on the throne of His glory, and the spirit of righteousness was poured out on Him, and the word of His mouth slays all the sinners, and all the unrighteous are destroyed from in front of His face.

3 And in that day all the kings and the mighty, and the exalted and those who hold the earth shall stand up and shall see and recognize that He sits on the throne of His glory, and that righteousness is judged before Him, and no lying word is spoken before Him.

4 Then pain will come on them as on a woman in labor, and she has pain in giving birth when her child enters the mouth of the womb, and she has pain in childbirth.

5 And one portion of them shall look at the other, and they shall be terrified, and they shall look downcast, and pain shall seize them, when they see that Son of Man sitting on the throne of His glory.

6 And the kings and the mighty and all who possess the earth shall bless and glorify and exalt Him who rules over all, who was hidden.

7 For from the beginning the Son of Man was hidden, and the Most High preserved Him in the presence of His might, and revealed Him to the elect.

8 And the congregation of the elect and holy shall be sown, and all the elect shall stand before Him on that day.

9 And all the kings and the mighty and the exalted and those who rule the earth shall fall down before Him on their faces, and worship and set their hope on that Son of Man, and petition Him and supplicate for mercy at His hands.

10 Nevertheless that Lord of spirits will so press them that they shall heavily go out from His presence, and their faces shall be filled with shame, and the darkness grows deeper on their faces.

11 And He will deliver them to the angels for punishment, to execute vengeance on them because they have oppressed His children and His elect.

12 And they shall be a spectacle for the righteous and for His elect. They shall rejoice over them, because the wrath of the Lord of spirits rests on them, and His sword is drunk with their blood.

13 The righteous and elect shall be saved on that day, and they shall never again see the face of the sinners and unrighteous.

14 And the Lord of spirits will abide over them, and they shall eat, lie down and rise up with the Son of Man for ever and ever.

15 The righteous and elect shall have risen from the earth, and ceased to be downcast and they will have been clothed with garments of life.

16 And these shall be the garments of life from the Lord of spirits; they shall not wear out nor will your glory pass away from before the Lord of spirits.

[Chapter 63]

1 In those days shall the mighty and the kings who possess the earth beg Him to grant them a little respite from His angels of punishment to whom they were delivered, that they might fall down and worship before the Lord of spirits, and confess their sins before Him.

2 And they shall bless and glorify the Lord of spirits, and say: 'Blessed is the Lord of spirits and the Lord of kings, and the Lord of the mighty and the Lord of the rich, and the Lord of glory and the Lord of wisdom,

3 And every secret is revealed in front of you. Your power is from generation to generation, and your glory for ever and ever. Deep and innumerable are all your secrets, and your righteousness is beyond reckoning.

4 We have now learned that we should glorify and bless the Lord of kings and Him who is King over all kings.'

5 And they shall say: 'Would that we had a respite to glorify and give thanks and confess our faith before His glory!

6 And now we long for a little respite but find it not. We are driven away and obtain it not: And light has vanished from before us, and darkness is our dwelling-place for ever and ever;

7 Because we have not believed in Him nor glorified the name of the Lord of spirits, but our hope was in the scepter of our kingdom, and in our own glory.

8 In the day of our suffering and tribulation He does not save and we find no respite for confession that our Lord is true in all His works, and in His judgments and His justice, and His judgments have no respect of persons.

9 We pass away from before His face on account of our works, and all our sins are judged in (in comparison to) righteousness.'

10 Now they shall say to themselves: 'Our souls are full of unrighteous gain, but what we have gained does not prevent us from descending from the midst of our worldly gain into the torment (burden) of Hell (Sheol).'

11 And after that their faces shall be filled with darkness and shame before that Son of Man, and they shall be driven from His presence, and the sword shall abide before His face in their midst.

12 Thus spoke the Lord of spirits: 'This is the ordinance and judgment with respect to the mighty and the kings and the exalted and those who possess the earth before the Lord of spirits.'

[Chapter 64]

1 And other forms I saw hidden in that place.

2 I heard the voice of the angel saying: 'These are the angels who descended to the earth, and revealed what was hidden to the children of men and seduced the children of men into committing sin.'

[Chapter 65]

1 And in those days Noah saw the earth that it had sunk down and its destruction was near.

2 And he arose from there and went to the ends of the earth, and cried aloud to his grandfather, Enoch.

3 And Noah said three times with an embittered voice: "Hear me, hear me, hear me." And I said to him: 'Tell me what it is that is falling out on the earth that the earth is in such evil plight and shaken, lest perchance I shall perish with it?'

4 And there was a great disturbance on the earth, and a voice was heard from heaven, and I fell on my face. And Enoch my grandfather came and stood by me, and said to me: 'Why have you cried to me with a bitter cry and weeping?'

5 A command has gone out from the presence of the Lord concerning those who dwell on the earth that their ruin is accomplished because they have learned all the secrets of the angels, and all the violence of the Satans (deceivers, accusers);

6 And all their powers - the most secret ones - and all the power of those who practice sorcery, and the power of witchcraft, and the power of those who make molten images for the whole earth.

7 And how silver is produced from the dust of the earth, and how soft metal originates in the earth.

8 For lead and tin are not produced from the earth like the first; it is a fountain that produces them;

9 And an angel stands in it, and that angel is preeminent.' And after that my grandfather Enoch took hold of me by my hand and lifted me up, and said to me:

10 'Go, for I have asked the Lord of spirits about this disturbance on the earth. And He said to me: "Because of their unrighteousness their judgment has been determined and shall not be withheld by Me for ever. Because of the sorceries which they have searched out and learned, the earth and those who dwell on it shall be destroyed."

11 And from these, they have no place of repentance forever, because they have shown them what was hidden, and they are the damned. But as for you, my son, the Lord of spirits knows that you are pure and guiltless of this reproach concerning the secrets.

12 And He has destined your name to be among the holy, and will preserve you among those who dwell on the earth; and has destined your righteous seed both for kingship and for great honors, and from your seed shall proceed a fountain of the righteous and holy without number for ever.

[Chapter 66]

1 And after that he showed me the angels of punishment who are prepared to come and let loose all the powers of the waters which are beneath in the earth in order to bring judgment and destruction on all who dwell on the earth.

2 And the Lord of spirits gave commandment to the angels who were going out, that they should not cause the waters to rise but should hold them in check; for those angels were in charge of the forces of the waters.

3 And I went away from the presence of Enoch.

[Chapter 67]

1 And in those days the word of God came to me, and He said to me: 'Noah, your lot has come up before Me, a lot without blame, a lot of love and righteousness.

2 And now the angels are making a wooden structure, and when they have completed that task I will place My hand on it and preserve it (keep it safe), and there shall come out of it the seed of life, and a change shall set in so that the earth will not remain without inhabitants.

3 And I will establish your seed before me for ever and ever, and I will spread abroad those who dwell with you; and the face of the earth will be fruitful. They shall be blessed and multiply on the earth in the name of the Lord.'

4 And He will imprison those angels, who have shown unrighteousness, in that burning valley which my grandfather Enoch had formerly shown to me in the west among the mountains of gold and silver and iron and soft metal and tin.

5 And I saw that valley in which there was a great earth quake and a tidal waves of the waters.

6 And when all this took place, from that fiery molten metal and from the convulsion thereof in that place, there was a smell of sulfur produced, and it was connected with those waters, and that valley of the angels who had led mankind astray burned beneath that ground.

7 And there were streams of fire throughout the valley, where these angels are punished who had led astray those who dwell on the earth.

8 But those waters shall in those days serve for the kings and the mighty and the exalted, and those who dwell on the earth, for the healing of the body, but for the punishment of the spirit. Their spirit is full of lust, that they will be punished in their body, for they have denied the Lord of spirits. They will see their punishment daily, and yet, they believe not in His name.

9 There will be a relationship between the punishment and change. As their bodies burn, a change will take place in their spirit for ever and ever; for before the Lord of spirits none shall utter an idle word.

10 For the judgment shall come on them, because they believe in the lust of their body and deny the Spirit of the Lord.

11 And the waters will change in those days; for when those angels are punished in these waters, the springs shall change, and when the angels ascend, this water of the springs shall change their temperature and become cold.

12 And I heard Michael answering and saying: 'This judgment in which the angels are judged is a testimony for the kings and the mighty who possess the earth.'

13 Because these waters of judgment minister to the healing of the body of the kings and the lust of their bodies; therefore they will not see and will not believe that those waters will change and become a fire which burns for ever.

[Chapter 68]

1 And after that my grandfather Enoch gave me the explanations of all the secrets in the book of the Parables which had been given to him, and he put them together for me in the words of the book of the Parables.

2 And on that day Michael answered Raphael and said: 'The power of the spirit grips me and makes me tremble because of the severity of the judgment of the secrets, and the judgment of the angels. Who can endure the severe judgment which has been executed, and before which they melt away?'

3 And Michael answered again, and said to Raphael: 'Who would not have a softened heart concerning it, and whose mind would not be troubled by this judgment against them because of those who have led them out?'

4 And it came to pass when he stood before the Lord of spirits, Michael said thus to Raphael: 'I will not defend them under the eye of the Lord; for the Lord of spirits has been angry with them because they act as if they were the Lord.

5 Therefore all that is hidden shall come on them for ever and ever; for no other angel or man shall have his portion in this judgment, but they alone have received their judgment for ever and ever.

[Chapter 69]

1 And after this judgment I will terrify and make them tremble because they have shown this to those who dwell on the earth.

2 And behold the names of those angels: the first of them is Samjaza; the second Artaqifa; and the third Armen, the fourth Kokabe, the fifth Turael; the sixth Rumjal; the seventh Danjal; the eighth Neqael; the ninth Baraqel; the tenth Azazel; the eleventh Armaros; the twelfth Batarjal; the thirteenth Busasejal; the fourteenth Hananel; the fifteenth Turel; and the sixteenth Simapesiel; the seventeenth Jetrel; the eighteenth Tumael; the nineteenth Turel; the twentieth Rumael; the twenty-first Azazyel;

3 And these are the chiefs of their angels and their names, and their leaders over hundreds, and leaders over fifties, and leaders over tens.

4 The name of the first Jeqon, that is, the one who led astray the sons of God, and brought them down to the earth, and led them astray through the daughters of men.

5 And the second was named Asbeel; he imparted to the holy sons of God evil counsel, and led them astray so that they defiled their bodies with the daughters of men.

6 And the third was named Gadreel; it is he who showed the children of men all the blows of death, and he led astray Eve, and showed the weapons of death to the sons of men; the shield and the coat of mail, and the sword for battle, and all the weapons of death to the children of men.

7 And from his hand they have proceeded against those who dwell on the earth from that day and for evermore.

8 And the fourth was named Penemue; he taught the children of men the bitter and the sweet, and he taught them all the secrets of their wisdom.

9 And he instructed mankind in writing with ink and paper, and thereby many sinned from eternity to eternity and until this day.

10 For men were not created for the purpose of confirming their good faith with pen and ink.

11 For men were created exactly like the angels, to the intent that they should continue pure and righteous; and death, which destroys everything, should not have taken hold of them, but through this their knowledge they are perishing, and through this power consumes them.

12 And the fifth was named Kasdeja; this is he who showed the children of men all the wicked smitings (blows) of spirits and demons, and the smitings (blows) of the embryo in the womb, that it may pass away, and the smitings (blows) of the soul the bites of the serpent, and the smitings (blows) which befall through the midday heat, the son of the serpent named Taba'et.

13 And this is the task of Kasbeel, the chief of the oath which he showed to the holy ones when he dwelt high above in glory, and its name is Biqa.

14 This (angel) requested Michael to show him the hidden name, that he might enunciate it in the oath,

15 So that those might quake before that name and oath who revealed all that was in secret to the children of men. And this is the power of this oath, for it is powerful and strong, and he placed this oath Akae in the hand of (under the control of) Michael.

16 And these are the secrets of this oath (God's promise, word) that heaven was suspended before the world was created, and for ever, and they are strong through his oath (word, promise).

17 And through it the earth was founded on the water, and from the secret recesses of the mountains come beautiful waters, from the creation of the world and to eternity.

18 And through that oath the sea was created, and as its foundation He set for it the sand against the time of its anger (rage) that it dare not pass beyond it from the creation of the world to eternity.

19 And through that oath are the depths made fast, and abide and stir not from their place from eternity to eternity.

20 And through that oath the sun and moon complete their course, and deviate not from their ordinance from eternity to eternity.

21 And through that oath the stars complete their course, and He calls them by their names, and they answer Him from eternity to eternity.

22 [And in like manner the spirits of the water, and of the winds, and of all kinds of spirits, and (their) paths from all the quarters of the winds respond to His command.]

(Author's note: Verse 22 is not complete in some translations.)

23 And there are preserved the voices of the thunder and the light of the lightning: and there are preserved the storehouses of the hail and the storehouses of the hoarfrost,

24 And the storehouses of the mist, and the storehouses of the rain and the dew. And all these believe and give thanks before the Lord of spirits, and glorify (Him) with all their power, and their food is in every act of thanksgiving; they thank and glorify and exalt the name of the Lord of spirits for ever and ever.

25 And this oath is mighty over them and through it they are preserved and their paths are preserved, and their course is not destroyed.

26 And there was great joy among them, and they blessed and glorified and exalted because the name of that Son of Man had been revealed to them.

27 And he sat on the throne of his glory, and the sum of judgment was given to the Son of Man. And he caused the sinners and all those who led the world astray to pass away and be destroyed from off the face of the earth.

28 They shall be bound with chains, and shut up and imprisoned in their place of assembly, and all their works vanish from the face of the earth.

29 And from that time forward, there shall be nothing corruptible; for that Son of Man has appeared, and has seated himself on the throne of his glory. And all evil shall pass away before his face, and the word of that Son of Man shall go out and be strong before the Lord of spirits.

[Chapter 70]

1 And it came to pass after this that during His lifetime His name was raised up to the Son of Man, and to the Lord of spirits from among those who dwell on the earth.

2 And He was raised aloft on the chariots of the spirit and His name vanished among them. And from that day I was no longer numbered among them; and He placed me between the two winds, between the North and the West, where the angels took the cords to measure the place for the elect and righteous for me.

3 And there I saw the first fathers and the righteous who dwell in that place from the beginning.

[Chapter 71]

1 And it came to pass after this that my spirit was translated (carried off) and it ascended into heaven; and I saw the sons of the holy angels (sons) of God. They were walking on flames of fire; their garments were white, and their faces shone like snow.

2 And I saw two rivers of fire, and the light of that fire shone like hyacinth, and I fell on my face before the Lord of spirits.

3 And the angel Michael, one of the archangels, seized me by my right hand, and lifted me up and led me out into all the secrets, and he showed me all the secrets of righteousness.

4 And he showed me all the secrets of the ends of heaven, and all the storehouses of all the stars, and all the lights, from where they proceed before the face of the holy ones.

5 And he translated (carried) my spirit into heaven of heavens, and I saw there as it were built of crystals, and between those crystals tongues of living fire.

6 My spirit saw circle of fire binding around the house of fire, and on its four sides were rivers full of living fire, and they encircled that house.

7 And round about were seraphim, cherubim, and ophannim; and these are they who sleep not and guard the throne of His glory.

8 And I saw angels who could not be counted, a thousand thousands, and ten thousand times ten thousand, encircling that house. And Michael, and Raphael, and Gabriel, and Phanuel, and the holy angels who are in heaven above, go in and out of that house.

9 And they came out from that house, and Michael and Gabriel, Raphael and Phanuel, and many holy angels without number.

10 And with them the Head of Days, His head white and pure as wool, and His raiment indescribable.

11 And I fell on my face, and my whole body melted, and my spirit was (transformed) transfigured. And I cried with a loud voice in the spirit of power, and I blessed and glorified and exalted.

12 And these blessings which came from my mouth were very pleasing before that Head of Days.

13 And the Head of Days came with Michael and Gabriel, Raphael and Phanuel, and thousands and ten thousands of angels without number.

14 And the angel came to me and greeted me with his voice, and said to me 'This is the Son of Man who is born to righteousness, and righteousness abides over him, and the righteousness of the Head of Days forsakes him not.'

15 And he said to me: 'He proclaims to you peace in the name of the world to come; for from there peace has proceeded since the creation of the world, and it shall be with you for ever and for ever and ever.

JOH 17:24 Father, I will that they also, whom thou hast given me, be with me where I am; that they may behold my glory, which thou hast given me: for thou lovest me before the foundation of the world.

16 And all shall walk in His ways since righteousness never forsook Him. Their dwelling-place shall be with Him and it will be their heritage, and they shall not be separated from Him for ever and ever and ever.

17 And so there shall be length of days with the Son of Man, and the righteous shall have peace and an upright way in the name of the Lord of spirits for ever and ever.'

HEB 4:3 For we which have believed do enter into rest, as he said, As I have sworn in my wrath, if they shall enter into my rest: although the works were finished from the foundation of the world.

[Chapter 72]

1 The book of the courses of the luminaries of heaven, the relations of each, according to their name, origin, and months (dominion and seasons) which Uriel, the holy angel who was with me, who is their guide, showed me; and he showed me all their laws (regulations) exactly as they are, and how it is with each of the years of the world and to eternity, until the new creation is accomplished which endures until eternity.

2 And this is the first law of the luminaries: the luminary the Sun has its rising in the eastern doors of heaven, and its setting in the western doors of heaven.

3 And I saw six doors in which the sun rises, and six doors in which the sun sets and the moon rises and sets in these doors, and the leaders of the stars and those whom they lead: six in the east and six in the west, and all following each other in accurately corresponding order.

4 There were also many windows to the right and left of these doors. And first there goes out the great luminary, named the Sun, and his sphere (orbit, disc) is like the sphere (orbit, disc) of heaven, and he is quite filled with illuminating and heating fire.

5 The chariot on which he ascends, the wind drives, and the sun goes down from heaven and returns through the north in order to reach the east, and is so guided that he comes to the appropriate door and shines in the face of heaven.

6 In this way he rises in the first month in the great door, which is the fourth.

7 And in that fourth door from which the sun rises in the first month are twelve windows, from which proceed a flame when they are opened in their season.

8 When the sun rises in heaven, he comes out through that fourth door, thirty mornings in succession, and sets accurately in the fourth door in the west of the heaven.

9 And during this period the day becomes daily longer and nights grow shorter to the thirtieth morning.

10 On that day the day is longer than the night by a ninth part, and the day amounts exactly to ten parts and the night to eight parts.

11 And the sun rises from that fourth door, and sets in the fourth and returns to the fifth door of the east thirty mornings, and rises from it and sets in the fifth door.

12 And then the day becomes longer by two parts and amounts to eleven parts, and the night becomes shorter and amounts to seven parts.

13 And it returns to the east and enters into the sixth door, and rises and sets in the sixth door one-and-thirty mornings on account of its sign.

14 On that day the day becomes longer than the night, and the day becomes double the night, and the day becomes twelve parts, and the night is shortened and becomes six parts.

15 And the sun mounts up to make the day shorter and the night longer, and the sun returns to the east and enters into the sixth door, and rises from it and sets thirty mornings.

16 And when thirty mornings are accomplished, the day decreases by exactly one part, and becomes eleven parts, and the night seven.

17 And the sun goes out from that sixth door in the west, and goes to the east and rises in the fifth door for thirty mornings, and sets in the west again in the fifth western door.

18 On that day the day decreases by two parts, and amounts to ten parts and the night to eight parts.

19 And the sun goes out from that fifth door and sets in the fifth door of the west, and rises in the fourth door for one-and-thirty mornings on account of its sign, and sets in the west.

20 On that day the day becomes equal with the night in length, and the night amounts to nine parts and the day to nine parts.

21 And the sun rises from that door and sets in the west, and returns to the east and rises thirty mornings in the third door and sets in the west in the third door.

22 And on that day the night becomes longer than the day, and night becomes longer than night, and day shorter than day until the thirtieth

morning, and the night amounts exactly to ten parts and the day to eight parts.

23 And the sun rises from that third door and sets in the third door in the west and returns to the east, and for thirty mornings rises in the second door in the east, and in like manner sets in the second door in the west of heaven.

24 And on that day the night amounts to eleven parts and the day to seven parts.

25 And the sun rises on that day from that second door and sets in the west in the second door, and returns to the east into the first door for one-and-thirty mornings, and sets in the first door in the west of heaven.

26 And on that day the night becomes longer and amounts to the double of the day: and the night amounts exactly to twelve parts and the day to six.

(Author's note: The day is divided into 18 sections of 90 minutes each.)

27 And the sun has traversed the divisions of his orbit and turns again on those divisions of his orbit, and enters that door thirty mornings and sets also in the west opposite to it.

28 And on that night has the night decreased in length by a ninth part, and the night has become eleven parts and the day seven parts.

29 And the sun has returned and entered into the second door in the east, and returns on those his divisions of his orbit for thirty mornings, rising and setting.

30 And on that day the night decreases in length, and the night amounts to ten parts and the day to eight.

31 And on that day the sun rises from that door, and sets in the west, and returns to the east, and rises in the third door for one-and-thirty mornings, and sets in the west of heaven.

32 On that day the night decreases and amounts to nine parts, and the day to nine parts, and the night is equal to the day and the year is exactly as to its days three hundred and sixty-four.

33 And the length of the day and of the night, and the shortness of the day and of the night arise through the course of the sun these distinctions are separated'.

34 So it comes that its course becomes daily longer, and its course nightly shorter.

35 And this is the law and the course of the great luminary which is named the sun, and his return as often as he returns sixty times and rises, for ever and ever.

36 And that which rises is the great luminary, and is so named according to its appearance, according as the Lord commanded.

37 As he rises, so he sets and decreases not, and rests not, but runs day and night, and his light is sevenfold brighter than that of the moon; but in regard to size, they are both equal.

[Chapter 73]

1 And after this law I saw another law dealing with the smaller luminary, which is named the Moon.

2 And her orbit is like the sphere (orbit, disc) of heaven, and her chariot in which she rides is driven by the wind, and light is given to her in measurement.

3 And her rising and setting change every month and her days are like the days of the sun, and when her light is uniformly (completely) full it amounts to the seventh part of the light of the sun.

4 And thus she rises. And her first phase in the east comes out on the thirtieth morning and on that day she becomes visible, and constitutes for you the first phase of the moon on the thirtieth day together with the sun in the door where the sun rises.

5 And the one half of her goes out by a seventh part, and her whole disc is empty, without light, with the exception of one-seventh part of it, and the fourteenth part of her light.

6 And when she receives one-seventh part of the half of her light, her light amounts to one-seventh part and the half thereof.

7 And she sets with the sun, and when the sun rises the moon rises with him and receives the half of one part of light, and in that night in the beginning of her morning in the beginning of the lunar day the moon sets with the sun, and is invisible that night with the fourteen parts and the half of one of them.

8 And she rises on that day with exactly a seventh part, and comes out and recedes from the rising of the sun, and in her remaining days she becomes bright in the remaining thirteen parts.

[Chapter 74]

1 And I saw another course, a law for her, and how according to that law she performs her monthly revolution.

2 And all these Uriel, the holy angel who is the leader of them all, showed to me, and their positions, and I wrote down their positions as he showed them to me, and I wrote down their months as they were, and the appearance of their lights until fifteen days were accomplished.

3 In single seventh parts she accomplishes all her light in the east, and in single seventh parts accomplishes all her darkness in the west.

4 And in certain months she alters her settings, and in certain months she pursues her own peculiar course.

5 In two months the moon sets with the sun: in those two middle doors the third and the fourth.

6 She goes out for seven days, and turns about and returns again through the door where the sun rises, and all her light is full; and she recedes from the sun, and in eight days enters the sixth door from which the sun goes out.

7 And when the sun goes out from the fourth door she goes out seven days, until she goes out from the fifth and turns back again in seven days into the fourth door and accomplishes all her light; and she recedes and enters into the first door in eight days.

8 And she returns again in seven days into the fourth door from which the sun goes out.

9 Thus I saw their positions, how the moons rose and the sun set in those days.

10 And if five years are added together the sun has an excess of thirty days, and all the days which accrue to it for one of those five years, when they are full, amount to 364 days.

11 And an excess of the sun and of the stars amounts to six days; in five years six days every year come to 30 days, and the moon falls behind the sun and stars to the number of 30 days.

12 And the sun and the stars bring in all the years exactly, so that they do not advance or delay their position by a single day to eternity; but complete the years with perfect justice in 364 days.

13 In three years there are 1,092 days, and in five years 1,820 days, so that in eight years there are 2,912 days.

14 For the moon alone the days amount in three years to 1,062 days, and in five years she falls 50 days behind to the sum of 1,770 there is five to be added 1,000 and 62 days.

15 And in five years there are 1,770 days, so that for the moon the days six in eight years amount to 21,832 days.

16 For in eight years she falls behind to the amount of 80 days, all the days she falls behind in eight years are 80.

17 And the year is accurately completed in conformity with their world-stations and the stations of the sun, which rise from the doors through which the sun rises and sets 30 days.

[Chapter 75]

1 And the leaders of the heads of the (ten) thousands, who are in charge of the whole creation and over all the stars, have also to do with the four days of the year which are not counted in the yearly calendar, being not separated from their office, according to the reckoning of the year, and these render service on the four days which are not counted in the reckoning of the year.

2 And because of them men go wrong in them, for those luminaries truly render service to the stations of the world, one in the first door, one on the third door of heaven, one in the fourth door, and one in the sixth door, and the exactness of the year is accomplished through its separate three hundred and sixty-four stations.

3 For the signs and the times and the years and the days the angel Uriel showed to me, whom the Lord of glory has set for ever over all the luminaries of heaven, in heaven and in the world, that they should rule on the face of heaven and be seen on the earth, and be leaders for the day via the sun and the night via the moon, and stars, and all the ministering creatures which make their revolution in all the chariots of heaven.

4 In like manner, twelve doors Uriel showed me, open in the sphere (disc) of the sun's chariot in heaven, through which the rays of the sun break out; and from them is warmth diffused over the earth, when they are opened at their appointed seasons.

5 And there are openings for the wind and the spirit of dew that when they are opened, stand open in heaven at the ends of the earth.

6 As for the twelve doors in the heaven, at the ends of the earth, out of which go out the sun, moon, and stars, and all the works of heaven in the east and in the west; there are many windows open to the left and right of them,

7 And one window at its appointed season produces warmth, corresponding to the doors from which the stars come out as He has commanded them; and in which they are set, corresponding to their number.

8 And I saw chariots in heaven, running in the world, above those doors in which the stars that never set.

9 And one is larger than all the rest, and it is that that makes its course through the entire world.

[Chapter 76]

1 At the ends of the earth I saw twelve doors open to all quarters of heaven, from which the winds go out and blow over the earth.

2 Three of them are open on the face of heaven, and three in the west; and three on the right of heaven, and three on the left.

3 And the three first are those of the east, and three are of the north, and three, after those on the left, of the south, and three of the west.

4 Through four of these come winds of blessing and prosperity (peace), and from those eight come hurtful winds; when they are sent, they bring destruction on all the earth and the water on it, and on all who dwell on it, and on everything which is in the water and on the land.

5 And the first wind from those doors, called the east wind, comes out through the first door which is in the east, inclining towards the south; from it desolation, drought, heat, and destruction come out .

6 And through the second door in the middle comes what is fitting (right, correct), and there come rain and fruitfulness and prosperity and dew. And through the third door which lies toward the north comes cold and drought.

7 And after these, comes out the south winds through three doors; through the first door of them inclining to the east comes out a hot wind.

8 And through the middle door next to it there comes out fragrant smells, and dew and rain, and prosperity and health.

9 And through the third door which lies to the west dew comes out and also rain, locusts and desolation.

10 And from the seventh door in the east comes the north winds, and dew, rain, locusts and desolation.

11 And from the center door come health and rain and dew and prosperity; and through the third door in the west come cloud and hoar-frost, and snow and rain, and dew and locusts.

12 And after these came the four west winds; through the first door adjoining the north come out dew and hoar-frost, and cold and snow and frost.

13 And from the center door come out dew and rain, and prosperity and blessing.

14 And through the last door which adjoins the south, come drought and desolation, and burning and destruction. And the twelve doors of the four quarters of heaven are therewith completed, and all their laws and all their plagues and all their benefactions have I shown to you, my son Methuselah.

[Chapter 77]

1 And the first quarter is called the east, because it is the first; and the second, the south, because the Most High will descend there. From there will He who is blessed for ever descend.

2 And the west quarter is named the diminished, because there all the luminaries of the heaven wane and go down.

3 And the fourth quarter, named the north, is divided into three parts: the first of them is for the dwelling of men; and the second contains seas of water, and the abyss (deep) and forests and rivers, and darkness and clouds; and the third part contains the garden of righteousness.

4 I saw seven high mountains, higher than all the mountains which are on the earth: and from here comes hoar-frost, and days, seasons, and years pass away.

5 I saw seven rivers on the earth larger than all the rivers. One of them coming from the west pours its waters into the Great Sea.

6 And these two come from the north to the sea and pour their waters into the Erythraean Sea in the east.

7 And the remaining four come out on the side of the north to their own sea, two of them to the Erythraean Sea, and two into the Great Sea and some say they discharge themselves there into the desert.

8 I saw seven great islands in the sea and in the mainland, two in the mainland and five in the Great Sea.

[Chapter 78]

1 And the names of the sun are the following: the first Orjares, and the second Tomas.

2 And the moon has four names: the first name is Asonja, the second Ebla, the third Benase, and the fourth Erae.

3 These are the two great luminaries; their spheres (disc) are like the sphere (disc) of the heaven, and the size of the spheres (disc) of both is alike.

4 In the sphere (disc) of the sun there are seven portions of light which are added to it more than to the moon, and in fixed measurements it is transferred until the seventh portion of the sun is exhausted.

5 And they set and enter the doors of the west, and make their revolution by the north, and come out through the eastern doors on the face of heaven.

6 And when the moon rises one-fourteenth part appears in heaven, and on the fourteenth day the moon's light becomes full.

7 And fifteen parts of light are transferred to her until the fifteenth day when her light is full, according to the sign of the year, and she becomes fifteen parts, and the moon grows by an additional fourteenth parts.

8 And as the moon's waning decreases on the first day to fourteen parts of her light, on the second to thirteen parts of light, on the third to twelve, on the fourth to eleven, on the fifth to ten, on the sixth to nine, on the seventh to eight, on the eighth to seven, on the ninth to six, on the tenth to five, on the eleventh to four, on the twelfth to three, on the thirteenth to two, on the fourteenth to the half of a seventh, and all her remaining light disappears wholly on the fifteenth.

9 And in certain months the month has twenty-nine days and once twenty-eight.

10 And Uriel showed me another law: when light is transferred to the moon, and on which side it is transferred to her by the sun.

11 During all the period during which the moon is growing in her light, she is transferring it to herself when opposite to the sun during fourteen days her light is full in heaven, and when she is ablaze throughout, her light is full in heaven.

12 And on the first day she is called the new moon, for on that day the light rises on her.

13 She becomes full moon exactly on the day when the sun sets in the west, and from the east she rises at night, and the moon shines the whole night through until the sun rises over against her and the moon is seen over against the sun.

14 On the side whence the light of the moon comes out, there again she wanes until all the light vanishes and all the days of the month are at an end, and her sphere (disc) is empty, void of light.

15 And three months she makes of thirty days, and at her time she makes three months of twenty-nine days each, in which she accomplishes her waning in the first period of time, and in the first door for one hundred and seventy-seven days.

16 And in the time of her going out she appears for three months consisting of thirty days each, and she appears for three months consisting of twenty-nine each.

17 By night she looks like a man for twenty days each time, and by day she appears like heaven, and there is nothing else in her save her light.

[Chapter 79]

1 And now, my son Methuselah, I have shown you everything, and the law of all the stars of heaven is completed.

2 And he showed me all the laws of these for every day, and for every season of every rule, and for every year, and for its going out, and for the order prescribed to it every month and every week.

3 And the waning of the moon which takes place in the sixth door, for in this sixth door her light is accomplished, and after that there is the beginning of the waning.

4 And the waning which takes place in the first door in its season, until one hundred and seventy-seven days are accomplished, calculated according to weeks, twenty-five weeks and two days.

5 She falls behind the sun and the order of the stars exactly five days in the course of one period, and when this place which you see has been traversed.

6 Such is the picture and sketch of every luminary which Uriel the archangel, who is their leader, showed to me.

[Chapter 80]

1 And in those days the angel Uriel answered and said to me: 'Behold, I have shown you everything, Enoch, and I have revealed everything to you

that you should see this sun and this moon, and the leaders of the stars of heaven and all those who turn them, their tasks and times and departures.

2 And in the days of the sinners the years shall be shortened, and their seed shall be tardy on their lands and fields, and all things on the earth shall alter, and shall not appear in their time. And the rain shall be kept back, and heaven shall withhold it.

3 And in those times the fruits of the earth shall be backward, and shall not grow in their time, and the fruits of the trees shall be withheld in their time.

4 And the moon shall alter her customs, and not appear at her time.

5 And in those days the sun shall be seen and he shall journey in the evening on the extremity of the great chariot in the west and shall shine more brightly than accords with the order of light.

6 And many rulers of the stars shall transgress their customary order. And these shall alter their orbits and tasks, and not appear at the seasons prescribed to them.

7 And the whole order of the stars shall be concealed from the sinners, and the thoughts of those on the earth shall err concerning them, and they shall be altered from all their ways, they shall err and take them to be gods.

8 And evil shall be multiplied on them, and punishment shall come on them so as to destroy all.'

[Chapter 81]

1 And he said to me: 'Enoch, look at these heavenly tablets and read what is written on them, and mark every individual fact.'

2 And I looked at the heavenly tablets, and read everything which was written on it and understood everything, and read the book of all the deeds of mankind, and of all the children of flesh; that shall be on the earth to the end of generations.

3 And I blessed the great Lord the King of glory for ever, in that He has made all the works of the world, and I exalted the Lord because of His patience, and blessed Him because of the children of men (sons of Abraham).

4 And then I said: 'Blessed is the man who dies in righteousness and goodness, concerning whom there is no book of unrighteousness written, and against whom no day of judgment shall be found.'

5 And the seven holy ones brought me and placed me on the earth before the door of my house, and said to me: 'Declare everything to your son Methuselah, and show to all your children that no flesh is righteous in the sight of the Lord, for He is their Creator.

6 For one year we will leave you with your son, until you give your last commands, that you may teach your children and record it for them, and testify to all your children; and in the second year they shall take you from their midst.

7 Let your heart be strong, for the good shall proclaim righteousness to the good; the righteous shall rejoice with the righteous, and shall wish one another well.

8 But the sinners shall die with the sinners, and the apostate shall go down with the apostate.

9 And those who practice righteousness shall die on account of the deeds of men, and be taken away on account of the deeds of the godless.'

10 And in those days they finished speaking to me, and I came to my people, blessing the Lord of the world.

[Chapter 82]

1 And now, my son Methuselah, all these things I am recounting to you and writing down for you! And I have revealed to you everything, and given you books concerning all these; so, my son Methuselah, preserve the books from your father's hand, and see that you deliver them to the generations of the world.

2 I have given wisdom to you and to your children, and those children to come, that they may give it to their children for generations. This wisdom namely that passes their understanding.

3 And those who understand it shall not sleep, but shall listen that they may learn this wisdom, and it shall please those that eat thereof better than good food.

4 Blessed are all the righteous, blessed are all those who walk in the way of righteousness and sin not as the sinners, in the numbering of all their days in which the sun traverses heaven, entering into and departing from the doors for thirty days with the heads of thousands of the order of the stars, together with the four which are within the calendar which divide the four portions of the year, which lead them and enter with them four days.

5 Owing to them men shall be at fault and not count them in the whole number of days of the year. Men shall be at fault, and not recognize them accurately.

6 For they belong to the calculations of the year and are truly recorded therein for ever, one in the first door and one in the third, and one in the fourth and one in the sixth, and the year is completed in three hundred and sixty-four days.

7 And the account of it is accurate and the recorded counting thereof is exact; for the luminaries, and months and festivals, and years and days, has Uriel shown and revealed to me, to whom the Lord of the whole creation of the world has subjected the host of heaven.

8 And he has power over night and day in heaven to cause the light to shine on men via the sun, moon, and stars, and all the powers of the heaven which revolve in their circular chariots. And these are the orders of the stars, which set in their places, and in their seasons and festivals and months.

9 And these are the names of those who lead them, who watch that they enter at their times, in their orders, in their seasons, in their months, in their periods of dominion, and in their positions.

10 Their four leaders who divide the four parts of the year enter first; and after them the twelve leaders of the orders who divide the months; and for the three hundred and sixty days there are heads over thousands who divide the days; and for the four days in the calendar there are the leaders which divide the four parts of the year.

11 And these heads over thousands are interspersed between leader and leader, each behind a station, but their leaders make the division.

12 And these are the names of the leaders who divide the four parts of the year which are ordained:

13 Milki'el, Hel'emmelek, and Mel'ejal, and Narel. And the names of those who lead them: Adnar'el, and Ijasusa'el, and 'Elome'el.

14 These three follow the leaders of the orders, and there is one that follows the three leaders of the orders which follow those leaders of stations that divide the four parts of the year. In the beginning of the year Melkejal rises first and rules, who is named Tam'aini and sun, and all the days of his dominion while he bears rule are ninety-one days.

15 And these are the signs of the days which are to be seen on earth in the days of his dominion: sweat, and heat; and calms; and all the trees bear fruit, and leaves are produced on all the trees, and the harvest of wheat, and the rose-flowers, and all the flowers which come out in the field, but the trees of the winter season become withered.

16 And these are the names of the leaders which are under them: Berka'el, Zelebs'el, and another who is added a head of a thousand, called Hilujaseph: and the days of the dominion of this leader are at an end.

17 The next leader after him is Hel'emmelek, whom one names the shining sun, and all the days of his light are ninety-one days.

18 And these are the signs of his days on the earth: glowing heat and dryness, and the trees ripen their fruits and produce all their fruits ripe and ready, and the sheep pair and become pregnant, and all the fruits of the earth are gathered in, and everything that is in the fields, and the winepress: these things take place in the days of his dominion.

19 These are the names, and the orders, and the leaders of those heads of thousands: Gida'ljal, Ke'el, and He'el, and the name of the head of a thousand which is added to them, Asfa'el: and the days of his dominion are at an end.

[Chapter 83]

1 And now, my son Methuselah, I will show you all my visions which I have seen, recounting them before you.

2 I saw two visions before I got married (took a wife), and the one was quite unlike the other: the first when I was learning to write: the second before I married (took) your mother, was when I saw a terrible vision.

3 And regarding them I prayed to the Lord. I had laid down in the house of my grandfather Mahalalel, when I saw in a vision how heaven collapsed and was carried off (removed, torn down) and fell to the earth.

4 And when it fell to the earth I saw how the earth was swallowed up in a great abyss, and mountains were suspended on mountains, and hills sank down on hills, and high trees were ripped from their stems, and hurled down and sunk in the abyss.

5 And then a word fell into my mouth, and I lifted up my voice to cry aloud, and said:

6 'The earth is destroyed.' And my grandfather Mahalalel woke me as I lay near him, and said to me: 'Why do you cry so, my son, and why do you make such moaning (lamentation)?'

7 And I recounted to him the whole vision which I had seen, and he said to me: 'You have seen a terrible thing , my son. Your dream (vision) is of a grave time and concerns the secrets of all the sin of the earth: it must sink into the abyss and be totally destroyed.

8 And now, my son, arise and pray to the Lord of glory, since you are a believer, that a remnant may remain on the earth, and that He may not destroy the whole earth.

9 My son, from heaven all this will come on the earth, and on the earth there will be great destruction.

10 After that I arose and prayed and implored and besought (God), and wrote down my prayer for the generations of the world, and I will show everything to you, my son Methuselah.

11 And when I had gone out below and seen the heaven, and the sun rising in the east, and the moon setting in the west, and a few stars, and the whole earth, and everything as He had known it in the beginning, then I blessed the Lord of judgment and exalted Him because He had made the sun to go out from the windows of the east, and he ascended and rose on the face of heaven, and set out and kept traversing the path shown to it.

[Chapter 84]

1 And I lifted up my hands in righteousness and blessed the Holy and Great One, and spoke with the breath of my mouth, and with the tongue of flesh,

which God has made for the children of the flesh of men, that they should speak therewith, and He gave them breath and a tongue and a mouth that they should speak therewith:

2 Blessed be you, O Lord, King, Great and mighty in your greatness, Lord of the whole creation of heaven, King of kings and God of the whole world. And your power and kingship and greatness abide for ever and ever, and throughout all generations your dominion and all heavens are your throne for ever, and the whole earth your footstool for ever and ever.

3 For you have made and you rule all things, and nothing is too hard for you, wisdom never departs from the place of your throne, nor turns away from your presence. You know and see and hear everything, and there is nothing hidden from you for you see everything.

4 And now the angels of your heavens are guilty of trespass, and on the flesh of men abide your wrath until the great day of judgment.

5 And now, O God and Lord and Great King, I implore and beseech you to fulfill my prayer, to leave me a posterity on earth, and not destroy all the flesh of man, and make the earth without inhabitant, so that there should be an eternal destruction.

6 And now, my Lord, destroy from the earth the flesh which has aroused your wrath, but the flesh of righteousness and uprightness establish as an eternal plant bearing seed forever, and hide not your face from the prayer of your servant, O Lord.'

[Author's note: In chapter 85 and following, a series of animals is mentioned. These seem to refer to nations or ethnicities. For example, the eagles may refer to the Roman empire, the Islamic nation is represented by the asses, Abraham may be the white bull, Jacob is a sheep, Egyptians are wolves, and so on. See Daniel Chapter 10 for other like imagery.

Other writers have attempted to be more specific. Starting with the concept of Noah's three sons, Shem, Ham and Japheth, giving rise to all the animals or nations in Chapter 89, they link the white bull to Abraham; Abraham's son, Ishmael, to the wild ass; Isaac to the white bull; Esau to the wild boar; Jacob to the white sheep; the Assyrians to lions; The small lambs with open eyes to the Essenes; Jesus to the "sheep with the big horn"; and in 90.17, the final twelve shepherds represent the Christian era.]

[Chapter 85]

1 And after this I saw another dream, and I will show the whole dream to you, my son.

2 And Enoch lifted up his voice and spoke to his son Methuselah: 'I will speak to you, my son, hear my words. Incline your ear to the dream (vision) of your father.

3 Before I married (took) your mother Edna, I saw in a vision on my bed, and behold a bull came out from the earth, and that bull was white.

4 And after it came out a heifer, and along with this later came out two bulls, one of them black and the other red.

5 And that black bull gored the red one and pursued him over the earth, and then I could no longer see that red bull. But that black bull grew and that heifer went with him, and I saw that many oxen proceeded from him which resembled and followed him.

6 And that cow, that first one, went from the presence of that first bull in order to seek that red one, but found him not, and mourned with a great lamentation and sought him.

7 And I looked until that first bull came to her and quieted (calmed) her, and from that time onward she cried no more.

8 And after that she bore another white bull, and after him she bore many bulls and black cows.

9 And I saw in my sleep that white bull likewise grew and became a great white bull, and from him proceeded many white bulls, and they resembled him. And they began to father many white bulls, which resembled them, one following another.

[Chapter 86]

1 And again I looked with my eyes as I slept, and I saw the heaven above, and behold a star fell from heaven, and it arose and ate and pastured among those oxen (bulls).

2 And after that I saw the large and the black oxen (bulls), and behold they all changed their stalls and pastures and their heifers (cattle) , and began to live with each other.

3 And again I saw in the vision, and looked towards heaven, and behold I saw many stars descend and cast themselves down from heaven to that first star, and they became bulls among those cattle and pastured with them.

4 And I looked at them and saw they all let out their private (sexual) members, like horses, and began to mount the cows of the bulls (oxen), and they all became pregnant and bore elephants, camels, and asses.

5 And all the bulls (oxen) feared them and were frightened of them, and began to bite with their teeth and to devour, and to gore with their horns.

6 And, moreover, they began to devour those oxen; and behold all the children of the earth began to tremble and shake before them and to flee from them.

[Chapter 87]

1 And again I saw how they began to gore each other and to devour each other, and the earth began to cry aloud.

2 And I raised my eyes again to heaven, and I saw in the vision, and behold there came out from heaven beings who were like white men, and four went out from that place and three others with them.

3 And those three that had come out last grasped me by my hand and took me up, away from the generations of the earth, and raised me up to a high place, and showed me a tower raised high above the earth, and all the hills were lower.

4 And one said to me: 'Remain here until you see everything that befalls those elephants, camels, and asses, and the stars and the oxen, and all of them.'

[Chapter 88]

1 And I saw one of those four who had come out first, and he seized that first star which had fallen from heaven, and bound it hand and foot and cast it into an abyss; now that abyss was narrow and deep, and horrible and dark.

2 And one of them drew a sword, and gave it to those elephants and camels and asses then they began to smite each other, and the whole earth shook because of them.

3 And as I was beholding in the vision one of those four who had come out stoned them from heaven, and gathered and took all the great stars whose private (sexual) members were like those of horses, and bound them all hand and foot, and threw them in an abyss of the earth.

[Chapter 89]

1 And one of those four went to that white bull and instructed him in a secret, and he was terrified: he was born a bull and became a man, and built for himself a great vessel and dwelt on it.

2 And three bulls dwelt with him in the vessel and they were covered over. And again I raised my eyes towards heaven and saw a high roof, with seven water torrents on it, and those torrents flowed with much water into an enclosure. And I looked again, and behold fountains were opened on the surface of that great enclosure, and the water began to bubble and swell and rise on the surface, and I saw that enclosure until all its surface was covered with water.

3 And the water, the darkness, and mist increased on it; and as I looked at the height of that water, the water had risen above the height of the enclosure, and was streaming over the enclosure, and it stood on the earth.

4 And all the cattle of the enclosure were gathered together until I saw how they sank and were swallowed up and perished in that water.

5 But that vessel floated on the water, while all the oxen (bulls) and elephants and camels and asses sank to the bottom with all the animals, so that I could no longer see them, and they were not able to escape, but perished and sank into the depths.

6 And again I watched in the vision until those water torrents were removed from that high roof, and the chasms of the earth were leveled up and other abysses were opened.

7 Then the water began to run down into these abysses, until the earth became visible; but that vessel settled on the earth, and the darkness retired and light appeared.

8 But that white bull which had become a man came out of that vessel, and the three bulls with him, and one of those three was white like that bull, and one of them was red as blood, and one black; and that white bull departed from them.

9 And they began to bring out beasts of the field and birds, so that there arose different genera: lions, tigers, wolves, dogs, hyenas, wild boars, foxes, squirrels, swine, falcons, vultures, kites, eagles, and ravens; and among them was born a white bull.

10 And they began to bite one another; but that white bull which was born among them fathered a wild ass and a white bull with it, and the wild asses multiplied.

11 But that bull which was born from him fathered a black wild boar and a white sheep; and the former fathered many boars, but the sheep gave birth to twelve sheep.

12 And when those twelve sheep had grown, they gave up one of them to the asses, and the asses again gave up that sheep to the wolves, and that sheep grew up among the wolves.

13 And the Lord brought the eleven sheep to live with it and to pasture with it among the wolves and they multiplied and became many flocks of sheep.

14 And the wolves began to fear them, and they oppressed them until they destroyed their little ones, and they threw their young into a deep river, but those sheep began to cry aloud on account of their little ones, and to complain to their Lord.

15 And a sheep which had been saved from the wolves fled and escaped to the wild asses; and I saw the sheep how they lamented and cried, and besought their Lord with all their might, until that Lord of the sheep descended at the voice of the sheep from a high abode, and came to them and pastured them.

16 And He called that sheep which had escaped the wolves, and spoke with it concerning the wolves that it should admonish them not to touch the sheep.

17 And the sheep went to the wolves according to the word of the Lord, and another sheep met it and went with it, and the two went and entered together into the assembly of those wolves, and spoke with them and admonished them not to touch the sheep from then on.

18 And on it I saw the wolves, and how they more harshly oppressed the sheep with all their power; and the sheep cried aloud.

19 And the Lord came to the sheep and they began to beat those wolves, and the wolves began to make lamentation; but the sheep became quiet and ceased to cry out.

20 And I saw the sheep until they departed from among the wolves; but the eyes of the wolves were blinded, and the wolves departed in pursuit of the sheep with all their power.

21 And the Lord of the sheep went with them, as their leader, and all His sheep followed Him.

22 And his face was dazzling and glorious and terrible to behold. But the wolves began to pursue those sheep until they reached a sea of water.

23 And that sea was divided, and the water stood on this side and on that before their face, and their Lord led them and placed Himself between them and the wolves.

24 And as those wolves had not yet seen the sheep, they proceeded into the midst of that sea, and the wolves followed the sheep, and those wolves ran after them into that sea.

25 And when they saw the Lord of the sheep, they turned to flee before His face, but that sea gathered itself together, and became as it had been created, and the water swelled and rose until it covered the wolves.

26 And I watched until all the wolves who pursued those sheep perished and were drowned.

27 But the sheep escaped from that water and went out into a wilderness, where there was no water and no grass; and they began to open their eyes and to see;

28 And I saw the Lord of the sheep pasturing them and giving them water and grass, and that sheep going and leading them.

29 And the sheep ascended to the summit of that high rock, and the Lord of the sheep sent it to them. And after that I saw the Lord of the sheep who

stood before them, and His appearance was great and terrible and majestic, and all those sheep saw Him and were afraid before His face.

30 And they all feared and trembled because of Him, and they cried to that sheep which was among them:

31 'We are not able to stand before our Lord or to behold Him.' And that sheep which led them again ascended to the summit of that rock, but the sheep began to be blinded and to wander from the way which he had showed them, but that sheep did not realize it.

32 And the Lord of the sheep was very angry with them, and that sheep discovered it, and went down from the summit of the rock, and came to the sheep, and found the greatest part of them blinded and fallen away.

33 And when they saw it they feared and trembled at its presence, and desired to return to their folds. And that sheep took other sheep with it, and came to those sheep which had fallen away, and began to slay them; and the sheep feared its presence, and thus that sheep brought back those sheep that had fallen away, and they returned to their folds.

34 And I saw in this vision until that sheep became a man and built a house for the Lord of the sheep, and placed all the sheep in that house.

35 And I saw until this sheep which had met that sheep which led them fell asleep (died); and I saw until all the great sheep perished and little ones arose in their place, and they came to a pasture, and approached a stream of water.

36 Then that sheep, their leader which had become a man, withdrew from them and fell asleep (died), and all the sheep looked for it (sought it) and cried over it with a great crying.

37 And I saw until they left off crying for that sheep and crossed that stream of water, and there arose the two sheep as leaders in the place of those which had led them and fallen asleep.

38 And I saw until the sheep came to a good place, and a pleasant and glorious land, and I saw until those sheep were satisfied; and that house stood among them in the (green) pleasant land.

39 And sometimes their eyes were opened, and sometimes blinded, until another sheep arose and led them and brought them all back, and their eyes were opened.

40 And the dogs and the foxes and the wild boars began to devour those sheep until the Lord of the sheep raised up another sheep, a ram from their midst, which led them.

41 And that ram began to butt on either side those dogs, foxes, and wild boars until he had destroyed them all.

42 And that sheep whose eyes were opened saw that ram, which was among the sheep, until it forsook its glory and began to butt those sheep, and trampled on them, and behaved itself unseemly.

43 And the Lord of the sheep sent the lamb to another lamb and raised it to being a ram and leader of the sheep instead of that ram which had forsaken its glory.

44 And it went to it and spoke to it alone, and raised it to being a ram, and made it the prince and leader of the sheep; but during all these things those dogs oppressed the sheep.

45 And the first ram pursued the second ram, and the second ram arose and fled before it; and I saw until those dogs pulled down the first ram.

46 And that second ram arose and led the little sheep. And those sheep grew and multiplied; but all the dogs, and foxes, and wild boars feared and fled before it, and that ram butted and killed the wild beasts, and those wild beasts had no longer any power among the sheep and robbed them no more of anything.

47 And that ram fathered many sheep and fell asleep; and a little sheep became ram in its place, and became prince and leader of those sheep.

48 And that house became great and broad, and it was built for those sheep: and a high and great tower was built on the house for the Lord of the sheep, and that house was low, but the tower was elevated and high, and the Lord of the sheep stood on that tower and they offered a full table before him.

49 And again I saw those sheep that they again erred and went many ways, and forsook that their house, and the Lord of the sheep called some from among the sheep and sent them to the sheep, but the sheep began to slay them.

50 And one of them was saved and was not slain, and it sped away and cried aloud over the sheep; and they sought to slay it, but the Lord of the sheep saved it from the sheep, and brought it up to me, and caused it to live there.

51 And many other sheep He sent to those sheep to testify to them and lament over them.

52 And after that I saw that when they forsook the house of the Lord and His tower they fell away entirely, and their eyes were blinded; and I saw the Lord of the sheep how He worked much slaughter among them in their herds until those sheep invited that slaughter and betrayed His place.

53 And He gave them over into the hands of the lions and tigers, and wolves and hyenas, and into the hand of the foxes, and to all the wild beasts, and those wild beasts began to tear in pieces those sheep.

54 And I saw that He forsook their house and their tower and gave them all into the hand of the lions, to tear and devour them, into the hand of all the wild beasts.

55 And I began to cry aloud with all my power, and to appeal to the Lord of the sheep, because the sheep were being devoured by all the wild beasts.

56 But He remained unmoved, though He saw it, and rejoiced that they were devoured and swallowed and robbed, and left them to be devoured in the hand of all the beasts.

57 And He called seventy shepherds, and gave those sheep to them that they might pasture them, and He spoke to the shepherds and their companions: 'Let each individual of you pasture the sheep from now on, and everything that I shall command you that do you.

58 And I will deliver them over to you duly numbered, and tell you which of them are to be destroyed-and them you will destroy.' And He gave over to them those sheep.

59 And He called another and spoke to him: 'Observe and mark everything that the shepherds will do to those sheep; for they will destroy more of them than I have commanded them.

60 And every excess and the destruction which will be done through the shepherds, record how many they destroy according to my command, and

how many according to their own caprice; record against every individual shepherd all the destruction he effects.

61 And read out before me by number how many they destroy, and how many they deliver over for destruction, that I may have this as a testimony against them, and know every deed of the shepherds, that I may comprehend and see what they do, whether or not they abide by my command which I have commanded them.

62 But they shall not know it, and you shall not declare it to them, nor admonish them, but only record against each individual all the destruction which the shepherds effect each in his time and lay it all before me.'

63 And I saw until those shepherds pastured in their season, and they began to slay and to destroy more than they were bidden, and they delivered those sheep into the hand of the lions.

64 And the lions and tigers ate and devoured the greater part of those sheep, and the wild boars ate along with them; and they burned that tower and demolished that house.

65 And I became very sorrowful over that tower because that house of the sheep was demolished, and afterwards I was unable to see if those sheep entered that house.

66 And the shepherds and their associates delivered over those sheep to all the wild beasts, to devour them, and each one of them received in his time a definite number, it was written by the other in a book how many each one of them destroyed of them.

67 And each one slew and destroyed many more than was prescribed; and I began to weep and lament on account of those sheep.

68 And thus in the vision I saw that one who wrote, how he wrote down every one that was destroyed by those shepherds, day by day, and carried up and laid down and showed actually the whole book to the Lord of the sheep - everything that they had done, and all that each one of them had made away with, and all that they had given over to destruction.

69 And the book was read before the Lord of the sheep, and He took the book from his hand and read it and sealed it and laid it down.

70 And I saw how the shepherds pastured for twelve hours, and behold three of those sheep turned back and came and entered and began to build up all that had fallen down of that house; but the wild boars tried to hinder them, but they were not able.

71 And they began again to build as before, and they raised up that tower, and it was named the high tower; and they began again to place a table before the tower, but all the bread on it was polluted and not pure.

72 And as touching all this the eyes of those sheep were blinded so that they saw not, and the eyes of their shepherds likewise were blinded; and they delivered them in large numbers to their shepherds for destruction, and they trampled the sheep with their feet and devoured them.

73 And the Lord of the sheep remained unmoved until all the sheep were dispersed over the field and mingled with the beasts, and the shepherds did not save them out of the hand of the beasts.

74 And this one who wrote the book carried it up, and showed it and read it before the Lord of the sheep, and implored Him on their account, and besought Him on their account as he showed Him all the doings of the shepherds, and gave testimony before Him against all the shepherds.

75 And he took the actual book and laid it down beside Him and departed.

[Chapter 90]

1 And I saw until that in this manner thirty-five shepherds undertook the pasturing of the sheep, and they completed their periods as did the first; and others received them into their hands, to pasture them for their period, each shepherd in his own period.

2 And after that I saw in my vision all the birds of heaven coming, the eagles, the vultures, the kites, the ravens; but the eagles led all the birds; and they began to devour those sheep, and to pick out their eyes and to devour their flesh.

3 And the sheep cried out because their flesh was being devoured by the birds, and as for me I looked and lamented in my sleep over that shepherd who pastured the sheep.

4 And I saw until those sheep were devoured by the dogs and eagles and kites, and they left neither flesh nor skin nor sinew remaining on them until

only their bones stood there; and their bones too fell to the earth and the sheep became few.

5 And I saw until that twenty-three had undertaken the pasturing and completed in their many periods fifty-eight times.

6 But behold lambs were borne by those white sheep, and they began to open their eyes and to see, and to cry to the sheep.

7 They cried to them, but they did not hearken to what they said to them, but were very deaf, and their eyes were very blinded.

8 And I saw in the vision how the ravens flew on those lambs and took one of those lambs, and dashed the sheep in pieces and devoured them.

9 And I saw until horns grew on those lambs, and the ravens cast down their horns; and I saw until there sprouted a great horn of one of those sheep, and their eyes were opened.

10 And it looked at them and their eyes opened, and it cried to the sheep, and the rams saw it and all ran to it.

11 And notwithstanding all this, those eagles and vultures and ravens and kites kept on tearing the sheep and swooping down on them and devouring them until the sheep remained silent, but the rams lamented and cried out.

12 And those ravens fought and battled with it and sought to lay low its horn, but they had no power over it.

13 All the eagles and vultures and ravens and kites were gathered together, and there came with them all the sheep of the field, they all came together, and helped each other to break that horn of the ram.

14 And I saw that man, who wrote down the names of the shepherds and brought them up before the Lord of the sheep, came, and he helped that ram and showed it everything; its help was coming down.

15 And I looked until that Lord of the sheep came to them angry, all those who saw him ran, and they all fell into the shadow in front of Him.

16 All the eagles and vultures and ravens and kites, gathered together and brought with them all the wild sheep, and they all came together and helped one another in order to dash that horn of the ram in pieces.

17 And I looked at that man, who wrote the book at the command of the Lord, until he opened that book of the destruction that those last twelve shepherds had done. And he showed, in front of the Lord of the sheep, that they had destroyed even more than those before them had.

18 And I looked and the Lord of the sheep came to them and took the Staff of His Anger and struck the Earth. And the Earth was split. And all the animals, and the birds of the sky, fell from those sheep and sank in the earth, and it closed over them.

19 And I saw until a great sword was given to the sheep, and the sheep proceeded against all the beasts of the field to slay them, and all the beasts and the birds of the heaven fled before their face. And I saw that man, who wrote the book according to the command of the Lord, until he opened that book concerning the destruction which those twelve last shepherds had wrought, and showed that they had destroyed much more than their predecessors, before the Lord of the sheep. And I saw until the Lord of the sheep came to them and took in His hand the staff of His wrath, and smote the earth, and the earth clave asunder, and all the beasts and all the birds of heaven fell from among those sheep, and were swallowed up in the earth and it covered them.

20 And I saw until a throne was erected in the pleasant land, and the Lord of the sheep sat Himself on it, and the other took the sealed books and opened those books before the Lord of the sheep.

21 And the Lord called those men, the seven first white ones, and commanded that they should bring before Him, beginning with the first star which led the way, all the stars whose private members were like those of horses, and they brought them all before Him.

22 And He said to that man who wrote before Him, being one of those seven white ones, and said to him: 'Take those seventy shepherds to whom I delivered the sheep, and who taking them on their own authority slew more than I commanded them.'

23 And behold they were all bound, I saw, and they all stood before Him.

24 And the judgment was held first over the stars, and they were judged and found guilty, and went to the place of condemnation, and they were cast into an abyss, full of fire and flaming, and full of pillars of fire.

25 And those seventy shepherds were judged and found guilty, and they were cast into that fiery abyss.

26 And I saw at that time how a like abyss was opened in the midst of the earth, full of fire, and they brought those blinded sheep, and they were all judged and found guilty and cast into this fiery abyss, and they burned; now this abyss was to the right of that house.

27 And I saw those sheep burning and their bones burning.

28 And I stood up to see until they folded up that old house; and carried off all the pillars, and all the beams and ornaments of the house were at the same time folded up with it, and they carried it off and laid it in a place in the south of the land.

29 And I saw until the Lord of the sheep brought a new house greater and loftier than that first, and set it up in the place of the first which had been folded up; all its pillars were new, and its ornaments were new and larger than those of the first, the old one which He had taken away, and all the sheep were within it.

30 And I saw all the sheep which had been left, and all the beasts on the earth, and all the birds of heaven, falling down and doing homage to those sheep and making petition to and obeying them in every thing.

31 And thereafter those three who were clothed in white and had seized me by my hand [who had taken me up before], and the hand of that ram also seizing hold of me, they took me up and set me down in the midst of those sheep before the judgment took place.

32 And those sheep were all white, and their wool was abundant and clean.

33 And all that had been destroyed and dispersed, and all the beasts of the field, and all the birds of heaven, assembled in that house, and the Lord of the sheep rejoiced with great joy because they were all good and had returned to His house.

34 And I saw until they laid down that sword, which had been given to the sheep, and they brought it back into the house, and it was sealed before the presence of the Lord, and all the sheep were invited into that house, but it held them not.

35 And the eyes of them all were opened, and they saw the good, and there was not one among them that did not see.

36 And I saw that the house was large and broad and very full.

37 And I saw that a white bull was born, with large horns and all the beasts of the field and all the birds of the air feared him and made petition to him all the time.

38 And I saw until all their generations were transformed, and they all became white bulls; and the first among them became a lamb, and that lamb became a great animal and had great black horns on its head; and the Lord of the sheep rejoiced over it and over all the oxen.

39 And I slept in their midst: And I awoke and saw everything.

40 This is the vision which I saw while I slept, and I awoke and blessed the Lord of righteousness and gave Him glory.

41 Then I wept greatly and my tears ceased not until I could no longer endure it; when I saw, they flowed on account of what I had seen; for everything shall come and be fulfilled, and all the deeds of men in their order were shown to me.

42 On that night I remembered the first dream, and because of it I wept and was troubled-because I had seen that vision.

[Author's note: As this section was interpreted from a Jewish point of reference, many have assumed the 'large horn' was Judas Maccabee. In the Christian frame of reference, the same symbol was Jesus Christ.]

[Note from editor: at this point, the time frame and text flow becomes non sequitur. It appears the codex was not kept in sequence here. Thus, the translated pages are out of sequence. The flow of time and occurrences seems to follow the pattern listed:

91:6 to 92.1 through 92:5 then jumps to 93:1. The flow then continues from 93:1 to 93:10 and then jumps to 91:7. From 91:7 the text continues to 91:19. It then picks up again at 93:11 and continues.

If one were to attempt to put this section into a time line, the interval would link together in some fashion resembling the following:

Ten Weeks of Judgment

WEEK 1 Antediluvian	Judgment & righteousness 93.3 Enoch's time
WEEK 2 flood	Judgment & cleansing 93.4 Noah's time and the great
WEEK 3	Righteousness is planted 93.5 Abraham's time
WEEK 4	Law for all generations 93.6 Moses' time
WEEK 5	House of Glory 93.7 Solomon's time
WEEK 6 time	Jesus ascends, temple burned, elect scattered 93.8 Jesus'
WEEK 7 Our time	Apostate generation Judgment of Fire 93.9 - 91.11
WEEK 8 Future time	A sword 91.12–13 New house, new heaven & earth
WEEK 9 time	The righteous judgment revealed 91.14 The judgment
WEEK 10	God's power is forever 91.15-16 Eternal time

When reading the text from this point to the end of chapter 93 one should keep this flow in mind.]

[Chapter 91]

1 And now, my son Methuselah, call to me all your brothers and gather together to me all the sons of your mother; for the word calls me, and the spirit is poured out on me, that I may show you everything that shall befall you for ever.'

2 And thereon Methuselah went and summoned to him all his brothers and assembled his relatives.

3 And he spoke to all the children of righteousness and said: 'Hear, you sons of Enoch, all the words of your father, and hearken, as you should, to the voice of my mouth; for I exhort you and say to you, beloved:

4 Love righteousness and walk in it, and draw near to righteousness without a double heart, and do not associate with those of a double heart, but walk in righteousness, my sons. And it shall guide you on good paths. And righteousness shall be your companion.'

5 'For I know that violence must increase on the earth, and a great punishment will be executed on the earth, it shall be cut off from its roots, and its whole construct will be destroyed.

6 And unrighteousness shall again be complete on the earth, and all the deeds of unrighteousness and of violence and sin shall prevail a second time.

7 And when sin and unrighteousness and blasphemy and violence in all kinds of deeds increase, and apostasy and transgression and uncleanness increase; a great chastisement shall come from heaven on all these, and the holy Lord will come out with wrath and chastisement to execute judgment on earth.

8 In those days violence shall be cut off from its roots, and the roots of unrighteousness together with deceit, and they shall be destroyed from under heaven.

9 And all the idols of the heathen shall be abandoned. And the temples burned with fire, and they shall remove them from the whole earth; and the heathen shall be cast into the judgment of fire, and shall perish in wrath and in grievous judgment for ever.

10 And the righteous shall arise from their sleep, and wisdom shall arise and be given to them.

11 And after that the roots of unrighteousness and those who plan violence and those who commit blasphemy shall be cut off, and the sinners shall be destroyed by the sword.

12 And after this there will be another week; **the eighth**, that of righteousness, and a sword will be given to it so that the Righteous Judgment may be executed on those who do wrong, and the sinners will be handed over into the hands of the righteous.

13 And, at its end, they will acquire Houses because of their righteousness, and a House will be built for the Great King in Glory, forever.

14 And after this, in the **ninth week**, the Righteous Judgment will be revealed to the whole world. And all the deeds of the impious will vanish from the whole Earth. And the world will be written down for destruction and all men will look to the Path of Uprightness.

15 And, after this, in the **tenth week**, in the seventh part, there will be an Eternal Judgment that will be executed on the Watchers and the Great Eternal Heaven that will spring from the midst of the Angels.

16 And the First Heaven will vanish and pass away and a New Heaven will appear, and all the Powers of Heaven will shine forever, with light seven times as bright.

17 And after this, there will be many weeks without number, forever, in goodness and in righteousness. And from then on sin will never again be mentioned.

18 And now I tell you, my sons, and show you, the paths of righteousness and the paths of violence. I will show them to you again that you may know what will come to pass.

19 And now, hearken to me, my sons, and walk in the paths of righteousness, and walk not in the paths of violence; for all who walk in the paths of unrighteousness shall perish for ever.'

[Chapter 92]

1 The book written by Enoch {Enoch indeed wrote this complete doctrine of wisdom, (which is) praised of all men and a judge of all the earth} for all my

children who shall live on the earth. And for the future generations who shall observe righteousness and peace.

2 Let not your spirit be troubled on account of the times; for the Holy and Great One has appointed days for all things.

3 And the righteous one shall arise from sleep, [Shall arise] and walk in the paths of righteousness, and all his path and conversation shall be in eternal goodness and grace.

4 He will be gracious to the righteous and give him eternal righteousness, and He will give him power so that he shall be (endowed) with goodness and righteousness. And he shall walk in eternal light.

5 And sin shall perish in darkness for ever, and shall no more be seen from that day for evermore.

[Chapter 93]

(Author's Note: Chapters 91 – 93 recount and expand on the events listed in the following weeks of prophecy. The explanation of the event are scattered in chapters 91 – 93, however, the list of events are stated clearly in the following list of week in chapter 93).

1 And after that Enoch both gave and began to recount from the books. And Enoch said:

2 'Concerning the children of righteousness and concerning the elect of the world, and concerning the plant of righteousness, I will speak these things. I Enoch will declare (them) to you, my sons, according to that which appeared to me in heavenly vision, and which I have known through the word of the holy angels, and have learned from heavenly tablets.'

3 And Enoch began to recount from the books and said: 'I was born the seventh in the first week, able judgment and righteousness still endured.

4 And after me there shall arise in the second week great wickedness, and deceit shall have sprung up; and in it there shall be the first end.

5 And in it a man shall be saved; and after it is ended unrighteousness shall grow up, and a law shall be made for the sinners. And after that in the third week at its close a man shall be elected as the plant of righteous judgment, and his posterity shall become the plant of righteousness for evermore.

6 And after that in the fourth week, at its close, visions of the holy and righteous shall be seen, and a law for all generations and an enclosure shall be made for them.

7 And after that in the fifth week, at its close, the house of glory and dominion shall be built for ever.

8 And after that in the sixth week, all who live in it shall be blinded, and the hearts of all of them shall godlessly forsake wisdom. And in it a man shall ascend; and at its close the house of dominion shall be burned with fire, and the whole race of the chosen root shall be dispersed.

9 And after that in the seventh week shall an apostate generation arise, and many shall be its deeds, and all its deeds shall be apostate.

10 And at its end shall be elected, the elect righteous of the eternal plant of righteousness shall be chosen to receive sevenfold instruction concerning all His creation.

11 For who is there of all the children of men that is able to hear the voice of the Holy One without being troubled? And who can think His thoughts? Who is there that can behold all the works of heaven?

12 And how should there be one who could behold heaven, and who is there that could understand the things of heaven and see a soul or a spirit and could tell of it, or ascend and see all their ends and think them or do like them?

13 And who is there of all men that could know what is the breadth and the length of the earth, and to whom has the measurement been shown of all of them?

14 Or is there any one who could discern the length of the heaven and how great is its height, and on what it is founded, and how great is the number of the stars, and where all the luminaries rest?

[Chapter 94]

1 And now I say to you, my sons, love righteousness and walk in it; because the paths of righteousness are worthy of acceptation, but the paths of unrighteousness shall suddenly be destroyed and vanish.

2 And to certain men of a generation shall the paths of violence and of death be revealed, and they shall hold themselves afar from them, and shall not follow them.

3 And now I say to you, the righteous, walk not in the paths of wickedness, nor in the paths of death, and draw not near to them, lest you be destroyed.

4 But seek and choose for yourselves righteousness and an elect life, and walk in the paths of peace, and you shall live and prosper.

5 And hold (keep) my words in the thoughts of your hearts, and permit them not to be erased from your hearts; for I know that sinners will tempt men to evilly entreat wisdom, so that no place may be found for her, and temptation will increase.

6 Woe to those who build unrighteousness and oppression and lay deceit as a foundation; for they shall be suddenly overthrown, and they shall have no peace.

7 Woe to those who build their houses with sin; for from all their foundations shall they be overthrown, and by the sword shall they fall. And those who acquire gold and silver shall suddenly perish in the judgment.

8 Woe to you, you rich, for you have trusted in your riches, and from your riches shall you depart, because you have not remembered the Most High in the days of your riches.

9 You have committed blasphemy and unrighteousness, and have become ready for the day of slaughter, and the day of darkness and the day of the great judgment.

10 Thus I speak and tell you: He who has created you will overthrow you, and for your fall there shall be no compassion, and your Creator will rejoice at your destruction.

11 And your righteousness shall be a reproach to the sinners and the godless in those days.

[Chapter 95]

1 Would that my eyes were rain clouds of water that I might weep over you, and pour down my tears as a cloud of water, that I might rest from my trouble of heart!

2 Who has permitted you to practice reproaches and wickedness? And so judgment shall overtake you, sinners.

3 You, righteous! Fear not the sinners, for again the Lord will deliver them into your hands, that you may execute judgment on them according to your desires.

4 Woe to you who speak against God (fulminate anathemas) which cannot be removed (reversed) - healing shall be far from you because of your sins.

5 Woe to you who repay your neighbor with evil; for you shall be repaid according to your works.

6 Woe to you, lying witnesses, and to those who weigh out injustice, for you shall suddenly perish.

7 Woe to you, sinners, for you persecute the righteous; for you shall be delivered up and persecuted because of injustice, and your yoke shall be heavy on you.

[Chapter 96]

1 Be hopeful, you righteous; for suddenly shall the sinners perish before you, and you shall have lordship over them, according to your desires.

2 And in the day of the tribulation of the sinners, your children shall mount and rise as eagles, and your nests shall be higher than the vultures'. You shall ascend as badgers and enter the crevices of the earth, and the clefts of the rock for ever before the unrighteous. And the satyrs (sirens) shall sigh and weep because of you.

3 Wherefore fear not, you that have suffered, for healing shall be your portion, and a bright light shall enlighten you, and the voice of rest you shall hear from heaven.

4 Woe to you, you sinners, for your riches make you appear like the righteous, but your hearts convict you of being sinners, and this fact shall be a testimony against you for a memorial of your evil deeds.

5 Woe to you who devour the finest of the wheat, and drink wine in large bowls (the best of waters), and tread under foot the lowly (humble) with your might.

6 Woe to you who drink water from every fountain (drink water all the time), for suddenly shall you be consumed and wither away, because you have forsaken the fountain of life.

(Author's note: the above reference is a euphemism for promiscuity.)

7 Woe to you who work unrighteousness and deceit and blasphemy; it shall be a memorial against you for evil.

8 Woe to you, you mighty, who with might oppress the righteous; for the day of your destruction is coming. Many and good days shall come to the righteous in those days - in the day of your judgment.

[Chapter 97]

1 Believe, you righteous, that the sinners will become a shame and perish in the day of unrighteousness.

2 Be it known to you, you sinners, that the Most High is mindful of your destruction, and the angels of heaven rejoice over your destruction.

3 What will you do, you sinners, and where shall you flee on that day of judgment, when you hear the voice of the prayer of the righteous?

4 You shall fare like to them, against whom these words shall be a testimony: "You have been companions of sinners."

5 And in those days the prayer of the righteous shall reach to the Lord, and for you the days of your judgment shall come.

6 And all the words of your unrighteousness shall be read out before the Great Holy One, and your faces shall be covered with shame, and He will reject every work which is grounded on unrighteousness.

7 Woe to you, you sinners, who live on the middle of the ocean and on the dry land, whose remembrance is evil against you.

8 Woe to you who acquire silver and gold in unrighteousness and say: "We have become rich with riches and have possessions; and have acquired everything we have desired.

9 And now let us do what we purposed, for we have gathered silver, and many are the servants in our houses and our granaries are full to the brim as if with water."

10 Yea, and like water your lies shall flow away; for your riches shall not abide but quickly depart (go up) from you, for you have acquired it all in unrighteousness, and you shall be given over to a great curse.

[Chapter 98]

1 And now I swear to you, to the wise and to the foolish, that you shall see (have) many experiences on the earth.

2 For you men shall put on more adornments than a woman, and colored garments more than a young woman, like royalty and in grandeur and in power, and in silver and in gold and in purple, and in splendor and in food they shall be poured out as water.

3 Therefore they shall have neither knowledge nor wisdom, and because of this they shall die together with their possessions; and with all their glory and their splendor, and in shame and in slaughter and in great destitution, their spirits shall be thrown into the furnace of fire.

4 I have sworn to you, you sinners, as a mountain has not become a slave, and a hill does not become the servant of a woman, even so sin has not been sent on the earth, but man of himself has created it, and they that commit it shall fall under a great curse.

5 And barrenness has not been given to the woman, but on account of the deeds of her own hands she dies without children.

6 I have sworn to you, you sinners, by the Holy Great One, that all your evil deeds are revealed in heaven, and that none of your wrong deeds (of oppression) are covered and hidden.

7 And do not think in your spirit nor say in your heart that you do not know and that you do not see that every sin is recorded every day in heaven in the presence of the Most High.

8 From now on, you know that all your wrongdoing that you do will be written down every day, until the day of your judgment.

9 Woe to you, you fools, for through your folly you shall perish; and you do not listen to the wise so no good will come to you against the wise,

10 And so and now, know you that you are prepared for the day of destruction. Therefore do not hope to live, you sinners, but you shall depart and die; for there will be no ransom for you; because you are prepared for the day of the great judgment, for the day of tribulation and great shame for your spirits.

11 Woe to you, you obstinate of heart, who work wickedness and eat blood. Where do you have good things to eat and to drink and to be filled? From all the good things which the Lord the Most High has placed in abundance on the earth; therefore you shall have no peace.

(Author's note: The above reference to eating blood may indicate cannibalism.)

12 Woe to you who love the deeds of unrighteousness; wherefore do you hope for good for yourselves? You know that you shall be delivered into the hands of the righteous, and they shall cut off your necks and slay you, and have no mercy on you.

13 Woe to you who rejoice in the distress of the righteous; for no grave shall be dug for you.

14 Woe to you who say the words of the wise are empty; for you shall have no hope of life.

15 Woe to you who write down lying and godless words; for they write down their lies so that men may hear them and act godlessly towards their neighbor. Therefore they shall have no peace but die a sudden death.

[Chapter 99]

1 Woe to you who do godless acts, and praise and honor lies; you shall perish, and no happy life shall be yours.

2 Woe to them who pervert the words of righteousness, and transgress the eternal law, and count themselves as sinless. They shall be trodden under foot on the earth.

3 In those days make ready, you righteous, to raise your prayers as a memorial, and place them as a testimony before the angels, that they may place the sin of the sinners for a reminder before the Most High.

4 In those days the nations shall be stirred up, and the families of the nations shall arise on the day of destruction.

5 And in those days the destitute shall go and throw their children out, and they shall abandon them, so that their children shall perish because of them. They shall abandon their children that are still babies (sucklings), and not return to them, and shall have no pity on their loved ones.

6 Again, I swear to you, you sinners, that sin is prepared for a day of unceasing bloodshed.

7 And they who worship stones, and carved images of gold and silver and wood and stone and clay, and those who worship impure spirits and demons, and all kinds of idols not according to knowledge, shall get no manner of help from them.

8 And they shall become godless by reason of the folly of their hearts, and their eyes shall be blinded through the fear of their hearts and through visions in their ambitions (dreams).

9 Through these they shall become godless and fearful; for they shall have done all their work with lies, and shall have worshiped a stone, therefore in an instant shall they perish.

10 But in those days blessed are all they who accept the words of wisdom, and understand them, and observe the paths of the Most High, and walk in the path of His righteousness, and become not godless with the godless, for they shall be saved.

11 Woe to you who spread evil to your neighbors, for you shall be slain in Hell.

12 Woe to you who make your foundation that of deceitful (sin) and lies, and who cause bitterness on the earth; for they shall thereby be utterly consumed.

13 Woe to you who build your houses through the hard labor of others, and all their building materials are the bricks and stones of sin; I tell you, you shall have no peace.

14 Woe to them who reject the measure and eternal inheritance of their fathers and whose souls follow after idols; for they shall have no rest.

15 Woe to them who do unrighteous acts and help oppression, and kill their neighbors until the day of the great judgment, for He will throw down your glory.

16 For He shall throw down your glory, and bring affliction on your hearts, and shall arouse His fierce anger, and destroy you all with the sword; and all the holy and righteous shall remember your sins.

[Chapter 100]

1 And in those days in one place the fathers together with their sons shall kill one another and brothers shall fall in death together until the streams flow with their blood.

2 For a man shall not withhold his hand from killing his sons and his sons' sons, and the sinner shall not withhold his hand from his honored brother, from dawn until sunset they shall kill one another.

3 And the horse shall walk up to the breast in the blood of sinners, and the chariot shall be submerged to its height.

REV 14:20 And the winepress was trodden without the city, and blood came out of the winepress, even unto the horse bridles, by the space of a thousand and six hundred furlongs.

4 In those days the angels shall descend into the secret places and gather together into one place all those who brought down sin and the Most High will arise on that day of judgment to execute great judgment among sinners.

5 And over all the righteous and holy He will appoint guardians from among the holy angels to guard them as the apple of an eye, until He makes an end of all wickedness and all sin, and even if the righteous sleep a long sleep, they have nothing to fear.

6 And the wise men will seek the truth and they and their sons will understand the words of this book, and recognize that their riches shall not be able to save them or overcome their sins.

7 Woe to you sinners, on the day of strong anguish, you who afflict the righteous and burn them with fire; you shall be requited according to your works.

8 Woe to you, you obstinate of heart, who watch in order to devise wickedness; therefore shall fear come on you and there shall be none to help you.

9 Woe to you, you sinners, on account of the words of your mouth, and on account of the deeds of your hands which your godlessness as caused, in blazing flames burning worse than fire shall you burn.

10 And now, know that the angels will ask Him in heaven about your deeds and from the sun and from the moon and from the stars they will ask about your sins because on the earth you execute judgment on the righteous.

11 And He will summon to testify against you every cloud and mist and dew and rain; for they shall all be withheld from falling on you, and they shall be mindful of your sins.

12 And now give gifts to the rain that it cease not from falling on you, nor the dew, when it has received gold and silver from you that it may fall. When the hoar-frost and snow with their chilliness, and all the snow storms with all their plagues fall on you, in those days you shall not be able to stand before them.

[Chapter 101]

1 Observe heaven, you children of heaven, and every work of the Most High, and fear Him and work no evil in His presence.

2 If He closes the windows of heaven, and withholds the rain and the dew from falling on the earth on your account, what will you do then?

3 And if He sends His anger on you because of your deeds, you cannot petition Him; for you spoke proud and arrogant words against His righteousness, therefore you shall have no peace.

4 Don't you see the sailors of the ships, how their ships are tossed back and forth by the waves, and are shaken by the winds, and are in great trouble?

5 And therefore they are afraid because all their nice possessions go on the sea with them, and they have bad feelings in their heart that the sea will swallow them and they will perish therein.

6 Are not the entire sea and all its waters, and all its movements, the work of the Most High, and has He not set limits to its actions, and confined it throughout by the sand?

7 And at His reproof it fears and dries up, and all its fish die and all that is in it; but you sinners that are on the earth fear Him not.

8 Has He not made heaven and the earth, and all that is in it ? Who has given understanding and wisdom to everything that moves on the earth and in the sea?

9 Do not the sailors of the ships fear the sea? Yet you sinners do not fear the Most High.

[Chapter 102]

1 In those days if He sent a horrible fire on you, where will you flee, and where will you find deliverance? And when He launches out His Word against you will you not be shaken and afraid?

2 And all the luminaries shall be shaken with great fear, and all the earth shall be afraid and tremble and be alarmed.

3 And all the angels shall execute their commands and shall seek to hide themselves from the presence of He who is Great in Glory, and the children of earth shall tremble and shake; and you sinners shall be cursed for ever, and you shall have no peace.

4 Fear you not, you souls of the righteous, and fear not you who have died in righteousness.

5 And don't grieve if your soul has descended in to the grave in grief, and that in your life you were not rewarded according to your goodness, but wait for the day of the judgment of sinners and for the day of cursing and chastisement.

6 And when you die the sinners will say about you: "As we die, so die the righteous, and what benefit do they reap for their deeds?

7 See, even as we, so do they die in grief and darkness, and what have they more than we? From now on we are equal.

8 And what will they receive and what will they see for ever? Look, they too have died, and from now on for ever shall they see no light."

9 I tell you, you sinners, you are content to eat and drink, and rob and sin, and strip men naked, and acquire wealth and see good days.

10 Have you seen the righteous how their end was peace, that no violence is found in them until their death?

11 Nevertheless they died and became as though they had not been, and their spirits descended into Hell in tribulation.

[Chapter 103]

1 Now, therefore, I swear to the righteous, by the glory of the Great and Honored and Mighty One who reigns, I swear to you, I know this mystery.

2 I have read the heavenly tablets, and have seen the holy books, and have found written in it and inscribed regarding them.

3 That all goodness and joy and glory are prepared for them, and written down for the spirits of those who have died in righteousness, and that much good shall be given to you in reward for your labors, and that your lot is abundant beyond the lot of the living.

4 And the spirits of you who have died in righteousness shall live and rejoice, and your spirits shall not perish, nor shall your memory from before the face of the Great One to all the generations of the world, therefore no longer fear their abuse.

5 Woe to you, you sinners, when you have died, if you die in the abundance of your sins, and woe to those who are like you and say regarding you: "Blessed are the sinners, they have seen all their days.

6 And how they have died in prosperity and in wealth, and have not seen tribulation or murder in their life; and they have died in honor, and judgment has not been executed on them during their life."

7 You know that their souls will be made to descend into Hell and they shall be wracked in great tribulation.

8 And into darkness and chains and a burning flame where there is harsh judgment your spirits shall enter, and the great judgment shall be for all the generations of the world. Woe to you, for you shall have no peace.

9 The righteous and good who are alive, do not say: "In our troubled days we have worked hard and experienced every trouble, and met with much evil and been afflicted, and have become few and our spirit small.

10 And we have been destroyed and have not found any to help us even with a word. We have been tortured and destroyed, and not expect to live from day to day.

11 We hoped to be the head and have become the tail. We have worked hard and had no satisfaction in our labor; and we have become the food of the sinners and the unrighteous, and they have laid their yoke heavily on us.

12 They have ruled over us and hated us and hit us, and to those that hated us we have bowed our necks but they pitied us not.

13 We desired to get away from them that we might escape and be at rest, but found no place where we should flee and be safe from them.

14 We complained to the rulers in our tribulation, and cried out against those who devoured us, but they did not pay attention to our cries and would not listen to our voice.

15 And they helped those who robbed us and devoured us and those who made us few; and they concealed their oppression (wrongdoing), and they did not remove from us the yoke of those that devoured us and dispersed us and murdered us, and they concealed their murder, and did not remember that they had lifted up their hands against us."

[Chapter 104]

1 I swear to you, that in heaven the angels remember you for good before the glory of the Great One.

2 And your names are written before the glory of the Great One. Be hopeful; for before you were put to shame through sickness and affliction; but now you shall shine as the lights of heaven,

471

3 You shall shine and you shall be seen, and the doors of heaven shall be opened to you. And in your cry, cry for judgment, and it shall appear to you; for all your tribulation shall be visited on the rulers, and on all who helped those who plundered you.

4 Be hopeful, and do not throw away your hopes for you shall have great joy as the angels of heaven.

5 What will you have to do ? You shall not have to hide on the day of the great judgment and you shall not be found as sinners, and the eternal judgment shall not come to you for all the generations, eternally.

6 And now fear not, you righteous, when you see the sinners growing strong and prospering in their ways; do not be their companions, but keep away from their violence.

7 For you shall become companions of the hosts of heaven. And, although you sinners say: "All our sins shall not be found out and be written down," nevertheless they shall write down all your sins every day.

8 And now I show to you that light and darkness, day and night, see all your sins.

9 Do not be godless in your hearts, and do not lie and do not change the words of righteousness, nor say that the words of the Holy Great One are lies, nor praise or rely on your idols; for all your lying and all your godlessness (leads not to) come not from righteousness but (leads to) from great sin.

10 And now I know this mystery, that sinners will alter and pervert the words of righteousness in many ways, and will speak wicked words, and lie, and practice great deceits, and write books concerning their words.

11 But when they write down all my words truthfully in their languages, and do not change or omit any of my words but write them all down truthfully - all that I first testified concerning them.

12 Then, I know another mystery, that books will be given to the righteous and the wise to produce joy and righteousness and much wisdom.

13 And to them the books shall be given, and they shall believe them and rejoice over them, and then all the righteous who have learned from them all the paths of righteousness shall be paid back.'

[Chapter 105]

1 In those days the Lord called them (the wise and righteous) to testify to the children of earth concerning their wisdom: Show it to them; for you are their guides, and a recompense over the whole earth.

2 For I and my son will be united with them for ever in the paths of righteousness in their lives; and you shall have peace: rejoice, you children of righteousness. Amen.

[Chapter 106]

Fragment of the Book of Noah

1 And after some days my son Methuselah took a wife for his son, Lamech, and she became pregnant by him and bore a son. And his body was white as snow and red as the blooming of a rose, and the hair of his head and his long curls were white as wool, and his eyes beautiful.

2 And when he opened his eyes, he lit up the whole house like the sun, and the whole house was very bright.

3 And on it he levitated (arose) in the hands of the midwife, opened his mouth, and conversed with the Lord of righteousness.

4 And his father, Lamech, was afraid of him and fled, and came to his father Methuselah. And he said to him: 'I have begotten a strange son, different and unlike man, and resembling the sons of the God of heaven; and his nature is different and he is not like us, and his eyes are as the rays of the sun, and his face is glorious.

5 And it seems to me that he did not spring from me but from the angels, and I fear that in his days a wonder may be performed on the earth.

6 And now, my father, I am here to ask you and beg you that you may go to Enoch, our father, and learn from him the truth, for his dwelling-place is among the angels."

7 And when Methuselah heard the words of his son, he came to me to the ends of the earth; for he had heard that I was there, and he cried aloud, and I heard his voice and I came to him. And I said to him: 'Behold, here am I, my son, why have you come to me? '

8 And he answered and said: 'Because of a great cause of anxiety have I come to you, and because of a disturbing vision have I approached.

9 And now, my father, hear me. To Lamech, my son, there has been born a son, the like of whom there is none other, and his nature is not like man's nature, and the color of his body is whiter than snow and redder than the bloom of a rose, and the hair of his head is whiter than white wool, and his eyes are like the rays of the sun, and he opened his eyes and the whole house lit up.

10 And he levitated (arose) in the hands of the midwife, and opened his mouth and blessed the Lord of heaven.

11 And his father Lamech became afraid and fled to me, and did not believe that he was sprung from him, but that he was in the likeness of the angels of heaven; and now I have come to you that you may make known to me the truth.'

12 And I, Enoch, answered and said to him: 'The Lord will do a new thing on the earth, and this I have already seen in a vision, and make known to you that in the generation of my father Jared some of the angels of heaven violated the word of the Lord. And they commit sin and broke the law, and have had sex (united themselves) with women and committed sin with them, and have married some of them, and have had children by them.

13 And they shall produce on the earth giants not according to the spirit, but according to the flesh, and there shall be a great punishment on the earth, and the earth shall be cleansed from all impurity.

14 There shall come a great destruction over the whole earth, and there shall be a flood (deluge) and a great destruction for one year.

15 And this son who has been born to you shall be left on the earth, and his three children shall be saved with him: when all mankind that are on the earth shall die, he and his sons shall be saved.

16 And now make known to your son, Lamech, that he who has been born is in truth his son, and call his name Noah; for he shall be left to you, and he and his sons shall be saved from the destruction, which shall come on the earth on account of all the sin and all the unrighteousness, which shall be full (completed) on the earth in his days.

17 And after that (flood) there shall be more unrighteousness than that which was done before on the earth; for I know the mysteries of the holy ones; for He, the Lord, has showed me and informed me, and I have read (them) in heavenly tablets.

[Chapter 107]

1 And I saw written about them that generation after generation shall transgress, until a generation of righteousness arises, and transgression is destroyed and sin passes away from the earth, and all manner of good comes on it.

2 And now, my son, go and make known to your son Lamech that this son, which has been born, is in truth his son, and this is no lie.'

3 And when Methuselah had heard the words of his father Enoch, for he had shown to him everything in secret, he returned and showed those things to him and called the name of that son Noah; for he will comfort the earth after all the destruction.

[Chapter 108]

1 Another book which Enoch wrote for his son Methuselah and for those who will come after him, and keep the law in the last days.

2 You who have done good shall wait for those days until an end is made of those who work evil; and an end of the power of the wrongdoers.

3 And wait until sin has passed away indeed, for their names shall be blotted out of the book of life and out of the holy books, and their (children) seed shall be destroyed for ever, and their spirits shall be killed, and they shall cry and lament in a place that is a chaotic desert, and they shall be burned in the fire; for there is no earth there.

4 I saw something there like an invisible cloud; because it was so deep I could not look over it, and I saw a flame of fire blazing brightly, and things like shining mountains circling and sweeping back and forth.

5 And I asked one of the holy angels who was with me and said to him: 'What is this bright thing (shining)? For it is not heaven but there was only the flame of a blazing fire, and the voice of weeping and crying and moaning, lamenting, and agony.'

6 And he said to me: 'This place which you see are where the spirits of sinners and blasphemers, and of those who work wickedness, are cast and the spirits of those who pervert everything that the Lord has spoken through the mouth of the prophets and even the prophecies (things that shall be).

7 For some of them are written and inscribed above in heaven, in order that the angels may read them and know that which shall befall the sinners, and the spirits of the humble, and of those who have afflicted their bodies, and been recompensed by God; and of those who have been abused (put to shame) by wicked men:

8 Who love God and loved neither gold nor silver nor any of the good things which are in the world, but gave over their bodies to torture.

9 Who, since they were born, longed not after earthly food, but regarded everything as a passing breath, and lived accordingly, and the Lord tried them much, and their spirits were found pure so that they should bless His name.

10 And all the blessings destined for them I have recounted in the books. And he has assigned them their reward, because they have been found to love heaven more than their life in the world, and though they were trodden under foot by wicked men, and experienced abuse and reviling from them and were put to shame, they blessed Me.

11 And now I will summon the spirits of the good who belong to the generation of light, and I will transform those who were born in darkness, who in the flesh were not rewarded with such honor as their faithfulness deserved.

12 And I will bring out in shining light those who have loved My holy name, and I will seat each on the throne of his honor.

MAT 19:28 And Jesus said unto them, Verily I say unto you, That you which have followed me, in the regeneration when the Son of man shall sit in the throne of his glory, you also shall sit upon twelve thrones, judging the twelve tribes of Israel.

13 And they shall shine for time without end; for righteousness is the judgment of God; because to the faithful He will give faithfulness in the habitation of upright paths.

14 And they shall see those who were born in darkness led into darkness, while the righteous shall shine. And the sinners shall cry aloud and see them shining, and they indeed will go where days and seasons are written down (prescribed) for them.'

THE BOOK OF JUBILEES
THE LITTLE GENESIS, THE APOCALYPSE OF MOSES

This is the history of how the days were divided and of the days of the law and of the testimony, of the events of the years, and of the weeks of years, of their Jubilees throughout all the years of the world, as the Lord spoke to Moses on Mount Sinai when he went up to receive the tablets of the law and the commandment, according to the voice of God when he said to him, "Go up to the top of the Mount."

[Chapter 1]

1 It happened in the first year of the exodus of the children of Israel out of Egypt, in the third month, on the sixteenth day of the month, that God spoke to Moses, saying, "Come up to Me on the Mountain, and I will give you two tablets of stone of the law and the commandment, which I have written, that you may teach them."

2 Moses went up into the mountain of God, and the glory of the Lord rested on Mount Sinai, and a cloud overshadowed it six days.

3 He called to Moses on the seventh day out of the middle of the cloud, and the appearance of the glory of the Lord was like a flame on the top of the mountain.

4 Moses was on the mountain forty days and forty nights, and God taught him the earlier and the later history of the division of all the days of the law and of the testimony.

5 He said, "Open your heart to every word which I shall speak to you on this mountain, and write them in a book in order that their generations may see how I have not forsaken them for all the evil which they have committed when they transgressed the covenant which I establish between Me and you for their generations this day on Mount Sinai.

6 It will come to pass when all these things come on them, that they will recognize that I am more righteous than they in all their judgments and in all their actions, and they will recognize that I have truly been with them.

7 Write all these words for yourself which I speak to you today, for I know their rebellion and their stubbornness, before I brought them into the land of

which I swore to their fathers, to Abraham and to Isaac and to Jacob, saying, " Unto your offspring will I give a land flowing with milk and honey.

8 They will eat and be satisfied, and they will turn to strange gods, to gods that cannot deliver them from any of their tribulation, and this witness shall be heard for a witness against them.

9 They will forget all My commandments, even all that I command them, and they will walk in the ways of the Gentiles, and after their uncleanness, and after their shame, and will serve their gods, and these will prove to them an offence and a tribulation and an sickness and a trap.

10 Many will perish and they will be taken captive, and will fall into the hands of the enemy, because they have forsaken My laws and My commandments, and the festivals of My covenant, and My sabbaths, and My holy place which I have made holy for Myself in their presence, and My tabernacle, and My sanctuary, which I have made holy for Myself in the midst of the land, that I should set My name on it, that it should reside there.

11 They will make themselves high places and places of worship and graven images. Each will worship graven images of his own making, Thus they will go astray. They will sacrifice their children to demons, and to all errors their hearts can work.

12 I will send witnesses to them that I may testify against them, but they will not hear. They will kill the witnesses. They will persecute those who seek the law, and they will abolish and change everything (in the Law) so as to work evil before My eyes.

13 I will hide My face from them. I will deliver them into the hand of the Gentiles. They will be captured like prey for their eating. I will remove them from the out of the land. I will scatter them among the Gentiles.

14 And they will forget My law and all My commandments and all My judgments. They will go astray regarding the observance of new moons, and sabbaths, and festivals, and jubilees, and laws.

15 After this they will turn to Me from among the Gentiles with all their heart and with all their soul and with all their strength, and I will gather them from among all the Gentiles, and they will seek me. I shall be found by them when they seek me with all their heart and with all their soul.

16 I will allow them to see abounding peace with righteousness. I will remove them, the plant of uprightness, with all My heart and with all My soul, and they shall be for a blessing and not for a curse, and they shall be the head and not the tail.

17 I will build My sanctuary among them, and I will dwell with them, and I will be their God and they shall be My people in truth and righteousness.

18 I will not forsake them nor fail them; for I am the Lord their God."

19 Moses fell on his face and prayed and said, 'O Lord my God, do not forsake Your people and Your inheritance, so that they should wander in the error of their hearts, and do not deliver them into the hands of their

enemies, the Gentiles, so that they should rule over them and cause them to sin against You.

20 Let your mercy, O Lord, be lifted up on Your people, and create in them an upright spirit, and let not the spirit of Beliar rule over them to accuse them before You, and to ensnare them from all the paths of righteousness, so that they may perish from before Your face.

21 But they are Your people and Your inheritance, which You have delivered with Your great power from the hands of the Egyptians, create in them a clean heart and a holy spirit, and let them not be ensnared in their sins from now on until eternity."

22 The Lord said to Moses, "I know their contrariness and their thoughts and their stubbornness, and they will not be obedient until they confess their own sin and the sin of their fathers.

23 After this they will turn to Me in all uprightness and with all their heart and with all their soul, and I will circumcise the foreskin of their heart and the foreskin of the heart of their offspring, and I will create in them a holy spirit, and I will cleanse them so that they shall not turn away from Me from that day to eternity.

24 And their souls will cling to Me and to all My commandments, and they will fulfill My commandments, and I will be their Father and they shall be My children.

25 They all shall be called children of the living God, and every angel and every spirit shall know, yes, they shall know that these are My children, and that I am their Father in uprightness and righteousness, and that I love them.

26 Write down for yourself all these words which I say to you on this mountain, from the first to the last, which shall come to pass in all the divisions of the days in the law and in the testimony and in the weeks and the jubilees to eternity, until I descend and dwell with them throughout eternity."

27 He said to the angel of the presence (of the Lord), "Write for Moses from the beginning of creation until My sanctuary has been built among them for all eternity.

28 The Lord will appear to the eyes of all, and all shall know that I am the God of Israel and the Father of all the children of Jacob, and King on Mount Zion for all eternity. And Zion and Jerusalem shall be holy."

29 The angel of the presence (of the Lord) who went before the camp of Israel took the tables of the divisions of the years, written from the time of the creation, concerning the law and the testimony of the weeks of the jubilees, according to the individual years, according to the numbering of all the jubilees, from the day of the new creation when the heavens and the earth shall be renewed and all their creation according to the powers of the heaven, and according to all the creation of the earth, until the sanctuary of

the Lord shall be made in Jerusalem on Mount Zion, and all the stars and planets be renewed for healing, peace, and blessing for all the elect of Israel, and that this is the way it may be from that day and to all the days of the earth.

[Chapter 2]

1 The angel of the presence (of the Lord) spoke to Moses according to the word of the Lord, saying, "Write the complete history of the creation, how in six days the Lord God finished all His works and all that He created, and kept Sabbath on the seventh day and made it holy for all ages, and appointed it as a sign for all His works.

2 For on the first day He created the heavens which are above and the earth and the waters and all the spirits which serve before him which are the angels of the presence (of the Lord), and the angels of sanctification, and the angels of the spirit of fire, and the angels of the spirit of the winds, and the angels of the spirit of the clouds, and of darkness, and of snow and of hail and of white frost, and the angels of the voices and of the thunder and of the lightning, and the angels of the spirits of cold and of heat, and of winter and of spring and of autumn and of summer and of all the spirits of his creatures which are in the heavens and on the earth, He created the bottomless pit and the darkness, evening and night, and the light, dawn and day, which He has prepared in the knowledge of His heart.

3 When we saw His works, we praised Him, and worshiped before Him because of all His works; for seven great works did He create on the first day.

4 On the second day He created the sky between the waters (above and below), and the waters were divided on that day. Half of them went up above the sky and half of them went down below the sky that was in the middle over the face of the whole earth. And this was the only work God created on the second day.

5 On the third day He commanded the waters to pass from off the face of the whole earth into one place, and the dry land to appear.

6 The waters did as He commanded them, and they receded from off the face of the earth into one place, and the dry land appeared.

7 On that day He created for them all the seas according to their separate gathering-places, and all the rivers, and the gatherings of the waters in the mountains and on all the earth, and all the lakes, and all the dew of the earth, and the seed which is sown, and all sprouting things, and fruit-bearing trees, and trees of the wood, and the garden of Eden, in Eden and throughout. These four great works God created on the third day.

8 On the fourth day He created the sun and the moon and the stars, and set them in the sky of the heaven, to give light on all the earth, and to rule over the day and the night, and divide the light from the darkness.

9 God appointed the sun to be a great sign on the earth for days and for sabbaths and for months and for feasts and for years and for sabbaths of years and for jubilees and for all seasons of the years.

10 And it divides the light from the darkness for prosperity that all things may prosper which sprout and grow on the earth. These three kinds He made on the fourth day.

11 On the fifth day He created great sea monsters in the depths of the waters, for these were the first things of flesh that were created by his hands, the fish and everything that moves in the waters, and everything that flies, the birds and all their kind.

12 And the sun rose above them to make them prosper, and the sun rose above everything that was on the earth, everything that sprouts out of the earth, and all fruit-bearing trees, and all flesh.

13 He created these three kinds on the fifth day. On the sixth day He created all the animals of the earth, and all cattle, and everything that moves on the earth.

14 After all this He created mankind. He created a man and a woman, and gave him dominion over all that is on the earth, and in the seas, and over everything that flies, and over beasts, and over cattle, and over everything that moves on the earth, and over the whole earth, and over all this He gave him dominion.

15 He created these four kinds on the sixth day. And there were altogether two and twenty kinds.

16 He finished all his work on the sixth day. That is all that is in the heavens and on the earth, and in the seas and in the abysses, and in the light and in the darkness, and in everything.

17 He gave us a great sign, the Sabbath day, that we should work six days, but keep Sabbath on the seventh day from all work.

18 All the angels of the presence (of the Lord), and all the angels of sanctification, these two great types of angels He has told to tell us to keep the Sabbath with Him in heaven and on earth.

19 And He said to us, "Look, I will separate to Myself a people from among all the peoples, and these shall keep the Sabbath day, and I will sanctify them to Myself as My people, and will bless them; as I have sanctified the Sabbath day and do sanctify it to Myself, even so will I bless them, and they shall be My people and I will be their God.

20 I have chosen the offspring of Jacob from among all that I have seen, and have written him down as My first-born son, and have sanctified him to Myself forever and ever; and I will teach them the Sabbath day, that they may keep Sabbath on it from all work."

21 He created in it a sign in accordance with which they should keep Sabbath with us on the seventh day, to eat and to drink, and to bless Him who has created all things as He has blessed and sanctified to Himself a

particular, exclusive people above all peoples, and that they should keep Sabbath together with us.

22 He caused His commands to rise up as a sweet odor acceptable before Him all the days.

23 There were two and twenty heads (representatives) of mankind from Adam to Jacob, and two and twenty kinds of work (creation) were made until the seventh day; this is blessed and holy; and the former also is blessed and holy; and this one serves with that one for sanctification and blessing.

24 Jacob and his offspring were granted that they should always be the blessed and holy ones of the first testimony and law, even as He had sanctified and blessed the Sabbath day on the seventh day.

25 He created heaven and earth and everything that He created in six days, and God made the seventh day holy, for all His works; therefore He commanded on its behalf that, whoever does any work on it shall die, and that he who defiles it shall surely die.

26 Because of this, command the children of Israel to observe this day that they may keep it holy and not do on it any work, and not to defile it, as it is holier than all other days.

27 And whoever profanes it shall surely die, and whoever does any work on it shall surely die eternally, that the children of Israel may observe this day throughout their generations, and not be rooted out of the land; for it is a holy day and a blessed day.

28 Every one who observes it and keeps Sabbath on it from all his work will be holy and blessed throughout all days as we are blessed.

29 Declare and say to the children of Israel the law of this day that they should keep Sabbath on it, and that they should not forsake it in the error of their hearts; and that it is not lawful to do any work on it which is not suitable, to do their own pleasure on it, and that they should not prepare anything to be eaten or drunk on it, and that it is not lawful to draw water, or bring in or take out through their gates any burden which they had not prepared for themselves on the sixth day in their dwellings.

30 They shall not bring or take anything from house to house on that day; for that day is more holy and blessed than any jubilee day of the jubilees; on this we kept Sabbath in the heavens before it was made known to any flesh to keep Sabbath on the earth.

31 The Creator of all things blessed it, but He did not sanctify all peoples and nations to keep Sabbath, but Israel alone, them alone He permitted to eat and drink and to keep Sabbath on the earth.

32 And the Creator of all things blessed this day which He had created for blessing and holiness and glory above all days.

33 This law and testimony was given to the children of Israel as a law forever to their generations.

[Chapter 3]

1 On the sixth day of the second week, according to the word of God, we brought to Adam all the beasts, and all the cattle, and all the birds, and everything that moves on the earth, and everything that moves in the water, according to their kinds, and according to their types, the beasts on the first day; the cattle on the second day; the birds on the third day; and all that moves on the earth on the fourth day; and that moves in the water on the fifth day.

2 And Adam named them all by their respective names. As he called them, so was their name.

3 On these five days Adam saw all these, male and female, according to every kind that was on the earth, but he was alone and found no helpmate.

4 The Lord said to us, "It is not good that the man should be alone, let us make a helpmate for him."

5 And the Lord our God caused a deep sleep to fall on him, and he slept, and He took from Adam a rib from among his ribs for the woman, and this rib was the origin of the woman. And He built up the flesh in its place, and built the woman.

6 He awakened Adam out of his sleep and on awakening he rose on the sixth day, and He brought her to him, and he knew her, and said to her, "This is now bone of my bones and flesh of my flesh; she shall be called my wife; because she was taken from her husband."

7 Therefore shall man and wife become one and therefore shall a man leave his father and his mother, and cling to his wife, and they shall be one flesh.

8 In the first week Adam was created, and from his rib, his wife. In the second week God showed her to him, and for this reason the commandment was given to keep in their defilement. A male should be purified in seven days, and for a female twice seven days.

9 After Adam had completed forty days in the land where he had been created, we brought him into the garden of Eden to till and keep it, but his wife we brought in on the eightieth day, and after this she entered into the garden of Eden.

10 And for this reason the commandment is written on the heavenly tablets in regard to her that gives birth, "If she bears a male, she shall remain unclean for seven days according to the first week of days, and thirty-three days shall she remain in the blood of her purifying, and she shall not touch any holy thing, nor enter into the sanctuary, until she completes these days which are decreed in the case of a male child.

11 But in the case of a female child she shall remain unclean two weeks of days, according to the first two weeks, and sixty-six days in the blood of her purification, and they will be in all eighty days."

12 When she had completed these eighty days we brought her into the Garden of Eden, for it is holier than all the earth besides and every tree that is planted in it is holy.

13 Therefore, there was ordained regarding her who bears a male or a female child the statute of those days that she should touch no holy thing, nor enter into the sanctuary until these days for the male or female child are completed.

14 This is the law and testimony that was written down for Israel, in order that they should observe it all the days.

15 In the first week of the first jubilee, Adam and his wife were in the garden of Eden for seven years tilling and keeping it, and we gave him work and we instructed him to do everything that is suitable for tillage.

16 And he tilled the garden, and was naked and did not realize it, and was not ashamed. He protected the garden from the birds and beasts and cattle. He gathered its fruit, and ate, and put aside that which was left over for himself and for his wife.

17 After the completion of exactly seven years there, and in the second month, on the seventeenth day of the month, the serpent came and approached the woman, and the serpent said to the woman, "Has God commanded you saying, you shall not eat of every tree of the garden?"

18 She said to it, God said to us, of all the fruit of the trees of the garden, eat; but of the fruit of the tree which is in the middle of the garden God said to us, you shall not eat of it, neither shall you touch it, or you shall die."

19 The serpent said to the woman, "You shall not surely die. God does know that on the day you shall eat of it, your eyes will be opened, and you will be as gods, and you will know good and evil.

20 And the woman saw the tree that it was beautiful and pleasant to the eye, and that its fruit was good for food, and she took of it and ate.

21 First, she covered her shame with fig leaves and then she gave the fruit to Adam and he ate, and his eyes were opened, and he saw that he was naked.

22 He took fig leaves and sewed them together, and made an apron for himself, and covered his shame.

23 God cursed the serpent, and was very angry at it forever.

24 And He was very angry with the woman, because she listened to the voice of the serpent, and ate; and He said to her, "I will vastly multiply your sorrow and your pains, in sorrow you will bring forth children, and your master shall be your husband, and he will rule over you."

25 To Adam also he said, " Because you have listened to the voice of your wife, and have eaten of the tree of which I commanded you not to eat, cursed be the ground for your sake, thorns and thistles shall it produce for you, and you will eat your bread in the sweat of your face, until you return to the earth from where you were taken; for earth you are, and to earth will you return."

26 And He made for them coats of skin, and clothed them, and sent them out from the Garden of Eden.

27 On that day on which Adam went out from the Garden, he offered as a sweet odor an offering, frankincense, incense, and sweet spice, and spices in the morning with the rising of the sun from the day when he covered his shame.

28 On that day was closed the mouth of all beasts, and of cattle, and of birds, and of whatever walks, and of whatever moves, so that they could no longer speak, for they had all spoken one with another with one dialect and with one language.

29 All flesh that was in the Garden of Eden He sent out of the Garden of Eden, and all flesh was scattered according to its kinds, and according to its types to the places that had been created for them.

30 Of all the beasts and cattle only to Adam alone He gave the ability to cover his shame.

31 Because of this, it is prescribed on the heavenly tablets as touching all those who know the judgment of the law, that they should cover their shame, and should not uncover themselves as the Gentiles uncover themselves.

32 On the new moon of the fourth month, Adam and his wife went out from the Garden of Eden, and they dwelt in the land of Elda in the land of their creation.

33 And Adam called the name of his wife Eve.

34 And they had no son until the first jubilee, and after this he knew her.

35 Now he tilled the land as he had been instructed in the Garden of Eden.

[Chapter 4]

1 In the third week in the second jubilee she gave birth to Cain, and in the fourth jubilee she gave birth to Abel, and in the fifth jubilee she gave birth to her daughter Awan.

2 In the first year of the third jubilee, Cain killed Abel because God accepted the sacrifice of Abel, and did not accept the offering of Cain.

3 And he killed him in the field, and his blood cried from the ground to heaven, complaining because he had killed him.

4 The Lord blamed Cain, because he had killed Abel, and He made him a fugitive on the earth because of the blood of his brother, and He cursed him on the earth.

5 Because of this it is written on the heavenly tablets, "Cursed is he who kills his neighbor treacherously, and let all who have seen and heard say,

'So be it', and the man who has seen and not reported it, let him be accursed as the one committing it."

6 For this reason we announce when we come before the Lord our God all the sin that is committed in heaven and on earth, and in light and in darkness, and everywhere.

7 And Adam and his wife mourned for Abel four weeks of years, and in the fourth year of the fifth week they became joyful, and Adam knew his wife again, and she gave birth to a son, and he called his name Seth, for he said "God has raised up a second offspring to us on the earth instead of Abel; for Cain killed him."

8 In the sixth week he begat his daughter Azura.

9 And Cain took Awan his sister to be his wife and she gave birth to Enoch at the close of the fourth jubilee.

10 In the first year of the first week of the fifth jubilee, houses were built on the earth, and Cain built a city, and called its name after the name of his son Enoch.

11 Adam knew Eve his wife and she gave birth to a total of nine sons. In the fifth week of the fifth jubilee Seth took Azura his sister to be his wife, and in the fourth year of the sixth week she gave birth to Enos.

12 He began to call on the name of the Lord on the earth.

13 In the seventh jubilee in the third week Enos took Noam his sister to be his wife, and she gave birth to a son in the third year of the fifth week, and he called his name Kenan.

14 At the close of the eighth jubilee Kenan took Mualeleth his sister to be his wife, and she gave birth to a son in the ninth jubilee, in the first week in the third year of this week, and he called his name Mahalalel.

15 In the second week of the tenth jubilee Mahalalel took to him to wife Dinah, the daughter of Barakiel the daughter of his father's brother, and she gave birth to a son in the third week in the sixth year, and he called his name Jared, for in his days the angels of the Lord descended on the earth, those who are named the Watchers, that they should instruct the children of men, and that they should do judgment and uprightness on the earth.

16 In the eleventh jubilee Jared took to himself a wife, and her name was Baraka, the daughter of Rasujal, a daughter of his father's brother, in the fourth week of this jubilee, and she gave birth to a son in the fifth week, in the fourth year of the jubilee, and he called his name Enoch.

17 He was the first among men that are born on earth who learned writing and knowledge and wisdom and who wrote down the signs of heaven according to the order of their months in a book, that men might know the seasons of the years according to the order of their separate months.

18 He was the first to write a testimony and he testified to the sons of men among the generations of the earth, and recounted the weeks of the jubilees, and made known to them the days of the years, and set in order the months and recounted the Sabbaths of the years as we made them, known to him.

19 And what was and what will be he saw in a vision of his sleep, as it will happen to the children of men throughout their generations until the day of judgment; he saw and understood everything, and wrote his testimony, and placed the testimony on earth for all the children of men and for their generations.

20 In the twelfth jubilee, in the seventh week of it, he took to himself a wife, and her name was Edna, the daughter of Danel, the daughter of his father's brother, and in the sixth year in this week she gave birth to a son and he called his name Methuselah.

21 He was with the angels of God these six jubilees of years, and they showed him everything that is on earth and in the heavens, the rule of the sun, and he wrote down everything.

22 And he testified to the Watchers, who had sinned with the daughters of men; for these had begun to unite themselves, so as to be defiled with the daughters of men, and Enoch testified against them all.

23 And he was taken from among the children of men, and we conducted him into the Garden of Eden in majesty and honor, and there he wrote down the condemnation and judgment of the world, and all the wickedness of the children of men.

24 Because of it God brought the waters of the flood on all the land of Eden; for there he was set as a sign and that he should testify against all the children of men, that he should recount all the deeds of the generations until the day of condemnation.

25 He burnt the incense of the sanctuary, even sweet spices acceptable before the Lord on the Mount.

26 For the Lord has four places on the earth, the Garden of Eden, and the Mount of the East, and this mountain on which you are this day, Mount Sinai, and Mount Zion which will be sanctified in the new creation for a sanctification of the earth; through it will the earth be sanctified from all its guilt and its uncleanness throughout the generations of the world.

27 In the fourteenth jubilee Methuselah took to himself a wife, Edna the daughter of Azrial, the daughter of his father's brother, in the third week, in the first year of this week, and he begat a son and called his name Lamech.

28 In the fifteenth jubilee in the third week Lamech took to himself a wife, and her name was Betenos the daughter of Baraki'il, the daughter of his father's brother, and in this week she gave birth to a son and he called his name Noah, saying, "This one will comfort me for my trouble and all my work, and for the ground which the Lord has cursed."

29 At the close of the nineteenth jubilee, in the seventh week in the sixth year of it, Adam died, and all his sons buried him in the land of his creation, and he was the first to be buried in the earth.

30 He lacked seventy years of one thousand years, because one thousand years are as one day in the testimony of the heavens. Therefore was it

written concerning the tree of knowledge, "On the day that you eat of it you shall die." Because of this he did not complete the one thousand years but instead he died during it.

31 At the close of this jubilee Cain was killed after him in the same year; because his house fell on him and he died in the middle of his house, and he was killed by its stones. With a stone he had killed Abel, and by a stone he was killed in righteous judgment.

32 For this reason it was ordained on the heavenly tablets, with the instrument with which a man kills his neighbor with the same shall he be killed. In the same manner that he wounded him, in like manner shall they deal with him."

33 In the twenty-fifth jubilee Noah took to himself a wife, and her name was Emzara, the daughter of Rake'el, the daughter of his father's brother, in the first year in the fifth week, and in the third year of it she gave birth to Shem, in the fifth year of it she gave birth to Ham, and in the first year in the sixth week she gave birth to Japheth.

[Chapter 5]

1 When the children of men began to multiply on the face of the earth and daughters were born to them, and the angels of God saw them on a certain year of this jubilee, that they were beautiful, and they took themselves wives of all whom they chose, and they gave birth to their sons and they were giants.

2 Because of them lawlessness increased on the earth and all flesh corrupted its way. Men and cattle and beasts and birds and everything that walked on the earth were all corrupted in their ways and their orders, and they began to devour each other. Lawlessness increased on the earth and the imagination and thoughts of all men were continually, totally evil.

3 God looked on the earth, and saw it was corrupt, and all flesh had corrupted its orders, and all that were on the earth had committed all manner of evil before His eyes.

4 He said that He would destroy man and all flesh on the face of the earth that He had created.

5 But Noah found grace before the eyes of the Lord.

6 And against the angels whom He had sent on the earth, He had boiling anger, and He gave commandment to root them out of all their dominion, and He commanded us to bind them in the depths of the earth, and look, they are bound in the middle of the earth, and are kept separate.

7 And against their sons went out a command from His mouth that they should be killed with the sword, and be left under heaven.

8 He said, "My spirit shall not always abide on man; for they also are flesh and their days shall be one hundred and twenty years."

9 He sent His sword into their presence that each should kill his neighbor, and they began to kill each other until they all fell by the sword and were destroyed from the earth.

10 And their fathers were witnesses of their destruction, and after this they were bound in the depths of the earth forever, until the day of the great condemnation, when judgment is executed on all those who have corrupted their ways and their works before the Lord.

11 He destroyed all wherever they were, and there was not one left of them whom He judged according to all their wickedness.

12 Through His work He made a new and righteous nature, so that they should not sin in their whole nature forever, but should be all righteous each in his own way always.

13 The judgment of all is ordained and written on the heavenly tablets in righteousness, even the judgment of all who depart from the path that is ordained for them to walk; and if they do not walk it, judgment is written down for every creature and for every kind.

14 There is nothing in heaven or on earth, or in light or in darkness, or in the abode of the dead or in the depth, or in the place of darkness that is not judged. All their judgments are ordained and written and engraved.

15 He will judge all, the great according to his greatness, and the small according to his smallness, and each according to his way.

16 He is not one who will regard the position of any person, nor is He one who will receive gifts, if He says that He will execute judgment on each.

17 If one gave everything that is on the earth, He will not regard the gifts or the person of any, nor accept anything at his hands, for He is a righteous judge.

18 Of the children of Israel it has been written and ordained, if they turn to him in righteousness He will forgive all their transgressions and pardon all their sins. It is written and ordained that He will show mercy to all who turn from all their guilt once each year.

19 And as for all those who corrupted their ways and their thoughts before the flood, no person was acceptable to God except Noah. His sons were saved in deference to him, and these God kept from the waters of the flood on his account; for Noah's heart was righteous in all his ways. He upheld the laws and did as God commanded him and he had not departed from anything that was ordained for him.

20 The Lord said that he would destroy everything on the earth, both men and cattle, and beasts, and birds of the air, and that which moves on the earth.

21 And He commanded Noah to make an ark, so that he might save himself from the waters of the flood.

22 And Noah made the ark in all respects as He commanded him, in the twenty-seventh jubilee of years, in the fifth week in the fifth year on the new moon of the first month.

23 He entered in the sixth year of it, in the second month, on the new moon of the second month, until the sixteenth; and he entered, and all that we brought to him, into the ark, and the Lord closed it from the outside on the seventeenth evening.

24 And the Lord opened seven floodgates of heaven, and He opened the mouths of the fountains of the great deep, seven mouths in number.

25 And the floodgates began to pour down water from the heaven forty days and forty closets, And the fountains of the deep also sent up waters, until the whole world was full of water.

26 The waters increased on the earth, by fifteen cubits (a cubit is about 18 inches) the waters rose above all the high mountains. And the ark was lift up from the earth. And it moved on the face of the waters.

27 And the water covered the face of the earth five months, which is one hundred and fifty days.

28 And the ark went and rested on the top of Lubar, one of the mountains of Ararat.

29 On the new moon in the fourth month the fountains of the great deep were closed and the floodgates of heaven were restrained; and on the new moon of the seventh month all the mouths of the bottomless gulfs of the earth were opened, and the water began to flow down into the deep below.

30 On the new moon of the tenth month the tops of the mountains were seen, and on the new moon of the first month the earth became visible.

31 The waters disappeared from the earth in the fifth week in the seventh year of it, and on the seventeenth day in the second month the earth was dry.

32 On the twenty-seventh of it he opened the ark, and sent out beasts, and cattle, and birds, and every moving thing.

[Chapter 6]

1 On the new moon of the third month he went out of the ark, and built an altar on that mountain.

2 And he made atonement for the earth, and took a kid and made atonement by its blood for all the guilt of the earth; for every thing that had been on it had been destroyed, except those that were in the ark with Noah.

3 He placed the fat of it on the altar, and he took an ox, and a goat, and a sheep and kids, and salt, and a turtle-dove, and the young of a dove, and placed a burnt sacrifice on the altar, and poured on it an offering mingled with oil, and sprinkled wine and sprinkled frankincense over everything, and caused a good and pleasing odor to arise, acceptable before the Lord.

4 And the Lord smelled the good and pleasing odor, and He made a covenant with Noah that there should not be any more floods to destroy the earth; that all the days of the earth seed-time and harvest should never cease; cold and heat, and summer and winter, and day and night should not change their order, nor cease forever.

5 "Increase and multiply on the earth, and become many, and be a blessing on it. I will inspire the fear of you and the dread of you in everything that is on earth and in the sea.

6 Look, I have given you all beasts, and all winged things, and everything that moves on the earth, and the fish in the waters, and all things for food; as the green herbs, I have given you all things to eat.

7 But you shall not eat anything live or with blood in it, for the life of all flesh is in the blood, or your blood of your lives will be required. At the hand of every man, at the hand of every beast will I require the blood of man.

8 Whoever sheds man's blood by man shall his blood be shed, for in the image of God He made man.

9 Increase, and multiply on the earth."

10 Noah and his sons swore that they would not eat any blood that was in any flesh, and he made a covenant before the Lord God forever throughout all the generations of the earth in this month.

11 Because of this He spoke to you that you should make a covenant with the children of Israel with an oath. In this month, on the mountain you should sprinkle blood on them because of all the words of the covenant, which the Lord made with them forever.

12 This testimony is written concerning you that you should observe it continually, so that you should not eat on any day any blood of beasts or birds or cattle during all the days of the earth, and the man who eats the blood of beast or of cattle or of birds during all the days of the earth, he and his offspring shall be rooted out of the land.

13 And you will command the children of Israel to eat no blood, so that their names and their offspring may be before the Lord our God continually.

14 There is no limit of days, for this law. It is forever. They shall observe it throughout their generations, so that they may continue supplicating on your behalf with blood before the altar; every day and at the time of morning and evening they shall seek forgiveness on your behalf perpetually before the Lord that they may keep it and not be rooted out.

15 And He gave to Noah and his sons a sign that there should not again be a flood on the earth.

16 He set His bow (a rainbow) in the cloud as a sign of the eternal covenant that there should never again be a flood on the earth to destroy it for all the days of the earth.

17 For this reason it is ordained and written on the heavenly tablets, that they should celebrate the feast of weeks in this month once a year, to renew the covenant every year.

18 This whole festival was celebrated in heaven from the day of creation until the days of Noah, which were twenty-six jubilees and five weeks of years. Noah and his sons observed it for seven jubilees and one week of years, until the day of Noah's death. From the day of Noah's death his sons did away with it until the days of Abraham, and they ate blood.

19 But Abraham observed it, and Isaac and Jacob and his children observed it up to your days, and in your days the children of Israel forgot it until you celebrated it anew on this mountain.

20 Command the children of Israel to observe this festival in all their generations for a commandment to them, one day in the year in this month they shall celebrate the festival.

21 For it is the feast of weeks and the feast of first-fruits, this feast is twofold and of a double nature, according to what is written and engraved concerning it, celebrate it.

22 For I have written in the book of the first law, in that which I have written for you, that you should celebrate it in its season, one day in the year, and I explained to you its sacrifices that the children of Israel should remember and should celebrate it throughout their generations in this month, the same day in every year.

23 On the new moon of the first month, and on the new moon of the fourth month, and on the new moon of the seventh month, and on the new moon of the tenth month are the days of remembrance, and the days of the seasons in the four divisions of the year. These are written and ordained as a testimony forever.

24 Noah ordained them for himself as feasts for the generations forever, so that they have become a memorial to him.

25 On the new moon of the first month he was told to make for himself an ark, and on that day the earth was dry and he saw from the opened ark, the earth. On the new moon of the fourth month the mouths of the depths of the bottomless pit beneath were closed.

26 On the new moon of the seventh month all the mouths of the abysses of the earth were opened, and the waters began to descend into them.

27 On the new moon of the tenth month the tops of the mountains were seen, and Noah was glad.

28 Because of this he ordained them for himself as feasts for a memorial forever, and thus are they ordained.

29 And they placed them on the heavenly tablets, each had thirteen weeks; from one to another passed their memorial, from the first to the second, and from the second to the third, and from the third to the fourth.

30 All the days of the commandment will be two and fifty weeks of days, and these will make the entire year complete. Thus it is engraved and ordained on the heavenly tablets.

31 And there is no neglecting this commandment for a single year or from year to year.

32 Command the children of Israel that they observe the years according to this counting, three hundred and sixty-four days, and these will constitute a complete year, and they will not disturb its time from its days and from its feasts; for every thing will fall out in them according to their testimony, and they will not leave out any day nor disturb any feasts.

33 But if they neglect and do not observe them according to His commandment, then they will disturb all their seasons and the years will be dislodged from this order, and they will neglect their established rules.

34 And all the children of Israel will forget and will not find the path of the years, and will forget the new moons, and seasons, and sabbaths and they will wrongly determine all the order of the years.

35 For I know and from now on will I declare it to you, and it is not of my own devising; for the book lies written in the presence of me, and on the heavenly tablets the division of days is ordained, or they forget the feasts of the covenant and walk according to the feasts of the Gentiles after their error and after their ignorance.

36 For there will be those who will assuredly make observations of the moon and how it disturbs the seasons and comes in from year to year ten days too soon.

37 For this reason the years will come upon them when they disturb (misinterpret) the order, and make an abominable day the day of testimony, and an unclean day a feast day, and they will confound all the days, the holy with the unclean, and the unclean day with the holy; for they will go wrong as to the months and sabbaths and feasts and jubilees.

38 For this reason I command and testify to you that you may testify to them; for after your death your children will disturb them, so that they will not make the year three hundred and sixty-four days only, and for this reason they will go wrong as to the new moons and seasons and sabbaths and festivals, and they will eat all kinds of blood with all kinds of flesh.

[Chapter 7]

1 In the seventh week in the first year of it, in this jubilee, Noah planted vines on the mountain on which the ark had rested, named Lubar, one of the Ararat Mountains, and they produced fruit in the fourth year, and he guarded their fruit, and gathered it in that year in the seventh month.

2 He made wine from it and put it into a vessel, and kept it until the fifth year, until the first day, on the new moon of the first month.

3 And he celebrated with joy the day of this feast, and he made a burnt sacrifice to the Lord, one young ox and one ram, and seven sheep, each a year old, and a kid of the goats, that he might make atonement thereby for himself and his sons.

4 He prepared the kid first, and placed some of its blood on the flesh that was on the altar that he had made, and all the fat he laid on the altar where he made the burnt sacrifice, and the ox and the ram and the sheep, and he laid all their flesh on the altar.

5 He placed all their offerings mingled with oil on it, and afterwards he sprinkled wine on the fire which had previously been made on the altar, and he placed incense on the altar and caused a sweet odor to rise up which was acceptable before the Lord his God.

6 And he rejoiced and he and his children drank the wine with joy.

7 It was evening, and he went into his tent, and being drunken he lay down and slept, and was uncovered in his tent as he slept.

8 And Ham saw Noah his father naked, and went out and told his two brothers (ridiculed his father to his two brothers) who were outside.

9 Shem took his garment and arose, he and Japheth, and they placed the garment on their shoulders and went backward and covered the shame of their father, and their faces were backward.

10 Noah awoke from sleep and knew all (abuse) that his younger son had done to him. He cursed him saying, "Cursed be Canaan; an enslaved servant shall he be to his brothers."

11 And he blessed Shem, and said, "Blessed be the Lord God of Shem, and Canaan shall be his servant.

12 God shall enlarge Japheth, and God shall dwell in the dwelling of Shem, and Canaan shall be his servant."

13 Ham knew that his father had cursed, him, his younger son, and he was displeased that he had cursed him, his son. And Ham parted from his father, he and his sons with him, Cush and Mizraim and Put and Canaan.

14 And he built for himself a city and called its name after the name of his wife Ne'elatama'uk.

15 Japheth saw it, and became envious of his brother, and he too built for himself a city, and he called its name after the name of his wife Adataneses.

16 Shem dwelt with his father Noah, and he built a city close to his father on the mountain, and he too called its name after the name of his wife Sedeqetelebab.

17 These three cities are near Mount Lubar; Sedeqetelebab in front of the mountain on its east; and Na'eltama'uk on the south; Adatan'eses towards the west.

18 These are the sons of Shem, Elam, and Asshur, and Arpachshad who was born two years after the flood, and Lud, and Aram.

19 The sons of Japheth, Gomer, Magog, Madai , Javan, Tubal and Meshech and Tiras, these are the descendants of Noah.

20 In the twenty-eighth jubilee Noah began to direct his sons in the ordinances and commandments, and all the judgments that he knew, and he exhorted his sons to observe righteousness, and to cover the shame of their flesh, and to bless their Creator, and honor father and mother, and love their neighbor, and guard their souls from fornication and uncleanness and all iniquity.

21 Because of these three things came the flood on the earth, namely, the fornication that the Watchers committed against the law of their ordinances when they went whoring after the daughters of men, and took themselves wives of all they chose, and they made the beginning of uncleanness.

22 And they begat sons, the Naphilim (Naphidim), and they were all dissimilar, and they devoured one another, and the Giants killed the Naphil, and the Naphil killed the Eljo, and the Eljo killed mankind, and one man killed one another.

23 Every one committed himself to crime and injustice and to shed much blood, and the earth was filled with sin.

24 After this they sinned against the beasts and birds, and all that moved and walked on the earth, and much blood was shed on the earth, and men continually desired only what was useless and evil.

25 And the Lord destroyed everything from the face of the earth. Because of the wickedness of their deeds, and because of the blood they had shed over all the earth, He destroyed everything. "

26 We were left, I and you, my sons, and everything that entered with us into the ark, and behold I see your works before me that you do not walk in righteousness, for in the path of destruction you have begun to walk, and you are turning one against another, and are envious one of another, and so it comes that you are not in harmony, my sons, each with his brother.

27 For I see the demons have begun their seductions against you and against your children and now I fear on your behalf, that after my death you will shed the blood of men on the earth, and that you, too, will be destroyed from the face of the earth.

28 For whoever sheds man's blood, and who ever eats the blood of any flesh, shall all be destroyed from the earth.

29 There shall be no man left that eats blood, or that sheds the blood of man on the earth, nor shall there be left to him any offspring or descendants living under heaven. Into the abode of the dead shall they go, and into the place of condemnation shall they descend, and into the darkness of the deep shall they all be removed by a violent death.

30 Do not smear blood on yourself or let it remain on you. Out of all the blood there shall be shed and out of all the days in which you have killed

any beasts or cattle or whatever flies on the earth you must do a good work to your souls by covering that which has been shed on the face of the earth.

31 You shall not be like him who eats blood, but guard yourselves that none may eat blood before you, cover the blood, for thus have I been commanded to testify to you and your children, together with all flesh.

32 Do not permit the soul (life) to be eaten with the flesh, that your blood, which is your life, may not be required at the hand of any flesh that sheds it on the earth.

33 For the earth will not be clean from the blood that has been shed on it, for only through the blood of him that shed it will the earth be purified throughout all its generations.

34 Now, my children, listen, have judgment and righteousness that you maybe planted in righteousness over the face of the whole earth, and your glory lifted up in the presence of my God, who spared me from the waters of the flood.

35 Look, you will go and build for yourselves cities, and plant in them all the plants that are on the earth, and moreover all fruit-bearing trees.

36 For three years the fruit of everything that is eaten will not be gathered, and in the fourth year its fruit will be accounted holy, offered as first fruit, acceptable before the Most High God, who created heaven and earth and all things.

37 Let them offer in abundance the first of the wine and oil as first-fruits on the altar of the Lord, who receives it, and what is left let the servants of the house of the Lord eat before the altar which receives it.

38 In the fifth year make the release so that you release it in righteousness and uprightness, and you shall be righteous, and all that you plant shall prosper. For this is how Enoch did it, the father of your father commanded Methuselah, his son, and Methuselah commanded his son Lamech, and Lamech commanded me all the things that his fathers commanded him.

39 I also will give you commandment, my sons, as Enoch commanded his son in the first jubilees, while still living, the seventh in his generation, he commanded and testified to his son and to his son's sons until the day of his death.

[Chapter 8]

1 In the twenty-ninth jubilee, in the beginning of first week, Arpachshad took to himself a wife and her name was Rasu'eja, the daughter of Susan, the daughter of Elam, and she gave birth to a son in the third year in this week, and he called his name Kainam.

2 The son grew, and his father taught him writing, and he went to seek for himself a place where he might seize a city for himself.

3 He found writing which former generations had carved on a rock, and he read what was on it, and he transcribed it and sinned because of it, for it contained the teaching of the Watchers, which they had used to observe the omens of the sun and moon and stars in all the signs of heaven.

4 He wrote it down and said nothing of it, for he was afraid to speak to Noah about it or he would be angry with him because of it.

5 In the thirtieth jubilee, in the second week, in the first year of it, he took to himself a wife, and her name was Melka, the daughter of Madai, the son of Japheth, and in the fourth year he begat a son, and called his name Shelah; for he said, "Truly I have been sent."

6 Shelah grew up and took to himself a wife, and her name was Mu'ak, the daughter of Kesed, his father's brother, in the one and thirtieth jubilee, in the fifth week, in the first year of it.

7 And she gave birth to a son in the fifth year of it, and he called his name Eber, and he took to himself a wife, and her name was Azurad, the daughter of Nebrod, in the thirty-second jubilee, in the seventh week, in the third year of it.

8 In the sixth year of it, she gave birth to a son, and he called his name Peleg, for in the days when he was born the children of Noah began to divide the earth among themselves, for this reason he called his name Peleg.

9 They divided it secretly among themselves, and told it to Noah.

10 In the beginning of the thirty-third jubilee they divided the earth into three parts, for Shem and Ham and Japheth, according to the inheritance of each, in the first year in the first week, when one of us (angels) who had been sent, was with them.

11 He called his sons, and they drew close to him, they and their children, and he divided the earth into the lots, which his three sons were to take in possession, and they reached out their hands, and took the writing out of the arms of Noah, their father.

12 There came out on the writing as Shem's lot the middle of the earth that he should take as an inheritance for himself and for his sons for the generations of eternity. From the middle of the mountain range of Rafa, from the mouth of the water from the river Tina, and his portion goes towards the west through the middle of this river, and it extends until it reaches the water of the abysses, out of which this river goes out and pours its waters into the sea Me'at, and this river flows into the great sea.

13 All that is towards the north is Japheth's, and all that is towards the south belongs to Shem. And it extends until it reaches Karaso, this is in the center of the tongue of land that looks towards the south.

14 His portion extends along the great sea, and it extends in a straight line until it reaches the west of the tongue that looks towards the south, for this sea is named the tongue of the Egyptian Sea.

15 And it turns from here towards the south towards the mouth of the great sea on the shore of its waters, and it extends to the west to Afra, and it extends until it reaches the waters of the river Gihon, and to the south of the waters of Gihon, to the banks of this river.

16 It extends towards the east, until it reaches the Garden of Eden, to the south of it and from the east of the whole land of Eden and of the whole east, it turns to the east and proceeds until it reaches the east of the mountain named Rafa, and it descends to the bank of the mouth of the river Tina.

17 This portion came out by lot for Shem and his sons, that they should possess it forever to his generations forever.

18 Noah rejoiced that this portion came out for Shem and for his sons, and he remembered all that he had spoken with his mouth in prophecy; for he had said, "Blessed be the Lord God of Shem and may the Lord dwell in the dwelling of Shem."

19 He knew that the Garden of Eden is the holy of holies, and the dwelling of the Lord, and Mount Sinai the center of the desert, and Mount Zion which is the center of the navel of the earth, these three were created as holy places facing each other.

20 And he blessed the God of gods, who had put the word of the Lord into his mouth, and the Lord forever.

21 And he knew that a blessed portion and a blessing had come to Shem and his sons and to their generations forever which was the whole land of Eden and the whole land of the Red Sea, and the whole land of the east and India, and on the Red Sea and the mountains of it, and all the land of Bashan, and all the land of Lebanon and the islands of Kaftur, and all the mountains of Sanir and Amana, and the mountains of Asshur in the north, and all the land of Elam, Asshur, and Babel, and Susan and Ma'edai, and all the mountains of Ararat, and all the region beyond the sea, which is beyond the mountains of Asshur towards the north, a blessed and spacious land, and all that is in it is very good.

22 Ham received the second portion, beyond the Gihon towards the south to the right of the Garden, and it extends towards the south and it extends to all the mountains of fire, and it extends towards the west to the sea of 'atel and it extends towards the west until it reaches the sea of Ma'uk which was that sea into which everything that is not destroyed descends.

23 It goes out towards the north to the limits of Gadir, and it goes out to the coast of the waters of the sea to the waters of the great sea until it draws near to the river Gihon, and goes along the river Gihon until it reaches the right of the Garden of Eden.

24 This is the land that came out for Ham as the portion which he was to occupy forever for himself and his sons to their generations forever.

25 Japheth received the third portion beyond the river Tina to the north of the outflow of its waters, and it extends north-easterly to the whole region of Gog, and to all the country east of it.

26 It extends northerly, and it extends to the mountains of Qelt towards the north, and towards the sea of Ma'uk, and it goes out to the east of Gadir as far as the region of the waters of the sea.

27 It extends until it approaches the west of Fara and it returns towards Aferag, and it extends easterly to the waters of the sea of Me'at.

28 It extends to the region of the river Tina in a northeasterly direction until it approaches the boundary of its waters towards the mountain Rafa, and it turns round towards the north.

29 This is the land that came out for Japheth and his sons as the portion of his inheritance that he should possess five great islands, and a great land in the north, for himself and his sons, for their generations forever.

30 But it is cold, and the land of Ham is hot, and the land of Shem is neither hot nor cold, but it is of blended cold and heat.

[Chapter 9]

1 Ham divided among his sons, and the first portion came out for Cush towards the east, and to the west of him for Mizraim, and to the west of him for Put, and to the west of him on the sea for Canaan.

2 Shem also divided among his sons, and the first portion came out for Elam and his sons, to the east of the river Tigris until it approaches the east, the whole land of India, and on the Red Sea on its coast, and the waters of Dedan, and all the mountains of Mebri and Ela, and all the land of Susan and all that is on the side of Pharnak to the Red Sea and the river Tina.

3 Asshur received the second Portion, all the land of Asshur and Nineveh and Shinar and to the border of India, and it ascends and skirts the river.

4 Arpachshad received the third portion, all the land of the region of the Chaldees to the east of the Euphrates, bordering on the Red Sea, and all the waters of the desert close to the tongue of the sea which looks towards Egypt, all the land of Lebanon and Sanir and Amana to the border of the Euphrates.

5 Aram received the fourth portion, all the land of Mesopotamia between the Tigris and the Euphrates to the north of the Chaldees to the border of the mountains of Asshur and the land of Arara.

6 Lud got the fifth portion, the mountains of Asshur and all surrounding to them until it reaches the Great Sea, and until it reaches the east of Asshur his brother.

7 Japheth also divided the land of his inheritance among his sons.

8 The first portion came out for Gomer to the east from the north side to the river Tina, and in the north there came out for Magog all the inner portions of the north until it reaches to the sea of Me'at.

9 Madai received as his portion that he should possess from the west of his two brothers to the islands, and to the coasts of the islands.

10 Javan got the fourth portion, every island and the islands that are towards the border of Lud.

11 For Tubal there came out the fifth portion in the middle of the tongue that approaches towards the border of the portion of Lud to the second tongue, to the region beyond the second tongue to the third tongue.

12 Meshech received the sixth portion, that is the entire region beyond the third tongue until it approaches the east of Gadir.

13 Tiras got the seventh portion, four great islands in the middle of the sea, which reach to the portion of Ham, and the islands of Kamaturi came out by lot for the sons of Arpachshad as his inheritance.

14 Thus the sons of Noah divided to their sons in the presence of Noah their father, and he bound them all by an oath, and invoked a curse on every one that sought to seize any portion which had not fallen to him by his lot.

15 They all said, "so be it; so be it " (amen and amen) for themselves and their sons forever throughout their generations until the day of judgment, on which the Lord God shall judge them with a sword and with fire for all the unclean wickedness of their errors, that they have filled the earth with, which are transgression, uncleanness and fornication and sin.

[Chapter 10]

1 In the third week of this jubilee the unclean demons began to lead astray the children of the sons of Noah, and to make them sin and to destroy them.

2 The sons of Noah came to Noah their father, and they told him about the demons that were leading astray and blinding and slaying his sons' sons.

3 And he prayed before the Lord his God, and said,

"God of the spirits of all flesh, who have shown mercy to me and have spared me and my sons from the waters of the flood,

and have not caused me to die as You did the sons of perdition; For Your grace has been great toward me,

and great has been Your mercy to my soul. Let Your grace be lifted up on my sons, and do not let the wicked spirits rule over them or they will destroy them from the earth.

4 But bless me and my sons, so that we may increase and multiply and replenish the earth.

5 You know how Your Watchers, the fathers of these spirits, acted in my day, and as for these spirits which are living, imprison them and hold them fast in the place of condemnation, and let them not bring destruction on the sons of your servant, my God; for these are like cancer and are created in order to destroy.

6 Let them not rule over the spirits of the living; for You alone can exercise dominion over them. And let them not have power over the sons of the righteous from now and forever."

7 And the Lord our God commanded us (angels) to bind all of them.

8 The chief of the spirits, Mastema, came and said, "Lord, Creator, let some of them remain before me, and let them listen to my voice, and do all that I shall say to them; for if some of them are not left to me, I shall not be able to execute the power of my will on the sons of men, for these are for corruption and leading astray before my judgment, for great is the wickedness of the sons of men."

9 He said, "Let one-tenth of them remain before him, and let nine-tenths of them descend into the place of condemnation."

10 He commanded one of us to teach Noah all their medicines, for He knew that they would not walk in uprightness, nor strive in righteousness.

11 We did according to all His words, all the malignant evil ones we bound in the place of condemnation and a tenth part of them we left that they might be subject in the presence of Satan on the earth.

12 We explained to Noah all the medicines of their diseases, together with their seductions, how he might heal them with herbs of the earth.

13 Noah wrote down all things in a book as we instructed him concerning every kind of medicine. Thus the evil spirits were precluded from hurting the sons of Noah.

14 He gave all that he had written to Shem, his eldest son, for he loved him greatly above all his sons.

15 And Noah slept with his fathers, and was buried on Mount Lubar in the land of Ararat.

16 Nine hundred and fifty years he completed in his life, nineteen jubilees and two weeks and five years.

17 In his life on earth he was greater than all the children of men except Enoch because of his righteousness he was perfect. For Enoch's office was ordained for a testimony to the generations of the world, so that he should recount all the deeds of generation to generation, until the day of judgment.

18 In the three and thirtieth jubilee, in the first year in the second week, Peleg took to himself a wife, whose name was Lomna the daughter of Sina'ar, and she gave birth to a son for him in the fourth year of this week, and he called his name Reu, for he said, "Look the children of men have become evil because the building a city and a tower in the land of Shinar was for an evil purpose."

19 For they departed from the land of Ararat eastward to Shinar, for in his days they built the city and the tower, saying, "Come, let us rise up by the tower into heaven."

20 They began to build, and in the fourth week they made brick with fire, and the bricks served them for stone,

and the clay with which they cemented them together was asphalt which comes out of the sea, and out of the fountains of water in the land of Shinar.

21 They built it, forty-three years were they building it. Its breadth was 203 bricks, and the height of a brick was the third of one; its height amounted to 5433 cubits and 2 palms, and the extent of one wall was thirteen times 600 feet and of the other thirty times 600 feet.

22 And the Lord our God said to us, "Look, they are one people, and they begin to do this, and now nothing will be withheld from them. Let us go down and confound their language, that they may not understand one another's speech, and they may be dispersed into cities and nations, and they will not be in agreement together with one purpose until the day of judgment."

23 And the Lord descended, and we descended with him to see the city and the tower that the children of men had built.

24 He confounded their language, and they no longer understood one another's speech, and they then ceased to build the city and the tower.

25 For this reason the whole land of Shinar is called Babel, because the Lord confounded all the language of the children of men there, and from that place they were dispersed into their cities, each according to his language and his nation.

26 Then, the Lord sent a mighty wind against the tower and it fell to the earth, and behold it was between Asshur and Babylon in the land of Shinar, and they called its name "Overthrow."

27 In the fourth week in the first year in the beginning of it in the four and thirtieth jubilee, were they dispersed from the land of Shinar.

28 Ham and his sons went into the land that he was to occupy, which he acquired as his portion in the land of the south.

29 Canaan saw the land of Lebanon to the river of Egypt was very good, and he did not go into the land of his inheritance to the west that is to the sea, and he dwelt in the land of Lebanon, eastward and westward from the border of Jordan and from the border of the sea.

30 Ham, his father, and Cush and Mizraim, his brothers, said to him, "You have settled in a land which is not yours, and which did not fall to us by lot, do not do so. If you do you and your sons will be conquered in the land and be accursed through a war. By war you have settled, and by war will your children fall, and you will be rooted out forever.

31 Do not live in the land of Shem, for to Shem and to his sons did it come by their lot.

32 Cursed are you, and cursed will you be beyond all the sons of Noah, by the curse by which we bound ourselves by an oath in the presence of the holy judge, and in the presence of Noah our father."

33 But he did not listen to them, and settled in the land of Lebanon from Hamath to the border of Egypt, he and his sons until this day. For this reason that land is named Canaan. And Japheth and his sons went towards the sea and settled in the land of their portion, and Madai saw the land of the sea and it did not please him, and he begged Ham and Asshur and Arpachshad, his wife's brother for a portion, and he dwelt in the land of Media, near to his wife's brother until this day.

34 And he called his and his son's dwelling-place, Media, after the name of their father Madai.

[Chapter 11]

1 In the thirty-fifth jubilee, in the third week, in the first year of it, Reu took to himself a wife, and her name was 'Ora, the daughter of 'Ur, the son of Kesed, and she gave birth to a son, and he called his name Seroh, in the seventh year of this week in this jubilee.

2 The sons of Noah began to war with each other, to take captives and kill each other, and to shed the blood of men on the earth, and to eat blood, and to build strong cities, and walls, and towers, and individuals began to exalt themselves above the nation, and to establish kingdoms, and to go to war, people against people, and nation against nation, and city against city, and all began to do evil, and to acquire arms, and to teach their sons war, and they began to capture cities, and to sell male and female slaves.

3 Ur, the son of Kesed, built the city of Ara of the Chaldees, and called its name after his own name and the name of his father.

4 And they made themselves molten images, and they worshipped the idols and the molten image they had made for themselves, and they began to make graven images and unclean and shadowy presence, and malevolent and malicious spirits assisted and seduced them into committing transgression and uncleanness.

5 Prince Mastema exerted himself to do all this, and he sent out other spirits, which were put under his control, to do all manner of wrong and sin, and all manner of transgression, to corrupt and destroy, and to shed blood on the earth.

6 For this reason he called the name of Seroh, Serug, for every one turned to do all manner of sin and transgression.

7 He grew up, and dwelt in Ur of the Chaldees, near to the father of his wife's mother, and he worshipped idols, and he took to himself a wife in the

thirty-sixth jubilee, in the fifth week, in the first year of it, and her name was Melka, the daughter of Kaber, the daughter of his father's brother.

8 She gave birth to Nahor, in the first year of this week, and he grew and dwelt in Ur of the Chaldees, and his father taught him the sciences of the Chaldees to divine and conjure, according to the signs of heaven.

9 In the thirty-seventh jubilee in the sixth week, in the first year of it, he took to himself a wife, and her name was 'Ijaska, the daughter of Nestag of the Chaldees.

10 And she gave birth to Terah in the seventh year of this week.

11 Prince Mastema sent ravens and birds to devour the seed that was sown in the land, in order to destroy the land, and rob the children of men of their labors. Before they could plow in the seed, the ravens picked it from the surface of the ground.

12 This is why he called his name Terah because the ravens and the birds reduced them to destitution and devoured their seed.

13 The years began to be barren, because of the birds, and they devoured all the fruit of the trees from the trees, it was only with great effort that they could harvest a little fruit from the earth in their days.

14 In this thirty-ninth jubilee, in the second week in the first year, Terah took to himself a wife, and her name was 'Edna, the daughter of Abram, the daughter of his father's sister.

15 In the seventh year of this week she gave birth to a son, and he called his name Abram, by the name of the father of his mother, for he had died before his daughter had conceived a son.

16 And the child began to understand the errors of the earth that all went astray after graven images and after uncleanness,

and his father taught him writing, and he was two weeks of years old, and he separated himself from his father, that he might not worship idols with him.

17 He began to pray to the Creator of all things that He might spare him from the errors of the children of men, and that his portion should not fall into error after uncleanness and vileness.

18 The time came for the sowing of seed in the land, and they all went out together to protect their seed against the ravens, and Abram went out with those that went, and the child was a lad of fourteen years.

19 A cloud of ravens came to devour the seed, and Abram ran to meet them before they settled on the ground, and cried to them before they settled on the ground to devour the seed, and said, "Descend not, return to the place from where you came," and they began to turn back.

20 And he caused the clouds of ravens to turn back that day seventy times, and of all the ravens throughout all the land where Abram was there settled not so much as one.

21 All who were with him throughout all the land saw him cry out, and all the ravens turn back, and his name became great in all the land of the Chaldees.

22 There came to him this year all those that wished to sow, and he went with them until the time of sowing ceased, and they sowed their land, and that year they brought enough grain home to eat and they were satisfied.

23 In the first year of the fifth week Abram taught those who made implements for oxen, the artificers in wood, and they made a vessel above the ground, facing the frame of the plow, in order to put the seed in it, and the seed fell down from it on the share of the plow, and was hidden in the earth, and they no longer feared the ravens.

24 After this manner they made vessels above the ground on all the frames of the plows, and they sowed and tilled all the land, according as Abram commanded them, and they no longer feared the birds.

[Chapter 12]

1 In the sixth week, in the seventh year of it, that Abram said to Terah his father, saying, "Father!"

2 He said, "Look, here am I, my son." He said, "What help and profit have we from those idols which you worship, and in the presence of which you bow yourself?

3 For there is no spirit in them. They are dumb forms, and they mislead the heart.

4 Do not worship them, Worship the God of heaven, who causes the rain and the dew to fall on the earth and does everything on the earth, and has created everything by His word, and all life is from His presence.

5 Why do you worship things that have no spirit in them?

For they are the work of men's hands, and you bear them on your shoulders, and you have no help from them, but they are a great cause of shame to those who make them, and they mislead the heart of those who worship them. Do not worship them."

6 His father said to him, "I also know it, my son, but what shall I do with a people who have made me serve them?

7 If I tell them the truth, they will kill me, because their soul clings to them so they worship them and honor them.

8 Keep silent, my son, or they will kill you." And these words he spoke to his two brothers, and they were angry with him and he kept silent.

9 In the fortieth jubilee, in the second week, in the seventh year of it, Abram took to himself a wife, and her name was Sarai, the daughter of his father, and she became his wife.

10 Haran, his brother, took to himself a wife in the third year of the third week, and she gave birth to a son in the seventh year of this week, and he called his name Lot.

11 Nahor, his brother, took to himself a wife.

12 In the sixtieth year of the life of Abram, that is, in the fourth week, in the fourth year of it, Abram arose in the night and burned the house of the idols, and he burned all that was in the house and no man knew it.

13 And they arose and sought to save their gods from the fire.

14 Haran hasted to save them, but the fire flamed over him, and he was burnt in the fire, and he died in Ur of the Chaldees before Terah his father, and they buried him in Ur of the Chaldees.

15 Terah went out from Ur of the Chaldees, he and his sons, to go into the land of Lebanon and into the land of Canaan, and he dwelt in the land of Haran, and Abram dwelt with Terah his father in Haran two weeks of years.

16 In the sixth week, in the fifth year of it, Abram sat up all night on the new moon of the seventh month to observe the stars from the evening to the morning, in order to see what would be the character of the year with regard to the rains, and he was alone as he sat and observed.

17 And a word came into his heart and he said, "All the signs of the stars, and the signs of the moon and of the sun are all in the hand of the Lord. Why do I search them out?

18 If He desires, He causes it to rain, morning and evening, and if He desires, He withholds it, and all things are in his hand."

19 He prayed in the night and said, "My God, God Most High, You alone are my God, and You and Your dominion have I chosen. And You have created all things, and all things that are the work of Your hands.

20 Deliver me from the hands of evil spirits who have dominion over the thoughts of men's hearts, and let them not lead me astray from You, my God. And establish me and my offspring forever so that we do not go astray from now and forever."

21 He said, "Shall I return to Ur of the Chaldees who are trying to find me? Should I return to them? Am I to remain here in this place? The right path is before You. Make it prosper in the hands of your servant that he may fulfill it and that I may not walk in the deceitfulness of my heart, O my God."

22 He stopped speaking and stopped praying, and then the word of the Lord was sent to him through me, saying, "Get out of your country, and from your kindred and from the house of your father and go to a land which I will show you, and I shall make you a great and numerous nation.

23 And I will bless you and I will make your name great,
and you will be blessed in the earth, and in You shall all families of the earth be blessed, and I will bless them that bless you, and curse them that curse you.

24 I will be a God to you and your son, and to your son's son, and to all your offspring, fear not, from now on and to all generations of the earth I am your God."

25 The Lord God said, "Open his mouth and his ears, that he may hear and speak with his mouth, with the language which has been revealed," for it had ceased from the mouths of all the children of men from the day of the overthrow of Babel.

26 And I opened his mouth, and his ears and his lips, and I began to speak with him in Hebrew in the tongue of the creation.

27 He took the books of his fathers, and these were written in Hebrew, and he transcribed them, and he began from then on to study them, and I made known to him that which he could not understand, and he studied them during the six rainy months.

28 In the seventh year of the sixth week he spoke to his father and informed him, that he would leave Haran to go into the land of Canaan to see it and return to him.

29 Terah his father said to him; "Go in peace. May the eternal God make your path straight. And the Lord be with you, and protect you from all evil, and grant to you grace, mercy and favor before those who see you, and may none of the children of men have power over you to harm you. Go in peace.

30 If you see a land pleasant to your eyes to dwell in, then arise and take me with you and take Lot with you, the son of Haran your brother as your own son, the Lord be with you.

31 Nahor your brother leave with me until you return in peace, and we go with you all together."

[Chapter 13]

1 Abram journeyed from Haran, and he took Sarai, his wife, and Lot, his brother Haran's son and they went to the land of Canaan, and he came into Asshur, and proceeded to Shechem, and dwelt near a tall oak.

2 He saw the land was very pleasant from the border of Hamath to the tall oak.

3 The Lord said to him, "To you and to your offspring I will give this land."

4 He built an altar there, and he offered on it a burnt sacrifice to the Lord, who had appeared to him.

5 He left from that place and went to the mountain Bethel on the west and Ai on the east, and pitched his tent there.

6 He saw the land was very wide and good, and everything grew on it, vines, and figs, and pomegranates, oaks, and ilexes, and turpentine and oil trees, and cedars and cypresses, and date trees, and all trees of the field, and there was water on the mountains.

7 And he blessed the Lord who had led him out of Ur of the Chaldees, and had brought him to this land.

8 In the first year, in the seventh week, on the new moon of the first month, he built an altar on this mountain, and called on the name of the Lord and said, "You, the eternal God, are my God."

9 He offered on the altar a burnt sacrifice to the Lord that He should be with him and not forsake him all the days of his life.

10 He left that place and went toward the south, and he came to Hebron and Hebron was built at that time, and he lived there two years, and he went from that place into the land of the south, to Bealoth, and there was a famine in the land.

11 Abram went into Egypt in the third year of the week, and he dwelt in Egypt five years before his wife was torn away from him.

12 Now, Tanais in Egypt was built seven years after Hebron.

13 When Pharaoh seized Sarai, the wife of Abram the Lord plagued Pharaoh and his house with great plagues because of Sarai, Abram's wife.

14 Abram was celebrated and admired because of his great possessions of sheep, and cattle, and donkeys, and horses, and camels, and menservants, and maidservants, and in silver and gold. Lot and his brother's son were also wealthy.

15 Pharaoh gave back Sarai, the wife of Abram, and he sent him out of the land of Egypt, and he journeyed to the place where he had pitched his tent at the beginning, to the place of the altar, with Ai on the east, and Bethel on the west, and he blessed the Lord his God who had brought him back in peace.

16 In the forty-first jubilee in the third year of the first week, that he returned to this place and offered on it a burnt sacrifice, and called on the name of the Lord, and said, "You, the most high God, are my God forever and ever."

17 In the fourth year of this week Lot parted from him, and Lot lived in Sodom, and the men of Sodom sinned greatly.

18 It grieved him in his heart that his brother's son had parted from him because Abram had no children.

19 After Lot had parted from him, in the fourth year of this week. In that year when Lot was taken captive, the Lord said to Abram, "Lift up your eyes from the place where you are dwelling, northward and southward, and westward and eastward.

20 All the land that you see I will give to you and to your offspring forever, and I will make your offspring as the sand of the sea, though a man may number the dust of the earth, yet your offspring shall not be numbered.

21 Arise, walk through the land in the length of it and the breadth of it, and see it all. To your offspring will I give it." And Abram went to Hebron, and lived there.

22 And in this year came Chedorlaomer, king of Elam, and Amraphel, king of Shinar, and Arioch king of Sellasar, and Tergal, king of nations, and killed the king of Gomorrah, and the king of Sodom fled, and many fell through wounds in the valley of Siddim, by the Salt Sea.

23 They took captive Sodom and Adam and Zeboim, and they took Lot captive, the son of Abram's brother, and all his possessions, and they went to Dan.

24 One who had escaped came and told Abram that his brother's son had been taken captive.

25 And Abram equipped his household servants for Abram, and for his offspring, a tenth of the first-fruits to the Lord, and the Lord ordained it as a law forever that they should give it to the priests who served before Him, that they should possess it forever.

26 There is no limit of days to this law, for He has ordained it for the generations forever that they should give to the Lord the tenth of everything, of the seed and of the wine and of the oil and of the cattle and of the sheep.

27 He gave it to His priests to eat and to drink with joy before Him.

28 The king of Sodom came and bowed down to him, and said, "Our Lord Abram, give to us the souls which you have rescued, but let the booty be yours."

29 And Abram said to him, "I lift up my hands to the Most High God, that from a thread to a shoe-latchet I shall not take anything that is yours so that you could never say, I have made Abram rich, except only what the young men, Aner and Eschol, and Mamre have eaten, and the portion of the men who went with me. These shall take their portion."

[Chapter 14]

1 After these things, in the fourth year of this week, on the new moon of the third month, the word of the Lord came to Abram in a dream, saying, "Fear not, Abram, I am your defender, and your reward will be very great."

2 He said, "Lord, Lord, what will you give me, seeing I go from here childless, and the son of Maseq, the son of my handmaid, Eliezer of Damascus, he will be my heir, and to me you have given no offspring."

3 He said to him, "This man will not be your heir, but one that will come out of your own bowels. He will be your heir."

4 And He brought him out abroad, and said to him, "Look toward heaven and number the stars if you are able to number them."

5 He looked toward heaven, and beheld the stars. And He said to him, "so shall your offspring be."

6 And he believed in the Lord, and it was counted to him as righteousness.

7 God said to him, "I am the Lord that brought you out of Ur of the Chaldees, to give you the land of the Canaanites to possess it forever, and I will be God to you and to your offspring after you."

8 He said, "Lord, Lord, how shall I know that I shall inherit it?"

9 God said to him, "Take Me a heifer of three years, and a goat of three years, and a sheep of three years, and a turtle-dove, and a pigeon."

10 And he took all these in the middle of the month and he dwelt at the oak of Mamre, which is near Hebron.

11 He built an altar there, and sacrificed all these. He poured their blood on the altar, and divided them in half, and laid them over against each other, but the birds he did not divide.

12 Birds came down on the pieces, and Abram drove them away, and did not permit the birds to touch them.

13 It happened, when the sun had set, that an ecstasy fell on Abram, and such a horror of great darkness fell on him, and it was said to Abram, "Know of a surety that your offspring shall be a stranger in a land that is not theirs, and they shall be brought into bondage, and afflicted for four hundred years.

14 The nation also to whom they will be in bondage will I judge, and after that they shall come out from that place with many possessions.

15 You will go to your fathers in peace, and be buried in a good old age.

16 But in the fourth generation they shall return here, for the iniquity of the Amorites is not yet full."

17 And he awoke from his sleep, and he arose, and the sun had set; and there was a flame, and a furnace was smoking, and a flame of fire passed between the pieces.

18 On that day the Lord made a covenant with Abram, saying, "To your offspring will I give this land, from the river of Egypt to the great river, the river Euphrates, the Kenites, the Kenizzites, the Kadmonites, the Perizzites, and the Rephaim, the Phakorites, and the Hivites, and the Amorites, and the Canaanites, and the Girgashites, and the Jebusites.

19 The day passed, and Abram offered the pieces, and the birds, and their fruit offerings, and their drink offerings, and the fire devoured them.

20 On that day we made a covenant with Abram, in the same way we had covenanted with Noah in this month; and Abram renewed the festival and laws for himself forever.

21 Abram rejoiced, and made all these things known to Sarai his wife. He believed that he would have offspring, but she did not bear.

22 Sarai advised her husband Abram, and said to him, "Go in to Hagar, my Egyptian maid, it may be that I shall build up offspring to you by her."

23Abram listened to the voice of Sarai his wife, and said to her, "Do so." And Sarai took Hagar, her maid, the Egyptian, and gave her to Abram, her husband, to be his wife.

24 He went in to her, and she conceived and gave birth to a son, and he called his name Ishmael, in the fifth year of this week; and this was the eighty-sixth year in the life of Abram.

[Chapter 15]

1 In the fifth year of the fourth week of this jubilee, in the third month, in the middle of the month, Abram celebrated the feast of the first-fruits of the grain harvest.

2 And he made new offerings on the altar, the first-fruits of the produce to the Lord, a heifer, and a goat, and a sheep on the altar as a burnt sacrifice to the Lord; their fruit offerings and their drink offerings he offered on the altar with frankincense.

3 The Lord appeared to Abram, and said to him, "I am God Almighty. Examine yourself and demonstrate yourself before me and be perfect.

4 I will make My covenant between Me and you, and I will multiply you greatly."

5 Abram fell on his face, and God talked with him, and said, "My law is with you, and you will be the father of many nations.

6 Neither shall your name any more be called Abram, but your name from now on, even forever, shall be Abraham.

7 For I have made you the father of many nations.

8 I will make you very great, and I will make you into nations, and kings shall come forth from you.

9 I shall establish My covenant between Me and you, and your offspring after you, throughout their generations, for an eternal covenant, so that I may be a God to you, and to your offspring after you.

10 You may possess the land where you have been a sojourner, the land of Canaan, and you will possess it forever, and I will be their God."

11 The Lord said to Abraham, "Keep my covenant, you and your offspring after you, and circumcise every male among you, and circumcise your foreskins, and it shall be a token of an eternal covenant between Me and you.

12 And the eighth day you shall circumcise the child, every male throughout your generations, him that is born in the house, or whom you

have bought with money from any stranger, whom you have acquired who is not of your offspring.

13 He that is born in your house shall surely be circumcised, and those whom you have bought with money shall be circumcised, and My covenant shall be in your flesh for an eternal ordinance.

14 The uncircumcised male who is not circumcised in the flesh of his foreskin on the eighth day, that soul shall be cut off from his people, for he has broken My covenant."

15 God said to Abraham, "As for Sarai your wife, her name shall no more be called Sarai, but Sarah shall be her name.

16 I will bless her, and give you a son by her, and I will bless him, and he shall become a nation, and kings of nations shall proceed from him."

17 Abraham fell on his face, and rejoiced, and said in his heart, "Shall a son be born to him that is a hundred years old, and shall Sarah, who is ninety years old, bring forth?"

18 Abraham said to God, "Oh, that Ishmael might live before you!"

19 God said, "Yea, and Sarah also shall bear you a son, and you will call his name Isaac, and I will establish My covenant with him, an everlasting covenant, and for his offspring after him.

20 And as for Ishmael also have I heard you, and behold I will bless him, and make him great, and multiply him greatly, and he shall beget twelve princes, and I will make him a great nation.

21 But My covenant will I establish with Isaac, whom Sarah shall bear to you this time next year."

22 God ceased speaking with him, and God went up from Abraham.

23 Abraham did according as God had said to him, and he took Ishmael his son, and all that were born in his house, and whom he had bought with his money, every male in his house, and circumcised the flesh of their foreskin.

24 On that same day was Abraham circumcised, and all the men of his house, and all those whom he had bought with money from the children of the stranger were circumcised with him.

25 This law is for all the generations forever, and there is no variance of days, and no omission of one day out of the eight days, for it is an eternal law, ordained and written on the heavenly tablets.

26 Every one that is born, the flesh of whose foreskin is not circumcised on the eighth day, does not belong to the children of the covenant which the Lord made with Abraham, but instead they belong to the children of destruction; nor is there any other sign on him that he is the Lord's, but he is destined to be destroyed and killed from the earth, and to be rooted out of the earth, for he has broken the covenant of the Lord our God.

27 All the angels of the presence (of the Lord) and all the angels of sanctification have been created already circumcised from the day of their creation, and before the angels of the presence (of the Lord) and the angels

of sanctification He has sanctified Israel, that they should be with Him and with His holy angels.

28 Command the children of Israel and let them observe the sign of this covenant for their generations as an eternal law, and they will not be rooted out of the land.

29 For the command is ordained for a covenant, that they should observe it forever among all the children of Israel.

30 For Ishmael and his sons and his brothers, and Esau, the Lord did not cause them to come to Him, and he did not choose them. Although they are the children of Abraham, He knew them, but He chose Israel to be His people.

31 He sanctified them, and gathered them from among all the children of men; for there are many nations and many peoples, and all are His, and over all nations He has placed spirits in authority to lead them astray from Him.

32 But over Israel He did not appoint any angel or spirit, for He alone is their ruler, and He will preserve them and require them at the hand of His angels and His spirits, and at the hand of all His powers in order that He may preserve them and bless them, that they may be His and He may be theirs from now on forever.

33 I announce to you that the children of Israel will not keep true to this law, and they will not circumcise their sons according to all this law; for in the flesh of their circumcision they will omit this circumcision of their sons, and all of the sons of Beliar will leave their sons uncircumcised as they were born.

34 There will be great wrath from the Lord against the children of Israel because they have forsaken His covenant and turned aside from His word, and provoked (God) and blasphemed, because they do not observe the ordinance of this law; for they have treated their genitalia like the Gentiles, so that they may be removed and rooted out of the land. And there will no more be pardon or forgiveness to them for all the sin of this eternal error.

[Chapter 16]

1 On the new moon of the fourth month we appeared to Abraham, at the oak of Mamre, and we talked with him, and we announced to him that Sarah, his wife, would give him a son.

2 And Sarah laughed, for she heard that we had spoken these words to Abraham. We warned her, and she became afraid, and denied that she had laughed because of the words.

3 We told her the name of her son, as his name is ordained and written in the heavenly tablets and it is Isaac.

4 We told her that when we returned to her at a set time, she would have conceived a son.

5 In this month the Lord executed his judgments on Sodom, and Gomorrah, and Zeboim, and all the region of the Jordan, and He burned them with fire and brimstone, and destroyed them and they are destroyed until this day, because of all their works. They are wicked and vast sinners, and they defile themselves and commit fornication in their flesh, and work uncleanness on the earth as I have told you.

6 In like manner, God will execute judgment on the places where they have done similar to the uncleanness of the Sodomites, and they will suffer a judgment like that of Sodom.

7 But for Lot, we made an exception, for God remembered Abraham, and sent him out from the place of the overthrow.

8 And he and his daughters committed sin on the earth, such as had not been on the earth since the days of Adam until his time, for the man had sex with his daughters.

9 It was commanded and engraved concerning all his offspring, on the heavenly tablets, to remove them and root them out, and to execute judgment on them like the judgment of Sodom, and to leave no offspring of that man on earth on the day of condemnation.

10 In this month Abraham moved from Hebron, and departed and lived between Kadesh and Shur in the mountains of Gerar.

11 In the middle of the fifth month he moved from that place, and lived at the Well of the Oath.

12 In the middle of the sixth month the Lord visited Sarah and did to her as He had spoken and she conceived.

13 And she gave birth to a son in the third month. In the middle of the month, at the time of which the Lord had spoken to Abraham, on the festival of the first-fruits of the harvest, Isaac was born.

14 Abraham circumcised his son on the eighth day, he was the first that was circumcised according to the covenant that is ordained forever.

15 In the sixth year of the fourth week we came to Abraham at the Well of the Oath, and we appeared to him.

16 We returned in the seventh month, and found Sarah with child before us and we blessed him, and we announced to him all the things that had been decreed concerning him, so that he should not die until he should beget six more sons and saw them before he died.

17 But in Isaac should his name and offspring be called, and that all the offspring of his sons should be Gentiles, and be counted with the Gentiles; but from the sons of Isaac one should become a holy offspring, and should not be counted among the Gentiles.

18 For he should become the portion (dowry) of the Most High, and all his offspring had fallen into the possession of God, that they should be to the Lord a people for His possession above all nations and that they should become a kingdom and priests and a holy nation.

19 We went our way, and we announced to Sarah all that we had told him, and they both rejoiced with very great joy.

20 He built there an altar to the Lord who had delivered him, and who was causing him to rejoice in the land of his sojourning, and he celebrated a festival of joy in this month for seven days, near the altar which he had built at the Well of the Oath.

21 He built tents for himself and for his servants on this festival, and he was the first to celebrate the feast of tabernacles on the earth.

22 During these seven days he brought a burnt offering to the Lord each day to the altar consisting of two oxen, two rams, seven sheep, one male goat, for a sin offering that he might atone thereby for himself and for his offspring.

23 As an offering of thanks he brought, seven rams, seven kids, seven sheep, and seven male goats, and their fruit offerings and their drink offerings; and he burnt all the fat of it on the altar, a chosen offering to the Lord for a sweet smelling odor.

24 Morning and evening he burnt fragrant substances, frankincense and incense, and sweet spice, and nard, and myrrh, and spice, and aromatic plants; all these seven he offered, crushed, mixed together in equal parts and pure.

25 And he celebrated this feast during seven days, rejoicing with all his heart and with all his soul, he and all those who were in his house, and there was no stranger with him, nor any that was uncircumcised.

26 He blessed his Creator who had created him in his generation, for He had created him according to His good pleasure. God knew and perceived that from him would arise the plant of righteousness for the eternal generations, and from him a holy offspring, so that it should become like Him who had made all things.

27 He blessed and rejoiced, and he called the name of this festival the festival of the Lord, a joy acceptable to the Most High God.

28 And we blessed him forever, and all his offspring after him throughout all the generations of the earth, because he celebrated this festival in its season, according to the testimony of the heavenly tablets.

29 For this reason it is ordained on the heavenly tablets concerning Israel, that they shall celebrate the feast of tabernacles seven days with joy, in the seventh month, acceptable before the Lord as a statute forever throughout their generations every year.

30 To this there is no limit of days; for it is ordained forever regarding Israel that they should celebrate it and dwell in tents, and set wreaths on their heads, and take leafy boughs, and willows from the brook.

31 Abraham took branches of palm trees, and the fruit of good and pleasing trees, and every day going round the altar with the branches seven times a day in the morning, he praised and gave thanks to his God for all things in joy.

[Chapter 17]

1 In the first year of the fifth week Isaac was weaned in this jubilee, and Abraham made a great banquet in the third month, on the day his son Isaac was weaned.

2 Ishmael, the son of Hagar, the Egyptian, was in front of Abraham, his father, in his place, and Abraham rejoiced and blessed God because he had seen his sons and had not died childless.

3 He remembered the words which He had spoken to him on the day that Lot had departed from him, and he rejoiced because the Lord had given him offspring on the earth to inherit the earth, and he blessed with all his mouth the Creator of all things.

4 Sarah saw Ishmael playing and dancing, and Abraham rejoicing with great joy, and she became jealous of Ishmael and said to Abraham, "Throw out this bondwoman and her son. The son of this bondwoman will not be heir with my son, Isaac."

5 And the situation was troubling to Abraham, because of his maidservant and because of his son, because he did not want to drive them from him.

6 God said to Abraham "Let it not be troubling in your sight, because of the child and because of the bondwoman. Listen to Sarah and to all her words and do them, for in Isaac shall your name and offspring be called.

7 But as for the son of this bondwoman I will make him a great nation, because he is of your offspring."

8 Abraham got up early in the morning, and took bread and a bottle of water, and placed them on the shoulders of Hagar and the child, and sent her away.

9 And she departed and wandered in the wilderness of Beersheba, and the water in the bottle was spent, and the child was thirsty, and was not able to go on, and fell down.

10 His mother took him and laid him under an olive tree, and went and sat her down over away from him at the distance of a bow-shot; for she said, "Let me not see the death of my child," and she sat and wept.

11 An angel of God, one of the holy ones, said to her, "Why do you weep, Hagar? Stand. Take the child, and hold him in your hand, for God has heard your voice, and has seen the child."

12 She opened her eyes, and she saw a well of water, and she went and filled her bottle with water, and she gave her child a drink, and she arose and went towards the wilderness of Paran.

13 And the child grew and became an archer, and God was with him, and his mother took him a wife from among the daughters of Egypt.

14 She (the wife) gave birth to a son, and he called his name Nebaioth; for she said, "The Lord was close to me when I called on him."

15 In the seventh week, in the first year of it, in the first month in this jubilee, on the twelfth of this month, there were voices in heaven regarding Abraham, that he was faithful in all that He told him, and that he loved the Lord, and that in every affliction he was faithful.

16 Prince Mastema came and said before God, "Look, Abraham loves Isaac his son, and he delights in him above all things, tell him to offer him as a burnt-offering on the altar, and You will see if he will do this command, and You will know if he is faithful in everyway that You test him.

17 The Lord knew that Abraham was faithful throughout all his afflictions, for He had tried him through his country and with famine, and had tried him with the wealth of kings, and had tried him again through his wife, when she was torn from him, and with circumcision; and had tried him through Ishmael and Hagar, his maid-servant, when he sent them away.

18 In everything that He had tried him, he was found faithful, and his soul was not impatient, and he was not slow to act, because he was faithful and a lover of the Lord.

[Chapter 18]

1 God said to him, "Abraham. Abraham." and he said, "Look, here am I."

2 He said, "Take your beloved son, Isaac, whom you love, and go to the high country, and offer him on one of the mountains which I will point out to you."

3 He got early in the morning and saddled his donkey, and took two young men with him, and Isaac his son, and split the wood of the burnt offering, and he went to the place on the third day, and he saw the place afar off.

4 He came to a well of water (near Mount Moriah), and he said to his young men, "You stay here with the donkey, and I and the lad shall go yonder, and when we have worshipped we shall come back to you."

5 He took the wood of the burnt-offering and laid it on Isaac his son, and he took the fire and the knife, and they went both of them together to that place.

6 Isaac said to his father, "Father" and he said, "Here am I, my son." He said to him, "Look, we have the fire, and the knife, and the wood, but where is the sheep for the burnt-offering, father?"

7 He said, "God will provide for himself a sheep for a burnt-offering, my son." And he neared the place of the mountain of God.

8 He built an altar, and he placed the wood on the altar, and bound Isaac his son, and placed him on the wood that was on the altar, and stretched out his hand to take the knife to kill Isaac, his son.

9 I stood in the presence of him, and before prince Mastema, (and the holy angels stood and wept over the altar as prince Mastema and his angels rejoiced and said "Isaac will be destroyed and we will see if Abraham is faithful), and the Lord said, "Command him not to lay his hand on the lad, nor to do anything to him, for I have shown that he fears the Lord."

10 I called to him from heaven, and said to him, "Abraham, Abraham." and he was terrified and said, "Here am I."

11 I said to him, "Lay not your hand on the lad, neither do anything to him; for now I have shown that you fear the Lord, and have not withheld your son, your first-born son, from me."

12 Prince Mastema was put to shame (and was bound by the angels); and Abraham lifted up his eyes and looked and saw a ram caught by his horns, and Abraham went and took the ram and offered it as a burnt-offering in place of his son.

13 Abraham called that place "The Lord has seen," so that it is said the Lord has seen. This is Mount Zion.

14 The Lord called Abraham by his name a second time from heaven, as he caused us to appear to speak to him in the name of the Lord.

15 He said, "By Myself have I sworn," said the Lord, "Because you have done this thing, and have not withheld your son, your beloved son, from Me, that in blessing I will bless you, and in multiplying I will multiply your offspring as the stars of heaven, and as the sand which is on the seashore.

16 Your offspring shall inherit the cities of their enemies, and in your offspring shall all nations of the earth be blessed. Because you have obeyed My voice, and I have shown to all that you are faithful to Me in all that I have said to you, "Go in peace."

17 Abraham went back to his young men, and they stood and went back together to Beersheba, and Abraham lived by the Well of the Oath.

18 And he celebrated this festival every year, seven days with joy, and he called it the festival of the Lord according to the seven days during which he went and returned in peace.

19 Accordingly, it has been ordained and written on the heavenly tablets regarding Israel and its children that they should observe this festival seven days with the joy of festival.

[Chapter 19]

1 In the first year of the first week in the forty-second jubilee, Abraham returned and lived across from Hebron, in Kirjath Arba for two weeks of years.

2 In the first year of the third week of this jubilee the days of the life of Sarah were completed, and she died in Hebron.

3 Abraham went to mourn over her and bury her, and we tested him to see if his spirit was patient and he had neither anger nor contempt in the words of his mouth, and he was found patient in this and was not disturbed.

4 In patience of spirit he discussed with the children of Heth that they should give him a place in which to bury his dead.

5 And the Lord gave him grace before all who saw him, and he asked the sons of Heth in gentleness, and they gave him the land of the double cave over beside Mamre, that is Hebron, for four hundred pieces of silver.

6 They said to him, "We shall give it to you for nothing," but he would not take it from them for nothing, for he gave the price of the place and paid the money in full. And he bowed down before them twice, and after this he buried his dead in the double cave.

7 All the days of the life of Sarah were one hundred and twenty-seven years, that is, two jubilees and four weeks and one year, these are the days of the years of the life of Sarah.

8 This is the tenth trial with which Abraham was tested, and he was found faithful and patient in spirit.

9 He did not say a single word regarding the rumor in the land of how God had said that He would give it to him and to his offspring after him, but instead he begged for a place there to bury his dead. Because he was found faithful, it was recorded on the heavenly tablets that he was the friend of God.

10 In the fourth year of it (this jubilee) he took a wife for his son Isaac and her name was Rebecca the daughter of Bethuel, the son of Nahor, the brother of Abraham the sister of Laban and daughter of Bethuel; and Bethuel was the son of Melca, who was the wife of Nahor, the brother of Abraham.

11 Abraham took to himself a third wife from among the daughters of his household servants, for Hagar had died before Sarah, and her name was

Keturah,. And she gave birth to six sons, Zimram, and Jokshan, and Medan, and Midian, and Ishbak, and Shuah, in the two weeks of years.

12 In the sixth week, in the second year of it, Rebecca gave birth to two sons of Isaac, Jacob and Esau.

13 And Jacob had no beard and was a straight and tall man who dwelt in tents, and Esau was a powerful a man of the field, and was hairy.

14 The youths grew, and Jacob learned to write, but Esau did not learn, for he was a man of the field and a hunter, and he learned war, and all his deeds were fierce.

15Abraham loved Jacob, but Isaac loved Esau.

16 And Abraham saw the deeds of Esau, and he knew that in Jacob should his name and offspring be called. He called Rebecca and gave commandment regarding Jacob, for he knew that she too loved Jacob much more than Esau.

17 He said to her, "My daughter, watch over my son Jacob, for he shall take my place on the earth. He shall be a blessing throughout the children of men and for the glory of all the offspring of Shem.

18 I know that the Lord will choose him to be a people (nation) and a possession to Himself, above all peoples that are on the face of the earth.

19 Isaac, my son, loves Esau more than Jacob, but I see that you truly love Jacob.

20 Add still further to your kindness to him, and regard him in love, for he shall be a blessing to us on the earth from now on to all generations of the earth.

21 Let your hands be strong and let your heart rejoice in your son Jacob, for I have loved him far beyond all my sons. He shall be blessed forever, and his offspring shall fill the whole earth.

22 If a man can number the sand of the earth, his offspring also shall be numbered.

23 And all the blessings with which the Lord has blessed me and my offspring shall belong to Jacob and his offspring always.

24 In his offspring shall my name be blessed, and the name of my fathers, Shem, Noah, Enoch, Mahalalel, Enos, Seth, and Adam. And these shall serve to lay the foundations of the heaven, and to strengthen the earth, and to renew all the stars and planets which are in the sky.

27 He called Jacob and kissed him in front of Rebecca, his mother, and blessed him, and said, "Jacob, my beloved son, whom my soul loves, may God bless you from above the sky, and may He give you all the blessings with which He blessed Adam, Enoch, Noah, and Shem; and all the things of which He told me, and all the things which He promised to give me, may He cause to be yours and your offspring forever, according to the days of heaven above the earth.

28 And the Spirits of Mastema shall not rule over you or over your offspring or turn you from the Lord, who is your God from now on forever.

29 May the Lord God be a father to you and may you be like His first-born son, and to the people always. Go in peace, my son."

30 And they both went out together from Abraham.

31 Rebecca loved Jacob, with all her heart and with all her soul, very much more than Esau, but Isaac loved Esau much more than Jacob.

[Chapter 20]

1 In the forty-second jubilee, in the first year of the seventh week, Abraham called Ishmael, and his twelve sons, and Isaac and his two sons, and the six sons of Keturah, and their sons.

2 And he commanded them that they should observe the way of the Lord, that they should work righteousness, and love each his neighbor, and act in this manner among all men, that they should each walk with regard to the ways of the Lord to do judgment and righteousness on the earth.

3 He also commanded them that they should circumcise their sons, according to the covenant, which God had made with them, and not deviate to the right or the left of all the paths which the Lord had commanded us, and that we should keep ourselves from all fornication and uncleanness.

4 He said, "If any woman or maid commits fornication among you, burn her with fire. And do not let them commit fornication with her with their eyes or their heart; and do not let them take to themselves wives from the daughters of Canaan, because the offspring of Canaan will be rooted out of the land."

5 He told them about the judgment on the giants, and the judgment on the Sodomites, how they had been judged because of their wickedness, and had died because of their fornication and uncleanness, and corruption through fornication together.

6 He said, "Guard yourselves from all fornication and uncleanness, and from all pollution of sin, or you will make our name a curse, and your whole life a shame, and all your sons to be destroyed by the sword, and you will become accursed like Sodom, and all that is left of you shall be as the sons of Gomorrah.

7 I implore you, my sons, love the God of heaven and cling to all His commandments.

8 Do not walk after their idols and after their ways of uncleanness, and do not make yourselves molten or graven gods. They are empty, and there is no spirit in them, for they are work of men's hands, and all who trust in them, trust in nothing.

9 Do not serve them, nor worship them, but serve the most high God, and worship Him continually, and hope for His presence always, and work

uprightness and righteousness before Him, that He may have pleasure in you and grant you His mercy, and send rain on you morning and evening, and bless all your works which you have performed on the earth, and bless your bread and your water, and bless the fruit of your womb and the fruit of your land, and the herds of your cattle, and the flocks of your sheep.

10 You will be for a blessing on the earth, and all nations of the earth will desire you, and bless your sons in my name, that they may be blessed as I am."

11 He gave to Ishmael and to his sons, and to the sons of Keturah, gifts, and sent them away from Isaac his son, and he gave everything to Isaac his son.

12 Ishmael and his sons, and the sons of Keturah and their sons, went together and settled from Paran to the border of Babylon in all the land that is toward the East facing the desert.

13 These mingled (intermarried) with each other, and their names were called Arabs, and Ishmaelites.

[Chapter 21]

1 In the sixth year of the seventh week of this jubilee Abraham called Isaac his son, and commanded him, saying, "I have become old. I do not know the day of my death but I am full of my days.

2 I am one hundred and seventy-five years old, and throughout all the days of my life I have remembered the Lord, and sought with all my heart to do His will, and to walk uprightly in all His ways.

3 My soul has hated idols. I have given my heart and spirit to the observance of the will of Him who created me.

4 For He is the living God, and He is holy and faithful, and He is righteous beyond all, and He is no respecter of men or of their gifts, for God is righteous, and executes judgment on all those who transgress His commandments and despise His covenant.

5 My son, observe His commandments and His law and His judgments, and do not walk after the abominations and after the graven images and after the molten images.

6 And eat no blood at all of animals or cattle, or of any bird that flies in the heaven.

7 If you kill a sacrificial animal as an acceptable peace offering, kill it, and pour out its blood on the altar. Place all the fat of the offering on the altar with fine flour and the meat offering mingled with oil with its drink offering. Place them all together on the altar of burnt offering. It is a sweet odor before the Lord.

8 You will offer the fat of the sacrifice of thanks offerings on the fire which is on the altar, and the fat which is on the belly, and all the fat on the inside,

behind the two kidneys, and all the fat that is on them, and lobes of the liver you will remove, together with the kidneys.

9 Offer all these for a sweet odor acceptable before the Lord, with its meat-offering and with its drink-offering, and the bread of the offering to the Lord.

10 Eat its meat on that day and on the second day, but do not let the sun go down on it until it is eaten. Let nothing be left over for the third day, for it is not acceptable. Let it no longer be eaten, and all who eat of it will bring sin on themselves, for thus I have found it written in the books of my forefathers, and in the words of Enoch, and in the words of Noah.

11 On all your offerings you will scatter salt, and do not let the salt of the covenant be lacking in all your offerings before the Lord.

12 As regards the wood of the sacrifices, beware to bring only these and no other wood to the altar in addition to these, cypress, bay, almond, fir, pine, cedar, savin, fig, olive, myrrh, laurel, and aspalathus.

13 Of these kinds of wood lay on the altar under the sacrifice, such as have been tested as to their appearance, and do not lay on it any split or dark wood, but only hard and clean wood, without fault, a healthy, new growth. Do not lay old wood on it, because there is no longer fragrance in it as before.

14 Besides these kinds of wood there is none other that you will place on the altar, for the fragrance is dispersed, and the smell of its fragrance will not go up to heaven.

15 Observe this commandment and do it, my son, that you may be upright in all your deeds.

16 Be clean in your body at all times. Wash yourself with water before you approach to offer on the altar. Wash your hands and your feet before you draw near to the altar, and when you are done sacrificing, wash your hands and feet again.

17 Let no blood appear on you or on your clothes. Be on your guard against blood, my son. Be on your guard continually and cover it with dust.

18 Do not eat any blood for it is the soul. Eat no blood whatsoever.

19 Take no payment for shedding the blood of man, or it will cause it to be shed without fear of punishment, without judgment. It is the blood that is shed that causes the earth to sin, and the earth cannot be cleansed from the blood of man except by the blood of he who shed it.

20 Take no present or gift for the blood of man, blood for blood, that you may be accepted before the Lord, the Most High God. He is the defense of the good, so that you may be preserved from all evil, and that He may withhold you from every kind of death.

21 I see, my son, all the works of the children of men are sin and wickedness, and all their deeds are uncleanness and an abomination and a pollution, and there is no righteousness in them.

22 Beware, or you will walk in their ways and tread in their paths, and commit a sin worthy of death before the Most High God. He will hide His face from you and give you back into the hands of your transgression, and root you out of the land, and your offspring likewise from under heaven, and your name and your offspring shall perish from the whole earth.

23 Turn away from all their deeds and all their uncleanness, and observe the laws of the Most High God, and do His will and be upright in all things.

24 If you do this, He will bless you in all your deeds, and will raise up from you a plant of righteousness through all the earth, throughout all generations of the earth, and my name and your name shall not be forgotten under heaven forever.

25 Go, my son in peace. May the Most High God, my God and your God, strengthen you to do His will, and may He bless all your offspring and the remainder of your offspring for the generations forever, with all righteous blessings, that you may be a blessing on all the earth."

26 And he went out from him rejoicing.

[Chapter 22]

1 In the first week in the forty-fourth jubilee, in the second year, that is, the year in which Abraham died, Isaac and Ishmael came from the Well of the Oath to celebrate the feast of weeks which is the feast of the first-fruits of the harvest to Abraham, their father, and Abraham rejoiced because his two sons had come.

2 Isaac had many possessions in Beersheba, and Isaac desired to go and see his possessions and to return to his father.

3 In those days Ishmael came to see his father, and they both came together, and Isaac offered a sacrifice for a burnt offering, and presented it on the altar of his father that he had made in Hebron.

4 He offered a thanks offering and made a feast of joy in the presence of Ishmael, his brother, and Rebecca made new cakes from the new grain, and gave them to Jacob, her son, to take them to Abraham, his father, from the first-fruits of the land, that he might eat and bless the Creator of all things before he died.

5 Isaac, also, sent Jacob to Abraham with an offering of his best for thanks so that he might eat and drink.

6 He ate and drank, and blessed the Most High God, who has created heaven and earth, who has made all the fat things of the earth, and given them to the children of men that they might eat and drink and bless their Creator.

7 "And now I give thanks to You, my God, because you have caused me to see this day, behold, I am one hundred three score and fifteen years, an old man and full of days, and all my days have been peace to me.

8 The sword of the adversary has not overcome me in all that You have given me and my children all the days of my life until this day.

9 My God, may Your mercy and Your peace be on Your servant, and on the offspring of his sons, that they may be to You a chosen nation and an inheritance from among all the nations of the earth from now on to all the days of the generations of the earth, to all the ages."

10 He called Jacob and said, "My son Jacob, may the God of all bless you and strengthen you to do righteousness, and His will before Him, and may He choose you and your offspring that you may become a people for His inheritance according to His will always.

11 My son, Jacob, draw near and kiss me." And he drew near and kissed him, and he said, "Blessed be my son Jacob and all the sons of God Most High, to all the ages. May God give to you an offspring of righteousness; and some of your sons may He sanctify throughout the whole earth. May nations serve you, and all the nations bow themselves before your offspring.

12 Be strong in the presence of men, and exercise authority over all the offspring of Seth. Then your ways and the ways of your sons will be justified, so that they shall become a holy nation.

13 May the Most High God give you all the blessings with which He has blessed me and He blessed Noah and Adam. May they rest on the sacred head of your offspring from generation to generation forever.

14 May He cleanse you from all unrighteousness and impurity so that you may be forgiven all the transgressions, which you have committed ignorantly. May He strengthen you, and bless you.

15 May you inherit the whole earth, and may He renew His covenant with you so that you may be to Him a nation for His inheritance for all the ages, and so that He may be to you and to your offspring a God in truth and righteousness throughout all the days of the earth.

16 My son Jacob, remember my words. Observe the commandments of Abraham, your father, separate yourself from the nations (gentiles), and do not eat with them. Do not emulate their works, and do not associate with them because their works are unclean, and all their ways are a pollution and an abomination and uncleanness.

17 They offer their sacrifices to the dead and they worship evil spirits, and they eat over the graves, and all their works are empty and nothingness.

18 They have no heart to understand and their eyes do not see what their works are, and how they go astray by saying to a piece of wood, "You are my God," and to a stone, "You are my Lord and you are my deliverer," because the stone and wood have no heart.

19 And as for you, my son Jacob, may the Most High God help you and the God of heaven bless you and remove you from their uncleanness and from all their error.

20 Jacob, be warned. Do not take a wife from any offspring of the daughters of Canaan, for all his offspring are to be rooted out of the earth.

21 Because of the transgression of Ham, Canaan erred, and all his offspring shall be destroyed from the earth including any remnant of it, and none springing from him shall exist except on the day of judgment.

22 And as for all the worshippers of idols and the profane, there shall be no hope for them in the land of the living, and no one on earth will remember them, for they shall descend into the abode of the dead, and they shall go into the place of condemnation. As the children of Sodom were taken away from the earth, so will all those who worship idols be taken away.

23 Fear not, my son Jacob. Be not dismayed, son of Abraham. May the Most High God preserve you from destruction, and may He deliver you from all the paths of error.

24 This house have I built for myself that I might put my name on it in the earth. It is given to you and to your offspring forever, and it will be named the house of Abraham. It is given to you and your offspring forever, for you will build my house and establish my name before God forever. Your offspring and your name will stand throughout all generations of the earth."

25 He ceased commanding him and blessing him.

26 The two lay together on one bed, and Jacob slept in the embracing arms of Abraham, his father's father, and he kissed him seven times, and his affection and his heart rejoiced over him.

27 He blessed him with all his heart and said, "The Most High God, the God of all, and Creator of all, who brought me out from Ur of the Chaldees that He might give me this land to inherit forever, that I might establish a holy offspring.

28 Blessed be the Most High forever."

29 And he blessed Jacob and said, "May Your grace and Your mercy be lift up on my son, over whom I rejoice with all my heart and my affection and on his offspring always.

30 Do not forsake him, nor diminish him from now to the days of eternity, and may Your eyes be opened on him and on his offspring, that You may preserve him, and bless him, and may sanctify him as a nation for Your inheritance. Bless him with all Your blessings from now to all the days of eternity, and renew Your covenant and Your grace with him and with his offspring according to all Your good pleasure to all the generations of the earth."

[Chapter 23]

1 He placed Jacob's two fingers on his eyes, and he blessed the God of gods, and he covered his face and stretched out his feet and slept the sleep of eternity, and was gathered to his fathers.

2 In spite of all this, Jacob was lying in his embracing arms, and knew not that Abraham, his father's father, was dead.

3 Jacob awoke from his sleep, and realized Abraham was cold as ice, and he said, "Father, father," but there was no answer, and he knew that he was dead.

4 He arose from his embracing arms and ran and told Rebecca, his mother, and Rebecca went to Isaac in the night, and told him and they went together, and Jacob with them, and a lamp was in his hand, and when they had gone in they found Abraham lying dead.

5 Isaac fell on the face of his father and wept and kissed him.

6 Ishmael, his son, heard the voices in the house of Abraham, and he arose, and went to Abraham his father, and wept over Abraham his father, he and all the house of Abraham, and they wept greatly.

7 His sons, Isaac and Ishmael, buried him in the double cave, near Sarah his wife, and all the men of his house, and Isaac and Ishmael, and all their sons, and all the sons of Keturah in their places wept for him forty days and then the days of weeping for Abraham were ended.

8 He lived three jubilees and four weeks of years, one hundred and seventy-five years, and completed the days of his life, being old and full of days.

9 For the days of the lives of their forefathers were nineteen jubilees; and after the Flood they began to grow less than nineteen jubilees, and to decrease in jubilees, and to grow old quickly, and to be full of their days because of the many types of hardships and the wickedness of their ways, with the exception of Abraham.

10 For Abraham was perfect in all his deeds with the Lord, and well-pleasing in righteousness all the days of his life. Yet, he did not complete four jubilees in his life, when he had grown old because of the wickedness in the world, and was full of his days.

11 All the generations which shall arise from this time until the day of the great judgment shall grow old quickly, before they complete two jubilees, and their knowledge shall forsake them because of their old age and all their knowledge shall vanish away.

12 In those days, if a man lives a jubilee and a-half of years, they shall say regarding him, "He has lived long," and the greater part of his days are pain and sorrow and hardship, and there is no peace. For calamity follows on calamity, and wound on wound, and hardship on hardship, and evil deeds on evil deeds, and illness on illness, and all judgments of destruction such as these, piled one on another, illness and overthrow, and snow and frost and ice, and fever, and chills, and mental and physical incapacity, and

famine, and death, and sword, and captivity, and all kinds of calamities and pains.

13 All of these shall come on an evil generation, which transgresses on the earth. Their works are uncleanness and fornication, and pollution and abominations.

14 Then they shall say, "The days of the forefathers were many, lasting a thousand years, and were good; but the days of our lives, if a man lives a long life are three score years and ten, and, if he is strong, four score years, and those evil, and there is no peace in the days of this evil generation."

15 In that generation the sons shall convict their fathers and their elders of sin and unrighteousness, and of the words of their mouths and the great wickedness which they perform, and concerning their forsaking the covenant which the Lord made between them and Him. They should observe and do all His commandments and His ordinances and all His laws, without departing either to the right hand or the left.

16 For all have done evil, and every mouth speaks sinfully and all their works are unclean and an abomination, and all their ways are pollution, uncleanness, and destruction.

17 The earth shall be destroyed because of all their works, and there shall be no fruit (seed) of the vine, and no oil; for their actions are altogether faithless, and they shall all perish together, beasts and cattle and birds, and all the fish of the sea, because of the children of men.

18 They shall quarrel with one another, the young with the old, and the old with the young, the poor with the rich, the lowly with the great, and the beggar with the prince, because of the law and the covenant; for they have forgotten the commandments, and covenant, and feasts, and months, and Sabbaths, and jubilees, and all judgments.

19 They shall use swords and war to turn them back to the way, but they shall not return until much blood has been shed on the earth, one by another.

20 Those who have escaped shall not return from their wickedness to the way of righteousness, but they shall all raise themselves to a high status through deceit and wealth, that they may each steal all that belongs of his neighbor, and they shall name the great name (of God), but not in truth and not in righteousness, and they shall defile the holy of holies with their uncleanness and the corruption of their pollution.

21 A great punishment shall come because of the deeds of this generation, and the Lord will give them over to the sword and to judgment and to slavery, and to be plundered and consumed.

22 And He will arouse the Gentile sinners against them, who have neither mercy nor compassion, and who shall respect no one, neither old nor young, nor any one, for they are more wicked, strong, and evil than all the children of men.

23 They shall use violence against Israel and shall violate Jacob, and much blood shall be shed on the earth, and there shall be none to gather the dead and none to bury them.

24 In those days they shall cry aloud, and call and pray that they may be saved from the hand of the sinners, the Gentiles. But none shall be excluded (none shall be saved).

25 The heads of the children shall be white with grey hair, and a child of three weeks shall appear old like a man of one hundred years, and their work and worth shall be destroyed by hardship and oppression.

26 In those days the children shall begin to study the laws, and to seek the commandments, and to return to the path of righteousness.

27 The days shall begin to grow many and increase among those children of men until their days draw close to one thousand years, and to a greater number of years than before age was recorded.

28 There shall be neither old man nor one who is aged, for all shall be as children and youths.

29 All their days shall be full and they shall live in peace and in joy, and there shall be neither Satan nor any evil destroyer because all their days shall be days of blessing and healing.

30 And at that time the Lord will heal His servants, and they shall rise up and see great peace, and drive out their adversaries. The righteous shall understand and be thankful, and rejoice with joy forever and ever, and they shall see all their judgments and all their curses enacted on their enemies.

31 Their bones shall rest in the earth, and their spirits shall have much joy, and they shall know that it is the Lord who executes judgment, and shows mercy to hundreds and thousands and to all that love Him.

32 Moses, write down these words. Write them and record them on the heavenly tablets for a testimony for the generations forever.

[Chapter 24]

1 It happened after the death of Abraham, that the Lord blessed Isaac his son, who arose from Hebron and went and dwelt at the Well of the Vision in the first year of the third week of this jubilee, seven years.

2 In the first year of the fourth week a famine began in the land, besides the first famine, which had been in the days of Abraham.

3 Jacob made lentil soup, and Esau came from the field hungry. He said to Jacob his brother, "Give me some of this red soup."

4 Jacob said to him, "Sell to me your birthright and I will give you bread, and also some of this lentil soup." And Esau said in his heart, "If I shall die what good is my birthright to me?"

5 He said to Jacob, "I give it to you." And Jacob said, "Swear to me, this day," and he swore to him.

6 And Jacob gave his brother Esau bread and soup, and he ate until he was satisfied, and Esau despised his birthright. For this reason was Esau's name called Edom (red), because of the red soup which Jacob gave him for his birthright.

7 And Jacob became the elder, and Esau was brought down from his dignity.

8 The famine covered the land, and Isaac departed to go down into Egypt in the second year of this week, and went to the king of the Philistines to Gerar, into the presence of Abimelech.

9 The Lord appeared to him and said to him, "Do not go down into Egypt. Dwell in the land that I shall tell you of, and sojourn in this land, and I will be with you and bless you.

10 For to you and to your offspring will I give all this land, and I will establish My oath which I swore to Abraham your father, and I will multiply your offspring as the stars of heaven, and will give to your offspring all this land.

11 And in your offspring shall all the nations of the earth be blessed, because your father obeyed My voice, and kept My ways and My commandments, and My laws, and My ordinances, and My covenant; and now do as you are told and dwell in this land."

12 And he dwelt in Gelar three weeks of years. And Abimelech commanded concerning him, and concerning all that was his, saying, "Any man that shall touch him or anything that is his shall surely die."

13 Isaac grew strong among the Philistines, and he got many possessions, oxen and sheep and camels and donkeys and a great household.

14 He sowed in the land of the Philistines and brought in a hundred-fold, and Isaac became very great, and the Philistines envied him.

15 Now all the wells that the servants of Abraham had dug during the life of Abraham, the Philistines had stopped them after the death of Abraham, and filled them with dirt.

16 Abimelech said to Isaac, "Go from us, for you are much mightier than we." Isaac departed from that place in the first year of the seventh week, and sojourned in the valleys of Gerar.

17 And they dug the wells of water again which the servants of Abraham, his father, had dug, and which the Philistines had filled after the death of Abraham his father, and he called their names as Abraham his father had named them.

18 The servants of Isaac dug a well in the valley, and found fresh, flowing water, and the shepherds of Gerar bickered with the shepherds of Isaac, saying, "The water is ours." Isaac called the name of the well "Perversity," because they had been perverse with us.

19 And they dug a second well, and they fought for that also, and he called its name "Enmity."

20 He left that place and they dug another well, and for that they did not fight, and he called the name of it "Room," and Isaac said, "Now the Lord has made room for us, and we have increased in the land."

21 And he went up from that place to the Well of the Oath in the first year of the first week in the forty-fourth jubilee.

22 The Lord appeared to him in the night of the new moon of the first month, and said to him, "I am the God of Abraham your father; fear not, for I am with you, and shall bless you and shall surely multiply your offspring as the sand of the earth, for the sake of Abraham my servant."

23 And he built an altar there, which Abraham his father had first built, and he called on the name of the Lord, and he offered sacrifice to the God of Abraham his father.

24 They dug a well and they found fresh, flowing water.

25 The servants of Isaac dug another well and did not find water, and they went and told Isaac that they had not found water, and Isaac said, "I have sworn this day to the Philistines and this thing has been announced to us."

26 And he called the name of that place the Well of the Oath, because there he had sworn to Abimelech and Ahuzzath, his friend, and also to Phicol, who was the commander and his host.

27 Isaac knew that day that he had sworn to them under pressure to make peace with them.

28 On that day Isaac cursed the Philistines and said, "Cursed be the Philistines to the day of wrath and indignation from among all nations. May God make them a disdain and a curse and an object of anger and indignation in the hands of the Gentile sinners and in the hands of the Kittim.

29 Whoever escapes the sword of the enemy and the Kittim, may the righteous nation root them out in judgment from under heaven. They shall be the enemies and foes of my children throughout their generations on the earth.

30 No part of them will remain. Not even one shall be spared on the day of the wrath of judgment. The offspring of the Philistines will experience destruction, rooting out, and expulsion from the earth and this is all that is in store for them. There shall not be a name or an offspring left on the earth for these Caphtorim (the seat of the Philistine state).

31 For though he rises up to heaven, he shall be brought down, and though he makes himself strong on earth, from there shall he be dragged out, and though he hide himself among the nations, even from that place shall he be rooted out.

32 Though he descends into the abode of the dead, his condemnation shall be great, and he shall have no peace there.

33 If he goes into captivity by the hands of those that seek his life they shall kill him on the way (to his imprisonment), and neither his name nor offspring shall be left on all the earth. Into an eternal curse shall he depart."

34 It is written and engraved concerning him on the heavenly tablets, that on the day of judgment he will be rooted out of the earth.

[Chapter 25]

1 In the second year of this week in this jubilee, Rebecca called Jacob her son, and spoke to him, saying, "My son, do not take a wife from the daughters of Canaan as Esau, your brother, who took two wives of the daughters of Canaan, and they have made my soul bitter with all their unclean acts, for all their actions are fornication and lust, and there is no righteousness in them, because their deeds are evil.

2 I love you greatly, my son, and my heart and my affection bless you every hour of the day and in every night.

3 Now, my son, listen to my voice, and do the will of your mother, and do not take a wife of the daughters of this land, but only from the house of my father, and of those related to my father.

4 If you will take you a wife of the house of my father, the Most High God will bless you, and your children shall be a righteous generation and a holy offspring." And then spoke Jacob to Rebecca, his mother, and said to her, "Look, mother, I am nine weeks of years old, and I have neither been with nor have I touched any woman, nor have I engaged myself to any, nor I have even thought of taking me wife of the daughters of Canaan.

5 For I remember, mother, the words of Abraham, our father, for he commanded me not to take a wife of the daughters of Canaan, but to take me a wife from the offspring of my father's house and from my kind folks.

6 I have heard before that daughters have been born to Laban, your brother, and I have set my heart on them to take a wife from among them.

7 For this reason I have guarded myself in my spirit against sinning or being corrupted in any way throughout all the days of my life; for with regard to lust and fornication, Abraham, my father, gave me many commands.

8 Despite all that he has commanded me, these two and twenty years my brother has argued with me, and spoken frequently to me and said, "My brother, take a wife that is a sister of my two wives," but I refused to do as he has done.

9 I swear before you mother, that all the days of my life I will not take me a wife from the daughters of the offspring of Canaan, and I will not act wickedly as my brother has done.

10 Do not be afraid mother, be assured that I shall do your will and walk in uprightness, and not corrupt my ways forever."

11 When she heard this, she lifted up her face to heaven and extended the fingers of her hands, and opened her mouth and blessed the Most High God, who had created the heaven and the earth, and she gave Him thanks and praise.

12 She said, "Blessed be the Lord God, and may His holy name be blessed forever and ever. He has given me Jacob as a pure son and a holy offspring; for he is Yours, and Yours shall his offspring be continually, throughout all the generations forever.

13 Bless him, O Lord, and place in my mouth the blessing of righteousness, that I may bless him."

14 At that hour, when the spirit of righteousness descended into her mouth, she placed both her hands on the head of Jacob, and said, "Blessed are You, Lord of righteousness and God of the ages, and may You bless him beyond all the generations of men.

15 My Son, may He give you the path of righteousness, and reveal righteousness to your offspring.

16 May He make your sons many during your life, and may they arise according to the number of the months of the year. And may their sons become many and great beyond the stars of heaven, and may their numbers be more than the sand of the sea.

17 May He give them this good and pleasing land, as He said He would give it to Abraham and to his offspring after him always, and may they hold it as a possession forever.

18 My son, may I see blessed children born to you during my life, and may all your offspring be blessed and holy.

19 And as you have refreshed your mother's spirit during her life, the womb of her that gave birth to you blesses you now. My affection and my heart (breasts) bless you and my mouth and my tongue greatly praise you.

20 Increase and spread over the earth. May your offspring be perfect in the joy of heaven and earth forever. May your offspring rejoice, and on the great day of peace may they have peace.

21 May your name and your offspring endure to all the ages, and may the Most High God be their God, and may the God of righteousness dwell with them, and may His sanctuary be built by you all the ages.

22 Blessed be he that blesses you, and all flesh that curses you falsely, may it be cursed."

23 And she kissed him, and said to him, "May the Lord of the world love you as the heart of your mother and her affection rejoice in you and bless you." And she ceased from blessing.

[Chapter 26]

1 In the seventh year of this week Isaac called Esau, his elder son, and said to him, " I am old, my son, and my sight is dim, and I do not know the day of my death.

2 Now, take your hunting weapons, your quiver, and your bow, and go out to the field, and hunt and catch me venison, my son, and make me flavorful meat, like my soul loves, and bring it to me that I may eat, and that my soul may bless you before I die."

3 But Rebecca heard Isaac speaking to Esau.

4 Esau went out early to the field to hunt and catch and bring home meat to his father.

5 Rebecca called Jacob, her son, and said to him, "Look, I heard Isaac, your father, speak to Esau, your brother, saying, "Hunt for me, and make me flavorful meat, and bring it to me that I may eat and bless you before the Lord before I die."

6 Now, my son, do as you are told and do as I command you. Go to your flock and fetch me two good kids of the goats, and I will make them good tasting meat for your father, like he loves, and you will bring it to your father that he may eat and bless you to the Lord before he dies."

7 Jacob said to Rebecca his mother, "Mother, I shall not withhold anything which my father would eat and which would please him, but I am afraid that he will recognize my voice and wish to touch me.

8 And you know that I am smooth, and Esau, my brother, is hairy, and I he will see me an evildoer because I am doing something that he has not told me to do and he will be very angry with me, and I shall bring on myself a curse, and not a blessing."

9 Rebecca, his mother, said to him, "Your curse be on me, my son, just do as you are told."

10 Jacob obeyed the voice of Rebecca, his mother, and went and brought back two good and fat goat kids, and brought them to his mother, and his mother made them tasty meat like he loved.

11 Rebecca took the good and pleasing clothes of Esau, her elder son, which was with her in the house, and she clothed Jacob, her younger son, with them, and she put the skins of the kids on his hands and on the exposed parts of his neck.

12 And she gave the meat and the bread, which she had prepared, to her son Jacob.

13 Jacob went in to his father and said, "I am your son. I have done as you asked me. Arise and sit and eat of that which I have caught, father, that your soul may bless me."

14 Isaac said to his son, "How have you found game so quickly, my son?"

15 Jacob said, "Because the Lord your God caused me to find."

16 Isaac said to him, "Come closer, that I may feel you, my son, and know if you are my son Esau or not."

17 Jacob went near to Isaac, his father, and he felt him and said, "The voice is Jacob's voice, but the hands are the hands of Esau," and he did not recognize him, because it was a decision from heaven to remove his power of perception and Isaac discerned not, because his hands were hairy as his brother Esau's, so Isaac blessed him.

18 He said, "Are you my son Esau? " and Jacob said, "I am your son," and Isaac said, "Bring it to me that I may eat of that which you have caught, my son, that my soul may bless you."

19 And Jacob brought it to him, and he ate, and Jacob brought him wine and he drank.

20 Isaac, his father, said to him, "Come close and kiss me, my son."

21 He came close and kissed Isaac. And he smelled the smell of his raiment, and he blessed Jacob and said, "Look, the smell of my son is as the smell of a full field which the Lord has blessed.

22 May the Lord give you of the dew of heaven and of the dew of the earth, and plenty of corn and oil. Let nations serve you and peoples bow down to you.

23 Be ruler over your brothers, and let your mother's sons bow down to you; and may all the blessings that the Lord has blessed me and blessed Abraham, my father, be imparted to you and to your offspring forever. Cursed be he that curses you, and blessed be he that blesses you."

24 It happened as soon as Isaac had made an end of blessing his son Jacob, that Jacob had went away from Isaac his father and hid himself.

25 Esau, his brother, came in from his hunting. And he also made flavorful meat, and brought it to his father and Esau said to his father, "Let my father arise, and eat of my venison that your soul may bless me."

26 Isaac, his father, said to him, "Who are you?" Esau said to him, "I am your first born, your son Esau. I have done as you have commanded me."

27 Isaac was very greatly surprised, and said, "Who is he that has hunted and caught and brought it to me, and I have eaten of all before you came, and have blessed him, and he shall be blessed, and all his offspring forever."

28 It happened when Esau heard the words of his father Isaac that he cried with a very loud and bitter cry, and said to his father, "Bless me also, father!"

29 Isaac said to him, "Your brother came with trickery, and has taken away your blessing."

30 He said, "Now I know why his name is Jacob. Behold, he has supplanted me these two times, he took away my birth-right, and now he has taken away my blessing."

31 Esau said, "Have you not reserved a blessing for me, father?" and Isaac answered and said to Esau, "Look, I have made him your lord, and all his brothers have I given to him for servants. I have strengthened him with plenty of corn and wine and oil. Now what shall I do for you, my son?"

32 Esau said to Isaac, his father, "Have you only one blessing, father? Please. Bless me, also, father."

33 Esau lifted up his voice and wept. And Isaac answered and said to him, "Far from the dew of the earth shall be your dwelling, and far from the dew of heaven from above.

34 By your sword will you live, and you will serve your brother.

35 It shall happen that when you become great, and do shake his yoke from off your neck, you will sin completely and commit a sin worthy of death, and your offspring shall be rooted out from under heaven."

36 Esau kept threatening Jacob because of the blessing his father blessed him with, and he said in his heart, "May the days of mourning for my father come now, so that I may kill my brother Jacob."

[Chapter 27]

1 Rebecca was told Esau's words in a dream, and Rebecca sent for Jacob her younger son, and said to him, "Look, Esau, your brother, will take vengeance on you and kill you.

2 Now, therefore, my son, do as you are told, and get up and flee to Laban, my brother, to Haran, and stay with him a few days until your brother's anger fades away, and he removes his anger from you, and forgets all that you have done. Then I will send for you to come from that place."

3 Jacob said, "I am not afraid. If he wishes to kill me, I will kill him."

4 But she said to him, "Let me not be bereft of both my sons on one day."

5 Jacob said to Rebecca, his mother, "Look, you know that my father has become old, and does not see because his eyes are dull. If I leave him he will think it is wrong. If I leave him and go away from you, my father will be angry and will curse me.

6 I will not go. When he sends me, only then will I go."

7 Rebecca said to Jacob, "I will go in and speak to him, and he will send you away."

8 Rebecca went in and said to Isaac, "I hate my life because of the two daughters of Heth, whom Esau has taken as wives. If Jacob take a wife from among the daughters of the land such as these, I could not live with it, because the daughters of Canaan are evil."

9 Isaac called Jacob and blessed him, and warned him and said to him, "Do not take you a wife of any of the daughters of Canaan. Arise and go to Mesopotamia, to the house of Bethuel, your mother's father, and take a wife from that place of the daughters of Laban, your mother's brother.

10 And God Almighty bless you and increase and multiply you that you may become a company of nations, and give you the blessings of my father, Abraham, to you and to your offspring after you, that you may inherit the

land that you travel in and all the land which God gave to Abraham. Go in peace, my son."

11 Isaac sent Jacob away, and he went to Mesopotamia, to Laban the son of Bethuel the Syrian, the brother of Rebecca, Jacob's mother.

12 It happened after Jacob had departed to Mesopotamia that the spirit of Rebecca was grieved for her son, and she wept.

13 Isaac said to Rebecca, "My sister, weep not because of Jacob, my son, for he goes in peace, and in peace will he return.

14 The Most High God will preserve him from all evil and will be with him. He will not forsake him all his days, for I know that his ways will be made to prosper in all things wherever he goes, until he return in peace to us, and we see him in peace. Fear not on his account, my sister, for he is on the upright path and he is a perfect man, and he is faithful and will not perish. Weep not."

15 Isaac comforted Rebecca because of her son Jacob, and blessed him.

16 Jacob went from the Well of the Oath to go to Haran on the first year of the second week in the forty-fourth jubilee, and he came to Luz on the mountains, that is, Bethel, on the new moon of the first month of this week, and he came to the place at dusk and turned from the way to the west of the road that is close, and that night he slept there, for the sun had set.

17 He took one of the stones of that place (as a pillow) and laid down under the tree, and he was journeying alone, and he slept.

18 Jacob dreamt that night, and saw a ladder set up on the earth, and the top of it reached to heaven, and he saw the angels of the Lord ascended and descended on it, and behold, the Lord stood on it.

19 And He spoke to Jacob and said, "I am the Lord God of Abraham, your father, and the God of Isaac. The land you are sleeping on I will give to you and to your offspring after you.

20 Your offspring shall be as the dust of the earth, and you will increase to the west and to the east, to the north and the south, and in you and in your offspring shall all the families of the nations be blessed.

21 Behold, I will be with you, and will keep you wherever you go. I will bring you into this land again in peace. I will not leave you until I do everything that I told you."

22 Jacob awoke from his sleep and said, "Truly this place is the house of the Lord, and I did not know it."

23 He was afraid and said, "I am afraid because this place is none other than the house of God, and this is the gate of heaven, and I did not know it."

24 Jacob got up early in the morning, and took the stone that he had placed under his head and set it up as a pillar for a sign. And he poured oil on the top of it. And he called the name of that place Bethel, but the name of the place was previously Luz.

25 And Jacob vowed a vow to the Lord, saying, "If the Lord will be with me, and will keep me in the way that I go, and give me bread to eat and clothes to put on, so that I come again to my father's house in peace, then the Lord shall be my God, and this stone which I have set up as a pillar for a sign in this place shall be the Lord's house, and of all that you gave me, I shall give the tenth to you, my God."

[Chapter 28]

1 He went on his journey, and came to the land of the east, to Laban, the brother of Rebecca, and he was with him, and Jacob served Laban for Rachel his daughter one week of years. In the first year of the third week of years he said to him, "Give me my wife, for whom I have served you seven years ," and Laban said to Jacob, "I will give you your wife."
2 Laban made a feast, and took Leah his elder daughter, and gave her to Jacob as a wife, and gave Leah Zilpah for a handmaid; and Jacob did not know, for he thought that she was Rachel.
3 He went in to her, and saw she was Leah; and Jacob was angry with Laban, and said to him, "Why have you done this to me?
4 Did I not serve you for Rachel and not for Leah? Why have you wronged me?
5 Take your daughter, and I will go. You have done evil to me." For Jacob loved Rachel more than Leah because Leah's eyes were weak, but her form was very beautiful. Rachel had beautiful eyes and a beautiful and very voluptuous form.
6 Laban said to Jacob, "It is not done that way in our country, we do not to give the younger before the elder." And it is not right to do this; for thus it is ordained and written in the heavenly tablets, that no one should give his younger daughter before the elder; but the elder one is given first and after her the younger. The man who does so will have guilt placed against him in heaven, and none is righteous that does this thing, for this deed is evil before the Lord.
7 Command the children of Israel that they not do this thing. Let them neither take nor give the younger before they have given the elder, for it is very wicked."
8 And Laban said to Jacob, "Let the seven days of the feast pass by, and I shall give you Rachel, that you may serve me another seven years, that you may pasture my sheep as you did in the former week (of years)."
9 On the day when the seven days of the feast of Leah had passed, Laban gave Rachel to Jacob, that he might serve him another seven years, and he gave Rachel, Bilhah, the sister of Zilpah, as a handmaid.

10 He served yet other seven years for Rachel, for Leah had been given to him for nothing, since it was Rachel he wanted.

11 And the Lord opened the womb of Leah, and she conceived and gave birth to a son for Jacob, and he called his name Reuben, on the fourteenth day of the ninth month, in the first year of the third week.

12 But the womb of Rachel was closed, for the Lord saw that Leah was hated and Rachel loved.

13 Again Jacob went in to Leah, and she conceived, and gave birth to a second son for Jacob, and he called his name Simeon, on the twenty-first of the tenth month, and in the third year of this week.

14 Again Jacob went in to Leah, and she conceived, and gave birth to a third son, and he called his name Levi, in the new moon of the first month in the sixth year of this week.

15 Again Jacob went in to her, and she conceived, and gave birth to a fourth son, and he called his name Judah, on the fifteenth of the third month, in the first year of the fourth week.

16 Because of all this Rachel envied Leah, for she did not bear a child, and she said to Jacob, "Give me children;" and Jacob said, "Have I withheld from you the fruits of your womb? Have I left you?"

17 And when Rachel saw that Leah had given birth to four sons for Jacob: Reuben and Simeon and Levi and Judah, she said to him, "Go in to Bilhah my handmaid, and she will conceive, and bear a son for me."

18 She gave him Bilhah, her handmaid, to wife. And he went in to her, and she conceived, and gave birth to a son, and he called his name Dan, on the ninth of the sixth month, in the sixth year of the third week.

19 Jacob went in again to Bilhah a second time, and she conceived, and gave birth to another son for Jacob, and Rachel called his name Napthali, on the fifth of the seventh month, in the second year of the fourth week.

20 When Leah saw that she had become sterile and could no longer have children, she envied Rachel, and she also gave her handmaid Zilpah to Jacob to wife, and she conceived, and gave birth to a son, and Leah called his name Gad, on the twelfth of the eighth month, in the third year of the fourth week.

21 He went in to her again, and she conceived and gave birth to a second son, and Leah called his name Asher, on the second of the eleventh month, in the fifth year of the fourth week.

22 Jacob went in to Leah, and she conceived, and gave birth to a son, and she called his name Issachar, on the fourth of the fifth month, in the fourth year of the fourth week, and she gave him to a nurse.

23 Jacob went in again to her, and she conceived, and gave birth to two children, a son and a daughter, and she called the name of the son Zabulon, and the name of the daughter Dinah, in the seventh day of the seventh month, in the sixth year of the fourth week.

24 The Lord was gracious to Rachel, and opened her womb, and she conceived, and gave birth to a son, and she called his name Joseph, on the new moon of the fourth month, in the sixth year in this fourth week.

25 In the days when Joseph was born, Jacob said to Laban, "Give me my wives and sons, and let me go to my father Isaac, and let me make a household for myself; for I have completed the years in which I have served you for your two daughters, and I will go to the house of my father."

26 Laban said to Jacob, "Stay with me and I will pay you wages, and pasture my flock for me again, and take your wages."

27 They agreed with one another that he should give him as his wages those of the lambs and kids which were born spotted black and white, these were to be his wages.

28 All the sheep brought out spotted and speckled and black, variously marked, and they brought out again lambs like themselves, and all that were spotted were Jacob's and those which were not spotted were Laban's.

29 Jacob's possessions multiplied greatly, and he possessed oxen and sheep and donkeys and camels, and men-servants and maid-servants.

30 Laban and his sons envied Jacob, and Laban took back his sheep from him, and he envied him and watched him for an opportunity to do evil.

[Chapter 29]

1 It happened when Rachel had given birth to Joseph, that Laban went to shear his sheep; for they were distant from him, a three-day journey.

2 Jacob saw that Laban was going to shear his sheep, and Jacob called Leah and Rachel, and spoke sweetly to them in order to convince them to come with him to the land of Canaan.

3 For he told them how he had seen everything in a dream. All that God had spoken to him that he should return to his father's house, and they said, "To every place where you go we will go with you."

4 Jacob blessed the God of Isaac his father, and the God of Abraham his father's father, and he arose and placed his wives and his children on donkeys, and took all his possessions and crossed the river, and came to the land of Gilead, and Jacob hid his intention from Laban and did not tell him.

5 In the seventh year of the fourth week Jacob turned his face toward Gilead in the first month, on the twenty-first of it.

6 Laban pursued and overtook Jacob in the mountain of Gilead in the third month, on the thirteenth of it. And the Lord did not permit him to injure Jacob for he appeared to him in a dream by night.

7 Laban spoke to Jacob. On the fifteenth of those days Jacob made a feast for Laban, and for all who came with him, and Jacob swore to Laban that day, and Laban also swore to Jacob, that neither should cross the mountain of Gilead to do evil to the other.

8 He made a heap (of stones) for a witness there; wherefore the name of that place is called, "The Heap of Witness," after this heap.

9 But before they used to call the land of Gilead the land of the Rephaim. The Rephaim were born giants whose height was ten, nine, eight, down to seven cubits.

10 Their dwelling place was from the land of the children of Ammon to Mount Hermon, and the seats of their kingdom were Karnaim and Ashtaroth, and Edrei, and Misur, and Beon.

11 The Lord destroyed them because of the evil of their deeds, for they were malevolent, and the Amorites were wicked and sinful. There is no people today which has committed the full range of their sins, and their life on the earth was shortened.

12 Jacob sent Laban away, and he departed into Mesopotamia, the land of the East, and Jacob returned to the land of Gilead.

13 He passed over the Jabbok in the ninth month, on the eleventh of it. On that day Esau, his brother, came to him, and he was reconciled to him, and departed from him to the land of Seir, but Jacob dwelt in tents.

14 In the first year of the fifth week in this jubilee he crossed the Jordan, and dwelt beyond the Jordan. He pastured his sheep from the sea of the heap to Bethshan, and to Dothan and to the forest of Akrabbim.

15 He sent his father Isaac all of his possessions such as clothing, and food, and meat, and drink, and milk, and butter, and cheese, and some dates of the valley.

16 Four times a year, he sent gifts to his mother Rebecca who was living at the tower of Abraham. He sent the gifts between the times of the months between plowing and reaping, and between autumn and the rain season, and between winter and spring.

17 For Isaac had returned from the Well of the Oath and gone up to the tower of his father Abraham, and he dwelt there apart from his son Esau.

18 For in the days when Jacob went to Mesopotamia, Esau took to himself a wife Mahalath, the daughter of Ishmael,
and he gathered together all the flocks of his father and his wives, and went up and dwelt on Mount Seir, and left Isaac his father at the Well of the Oath alone.

19 And Isaac went up from the Well of the Oath and dwelt in the tower of Abraham his father on the mountains of Hebron, and that is where Jacob sent all that he did send to his father and his mother from time to time, all they needed, and they blessed Jacob with all their heart and with all their soul.

[Chapter 30]

1 In the first year of the sixth week he went up to Salem, to the east of Shechem, in the fourth month, and he went in peace. Shechem, the son of Hamor, the Hivite, the prince of the land carried off Dinah, the daughter of Jacob, into the house, and he had sex with her and defiled her. She was a little girl, a child of twelve years.

2 He begged his father and her brothers that she might be given to him as a wife.

3 Jacob and his sons were very angry because of the men of Shechem, for they had defiled Dinah, their sister. They spoke to them while planning evil acts and they dealt deceitfully with them and tricked them.

4 Simeon and Levi came unexpectedly to Shechem and executed judgment on all the men of Shechem, and killed all the men whom they found in it. They did not leave a single one remaining in it. They killed all in hand to hand battle because they had dishonored their sister Dinah.

5 Let it not again be done from now on that a daughter of Israel be defiled. Judgment is ordained in heaven against them that they should destroy all

the men of the Shechemites with the sword because they had committed shame in Israel.

6 The Lord delivered them into the hands of the sons of Jacob that they might exterminate them with the sword and execute judgment on them. That it might not again be done in Israel that a virgin of Israel should be defiled.

7 If there is any man in Israel who wishes to give his daughter or his sister to any man who is of the offspring of the Gentiles he shall surely die. They shall stone him, for he has committed shame in Israel. They shall burn the woman with fire, because she has dishonored the name of the house of her father, and she shall be rooted out of Israel.

8 Do not let an adulteress and let no uncleanness be found in Israel throughout all the days of the generations of the earth. For Israel is holy to the Lord, and every man who has defiled it shall surely die. They shall stone him.

9 For it has been ordained and written in the heavenly tablets regarding all the offspring of Israel. He who defiles it shall surely die. He shall be killed by stoning. There is no limit of days for this law. There is no remission, and no atonement.

10 The man who has defiled his daughter shall be rooted out from every corner of all Israel, because he has given of his offspring to Moloch (a pagan God, the worship of which involved burning the child alive), and committed impurity and defiled his child.

11 Moses, command the children of Israel and exhort them not to give their daughters to the Gentiles, and not to take for their sons any of the daughters of the Gentiles, for this is abominable before the Lord.

12 It is because of this that I have written all the deeds of the Shechemites, which they committed against Dinah, and placed them in the words of the Law for you. I have also written how the sons of Jacob spoke, saying, "We will not give our daughter to a man who is uncircumcised, for that is a reproach to us."

13 It is a reproach to Israel that anyone take the daughters of the Gentiles, for this is unclean and abominable to Israel.

14 Israel will not be free from this uncleanness if it has a wife of the daughters of the Gentiles, or has given any of its daughters to a man who is of any of the Gentiles.

15 There will be plague upon plague, and curse upon curse, and every judgment and plague and curse will come if he does this thing, or if they ignore those who commit uncleanness, or defile the sanctuary of the Lord, or those who profane His holy name. If any of these happen the whole nation together will be judged for all the uncleanness and profanation of this man.

16 There will be no judging people by their position and no receiving fruits, or offerings, or burnt-offerings, or fat, or the fragrance of sweet odor from his hands. It will be unacceptable and so warn every man and woman in Israel who defiles the sanctuary.

17 For this reason I have commanded you, saying, "Give this testimony to Israel, see how the Shechemites and their sons fared? See how they were delivered into the hands of two sons of Jacob, and they killed them under torture? It was counted to them for righteousness, and it is written down to them for righteousness.

18 The offspring of Levi were chosen for the priesthood, and to be Levites, that they might minister before the Lord, as we do, continually. Levi and his sons will be blessed forever, for he was zealous to execute righteousness and judgment and vengeance on all those who arose against Israel.

19 So they wrote a testimony in his favor of blessing and righteousness on the heavenly tablets in the presence of the God of all.

20 We remember the righteousness that the man fulfilled during his life, throughout the years, until a thousand generations they will record it. It will come to him and to his descendants after him, and he has been recorded on the heavenly tablets as a friend and a righteous man.

21 All this account I have written for you, and have commanded you to tell the children of Israel, so that they will not commit sin nor transgress the laws nor break the covenant which has been ordained for them. They should fulfill it and be recorded as friends (of God).

22 But if they transgress and work uncleanness in any way, they will be recorded on the heavenly tablets as adversaries (of God), and they will be blotted out of the book of life. Instead, they will be recorded in the book of those who will be destroyed and with those who will be rooted out of the earth.

23 On the day when the sons of Jacob killed Shechem it was written in the record in their favor in heaven that they had executed righteousness and uprightness and vengeance on the sinners, and it was written for a blessing.

24 They brought Dinah, their sister, out of the house of Shechem. They took everything that was in Shechem captive. They took their sheep and their oxen and their donkeys, and all their wealth, and all their flocks, and brought them all to Jacob their father.

25 He reproached them because they had put the city to the sword for he feared those who dwelt in the land, the Canaanites and the Perizzites.

26 The dread of the Lord was on all the cities that are near Shechem. They did not fight or chase after the sons of Jacob, for terror had fallen on them.

[Chapter 31]

1 On the new moon of the month, Jacob spoke to all the people of his house, saying, "Purify yourselves and change your clothes, and let us get up and go to Bethel where I vowed a vow to Him on the day when I fled from Esau my brother. Let us do this because God has been with me and brought me into this land in peace. You must put away the strange gods that you raise among you."

2 They gave up the strange gods and that which was in their ears and which was on their necks and the idols which Rachel stole from Laban her father she gave wholly to Jacob. And he burnt and broke them to pieces and destroyed them, and hid them under an oak, which is in the land of Shechem.

3 He went up on the new moon of the seventh month to Bethel. And he built an altar at the place where he had slept, and he set up a pillar there, and he sent word to his father, Isaac, and his mother, Rebecca. He asked to come to Isaac. There, Jacob wished to offer his sacrifice.

4 Isaac said, "Let my son, Jacob, come, and let me see him before I die."

5 Jacob went to his father, Isaac, and his mother, Rebecca, to the house of his father Abraham, and he took two of his sons with him, Levi and Judah.

6 Rebecca came out from the tower to the front of it to kiss Jacob and embrace him, for her spirit had revived when she heard, "Look Jacob your son has come," and she kissed him.

7 She saw his two sons and she recognized them. She said to him, "Are these your sons, my son?" and she embraced them and kissed them, and blessed them, saying, "In you shall the offspring of Abraham become illustrious, and you shall prove a blessing on the earth."

8 Jacob went in to Isaac his father, to the room where he lay, and his two sons were with him. He took his father's hand, stooped down, he kissed him. Isaac held on to the neck of Jacob his son, and wept on his neck.

9 The darkness left the eyes of Isaac, and he saw the two sons of Jacob, Levi, and Judah. And he said, "Are these your sons, my son? Because they look like you."

10 He said to Isaac, "They were truly my sons, and you have clearly seen that they are truly my sons."

11 They came near to him, and he turned and kissed them and embraced them both together.

12 The spirit of prophecy came down into his mouth, and he took Levi by his right hand and Judah by his left.

13 He turned to Levi first, and began to bless him first, and said to him, "May the God of all, the very Lord of all the ages, bless you and your children throughout all the ages.

14 May the Lord give to you and your offspring greatness and great glory from among all flesh. May the Lord cause you and your offspring to draw near to Him to serve in His sanctuary like the angels of the presence (of the

Lord) and as the holy ones. The offspring of your sons shall be for the glory and greatness and holiness of God. May He make them great throughout all the ages. They shall be judges and princes, and chiefs of all the offspring of the sons of Jacob. They shall speak the word of the Lord in righteousness, and they shall judge all His judgments in righteousness.

15 They shall declare My ways to Jacob and My paths to Israel. The blessing of the Lord shall be given in their mouths to bless all the offspring of the beloved.

16 Your mother has called your name Levi, and rightly has she called your name. You will be joined to the Lord and be the companion of all the sons of Jacob. Let His table be your table, and let your sons eat from it. May your table be full throughout all generations, and let your food not fail in all the ages.

17 Let all who hate you fall down before you, and let all your adversaries be rooted out and perish. Blessed be he that blesses you, and cursed be every nation that curses you."

18 To Judah he said, "May the Lord give you strength and power to put all that hate you under your feet. You and one of your sons will be a prince over the sons of Jacob. May your name and the name of your sons go out across every land and region.

19 Then shall the Gentiles fear you, and all the nations and people shall shake (with fear of you). In you will be the help of Jacob, and in you will be found the salvation of Israel.

20 When you sit on the throne, which honors of your righteousness, there shall be great peace for all the offspring of the sons of the beloved. Blessed be he that blesses you, and cursed be all that hate you, afflict you, or curse you. They shall be rooted out and destroyed from the earth."

21 He turned, kissed him again, and embraced him, and rejoiced greatly because he had seen the sons of his son, Jacob, clearly and truly.

22 He stepped out from between his feet and fell down. He bowed down to him, and blessed them. He rested there with Isaac, his father, that night, and they ate and drank with joy.

23 He made the two sons of Jacob sleep, the one on his right hand and the other on his left. It was counted to him for righteousness.

24 Jacob told his father everything during the night about how the Lord had shown him great mercy, and how he had caused him to prosper in all his ways, and how he protected him from all evil.

25 Isaac blessed the God of his father Abraham, who had not withdrawn his mercy and his righteousness from the sons of his servant Isaac.

26 In the morning, Jacob told his father, Isaac, the vow, which he had vowed to the Lord. He told him of the vision which he had seen, and that he had built an altar. He told him that everything was ready for the sacrifice to be made before the Lord as he had vowed. He had come to set him on a donkey.

27 Isaac said to Jacob his son, "I am not able to go with you, for I am old and not able to endure the way. Go in peace, my son. I am one hundred and sixty-five years this day. I am no longer able to journey. Set your mother on a donkey and let her go with you.

28 I know that you have come on my account, my son. May this day be blessed on which you have seen me alive, and I also have seen you, my son.

29 May you prosper and fulfill the vow that you have vowed. Do not put off your vow, for you will be called to account for the vow. Now hurry to perform it, and may He who has made all things be pleased. It is to Him you have vowed the vow."

30 He said to Rebecca, "Go with Jacob your son," and Rebecca went with Jacob her son, and Deborah with her, and they came to Bethel.

31 Jacob remembered the prayer with which his father had blessed him and his two sons, Levi and Judah. He rejoiced and blessed the God of his fathers, Abraham and Isaac.

32 He said, "Now I know that my sons and I have an eternal hope in the God of all." Thus is it ordained concerning the two. They recorded it as an eternal testimony to them on the heavenly tablets how Isaac blessed his sons.

[Chapter 32]

1 That night he stayed at Bethel, and Levi dreamed that they had ordained and made his sons and him the priests of the Most High God forever. Then he awoke from his sleep and blessed the Lord.

2 Jacob rose early in the morning, on the fourteenth of this month, and he gave a tithe for all that came with him, both of men and cattle, both of gold and every vessel and garment. Yes, he gave tithes of all.

3 In those days Rachel became pregnant with her son Benjamin. Jacob counted his sons starting from him and going to the oldest and Levi fell to the portion of the Lord. (Levi was the third son – three is the number of spiritual completeness.) His father clothed him in the garments of the priesthood and filled his hands.

4 On the fifteenth of this month, he brought fourteen oxen from among the cattle, and twenty-eight rams, and forty-nine sheep, and seven lambs, and twenty-one kids of the goats to the altar as a burnt-offering on the altar of sacrifice. The offering was well pleasing and a sweet odor before God.

5 This was his offering, done in acknowledgement of the vow in which he had promised that he would give a tenth, with their fruit-offerings and their drink- offerings.

6 When the fire had consumed it, he burnt incense over the fire, and for a thank-offering he sacrificed two oxen and four rams and four sheep, four male goats, and two sheep of a year old, and two kids of the goats. This he did daily for seven days.

7 He, his men, and all his sons were eating this with joy during seven days and blessing and thanking the Lord, who had delivered him out of all his tribulation and had given him His promise.

8 He tithed all the clean animals, and made a burnt sacrifice, but he did not give the unclean animals to Levi his son. He gave him (responsibility for) all the souls of the men. Levi acted in the priestly office at Bethel in the presence of Jacob his father, in preference to his ten brothers. He was a priest there, and Jacob gave his vow, and he gave a tithe to the Lord again and sanctified it, and it became holy to Him.

9 For this reason it is ordained on the heavenly tablets as a law for the offering of the tithe should be eaten in the presence of the Lord every year, in the place where it is chosen that His name should live and reside. This law has no limit of days forever.

10 This law is written so that it may be fulfilled every year. The second tithe should be eaten in the presence of the Lord, in the place where it has been chosen, and nothing shall be left over from it from this year to the following year.

11 In its year shall the seed be eaten until the days of the gathering of the seed of the year. The wine shall be consumed until the days of the wine, and the oil until the days of its season.

12 All that is left of it and all that becomes old will be regarded as spoiled, let it be burnt with fire, for it is unclean.

13 Let them eat it together in the sanctuary, and let them not permit it to become old.

14 All the tithes of the oxen and sheep shall be holy to the Lord, and shall belong to His priests. They will eat before Him from year to year, for thus is it ordained and written on the heavenly tablets regarding the tithe.

15 On the following night, on the twenty-second day of this month, Jacob resolved to build that place and to surround the court with a wall, and to sanctify it and make it holy forever, for himself and his children after him.

16 The Lord appeared to him by night and blessed him and said to him, "Your name shall not be called Jacob, but they will call your name Israel."

17 And He said to him again, "I am the Lord who created the heaven and the earth, and I will increase you and multiply you greatly, and kings shall come forth from you, and they shall be judges everywhere the foot of the sons of men have walked.

18 I will give to your offspring all the earth that is under heaven. They shall judge all the nations, as they desire. After that they shall possess the entire earth and inherit it forever."

19 And He finished speaking with him, and He went up from him.

20 Jacob watched until He had ascended into heaven.

21 In a vision at night he saw an angel descend from heaven with seven tablets in his hands, and he gave them to Jacob, and he read them and knew all that was written on it that would happen to him and his sons throughout all the ages.

22 He showed him all that was written on the tablets, and said to him, "Do not build on this place, and do not make it an eternal sanctuary, and do not live here. This is not the place. Go to the house of Abraham your father and live with Isaac, your father, until the day he dies.

23 For in Egypt you will die in peace, and in this land you will be buried with honor in the sepulcher of your fathers, with Abraham and Isaac.

24 Do not fear. As you have seen and read it shall all be. Write down everything that you have seen and read."

25 Jacob said, "Lord, how can I remember all that I have read and seen?" He said to him, "I will bring all things to your remembrance."

26 He ascended from Jacob, and Jacob awoke from his sleep. He remembered everything that he had read and seen, and he wrote down all the words.

27 He celebrated there yet another day, and he sacrificed on that day as he had sacrificed on all the former days. He called its name "Addition," because this day was added, and the former days he called "The Feast."

28 It was made known and revealed to him and it is written on the heavenly tablets that he should celebrate the day, and add it to the seven days of the feast.

29 Its name was called "Addition," because that it was recorded among the days of the feast days, according to the number of the days of the year.

30 In the night, on the twenty-third of this month, Deborah, Rebecca's nurse died, and they buried her beneath the city under the oak of the river. He called the name of this place, "The river of Deborah," and he called the oak, "The oak of the mourning of Deborah."

31 Rebecca departed and returned to her house, to his father Isaac. Jacob sent rams and sheep and male goats by her so that she should prepare a meal for his father such as he desired.

32 He followed his mother until he came to the land of Kabratan, and he lived there.

33 Rachel gave birth to a son in the night, and called his name "son of my sorrow", for she broke down while giving birth to him, but his father called his name Benjamin. This happened on the eleventh day of the eighth month in the first of the sixth week of this jubilee.

34 Rachel died there and she was buried in the land of Ephrath, the same is Bethlehem, and Jacob built a pillar on the grave of Rachel, on the road above her grave.

[Chapter 33]

1 Jacob went and lived to the south of Magdaladra'ef. He and Leah, his wife, went to his father, Isaac, on the new moon of the tenth month.

2 Reuben saw Bilhah, Rachel's maid, the concubine of his father, bathing in water in a secret place, and he loved her.

3 He hid himself at night, and he entered the house of Bilhah at night. He found her sleeping alone on a bed in her house.

4 He had sex with her. She awoke and saw that is was Reuben lying with her in the bed. She uncovered the border of her covering and grabbed him and cried out when she discovered that it was Reuben.

5 She was ashamed because of him and released her hand from him, and he fled.

6 Because of this, she mourned greatly and did not tell it to any one.

7 When Jacob returned and sought her, she said to him, "I am not clean for you. I have been defiled in regard to you. Reuben has defiled me, and has had sex with me in the night. I was asleep and did not realize he was there until he uncovered my skirt and had sex with me."

8 Jacob was very angry with Reuben because he had sex with Bilhah, because he had uncovered his father's skirt.

9 Jacob did not approach her again because Reuben had defiled her. And as for any man who uncovers his father's skirt his deed is greatly wicked, for he is disgusting to the Lord.

10 For this reason it is written and ordained on the heavenly tablets that a man should not lie with his father's wife, and should not uncover his father's skirt. This is unclean and they shall surely die together, the man who lies with his father's wife and the woman also, for they have committed uncleanness on the earth.

11 There shall be nothing unclean before our God in the nation that He has chosen for Himself as a possession.

12 Again, it is written a second time, "Cursed be he who lies with the wife of his father, for he has uncovered his father's shame." All the holy ones of the Lord said, "So be it. So be it."

13 "Moses, command the children of Israel so that they observe this word. It entails a punishment of death. It is unclean, and there is no atonement forever for the man who has committed this. He is to be put to death. Kill him by stoning. Root him out from among the people of our God.

14 No man who does so in Israel will be permitted to remain alive a single day on the earth. He is abominable and unclean.

15 Do not let them say, "Reuben was granted life and forgiveness after he had sex with his father's concubine, although she had a husband, and her husband, Jacob, his father, was still alive."

16 Until that time the ordinance and judgment and law had not been revealed in its completeness for all. In your days it has been revealed as a law of seasons and of days. It is an everlasting law for all generations forever. For this law has no limit of days, and no atonement for it.

17 They must both be rooted out of the entire nation. On the day they committed it they shall be killed.

18 Moses, write it down for Israel that they may observe it, and do according to these words, and not commit a sin punishable by death. The Lord our God is judge, who does not respect persons (position) and accepts no gifts.

19 Tell them these words of the covenant, that they may hear and observe, and be on their guard with respect to them, and not be destroyed and rooted out of the land; for an uncleanness, and an abomination, and a contamination, and a pollution are all they who commit it on the earth before our God.

20 There is no greater sin on earth than fornication that they commit. Israel is a holy nation to the Lord its God, and a nation of inheritance. It is a priestly and royal nation and for His own possession. There shall appear no such uncleanness among the holy nation.

21 In the third year of this sixth week, Jacob and all his sons went and lived in the house of Abraham, near Isaac his father and Rebecca his mother.

22 These were the names of the sons of Jacob, the first-born

Reuben, Simeon, Levi, Judah, Issachar, Zebulon, which are the sons of Leah. The sons of Rachel are Joseph and Benjamin. The sons of Bilhah are Dan and Naphtali; and the sons of Zilpah, Gad and Asher. Dinah is the daughter of Leah, the only daughter of Jacob.

23 They came and bowed themselves to Isaac and Rebecca. When they saw them they blessed Jacob and all his sons, and Isaac rejoiced greatly, for he saw the sons of Jacob, his younger son and he blessed them.

[Chapter 34]

1 In the sixth year of this week of the forty-fourth jubilee Jacob sent his sons and his servants to pasture their sheep in the pastures of Shechem.

2 The seven kings of the Amorites assembled themselves together (to fight) against them and kill them. They hid themselves under the trees, to take their cattle as booty.

3 Jacob, Levi, Judah and Joseph were in the house with Isaac their father, for his spirit was sorrowful, and they could not leave him. Benjamin was the youngest, and for this reason he remained with his father.

4 The king of Taphu, the king of Aresa, the king of Seragan, the king of Selo, the king of Ga'as, the king of Bethoron, the king of Ma'anisakir, and all those who dwell in these mountains and who dwell in the woods in the land of Canaan came.

5 They announced to Jacob saying, "Look, the kings of the Amorites have surrounded your sons, and plundered their herds."

6 And he left his house, he and his three sons and all the servants of his father, and his own servants, and he went against them with six thousand men, who carried swords.

7 He killed them in the pastures of Shechem, and pursued those who fled, and he killed them with the edge of the sword, and he killed Aresa and Taphu and Saregan and Selo and Amani sakir and Gaga'as, and he recovered his herds.

8 He conquered them, and imposed tribute on them that they should pay him five fruit products of their land. He built (the cities of) Robel and Tamnatares.

9 He returned in peace, and made peace with them, and they became his servants until the day that he and his sons went down into Egypt.

10 In the seventh year of this week he sent Joseph from his house to the land of Shechem to learn about the welfare of his brothers. He found them in the land of Dothan.

11 They dealt treacherously with him, and formed a plot against him to kill him, but they changed their minds and sold him to Ishmaelite merchants. They brought him down into Egypt, and they sold him to Potiphar, the eunuch of Pharaoh, the chief of the cooks and priest of the city of Elew."

12 The sons of Jacob slaughtered a kid, and dipped Joseph's coat in the blood and sent it to Jacob their father on the tenth of the seventh month.

13 They brought it to him in the evening and he mourned all that night. He became feverish with mourning for Joseph's death, and he said, "An evil beast has devoured Joseph". All the members of his house mourned and grieved with him that day.

14 His sons and his daughter got up to comfort him, but he refused to be comforted for his son.

15 On that day Bilhah heard that Joseph had perished, and she died mourning him. She was living in Qafratef, and Dinah, his daughter, died after Joseph had perished.

16 There were now three reasons for Israel to mourn in one month. They buried Bilhah next to the tomb of Rachel, and Dinah, his daughter. They were (all) buried there.

17 He mourned for Joseph one year, and did not cease, for he said, "Let me go down to my grave mourning for my son."

18 For this reason it is ordained for the children of Israel that they should remember and mourn on the tenth of the seventh month. On that day the news came which made Jacob weep for Joseph. On this day they should

make atonement for their sins for themselves with a young goat on the tenth of the seventh month, once a year, for they had grieved the sorrow of their father regarding Joseph his son.

19 This day, once a year, has been ordained that they should grieve on it for their sins, and for all their transgressions and for all their errors, so that they might cleanse themselves.

20 After Joseph perished, the sons of Jacob took to themselves wives. The name of Reuben's wife is Ada; and the name of Simeon's wife is Adlba'a, a Canaanite. The name of Levi's wife is Melka, of the daughters of Aram, of the offspring of the sons of Terah. The name of Judah's wife is Betasu'el, a Canaanite. The name of Issachar's wife is Hezaqa, and the name of Zabulon's wife is Ni'iman. The name of Dan's wife is Egla. The name of Naphtali's wife is Rasu'u, of Mesopotamia. The name of Gad's wife is Maka. The name of Asher's wife is Ijona. The name of Joseph's wife is Asenath, the Egyptian. The name of Benjamin's wife is Ijasaka.

21 And Simeon repented, and took a second wife from Mesopotamia as his brothers had done.

[Chapter 35]

1 In the first year of the first week of the forty-fifth jubilee Rebecca called Jacob, her son, and commanded him regarding his father and regarding his brother, that he should honor them all the days of his life.

2 Jacob said, "I will do everything you have commanded. I will honor them. This will be honor and greatness to me, and righteousness before the Lord.

3 Mother, you know from the time I was born until this day, all my deeds and all that is in my heart. I always think good concerning all.

4 Why should I not do this thing which you have commanded me, that I should honor my father and my brother?

5 Tell me, mother, what perversity have you seen in me and I shall turn away from it, and mercy will be on me."

6 She said to him, "My son, in all my days I have not seen any perverseness in you, but only upright deeds. Yet, I will tell you the truth, my son, I shall die this year. I shall not survive this year in my life. I have seen the day of my death in a dream. I should not live beyond a hundred and fifty-five years. I have completed all the days that I am to live my life."

7 Jacob laughed at the words of his mother because his mother had said she should die. She was sitting across from him in possession of her strength, and she was still strong. She came and went (as she wished). She could see well, and her teeth were strong. No sickness had touched her all the days of her life.

8 Jacob said to her, "If my days of life are close to yours and my strength remains with me as your strength has, I would be blessed, mother. You will not die. You are simply joking with me regarding your death."

9 She went in to Isaac and said to him, " I make one request of you. Make Esau swear that he will not injure Jacob, nor pursue him with intent to harm him. You know Esau's thoughts have been perverse from his youth, and there is no goodness in him. He desires to kill him after you die.

10 You know all that he has done since the day Jacob, his brother, went to Haran until this day. He has forsaken us with his whole heart, and has done evil to us. He has stolen your flocks and carried off all your possessions while you watched.

11 When we asked him and begged him for what was our own, he did as a man (stranger) who was taking pity on us (giving a token like one giving alms to a beggar).

12 He is bitter against you because you blessed Jacob, your perfect and upright son. There is no evil but only goodness in Jacob. Since he came from Haran to this day he has not robbed us of anything. He always brings us everything in its season. He rejoices and blesses us with all his heart when we take his hands. He has not parted from us since he came from Haran until this day, and he remains with us continually at home honoring us."

13 Isaac said to her, "I also know and see the deeds of Jacob who is with us, how he honors us with all his heart. Before, I loved Esau more than Jacob because he was the first-born, but now I love Jacob more than Esau, for Esau has done many evil deeds, and there is no righteousness in him. All his ways are unrighteousness and violence.

14 My heart is troubled because of all his deeds. Neither he nor his offspring will be exempt because they are those who will be destroyed from the earth and who will be rooted out from under heaven. He and his children have forsaken the God of Abraham and gone after his wives (wives' gods) and after their uncleanness and after their error.

15 You told me to make him swear that he will not kill Jacob his brother, but even if he swears, he will not abide by his oath. He will not do good but evil only.

16 If he desires to kill Jacob, his brother, then into Jacob's hands he will be given. He will not escape from Jacob's hands.

17 Do not be afraid for Jacob, for the guardian of Jacob is great, powerful, honored, and praised more than the guardian of Esau."

18 Rebecca called for Esau and he came to her, and she said to him, "I have a request of you, my son. Promise to do it, my son."

19 He said, "I will do everything that you say to me, and I will not refuse your request."

20 She said to him, "I ask you that the day I die, you will take me in and bury me near Sarah, your father's mother, and that you and Jacob will love each other and that neither will desire evil against the other, but (have)

mutual love only. Do this so you will prosper, my son, and be honored in the all of the land, and no enemy will rejoice over you. You will be a blessing and a mercy in the eyes of all those that love you."

21 He said, "I will do all that you have told me. I shall bury you on the day you die near Sarah, my father's mother, as you have desired that her bones may be near your bones.

22 Jacob, my brother, I shall love above all flesh. I have only one brother in all the earth but him. It is only what is expected of me. It is no great thing if I love him, for he is my brother, and we were sown together in your body, and together came we out from your womb. If I do not love my brother, whom shall I love?

23 I beg you to exhort Jacob concerning me and concerning my sons, for I know that he will assuredly be king over me and my sons, for on the day my father blessed him he made him the higher and me the lower.

24 I swear to you that I shall love him, and not desire evil against him all the days of my life but good only."

25 And he swore to her regarding all this matter. While Esau was there, she called Jacob and gave him her orders according to the words that she had spoken to Esau.

26 He said, "I shall do your pleasure, believe me that no evil will proceed from me or from my sons against Esau. I shall be first in nothing except in love only."

27 She and her sons ate and drank that night, and she died, three jubilees and one week and one year old on that night. Her two sons, Esau and Jacob, buried her in the double cave near Sarah, their father's mother.

[Chapter 36]

1 In the sixth year of this week Isaac called his two sons Esau and Jacob, and they came to him, and he said to them, "My sons, I am going the way of my fathers, to the eternal house where my fathers are.

2 Bury me near Abraham my father, in the double cave in the field of Ephron the Hittite, where Abraham purchased a sepulcher to bury in. Bury me in the sepulcher I dug for myself.

3 I command you, my sons, to practice righteousness and uprightness on the earth, so that the Lord may do to you what he said he would do to Abraham and to his offspring.

4 Love one another. Love your brothers as a man who loves his own soul. Let each seek how he may benefit his brother, and act together on the earth. Let them love each other as their own souls.

5 I command and warn you to reject idols. Hate them, and do not love them. They are fully deceptive to those that worship them and for those that bow down to them.

6 Remember the Lord God of Abraham, your father, and how I worshipped Him and served Him in righteousness and in joy, that God might multiply you and increase your offspring as the multitude of stars in heaven, and establish you on the earth as the plant of righteousness, which will not be rooted out to all the generations forever.

7 And now I shall make you swear a great oath, for there is no oath which is greater than that which is by the name glorious, honored, great, splendid, wonderful and mighty, which created the heavens and the earth and all things together, that you will fear Him and worship Him.

8 Each will love his brother with affection and righteousness. Neither will desire to do evil against his brother from now on forever all the days of your life so that you may prosper in all your deeds and not be destroyed.

9 If either of you plans evil against his brother, know that he that plans evil shall fall into his brother's hand, and shall be rooted out of the land of the living, and his offspring shall be destroyed from under heaven.

10 But on that day there will be turbulence, curses, wrath, anger, and will He burn his land and his city and all that is his with a devouring fire like the fire He sent to burn Sodom and he shall be blotted out of the book of the discipline of the children of men, and he will not be recorded in the book of life. He shall be added in the book of destruction. He shall depart into eternal curses. Their condemnation may be always renewed in hate and in curses and in wrath and in torment and in anger and in plagues and in disease forever.

11 My sons, this, I say and testify to you, will be the result according to the judgment which shall come on the man who wishes to injure his brother."

12 Then he divided all his possessions between the two on that day, and he gave the larger portion to him that was the first-born, and the tower and all that was around it, and all that Abraham possessed at the Well of the Oath.

13 He said, "This larger portion I will give to the first-born."

14 Esau said, "I have sold and relinquished my birthright to Jacob. Let it be given to him. I have nothing to say regarding it, for it is his."

15 Isaac said, "May a blessing rest on you, my sons, and on your offspring this day. You have given me rest, and my heart is not pained concerning the birthright, or that you should work wickedness because of it.

16 May the Most High God bless the man and his offspring forever that does righteousness."

17 He stopped commanding them and blessing them, and they ate and drank together in front of him, and he rejoiced because there was one mind between them, and they went out from him and rested that day and slept.

18 Isaac slept on his bed that day rejoicing. He slept the eternal sleep, and died one hundred and eighty years old. He lived twenty-five weeks and five years; and his two sons, Esau and Jacob, buried him.

19 After that Esau went to the land of Edom, to the mountains of Seir, and lived there.

20 Jacob lived in the mountains of Hebron, in the high place of the land in which his father Abraham had journeyed. He worshipped the Lord with all his heart. He had divided the days of his generations according to the commands he had seen.

21 Leah, his wife, died in the fourth year of the second week of the forty-fifth jubilee, and he buried her in the double cave near Rebecca his mother to the left of the grave of Sarah, his father's mother. All her sons and his sons came to mourn over Leah, his wife, with him and to comfort him regarding her. He was lamenting her for he loved her greatly after Rachel, her sister, died. She was perfect and upright in all her ways and she honored Jacob. All the days that she lived with him he did not hear from her mouth a harsh word, for she was gentle, peaceable, upright and honorable.

22 And he remembered all the deeds she had done during her life and he lamented her greatly. He loved her with all his heart and with all his soul.

[Chapter 37]

1 On the day that Isaac, the father of Jacob and Esau died, the sons of Esau heard that Isaac had given the elder's portion to his younger son, Jacob, and they were very angry.

2 They argued with their father, saying, "Why has your father given Jacob the portion of the elder and passed you over even though you are the elder and Jacob the younger?"

3 He said to them, "Because I sold my birthright to Jacob for a small portion of lentils (lentil soup), and on the day my father sent me to hunt, catch, and bring him something that he should eat and bless me, Jacob came with deceit and brought my father food and drink. My father blessed him and put me under his hand.

4 Now our father has caused Jacob and me to swear that we shall not devise evil plans against his brother (each other), and that we shall continue in love and in peace each with his brother and not make our ways corrupt."

5 They said to him, "We shall not listen to you to make peace with him. We are stronger than him and we are more powerful than he is. We shall depose him and kill him, and destroy him and his sons. If you will not go with us, we shall hurt you also.

6 Listen! Let us send to Aram, Philistia, Moab, and Ammon. Let us take chosen men who are trained in battle, and let us go against him and do battle with him. Let us exterminate him from the earth before he grows strong."

7 Their father said to them, "Do not go and do not make war with him or you shall fall before him."

8 They said to him, "This is how you have acted from your youth until this day. You have continued to put your neck under his yoke. We shall not listen to these words."

9 Then they sent to Aram, and to Aduram to the friend of their father, and they also hired one thousand chosen men of war.

10 And there came to them from Moab and from the children of Ammon, those who were hired, one thousand chosen men, and from Philistia, one thousand chosen warriors, and from Edom and from the Horites one thousand chosen warriors, and from the Kittim mighty warriors.

11 They said to their father, "Go out with them and lead them or else we shall kill you."

12 And he was filled with boiling anger on seeing that his sons were forcing him to go before them to lead them against Jacob, his brother.

13 But afterward he remembered all the evil that lay hidden in his heart against Jacob his brother, and he did not remember the oath he had sworn to his father and to his mother that he would plan no evil against Jacob, his brother, all his days.

14 Because Jacob was in mourning for his wife Leah, he did not know they were coming to battle against him until they approached the tower with four thousand soldiers and chosen warriors. The men of Hebron sent to him saying, "Look your brother has come against you to fight. He has with him four thousand men carrying swords, shields, and weapons." They told him this because they loved Jacob more than Esau.

15 So they told him, for Jacob was a more gracious and merciful man than Esau.

16 But Jacob would not believe until they came very near to the tower.

17 He closed the gates of the tower; and he stood on the battlements and spoke to his brother Esau and said, "Noble is the comfort you have come to give me concerning the death of my wife. Is this the oath that you swore to your father and again to your mother before they died? You have broken the oath, and on the moment that you swore to your father you were condemned."

18 Then Esau answered and said to him, "Neither the children of men nor the beasts of the earth have sworn an oath of righteousness and kept it forever. Every day they lay evil plans one against another regarding how they might kill their adversary or foe.

19 You will hate my children and me forever, so there is no observing the tie of brotherhood with you.

20 Hear these words that I declare to you. If the boar can change its skin and make its bristles as soft as wool, or if it can cause horns to sprout out on its head like the horns of a stag or of a sheep, then will I observe the tie of brotherhood with you. Like breasts separate themselves from their mother (and fight), you and I have never been brothers.

21 If the wolves make peace with the lambs and not devour or do them violence, and if their hearts are towards them for good, then there shall be peace in my heart towards you. If the lion becomes the friend of the ox and makes peace with him and if he is bound under one yoke with him and plows with him, then will I make peace with you.

22 When the raven becomes white as the raza (a white bird?), then know that I have loved you and shall make peace with you. You will be rooted out, and your sons shall be rooted out, and there shall be no peace for you."

23 Jacob saw that Esau had decided in his heart to do evil toward him, and that he desired with all his soul to kill him. Jacob saw that Esau had come pouncing like the wild boar which charges the spear that is set to pierce and kill it, and yet does not even slow down. Then he spoke to his own people and to his servants and told them that Esau and his men were going to attack him and all his companions.

[Chapter 38]

1 After that Judah spoke to Jacob, his father, and said to him, "Bend your bow, father, and send forth your arrows and bring down the adversary and kill the enemy. You have the power to do it. We will not kill your brother because he is your kin and he is like you, so we will honor his life."

2 Then Jacob bent his bow and sent forth the arrow and struck Esau, his brother, on the right side of his chest and killed him.

3 And again he sent forth an arrow and struck Adoran the Aramaean, on the left side of his chest, and it drove him backward and killed him. Then the sons of Jacob and their servants went out, dividing themselves into companies on the four sides of the tower.

4 Judah went out in front. Naphtali and Gad along with fifty servants went to the south side of the tower, and they killed all they found before them. Not one individual escaped.

5 Levi, Dan, and Asher went out on the east side of the tower along with fifty men, and they killed the warriors of Moab and Ammon.

6 Reuben, Issachar, and Zebulon went out on the north side of the tower along with fifty men and they killed the warriors of the Philistines.

7 Reuben's son, Simeon, Benjamin, and Enoch went out on the west side of the tower along with fifty men and they killed four hundred men, stout warriors of Edom and of the Horites. Six hundred fled, and four of the sons of Esau fled with them, and left their father lying killed, as he had fallen on the hill that is in Aduram.

8 And the sons of Jacob pursued them to the mountains of Seir. And Jacob buried his brother on the hill that is in Aduram, and he returned to his house.

9 The sons of Jacob crushed the sons of Esau in the mountains of Seir, and made them bow their necks so that they became servants of the sons of Jacob.

10 They sent a message to their father to inquire whether they should make peace with them or kill them.

11 Jacob sent word to his sons that they should make peace. They made peace with them but also placed the yoke of servitude on them, so that they paid tribute to Jacob and to his sons always.

12 And they continued to pay tribute to Jacob until the day that he went down to Egypt.

13 The sons of Edom have not escaped the yoke of servitude imposed by the twelve sons of Jacob until this day.

14 These are the kings that reigned in Edom before there was any king over the children of Israel (until this day) in the land of Edom.

15 And Balaq, the son of Beor, reigned in Edom, and the name of his city was Danaba. Balaq died, and Jobab, the son of Zara of Boser, ruled in his place.

16 Jobab died, and Asam, of the land of Teman, ruled in his place.

17 Asam died, and Adath, the son of Barad, who killed Midian in the field of Moab, ruled in his place, and the name of his city was Avith.

18 Adath died, and Salman, from Amaseqa, ruled in his place.

19 Salman died, and Saul of Ra'aboth by the river, ruled in his place. Saul died, and Ba'elunan, the son of Achbor, ruled in his place.

20 Ba'elunan, the son of Achbor died, and Adath ruled in his place, and the name of his wife was Maitabith, the daughter of Matarat, the daughter of Metabedza'ab. These are the kings who reigned in the land of Edom.

[Chapter 39]

1 Jacob lived in the land that his father journeyed in, which is the land of Canaan.

2 These are the generations of Jacob. Joseph was seventeen years old when they took him down into the land of Egypt, and Potiphar, a eunuch of Pharaoh, the chief cook, bought him.

3 He made Joseph the manager over Potiphar's entire house and the blessing of the Lord came on the house of the Egyptian because of Joseph. And the Lord caused him to prosper in all that he did.

4 The Egyptian turned everything over to the hands of Joseph because he saw that the Lord was with him, and that the Lord caused him to prosper him in all that he did.

5 Joseph's appearance was beautiful, and his master's wife watched Joseph, and she loved him and wanted him to have sex with her.

6 But he did not surrender his soul because he remembered the Lord and the words which Jacob, his father, used to read to him from the writings of Abraham, that no man should commit fornication with a woman who has a husband. For him the punishment of death has been ordained in the heavens before the Most High God, and the sin will be recorded against him in the eternal books, which are always in the presence of the Lord.

7 Joseph remembered these words and refused to have sex with her.

8 And she begged him for a year, but he refused and would not listen.

9 But while he was in the house she embraced him and held him tightly in order to force him to sleep with her. She closed the doors of the house and held on to him, but he left his garment in her hands and broke through the door and ran out from her presence.

10 The woman saw that he would not sleep with her, and she slandered him in the presence of his master, saying "Your Hebrew servant, whom you love, sought to force me to have sex with him. When I shouted for help he

fled and left his garment in my hands. I tried to stop him but he broke through the door."

11 When the Egyptian saw Joseph's garment and the broken door, and heard the words of his wife, he threw Joseph into prison and put him in the place where the prisoners of the king were kept.

12 He was there in the prison, and the Lord gave Joseph favor in the sight of the chief of the prison guards and caused him to have compassion for Joseph, because he saw that the Lord was with him, and that the Lord made all that he did to prosper.

13 He turned over all things into his hands, and the chief of the prison guards knew of nothing that was going on in the prison, because Joseph did everything for him, and the Lord perfected it. He remained there two years.

14 In those days Pharaoh, king of Egypt, was very angry at his two eunuchs, the chief butler, and the chief baker. He put them in the prison facility of the house of the chief cook, where Joseph was kept.

15 The chief of the prison guards appointed Joseph to serve them, and he served them.

16 They both dreamed a dream, the chief butler and the chief baker, and they told it to Joseph.

17 As he interpreted to them so it happened to them, and Pharaoh restored the chief butler to his office and he killed the chief baker as Joseph had interpreted to them.

18 But the chief butler forgot Joseph was in the prison, although he had informed him of what would happen to him. He did not remember to inform Pharaoh of how Joseph had told him (about his dream), because he forgot.

[Chapter 40]

1 In those days Pharaoh dreamed two dreams in one night concerning a famine that was to be in all the land, and he awoke from his sleep and called all the magicians and interpreters of dreams that were in Egypt. He told them his two dreams but they were not able to tell him what they meant.

2 Then the chief butler remembered Joseph and told the king of him, and he brought him out from the prison, and the king told his two dreams to him.

3 He said before Pharaoh that his two dreams were one, and he said to him, "Seven years shall come in which there shall be plenty in all the land of Egypt, but after that, seven years of famine. Such a famine as has not been in all the land.

4 Now, let Pharaoh appoint administrators in all the land of Egypt, and let them store up food in every city throughout all the years of plenty, and

there will be food for the seven years of famine, and those of the land will not perish through the famine, even though it will be very severe."

5 The Lord gave Joseph favor and mercy in the eyes of Pharaoh. Pharaoh said to his servants, "We shall not find such a wise and prudent man like this man, because the spirit of the Lord is with him."

6 And he appointed Joseph the second in command in his entire kingdom and gave him authority over all Egypt, and placed him on the second chariot of Pharaoh to ride.

7 And he clothed him with fine linen clothes, and he put a gold chain around his neck, and a crier proclaimed before him "El" "El wa Abirer," and he placed a ring on his hand and made him ruler over all his house, and lifted him up before the people, and said to him, "Only on the throne shall I be greater than you."

8 Joseph ruled over all the land of Egypt, and all the governors of Pharaoh, and all his servants, and all those who did the king's business loved him because he walked in uprightness, because he was without pride and arrogance. He did not judge people by their position, and did not accept gifts, but he judged all the people of the land in uprightness.

9 The land of Egypt was at peace before Pharaoh because of Joseph, because the Lord was with him, and the Lord gave him favor and mercy for all his generations before all those who knew him and those who heard of him, and Pharaoh's kingdom was run efficiently, and there was no Satan (adversary) and no evil person in it.

10 And the king called Joseph's name Sephantiphans, and gave Joseph the daughter of Potiphar, the daughter of the priest of Heliopolis, the chief cook to marry.

11 On the day that Joseph stood before Pharaoh he was thirty years old.

12 In that year Isaac died. Things transpired as Joseph had said in the interpretation of Pharaoh's dream and there were seven years of plenty over all the land of Egypt, and the land of Egypt abundantly produced, one measure producing eighteen hundred measures.

13 Joseph gathered food into every city until they were full of grain and they could no longer count or measure it because of its multitude.

[Chapter 41]

1 In the forty-fifth jubilee, in the second week, and in the second year, Judah took his first-born Er, a wife from the daughters of Aram, named Tamar.

2 But he hated her, and did not have sex with her, because her mother was of the daughters of Canaan, and he wished to take him a wife of the lineage of his mother, but Judah, his father, would not permit him to do that.

3 Er, the first-born of Judah, was wicked, and the Lord killed him.

4 And Judah said to Onan, his brother, "Go in to your brother's wife and perform the duty of a husband's brother to her, and raise up offspring to your brother."

5 Onan knew that the offspring would not be his, but his brother's only, and he went into the house of his brother's wife, and spilt his seed (ejaculates) on the ground, and he was wicked in the eyes of the Lord, and He killed him.

6 Judah said to Tamar, his daughter-in-law, "Remain in your father's house as a widow until Shelah, my son has grown up, and I shall give you to him to wife."

7 He grew up, but Bedsu'el, the wife of Judah, did not permit her son Shelah to marry. Bedsu'el, Judah's wife, died in the fifth year of this week.

8 In the sixth year Judah went up to shear his sheep at Timnah.

9 And they told Tamar, "Look, your father-in-law is going up to Timnah to shear his sheep." And she took off her widow's clothes, and put on a veil, and adorned herself, and sat in the gate connecting the road to Timnah.

10 As Judah was going along he saw her, and thought she was a prostitute, and he said to her, "Let me come in to you," and she said to him, "Come in," and he went in.

11 She said to him, "Give me my pay," and he said to her, "I have nothing with me except my ring that is on my finger, my necklace, and my staff which is in my hand."

12 She said to him, "Give them to me until you send me my pay." And he said to her, "I will send to you a kid of the goats", and he gave her his ring, necklace, and staff, and she conceived by him.

13 Judah went to his sheep, and she went to her father's house.

14 Judah sent a kid of the goats by the hand of his shepherd, an Adullamite, but he could not find her, so he asked the people of the place, saying, "Where is the prostitute who was here?"

15 They said to him, "There is no prostitute here with us." And he returned and informed Judah that he had not found her, "I asked the people of the place, and they said to me, "There is no prostitute here." "

16 He said, "If you see her give the kids to her or we become a cause of ridicule." And when she had completed three months, it was revealed that she was with child, and they told Judah, saying, "Look Tamar, your daughter-in-law, is with child by whoredom."

17 And Judah went to the house of her father, and said to her father and her brothers, "Bring her out, and let them burn her, for she has committed uncleanness in Israel."

18 It happened when they brought her out to burn her that she sent to her father-in-law the ring and the necklace, and the staff, saying, "Tell us whose are these, because by him am I with child."

19 Judah acknowledged, and said, "Tamar is more righteous than I am.

20 Do not let them burn her." For that reason she was not given to Shelah, and he did not again approach her and after that she gave birth to two sons, Perez and Zerah, in the seventh year of this second week.

21 At this time the seven years of fruitfulness were completed, of which Joseph spoke to Pharaoh.

22 Judah acknowledged the evil deed that he had done because he had sex with his daughter-in-law, and he hated himself for it.

23 He acknowledged that he had transgressed and gone astray, because he had uncovered the skirt of his son, and he began to lament and to supplicate before the Lord because of his transgression.

24 We told him in a dream that it was forgiven him because he supplicated earnestly, and lamented, and did not commit the act again.

25 And he received forgiveness because he turned from his sin and from his ignorance, because he transgressed greatly before our God. Every one that acts like this, every one who has sex with his mother-in-law, let them burn him alive with fire. Because there is uncleanness and pollution on them, let them burn them alive.

26 Command the children of Israel that there should be no uncleanness among them, because every one who has sex with his daughter-in-law or with his mother-in-law has committed

uncleanness. Let them burn the man who has had sex with her with fire, and likewise burn the woman, so that God will turn away wrath and punishment from Israel.

27 We told Judah that his two sons had not had sex with her, and for this reason his offspring was established for a second generation, and would not be rooted out.

28 For in single-mindedness he had gone and sought for punishment, namely, according to the judgment of Abraham, which he had commanded his sons. Judah had sought to burn her alive.

[Chapter 42]

1 In the first year of the third week of the forty-fifth jubilee the famine began to come into the land, and the rain refused to be given to the earth. None whatsoever fell.

2 The earth became barren, but in the land of Egypt there was food, because Joseph had gathered the seed of the land in the seven years of plenty and had preserved it.

3 The Egyptians came to Joseph that he might give them food, and he opened the storehouses where the grain of the first year was stored, and he sold it to the people of the land for gold.

4 Jacob heard there was food in Egypt, and he sent his ten sons that they should procure food for him in Egypt, and they arrived among those that went there, but Benjamin he did not send.

5 Joseph recognized them, but they did not recognize him. He spoke to them and questioned them, and he said to them, "Are you not spies and have you not come to explore ways to enter this land?"

6 And he put them in custody.

7 After that, he set them free again, and detained Simeon alone and sent his nine brothers away.

8 He filled their sacks with corn, and he put their gold back in their sacks, and they did not know it. Joseph then commanded them to bring their younger brother, because they had told him their father was living and also their younger brother.

9 They went up from the land of Egypt and they came to the land of Canaan. There they told their father all that had happened to them, and how the ruler of the country had spoken rudely to them, and had seized Simeon until they should bring Benjamin.

10 Jacob said, "You have taken my children from me! Joseph is gone and Simeon also is gone, and now you will take Benjamin away. I am the victim of your wickedness."

11 He said, "My son will not go down with you because fate may have it that he would fall sick. Their mother gave birth to two sons, and one has died, and this one also you will take from me. If, by fate, he took a fever on the road, you would turn my old age to sorrow and death."

12 He saw that every man's money had been returned to him in his sack, and for this reason he feared to send him.

13 The famine increased and became grievous in the land of Canaan, and in all lands except in the land of Egypt. Egypt had food because many of the children of the Egyptians had stored up their seed for food from the time when they saw Joseph gathering seed together and putting it in storehouses and preserving it for the years of famine.

14 The people of Egypt fed themselves on it during the first year of their famine but when Israel saw that the famine was very serious in the land, and that there was no deliverance, he said to his sons, "Go again, and procure food for us so that we will not die."

15 They said, "We shall not go unless our youngest brother go with us!"

16 Israel saw that if he did not send Benjamin with them, they would all perish because of the famine.

17 Reuben said, "Give him to me, and if I do not bring him back to you, kill my two sons in payment for his soul." Israel said to Reuben, "He shall not go with you."

18 Judah came near and said, "Send him with me, and if I do not bring him back to you, let me bear your blame all the days of my life."

19 He sent him with them in the second year of this week on the first day of the month.

20 They all came to the land of Egypt, and they had presents in their hands of sweet spice, almonds, turpentine nuts, and pure honey.

21 And they went and stood before Joseph, and he saw Benjamin his brother, and he knew him, and said to them, "Is this your youngest brother?" They said to him, "It is he."

22 He said, "The Lord be gracious to you, my son!" And he sent Benjamin into his house and he brought out Simeon to them. Joseph made a feast for them, and they presented to him the gifts that they had brought in their hands.

23 They ate before Joseph and he gave them all a portion of food, but the portion of food given to Benjamin was seven times larger than any of theirs.

24 And they ate and drank and got up and remained with their donkeys.

25 Joseph devised a plan whereby he might learn their thoughts as to whether they desired peace or not. He said to the steward who was over his house, "Fill all their sacks with food. Place their money back in their vessels. Put my cup, the silver cup out of which I drink, in the sack of the youngest and send them away."

[Chapter 43]

1 He did as Joseph had told him, and filled all their sacks with food for them and put their money back into their sacks, and put the cup in Benjamin's sack.

2 Early in the morning they departed, and it happened that when they had gone from that place, Joseph said to the steward of his house, "Pursue them, run and seize them, and say, 'You have repaid my kindness with evil. You have stolen from me the silver cup out of which my lord drinks.'

3 Bring me back their youngest brother. Go! Get him quickly before I go to my seat of judgment (judge you guilt of disobeying an order). "

4 He ran after them and said the words as he was told. They said to him, "God forbid that your servants should do this thing, and steal any utensil or money from the house of your lord, like the things we found in our sacks the first time we, your servants, came back from the land of Canaan.

5 We have not stolen any utensil. How could we? Look here in our sacks and search, and wherever you find the cup in the sack of any man among us, let him be killed, and we and our donkeys will serve your lord."

6 He said to them, "Not so. If I find it, the man whose sack I find it in I shall take as a servant, and the rest of you shall return in peace to your house."

7 He was searching in their vessels, beginning with the eldest and ending with the youngest, when it was found in Benjamin's sack.

8 They ripped their garments in frustration, and placed their belongings back on their donkeys, and returned to the city and came to the house of Joseph. They all bowed themselves with their faces to the ground in front of him.

9 Joseph said to them, "You have done evil." They said, "What shall we say and how shall we defend ourselves? Our lord has discovered the transgression of his servants; and now we and our donkeys are the servants of our lord."

10 Joseph said to them, "I too fear the Lord. As for you, go to your homes and let your brother be my servant, because you have done evil. I delight in this cup as no one else delights in his cup and yet you have stolen it from me."

11 Judah said, "O my lord, I pray you to let your servant speak a word in my lord's ear. Your servant's mother had two sons for our father. One went away and was lost, and has not been found since. This one alone is left of his mother, and your servant our father loves him. He would die if the lad were lost to him.

12 When we go to your servant our father, and the lad is not with us, it will happen that he will die. We will have brought so much sorrow on our father it will bring his death.

13 Now rather let me, your servant, stay here as a bondsman to my lord instead of the boy. Let the lad go with his brothers, because I will stand in for him at the hand of your servant our father. If I do not bring him back, your servant will bear the blame of our father forever."

14 Joseph saw that they were all in accord in doing good to one another. Then, he could not refrain himself, and he told them that he was Joseph.

15 And he conversed with them in the Hebrew tongue and hugged their necks and wept.

16 At first they did not recognize him and then they began to weep. He said to them, "Do not weep for me, but hurry and bring my father to me. See, it is my mouth that speaks and the eyes of my brother Benjamin see me.

17 Pay attention. This is the second year of the famine, and there are still five years to come without harvest or fruit of trees or plowing.

18 You and your households come down quickly, so that you won't die because of the famine. Do not be grieved for your possessions, because the Lord sent me before you to set things in order that many people might live.

19 Tell my father that I am still alive. You see that the Lord has made me as a father to Pharaoh, and ruler over his house and over all the land of Egypt.

20 Tell my father of all my glory, and all the riches and glory that the Lord has given me."

21 By the command of Pharaoh's mouth, he gave them chariots and provisions for the way, and he gave them all multi-colored raiment and silver.

22 He sent corn, raiment, silver, and ten donkeys that carried all of this to his father, and he sent them away.

23 They went up and told their father that Joseph was alive, and was measuring out corn to all the nations of the earth, and that he was ruler over all the land of Egypt.

24 But their father did not believe it, because he was not in his right mind. But when he saw the wagons, which Joseph had sent, the life of his spirit revived, and he said, "It is enough for me if Joseph lives. I will go down and see him before I die."

[Chapter 44]

1 Israel took his journey from Haran's house on the new moon of the third month, and he stopped at the Well of the Oath on the way and he offered a sacrifice to the God of his father Isaac on the seventh of this month.

2 Jacob remembered the dream that he had at Bethel, and he feared to go down into Egypt.

3 He was thinking of sending word to Joseph to come to him because he did not want to go down. He remained there seven days, hoping fate would permit him to see a vision as to whether he should remain or go down.

4 He celebrated the harvest festival of the first-fruits with old grain, because in all the land of Canaan there was not a handful of seed in the ground because the famine was affecting all the beasts, and cattle, and birds, and all men.

5 On the sixteenth the Lord appeared to him, and said to him, "Jacob, Jacob," and he said, "Here I am."

6 And He said to him, "I am the God of your fathers, the God of Abraham and Isaac. Do not be afraid to go down into Egypt, because I will be there to make you a great nation. I will go down with you, and I will bring you up again. You will be buried in this land and Joseph will put his hands on your eyes (to close them in death). Do not be afraid. Go down into Egypt."

7 And his sons got up and placed their father and their possessions on wagons.

8 Israel got up from the Well of the Oath on the sixteenth of this third month, and he went to the land of Egypt.

9 Israel sent Judah before him to his son Joseph to examine the Land of Goshen, because Joseph had told his brothers that they should come and live there so they could be near him.

10 This was the best land in Egypt. It was near to him and suitable for all of the cattle they had.

11 These are the names of the sons of Jacob who went into Egypt with Jacob their father; Reuben, the First-born of Israel and his sons Enoch, and Pallu, and Hezron and Carmi, making five.

12 Simeon and his sons Jemuel, and Jamin, and Ohad, and Jachin, and Zohar, and Shaul, the son of the Zephathite woman, making seven.

13 Levi and his sons Gershon, and Kohath, and Merari, making four.

14 Judah and his sons Shela, and Perez, and Zerah, making four.

15 Issachar and his sons Tola, and Phua, and Jasub, and Shimron, making five.

16 Zebulon and his sons Sered, and Elon, and Jahleel, making four.

17 These are the sons of Jacob and their sons whom Leah bore to Jacob in Mesopotamia, six, and their one sister, Dinah and all the souls of the sons of Leah, and their sons, who went with Jacob their father into Egypt. Twenty-nine souls, and Jacob, making thirty, were the number of people that went into Egypt.

18 And the sons of Zilpah, Leah's handmaid, the wife of Jacob, who bore to Jacob Gad and Ashur and their sons who went with him into Egypt.

19 The sons of Gad are Ziphion, and Haggi, and Shuni, and Ezbon, and Eri, and Areli, and Arodi, which make eight souls in total. The sons of Asher are Imnah, and Ishvah, and Ishvi, and Beriah, and Serah, and their one sister, which makes six in total.

20 All the souls were fourteen, and all those of Leah were forty-four.

21 The sons of Rachel, the wife of Jacob are Joseph and Benjamin.

22 There were born to Joseph in Egypt before his father came into Egypt, those whom Asenath, daughter of Potiphar, priest of Heliopolis gave birth to him, Manasseh, and Ephraim. The wife and children of Joseph totaled three.

23 The sons of Benjamin, Bela and Becher and Ashbel, Gera, and Naaman, and Ehi, and Rosh, and Muppim, and Huppim, and Ard with Benjamin totaled eleven.

24 And all the souls of Rachel were fourteen.

25 And the sons of Bilhah, the handmaid of Rachel, the wife of Jacob, whom she gave birth to Jacob, were Dan and Naphtali. These are the names of their sons who went with them into Egypt.

26 The sons of Dan were Hushim, and Samon, and Asudi. and "Ijaka, and Salomon, all totaling six.

27 All but one died the year in which they entered into Egypt, and there was left to Dan only Hushim.

28 These are the names of the sons of Naphtali: Jahziel, and Guni and Jezer, and Shallum, and 'Iv.

29 And 'Iv, who was born after the years of famine, died in Egypt.

30 All the souls (offspring) of Rachel were twenty-six.

31 All the souls (offspring) of Jacob, which went into Egypt, were seventy souls.

32 These are his children and his children's children, in all seventy, but five died in Egypt in the time of Joseph's rule and they had no children.

33 In the land of Canaan two sons of Judah died, Er and Onan, and they had no children, and the children of Israel buried those who died, and they were counted among the seventy Gentile nations.

[Chapter 45]

1 On the new moon of the fourth month, in the second year of the third week of the forty-fifth jubilee, Israel went into the country of Egypt, to the land of Goshen.

2 Joseph went to meet his father, Jacob, in the land of Goshen, and he hugged his father's neck and wept.

3 Israel said to Joseph, "Now that I have seen you let me die and may the Lord God of Israel, the God of Abraham, and the God of Isaac, who has not withheld His mercy and His grace from His servant Jacob, be blessed.

4 It is enough for me to have seen your face while I am yet alive. Yes, this is the true vision which I saw at Bethel.

5 Blessed be the Lord my God forever and ever, and blessed be His name."

6 Joseph and his brothers ate bread in the presence of their father and drank wine, and Jacob rejoiced with very great joy because he saw Joseph eating with his brothers and drinking in the presence of him, and he blessed the Creator of all things who had preserved him, and had preserved for him his twelve sons.

7 Joseph had given his father and his brothers as a gift the right of dwelling in the land of Goshen and in Rameses and the entire region around it, which he ruled over in the presence of Pharaoh.

8 Israel and his sons dwelt in the land of Goshen, the best part of the land of Egypt, and Israel was one hundred and thirty years old when he came into Egypt. Joseph nourished his father and his brothers and also their possessions (servants) with bread as much as they needed for the seven years of the famine.

9 The land of Egypt became available for purchase because of the famine, and Joseph acquired all the land of Egypt for Pharaoh in return for food, and he got possession of the people and their cattle and everything for Pharaoh.

10 The years of the famine were completed, and Joseph gave the people in the land seed and food that they might sow the land in the eighth year, because the river had overflowed all the land of Egypt.

11 For in the seven years of the famine it had not overflowed and had irrigated only a few places on the banks of the river, but now it overflowed and the Egyptians sowed the land, and it produced much corn that year.

12 This was the first year of the fourth week of the forty-fifth jubilee. Joseph took one-fifth of the corn of the harvest for the king and left four parts for them for food and for seed, and Joseph made it a law for Egypt until this day.

13 Israel lived in the land of Egypt seventeen years, and all the days which he lived were three jubilees, one hundred and forty-seven years, and he died in the fourth year of the fifth week of the forty-fifth jubilee.

14 Israel blessed his sons before he died and told them everything that they would go through in the land of Egypt. He revealed to them what they would live through in the last days, and he blessed them and gave Joseph two portions of the land.

15 He slept with his fathers, and he was buried in the double cave in the land of Canaan, near Abraham his father, in the grave which he dug for himself in the land of Hebron.

16 And he gave all his books and the books of his fathers to Levi, his son so that he might preserve them and replicate them for his children until this day.

[Chapter 46]

1 It happened that after the death of Jacob the children of Israel continued to multiply in the land of Egypt, and they became a great nation, and they were in one accord of heart, so that brother loved brother and every man helped his brother. They increased abundantly and multiplied greatly, ten weeks of years, all the days of the life of Joseph.

2 There was neither Satan nor any evil in all the days of the life of Joseph after his father, Jacob (had died), because all the Egyptians respected the children of Israel all the days of the life of Joseph.

3 Joseph died, being a hundred and ten years old. He lived seventeen years in the land of Canaan, and ten years he was a servant, and three years in prison, and eighty years he was under the king, ruling all the land of Egypt.

4 He died and so did all his brothers and all of that generation. But, he commanded the children of Israel before he died that they should carry his bones with them when they went out from the land of Egypt.

5 And he made them swear regarding his bones, because he knew that the Egyptians would not bring his bones out of Egypt or bury him in the land of

Canaan, because while dwelling in the land of Assyria, king Makamaron, the king of Canaan, fought against Egypt in the valley and killed the king of Egypt there, and pursued the Egyptians to the gates of "Ermon.

6 But he was not able to enter, because another king, a new king, had become king of Egypt, and he was stronger than he (Makamaron), and he returned to the land of Canaan, and the gates of Egypt were closed so that none came or went from Egypt.

7 Joseph died in the forty-sixth jubilee, in the sixth week, in the second year, and they buried him in the land of Egypt, and all his brothers died after him.

8 The king of Egypt went to war against the king of Canaan in the forty-seventh jubilee, in the second week in the second year, and the children of Israel brought out all the bones of the children of Jacob except the bones of Joseph, and they buried them in the field in the double cave in the mountain.

9 Then, most of them returned to Egypt, but a few of them remained in the mountains of Hebron, and Amram your father remained with them.

10 The king of Canaan was victorious over the king of Egypt, and he closed the gates of Egypt.

11 He devised an evil plan against the children of Israel to afflict them. He said to the people of Egypt, "Look, the people of the children of Israel have increased and multiplied more than we.

12 Let us use wisdom and deal with them before they become too many. Let us make them our slaves before we go to war and they rise up against us on the side of our enemies. Before they leave and fight against us let us do this because their hearts and faces (allegiances) are towards the land of Canaan."

13 He set over them taskmasters to enforce slavery, and they built strong cities for Pharaoh, Pithom, and Raamses and they built all the walls and all the fortifications, which had fallen in the cities of Egypt.

14 They enslaved them with harshness, and the more they were evil toward them, the more they increased and multiplied.

15 And the people of Egypt despised the children of Israel.

[Chapter 47]

1 In the seventh week, in the seventh year, in the forty-seventh jubilee, your father went out from the land of Canaan, and you (Moses) were born in the fourth week, in the sixth year of it, in the forty-eighth jubilee; this was the time of tribulation for the children of Israel.

2 Pharaoh, the king of Egypt, issued a command ordering them to throw all their newborn male children into the river.

3 And they threw them into the river for seven months until the day that you were born. It is said that your mother hid you for three months.

4 She made an ark for you, and covered it with pitch and tar, and placed it in the reeds on the bank of the river. She placed you in it seven days. Your mother came by night and nursed you. By day Miriam, your sister, guarded you from the birds.

5 In those days Tharmuth, the daughter of Pharaoh, came to bathe in the river, and she heard you crying. She told her maids to bring you out, and they brought you to her.

6 She took you out of the ark, and she had compassion on you.

7 Your sister said to her, "Shall I go and call to you one of the Hebrew women to nurse this baby for you?" And she said to her, "Go."

8 Your sister went and called your mother, Jochebed, and Pharaoh's daughter gave her wages (employed her), and she nursed you.

9 Afterwards, when you grew up, they brought you to the daughter of Pharaoh, and you became her son. Amram, your father, taught you writing. After you had completed three weeks (twenty-seven years) they brought you into the royal court.

10 You were three weeks of years at court until the time when you went out from the royal court and saw an Egyptian beating your friend who was of the children of Israel, and you killed him and hid him in the sand.

11 On the second day you came across two children of Israel quarreling together, and you asked the one who was doing wrong, "Why did you hit your brother?"

12 He was angry and indignant, and said, "Who made you a prince and a judge over us?

13 Do you want to kill me like you killed the Egyptian yesterday?" You were afraid and you fled on because of these words.

[Chapter 48]

1 In the sixth year of the third week of the forty-ninth jubilee you fled and went to live in the land of Midian for five weeks and one year. You returned to Egypt in the second week in the second year in the fiftieth jubilee.

2 You know what He said to you on Mount Sinai, and what prince Mastema desired to do with you when you returned to Egypt.

3 Did he (Mastema) not seek to kill you with all his power and to deliver the Egyptians from your hand when he saw that you were sent to execute judgment and to take revenge on the Egyptians?

4 But I delivered you out of his hand, and you performed the signs and wonders which you were sent to perform in Egypt against Pharaoh, and against all of his household, and against his servants and his people.

5 The Lord exacted a great vengeance on them for Israel's sake, and struck them through the plagues of blood, frogs, lice, dog-flies, malignant boils, breaking out in pustules, the death of their cattle, and the plague of hailstones. He destroyed everything that grew from them by plagues of locusts, which devoured the remainder left by the hail, and by darkness, and by the death of the first-born of men and animals. The Lord took vengeance on all of their idols and burned them with fire.

6 Everything was sent through your hand, that you should declare these things before they were done. You spoke with the king of Egypt in the presence of all his servants and in the presence of his people and everything took place according to your words. Ten great and terrible judgments came on the land of Egypt so that you might execute vengeance on Egypt for Israel.

7 And the Lord did everything for Israel's sake according to His covenant, which he had ordained with Abraham. He took vengeance on them because they had brought them by force into bondage.

8 Prince Mastema stood against you, and sought to deliver you into the hands of Pharaoh. He helped the Egyptian sorcerers when they stood up and committed the evil acts they did in your presence. Indeed, we permitted them to work, but the remedies we did not allow to be worked by their hands.

9 The Lord struck them with malignant ulcers (hemorrhoids?), and they were not able to stand. They could not perform a single sign because we destroyed them.

10 Even after all of these signs and wonders, prince Mastema was not put to shame because he took courage and cried to the Egyptians to pursue you with all the power the Egyptians had, with their chariots, and with their horses, and with all the hosts of the peoples of Egypt.

11 But I stood between the Egyptians and Israel, and we delivered Israel out of his hand, and out of the hand of his people. The Lord brought them through the middle of the sea as if it were dry land.

12 The Lord our God threw all the people whom he (Mastema) brought to pursue Israel into the middle of the sea, into the depths of the bottomless pit, beneath the children of Israel, even as the people of Egypt had thrown their (Israel's) children into the river. He took vengeance on one million of them. In addition to one thousand strong and energetic men were destroyed

because of the death of the suckling children of your people, which they had thrown into the river.

13 On the fourteenth day and on the fifteenth and on the sixteenth and on the seventeenth and on the eighteenth days, prince Mastema was bound and imprisoned and placed behind the children of Israel so that he might not accuse them.

14 On the nineteenth day we let them (Mastema and his demons) loose so that they might help the Egyptians pursue the children of Israel.

15 He hardened their hearts and made them stubborn, and the plan was devised by the Lord our God that He might strike the Egyptians and throw them into the sea.

16 On the fourteenth day we bound him that he might not accuse the children of Israel on the day when they asked the Egyptians for vessels and garments, vessels of silver, and vessels of gold, and vessels of bronze, in order to exact from the Egyptians a price in return for the bondage they had been forced to serve.

17 We did not lead the children of Israel from Egypt empty handed.

[Chapter 49]

1 Remember the commandment which the Lord commanded you concerning the Passover. You should celebrate it in its season on the fourteenth day of the first month. You should kill the sacrifice before evening. They should eat it by night on the evening of the fifteenth from the time of the setting of the sun.

2 Because on this night, at the beginning of the festival and the beginning of the joy, you were eating the Passover (lamb) in Egypt, when all the powers of Mastema had been let loose to kill all the first-born in the land of Egypt, from the first-born of Pharaoh to the first-born of the captive maid-servant in the mill, and even the first-born of the cattle.

3 This is the sign that the Lord gave them, in every house on the door post on which they saw the blood of a lamb of the first year they should not enter to kill, but should pass by it, that all those should be exempt that were in the house because the sign of the blood was on its door posts.

4 And the powers of the Lord did everything as the Lord commanded them, and they passed by all the children of Israel, and the plague did not come on them to destroy them, cattle, man, or dog.

5 The plague was oppressive in Egypt, and there was no house in Egypt where there was not one dead, and weeping, and lamentation.

6 All Israel was eating the flesh of the paschal lamb, and drinking the wine, and was praising, and blessing, and giving thanks to the Lord God of their

fathers, and they were ready to get out from under the yoke of Egypt and the evil bondage.

7 Remember this day all the days of your life. Observe it from year to year all the days of your life, once a year, on its day, according to all the law of it. Do not forsake it from day to day, or from month to month.

8 It is an eternal law, and engraved on the heavenly tablets regarding all the children of Israel that they should observe it on its day once a year, every year, throughout all their generations. There is no limit of days, for this is a law forever.

9 The man who is free from uncleanness, and does not come to observe Passover on the occasion of its day and does not bring an acceptable offering before the Lord to eat and to drink before the Lord on the day of its festival will be guilty. If he is clean and close at hand (near the temple) and does not come, he shall be cut off because he did not offer the offering of the Lord in its appointed season. He shall take the guilt on himself.

10 Let the children of Israel come and observe the passover on the day of its fixed time, on the fourteenth day of the first month, between the evenings, from the third part of the day to the third part of the night, for two portions of the day are given to the light, and a third part to the evening.

11 The Lord commanded you to observe it between the evenings.

12 And it is not permissible to kill the sacrifice during any period of light, but only during the period bordering on the evening, and let them eat it at the time of the evening, until the third part of the night. Whatever is left over of all its flesh from the third part of the night and onwards is to be burned with fire.

13 They shall not cook it with water (boil or seethe it), nor shall they eat it raw, but roast it on the fire. They shall eat it with care, making sure its head with the inwards and its feet are roasted with fire, and they shall not break any bone of it, for of the children of Israel no bone shall be crushed.

14 For this reason the Lord commanded the children of Israel to observe the passover on the day of its fixed time, and they shall not break a bone of it, because it is a festival day He commanded. There was no passing over from any other day or any other month, but on the exact day let the festival be observed.

15 Command the children of Israel to observe the passover throughout their days, every year, once a year on the day of its fixed time, and it shall be a memorial well pleasing in the presence of the Lord, and no plague shall come on them to kill or to strike in that year in which they celebrate the passover in its season in every respect according to His command.

16 And they shall not eat it outside the sanctuary of the Lord, but before the sanctuary of the Lord, and all the people of the congregation of Israel shall celebrate it in its appointed season.

17 Every man twenty years of age and upward, who has come on the day of the Passover shall eat it in the sanctuary of your God before the Lord. This is how it is written and ordained. They should eat it in the sanctuary of the Lord.

18 When the children of Israel come into the land of Canaan that they are to possess, set up the tabernacle (tent) of the Lord within the land occupied by one of their tribes until the sanctuary of the Lord has been built in the land. There, let them come and celebrate the passover at tabernacle of the Lord, and let them kill it before the Lord from year to year.

19 When the house of the Lord has been built in the land of their inheritance, they shall go there and kill the Passover (lamb) in the evening, at sunset, at the third part of the day.

20 They shall offer its blood on the threshold of the altar, and shall place its fat on the fire, which is on the altar, and they shall eat its flesh roasted with fire in the yard of the house, which has been sanctified in the name of the Lord.

21 They may not celebrate the passover in their cities, nor in any place except at the tabernacle of the Lord, or before His house where His name has dwelt. They shall not stray from the Lord.

22 Moses, command the children of Israel to observe the ordinances of the passover, as it was commanded to you. Declare to them every year the purpose and time of the festival of unleavened bread. They should eat unleavened bread seven days. They should observe its festival and bring an offering every day during those seven days of joy before the Lord on the altar of your God.

23 Celebrate this festival with haste as when you went out from Egypt and you entered into the wilderness of Shur, because on the shore of the sea you completed it (the exodus).

[Chapter 50]

1 I made this law known to you the days of the Sabbaths in the desert of Sinai, between Elim and Sinai.

2 I told you of the Sabbaths of the land on Mount Sinai, and I told you of the jubilee years in the sabbaths of years, but have I not told you the year of it until you enter the land which you are to possess.

3 Keep the sabbaths of the land while they live on it, and they shall know the jubilee year.

4 I have ordained for you the year of weeks and the years and the jubilees. There are forty-nine jubilees from the days of Adam until this day, and one week and two years, and there are forty years yet to come for learning the

commandments of the Lord, until they pass over into the land of Canaan, crossing the Jordan to the west.

5 The jubilees shall pass by until Israel is cleansed from all guilt of fornication, and uncleanness, and pollution, and sin, and error, and it dwells with confidence in all the land. There shall be no more Satan or any evil one, and the land shall be clean from that time forever.

6 I have written down the commandment for them regarding the Sabbaths and all the judgments of its laws for you.

7 Six days will you labor, but the seventh day is the Sabbath of the Lord your God.

8 You shall do no manner of work in it, you and your sons, and your menservants and your maidservants, and all your cattle and travelers also who lodge with you. The man that does any work on it shall die. Whoever desecrates that day, whoever has sex with his wife, whoever says he will do something on it, or he that will set out on a journey on it in regard to any buying or selling, or whoever draws water on it which he had not prepared for himself on the sixth day, and whoever takes up any burden to carry it out of his tent or out of his house shall die.

9 You shall do no work whatsoever on the Sabbath day except what you have prepared for yourselves on the sixth day, so as to eat, and drink, and rest. Keep Sabbath free from all work on that day. It is to bless the Lord your God, who has given you a day of festival and a holy day, and a day of the holy kingdom. This is a day for Israel among all their days forever.

10 Great is the honor which the Lord has given to Israel that they should eat, drink, and be satisfied on this festival day. Rest on it from all labor, which belongs to the labor of the children of men, except burning frankincense and bringing offerings and sacrifices before the Lord for days and for Sabbaths.

11 Only this work shall be done on the Sabbath days in the sanctuary of the Lord your God so that they may atone for Israel with sacrifice continually from day to day for a memorial pleasing before the Lord, so that He may always receive them from day to day according to what you have been commanded.

12 Every man who does any work on it, or takes a trip, or tills his farm, whether in his house or any other place, and whoever lights a fire, or rides a beast, or travels by ship on the sea shall die. And whoever strikes or kills anything, or slaughters a beast or a bird, or whoever catches an animal or a bird or a fish, or whoever fasts or makes war on the Sabbaths, the man who does any of these things on the Sabbath shall die. This is done so that the children of Israel will observe the Sabbaths according to the commandments regarding the Sabbaths of the land. It is written in the tablets, which He gave into my hands that I should write out for you the laws of the seasons, and the seasons according to the division of their days.

This completes the account of the division of the days.

CLEMENT OF ROME

First Epistle

THE FIRST EPISTLE OF CLEMENT TO THE CORINTHIANS

1Clem prologue:1

The Church of God which sojourns in Rome to the Church of God which sojourns in Corinth, to them which are called and sanctified by the will of God through our Lord Jesus Christ. Grace to you and peace from Almighty God through Jesus Christ be multiplied.

1Clem 1:1

By reason of the sudden and repeated calamities and reverses which are befalling us, brethren, we consider that we have been somewhat tardy in giving heed to the matters of dispute that have arisen among you, dearly beloved, and to the detestable and unholy sedition, so alien and strange to the elect of God, which a few headstrong and self-willed persons have kindled to such a pitch of madness that your name, once revered and renowned and lovely in the sight of all men, has been greatly reviled.

1Clem 1:2

For who that had sojourned among you did not approve your most virtuous and steadfast faith? Who did not admire your sober and forbearing piety in Christ? Who did not publish abroad your magnificent disposition of hospitality? Who did not congratulate you on your perfect and sound knowledge?

1Clem 1:3

For you did all things without respect of persons, and you walked after the ordinances of God, submitting yourselves to your rulers and rendering to the older men among you the honor which is their due.

On the young too you enjoined modest and seemly thoughts: and the women you charged to perform all their duties in a blameless and seemly and pure conscience, cherishing their own husbands, as is meet; and you taught them to keep in the rule of obedience, and to manage the affairs of their household in seemliness, with all discretion.

1Clem 2:1

And you were all lowly in mind and free from arrogance, yielding rather than claiming submission, more glad to give than to receive, and content with the provisions which God supplies. And giving heed unto His words, you laid them up diligently in your hearts, and His sufferings were before your eyes.

1Clem 2:2

Thus a profound and rich peace was given to all, and an insatiable desire of doing good. An abundant outpouring also of the Holy Spirit fell upon all;

1Clem 2:3

and, being full of holy counsel, in excellent zeal and with a pious confidence you stretched out your hands to Almighty God, supplicating Him to be propitious, if unwillingly you had committed any sin.

1Clem 2:4

you had conflict day and night for all the brotherhood, that the number of His elect might be saved with fearfulness and intentness of mind.

1Clem 2:5

You were sincere and simple and free from malice one towards another.

1Clem 2:6

Every sedition and every schism was abominable to you. you mourned over the transgressions of your neighbors: you judged their shortcomings to be your own.

1Clem 2:7

you repented not of any well-doing, but were ready unto every good work.

1Clem 2:8

Being adorned with a most virtuous and honorable life, you performed all your duties in the fear of Him. The commandments and the ordinances of the Lord were written on the tablets of your hearts.

1Clem 3:1

All glory and enlargement was given unto you, and that was fulfilled which is written My beloved ate and drank and was enlarged and waxed fat and kicked.

1Clem 3:2

Hence come jealousy and envy, strife and sedition, persecution and tumult, war and captivity.

1Clem 3:3

So men were stirred up, the mean against the honorable, the ill reputed against the highly reputed, the foolish against the wise, the young against the elder.

1Clem 3:4

For this cause righteousness and peace stand aloof, while each man has forsaken the fear of the Lord and become purblind in the faith of Him, neither walketh in the ordinances of His commandments nor liveth according to that which becometh Christ, but each goeth after the lusts of his evil heart, seeing that they have conceived an unrighteous and ungodly jealousy, through which also death entered into the world.

1Clem 4:1

For so it is written, And it came to pass after certain days that Cain brought of the fruits of the earth a sacrifice unto God, and Abel he also brought of the firstlings of the sheep and of their fatness.

1Clem 4:2

And God looked upon Abel and upon his gifts, but unto Cain and unto his sacrifices He gave no heed.

1Clem 4:3

And Cain was very sorrowful, and his countenance fell.

1Clem 4:4

And God said unto Cain, Wherefore art you very sorrowful and wherefore did thy countenance fall? If you hast offered aright and hast not divided aright, didst you not sin? Hold thy peace.

1Clem 4:5
Unto you shall he turn, and you shall rule over him. {This last
phrase has also been translated: Be at peace: your offering
returns to thyself, and you shall again possess it.}

1Clem 4:6
And Cain said unto Abel his brother, Let us go over unto the plain.
And it came to pass, while they Were in the plain, that Cain rose up
against Abel his brother and slew him.

1Clem 4:7
you see, brethren, jealousy and envy wrought a brother's murder.

1Clem 4:8
By reason of jealousy our father Jacob ran away from the face of Esau
his brother.

1Clem 4:And jealousy caused Joseph to be persecuted even unto death, and
to come
even unto bondage.

1Clem 4:10
Jealousy compelled Moses to flee from the face of Pharaoh king of
Egypt while it was said to him by his own countryman, Who made you
a judge or a decider over us, Would you slay me, even as
yesterday you murdered the Egyptian?
1Clem 4:11
By reason of jealousy Aaron and Miriam were lodged outside the camp.

1Clem 4:12
Jealousy brought Dathan and Abiram down alive to hades, because they
made sedition against Moses the servant of God.

1Clem 4:13
By reason of jealousy David was envied not only by the Philistines,
but was persecuted also by Saul [king of Israel].

1Clem 5:1
But, to pass from the examples of ancient days, let us come to those
champions who lived nearest to our time. Let us set before us the
noble examples which belong to our generation.

1Clem 5:2
By reason of jealousy and envy the greatest and most righteous

pillars of the Church were persecuted, and contended even unto death.

1Clem 5:3
Let us set before our eyes the good Apostles.

1Clem 5:4
There was Peter who by reason of unrighteous jealousy endured not one not one but many labors, and thus having borne his testimony went to his appointed place of glory.

1Clem 5:5
By reason of jealousy and strife Paul by his example pointed out the prize of patient endurance. After that he had been seven times in bonds, had been driven into exile, had been stoned, had preached in the East and in the West, he won the noble renown which was the reward of his faith,

1Clem 5:6
having taught righteousness unto the whole world and having reached the farthest bounds of the West; and when he had borne his testimony before the rulers, so he departed from the world and went unto the holy place, having been found a notable pattern of patient endurance.

1Clem 6:1
   Unto these men of holy lives was gathered a vast multitude of the elect, who through many indignities and tortures, being the victims of jealousy, set a brave example among ourselves.

1Clem 6:2
By reason of jealousy women being persecuted, after that they had suffered cruel and unholy insults as Danaids and Dircae, safely reached the goal in the race of faith, and received a noble reward, feeble though they were in body.

1Clem 6:3
Jealousy has estranged wives from their husbands and changed the saying of our father Adam, This now is bone of my bones and flesh of my flesh.

1Clem 6:4
Jealousy and strife have overthrown great cities and uprooted great nations.

1Clem 7:1

These things, dearly beloved, we write, not only as admonishing you, but also as putting ourselves in remembrance. For we are in the same lists, and the same contest awaits us.

1Clem 7:2

Wherefore let us forsake idle and vain thoughts; and let us conform to the glorious and venerable rule which has been handed down to us;

1Clem 7:3

and let us see what is good and what is pleasant and what is acceptable in the sight of Him that made us.

1Clem 7:4

Let us fix our eyes on the blood of Christ and understand how precious it is unto His Father, because being shed for our salvation it won for the whole world the grace of repentance.

1Clem 7:5

Let us review all the generations in turn, and learn how from generation to generation the Master has given a place for repentance unto them that desire to turn to Him.

1Clem 7:6

Noah preached repentance, and they that obeyed were saved.

1Clem 7:7

Jonah preached destruction unto the men of Nineveh; but they, repenting of their sins, obtained pardon of God by their supplications and received salvation, albeit they were aliens from God.

1Clem 8:1

The ministers of the grace of God through the Holy Spirit spoke concerning repentance.

1Clem 8:2

Yea and the Master of the universe Himself spoke concerning repentance with an oath:

1Clem 8:3

for, as I live says the Lord, I desire not the death of the sinner, so much as his repentance,

1Clem 8:4
and He added also a merciful judgment: Repent you, O house of
Israel, of your iniquity; say unto the sons of My people, Though
your sins reach from the earth even unto the heaven, and though
they be redder than scarlet and blacker than sackcloth, and you turn
unto Me with your whole heart and say Father, I will give ear unto
you as unto a holy people.

1Clem 8:5
And in another place He said on this wise, Wash, be you clean. Put
away your iniquities from your souls out of My sight. Cease from
your iniquities; learn to do good; seek out judgment; defend him
that is wronged: give judgment for the orphan, and execute
righteousness for the widow; and come and let us reason together,
said He; and though your sins be as crimson, I will make them
white as snow; and though they be as scarlet, I will make them
white as wool. And if you be willing and will hearken unto Me, you
shall eat the good things of the earth; but if you be not willing,
neither hearken unto Me, a sword shall devour you; for the mouth of
the Lord has spoken these things.

1Clem 8:6
Seeing then that He desires all His beloved to be partakers of
repentance, He confirmed it by an act of His almighty will.

1Clem 9:1
   Wherefore let us be obedient unto His excellent and glorious will;
and presenting ourselves as suppliants of His mercy and goodness, let
us fall down before Him and betake ourselves unto His compassions,
forsaking the vain toil and the strife and the jealousy which leads
unto death.

1Clem 9:2
Let us fix our eyes on them that ministered perfectly unto His
excellent glory.

1Clem 9:3
Let us set before us Enoch, who being found righteous in obedience
was translated, and his death was not found.

1Clem 9:4
Noah, being found faithful, by his ministration preached regeneration
unto the world, and through him the Master saved the living creatures

that entered into the ark in concord.

1Clem 10:1
Abraham, who was called the 'friend,' was found faithful in that he
rendered obedience unto the words of God.

1Clem 10:2
He through obedience went forth from his land and from his kindred
and from his father's house, that leaving a scanty land and a feeble
kindred and a mean house he might inherit the promises of God.

1Clem 10:3
For He said unto him Go forth from thy land and from thy kindred
and from thy father's house unto the land which I shall show you,
and I will make you into a great nation, and I will bless you and
will magnify thy name, and you shall be blessed. And I will bless
them that bless you, and I will curse them that curse you; and in
you shall all the tribes of the earth be blessed.

1Clem 10:4
And again, when he was parted from Lot, God said unto him Look up
with your eyes, and behold from the place where you now art, unto
the north and the south and the sunrise and the sea; for all the
land which you see, I will give it unto you and to thy seed for
ever;

1Clem 10:5
and I will make thy seed as the dust of the earth. If any man can
count the dust of the earth, then shall thy seed also be counted.

1Clem 10:6
And again He said; God led Abraham forth and said unto him, Look
up unto the heaven and count the stars, and see whether you canst
number them. So shall thy seed be. And Abraham believed God, and it
was reckoned unto him for righteousness.

1Clem 10:7
For his faith and hospitality a son was given unto him in old age,
and by obedience he offered him a sacrifice unto God on one of the
mountains which He showed him.

1Clem 11:1
For his hospitality and godliness Lot was saved from Sodom, when all
the country round about was judged by fire and brimstone; the Master

having thus fore shown that He forsakes not them which set their hope on Him, but appoints unto punishment and torment them which swerve aside.

1Clem 11:2
For when his wife had gone forth with him, being otherwise minded and not in accord, she was appointed for a sign hereunto, so that she became a pillar of salt unto this day, that it might be known unto all men that they which are double-minded and they which doubt concerning the power of God are set for a judgment and for a token unto all the generations.

1Clem 12:1
   For her faith and hospitality Rahab the harlot was saved.

1Clem 12:2
For when the spies were sent forth unto Jericho by Joshua the son of Nun, the king of the land perceived that they were come to spy out his country, and sent forth men to seize them, that being seized they might be put to death.

1Clem 12:3
So the hospitable Rahab received them and hid them in the upper chamber under the flax stalks.

1Clem 12:4
And when the messengers of the king came near and said, The spies of our land entered in unto you: bring them forth, for the king so ordereth: then she answered, The men truly, whom you seek, entered in unto me, but they departed forthwith and are sojourning on the way; and she pointed out to them the opposite road.

1Clem 12:5
And she said unto the men, Of a surety I perceive that the Lord your God delivered this city unto you; for the fear and the dread of you is fallen upon the inhabitants thereof. When therefore it shall come to pass that you take it, save me and the house of my father.

1Clem 12:6
And they said unto her, It shall be even so as you hast spoken unto us. Whensoever therefore you perceives that we are coming, you shall gather all thy folk beneath thy roof and they shall be

saved; for as many as shall be found without the house shall
perish.

1Clem 12:7
And moreover they gave her a sign, that she should hang out from her
house a scarlet thread, thereby showing beforehand that through the
blood of the Lord there shall be redemption unto all them that
believe and hope on God.

1Clem 12:8
you see, dearly beloved, not only faith, but prophecy, is found in the
woman.

1Clem 13:1
   Let us therefore be lowly minded, brethren, laying aside all
arrogance and conceit and folly and anger, and let us do that which
is written. For the Holy Ghost said, Let not the wise man boast in
his wisdom, nor the strong in his strength, neither the rich in his
riches; but he that boasts let him boast in the Lord, that he may
seek Him out, and do judgment and righteousness most of all
remembering the words of the Lord Jesus which He spoke, teaching
forbearance and long-suffering:

1Clem 13:2
for thus He spoke Have mercy, that you may receive mercy: forgive,
that it may be forgiven to you. As you do, so shall it be done to
you. As you give, so shall it be given unto you. As you judge, so
shall you be judged. As you show kindness, so shall kindness be
showed unto you. With what measure you mete, it shall be measured
withal to you.

1Clem 13:3
With this commandment and these precepts let us confirm ourselves,
that we may walk in obedience to His hallowed words, with lowliness
of mind.

1Clem 13:4
For the holy word said, Upon whom shall I look, save upon him that
is gentle and quiet and feared My oracles?

1Clem 14:1
   Therefore it is right and proper, brethren, that we should be
obedient unto God, rather than follow those who in arrogance and
unruliness have set themselves up as leaders in abominable jealousy.

1Clem 14:2
For we shall bring upon us no common harm, but rather great peril, if
we surrender ourselves recklessly to the purposes of men who launch
out into strife and seditions, so as to estrange us from that which
is right.

1Clem 14:3
Let us be good one towards another according to the compassion and
sweetness of Him that made us. For it is written:

1Clem 14:4
The good shall be dwellers in the land, and the innocent shall be
left on it but they that transgress shall be destroyed utterly from
it.

1Clem 14:5
And again He said I saw the ungodly lifted up on high and exalted
as the cedars of Lebanon. And I passed by, and behold he was not;
and sought out his place, and I found it not. Keep innocence and
behold uprightness; for there is a remnant for the peaceful man.

1Clem 15:1
   Therefore let us cleave unto them that practice peace with
godliness, and not unto them that desire peace with dissimulation.

1Clem 15:2
For He said in a certain place This people honored Me with their
lips, but their heart is far from Me,

1Clem 15:3
and again, they blessed with their mouth, but they cursed with
their heart.

1Clem 15:4
And again He said, They loved Him with their mouth, and with their
tongue they lied unto Him; and their heart was not upright with
Him, neither were they steadfast in His covenant.

1Clem 15:5
For this cause let the deceitful lips be made dumb which speak
iniquity against the righteous. And again May the Lord utterly
destroy all the deceitful lips, the tongue that speaks proud

things, even them that say, Let us magnify our tongue; our lips are
our own; who is lord over us?

1Clem 15:6
For the misery of the needy and for the groaning of the poor I will
now arise, said the Lord. I will set him in safety; I will deal
boldly by him.

1Clem 16:1
  For Christ is with them that are lowly of mind, not with them that
exalt themselves over the flock.

1Clem 16:2
The scepter of the majesty of God, even our Lord Jesus Christ, came
not in the pomp of arrogance or of pride, though He might have done
so, but in lowliness of mind, according as the Holy Spirit spoke
concerning Him.

1Clem 16:3
For He said Lord, who believed our report? and to whom was the arm
of the Lord revealed? We announced Him in His presence. As a child
was He, as a root in a thirsty ground. There is no form in Him,
neither glory. And we beheld Him, and He had no form nor
comeliness, but His form was mean, lacking more than the form of
men. He was a man of stripes and of toil, and knowing how to bear
infirmity: for His face is turned away. He was dishonored and held
of no account.

1Clem 16:4
He bore our sins and suffers pain for our sakes: and we
accounted Him to be in toil and in stripes and in affliction.

1Clem 16:5
And He was wounded for our sins and has been afflicted for our
iniquities. The chastisement of our peace is upon Him. With His
bruises we were healed.

1Clem 16:6
We all went astray like sheep, each man went astray in his own
path:

1Clem 16:7
and the Lord delivered Him over for our sins. And He opened not
His mouth, because He is afflicted. As a sheep He was led to

slaughter; and as a lamb before his shearer is dumb, so opened He not His mouth. In His humiliation His judgment was taken away.

1Clem 16:8
His generation who shall declare? For His life is taken away from the earth.

1Clem 16:9
For the iniquities of my people He is come to death.

1Clem 16:10
And I will give the wicked for His burial, and the rich for His death; for He wrought no iniquity, neither was guile found in His mouth. And the Lord desired to cleanse Him from His stripes.

1Clem 16:11
If you offer for sin, your soul shall see along lived seed.

1Clem 16:12
And the Lord desired to take away from the toil of His soul, to show Him light and to mould Him with understanding, to justify a Just One that is a good servant unto many. And He shall bear their sins.

1Clem 16:13
Therefore He shall inherit many, and shall divide the spoils of the strong; because His soul was delivered unto death, and He was reckoned unto the transgressors;

1Clem 16:14
and He bare the sins of many, and for their sins was He delivered up.

1Clem 16:15
And again He Himself said; But I am a worm and no man, a reproach of men and an outcast of the people.

1Clem 16:16
All they that beheld me mocked at me; they spoke with their lips; they wagged their heads, saying, He hoped on the Lord; let Him deliver him, or let Him save him, for He desired him.

1Clem 16:17

you see, dearly beloved, what is the pattern that has been given unto us; for, if the Lord was thus lowly of mind, what should we do, who through Him have been brought under the yoke of His grace?

1Clem 17:1

Let us be imitators also of them which went about in goatskins and sheepskins, preaching the coming of Christ. We mean Elijah and Elisha and likewise Ezekiel, the prophets, and besides them those men also that obtained a good report.

1Clem 17:2

Abraham obtained an exceeding good report and was called the friend of God; and looking steadfastly on the glory of God, he said in lowliness of mind, But I am dust and ashes.

1Clem 17:3

Moreover concerning Job also it is thus written; And Job was righteous and unblamable, one that was true and honored God and abstained from all evil.

1Clem 17:4

Yet he himself accused himself saying, No man from filth; no, not though his life be but for a day.

1Clem 17:5

Moses was called faithful in all His house, and through his ministration God judged Egypt with the plagues and the torments which befell them. Howbeit he also, though greatly glorified, yet spoke no proud words, but said, when an oracle was given to him at the bush, Who am I, that Thou send me?

1Clem 17:6

Nay, I am feeble of speech and slow of tongue. And again he said, But I am smoke from the pot.

1Clem 18:1

But what must we say of David that obtained a good report? of whom God said, I have found a man after My heart, David the son of Jesse: with eternal mercy have I anointed him.

1Clem 18:2

Yet he too said unto God Have mercy upon me, O God, according to Your great mercy; and according to the multitude of Your compassions, blot out mine iniquity.

1Clem 18:3
Wash me yet more from mine iniquity, and cleanse me from my sin.
For I acknowledge mine iniquity, and my sin is ever before me.
Against Thee only did I sin, and I wrought evil in Your sight; that
You may be justified in Your words, and may conquer in Your
pleading.

1Clem 18:4
For behold, in iniquities was I conceived, and in sins did my
mother bear me. For behold You hast loved truth: the dark and
hidden things of Your wisdom hast You showed unto me.

1Clem 18:5
You shall sprinkle me with hyssop, and I shall be made clean. You
shall wash me, and I shall become whiter than snow.

1Clem 18:6
You shall make me to hear of joy and gladness. The bones which
have been humbled shall rejoice.

1Clem 18:7
Turn away Your face from my sins, and blot out all mine iniquities.

1Clem 18:8
Make a clean heart within me, O God, and renew a right spirit in
mine inmost parts. Cast me not away from Your presence, and take not
Your Holy Spirit from me.

1Clem 18:9
Restore unto me the joy of Your salvation, and strengthen me with a
princely spirit.

1Clem 18:10
I will teach sinners Your ways, and godless men shall be converted
unto Thee.

1Clem 18:11
Deliver me from blood guiltiness, O God, the God of my salvation.
My tongue shall rejoice in Your righteousness.

1Clem 18:12
Lord, You shall open my mouth, and my lips shall declare Your

praise.

1Clem 18:13
For, if You had desired sacrifice, I would have given it: in
whole burnt offerings You wilt have no pleasure.

1Clem 18:14
A sacrifice unto God is a contrite spirit; a contrite and humbled
heart God will not despise.

1Clem 19:1
   The humility therefore and the submissiveness of so many and so
great men, who have thus obtained a good report, has through
obedience made better not only us but also the generations which were
before us, even them that received His oracles in fear and truth.

1Clem 19:2
Seeing then that we have been partakers of many great and glorious
doings, let us hasten to return unto the goal of peace which has
been handed down to us from the beginning, and let us look
steadfastly unto the Father and Maker of the whole world, and hold fast
unto His splendid and excellent gifts of peace and benefits.

1Clem 19:3
Let us behold Him in our mind, and let us look with the eyes of our
soul unto His long-suffering will. Let us note how free from anger He
is towards all His creatures.

1Clem 20:1
   The heavens are moved by His direction and obey Him in peace.

1Clem 20:2
Day and night accomplish the course assigned to them by Him, without
hindrance one to another.

1Clem 20:3
The sun and the moon and the dancing stars according to His
appointment circle in harmony within the bounds assigned to them,
without any swerving aside.

1Clem 20:4
The earth, bearing fruit in fulfillment of His will at her proper
seasons, puts forth the food that supplies abundantly both men
and beasts and all living things which are thereupon, making no

dissension, neither altering anything which He has decreed.

1Clem 20:5
Moreover, the inscrutable depths of the abysses and the unutterable
statutes of the nether regions are constrained by the same
ordinances.

1Clem 20:6
The basin of the boundless sea, gathered together by His workmanship
into it's reservoirs, passes not the barriers wherewith it is
surrounded; but even as He ordered it, so it doeth.

1Clem 20:7
For He said, So far shall you come, and thy waves shall be broken
within you.

1Clem 20:8
The ocean which is impassable for men, and the worlds beyond it, are
directed by the same ordinances of the Master.

1Clem 20:9
The seasons of spring and summer and autumn and winter give way in
succession one to another in peace.

1Clem 20:10
The winds in their several quarters at their proper season fulfill
their ministry without disturbance; and the ever flowing fountains,
created for enjoyment and health, without fail give their breasts
which sustain the life for men. Yea, the smallest of living things
come together in concord and peace.

1Clem 20:11
All these things the great Creator and Master of the universe ordered
to be in peace and concord, doing good unto all things, but far
beyond the rest unto us who have taken refuge in His compassionate
mercies through our Lord Jesus Christ,

1Clem 20:12
to whom be the glory and the majesty for ever and ever. Amen.

1Clem 21:1
  Look you, brethren, lest His benefits, which are many, turn unto
judgment to all of us, if we walk not worthily of Him, and do those

things which are good and well pleasing in His sight with concord.

1Clem 21:2
For He said in a certain place, The Spirit of the Lord is a lamp
searching the closets of the belly.

1Clem 21:3
Let us see how near He is, and how that nothing escapes Him of our
thoughts or our devices which we make.

1Clem 21:4
It is right therefore that we should not be deserters from His will.

1Clem 21:5
Let us rather give offense to foolish and senseless men who exalt
themselves and boast in the arrogance of their words, than to God.

1Clem 21:6
Let us fear the Lord Jesus [Christ], whose blood was given for us.
Let us reverence our rulers; let us honor our elders; let us instruct
our young men in the lesson of the fear of God. Let us guide our
women toward that which is good:

1Clem 21:7
let them show forth their lovely disposition of purity; let them
prove their sincere affection of gentleness; let them make manifest
the moderation of their tongue through their silence; let them show
their love, not in factious preferences but without partiality
towards all them that fear God, in holiness. Let our children be
partakers of the instruction which is in Christ:

1Clem 21:8
let them learn how lowliness of mind prevailed with God, what power
chaste love has with God, how the fear of Him is good and great and
saved all them that walk therein in a pure mind with holiness.

1Clem 21:9
For He is the searcher out of the intents and desires; whose breath
is in us, and when He listed, He shall take it away.

1Clem 22:1
   Now all these things the faith which is in Christ confirmed: for He
Himself through the Holy Spirit thus invite thus: Come, my
children, hearken unto Me, I will teach you the fear of the Lord.

1Clem 22:2
What man is he that desired life and loved to see good days?

1Clem 22:3
Make thy tongue to cease from evil, and thy lips that they speak no guile.

1Clem 22:4
Turn aside from evil and do good.

1Clem 22:5
Seek peace and ensue it.

1Clem 22:6
The eyes of the Lord are over the righteous, and His ears are turned to their prayers. But the face of the Lord is upon them that do evil, to destroy their memorial from the earth.

1Clem 22:7
The righteous cried out, and the Lord heard him, and delivered him from all his troubles. Many are the troubles of the righteous, and the Lord shall deliver him from them all.

1Clem 22:8
And again Many are the stripes of the sinner, but them that set their hope on the Lord mercy shall compass about.

1Clem 23:1
   The Father, who is pitiful in all things, and ready to do good, has compassion on them that fear Him, and kindly and lovingly bestowed His favors on them that draw nigh unto Him with a single mind.

1Clem 23:2
Therefore let us not be double-minded, neither let our soul indulge in idle humors respecting His exceeding and glorious gifts.

1Clem 23:3
Let this scripture be far from us where He said Wretched are the double-minded, Which doubt in their soul and say, These things we did hear in the days of our fathers also, and behold we have grown old, and none of these things has befallen us.

1Clem 23:4

you fools, compare yourselves unto a tree; take a vine. First it
sheds its leaves, then a shoot cometh, then a leaf, then a
flower, and after these a sour berry, then a full ripe grape. you
see that in a little time the fruit of the tree attained unto
mellowness.

1Clem 23:5

Of a truth quickly and suddenly shall His will be accomplished, the
scripture also bearing witness to it, saying He shall come quickly
and shall not tarry; and the Lord shall come suddenly into His
temple, even the Holy One, whom you expect.

1Clem 24:1

Let us understand, dearly beloved, how the Master continually
showed unto us the resurrection that shall be hereafter; whereof He
made the Lord Jesus Christ the firstfruit, when He raised Him from
the dead.

1Clem 24:2

Let us behold, dearly beloved, the resurrection which happened at
its proper season.

1Clem 24:3

Day and night show unto us the resurrection. The night fell
asleep, and day arose; the day departed, and night cometh on.

1Clem 24:4

Let us mark the fruits, how and in what manner the sowing took
place.

1Clem 24:5

The sower went forth and casted into the earth each of the
seeds; and these falling into the earth dry and bare decay: then out
of their decay the mightiness of the Master's providence raised them
up, and from being one they increase manifold and bear fruit.

1Clem 25:1

Let us consider the marvelous sign which is seen in the regions of
the east, that is, in the parts about Arabia.

1Clem 25:2

There is a bird, which is named the phoenix. This, being the only
one of its kind, lived for five hundred years; and when it has now

reached the time of its dissolution that it should die, it made for itself a coffin of frankincense and myrrh and the other spices, into the which in the fullness of time it entered, and so it died.

1Clem 25:3
But, as the flesh rotted, a certain worm is engendered, which is nurtured from the moisture of the dead creature and put forth wings. Then, when it is grown lusty, it took up that coffin where are the bones of its parent, and carrying them journeyed from the country of Arabia even unto Egypt, to the place called the City of the Sun;

1Clem 25:4
and in the daytime in the sight of all, flying to the altar of the Sun, it bathed them thereupon; and this done, it set forth to return.

1Clem 25:5
So the priests examine the registers of the times, and they find that it has come when the five hundredth year is completed.

1Clem 26:1
   Do we then think it to be a great and marvelous thing, if the Creator of the universe shall bring about the resurrection of them that have served Him with holiness in the assurance of a good faith, seeing that He showed to us even by a bird the magnificence of His promise?

1Clem 26:2
For He said in a certain place And You shall raise me up, and I will praise Thee; and; I went to rest and slept, I was awaked, for You art with me.

1Clem 26:3
And again Job said And You shall raise this my flesh which has endured all these things.

1Clem 27:1
   With this hope therefore let our souls be bound unto Him that is faithful in His promises and that is righteous in His judgments.

1Clem 27:2
He that commanded not to lie, much more shall He Himself not lie:

for nothing is impossible with God save to lie.

1Clem 27:3
Therefore let our faith in Him be kindled within us, and let us
understand that all things are nigh unto Him.

1Clem 27:4
By a word of His majesty He compacted the universe; and by a word He
can destroy it.

1Clem 27:5
Who shall say unto Him, What hast you done? or who shall resist
the might of His strength? When He listeth, and as He listeth, He
will do all things; and nothing shall pass away of those things that
He has decreed.

1Clem 27:6
All things are in His sight, and nothing escaped His counsel,

1Clem 27:7
seeing that The heavens declare the glory of God, and the firmament
proclaimed His handiwork. Day uttered word unto day, and night
proclaimed knowledge unto night; and there are neither words nor
speeches, whose voices are not heard.

1Clem 28:1
   Since therefore all things are seen and heard, let us fear Him and
forsake the abominable lusts of evil works, that we maybe shielded by
His mercy from the coming judgments.

1Clem 28:2
For where can any of us escape from His strong hand? And what world
will receive any of them that desert from His service?

1Clem 28:3
For the holy writing said in a certain place Where shall I go, and
where shall I be hidden from Your face? If I ascend into the heaven,
You art there; if I depart into the farthest parts of the earth,
there is Your right hand; if I make my bed in the depths, there is
Your Spirit.

1Clem 28:4
Whither then shall one depart, or where shall one flee, from Him that
embraced the universe?

1Clem 29:1

Let us therefore approach Him in holiness of soul, lifting up pure and undefiled hands unto Him, with love towards our gentle and compassionate Father who made us an elect portion unto Himself.

1Clem 29:2
For
thus it is written: When the Most High divided the nations, when He dispersed the sons of Adam, He fixed the boundaries of the nations according to the number of the angels of God. His people Jacob became the portion of the Lord, and Israel the measurement of His inheritance.

1Clem 29:3
And in another place He said, Behold, the Lord took for Himself a nation out of the midst of the nations, as a man took the first fruits of his threshing floor; and the holy of holies shall come forth from that nation.

1Clem 30:1

Seeing then that we are the special portion of a Holy God, let us do all things that pertain unto holiness, forsaking evil speakings, abominable and impure embraces, drunkennesses and tumults and hateful lusts, abominable adultery, hateful pride.

1Clem 30:2
For God, He said, resisted the proud, but gave grace to the lowly.

1Clem 30:3
Let us therefore hold fast unto those to whom grace is given from God. Let us clothe ourselves in concord, being lowly-minded and temperate, holding ourselves aloof from all back biting and evil speaking, being justified by works and not by words.

1Clem 30:4
For He said, He that said much shall hear also again. Doth the ready talker think to be righteous?

1Clem 30:5
Blessed is the offspring of a woman that lived but a short time. Be not you abundant in words.

1Clem 30:6
Let our praise be with God, and not of ourselves: for God hated them that praise themselves.

1Clem 30:7
Let the testimony to our well doing be given by others, as it was given unto our fathers who were righteous.

1Clem 30:8
Boldness and arrogance and daring are for them that are accursed of God; but forbearance and humility and gentleness are with them that are blessed of God.

1Clem 31:1
Let us therefore hold fast unto His blessing, and let us see what are the ways of blessing. Let us study the records of the things that have happened from the beginning.

1Clem 31:2
Wherefore was our father Abraham blessed? Was it not because he wrought righteousness and truth through faith?

1Clem 31:3
Isaac with confidence, as knowing the future, was led a willing sacrifice.

1Clem 31:4
Jacob with humility departed from his land because of his brother, and went unto Laban and served; and the twelve tribes of Israel were given unto him.

1Clem 32:1
If any man will consider them one by one in sincerity, he shall understand the magnificence of the gifts that are given by Him.

1Clem 32:2
For of Jacob are all the priests and Levites who minister unto the altar of God; of him is the Lord Jesus as concerning the flesh; of him are kings and rulers and governors in the line of Judah; yea and the rest of his tribes are held in no small honor, seeing that God promised saying, Your seed shall be as the stars of heaven.

1Clem 32:3

They all therefore were glorified and magnified, not through themselves or their own works or the righteous doing which they wrought, but through His will.

1Clem 32:4
And so we, having been called through His will in Christ Jesus, are not justified through ourselves or through our own wisdom or understanding or piety or works which we wrought in holiness of heart, but through faith, whereby the Almighty God justified all men that have been from the beginning; to whom be the glory for ever and ever. Amen.

1Clem 33:1
What then must we do, brethren? Must we idly abstain from doing good, and forsake love? May the Master never allow this to befall us at least; but let us hasten with urgency and zeal to accomplish every good work.

1Clem 33:2
For the Creator and Master of the universe Himself rejoiced in His works.

1Clem 33:3
For by His exceeding great might He established the heavens, and in His incomprehensible wisdom He set them in order. And the earth He separated from the water that surrounded it, and He set it firm on the sure foundation of His own will; and the living creatures which walk upon it He commanded to exist by His ordinance. Having before created the sea and the living creatures therein, He enclosed it by His own power.

1Clem 33:4
Above all, as the most excellent and exceeding great work of His intelligence, with His sacred and faultless hands He formed man in the impress of His own image.

1Clem 33:5
For thus said God Let us make man after our image and after our likeness. And God made man; male and female made He them.

1Clem 33:6
So having finished all these things, He praised them and blessed them and said, Increase and multiply.

1Clem 33:7
We have seen that all the righteous were adorned in good works. Yea,
and the Lord Himself having adorned Himself with worlds rejoiced.

1Clem 33:8
Seeing then that we have this pattern, let us conform ourselves with
all diligence to His will; let us with all our strength work the work
of righteousness.

1Clem 34:1
   The good workman received the bread of his work with boldness, but
the slothful and careless dared not look his employer in the face.

1Clem 34:2
It is therefore needful that we should be zealous unto well doing,
for of Him are all things:

1Clem 34:3
since He forewarned us saying, Behold, the Lord, and His reward is
before His face, to recompense each man according to his work.

1Clem 34:4
He exhorted us therefore to believe on Him with our whole heart, and
to be not idle nor careless unto every good work.

1Clem 34:5
Let our boast and our confidence be in Him: let us submit ourselves
to His will; let us mark the whole host of His angels, how they stand
by and minister unto His will.

1Clem 34:6
For the scripture said, Ten thousands of ten thousands stood by
Him, and thousands of thousands ministered unto Him: and they cried
aloud, Holy, holy, holy is the Lord of Sabaoth; all creation is
full of His glory.

1Clem 34:7
Yea, and let us ourselves then, being gathered together in concord
with intentness of heart, cry unto Him as from one mouth earnestly
that we may be made partakers of His great and glorious promises.

1Clem 34:8
For He said, Eye has not seen and ear has not heard, and it has

not entered into the heart of man what great things He has
prepared for them that patiently await Him.

1Clem 35:1
How blessed and marvelous are the gifts of God, dearly beloved!!

1Clem 35:2
Life in immortality, splendor in righteousness, truth in boldness,
faith in confidence, temperance in sanctification! And all these
things fall under our apprehension.

1Clem 35:3
What then, think you, are the things preparing for them that patiently
await Him? The Creator and Father of the ages, the All holy One
Himself knew their number and their beauty.

1Clem 35:4
Let us therefore contend, that we may be found in the number of those
that patiently await Him, to the end that we may be partakers of His
promised gifts.

1Clem 35:5
But how shall this be, dearly beloved? If our mind be fixed through
faith towards God; if we seek out those things which are well
pleasing and acceptable unto Him; if we accomplish such things as
beseem His faultless will, and follow the way of truth, casting off
from ourselves all unrighteousness and iniquity, covetousness,
strifes, malignity and deceits, whisperings and backbitings, hatred
of God, pride and arrogance, vainglory and inhospitality.

1Clem 35:6
For they that do these things are hateful to God; and not only they
that do them, but they also that consent unto them.

1Clem 35:7
For the scripture said, But unto the sinner said God, Wherefore
do you declare Mine ordinances, and take My covenant upon thy
lips?

1Clem 35:8
Yet You didst hate instruction and didst cast away My words behind
you. If you saw a thief you didst keep company with him, and
with the adulterers you didst set thy portion. Your mouth

multiplied wickedness and thy tongue wove deceit. You sat and
spoke against thy brother, and against the son of thy mother you
didst lay a stumbling block.

1Clem 35:9
These things You hast done, and I kept silence. You thought
unrighteous man, that I should be like unto you.

1Clem 35:10
I will convict you and will set you face to face with thyself.

1Clem 35:11
Now understand you these things, you that forget God, lest at any
time He seize you as a lion, and there be none to deliver.

1Clem 35:12
The sacrifice of praise shall glorify Me, and there is the way
wherein I will show him the salvation of God.

1Clem 36:1
   This is the way, dearly beloved, wherein we found our salvation,
even Jesus Christ the High priest of our offerings, the Guardian and
Helper of our weakness.

1Clem 36:2
Through Him let us look steadfastly unto the heights of the heavens;
through Him we behold as in a mirror His faultless and most excellent
visage; through Him the eyes of our hearts were opened; through Him
our foolish and darkened mind sprung up unto the light; through
Him the Master willed that we should taste of the immortal knowledge
Who being the brightness of His majesty is so much greater than
angels, as He has inherited a more excellent name.

1Clem 36:3
For so it is written Who made His angels spirits and His
ministers aflame of fire

1Clem 36:4
but of His Son the Master said thus, You art My Son, I this day
have begotten you. Ask of Me, and I will give Thee the Gentiles
for Your inheritance, and the ends of the earth for Your
possession.

1Clem 36:5

And again He said unto Him Sit You on My right hand, until I make Your enemies a footstool for Your feet.

1Clem 36:6
Who then are these enemies? They that are wicked and resist His will.

1Clem 37:1
   Let us therefore enlist ourselves, brethren, with all earnestness in His faultless ordinances.

1Clem 37:2
Let us mark the soldiers that are enlisted under our rulers, how exactly, how readily, how submissively, they execute the orders given them.

1Clem 37:3
All are not prefects, nor rulers of thousands, nor rulers of hundreds, nor rulers of fifties, and so forth; but each man in his own rank executed the orders given by the king and the governors.

1Clem 37:4
The great without the small cannot exist, neither the small without the great. There is a certain mixture in all things, and therein is utility.

1Clem 37:5
Let us take our body as an example. The head without the feet is nothing; so likewise the feet without the head are nothing: even the smallest limbs of our body are necessary and useful for the whole body: but all the members conspire and unite in subjection, that the whole body maybe saved.

1Clem 38:1
   So in our case let the whole body be saved in Christ Jesus, and let each man be subject unto his neighbor, according as also he was appointed with his special grace.

1Clem 38:2
Let not the strong neglect the weak; and let the weak respect the strong. Let the rich minister aid to the poor; and let the poor give thanks to God, because He has given him one through whom his wants may be supplied. Let the wise display his wisdom, not in words, but

in good works. He that is lowly in mind, let him not bear testimony
to himself, but leave testimony to be borne to him by his neighbor.
He that is pure in the flesh, let him be so, and not boast, knowing
that it is Another who bestowed his continence upon him.

1Clem 38:3
Let us consider, brethren, of what matter we were made; who and what
manner of beings we were, when we came into the world; from what a
sepulchre and what darkness He that molded and created us brought us
into His world, having prepared His benefits aforehand ere ever we
were born.

1Clem 38:4
Seeing therefore that we have all these things from Him, we ought in
all things to give thanks to Him, to whom be the glory for ever and
ever. Amen.

1Clem 39:1
   Senseless and stupid and foolish and ignorant men jeer and mock at
us, desiring that they themselves should be exalted in their
imaginations.

1Clem 39:2
For what power has a mortal? or what strength has a child of earth?

1Clem 39:3
For it is written; There was no form before mine eyes; only I heard
a breath and a voice.

1Clem 39:4
What then? Shall a mortal be clean in the sight of the Lord; or
shall a man be unblamable for his works? seeing that He is
distrustful against His servants and noted some perversity against
His angels.

1Clem 39:5
Nay, the heaven is not clean in His sight. Away then, you that dwell
in houses of clay, whereof, even of the same clay, we ourselves are
made. He smote them like a moth, and from morn to even they are no
more. Because they could not succor themselves, they perished.

1Clem 39:6
He breathed on them and they died, because they had no wisdom.

1Clem 39:7
But call you, if perchance one shall obey you, or if you shall
see one of the holy angels. For wrath killed the foolish man, and
envy slayed him that has gone astray.

1Clem 39:8
And I have seen fools throwing out roots, but forthwith their
habitation was eaten up.

1Clem 39:9
Far be their sons from safety. May they be mocked at the gates of
inferiors, and there shall be none to deliver them. For the things
which are prepared for them, the righteous shall eat; but they
themselves shall not be delivered from evils.

1Clem 40:1
   Forasmuch then as these things are manifest beforehand, and we have
searched into the depths of the Divine knowledge, we ought to do all
things in order, as many as the Master has commanded us to perform
at their appointed seasons.

1Clem 40:2
Now the offerings and ministrations He commanded to be performed with
care, and not to be done rashly or in disorder, but at fixed times
and seasons.

1Clem 40:3
And where and by whom He would have them performed, He Himself
fixed
by His supreme will: that all things being done with piety according
to His good pleasure might be acceptable to His will.

1Clem 40:4
They therefore that make their offerings at the appointed seasons are
acceptable and blessed: for while they follow the institutions of
the Master they cannot go wrong.

1Clem 40:5
For unto the high priest his proper services have been assigned, and
to the priests their proper office is appointed, and upon the Levites
their proper ministrations are laid. The layman is bound by the
layman's ordinances.

1Clem 41:1

Let each of you, brethren, in his own order give thanks unto God, maintaining a good conscience and not transgressing the appointed rule of his service, but acting with all seemliness.

1Clem 41:2

Not in every place, brethren, are the continual daily sacrifices offered, or the freewill offerings, or the sin offerings and the trespass offerings, but in Jerusalem alone. And even there the offering is not made in every place, but before the sanctuary in the court of the altar; and this too through the high priest and the afore said ministers, after that the victim to be offered has been inspected for blemishes.

1Clem 41:3

They therefore who do any thing contrary to the seemly ordinance of His will receive death as the penalty.

1Clem 41:4

you see, brethren, in proportion as greater knowledge has been vouchsafed unto us, so much the more are we exposed to danger.

1Clem 42:1

The Apostles received the Gospel for us from the Lord Jesus Christ; Jesus Christ was sent forth from God.

1Clem 42:2

So then Christ is from God, and the Apostles are from Christ. Both therefore came of the will of God in the appointed order.

1Clem 42:3

Having therefore received a charge, and having been fully assured through the resurrection of our Lord Jesus Christ and confirmed in the word of God with full assurance of the Holy Ghost, they went forth with the glad tidings that the kingdom of God should come.

1Clem 42:4

So preaching everywhere in country and town, they appointed their firstfruits, when they had proved them by the Spirit, to be bishops and deacons unto them that should believe.

1Clem 42:5

And this they did in no new fashion; for indeed it had been written concerning bishops and deacons from very ancient times; for thus

said the scripture in a certain place, I will appoint their
bishops in righteousness and their deacons in faith.

1Clem 43:1
   And what marvel, if they which were entrusted in Christ with such a
work by God appointed the aforesaid persons? seeing that even the
blessed Moses who was a faithful servant in all His house recorded
for a sign in the sacred books all things that were enjoined upon
him. And him also the rest of the prophets followed, bearing witness
with him unto the laws that were ordained by him.

1Clem 43:2
For he, when jealousy arose concerning the priesthood, and there was
dissension among the tribes which of them was adorned with the
glorious name, commanded the twelve chiefs of the tribes to bring to
him rods inscribed with the name of each tribe. And he took them and
tied them and sealed them with the signet rings of the chiefs of the
tribes, and put them away in the tabernacle of the testimony on the
table of God.

1Clem 43:3
And having shut the tabernacle he sealed the keys and likewise also
the doors.

1Clem 43:4
And he said unto them, Brethren, the tribe whose rod shall bud, this
has God chosen to be priests and ministers unto Him.

1Clem 43:5
Now when morning came, he called together all Israel, even the six
hundred thousand men, and showed the seals to the chiefs of the
tribes and opened the tabernacle of the testimony and drew forth the
rods. And the rod of Aaron was found not only with buds, but also
bearing fruit.

1Clem 43:6
What think you, dearly beloved? Did not Moses know beforehand that
this would come to pass? Assuredly he knew it. But that disorder
might not arise in Israel, he did thus, to the end that the Name of
the true and only God might be glorified: to whom he the glory for
ever and ever. Amen...

1Clem 44:1

And our Apostles knew through our Lord Jesus Christ that there would be strife over the name of the bishop's office.

1Clem 44:2
For this cause therefore, having received complete foreknowledge, they appointed the aforesaid persons, and afterwards they provided a continuance, that if these should fall asleep, other approved men should succeed to their ministration. Those therefore who were appointed by them, or afterward by other men of repute with the consent of the whole Church, and have ministered unblamably to the flock of Christ in lowliness of mind, peacefully and with all modesty, and for long time have borne a good report with all these men we consider to be unjustly thrust out from their ministration.

1Clem 44:3
For it will be no light sin for us, if we thrust out those who have offered the gifts of the bishop's office unblamably and holily.

1Clem 44:4
Blessed are those presbyters who have gone before, seeing that their departure was fruitful and ripe: for they have no fear lest any one should remove them from their appointed place.

1Clem 44:5
For we see that you have displaced certain persons, though they were living honorably, from the ministration which had been respected by them blamelessly.

1Clem 45:1
  Be you contentious, brethren, and jealous about the things that pertain unto salvation.

1Clem 45:2
you have searched the scriptures, which are true, which were given through the Holy Ghost;

1Clem 45:3
and you know that nothing unrighteous or counterfeit is written in them. you will not find that righteous persons have been thrust out by holy men.

1Clem 45:4
Righteous men were persecuted, but it was by the lawless; they were imprisoned, but it was by the unholy. They were stoned by

transgressors: they were slain by those who had conceived a
detestable and unrighteous jealousy.

1Clem 45:5
Suffering these things, they endured nobly.

1Clem 45:6
For what must we say, brethren? Was Daniel cast into the lions' den
by them that feared God?

1Clem 45:7
Or were Ananias and Azarias and Misael shut up in the furnace of fire
by them that professed the excellent and glorious worship of the Most
High? Far be this from our thoughts. Who then were they that did
these things? Abominable men and full of all wickedness were stirred
up to such a pitch of wrath, as to bring cruel suffering upon them
that served God in a holy and blameless purpose, not knowing that the
Most High is the champion and protector of them that in a pure
conscience serve His excellent Name: unto whom be the glory for ever
and ever. Amen.

1Clem 45:8
But they that endured patiently in confidence
inherited glory and honor; they were exalted, and had their names
recorded by God in their memorial for ever and ever. Amen.

1Clem 46:1
  To such examples as these therefore, brethren, we also ought to
hold fast.

1Clem 46:2
For it is written; Hold fast unto the saints, for they that hold fast
unto them shall be sanctified.

1Clem 46:3
And again He said in another place; With the guiltless man you
shall be guiltless, and with the elect you shall be elect, and
with the crooked you shall deal crookedly.

1Clem 46:4
Let us therefore hold fast to the guiltless and righteous: and these
are the elect of God.

1Clem 46:5
Wherefore are there strifes and wraths and factions and divisions and war among you?

1Clem 46:6
Have we not one God and one Christ and one Spirit of grace that was shed upon us? And is there not one calling in Christ?

1Clem 46:7
Wherefore do we tear and rend asunder the members of Christ, and stir up factions against our own body, and reach such a pitch of folly, as to forget that we are members one of another?

1Clem 46:8
Remember the words of Jesus our Lord: for He said, Woe unto that man; it were good for him if he had not been born, rather than that at he should offend one of Mine elect. It were better for him that a millstone were hanged about him, and be cast into the sea, than that he should pervert one of Mine elect.

1Clem 46:9
Your division has perverted many; it has brought many to despair, many to doubting, and all of us to sorrow. And your sedition still continued.

1Clem 47:1
   Take up the epistle of the blessed Paul the Apostle.

1Clem 47:2
What wrote he first unto you in the beginning of the Gospel?

1Clem 47:3
Of a truth he charged you in the Spirit concerning himself and Cephas and Apollos, because that even then you had made parties.

1Clem 47:4
Yet that making of parties brought less sin upon you; for you were partisans of Apostles that were highly reputed, and of a man approved in their sight.

1Clem 47:5
But now mark you, who they are that have perverted you and diminished the glory of your renowned love for the brotherhood.

1Clem 47:6
It is shameful, dearly beloved, yes, utterly shameful and unworthy of
your conduct in Christ, that it should be reported that the very
steadfast and ancient Church of the Corinthians, for the sake of one
or two persons, made sedition against its presbyters.

1Clem 47:7
And this report has reached not only us, but them also which differ
from us, so that you even heap blasphemies on the Name of the Lord by
reason of your folly, and moreover create peril for yourselves.

1Clem 48:1
   Let us therefore root this out quickly, and let us fall down before
the Master and entreat Him with tears, that He may show Himself
propitious and be reconciled unto us, and may restore us to the
seemly and pure conduct which belonged to our love of the brethren.

1Clem 48:2
For this is a gate of righteousness opened unto life, as it is
written; Open me the gates of righteousness, that I may enter in
thereby and preach the Lord.

1Clem 48:3
This is the gate of the Lord; the righteous shall enter in
thereby.

1Clem 48:4
Seeing then that many gates are opened, this is that gate which is in
righteousness, even that which is in Christ, whereby all are blessed
that have entered in and direct their path in holiness and
righteousness, performing all things without confusion.

1Clem 48:5
Let a man be faithful, let him be able to expound a deep saying, let
him be wise in the discernment of words, let him be strenuous in
deeds, let him be pure;

1Clem 48:6
for so much the more ought he to be lowly in mind, in proportion as
he seemed to be the greater; and he ought to seek the common
advantage of all, and not his own.

1Clem 49:1

Let him that has love in Christ fulfill the commandments of Christ.

1Clem 49:2
Who can declare the bond of the love of God?

1Clem 49:3
Who is sufficient to tell the majesty of its beauty?

1Clem 49:4
The height, where unto love exalted, is unspeakable.

1Clem 49:5
Love joined us unto God; love covered a multitude of sins; love
endured all things, is long-suffering in all things. There is
nothing coarse, nothing arrogant in love. Love has no divisions,
love made no seditions, love doeth all things in concord. In love
were all the elect of God made perfect; without love nothing is well
pleasing to God:

1Clem 49:6
in love the Master took us unto Himself; for the
love which He had toward us, Jesus Christ our Lord has given His
blood for us by the will of God, and His flesh for our flesh and His
life for our lives.

1Clem 50:1
   you see, dearly beloved, how great and marvelous a thing is love, and
there is no declaring its perfection.

1Clem 50:2
Who is sufficient to be found therein, save those to whom God shall
vouchsafe it? Let us therefore entreat and ask of His mercy, that we
may be found blameless in love, standing apart from the factiousness
of men. All the generations from Adam unto this day have passed
away: but they that by God's grace were perfected in love dwell in
the abode of the pious; and they shall be made manifest in the
visitation of the Kingdom of God.

1Clem 50:3
For it is written; Enter into the closet for a very little while
until Mine anger and Mine wrath shall pass away, and I will
remember a good day and will raise you from your tombs.

1Clem 50:4

Blessed were we, dearly beloved, if we should be doing the
commandments of God in concord of love, to the end that our sins may
through love be forgiven us.

1Clem 50:5
For it is written; Blessed are they whose iniquities are forgiven,
and whose sins are covered. Blessed is the man to whom the Lord
shall impute no sin, neither is guile in his mouth.

1Clem 50:6
This declaration of blessedness was pronounced upon them that have
been elected by God through Jesus Christ our Lord, to whom be the
glory for ever and ever. Amen.

1Clem 51:1
   For all our transgressions which we have committed through any of
the wiles of the adversary, let us entreat that we may obtain
forgiveness. Yea and they also, who set themselves up as leaders of
faction and division, ought to look to the common ground of hope.

1Clem 51:2
For such as walk in fear and love desire that they themselves should
fall into suffering rather than their neighbors; and they pronounce
condemnation against themselves rather than against the harmony which
has been handed down to us nobly and righteously.

1Clem 51:3
For it is good for a man to make confession of his trespasses rather
than to harden his heart, as the heart of those was hardened who made
sedition against Moses the servant of God; whose condemnation was
clearly manifest,

1Clem 51:4
for they went down to hades alive, and Death shall be their
shepherd.

1Clem 51:5
Pharaoh and his host and all the rulers of Egypt, their chariots
and their horsemen, were overwhelmed in the depths of the Red Sea,
and perished for none other reason but because their foolish hearts
were hardened after that the signs and the wonders had been wrought
in the land of Egypt by the hand of Moses the servant of God.

1Clem 52:1

The Master, brethren, has need of nothing at all. He desired not anything of any man, save to confess unto Him.

1Clem 52:2

For the elect David said; I will confess unto the Lord, and it shall please Him more than a young calf that grew horns and hoofs. Let the poor see it, and rejoice.

1Clem 52:3

And again He said; Sacrifice to God a sacrifice of praise, and pay thy vows to the Most High: and call upon Me in the day of your affliction, and I will deliver you, and you shall glorify Me.

1Clem 52:4

For a sacrifice unto God is a broken spirit.

1Clem 53:1

For you know, and know well, the sacred scriptures, dearly beloved, and you have searched into the oracles of God. We write these things therefore to put you in remembrance.

1Clem 53:2

When Moses went up into the mountain and had spent forty days and forty nights in fasting and humiliation, God said unto him; Moses, Moses, come down , quickly hence, for My people whom you lead forth from the land of Egypt have wrought iniquity: they have transgressed quickly out of the way which you didst command unto them: they have made for themselves molten images.

1Clem 53:3

And the Lord said unto him; I have spoken unto you once and twice, saying, I have seen this people, and behold it is stiff-necked. Let Me destroy them utterly, and I will blot out their name from under heaven, and I will make of you a nation great and wonderful and numerous more than this.

1Clem 53:4

And Moses said; Nay, not so, Lord Forgive this people their sin, or blot me also out of the book of the living.

1Clem 53:5

O mighty love! O unsurpassable perfection! The servant is bold with his Master; he asked forgiveness for the multitude, or he demanded that himself also be blotted out with them.

1Clem 54:1

Who therefore is noble among you? Who is compassionate? Who is fulfilled with love?

1Clem 54:2

Let him say; If by reason of me there be faction and strife and divisions, I retire, I depart, whither you will, and I do that which is ordered by the people: only let the flock of Christ be at peace with its duly appointed presbyters.

1Clem 54:3

He that shall have done this, shall win for himself great renown in Christ, and every place will receive him: for the earth is the Lord's and the fullness thereof.

1Clem 54:4

Thus have they done and will do, that live as citizens of that kingdom of God which brings no regrets.

1Clem 55:1

But, to bring forward examples of Gentiles also; many kings and rulers, when some season of pestilence pressed upon them, being taught by oracles have delivered themselves over to death, that they might rescue their fellow citizens through their own blood. Many have retired from their own cities, that they might have no more seditions.

1Clem 55:2

We know that many among ourselves have delivered themselves to bondage, that they might ransom others. Many have sold themselves to slavery, and receiving the price paid for themselves have fed others.

1Clem 55:3

Many women being strengthened through the grace of God have performed many manly deeds.

1Clem 55:4

The blessed Judith, when the city was beleaguered, asked of the elders that she might be suffered to go forth into the camp of the aliens.

1Clem 55:5
So she exposed herself to peril and went forth for love of her
country and of her people which were beleaguered; and the Lord
delivered Holophernes into the hand of a woman.

1Clem 55:6
To no less peril did Esther also, who was perfect in faith, expose
herself, that she might deliver the twelve tribes of Israel, when
they were on the point to perish. For through her fasting and her
humiliation she entreated the all seeing Master, the God of the
ages; and He, seeing the humility of her soul, delivered the people
for whose sake she encountered the peril.

1Clem 56:1
   Therefore let us also make intercession for them that are in any
transgression, that forbearance and humility may be given them, to
the end that they may yield not unto us, but unto the will of God.
For so shall the compassionate remembrance of them with God and the
saints be fruitful unto them, and perfect.

1Clem 56:2
Let us accept chastisement, whereat no man ought to be vexed, dearly
beloved. The admonition which we give one to another is good and
exceeding useful; for it joined us unto the will of God.

1Clem 56:3
For thus said the holy word; The Lord has indeed chastened me,
and has not delivered me over unto death.

1Clem 56:4
For whom the Lord loved He chastened, and scourged every son
whom He received.

1Clem 56:5
For the righteous, it is said, shall chasten me in mercy and
shall reprove me, but let not the mercy of sinners anoint my head.

1Clem 56:6
And again He said; Blessed is the man whom the Lord has reproved,
and refuse not you the admonition of the Almighty. For He caused
pain, and he restored again:

1Clem 56:7
He has smitten, and His hands have healed.

1Clem 56:8
Six times shall He rescue you from afflictions and at the seventh
no evil shall touch you.

1Clem 56:9
In famine he shall deliver you from death, and in war He shall
release you from the arm of the sword.

1Clem 56:10
And from the scourge of the tongue He shall hide you and you
shall not be afraid when evils approach.

1Clem 56:11
You shall laugh at the unrighteous and wicked, and of the wild
beasts you shall not be afraid.

1Clem 56:12
For wild beasts shall be at peace with you.

1Clem 56:13
Then shall you know that thy house shall be at peace: and the
abode of thy tabernacle shall not go wrong,

1Clem 56:14
and you shall know that thy seed is many, and thy children as the
plenteous herbage of the field.

1Clem 56:15
And you shall come to the grave as ripe corn reaped in due season,
or as the heap of the threshing floor gathered together at the
right time.

1Clem 56:16
you see, dearly beloved, how great protection there is for them that
are chastened by the Master: for being a kind father He chastened
us to the end that we may obtain mercy through His holy chastisement.

1Clem 57:1
  you therefore that laid the foundation of the sedition, submit
yourselves unto the presbyters and receive chastisement unto
repentance, bending the knees of your heart.

1Clem 57:2
Learn to submit yourselves, laying aside the arrogant and proud
stubbornness of your tongue. For it is better for you to be found
little in the flock of Christ and to have your name on God's roll,
than to be had in exceeding honor and yet be cast out from the hope
of Him.

1Clem 57:3
For thus said the All virtuous Wisdom; Behold I will pour out for
you a saying of My breath, and I will teach you My word.

1Clem 57:4
Because I called and you obeyed not, and I held out words and you
heeded not, but made My councils of none effect, and were
disobedient unto My reproofs; therefore I also will laugh at your
destruction, and will rejoice over you when ruin cometh upon you,
and when confusion overtook you suddenly, and your overthrow is
at hand like a whirlwind,

1Clem 57:5
or when you call upon Me, yet will I not here you. Evil men shall
seek me and not find me: for they hated wisdom, and chose not the
fear of the Lord, neither would they give head unto My councils,
but mocked at My reproofs.

1Clem 57:6
Therefore they shall eat the fruits of their own way, and shall be
filled with their own ungodliness.

1Clem 57:7
For because they wronged babes, they shall be slain, and
inquisition shall destroy the ungodly. But he that heard Me shall
dwell safely trusting in hope, and shall be quiet from all fear of
all evil.

1Clem 58:1
  Let us therefore be obedient unto His most holy and glorious Name,
thereby escaping the threatenings which were spoken of old by the
mouth of Wisdom against them which disobey, that we may dwell safely,
trusting in the most holy Name of His majesty.

1Clem 58:2
Receive our counsel, and you shall have no occasion of regret. For as
God lived, and the Lord Jesus Christ lived, and the Holy Spirit,

who are the faith and the hope of the elect, so surely shall he, who
with lowliness of mind and instant in gentleness has without
regretfulness performed the ordinances and commandments that are
given by God, be enrolled and have a name among the number of them
that are saved through Jesus Christ, through whom is the glory unto
Him for ever and ever. Amen.

1Clem 59:1
   But if certain persons should be disobedient unto the words spoken
by Him through us, let them understand that they will entangle
themselves in no slight transgression and danger;

1Clem 59:2
but we shall be guiltless of this sin. And we will ask, with
insistency of prayer and supplication, that the Creator of the universe
may guard intact unto the end the number that has been numbered of
His elect throughout the whole world, through His beloved Son Jesus
Christ, through whom He called us from darkness to light, from
ignorance to the full knowledge of the glory of His Name.

1Clem 59:3
   [Grant unto us, Lord,] that we may set our hope on Your Name which is
the primal source of all creation, and open the eyes of our hearts,
that we may know Thee, who alone abide Highest in the lofty, Holy
in the holy; who lays low in the insolence of the proud, who
set the lowly on high, and brings the lofty low; who
makes rich and makes poor; who kills and makes alive; who
alone art the Benefactor of spirits and the God of all flesh; who
looks into the abysses, who sees the works of man; the rescuer
of them that are in peril, the Savior of them that are in
despair; The Creator and Overseer of every spirit; who multiplies
the nations upon earth, and hast chosen out from all men those that
love Thee through Jesus Christ, Your beloved Son, through whom You
didst instruct us, didst sanctify us, didst honor us.

1Clem 59:4
We beseech Thee, Lord and Master, to be our help and succor. Save
those among us who are in tribulation; have mercy on the lowly; lift
up the fallen; show Thyself unto the needy; heal the ungodly; convert
the wanderers of Your people; feed the hungry; release our prisoners;
raise up the weak; comfort the fainthearted. Let all the Gentiles
know that You art the God alone, and Jesus Christ is Your Son, and
we are Your people and the sheep of Your pasture.

1Clem 60:1
You through Your operations didst make manifest the everlasting
fabric of the world. You, Lord, didst create the earth. You that
art faithful throughout all generations, righteous in Your judgments,
marvelous in strength and excellence, You that art wise in creating
and prudent in establishing that which You hast made, that art good
in the things which are seen and faithful with them that trust on
Thee, pitiful and compassionate, forgive us our iniquities and our
unrighteousnesses and our transgressions and shortcomings.

1Clem 60:2
Lay not to our account every sin of Your servants and Your handmaids,
but cleanse us with the cleansing of Your truth, and guide our steps
to walk in holiness and righteousness and singleness of heart
and to do such things as are good and well pleasing in Your sight
and in the sight of our rulers.

1Clem 60:3
Yea, Lord, make Your face to shine upon us in peace for our good,
that we may be sheltered by Your mighty hand and delivered from
every sin by Your uplifted arm. And deliver us from them that
hate us wrongfully.

1Clem 60:4
Give concord and peace to us and to all that dwell on the earth, as
You gave to our fathers, when they called on Thee in faith
and truth with holiness, [that we may be saved,] while we render
obedience to Your almighty and most excellent Name, and to our
rulers and governors upon the earth.

1Clem 61:1
You, Lord and Master, hast given them the power of sovereignty
through Your excellent and unspeakable might, that we knowing the
glory and honor which You hast given them may submit ourselves unto
them, in nothing resisting Your will. Grant unto them therefore, O
Lord, health peace, concord, stability, that they may administer the
government which You hast given them without failure.

1Clem 61:2
For You, O heavenly Master, King of the ages, give to the sons of
men glory and honor and power over all things that are upon the
earth. Do You, Lord, direct their counsel according to that which
is good and well pleasing in Your sight, that, administering in peace

and gentleness with Godliness the power which You hast given them, they may obtain Your favor.

1Clem 61:3
O You, who alone art able to do these things and things far more exceeding good than these for us, we praise Thee through the High priest and Guardian of our souls, Jesus Christ, through whom be the glory and the majesty unto Thee both now and for all generations and for ever and ever. Amen.

1Clem 62:1
As touching those things which befit our religion and are most useful for a virtuous life to such as would guide [their steps] in holiness and righteousness, we have written fully unto you, brethren.

1Clem 62:2
For concerning faith and repentance and genuine love and temperance and sobriety and patience we have handled every argument, putting you in remembrance, that you ought to please Almighty God in righteousness and truth and long suffering with holiness, laying aside malice and pursuing concord in love and peace, being instant in gentleness; even as our fathers, of whom we spoke before, pleased Him, being lowly minded toward their Father and God and Creator and towards all men.

1Clem 62:3
And we have put you in mind of these things the more gladly, since we knew well that we were writing to men who are faithful and highly accounted and have diligently searched into the oracles of the teaching of God.

1Clem 63:1
Therefore it is right for us to give heed to so great and so many examples and to submit the neck and occupying the place of obedience to take our side with them that are the leaders of our souls, that ceasing from this foolish dissension we may attain unto the goal which lies before us in truthfulness, keeping aloof from every fault.

1Clem 63:2
For you will give us great joy and gladness, if you render obedience unto the things written by us through the Holy Spirit, and root out the unrighteous anger of your jealousy, according to the entreaty which we have made for peace and concord in this letter.

1Clem 63:3
And we have also sent faithful and prudent men that have walked among us from youth unto old age unblamably, who shall also be witnesses between you and us.

1Clem 63:4
And this we have done that you might know that we have had, and still have, every solicitude that you should be speedily at peace.

1Clem 64:1
Finally may the All seeing God and Master of spirits and Lord of all flesh, who chose the Lord Jesus Christ, and us through Him for a peculiar people, grant unto every soul that is called after His excellent and holy Name faith, fear, peace, patience, long-suffering, temperance, chastity and soberness, that they may be well pleasing unto His Name through our High priest and Guardian Jesus Christ, through whom unto Him be glory and majesty, might and honor, both now and for ever and ever. Amen.

1Clem 65:1
Now send you back speedily unto us our messengers Claudius Ephebus and Valerius Bito, together with Fortunatus also, in peace and with joy, to the end that they may the more quickly report the peace and concord which is prayed for and earnestly desired by us, that we also may the more speedily rejoice over your good order.

1Clem 65:2
The grace of our Lord Jesus Christ be with you and with all men in all places who have been called by God and through Him, through whom be glory and honor, power and greatness and eternal dominion, unto Him, from the ages past and forever and ever. Amen.

The Shepherd of Hermas

Vision 1

1:1 The master, who raised me sold me to a lady, Rhoda in Rome. After many years, I met her again, and began to love her as a sister.

1:2 After a period of time I saw her bathing in the river Tiber; and I gave her my hand, and led her out of the river. When I saw her beauty, I thought to myself, "I would be happy if I had such a one as a wife both because of her beauty and character." I merely thought about this and nothing more.

1:3 After a while, as I was travelling to Cumae, and praising God because of his creatures, for their greatness and beauty and power. As I walked I fell asleep. And a Spirit took me, and lifted me away through a land that had no path and through which no man could pass. The place has cliffs, and was broken into clefts by rivers. When I had crossed the river, I came into the level country, and knelt down, and began to pray to the Lord and to confess my sins.

1:4 Now, while I prayed, heaven was opened, and I saw the lady, whom I had desired, greeting me from heaven, saying, "Good day, Hermas."

1:5 And, looking at her, I said to her, "Lady, what are you doing here?" Then she answered me, "I was taken up, that I might convict you of your sins before the Lord."

1:6 I said to her, "Dost you now convict me?" "Nay, not so," said she, "but hear the words, that I shall say to you. God, Who dwelled in the heavens, and created out of nothing the things which are, and increased and multiplied them for His holy Church's sake, is wroth with you, for that you didst sin against me."

1:7 I answered her and said, "Sin against you? In what way? Did I ever speak an unseemly word unto you? Did I not always regard you as a goddess? Did I not always respect you as a sister? How couldst you falsely charge me, lady, with such villainy and uncleanness?

1:8 "Laughing she said unto me, "The desire after evil entered into your heart. No, think you not that it is an evil deed for a righteous man, if the evil desire should enter into his heart? It is indeed a sin and a great one too," said she; "for the righteous man entertained righteous purposes. While then his purposes are righteous, his repute stands steadfast in the heavens, and he finds the Lord easily propitiated in all that he does. But they that entertain evil purposes in their hearts, bring upon themselves death an captivity, especially they that claim for themselves this present work and boast in its riches, and hold fast not to the good things that are to come.

1:9 Their souls shall rue it, seeing that they have no hope, but have abandoned themselves and their life. But do you pray unto God and He shall heal your own sins, and those of thy whole house, and of all the saints."

2:1 As soon as she had spoken these words the heavens were shut and I was given over to horror and grief Then I said within myself "If this sin is recorded against me, how can I be saved? Or how shall I propitiate God for my sins which are full-blown? Or with which words shall I entreat the Lord that He may be propitious unto me?

2:2 While I was advising and discussing these matters in my heart, I see, before me a great white chair of snow-white wool; and there came an aged lady in glistening raiment, having a book in her hands, and she sat down alone, and she saluted me, "Good morrow, Hermas." Then I grieved and weeping, said, "Good morrow, lady."

2:3 And she said to me "Why so gloomy, Hermas, you that art patient and good-tempered and art always smiling? Why so downcast in thy looks, and far from cheerful?" And I said to her, "Because of an excellent lady's saying that I had sinned against her."

2:4 Then she said, "Far be this thing from the servant of God! Nevertheless the thought did enter into thy heart concerning her. Now to the servants of God such a purpose brings sin. For it is an evil and mad purpose to overtake a devout spirit that has been already approved, that it should desire an evil deed, and especially if it be Hermas the temperate, who abstained from every evil desire, and is full of all simplicity and of great guilelessness.

3:1 "Yet it is not for this that God is wroth with you, but that you may convert thy family, that has done wrong against the Lord and against you their parents. But out of fondness for thy children you didst not admonish thy family, but didst suffer it to become fearfully corrupt. Therefore the Lord is wroth with you. But He will heal all thy past sins, which have been committed in thy family; for by reason of their sins and iniquities you hast been corrupted by the affairs of this world.

3:2 But the great mercy of the Lord had pity on you and thy family, and will strengthen you, and establish you in His glory. Only be not you careless, but take courage, and strengthen thy family. For as the smith hammering his work conquers the task which he wills, so also doth righteous discourse repeated daily conquer all evil. Cease not therefore to reprove thy children; for I know that if they shall repent with all their heart, they shall be written in the books of life with the saints."

3:3 After these words of hers had ceased, she said unto me, "Wilt you listen to me as I read?" Then say I, "Yes, lady." She said to me, "Be attentive, and hear the glories of God" I listened with attention and with wonder to that which I had no power to remember; for all the words were terrible, such as man cannot bear. The last words however I remembered, for they were suitable for us and gentle.

3:4 "Behold, the God of Hosts, Who by His invisible and mighty power and by His great wisdom created the world, and by His glorious purpose clothed His creation with comeliness, and by His strong word fixed the heaven, and founded the earth upon the waters, and by His own wisdom and providence formed His holy Church, which also He blessed-behold, He removed the heavens and the mountains and the hills and the seas, and all things are made level for His elect, that He may fulfill to them the promise which He promised with great glory and rejoicing, if so be that they shall keep the ordinances of God, which they received, with great faith."

4:1 When then she finished reading and arose from her chair, there came four young men, and they took away the chair, and departed towards the East.

4:2 Then she called me unto her, and she touched my breast, and said to me, "Did my reading please you?" And I say unto her, "Lady, these last words please me, but the former were difficult and hard." Then she spoke to me, saying, "These last words are for the righteous, but the former are for the heathen and the rebellious."

4:3 While she yet spoke with me, two men appeared, and took her by the arms, and they departed, whither the chair also had gone, towards the East. And she smiled as she departed and, as she was going, she said to me, "Play the man, Hermas."

Vision 2

1[5]:1 I was on the way to Cumae, at the same season as last year, and called to mind my last year's vision as I walked; and again a Spirit took me, and carried me away to the same place as last year.

1[5]:2 When then I arrived at the place, I fell upon my knees, and began to pray to the Lord, and to glorify His name, for that he counted me worthy, and made known unto me my former sins.

1[5]:3 But after I had risen up from prayer, I behold before me the aged lady, whom also I had seen last year, walking and reading a little book. And she said to me, "Canst you report these things to the elect of God?" I say unto her, "Lady, I cannot recollect so much; but give me the little book, that I may copy it." "Take it," said she, "and be sure and return it to me."

1[5]:4 I took it, and retiring to a certain spot in the country I copied it letter for letter: for I could not make out the syllables. When then I had finished the letters of the book, suddenly the book was snatched out of my hand; but by whom I did not see.

2[6]:1 Now after fifteen days, when I had fasted and entreated the Lord earnestly, the knowledge of the writing was revealed to me. And this is what was written:--

2[6]:2 "Your seed, Hermas, have sinned against God, and have blasphemed the Lord, and have betrayed their parents through great wickedness, yea, they have got the name of betrayers of parents, and yet they did not profit by their betrayal; and they still further added to their sins wanton deeds and reckless wickedness; and so the measure of their transgressions was filled up.

2[6]:3 But make these words known to all thy children, and to thy wife who shall be as thy sister; for she too refrained not from using her tongue, wherewith she doeth evil. But, when she hears these words, she will refrain, and will find mercy.

2[6]:4 After that you hast made known unto them all these words, which the Master commanded me that they should be revealed unto you, then all their sins which they sinned aforetime are forgiven to them; yea, and to all the saints that have sinned unto this day, if they repent with their whole heart, and remove double-mindedness from their heart.

2[6]:5 For the Master swore by His own glory, as concerning His elect; that if, now that this day has been set as a limit, sin shall hereafter be committed, they shall not find salvation; for repentance for the righteous has an end; the days of repentance are accomplished for all the saints; whereas for the Gentiles there is repentance until the last day.

2[6]:6 You shall therefore say unto the elders of the Church, that they direct their paths in righteousness, that they may receive in full the promises with abundant glory.

2[6]:7 you therefore that work righteousness be steadfast, and be not double-minded, that you may have admission with the holy angels. Blessed are you, as many as endure patiently the great tribulation that cometh, and as many as shall not deny their life.

2[6]:8 For the Lord swear concerning His Son, that those who denied their Lord should be rejected from their life, even they that are now about to deny Him in the coming days; but to those who denied Him aforetime, to them mercy was given of His great loving kindness.

3[7]:1 "But do you, Hermas, no longer bear a grudge against thy children, neither suffer thy sister to have her way, so that they may be purified from their former sins. For they shall be chastised with a righteous chastisement, unless you bear a grudge against them thyself. The bearing of a grudge worked death. But you, Hermas, hast had great tribulations of your own, by reason of the transgressions of thy family, because you had no care for them. For you was neglectful of them, and was mixed up with your evil transactions.

3[7]:2 But herein is thy salvation, in that you didst not depart from the living God, and in thy simplicity and thy great continence. These have saved you, if you abide therein; and they save all who do such things, and walk in guilelessness and simplicity. These men prevail over all wickedness, and continue unto life eternal.

3[7]:3 Blessed are all they that work righteousness. They shall never be destroyed.

3[7]:4 But you shall say to Maximus, "Behold tribulation cometh (upon you), if you think fit to deny a second time. The Lord is nigh unto them that turn unto him, as it is written in Eldad and Modat, who prophesied to the people in the wilderness."

4[8]:1 Now, brethren, a revelation was made unto me in my sleep by a youth of exceeding fair form, who said to me, "Whom think you the aged woman, from whom you received the book, to be?" I say, "The Sibyl" "You art wrong," said he, "she is not." "Who then is she?" I say. "The Church," said he. I said unto him, "Wherefore then is she aged?" "Because," said he, "she was created before all things; therefore is she aged; and for her sake the world was framed."

4[8]:2 And afterwards I saw a vision in my house. The aged woman came, and asked me, if I had already given the book to the elders. I said that I had not given it. "You hast done well," she said, "for I have words to add. When then I shall have finished all the words, it shall be made known by thy means to all the elect.

4[8]:3 You shall therefore write two little books, and shall send one to Clement, and one to Grapte. So Clement shall send to the foreign cities, for this is his duty; while Grapte shall instruct the widows and the orphans. But you shall read (the book) to this city along with the elders that preside over the Church.

Vision 3

1[9]:1 The third vision, which I saw, brethren, was as follows.

1[9]:2 After fasting often, and entreating the Lord to declare unto me the revelation which He promised to show me by the mouth of the aged woman, that very night the aged woman was seen of me, and she said to me, "Seeing that you art so importunate and eager to know all things, come into the country where you abide, and about the fifth hour I will appear, and will show you what you ought to see."

1[9]:3 I asked her, saying, "Lady, to what part of the country?" "Where you wilt," said she. I selected a beautiful and retired spot; but before I spoke to her and named the spot, she said to me, "I will come, whither you will."

1[9]:4 I went then, brethren, into the country, and I counted up the hours, and came to the place where I appointed her to come, and I see an ivory couch placed there, and on the couch there lay a linen cushion, and on the cushion was spread a coverlet of fine linen of flax.

1[9]:5 When I saw these things so ordered, and no one in the place, I was amazed, and a fit of trembling seized me, and my hair stood on end; and a fit of shuddering came upon me, because I was alone. When then I recovered myself, and remembered the glory of God, and took courage, I knelt down and confessed my sins to the Lord once more, as I had done on the former occasion.

1[9]:6 Then she came with six young men, the same whom I had seen before, and she stood by me, and listened attentively to me, as I prayed and confessed my sins to the Lord. And she touched me, and said: "Hermas, make an end of constantly entreating for thy sins; entreat also for righteousness, that you may take some part forthwith to thy family."

1[9]:7 Then she raised me by the hand, and led me to the couch, and said to the young men, "Go you, and build."

1[9]:8 And after the young men had retired and we were left alone, she said to me, "Sit down here." I say to her, "Lady, let the elders sit down first." "Do as I bid you," said she, "sit down."

1[9]:9 When then I wanted to sit down on the right side, she would not allow me, but beckoned me with her hand that I should sit on the left side. As then I was musing thereon, and was sad because she would not permit me to sit on the right side, she said to me, "Art you sad, Hermas? The place on the right side is for others, even for those who have already been well-pleasing to God, and have suffered for the Name's sake. But you lack much that you should sit with them; but as you abide in thy simplicity, even so, and you shall sit with them, you and as many as shall have done their deeds, and have suffered what they suffered."

2[10]:1 "What did they suffer?" say I. "Listen," said she. "Stripes, imprisonments, great tribulations, crosses, wild beasts, for the Name's sake. Therefore to them belongs the right side of the Holiness--to them, and to all who shall suffer for the Name. But for the rest is the left side. Howbeit, to both, to them that sit on the right, and to them that sit on the left, are the same gifts, and the same promises, only they sit on the right and have a certain glory.

2[10]:2 You indeed art very desirous to sit on the right with them, but thy shortcomings are many; yet you shall be purified from thy shortcomings; yea, and all that are not double-minded shall be purified from all their sins unto this day."

2[10]:3 When she had said this, she wished to depart; but, falling at her feet, I entreated her by the Lord that she would show me the vision which she promised.

2[10]:4 Then she again took me by the hand, and raised me, and seated me on the couch at the left hand, while she herself sat on the right. And lifting up a certain glistening rod, she said to me, "See you a great thing?" I say to her, "Lady, I see nothing." She said to me, "Look you; do you not see in front of you a great tower being built upon the waters, of glistening square stones?"

2[10]:5 Now the tower was being built foursquare by the six young men that came with her. And countless other men were bringing stones, some of them from the deep, and others from the land, and were handing them to the six young men. And they took them and built.

2[10]:6 The stones that were dragged from the deep they placed in every case, just as they were, into the building, for they had been shaped, and they fitted in their joining with the other stones; and they adhered so closely one with another that their joining could not possibly be detected; and the building of the tower appeared as if it were built of one stone.

2[10]:7 But of the other stones which were brought from the dry land, some they threw away, and some they put into the building; and others they broke in pieces, and threw to a distance from the tower.

2[10]:8 Now many other stones were lying round the tower, and they did not use them for the building; for some of them were mildewed, and others had cracks in them, and others were too short, and others were white and round, and did not fit into the building.

2[10]:9 And I saw other stones thrown to a distance from the tower, and coming to the way, and yet not staying in the way, but rolling to where there was no way; and others falling into the fire and burning there; and others falling near the waters, and yet not able to roll into the water, although they desired to roll and to come to the water.

3[11]:1 When she had shown me these things, she wished to hurry away. I say to her, "Lady, what advantage is it to me to have seen these things, and yet not to know what the things mean? "She answered and said unto me, "You art an over-curious fellow, in desiring to know all that concerns the tower." "Yea, lady," I said, "that I may announce it to my brethren, and that they [may be the more gladdened and] when they hear [these things] they may know the Lord in great glory." Then said she,

3[11]:2 "Many shall hear; but when they hear, some of them shall be glad, and others shall weep. Yet even these latter, if they hear and repent, shall likewise be glad. Hear you therefore the parables of the tower; for I will reveal all things unto you. And trouble me no more about revelation; for these revelations have an end, seeing that they have been completed. Nevertheless you wilt not cease asking for revelations; for you art shameless."

3[11]:3 The tower, which you see building, is myself, the Church, which was seen of you both now and aforetime. Ask, therefore, what you will concerning the tower, and I will reveal it unto you, that you may rejoice with the saints."

3[11]:4 I say unto her, "Lady, since you didst hold me worthy once for all, that you should reveal all things to me, reveal them." Then she said to me, "Whatsoever is possible to be revealed to you, shall be revealed. Only let thy heart be with God, and doubt not in thy mind about that which you sees."

3[11]:5 I asked her, "Wherefore is the tower built upon waters, lady?" "I told you so before," said she, "and indeed you do enquire diligently. So by thy enquiry you discovered the truth. Hear then why the tower is built upon waters; it is because your life is saved and shall be saved by water. But the tower has been founded by the word of the Almighty and Glorious Name, and is strengthened by the unseen power of the Master."

4[12]:1 I answered and said unto her, "Lady, this thing is great and marvelous. But the six young men that build, who are they, lady?" "These are the holy angels of God, that were created first of all, unto whom the Lord delivered all His creation to increase and to build it, and to be masters of all creation. By their hands therefore the building of the tower will be accomplished."

4[12]:2 "And who are the others who are bringing the stones in?" "They also are holy angels of God; but these six are superior to them. The building of the tower then shall be accomplished, and all alike shall rejoice in the (completed) circle of the tower, and shall glorify God that the building of the tower was accomplished."

4[12]:3 I enquired of her, saying, "Lady, I could wish to know concerning the end of the stones, and their power, of what kind it is." She answered and said unto me, "It is not that you of all men art especially worthy that it should be revealed to you; for there are others before you, and better than you art, unto whom these visions ought to have been revealed. But that the name of God may be glorified, it has been revealed to you, all shall be revealed, for the sake of the doubtful-minded, who question in their hearts whether these things are so or not. Tell them that all these things are true, and that there is nothing beside the truth, but that all are steadfast, and valid, and established on a firm foundation.

5[13]:1 "Hear now concerning the stones that go to the building The stones that are squared and white, and that fit together in their joints, these are the apostles and bishops and teachers and deacons, who walked after the holiness of God, and exercised their office of bishop and teacher and deacon in purity and sanctity for the elect of God, some of them already fallen on sleep, and others still living. And because they always agreed with one another, they both had peace among themselves and listened one to another. Therefore their joinings fit together in the building of the tower."

5[13]:2 "But they that are dragged from the deep, and placed in the building, and that fit together in their joinings with the other stones that are already built in, who are they?" "These are they that suffered for the name of the Lord."

5[13]:3 "But the other stones that are brought from the dry land, I would fain know who these are, lady." She said, "Those that go to the building, and yet are not hewn, these the Lord has approved because they walked in the uprightness of the Lord, and rightly performed His commandments."

5[13]:4 "But they that are brought and placed in the building, who are they?"

"They are young in the faith, and faithful; but they are warned by the angels to do good, because wickedness was found in them."

5[13]:5 "But those whom they rejected and threw away, who are they?" "These have sinned, and desire to repent, therefore they were not cast to a great distance from the tower, because they will be useful for the building, if they repent. They then that shall repent, if they repent, will be strong in the faith, if they repent now while the tower is building. But if the building shall be finished, they have no more any place, but shall be castaways. This privilege only they have, that they lie near the tower.

5[13]:1 But wouldst you know about them that are broken in pieces, and cast away far from the tower? These are the sons of lawlessness. They received the faith in hypocrisy, and no wickedness was absent from them. Therefore they have not salvation, for they are not useful for building by reason of their wickednesses. Therefore they were broken up and thrown far away by reason of the wrath of the Lord, for they excited Him to wrath.

5[13]:2 But the rest whom you hast seen lying in great numbers, not going to the building, of these they that are mildewed are they that knew the truth, but did not abide in it, nor hold fast to the saints. Therefore they are useless."

5[13]:3 "But they that have the cracks, who are they?" "These are they that have discord in their hearts against one another, and are not at peace among themselves; who have an appearance of peace, but when they depart from one another, their wickednesses abide in their hearts. These are the cracks which the stones have.

5[13]:4 But they that are broken off short, these have believed, and have their greater part in righteousness, but have some parts of lawlessness; therefore they are too short, and are not perfect."

5[13]:5 "But the white and round stones, which did not fit into the building, who are they, lady?" She answered and said to me, "How long art you foolish and stupid, and enquire everything, and understand nothing? These are they that have faith, but have also riches of this world. When tribulation cometh, they deny their Lord by reason of their riches and their business affairs."

5[13]:6 And I answered and said unto her, "When then, lady, will they be useful for the building?" "When," she replied, "their wealth, which led their souls astray, shall be cut away, then will they be useful for God. For just as the round stone, unless it be cut away, and lose some portion of itself, cannot become square, so also they that are rich in this world, unless their riches be cut away, cannot become useful to the Lord.

5[13]:7 Learn first from thyself When you had riches, you was useless; but now you art useful and profitable unto life. Be you useful unto God, for you thyself also art taken from the same stones.

7[15]:1 "But the other stones which you saw cast far away from the tower and falling into the way and rolling out of the way into the regions where there is no way, these are they that have believed, but by reason of their double heart they abandon their true way. Thus thinking that they can find a better way, they go astray and are sore distressed, as they walk about in the regions where there is no way.

7[15]:2 But they that fall into the fire and are burned, these are they that finally rebelled from the living God, and it no more entered into their hearts to repent by reason of the lusts of their wantonness and of the wickednesses which they wrought.

7[15]:3 But the others, which are near the waters and yet cannot roll into the water, would you know who are they? These are they that heard the word, and would be baptized unto the name of the Lord. Then, when they call to their remembrance the purity of the truth, they change their minds, and go back again after their evil desires."

7[15]:4 So she finished the explanation of the tower.

7[15]:5 Still importunate, I asked her further, whether for all these stones that were rejected and would not fit into the building of the tower that was repentance, and they had a place in this tower. "They can repent," she said, "but they cannot be fitted into this tower.

7[15]:6 Yet they shall be fitted into another place much more humble, but not until they have undergone torments, and have fulfilled the days of their sins. And they shall be changed for this reason, because they participated in the Righteous Word; and then shall it befall them to be relieved from their torments, if the evil deeds, that they have done, come into their heart; but if these come not into their heart, they are not saved by reason of the hardness of their hearts."

8[16]:1 When then I ceased asking her concerning all these things, she said to me; "Would you see something else?" Being very desirous of beholding, I was greatly rejoiced that I should see it.

8[16]:2 She looked upon me, and smiled, and she said to me, "See you seven women round the tower?" "I see them, lady," say I. "This tower is supported by them by commandment of the Lord.

8[16]:3 Hear now their employments. The first of them, the woman with the strong hands, is called Faith; through her are saved the elect of God.

8[16]:4 And the second, that is girded about and looked like a man, is called Continence; she is the daughter of Faith. Whosoever then shall follow her, becomes happy in his life, for he shall refrain from all evil deeds, believing that, if he refrain from every evil desire, he shall inherit eternal life."

8[16]:5 "And the others, lady, who be they?" "They are daughters one of the other. The name of the one is Simplicity, of the next, Knowledge, of the next, Guilelessness, of the next, Reverence, of the next, Love. When then you shall do all the works of their mother, you canst live."

8[16]:6 "I would fain know, lady," I say, "what power each of them possessed." "Listen then," said she, "to the powers which they have.

8[16]:7 Their powers are mastered each by the other, and they follow each other, in the order in which they were born. From Faith is born Continence, from Continence Simplicity, from Simplicity Guilelessness, from Guilelessness Reverence, from Reverence Knowledge, from Knowledge Love. Their works then are pure and reverent and divine.

8[16]:8 Whosoever therefore shall serve these women, and shall have strength to master their works, shall have his dwelling in the tower with the saints of God."

8[16]:9 Then I asked her concerning the seasons, whether the consummation is even now. But she cried aloud, saying, "Foolish man, see you not that the tower is still a-building? Whenever therefore the tower shall be finished building, the end cometh; but it shall be built up quickly. Ask me no more questions: this reminder is sufficient for you and for the saints, and is the renewal of your spirits.

8[16]:10 But it was not revealed to thyself alone, but in order that you might show these things unto all. After three days--

8[16]:11 for you must understand first, and I charge you, Hermas, first with these words, which I am about to speak to you--(I charge you to) tell all these things into the ears of the saints, that hearing them and doing them they may be purified from their wickednesses, and thyself also with them."

9[17]:1 "Hear me, my children. I brought you up in much simplicity and guilelessness and reverence, through the mercy of the Lord, Who instilled righteousness into you, that you might be justified and sanctified from all wickedness and all crookedness. But you will not to cease from your wickedness.

9[17]:2 Now then hear me and be at peace among yourselves, and have regard one to another, and assist one another, and do not partake of the creatures of God alone in abundance, but share them also with those that are in want.

9[17]:3 For some men through their much eating bring weakness on the flesh, and injure their flesh: whereas the flesh of those who have nought to eat is injured by their not having sufficient nourishment, and their body is ruined.

9[17]:4 This exclusiveness therefore is hurtful to you that have and do not share with them that are in want.

9[17]:5 Look you to the judgment that cometh. you then that have more than enough, seek out them that are hungry, while the tower is still unfinished; for after the tower is finished, you will desire to do good, and will find no place for it.

9[17]:6 Look you therefore, you that exult in your wealth, lest they that are in want shall moan, and their moaning shall go up unto the Lord, and you with your [abundance of good things be shut outside the door of the tower.

9[17]:7 Now therefore I say unto you that are rulers of the Church, and that occupy the chief seats; be not you like unto the sorcerers. The sorcerers indeed carry their drugs in boxes, but you carry your drug and your poison in your heart.

9[17]:8 you are case-hardened, and you will not cleanse your hearts and mix your wisdom together in a clean heart, that you may obtain mercy from the Great King.

9[17]:9 Look you therefore, children, lest these divisions of yours deprive you of your life.

9[17]:10 How is it that you wish to instruct the elect of the Lord, while you yourselves have no instruction? Instruct one another therefore, and have peace among yourselves, that I also may stand gladsome before the Father, and give an account concerning you all to your Lord."

10[18]:1 When then she ceased speaking with me, the six young men, who were building, came, and took her away to the tower, and other four lifted the couch, and took it also away to the tower. I saw not the face of these, for they were turned away.

10[18]:2 And, as she went, I asked her to reveal to me concerning the three forms, in which she had appeared to me. She answered and said to me; "As concerning these things you must ask another, that they may be revealed to you."

10[18]:3 Now she was seen of me, brethren, in my first vision of last year, as a very aged woman and seated on a chair.

10[18]:4 In the second vision her face was youthful, but her flesh and her hair were aged, and she spoke to me standing; and she was more gladsome than before.

10[18]:5 But in the third vision she was altogether youthful and of exceeding great beauty, and her hair alone was aged; and she was gladsome exceedingly and seated on a couch. Touching these things I was very greatly anxious to learn this revelation.

10[18]:6 And I see the aged woman in a vision of the night, saying to me, "Every enquiry needs humility. Fast therefore, and you shall receive what you ask from the Lord."

10[18]:7 So I fasted one day; and that very night there appeared unto me a young man, and he said to me, "Seeing that you ask me revelations offhand with entreaty, take heed lest by thy much asking you injure thy flesh.

10[18]:8 Sufficient for you are these revelations. Canst you see mightier revelations than those you hast seen?"

10[18]:9 I say unto him in reply, "Sir, this one thing alone I ask, concerning the three forms of the aged woman, that a complete revelation may be vouchsafed me." He said to me in answer, How long are you without understanding? It is your double-mindedness that made you of no understanding, and because your heart is not set towards the Lord."

10[18]:10 I answered and said unto him again, "From you, Sir, we shall learn the matters more accurately."

11[19]:1 Listen," said he, "concerning the three forms, of which you enquire.

11[19]:2 In the first vision wherefore did she appear to you an aged woman and seated on a chair? Because your spirit was aged, and already decayed, and had no power by reason of your infirmities and acts of double-mindedness.

11[19]:3 For as aged people, having no longer hope of renewing their youth, expect nothing else but to fall asleep, so you also, being weakened with the affairs of this world gave yourselves over to repining, and cast not your cares on the Lord; but your spirit was broken, and you were aged by your sorrows."

11[19]:4 "Wherefore then she was seated on a chair, I would fain know, Sir." "Because every weak person sits on a chair by reason of his weakness, that the weakness of his body may be supported. So you hast the symbolism of the first vision."

12[20]:1 "But in the second vision you saw her standing, and with her countenance more youthful and more gladsome than before; but her flesh and her hair aged. Listen to this parable also," said he.

12[20]:2 "Imagine an old man, who has now lost all hope of himself by reason of his weakness and his poverty, and expected nothing else save the last day of his life. Suddenly an inheritance is left him. He heard the news, rose up and full of joy clothes himself with strength, and no longer lied down, but stood up, and his spirit, which was now broken by reason of his former circumstances, is renewed again, and he no longer sat, but took courage; so also was it with you, when you heard the revelation which the Lord revealed unto you.

12[20]:3 For He had compassion on you, and renewed your spirits, and you laid aside your maladies, and strength came to you, and you were made powerful in the faith, and the Lord rejoiced to see you put on your strength. And therefore He showed you the building of the tower; yea, and other things also shall He show you, if with your whole heart you be at peace among yourselves.

13[21]:1 But in the third vision you saw her younger and fair and gladsome, and her form fair.

13[21]:2 For just as when to some mourner cometh some piece of good tidings, immediately he forgot his former sorrows, and admitted nothing but the tidings which he has heard, and is strengthened thenceforth unto that which is good, and his spirit is renewed by reason of the joy which he has received; so also you have received a renewal of your spirits by seeing these good things.

13[21]:3 And whereas you saw her seated on a couch, the position is a firm on; for the couch has four feet and stood firmly; for the world too Is upheld by means of four elements.

13[21]:4 They then that have fully repented shall be young again, and founded firmly, seeing that they have repented with their whole heart. There you hast the revelation entire and complete. You shall ask nothing more as touching revelation-- but if anything be lacking still, it shall be revealed unto you."

Vision 4

1[22]:1 The fourth vision which I saw, brethren, twenty days after the former vision which came unto me, for a type of the impending tribulation.

1[22]:2 I was going into the country by the Companion Way. From the high road, it is about ten stades; and the place is easy for traveling.

1[22]:3 While then I am walking alone, I entreat the Lord that He will accomplish the revelations and the visions which He showed me through His holy Church, that He may strengthen me and may give repentance to His servants which have stumbled, that His great and glorious Name may be glorified, for that He held me worthy that He should show me His marvels.

1[22]:4 And as I gave glory and thanksgiving to Him, there answered me as it were the sound of a voice, "Be not of doubtful mind, Hermas." I began to question in myself and to say, "How can I be of doubtful mind, seeing that I am so firmly founded by the Lord, and have seen glorious things?"

1[22]:5 And I went on a little, brethren, and behold, I see a cloud of dust rising as it were to heaven, and I began to say within myself, "Can it be that cattle are coming, and raising a cloud of dust?" for it was just about a stade from me.

1[22]:6 As the cloud of dust waxed greater and greater, I suspected that it was something supernatural. Then the sun shone out a little, and behold, I see a huge beast like some sea-monster, and from its mouth fiery locusts issued forth. And the beast was about a hundred feet in length, and its head was as it were of pottery.

1[22]:7 And I began to weep, and to entreat the Lord that He would rescue me from it. And I remembered the word which I had heard, "Be not of doubtful mind, Hermas."

1[22]:8 Having therefore, brethren, put on the faith of the Lord and called to mind the mighty works that He had taught me, I took courage and gave myself up to the beast. Now the beast was coming on with such a rush, that it might have ruined a city.

1[22]:9 I come near it, and, huge monster as it was, it stretched itself on the ground, and merely put forth its tongue, and stirred not at all until I had passed by it.

1[22]:10 And the beast had on its head four colors; black then fire and blood color, then gold, then white.

2[23]:1 Now after I had passed the beast, and had gone forward about thirty feet, behold, there met me a virgin arrayed as if she were going forth from a bridal-chamber all in white and with white sandals, veiled up to her forehead, and her head-covering consisted of a turban, and her hair was white.

2[23]:2 I knew from the former Visions that it was the Church, and I became more cheerful. She saluted me, saying, "Good morrow, my good man"; and I saluted her in turn, "Lady, good morrow."

2[23]:3 She answered and said unto me, "Did nothing meet you? "I say unto her, Lady, such a huge beast, that could have destroyed whole peoples: but, by the power of the Lord and by His great mercy, I escaped it."

2[23]:4 "You didst escape it well," said she, "because you didst cast thy care upon God, and didst open thy heart to the Lord, believing that you can be saved by nothing else but by His great and glorious Name. Therefore the Lord sent His angel, which is over the beasts, whose name is Segri, and shut his mouth that it might not hurt you. You hast escaped a great tribulation by reason of thy faith, and because, though you saw so huge a beast, you didst not doubt in thy mind.

2[23]:5 Go therefore, and declare to the elect of the Lord His mighty works, and tell them that this beast is a type of the great tribulation which is to come. If therefore you prepare yourselves beforehand, and repent (and turn) unto the Lord with your whole heart, you shall be able to escape it, if your heart be made pure and without blemish, and if for the remaining days of your life you serve the Lord blamelessly. Cast your cares upon the Lord and He will set them straight.

2[23]:6 Trust you in the Lord, you men of doubtful mind, for He can do all things, yea, He both turned away His wrath from you, and again He sent forth His plagues upon you that are of doubtful mind. Woe to them that hear these words and are disobedient; it were better for them that they had not been born."

3[24]:1 I asked her concerning the four colors, which the beast had upon its head. Then she answered me and said, "Again you art curious about such matters." "Yes, lady," said I, "make known unto me what these things are."

3[24]:2 "Listen," said she; "the black is this world in which you dwell;

3[24]:3 and the fire and blood color showed that this world must perish by blood and fire;

3[24]:4 and the golden part are you that has escaped from this world. For as the gold is tested by the fire and is made useful, so you also [that dwell in it] are being tested in yourselves. you then that abide and pass through the fire will be purified by it. For as the old loses its dross. so you also shall cast away all sorrow and tribulation, and shall be purified, and shall be useful for the building of the tower.

3[24]:5 But the white portion is the coming age, in which the elect of God shall dwell; because the elect of God shall be without spot and pure unto life eternal.

3[24]:6 Wherefore cease not you to speak in the ears of the saints. you have now the symbolism also of the tribulation which is coming in power. But if you be willing, it shall be nothing. Remember you the things that are written beforehand."

3[24]:7 With these words she departed, and I saw not in what direction she departed; for a noise was made: and I turned back in fear, thinking that the beast was coming.

Vision 5

5[25]:1 As I prayed in the house, and sat on the couch, there entered a man glorious in his visage, in the garb of a shepherd, with a white skin wrapped about him, and with a wallet on his shoulders and a staff in his hand. And he saluted me, and I saluted him in return.

5[25]:2 And he immediately sat down by my side, and he said unto me, "I was sent by the most holy angel, that I might dwell with you the remaining days of thy life."

5[25]:3 I thought he came to tempt me, and I say unto him, "Why, who art you? For I know," say I, "unto whom I was delivered." He said to me, "Dost you not recognize me?" "No," I say. "I," said he, "am the shepherd, unto whom you were delivered."

5[25]:4 While he was still speaking, his form was changed, and I recognized him as being the same, to whom I was delivered; and straightway I was confounded, and fear seized me, and I was altogether overwhelmed with distress that I had answered him so wickedly and senselessly.

5[25]:5 But he answered and said unto me, "Be not confounded, but strengthen thyself in my commandments which I am about to command you. For I was sent," said he, "that I might show you again all the things which you didst see before, merely the heads which are convenient for you. First of all, write down my commandments and my parables; and the other matters you shall write down as I shall show them to you. The reason why," said he, "I command you to write down first the commandments and parables is, that you may read them off-hand, and may be able to keep them."

5[25]:6 So I wrote down the commandments and parables, as he commanded me.

5[25]:7 If then, when you hear them, you keep them and walk in them, and do them with a pure heart, you shall receive from the Lord all things that He promised you; but if, when you hear them, you do not repent, but still add to your sins, you shall receive from the Lord the opposite. All these the shepherd, the angel of repentance commanded me to write.

Mandate 1

1[26]:1 "First of all, believe that God is One, even He who created all things and set them in order, and brought all things from non-existence into being, Who comprehends all things, being alone incomprehensible.

1[26]:2 Believe Him therefore, and fear Him, and in this fear be continent. Keep these things, and you shall cast off all wickedness from thyself, and shall clothe thyself with every excellence of righteousness, and shall live unto God, if you keep this commandment."

Mandate 2

1[27]:1 He said to me; "Keep simplicity and be guileless, and you shall be as little children, that know not the wickedness which destroyed the life of men.

1[27]:2 First of all, speak evil of no man, neither take pleasure in listening to a slanderer. Otherwise you that hear too shall be responsible for the sin of him that speaks the evil, if you believe the slander, which you hear; for in believing it you thyself also wilt have a grudge against thy brother. So then shall you be responsible for the sin of him that speaks the evil.

1[27]:3 Slander is evil; it is a restless demon, never at peace, but always having its home among factions. Refrain from it therefore, and you shall have success at all times with all men.

1[27]:4 But clothe thyself in reverence, wherein is no evil stumbling-block, but all things are smooth and gladsome. Work that which is good, and of thy labors, which God gives you, give to all that are in want freely, not questioning to whom you shall give, and to whom you shall not give. Give to all; for to all God desires that there should be given of His own bounties.

1[27]:5 They then that receive shall render an account to God why they received it, and to what end; for they that receive in distress shall not be judged, but they that receive by false pretence shall pay the penalty.

1[27]:6 He then that gives is guiltless; for as he received from the Lord the ministration to perform it, he has performed it in sincerity, by making no distinction to whom to give or not to give. This ministration then, when sincerely performed, becomes glorious in the sight of God. He therefore that ministered thus sincerely shall live unto God.

1[27]:7 Therefore keep this commandment, as I have told you, that your own repentance and that of thy household may be found to be sincere, and [thy] heart pure and undefiled."

Mandate 3

1[28]:1 Again he said to me; "Love truth, and let nothing but truth proceed out of thy mouth, that the Spirit which God made to dwell in this flesh, may be found true in the sight of all men; and thus shall the Lord, Who dwelt in you, be glorified; for the Lord is true in every word, and with Him there is no falsehood.

1[28]:2 They therefore that speak lies set the Lord at nought, and become robbers of the Lord, for they do not deliver up to Him the deposit which they received. For they received of Him a spirit free from lies. This if they shall return a lying spirit, they have defiled the commandment of the Lord and have become robbers."

1[28]:3 When then I heard these things, I wept bitterly. But seeing me weep he said, "Why weep you?" "Because, Sir," say I "I know not if I can be saved." "Why so?" said he. "Because, Sir," I say, "never in my life spoke I a true word, but I always lied deceitfully with all men and dressed up my falsehood as truth before all men; and no man ever contradicted me, but confidence was placed in my word. How then, Sir," say I, "can I live, seeing that I have done these things?"

1[28]:4 "Your supposition," he said, "is right and true, for it behooved you as a servant of God to walk in truth, and no complicity with evil should abide with the Spirit of truth, nor bring grief to the Spirit which is holy and true." "Never, Sir," say I, "heard I clearly words such as these."

1[28]:5 "Now then," said he, "you heard Guard them, that the former falsehoods also which you spake in thy business affairs may themselves become credible, now that these are found true; for they too can become trustworthy. If you keep these things, and from henceforward speak nothing but truth, you shall be able to secure life for thyself And whosoever shall hear this command, and abstain from falsehood, that most pernicious habit, shall live unto God."

Mandate 4

1[29]:1 "I charge you, "said he, "to keep purity, and let not a thought enter into thy heart concerning another's wife, or concerning fornication, or concerning any such like evil deeds; for in so doing you commit a great sin. But remember your own wife always, and you shall never go wrong.

1[29]:2 For should this desire enter into your heart, you wilt go wrong, and should any other as evil as this, you commit sin. For this desire in a servant of God is a great sin; and if any man doeth this evil deed, he worked out death for himself.

1[29]:3 Look to it therefore. Abstain from this desire; for, where holiness dwells, there lawlessness ought not to enter into the heart of a righteous man."

1[29]:4 I say to him, "Sir, permit me to ask you a few more questions" "Say on," said he. "Sir," say I, "if a man who has a wife that is faithful in the Lord detect her in adultery, doth the husband sin in living with her?"

1[29]:5 "So long as he is ignorant," said he, "he sinned not; but if the husband know of her sin, and the wife repent not, but continue in her fornication, and her husband live with her, he makes himself responsible for her sin and an accomplice in her adultery."

1[29]:6 "What then, Sir," say I, "shall the husband do, if the wife continue in this case?" "Let him divorce her," said he, "and let the husband abide alone: but if after divorcing his wife he shall marry another, he likewise commits adultery."

1[29]:7 "If then, Sir," say I, "after the wife is divorced, she repent and desire to return to her own husband, shall she not be received?"

1[29]:8 "Certainly," said he, "if the husband received her not, he sinned and brings great sin upon himself; nay, one who has sinned and repented must be received, yet not often; for there is but one repentance for the servants of God. For the sake of her repentance therefore the husband ought not to marry. This is the manner of acting enjoined on husband and wife.

1[29]:9 Not only," said he, "is it adultery, if a man pollute his flesh, but whosoever doeth things like unto the heathen commits adultery. If therefore in such deeds as these likewise a man continue and repent not, keep away from him, and live not with him. Otherwise, you also art a partaker of his sin.

1[29]:10 For this cause you were enjoined to remain single, whether husband or wife; for in such cases repentance is possible.

1[29]:11 I," said he, "am not giving an excuse that this matter should be concluded thus, but to the end that the sinner should sin no more. But as concerning his former sin, there is One Who is able to give healing; it is He Who has authority over all things."

2[30]:1 I asked him again, saying, "Seeing that the Lord held me worthy that you should always dwell with me, suffer me still to say a few words, since I understand nothing, and my heart has been made dense by my former deeds. Make me to understand, for I am very foolish, and I apprehend absolutely nothing."

2[30]:2 He answered and said unto me, "I," said he, "preside over repentance, and I give understanding to all who repent. No, think you not," said he, "that this very act of repentance is understanding? To repent is great understanding," said he. "For the man that has sinned understands that he has done evil before the Lord, and the deed which he has done enters into his heart, and he repents, and doeth no more evil, but doeth good lavishly, and humbles his own soul and puts it to torture because it sinned. You see then that repentance is great understanding."

2[30]:3 "It is on this account therefore, Sir," say I, "that I enquire everything accurately of you; first, because I am a sinner; secondly, because I know not what deeds I must do that I may live, for my sins are many and various."

2[30]:4 "You shall live," said he, "if you keep my commandments and walk in them and whosoever shall hear these commandments and keep them, shall live unto God."

3[31]:1 "I will still proceed, Sir," say I, "to ask a further question." "Speak on," said he. "I have heard, Sir," say I, "from certain teachers, that there is no other repentance, save that which took place when we rent down into the water and obtained remission of our former sins."

3[31]:2 He said to me; "You hast well heard; for so it is. For he that has received remission of sins ought no longer to sin, but to dwell in purity.

3[31]:3 But, since you enquire all things accurately, I will declare unto you this also, so as to give no excuse to those who shall hereafter believe or those who have already believed, on the Lord. For they that have already believed, or shall hereafter believe, have not repentance for sins, but have only remission of their former sins.

3[31]:4 To those then that were called before these days the Lord has appointed repentance. For the Lord, being a discerner of hearts and foreknowing all things, perceived the weakness of men and the manifold wiles of the devil, how that he will be doing some mischief to the servants of God, and will deal wickedly with them.

3[31]:5 The Lord then, being very compassionate, had pity on His handiwork, and appointed this (opportunity of) repentance, and to me was given the authority over this repentance.

3[31]:6 But I say unto you," said he, "if after this great and holy calling any one, being tempted of the devil, shall commit sin, he has only one (opportunity of) repentance. But if he sin off-hand and repent, repentance is unprofitable for such a man; for he shall live with difficulty."

3[31]:7 I say unto him, "I was quickened unto life again, when I heard these things from you so precisely. For I know that, if I shall add no more to my sins, I shall be saved." "You shall be saved," he said, "you and all, as many as shall do these things."

4[32]:1 I asked him again, saying, "Sir, since once you do bear with me, declare unto me this further matter also." "Say on," said he. "If a wife, Sir," say I, "or, it may be, a husband fall asleep, and one of them marry, doth the one that marries sin?"

4[32]:2 "He sins not," said he, "but if he remain single, he invests himself with more exceeding honor and with great glory before the Lord; yet even if he should marry, he sins not.

4[32]:3 Preserve purity and holiness therefore, and you shall live unto God. All these things, which I speak and shall hereafter speak unto you, guard from this time forward, from the day when you was committed unto me, and I will dwell in thy house.

4[32]:4 But for thy former transgressions there shall be remission, if you keep my commandments. Yea, and all shall have remission, if they keep these my commandments, and walk in this purity."

Mandate 5

1[33]:1 "Be you long-suffering and understanding," he said, "and you shall have the mastery over all evil deeds, and shall work all righteousness.

1[33]:2 For if you art long-suffering, the Holy Spirit that abides in you shall be pure, not being darkened by another evil spirit, but dwelling in a large room shall rejoice and be glad with the vessel in which he dwells, and shall serve God with much cheerfulness, having prosperity in himself.

1[33]:3 But if any angry temper approach, forthwith the Holy Spirit, being delicate, is straitened, not having [the] place clear, and seeks to retire from the place; for he is being choked by the evil spirit, and has no room to minister unto the Lord, as he desires, being polluted by angry temper. For the Lord dwells in long-suffering, but the devil in angry temper.

1[33]:4 Thus that both the spirits then should be dwelling together is inconvenient and evil for that man in whom they dwell.

1[33]:5 For if you take a little wormwood, and pour it into a jar of honey, is not the whole of the honey spoiled, and all that honey ruined by a very small quantity of wormwood? For it destroyed the sweetness of the honey, and it no longer has the same attraction for the owner, because it is rendered bitter and has lost its use. But if the wormwood be not put into the honey, the honey is found sweet and becomes useful to its owner.

1[33]:6 You see [then] that long-suffering is very sweet, beyond the sweetness of honey, and is useful to the Lord, and He dwells in it. But angry, temper is bitter and useless. If then angry temper be mixed with long-suffering, long-suffering is polluted and the man's intercession is no longer useful to God."

1[33]:7 "I would fain know, Sir," say I, "the working of angry temper, that I may guard myself from it." "Yea, verily," said he, "if you guard not thyself from it--you and thy family--you hast lost all thy hope. But guard thyself from it; for I am with you. Yea, and all men shall hold aloof from it, as many as have repented with their whole heart. For I will be with them and will preserve them; for they all were justified by the most holy angel.

2[34]:1 "Hear now," said he, "the working of angry temper, how evil it is, and how it subverts the servants of God by its own working, and how it leads them astray from righteousness. But it doth not lead astray them that are full in the faith, nor can it work upon them, because the power of the Lord is with them; but them that are empty and double-minded it leads astray.

2[34]:2 For when it sees such men in prosperity it insinuates itself into the heart of the man, and for no cause whatever the man or the woman is embittered on account of worldly matters, either about meats, or some triviality, or about some friend, or about giving or receiving, or about follies of this kind. For all these things are foolish and vain and senseless and inexpedient for the servants of God.

2[34]:3 But long-suffering is great and strong, and has a mighty and vigorous power, and is prosperous in great enlargement, gladsome, exultant, free from care, glorifying the Lord at every season, having no bitterness in itself, remaining always gentle and tranquil. This long-suffering therefore dwells with those whose faith is perfect.

2[34]:4 But angry temper is in the first place foolish, fickle and senseless; then from foolishness is engendered bitterness, and from bitterness wrath, and from wrath anger, and from anger spite; then spite being composed of all these evil elements becomes a great sin and incurable.

2[34]:5 For when all these spirits dwell in one vessel, where the Holy Spirit also dwells, that vessel cannot contain them, but overflows.

2[34]:6 The delicate spirit therefore, as not being accustomed to dwell with an evil spirit nor with harshness, departs from a man of that kind, and seeks to dwell with gentleness and tranquility.

2[34]:7 Then, when it has removed from that man, in whom it dwells, that man becomes emptied of the righteous spirit, and henceforward, being filled with the evil spirits, he is unstable in all his actions, being dragged about hither and thither by the evil spirits, and is altogether blinded and bereft of his good intent. Thus then it happens to all persons of angry temper.

2[34]:8 Refrain therefore from angry temper, the most evil of evil spirits. But clothe thyself in long-suffering, and resist angry temper and bitterness, and you shall be round in company with the holiness which is beloved of the Lord. See then that you never neglect this commandment; for if you master this commandment, you shall be able likewise to keep the remaining commandments, which I am about to give you. Be strong in them and endowed with power; and let all be endowed with power, as many as desire to walk in them."

Mandate 6

1[35]:1 I charged you," said he, "in my first commandment to guard faith and fear and temperance." "Yes, Sir," say I. "But now," said he, "I wish to show you their powers also, that you mayest understand what is the power and effect of each one of them. For their effects are two fold. Now they are prescribed alike to the righteous and the unrighteous.

1[35]:2 Do you therefore trust righteousness, but trust not unrighteousness; for the way of righteousness is straight, but the way of unrighteousness is crooked. But walk you in the straight [and level] path, and leave the crooked one alone.

1[35]:3 For the crooked way has no tracks, but only pathlessness and many stumbling stones, and is rough and thorny. So it is therefore harmful to those who walk in it.

1[35]:4 But those who walk in the straight way walk on the level and without stumbling: for it is neither rough nor thorny. You seest then that it is more expedient to walk in this way."

1[35]:5 "I am pleased, Sir," say I, "to walk in this way." "You shall walk," he said, "yea, and whosoever shall turn unto the Lord with his whole heart shall walk in it.

2[36]:1 "Hear now," said he, "concerning faith. There are two angels with a man, one of righteousness and one of wickedness."

2[36]:2 "How then, Sir," say I, "shall I know their workings, seeing that both angels dwell with me?"

2[36]:3 "Hear," said he, "and understand their workings. The angel of righteousness is delicate and bashful and gentle and tranquil. When then this one enters into thy heart, forthwith he speaketh with you of righteousness, of purity, of holiness, and of contentment, of every righteous deed and of every glorious virtue. When all these things enter into thy heart, know that the angel of righteousness is with you. [These then are the works of the angel of righteousness.] Trust him therefore and his works.

2[36]:4 Now see the works of the angel of wickedness also. First of all, he is quick tempered and bitter and senseless, and his works are evil, overthrowing the servants of God. Whenever then he entereth into thy heart, know him by his works."

2[36]:5 "How I shall discern him, Sir," I reply, "I know not." Listen," said he. "When a fit of angry temper or bitterness comes upon you, know that he is in you. Then the desire of much business and the costliness of many viands and drinking bouts and of many drunken fits and of various luxuries which are unseemly, and the desire of women, and avarice, and haughtiness and boastfulness, and whatsoever things are akin and like to these--when then these things enter into thy heart, know that the angel of wickedness is with you.

2[36]:6 Do you therefore, recognizing his works, stand aloof from him, and trust him in nothing, for his works are evil and inexpedient for the servants of God. Here then you hast the workings of both the angels. Understand them, and trust the angel of righteousness.

2[36]:7 But from the angel of wickedness stand aloof, for his teaching is evil in every matter; for though one be a man of faith, and the desire of this angel enter into his heart, that man, or that woman, must commit some sin.

2[36]:8 And if again a man or a woman be exceedingly wicked, and the works of the angel of righteousness come into that man's heart, he must of necessity do something good.

2[36]:9 You see then," said he, "that it is good to follow the angel of righteousness, and to bid farewell to the angel of wickedness.

2[36]:10 This commandment declares what concerns faith, that you may trust the works of the angel of righteousness, and doing them may live unto God. But believe that the works of the angel of wickedness are difficult; so by not doing them you shall live unto God."

Mandate 7

1[37]:1 "Fear the Lord," said he, "and keep His commandments. So keeping the commandments of God you shall be powerful in every deed, and thy doing shall be incomparable. For whilst you fear the Lord, you shall do all things well. But this is the fear wherewith you ought to be afraid, and you shall be saved.

1[37]:2 But fear not the devil; for, if you fear the Lord, you shall be master over the devil, for there is no power in him. [For] in whom is no power, neither is there fear of him; but in whom power is glorious, of him is fear likewise. For every one that has power has fear, whereas he that has no power is despised of all.

1[37]:3 But fear you the works of the devil, for they are evil. While then you fear the Lord, you wilt fear the works of the devil, and wilt not do them, but abstain from them.

1[37]:4 Fear therefore is of two kinds. If you desire to do evil, fear the Lord, and you shall not do it. If again you desire to do good, fear the Lord and you shall do it. Therefore the fear of the Lord is powerful and great and glorious. Fear the Lord then, and you shall live unto Him; yea, and as many of them that keep His commandments as shall fear Him, shall live unto God."

1[37]:5 "Wherefore, Sir," say I, "didst you say concerning those that keep His commandments, "They shall live unto God"?" "Because," said he, "every creature fears the Lord, but not every one keeps His commandments. Those then that fear Him and keep His commandments, they have life unto God; but they that keep not His commandments have no life in them."

Mandate 8

1[38]:1 "I told you," said he, "that the creatures of God are twofold; for temperance also is twofold. For in some things it is right to be temperate, but in other things it is not right."

1[38]:2 "Make known unto me, Sir," say I, "in what things it is right to be temperate, and in what things it is not right." "Listen," said he. "Be temperate as to what is evil, and do it not; but be not temperate as to what is good, but do it. For if you be temperate as to what is good, so as not to do it, you commits a great sin; but if you be temperate as to what is evil, so as not to do it, you doest great righteousness. Be temperate therefore in abstaining from all wickedness, and do that which is good."

1[38]:3 "What kinds of wickedness, Sir," say I, "are they from which we must be temperate and abstain?" "Listen," said he; "from adultery and fornication, from the lawlessness of drunkenness, from wicked luxury, from many viands and the costliness of riches, and vaunting and haughtiness and pride, and from falsehood and evil speaking and hypocrisy, malice and all blasphemy.

1[38]:4 These works are the most wicked of all in the life of men. From these works therefore the servant of God must be temperate and abstain; for he that is not temperate so as to abstain from these cannot live unto God. Listen then to what follows upon these."

1[38]:5 "Why, are there still other evil deeds, Sir?" say I. "Aye, said he, "there are many, from which the servant of God must be temperate and abstain; theft, falsehood, deprivation, false witness, avarice, evil desire, deceit, vainglory, boastfulness, and whatsoever things are like unto these.

1[38]:6 Think you not that these things are wrong, yea, very wrong," [said he,] "for the servants of God? In all these things he that serves God must exercise temperance. Be you temperate, therefore, and refrain from all these things, that you may live unto God, and be enrolled among those who exercise self-restraint in them. These then are the things from which you should restrain thyself

1[38]:7 Now hear," said he, "the things, in which you should not exercise self restraint, but do them. Exercise no self-restraint in that which is good, but do it."

1[38]:8 "Sir," say I, "show me the power of the good also, that I may walk in them and serve them, that doing them it may be possible for me to be saved." "Hear," said he, "the works of the good likewise, which you must do, and towards which you must exercise no self-restraint.

1[38]:9 First of all, there is faith, fear of the Lord, love, concord, words of righteousness, truth, patience; nothing is better than these in the life of men. If a man keep these, and exercise not self-restraint from them, he becomes blessed in his life.

1[38]:10 Hear now what follow upon these; to minister to widows, to visit the orphans and the needy, to ransom the servants of God from their afflictions, to be hospitable (for in hospitality benevolence from time to time has a place), to resist no man, to be tranquil, to show yourself more submissive than all men, to reverence the aged, to practice righteousness, to observe brotherly feeling, to endure injury, to be long-suffering, to bear no grudge, to exhort those who are sick at soul, not to cast away those that have stumbled from the faith, but to convert them and to put courage Into them, to reprove sinners, not to oppress debtors and indigent persons, and whatsoever actions are like these.

1[38]:11 Do these things," said he, "seem to you to be good?" "Why, what, Sir," say I, "can be better than these?" "Then walk in them," said he, "and abstain not from them, and you shall live unto God.

1[38]:12 Keep this commandment therefore. If you do good and abstain not from it, you shall live unto God; yea, and all shall live unto God who act so. And again if you do not evil, and abstain from it, you shall live unto God; yea, and all shall live unto God, who shall keep these commandments, and walk in them."

Mandate 9

1[39]:1 He said to me; "Remove from thyself a doubtful mind and doubt not at all whether to ask of God, saying within thyself, "How can I ask thing of the Lord and receive it, seeing that I have committed so many sins against Him?"

1[39]:2 Reason not thus, but turn to the Lord with thy whole heart, and ask of Him nothing wavering, and you shall know His exceeding compassion, that He will surely not abandon you, but will fulfill the petition of thy soul.

1[39]:3 For God is not as men who bear a grudge, but Himself is without malice and has compassion on His creatures.

1[39]:4 Do you therefore cleanse thy heart from all the vanities of this life, and from the things mentioned before; and ask of the Lord, and you shall receive all things, and shall lack nothing of all thy petitions, if you ask of the Lord nothing wavering.

1[39]:5 But if you waver in thy heart, you shall surely receive none of thy petitions. For they that waver towards God, these are the doubtful-minded, and they never obtain any of their petitions.

1[39]:6 But they that are complete in the faith make all their petitions trusting in the Lord, and they receive, because they ask without wavering, nothing doubting; for every doubtful-minded man, if he repent not, shall hardly be saved.

1[39]:7 Cleanse therefore thy heart from doubtful-mindedness, and put on faith, for it is strong, and trust God that you wilt receive all thy petitions which you ask; and if after asking anything of the Lord, you receive thy petition somewhat tardily, be not of doubtful mind because you didst not receive the petition of thy soul at once. For assuredly it is by reason of some temptation or some transgression, of which you art ignorant, that you receive thy petition so tardily.

1[39]:8 Do you therefore cease not to make thy soul's petition, and you shall receive it. But if you grow weary, and doubt as you ask, blame yourself and not Him that gave unto you. See to this doubtful-mindedness; for it is evil and senseless, and uproots many from the faith, yea, even very faithful and strong men. For indeed this doubtful-mindedness is a daughter of the devil, and works great wickedness against the servants of God.

1[39]:9 Therefore despise doubtful-mindedness and gain the mastery over it in everything, clothing yourself with faith which is strong and powerful. For faith promises all things, accomplishes all things; but doubtful-mindedness, as having no confidence in itself, fails in all the works which it doeth.

1[39]:10 You see then," said he, "that faith is from above from the Lord, and has great power; but doubtful-mindedness is an earthly spirit from the devil, and has no power.

1[39]:11 Do you therefore serve that faith which has power, and hold aloof from the doubtful-mindedness which has no power; and you shall live unto God; yea, and all those shall live unto God who are so minded."

Mandate 10

1[40]:1 "Put away sorrow from yourself," said he, "for she is the sister of doubtful-mindedness and of angry temper."

1[40]:2 "How, Sir," say I, "is she the sister of these? For angry temper seems to me to be one thing, doubtful-mindedness another, sorrow another." "You art a foolish fellow," said he, "[and] perceives not that sorrow is more evil than all the spirits, and is most fatal to the servants of God, and beyond all the spirits destroys a man, and crushes out the Holy Spirit and yet again saves it."

1[40]:3 "I, Sir," say I, "am without understanding, and I understand not these parables. For how it can crush out and again save, I do not comprehend."

1[40]:4 "Listen," said he. "Those who have never investigated concerning the truth, nor enquired concerning the deity, but have merely believed, and have been mixed up in business affairs and riches and heathen friendships, and many other affairs of this world--as many, I say, as devote themselves to these things, comprehend not the parables of the deity; for they are darkened by these actions, and are corrupted and become barren.

1[40]:5 As good vineyards, when they are treated with neglect, are made barren by the thorns and weeds of various kinds, so men who after they have believed fall into these many occupations which were mentioned before, lose their understanding and comprehend nothing at all concerning righteousness; for if they hear concerning the deity and truth, their mind is absorbed in their occupations, and they perceive nothing at all.

1[40]:6 But they that have the fear of God, and investigate concerning deity and truth, and direct their heart towards the Lord, perceive and understand everything that is said to them more quickly, because they have the fear of the Lord in themselves; for where the Lord dwells, there too is great understanding. Hold fast therefore unto the Lord, and you shall understand and perceive all things.

2[41]:1 "Hear now, senseless man," said he, "How sorrow crushes out the Holy Spirit, and again saves it.

2[41]:2 When the man of doubtful mind sets his hand to any action, and fails in it owing to his doubtful-mindedness, grief at this enters into the man, and grieves the Holy Spirit, and crushes it out.

2[41]:3 Then again when angry temper cleaves to a man concerning any matter, and he is much embittered, again sorrow enters into the heart of the man that was ill-tempered, and he is grieved at the deed which he has done, and repents that he did evil.

2[41]:4 This sadness therefore seems to bring salvation, because he repented at having done the evil. So both the operations sadden the Spirit; first, the doubtful mind saddens the Spirit, because it succeeded not in its business, and the angry temper again, because it did what was evil. Thus both are saddening to the Holy Spirit, the doubtful mind and the angry temper.

2[41]:5 Put away therefore from yourself sadness, and afflict not the Holy Spirit that dwells in you, lest haply He intercede with God [against you], and depart from you.

2[41]:6 For the Spirit of God, that was given unto this flesh, endures not sadness neither constraint.

3[42]:1 "Therefore clothe yourself in cheerfulness, which has favor with Cod always, and is acceptable to Him, and rejoice in it. For every cheerful man works good, and thinks good, and despises sadness;

3[42]:2 but the sad man is always committing sin. In the first place he commits sin, because he grieves the Holy Spirit, which was given to the man being a cheerful spirit; and in the second place, by grieving the Holy Spirit he doeth lawlessness, in that he doth not intercede with neither confess unto God. For the intercession of a sad man has never at any time power to ascend to the altar of God."

3[42]:3 "Wherefore," say I, "doth not the intercession of him that is saddened ascend to the altar?" "Because," said he, "sadness is seated at his heart. Thus sadness mingled with the intercession doth not suffer the intercession to ascend pure to the altar. For as vinegar when mingled with wine in the same (vessel) has not the same pleasant taste, so likewise sadness mingled with the Holy Spirit has not the same intercession.

3[42]:4 Therefore cleanse yourself from this wicked sadness, and you shall live unto God; yea, and all they shall live unto God, who shall cast away sadness from themselves and clothe themselves in all cheerfulness."

Mandate 11

1[43]:1 He showed me men seated on a couch, and another man seated on a chair. And he said to me, "See you those that are seated on the couch?" "I see them, Sir," say I. "These," said he, "are faithful, but he that sits on the chair is a false prophet who destroys the mind of the servants of God--I mean, of the doubtful-minded, not of the faithful.

1[43]:2 These doubtful-minded ones then come to him as to a soothsayer and enquire of him what shall befall them. And he, the false prophet, having no power of a divine Spirit in himself, speaks with them according to their enquiries [and according to the lusts of their wickedness], and fills their souls as they themselves wish.

1[43]:3 For being empty himself he gives empty answers to empty enquirers; for what-ever enquiry may be made of him, he answers according to the emptiness of the man. But he speaks also some true words; for the devil fills him with his own spirit, if so be he shall be able to break down some of the righteous.

1[43]:4 So many therefore as are strong in the faith of the Lord, clothed with the truth, hold fast not to such spirits, but hold aloof from them; but as

665

many as are doubters and frequently change their minds, practice soothsaying like the Gentiles, and bring upon themselves greater sin by their idolatries. For he that consults a false prophet on any matter is an idolater and emptied of the truth, and senseless.

1[43]:5 For no Spirit given of God needs to be consulted; but, having the power of deity, speaks all things of itself, because it is from above, even from the power of the divine Spirit.

1[43]:6 But the spirit which is consulted, and speaks according to the desires of men, is earthly and fickle, having no power; and it speaks not at all, unless it be consulted."

1[43]:7 "How then, Sir," say I, "shall a man know who of them is a prophet, and who a false prophet?" "Hear," said he, "concerning both the prophets; and, as I shall tell you, so shall you test the prophet and the false prophet. By his life test the man that has the divine Spirit.

1[43]:8 In the first place, he that has the [divine] Spirit, which is from above, is gentle and tranquil and humble-minded, and abstains from all wickedness and vain desire of this present world, and holds himself inferior to all men, and gives no answer to any man when enquired of, nor speaks in solitude (for neither doth the Holy Spirit speak when a man wishes Him to speak); but the man speaks then when God wishes him to speak.

1[43]:9 When then the man who has the divine Spirit cometh into an assembly of righteous men, who have faith in a divine Spirit, and intercession is made to God by the gathering of those men, then the angel of the prophetic spirit, who is attached to him, fills the man, and the man, being filled with the Holy Spirit, speaks to the multitude, according as the Lord wills.

1[43]:10 In this way then the Spirit of the deity shall be manifest. This then is the greatness of the power as touching the Spirit of the deity of the Lord.

1[43]:11 Hear now," said he, "concerning the earthly and vain spirit, which has no power but is foolish.

1[43]:12 In the first place, that man who seems to have a spirit exalts himself, and desires to have a chief place, and straight-way he is impudent and shameless and talkative and conversant in many luxuries and in many other deceits and receives money for his prophesying, and if he receives not, he prophesies not. Now can a divine Spirit receive money and prophesy? It is not possible for a prophet of God to do this, but the spirit of such prophets is earthly.

1[43]:13 In the next place, it never approaches an assembly of righteous men; but avoids them, and clings to the doubtful-minded and empty, and prophesies to them in corners, and deceives them, speaking all things in emptiness to gratify their desires; for they too are empty whom it answers. For the empty vessel placed together with the empty is not broken, but they agree one with the other.

1[43]:14 But when he comes into an assembly full of righteous men who have a Spirit of deity, and intercession is made from them, that man is emptied, and the earthly spirit flees from him in fear, and that man is struck dumb and is altogether broken in pieces, being unable to utter a word.

1[43]:15 For, if you pack wine or oil into a closet, and place an empty vessel among them, and again desire to unpack the closet, the vessel which you place there empty, empty in like manner you will find it. Thus also the empty prophets, whenever they come unto the spirits of righteous men, are found just such as they came.

1[43]:16 I have given you the life of both kinds of prophets. Therefore test, by his life and his works, the man who says that he is moved by the Spirit.

1[43]:17 But do you trust the Spirit that cometh from God, and has power; but in the earthly and empty spirit put no trust at all; for in it there is no power, for it cometh from the devil.

1[43]:18 Listen [then] to the parable which I shall tell you. Take a stone, and throw it up to heaven--see if you can reach it; or again, take a squirt of water, and squirt it up to heaven--see if you can bore through the heaven."

1[43]:19 "How, Sir," say I, "can these things be? For both these things which you hast mentioned are beyond our power." "Well then," said he, "just as these things are beyond our power, so likewise the earthly spirits have no power and are feeble.

1[43]:20 Now take the power which cometh from above. The hail is a very, small grain, and yet, when it falls on a man's head, what pain it causes! Or again, take a drop which falls on the ground from the tiles, and bores through the stone.

1[43]:21 You see then that the smallest things from above falling on the earth have great power. So likewise the divine Spirit coming from above is powerful. This Spirit therefore trust, but from the other hold aloof."

Mandate 12

1[44]:1 He said to me; "Remove from yourself all evil desire, and clothe yourself in the desire which is good and holy; for clothed with this desire you shall hate the evil desire, and shall bridle and direct it as you wilt.

1[44]:2 For the evil desire is wild, and only tamed with difficulty; for it is terrible, and by its wildness is very costly to men; more especially if a servant of God get entangled in it, and have no understanding, he is put to fearful costs by it. But it is costly to such men as are not clothed in the good desire, but are mixed up with this life "These men then it hands over to death."

1[44]:3 "Of what sort, Sir," say I, "are the works of the evil desire, which hand over men to death? Make them known to me, that I may hold aloof from them." Listen," [said he,] "through what works the evil desire brings death to the servants of God.

2[45]:1 "Before all is desire for the wife or husband of another, and for extravagance of wealth, and for many needless dainties, and for drinks and other luxuries, many and foolish. For even luxury is foolish and vain for the servants of God.

2[45]:2 These desires then are evil, and bring death to the servants of God. For this evil desire is a daughter of the devil. you must, therefore, abstain from the evil desires, that so abstaining you may live unto God.

2[45]:3 But as many as are mastered by them, and resist them not, are done to death utterly; for these desires are deadly.

2[45]:4 But do you clothe yourself in the desire of righteousness, and, having armed yourself with the fear of the Lord, resist them. For the fear of God dwells in the good desire. If the evil desire shall see you armed with the fear of God and resisting itself, it shall flee far from you, and shall no more be seen of you, being in fear of your arms.

2[45]:5 Do you therefore, when you art crowned for thy victory over it, come to the desire of righteousness, and deliver to her the victor's prize which you hast received, and serve her, according as she herself desires. If you serve the good desire, and art subject to her, you shall have power to master the evil desire, and to subject her, according as you wilt."

3[46]:1 "I would fain know, Sir," say I, "in what ways I ought to serve the good desire." "Listen," said he; "practice righteousness and virtue, truth and the fear of the Lord, faith and gentleness, and as many good deeds as are like these. Practicing these you shall be well-pleasing as a servant of God, and shall live unto Him; yea, and every one who shall serve the good desire shall live unto God."

3[46]:2 So he completed the twelve commandments, and he said to me; You hast these commandments; walk in them, and exhort thy hearers that their repentance may become pure for the rest of the days of their life.

3[46]:3 This ministration, which I give you, fulfill you with all diligence to the end, and you shall effect much. For you shall find favor among those who are about to repent, and they shall obey thy words. For I will be with you, and will compel them to obey you."

3[46]:4 I say to him; "Sir, these commandments are great and beautiful and glorious, and are able to gladden the heart of the man who is able to observe them. But I know not whether these commandments can be kept by a man, for they are very hard."

3[46]:5 He answered and said unto me; "If you set it before yourself that they can be kept, you wilt easily keep them, and they will not be hard; but if it once enter into thy heart that they cannot be kept by a man, you wilt not keep them.

3[46]:6 But now I say unto you; if you keep them not. but neglect them you shall not have salvation, neither thy children nor thy household, since you hast already pronounced judgment against yourself that these commandments cannot be kept by a man."

4[47]:1 And these things he said to me very angrily, so that I was confounded, and feared him exceedingly; for his form was changed, so that a man could not endure his anger.

4[47]:2 And when he saw that I was altogether disturbed and confounded, he began to speak more kindly [and cheerfully] to me, and he said; "Foolish fellow, void of understanding and of doubtful mind, perceives you not the glory of God, how great and mighty and marvelous it is, how that He created the world for man's sake, and subjected all His creation to man, and gave all authority to him, that he should be master over all things under the heaven?

4[47]:3 If then," [he said,] "man is lord of all the creatures of God and masters all things, cannot he also master these commandments Aye," said he, "the man that has the Lord in his heart can master [all things and] all these commandments.

4[47]:4 But they that have the Lord on their lips, while their heart is hardened, and are far from the Lord, to them these commandments are hard and inaccessible.

4[47]:5 Therefore do you, who are empty and fickle in the faith, set your Lord in your heart, and you shall perceive that nothing is easier than these commandments, nor sweeter, nor more gentle.

4[47]:6 Be you converted, you that walk after the commandments of the devil, (the commandments which are so) difficult and bitter and wild and riotous; and fear not the devil, for there is no power in him against you.

4[47]:7 For I will be with you, I, the angel of repentance, who have the mastery over him. The devil has fear alone, but his fear has no force. Fear him not therefore; and he will flee from you."

5[48]:1 I say to him, "Sir, listen to a few words from me." "Say what you wilt," said he. "Man, Sir," I say, "is eager to keep the commandments of God, and there is no one that asks not of the Lord that he may be strengthened in His commandments, and be subject to them; but the devil is hard and overmasters them."

5[48]:2 "He cannot," said he, "overmaster the servants of God, who set their hope on Him with their whole heart. The devil can wrestle with them, but he cannot overthrow them. If then you resist him, he will be vanquished and will flee from you disgraced. But as many," said he, "as are utterly empty, fear the devil as if he had power.

5[48]:3 When a man has filled amply sufficient jars with good wine, and among these jars a few are quite empty, he comes to the jars, and does not examine the full ones, for he knows that they are full; but he examines the empty ones, fearing lest they have turned sour. For empty jars soon turn sour, and the taste of the wine is spoilt.

5[48]:4 So also the devil cometh to all the servants of God tempting them. As many then as are complete in the faith, oppose him mightily, and he departs from them, not having a place where he can find an entrance. So he cometh next to the empty ones, and finding a place goes into them, and further he doeth what he wills in them, and they become submissive slaves to him.

6[49]:1 "But I, the angel of repentance, say unto you; Fear not the devil; for I was sent," said he, "to be with you who repent with your whole heart, and to strengthen you in the faith.

6[49]:2 Believe, therefore, on God, you who by reason of your sins have despaired of your life, and are adding to your sins, and weighing down your life; for if you turn unto the Lord with your whole heart, and work righteousness the remaining days of your life, and serve Him rightly according to His will, He will give healing to your former sins, and you shall have power to master the works of the devil. But of the threatening of the devil fear not at all; for he is unstrung, like the sinews of a dead man.

6[49]:3 Hear me therefore, and fear Him, Who is able to do all things, to save and to destroy, and observe these commandments, and you shall live unto God."

6[49]:4 I say to him, "Sir, now am I strengthened in all the ordinances of the Lord, because you art with me; and I know that you wilt crush all the power of the devil, and we shall be masters over him, and shall prevail over all his works. And I hope, Sir, that I am now able to keep these commandments which you hast commanded, the Lord enabling me."

6[49]:5 "You shall keep them," said he, "if thy heart be found pure with the Lord; yea, and all shall keep them, as many as shall purify their hearts from the vain desires of this world, and shall live unto God."

Parables Which He spoke With Me

Parable 1

1[50]:1 He said to me; "you know that you, who are the servants of God, are dwelling in a foreign land; for your city is far from this city. If then you know your city, in which you shall dwell, why do you here prepare fields and expensive displays and buildings and dwelling-chambers which are superfluous?

1[50]:2 He, therefore, that prepares these things for this city does not purpose to return to his own city.

1[50]:3 O foolish and double-minded and miserable man, perceives you not that all these things are foreign, and are under the power of another For the lord of this city shall say, "I do not wish you to dwell in my city; go forth from this city, for you do not conform to my laws."

1[50]:4 You, therefore who hast fields and dwellings and many other possessions, when you art cast out by him, what wilt you do with thy field and thy house am all the other things that you prepared for yourself? For the lord of this country said to you justly, "Either conform to my laws, or depart from my country."

1[50]:5 What then shall you do, who art under law in your own city? For the sake of thy fields and the rest of thy possessions wilt you altogether repudiate thy law, and walk according to the law of this city? Take heed, lest it be inexpedient to repudiate the law; for if you should desire to return again to thy city, you shall surely not be received [because you didst repudiate the law of the city], and shall be shut out from it.

1[50]:6 Take heed therefore; as dwelling in a strange land prepare nothing more for yourself but a competency which is sufficient for you, and make ready that, whenever the master of this city may desire to cast you out for your opposition to his law, you may go forth from his city and depart into your own city and use your own law joyfully, free from all insult.

1[50]:7 Take heed therefore, you that serve God and have Him in your heart: work the "works of God being mindful of His commandments and of the promises which He made, and believe Him that He will perform them, if His commandments be kept.

1[50]:8 Therefore, instead of fields buy you souls that are in trouble, as each is able, and visit widows and orphans, and neglect them not; and spend your riches and all your displays, which you received from God, on fields and houses of this kind.

1[50]:9 For to this end the Master enriched you, that you might perform these ministrations for Him. It is much better to purchase fields [and possessions] and houses of this kind, which you wilt find in your own city, when you visit it.

1[50]:10 This lavish expenditure is beautiful and joyous, not bringing sadness or fear, but bringing joy. The expenditure of the heathen then practice not you; for it is not convenient for you the servants of God.

1[50]:11 But practice your own expenditure, in which you can rejoice; and do not corrupt, neither touch that which is another man's, nor lust after it for it is wicked to lust after other men's possessions. But perform your own task, and you shall be saved."

Parable 2

1[51]:1 As I walked in the field, and noticed an elm and a vine, and was distinguishing them and their fruits, the shepherd appears to me and said; "What art you meditating within yourself?" "I am thinking, [Sir,]" say I, "about the elm and the vine, that they are excellently suited the one to the other."

1[51]:2 "These two trees," said he, "are appointed for a type to the servants of God." "I would fain know, [Sir,]" say I, "the type contained in these trees, of which you speak." "See you," said he, "the elm and the vine ?" "I see them, Sir," say I.

1[51]:3 "This vine," said he, "bears fruit, but the elm is an unfruitful stock. Yet this vine, except it climb up the elm, cannot bear much fruit when it is spread on the ground; and such fruit as it bears is rotten, because it is not suspended upon the elm. When then the vine is attached to the elm, it bears fruit both from itself and from the elm.

1[51]:4 You see then that the elm also bears [much] fruit, not less than the vine, but rather more." How more, Sir?" say I. "Because," said he, "the vine, when hanging upon the elm, bears its fruit in abundance, and in good condition; but, when spread on the ground, it bears little fruit, and that rotten. This parable therefore is applicable to the servants of God, to poor and to rich alike."

1[51]:5 "How, Sir?" say I; "instruct me." "Listen," said he; the rich man has much wealth, but in the things of the Lord he is poor, being distracted about his riches, and his confession and intercession with the Lord is very scanty; and even that which he gives is mall and weak and has not power above. When then the rich man goes up to the poor, and assists him in his needs, believing that for what he doth to the poor man he shall be able to obtain a reward with God--because the poor man is rich in intercession [and confession], and his intercession has great power with God--the rich man then supplies all things to the poor man without wavering.

1[51]:6 But the poor man being supplied by the rich makes intercession for him, thanking God for him that gave to him. And the other is still more zealous to assist the poor man, that he may be continuous in his life: for he knows that the intercession of the poor man is acceptable and rich before God.

1[51]:7 They both then accomplish their work; the poor man makes intercession, wherein he is rich [which he received of the Lord]; this he renders again to the Lord Who supplies him with it. The rich man too in like manner furnishes to the poor man, nothing doubting, the riches which he received from the Lord. And this work great and acceptable with God, because (the rich man) has understanding concerning his riches, and works for the poor man from the bounties of the Lord, and accomplishes the ministration of the Lord rightly.

1[51]:8 In the sight of men then the elm seems not to bear fruit, and they know not, neither perceive, that if there cometh a drought the elm having water nurtures the vine, and the vine having a constant supply of water bears fruit two fold, both for itself and for the elm. So likewise the poor, by interceding with the Lord for the rich, establish their riches, and again the rich, supplying their needs to the poor, establish their souls.

1[51]:9 So then both are made partners in the righteous work. He then that doeth these things shall not be abandoned of God, but shall be written in the books of the living.

1[51]:10 Blessed are the rich, who understand also that they are enriched from the Lord. For they that have this mind shall be able to do some good work."

Parable 3

1[52]:1 He showed me many trees which had no leaves, but they seemed to me to be, as it were, withered; for they were all alike. And he said to me; "See you these trees?" "I see them, Sir," I say, "they are all alike, and are withered." He answered and said to me; "These trees that you see are they that dwell in this world."

1[52]:2 "Wherefore then, Sir," say I, "are they as if they were withered, and alike?" "Because," said he, "neither the righteous are distinguishable, nor the sinners in this world, but they are alike. For this world is winter to the righteous, and they are not distinguishable, as they dwell with the sinners.

1[52]:3 For as in the winter the trees, having shed their leaves, are alike, and are not distinguishable, which are withered, and which alive, so also in this world neither the just nor the sinners are distinguishable, but they are all alike."

Parable 4

1[53]:1 He showed me many trees again, some of them sprouting, and others withered, and he said to me; "See you," said he, "these trees?" "I see them, Sir," say I, "some of them sprouting, and others withered."

1[53]:2 "These trees," said he, "that are sprouting are the righteous, who shall dwell in the world to come; for the world to come is summer to the righteous, but winter to the sinners. When then the mercy of the Lord shall shine forth, then they that serve God shall be made manifest; yea, and all men shall be made manifest.

1[53]:3 For as in summer the fruits of each several tree are made manifest, and are recognized of what sort they are, so also the fruits of the righteous shall be manifest, and all [even the very smallest] shall be known to be flourishing in that world.

1[53]:4 But the Gentiles and the sinners, just as you saw the trees which were withered, even such shall they be found, withered and unfruitful in that world, and shall be burnt up as fuel, and shall be manifest, because their practice in their life has been evil. For the sinners shall be burned, because they sinned and repented not; and the Gentiles shall be burned, because they knew not Him that created them.

1[53]:5 Do you therefore bear fruit, that in that summer thy fruit may be known. But abstain from overmuch business, and you shall never fill into any sin. For they that busy themselves overmuch, sin much also, being distracted about their business, and in no wise serving their own Lord.

1[53]:6 How then," said he, "can such a man ask anything of the Lord and receive it, seeing that he serves not the Lord? [For] they that serve Him, these shall receive their petitions, but they that serve not the Lord, these shall receive nothing.

1[53]:7 But if any one work one single action, he is able also to serve the Lord; for his mind shall not be corrupted from (following) the Lord, but he shall serve Him, because he keeps his mind pure.

1[53]:8 If therefore you doest these things, you shall be able to bear fruit unto the world to come; yea, and whosoever shall do these things, shall bear fruit."

Parable 5

1[54]:1 As I was fasting and seated on a certain mountain, and giving thanks to the Lord for all that He had done unto me, I see the shepherd seated by me and saying; "Why hast you come hither in the early morn?" "Because, Sir," say I, "I am keeping a station."

1[54]:2 "What," said he, "is a station?" "I am fasting, Sir," say I. "And what," said he, "is this fast [that you are fasting]?" "As I was accustomed, Sir," say I, "so I fast."

1[54]:3 "you know not," said he, "how to fast unto the Lord, neither is this a fast, this unprofitable fast which you make unto Him." "wherefore, Sir," say I, "say you this?" "I tell you," said he, "that this is not a fast, wherein you think to fast; but I will teach you what is a complete fast and acceptable to the Lord. Listen," said he;

1[54]:4 "God desires not such a vain fast; for by so fasting unto God you shall do nothing for righteousness. But fast you [unto God] such a fast as this;

1[54]:5 do no wickedness in thy life, and serve the Lord with a pure heart; observe His commandments and walk in His ordinances, and let no evil desire rise up in thy heart; but believe God. Then, if you shall do these things, and fear Him, and control yourself from every evil deed, you shall live unto God; and if you do these things, you shall accomplish a great fast, and one acceptable to God.

2[55]:1 "Hear the parable which I shall tell you relating to fasting.

2[55]:2 A certain man had an estate, and many slaves, and a portion of his estate he planted as a vineyard; and choosing out a certain slave who was trusty and well-pleasing (and) held in honor, he called him to him and said unto him; "Take this vineyard [which I have planted], and fence it [till I come], but do nothing else to the vineyard. Now keep this my commandment, and you shall be free in my house." Then the master of the servant went away to travel abroad.

2[55]:3 When then he had gone away, the servant took and fenced the vineyard; and having finished the fencing of the vineyard, he noticed that the vineyard was full of weeds.

2[55]:4 So he reasoned within himself, saying, "This command of my lord I have carried out I will next dig this vineyard, and it shall be neater when it is dug; and when it has no weeds it will yield more fruit, because not choked by the weeds." He took and dug the vineyard, and all the weeds that were in the vineyard he plucked up. And that vineyard became very neat and flourishing, when it had no weeds to choke it.

2[55]:5 After a time the master of the servant [and of the estate] came, and he went into the vineyard. And seeing the vineyard fenced neatly, and dug as well, and [all] the weeds plucked up, and the vines flourishing, he rejoiced [exceedingly] at what his servant had done.

2[55]:6 So he called his beloved son, who was his heir, and the friends who were his advisers, and told them what he had commanded his servant, and how much he had found done. And they rejoiced with the servant at the testimony which his master had borne to him.

2[55]:7 And he said to them; "I promised this servant his freedom, if he should keep the commandment which I commanded him; but he kept my commandment and did a good work besides to my vineyard, and pleased me greatly. For this work therefore which he has done, I desire to make him joint-heir with my son, because, when the good thought struck him, he did not neglect it, but fulfilled it."

2[55]:8 In this purpose the son of the master agreed with him, that the servant should be made joint-heir with the son.

2[55]:9 After some few days, his master made a feast, and sent to him many dainties from the feast. But when the servant received [the dainties sent to him by the master], he took what was sufficient for him, and distributed the rest to his fellow servants.

2[55]:10 And his fellow-servants, when they received the dainties, rejoiced, and began to pray for him, that he might find greater favor with the master, because he had treated them so handsomely.

2[55]:11 All these things which had taken place his master heard, and again rejoiced greatly at his deed. So the master called together again his friends and his son, and announced to them the deed that he had done with regard to his dainties which he had received; and they still more approved of his resolve, that his servant should be made joint-heir with his son."

3[56]:1 I say, "Sir, I understand not these parables, neither can I apprehend them, unless you explain them for me."

3[56]:2 "I will explain everything to you," said he; "and will show you whatsoever things I shall speak with you. Keep the commandments of the Lord, and you shall be well-pleasing to God, and shall be enrolled among the number of them that keep His commandments.

3[56]:3 But if you do any good thing outside the commandment of God, you shall win for yourself more exceeding glory, and shall be more glorious in the sight of God than you would otherwise have been. If then, while you keep the commandments of God, you add these services likewise, you shall rejoice, if you observe them according to my commandment."

3[56]:4 I say to him, "Sir, whatsoever you command me, I will keep it; for I know that you art with me." "I will be with you," said he, "because you hast so great zeal for doing good; yea, and I will be with all," said he, "whosoever have such zeal as this.

3[56]:5 This fasting," said he, "if the commandments of the Lord are kept, is very good. This then is the way, that you shall keep this fast which you art about to observe].

3[56]:6 First of all, keep yourself from every evil word and every evil desire, and purify thy heart from all the vanities of this world. If you keep these things, this fast shall be perfect for you.

3[56]:7 And thus shall you do. Having fulfilled what is written, on that day on which you fastest you shall taste nothing but bread and water; and from thy meats, which you would have eaten, you shall reckon up the amount of that day's expenditure, which you would have incurred, and shall give it to a widow, or an orphan, or to one in want, and so shall you humble thy soul, that he that has received from thy humiliation may satisfy his own soul, and may pray for you to the Lord.

3[56]:8 If then you shall so accomplish this fast, as I have commanded you, thy sacrifice shall be acceptable in the sight of God, and this fasting shall be recorded; and the service so performed is beautiful and joyous and acceptable to the Lord.

3[56]:9 These things you shall so observe, you and thy children and thy whole household; and, observing them, you shall be blessed; yea, and all those, who shall hear and observe them, shall be blessed, and whatsoever things they shall ask of the Lord, they shall receive."

4[57]:1 I entreated him earnestly, that he would show me the parable of the estate, and of the master, and of the vineyard, and of the servant that fenced the vineyard, [and of the fence,] and of the weeds which were plucked up out of the vineyard, and of the son, and of the friends, the advisers. For I understood that all these things are a parable.

4[57]:2 But he answered and said unto me; "You art exceedingly importunate in enquiries. You ought not," [said he,] "to make any enquiry at all; for if it be right that a thing be explained unto you, it shall be explained." I say to him; "Sir, whatsoever things you show unto me and do not explain, I shall have seen them in vain, and without understanding what they are. In like manner also, if you speak parables to me and interpret them not, I shall have heard a thing in vain from you."

4[57]:3 But he again answered, and said unto me; "Whosoever," said he, "is a servant of God, and has his own Lord in his heart, asks understanding of Him, and receives it, and interprets every parable, and the words of the Lord which are spoken in parables are made known unto him. But as many as are sluggish and idle in intercession, these hesitate to ask of the Lord.

4[57]:4 But the Lord is abundant in compassion, and gives to them that ask of Him without ceasing. But you who hast been strengthened by the holy angel, and hast received from him such (powers of intercession and art not idle, wherefore do you not ask understanding of the Lord, and obtain it from Him)."

4[57]:5 I say to him, "Sir, I that have you with me have (but) need to ask you and enquire of you; for you show me all things, and speak with me; but if I had seen or heard them apart from you I should have asked of the Lord, that they might be shown to me."

5[58]:1 "I told you just now," said he, "that you art unscrupulous and importunate, in enquiring for the interpretations of the parables. But since you art so obstinate, I will interpret to you the parable of the estate and all the accompaniments thereof, that you may make them known unto all. Hear now," said he, "and understand them.

5[58]:2 The estate is this world, and the lord of the estate is He that created all things, and set them in order, and endowed them with power; and the servant is the Son of God, and the vines are this people whom He Himself planted;

5[58]:3 and the fences are the [holy] angels of the Lord who keep together His people; and the weeds, which are plucked up from the vineyard, are the transgressions of the servants of God; and the dainties which He sent to him from the feast are the commandments which He gave to His people through His Son; and the friends and advisers are the holy angels which were first created; and the absence of the master is the time which remains over until His coming."

5[58]:4 I say to him; "Sir, great and marvelous are all things and all things are glorious; was it likely then," say I, "that I could have apprehended them?" "Nay, nor can any other man, though he be full of understanding, apprehend them." "Yet again, Sir," say I, "explain to me what I am about to enquire of you."

5[58]:5 "Say on," he said, "if you desire anything." "Wherefore, Sir,]" say I, "is the Son of God represented in the parable in the guise of a servant?"

6[59]:1 "Listen," said he; "the Son of God is not represented in the guise of a servant, but is represented in great power and lordship." "How, Sir?" say I; "I comprehend not."

6[59]:2 "Because," said he, "God planted the vineyard, that is, He created the people, and delivered them over to His Son. And the Son placed the angels in charge of them, to watch over them; and the Son Himself cleansed their sins, by laboring much and enduring many toils; for no one can dig without toil or labor.

6[59]:3 Having Himself then cleansed the sins of His people, He showed them the paths of life, giving them the law which He received from His Father. You see," said he, "that He is Himself Lord of the people, having received all power from His Father.

6[59]:4 But how that the lord took his son and the glorious angels as advisers concerning the inheritance of the servant, listen.

6[59]:5 The Holy Pre-existent Spirit. Which created the whole creation, God made to dwell in flesh that He desired. This flesh, therefore, in which the Holy Spirit dwelt, was subject unto the Spirit, walking honorably in holiness and purity, without in any way defiling the Spirit.

6[59]:6 When then it had lived honorably in chastity, and had labored with the Spirit, and had cooperated with it in everything, behaving itself boldly and bravely, He chose it as a partner with the Holy Spirit; for the career of this flesh pleased [the Lord], seeing that, as possessing the Holy Spirit, it was not defiled upon the earth.

6[59]:7 He therefore took the son as adviser and the glorious angels also, that this flesh too, having served the Spirit unblamably, might have some place of sojourn, and might not seem to hare lost the reward for its service; for all flesh, which is found undefiled and unspotted, wherein the Holy Spirit dwelt, shall receive a reward.

6[59]:8 Now you hast the interpretation of this parable also."

7[60]:1 "I was right glad, Sir," say I, "to hear this interpretation." "Listen now," said he, "Keep this thy flesh pure and undefiled, that the Spirit which dwells in it may bear witness to it, and thy flesh may be justified.

7[60]:2 See that it never enter into your heart that this flesh of your is perishable, and so you abuse it in some defilement. [For] if you defile thy flesh, you shall defile the Holy Spirit also; but if you defile the flesh, you shall not live."

7[60]:3 "But if, Sir," say I, "there has been any ignorance in times past, before these words were heard, how shall a man who has defiled his flesh be saved?" "For the former deeds of ignorance," said he, "God alone has power to give healing; for all authority is His.

7[60]:4 [But now keep yourself, and the Lord Almighty, Who is full of compassion, will give healing for thy former deeds of ignorance,] if henceforth you defile not thy flesh, neither the Spirit; for both share in common, and the one cannot be defiled without the other. Therefore keep both pure, and you shall live unto God."

Parable 6

1[61]:1 As I sat in my house, and glorified the Lord for all things that I had seen, and was considering concerning the commandments, how that they were beautiful and powerful and gladsome and glorious and able to save a man's soul, I said within myself; "Blessed shall I be, if I walk in these commandments; yea, and whosoever shall walk in them shall be blessed."

1[61]:2 As I spoke these things within myself, I see him suddenly seated by me, and saying as follows; "Why art you of a doubtful mind concerning the commandments, which I commanded you? They are beautiful. Doubt not at all; but clothe yourself in the faith of the Lord, and you shall walk in them. For I will strengthen you in them.

1[61]:3 These commandments are suitable for those who meditate repentance; for if they walk not in them, their repentance is in vain.

1[61]:4 you then that repent, cast away the evil doings of this world which crush you; and, by putting on every excellence of righteousness, you shall be able to observe these commandments, and to add no more to your sins. If then you add no further sin at all, you will depart from your former sins.

Walk then in these my commandments, and you shall live unto God. These things have [all] been told you from me."

1[61]:5 And after he had told these things to me, he said to me, "Let us go into the country, and I will show you the shepherds of the sheep." "Let us go, Sir," say I. And we came to a certain plain, and he shows me a young man, a shepherd, clothed in a light cloak, of saffron color;

1[61]:6 and he was feeding a great number of sheep, and these sheep were, as it were, well fed and very frisky, and were gladsome as they skipped about hither and thither; and the shepherd himself was all gladsome over his flock; and the very visage of the shepherd was exceedingly gladsome; and he ran about among the sheep.

2[62]:1 And he said to me; "See you this shepherd?" "I see him Sir," I say. "This," said he, "is the angel of self-indulgence and of deceit. He crushes the souls of the servants of God, and perverts them from the truth, leading them astray with evil desires, wherein they perish.

2[62]:2 For they forget the commandments of the living God, and walk in vain deceits and acts of self-indulgence, and are destroyed by this angel, some of them unto death, and others unto corruption."

2[62]:3 I say to him, "Sir, I comprehend not what means "unto death," and what "unto corruption". "Listen," said he; "the sheep which you saw gladsome and skipping about, these are they who have been turned asunder from God utterly, and have delivered themselves over to the lusts of this world. In these, therefore, there is not repentance unto life. For the Name of God is being blasphemed through them. The life of such persons is death.

2[62]:4 But the sheep, which you saw not skipping about, but feeding in one place, these are they that have delivered themselves over to acts of self-indulgence and deceit, but have not uttered any blasphemy against the Lord. These then have been corrupted from the truth. In these there is hope of repentance, wherein they can live. Corruption then has hope of a possible renewal, but death has eternal destruction."

2[62]:5 Again we went forward a little way, and he showed me a great shepherd like a wild man in appearance, with a white goatskin thrown about him; and he had a kind of wallet on his shoulders, and a staff very hard and with knots in it, and a great whip. And his look was very sour, so that I was afraid of him because of his look.

2[62]:6 This shepherd then kept receiving from the young man, the shepherd, those sheep that were frisky and well fed, but not skipping about, and putting them in a certain spot, which was precipitous and covered with thorns and briars, so that the sheep could not disentangle themselves from the thorns and briars, but [became entangled among the thorns and briars.

2[62]:7 And so they] pastured entangled in the thorns and briars, and were in great misery with being beaten by him; and he kept driving them about to and fro, and giving them no rest, and all together those sheep had not a happy time.

3[63]:1 When then I saw them so lashed with the whip and vexed, I was sorry for their sakes, because they were so tortured and had no rest at all.

3[63]:2 I say to the shepherd who was speaking with me; "Sir, who is this shepherd, who is [so] hard-hearted and severe, and has no compassion at all for these sheep?" "This," said he, "is the angel of punishment, and he is one of the just angels, and presides over punishment.

3[63]:3 So he receives those who wander away from God, and walk after the lusts and deceits of this life, and punishes them, as they deserve, with fearful and various punishments."

3[63]:4 "I would fain learn, Sir," said I, "of what sort are these various punishments." "Listen," said he; "the various tortures and punishments are tortures belonging to the present life; for some are punished with losses, and others with want, and others with divers maladies, and others with [every kind] of unsettlement, and others with insults from unworthy persons and with suffering in many other respects.

3[63]:5 For many, being unsettled in their plans, set their hands to many things, and nothing ever goes forward with them. And then they say that they do not prosper in their doings, and it doth not enter into their hearts that they have done evil deeds, but they blame the Lord.

3[63]:6 When then they are afflicted with every kind of affliction, then they are delivered over to me for good instruction, and are strengthened in the faith of the Lord, and serve the Lord with a pure heart the remaining days of their life. But, if they repent, the evil works which they have done rise up in their hearts, and then they glorify God, saying that He is a just Judge, and that they suffered justly each according to his doings. And they serve the Lord thenceforward with a pure heart, and are prosperous in all their doings, receiving from the Lord whatsoever things they may ask; and then they glorify the Lord because they were delivered over unto me, and they no longer suffer any evil thing."

3[63]:1 I say unto him; "Sir, declare unto me this further matter." "What enquire you yet?" said he. "Whether, Sir," say I, "they that live in self-indulgence and are deceived undergo torments during the same length of time as they live in self-indulgence and are deceived." He said to me, "They undergo torments for the same length of time."

3[63]:2 "Then, Sir," say I, "they undergo very slight torments; for those who are living thus in self-indulgence and forget God ought to have been tormented seven-fold."

3[63]:3 He said to me, "You art foolish, and comprehend not the power of the torment" "True," say I, "for if I had comprehended it, I should not have asked you to declare it to me." "Listen," said he, "to the power of both, [of the self-indulgence and of the torment].

3[63]:4 The time of the self-indulgence and deceit is one hour. But an hour of the torment has the power of thirty days. If then one live in self indulgence and be deceived for one day, and be tormented for one day, the day of the torment is equivalent to a whole year. For as many days then as a man lives in self-indulgence, for so many years is he tormented. You see then," said he, "that the time of the self-indulgence and deceit is very short, but the time of the punishment and torment is long."

5[65]:1 "Inasmuch, Sir," say I, "as I do not quite comprehend concerning the time of the deceit and self-indulgence and torment, show me more clearly."

5[65]:2 He answered and said unto me; "Your stupidity clings to you; and you wilt not cleanse thy heart and serve God Take heed," [said he,] "lest haply the time be fulfilled, and you be found in thy foolishness. Listen then," [said he,] "even as you wish, that you may comprehend the matter.

5[65]:3 He that lives in self-indulgence and is deceived for one day, and doeth what he wishes, is clothed in much folly and comprehended not the thing which he doeth; for on the morrow he forgets what he did the day before. For self-indulgence and deceit have no memories, by reason of the folly, wherewith each is clothed; but when punishment and torment cling to a man for a single day, he is punished and tormented for a whole year long; for punishment and torment have long memories.

5[65]:4 So being tormented and punished for the whole year, the man remembers at length the self-indulgence and deceit, and perceives that it is on their account that he is suffering these ills. Every man, therefore, that lives in self-indulgence and is deceived, is tormented in this way because, though possessing lire, they have delivered themselves over unto death."

5[65]:5 "What kinds of self-indulgence, Sir," say I, "are harmful?" "Every action," said he, "is self-indulgence to a man, which he does with pleasure; for the irascible man, when he gives the reins to his passion, is self-indulgent; and the adulterer and the drunkard and the slanderer and the liar and the miser and the defrauder and he that doeth things akin to these, gives the reins to his peculiar passion; therefore he is self-indulgent in his action.

5[65]:6 All these habits of self-indulgence are harmful to the servants of God; on account of these deceits therefore they so suffer who are punished and tormented.

5[65]:7 But there are habits of self-indulgence like-wise which save men; for many are self-indulgent in doing good, being carried away by the pleasure it gives to themselves. This self-indulgence then is expedient for the servants of God, and brings life to a man of this disposition; but the harmful self-indulgences afore-mentioned bring to men torments and punishments; and if they continue in them and repent not, they bring death upon themselves."

Parable 7

1[66]:1 After a few days I saw him on the same plain, where also I had seen the shepherds, and he said to me, "What seek you?" "I am here, Sir," say I, "that you may bid the shepherd that punishes go out of my house; for he afflicts me much." "It is necessary for you," said he, "to be afflicted; for so," said he, "the glorious angel ordered as concerning you, for he wishes you to be proved." "Why, what so evil thing have I done, Sir," say I, "that I should be delivered over to this angel?"

1[66]:2 "Listen," said he. "Your sins are many, yet not so many that you should be delivered over to this angel; but thy house has committed great iniquities and sins, and the glorious angel was embittered at their deeds, and for this cause he bade you be afflicted for a certain time, that they also might repent and cleanse themselves from every lust of this world. When therefore they shall repent and be cleansed, then shall the angel of punishment depart."

1[66]:3 I say to him; "Sir, if they perpetrated such deeds that the glorious angel is embittered, what have I done?" "They cannot be afflicted otherwise," said he, "unless you, the head of the [whole] house, be afflicted; for if you be afflicted, they also of necessity will be afflicted; but if you be prosperous, they can suffer no affliction."

1[66]:4 "But behold, Sir," say I, "they have repented with their whole heart." "I am quite aware myself," said he, "that they have repented with their whole heart; well, think you that the sins of those who repent are forgiven forthwith? Certainly not; but the person who repents must torture his own soul, and must be thoroughly humble in his every action, and be afflicted with all the divers kinds of affliction; and if he endure the afflictions which come upon him, assuredly He Who created all things and endowed them with power will be moved with compassion and will bestow some remedy.

1[66]:5 And this (will God do), if in any way He perceive the heart of the penitent pure from every evil thing. But it is expedient for you and for thy house that you should be afflicted now. But why speak I many words to you? You must be afflicted as the angel of the Lord commanded, even he that delivered you unto me; and for this give thanks to the Lord, in that He deemed you worthy that I should reveal unto you beforehand the affliction, that foreknowing it you might endure it with fortitude."

1[66]:6 I say to him; "Sir, be you with me, and I shall be able to endure all affliction [easily]." "I will be with you," said he; "and I will ask the angel that punishs to afflict you more lightly; but you shall be afflicted for a short time, and you shall be restored again to thy house. Only continue to be humble and to minister unto the Lord with a pure heart, you and thy children and thy house, and walk in my commandments which I command you, and thus it will be possible for thy repentance to be strong and pure.

1[66]:7 And if you keep these commandments with thy household, all affliction shall hold aloof from you; yea, and affliction," said he, "shall hold aloof from all whosoever shall walk in these my commandments."

Parable 8

1[67]:1 He showed me a [great] willow, overshadowing plains and mountains, and under the shadow of the willow all have come who are called by the name of the Lord.

1[67]:2 And by the willow there stood an angel of the Lord, glorious and very tall, having a great sickle, and he was lopping branches from the willow, and giving them to the people that sheltered beneath the willow; and he gave them little rods about a cubit long.

1[67]:3 And after all had taken the rods, the angel laid aside the sickle, and the tree was sound, just as I had seen it.

1[67]:4 Then I marveled within myself, saying, "How is the tree sound after so many branches have been lopped off?" The shepherd said to me, "Marvel not that the tree remained sound, after so many branches were lopped off but wait until you see all things, and it shall be shown to you what it is."

1[67]:5 The angel who gave the rods to the people demanded them back from them again, and according as they had received them, so also they were summoned to him, and each of them returned the several rods. But the angel of the Lord took them, and examined them.

1[67]:6 From some he received the rods withered and eaten as it were by grubs: the angel ordered those who gave up rods like these to stand apart.

1[67]:7 And others gave them up withered, but not grub-eaten; and these again he ordered to stand apart.

1[67]:8 And others gave them up half-withered; these also stood apart.

1[67]:9 And others gave up their rods half-withered and with cracks; these also stood apart.

1[67]:10 And others gave up their rods green and with cracks; these also stood apart. And others gave up their rods one half withered and one half green; these also stood apart.

1[67]:11 And others brought their rods two parts of the rod green, and the third part withered; these also stood apart. And others gave them up two parts withered, and the third part green; these also stood apart.

1[67]:12 And others gave up their rods nearly all green, but a very small portion of their rods was withered, just the end; but they had cracks in them; these also stood apart.

1[67]:13 And in those of others there was a very small portion green, but the rest of the rods was withered; these also stood apart.

1[67]:14 And others came bringing their rods green, as they received them from the angel; and the most part of the multitude gave up their rods in this state; and the angel rejoiced exceedingly at these; these also stood apart.

1[67]:15 And others gave up their rods green and with shoots, these also stood apart; and at these again the angel rejoiced exceedingly.

1[67]:16 And others gave up their rods green and with shoots; and their shoots had, as it were, a kind of fruit. And those men were exceeding gladsome, whose rods were found in this state. And over them the angel exulted, and the shepherd was very gladsome over them.

2[68]:1 And the angel of the Lord commanded crowns to be brought. And crowns were brought, made as it were of palm branches; and he crowned the men that had given up the rods which had the shoots and some fruit, and sent them away into the tower.

2[68]:2 And the others also he sent into the tower, even those who had given up the rods green and with shoots, but the shoots were without fruit; and he set a seal upon them.

2[68]:3 And all they that went into the tower had the same raiment, white as snow.

2[68]:4 And those that had given up their rods green as they received them, he sent away, giving them a [white] robe, and seals.

2[68]:5 After the angel had finished these things, he said to the shepherd; "I go away; but these you shall send away to (their places within) the walls, according as each deserves to dwell; but examine their rods carefully), and so send them away. But be careful in examining them. Take heed lest any escape you," said he. "Still if any escape you, I will test them at the altar." When he had thus spoken to the shepherd, he departed.

2[68]:6 And, after the angel had departed, the shepherd said to me; "Let us take the rods of all and plant them, to see whether any of them shall be able to live." I say unto him, "Sir, these withered things, how can they live?"

2[68]:7 He answered and said unto me; "This tree is a willow, and this class of trees clings to life. If then the rods shall be planted and get a little moisture, many of them will live. And afterwards let us try to pour some water also over them. If any of them shall be able to live, I will rejoice with it; but if it live not, I at least shall not be found neglectful."

2[68]:8 So the shepherd bade me call them, just as each one of them was stationed. And they came row after row, and they delivered up the rods to the shepherd. And the shepherd took the rods, and planted them in rows, and after he had planted them, he poured much water over them, so that the rods could not be seen for the water.

2[68]:9 And after he had watered the rods, he said to me; "Let us go now. and after days let us return and inspect all the rods; for He Who created this tree wills that all those who have received rods from this tree should live. And I myself hope that these little rods, after they have got moisture and been watered, will live the greater part of them."

3[69]:1 I say to him; "Sir, inform me what this tree is. For I am perplexed herewith, because, though so many branches were cut off, the tree is sound, and nothing appears to have been cut from it; I am therefore perplexed thereat."

3[69]:2 "Listen," said he; "this great tree which overshadows plains and mountains and all the earth is the law of God which was given to the whole world; and this law is the Son of Cod preached unto the ends of the earth. But the people that are under the shadow are they that have heard the preaching, and believed on Him;

3[69]:3 but the great and glorious angel is Michael, who has the power over this people and is their captain. For this is he that puts the law into the hearts of the believers; therefore he himself inspects them to whom he gave it, to see whether they have observed it.

3[69]:4 But you see the rods of every one; for the rods are the law. You see these many rods rendered useless, and you shall notice all those that have not observed the law, and shall see the abode of each severally."

3[69]:5 I say unto him; "Sir, wherefore did he send away some into the tower, and leave others for you?" "As many," said he, "as transgressed the law which they received from him, these he left under my authority for repentance; but as many as already satisfied the law and have observed it, these he has under his own authority."

3[69]:6 "Who then, Sir," say I, "are they that have been crowned and go into the tower?" ["As many," said he, "as wrestled with the devil and overcame him in their wrestling, are crowned:] these are they that suffered for the law.

3[69]:7 But the others, who likewise gave up their rods green and with shoots, though not with fruit, are they that were persecuted for the law, but did not suffer nor yet deny their law.

3[69]:8 But they that gave them up green just as they received them, are sober and righteous men, who walked altogether in a pure heart and have kept the commandments of the Lord. But all else you shall know, when I have examined these rods that have been planted and watered."

4[70]:1 And after a few days we came to the place, and the shepherd sat down in the place of the angel, while I stood by him. And he said to me; "Gird yourself with a garment of raw flax, and minister to me." So I girded myself with a clean garment of raw flax made of coarse material.

4[70]:2 And when he saw me girded and ready to minister to him "Call," said he, "the men whose rods have been planted, according to the rank as each presented their rods." And I went away to the plain, and called them all; and they stood all of them according to their ranks.

4[70]:3 He said to them; "Let each man pluck out his own rod, and bring it to me." Those gave them up first, who had the withered and chipped rods, and they were found accordingly withered and chipped. He ordered them to stand apart.

4[70]:4 Then those gave them up, who had the withered but not chipped; and some of them gave up the rods green, and others withered and chipped as by grubs. Those then that gave them up green he ordered to stand apart; but those that gave them up withered and chipped he ordered to stand with the first.

4[70]:5 Then those gave them up who had the half-withered and with cracks; and many of them gave them up green and without cracks; and some gave them up green and with shoots, and fruits on the shoots, such as those had who went into the tower crowned; and some gave them up withered and eaten, and some withered and uneaten, and some such as they were, half-withered and with cracks. He ordered them to stand each one apart, some in their proper ranks, and others apart.

5[71]:1 Then those gave them up who had their rods green, but with cracks. These all gave them up green, and stood in their own company. And the shepherd rejoiced over these, because they all were changed and had put away their cracks.

5[71]:2 And those gave them up likewise who had the one half green and the other half withered. The rods of some were found entirely green, of some half-withered, of some withered and eaten, and of some green and with shoots. These were all sent away each to his company.

5[71]:3 Then those gave them up who had two parts green and the third withered; many of them gave them up green, and many half-withered, and others withered and eaten. These all stood in their own company.

5[71]:4 Then those gave them up who had two parts withered and the third part green. Many of them gave them up half-withered, but some withered and eaten, others half-withered and with cracks, and a few green. These all stood in their own company.

5[71]:5 Then those gave them up who had their rods green, but a very small part [withered] and with cracks. Of these some gave them up green, and others green and with shoots. These also went away to their own company.

5[71]:6 Then those gave them up who had a very small part green and the other parts withered. The rods of these were found for the most part green and with shoots and fruit on the shoots, and others altogether green. At these rods the shepherd rejoiced very [greatly], because they were found so. And these went away each to his own company.

6[72]:1 After [the shepherd] had examined the rods of all, he said to me, "I told you that this tree clings to life. See you," said he, "how many repented and were saved?" "I see, Sir," say I. "It is," said he, that you may see the abundant compassion of the Lord, how great and glorious it is, and He has given (His) Spirit to those that are worthy of repentance."

6[72]:2 "Wherefore then, Sir," say I, "did they not all repent?" "To those, whose heart He saw about to become pure and to serve Him with all the heart, to them He gave repentance; but those whose craftiness and wickedness He saw, who intend to repent in hypocrisy, to them He gave not repentance, lest haply they should again profane His name."

6[72]:3 I say unto him, "Sir, now then show me concerning those that have given up their rods, what manner of man each of them is, and their abode, that when they hear this, they that believed and have received the seal and have broken it and did not keep it sound may fully understand what they are doing, and repent, receiving from you a seal, and may glorify the Lord, that He had compassion upon them and sent you to renew their spirits."

6[72]:4 "Listen," said he; "those whose rods were found withered and grub-eaten, these are the renegades and traitors to the Church, that blasphemed the Lord in their sins, and still further were ashamed of the Name of the Lord, which was invoked upon them. These then perished altogether unto God. But you see how not one of them repented, although they heard the words which you spoke to them, which I commanded you. From men of this kind life departed.

6[72]:5 But those that gave up the withered and undecayed (rods), these also are near them; for they were hypocrites, and brought in strange doctrines, and perverted the servants of God, especially them that had sinned, not permitting them to repent, but persuading them with their foolish doctrines. These then have hope of repenting.

6[72]:6 But you see that many of them have indeed repented from the time when you speak to them my commandments; yea, and (others) still will repent. And as many as shall not repent, have lost their life; but as many of them as repented, became good; and their dwelling was placed within the first walls, and some of them even ascended into the tower. You see then," [said he,] "that repentance from sins brings life, but not to repent brings death.

7[73]:1 "But as many as gave up (the rods) half-withered, and with cracks in them, hear also concerning these. Those whose rods were half-withered throughout are the double-minded; for they neither live nor are dead.

7[73]:2 But those that have them half-withered and cracks in them, these are both double-minded and slanderers, and are never at peace among themselves but always causing dissensions. Yet even to these," [said he,] "repentance is given. You see," [said he,] "that some of them have repented; and there is still," said he, "hope of repentance among them.

7[73]:3 And as many of them," said he, "as have repented, have their abode within the tower; but as many of them as have repented tardily shall abide within the walls; and as many as repent not, but continue in their doings, shall die the death.

7[73]:4 But they that have given up their rods green and with cracks, these were found faithful and good at all times, [but] they have a certain emulation one with another about first places and about glory of some kind or other; but all these are foolish in having (emulation) one with another about first places.

7[73]:5 Yet these also, when they heard my commandments, being good, purified themselves and repented quickly. They have their habitation, therefore, within the tower. But if any one shall again turn to dissension, he shall be cast out from the tower and shall lose his life.

7[73]:6 Life is for all those that keep the commandments of the Lord. But in the commandments there is nothing about first places, or about glory of any kind, but about long-suffering and humility in man. In such men, therefore, is the life of the Lord, but in factious and lawless men is death.

8[74]:1 "But they that gave up their rods half green and half withered, these are they that are mixed up in business and hold fast not to the saints. Therefore the one half of them lives , but the other half is dead.

8[74]:2 Many then when they heard my commandments repented. As many then as repented, have their abode within the tower. But some of them altogether stood aloof These then have no repentance; for by reason of their business affairs they blasphemed the Lord and denied Him. So they lost their life for the wickedness that they committed.

8[74]:3 But many of them were doubtful-minded. These still have place for repentance, if they repent quickly, and their dwelling shall be within the tower; and if they repent tardily, they shall dwell within the walls; but if they repent not, they too have lost their life.

8[74]:4 But they that have given up two parts green and the third part withered, these are they that have denied with manifold denials.

8[74]:5 Many of them therefore repented and departed to dwell inside the tower; but many utterly rebelled from God; these lost their life finally. And some of them were double-minded and caused dissensions. For these then there is repentance, if they repent speedily and continue not in their pleasures; but if they continue in their doings, they likewise procure for themselves death.

9[75]:1 "But they that have given up their rods two thirds withered and one third green, these are men who have been believers, but grew rich and became renowned among the Gentiles. They clothed themselves with great pride and became high-minded, and abandoned the truth and did not hold fast to the righteous, but lived together after the manner of the Gentiles, and this path appeared the more pleasant unto them; yet they departed not from God, but continued in the faith, though they wrought not the works of the faith.

9[75]:2 Many of them therefore repented, and they had their habitation within the tower.

9[75]:3 But others at the last living with the Gentiles, and being corrupted by the vain opinions of the Gentiles, departed from God, and worked the works of the Gentiles. These therefore were numbered with the Gentiles.

9[75]:4 But others of them were doubtful-minded, not hoping to be saved by reason of the deeds that they had done; and others were double-minded and made divisions among themselves. For these then that were double-minded by reason of their doings there is still repentance; but their repentance ought to be speedy, that their dwelling may be within the tower; but for those who repent not, but continue in their pleasures, death is nigh.

10[76]:1 "But they that gave up their rods green, yet with the extreme ends withered and with cracks; these were found at all times good and faithful and glorious in the sight of God, but they sinned to a very slight degree by reason of little desires and because they had somewhat against one another. But, when they heard my words, the greater part quickly repented, and their dwelling was assigned within the tower.

10[76]:2 But some of them were double-minded, and some being double-minded made a greater dissension. In these then there is still a hope of repentance, because they were found always good; and hardly shall one of them die.

10[76]:3 But they that gave up their rods withered, yet with a very small part green, these are they that believed, but practiced the works of lawlessness. Still they never separated from God, but bore the Name gladly, and gladly received into their houses the servants of God. So hearing of this repentance they repented without wavering, and they practice all excellence and righteousness.

10[76]:4 And some of them even suffer persecution willingly, knowing the deeds that they did.'All these then shall have their dwelling within the tower."

11[77]:1 And after he had completed the interpretations of all the rods, he said unto me; "Go, and tell all men to repent, and they shall live unto God; for the Lord in His compassion sent me to give repentance to all, though some of them do not deserve it for their deeds; but being long-suffering the Lord wills them that were called through His Son to be saved."

11[77]:2 I say to him; "Sir, I hope that all when they hear these words will repent; for I am persuaded that each one, when he fully knows his own deeds and fears God, will repent."

11[77]:3 He answered and said unto me; "As many," [said he,] "as [shall repent] from their whole heart [and] shall cleanse themselves from all the evil deeds aforementioned, and shall add nothing further to their sins, shall receive healing from the Lord for their former sins, unless they be double-minded concerning these commandments, and they shall live unto God. [But as many," said he, "as shall add to their sins and walk in the lusts of this world, shall condemn themselves to death.]

11[77]:4 But do you walk in my commandments, and live [unto God; yea, and as many as shall walk in them and shall do rightly, shall live unto God."]

11[77]:5 Having shown me all these things [and told me them] he said to me; "Now the rest will I declare (unto you) after a few days."

Parable 9

1[78]:1 After I had written down the commandments and parables of the shepherd, the angel of repentance, he came to me and said to me; "I wish to show you all things that the Holy Spirit, which spoke with you in the form of the Church, showed unto you. For that Spirit is the Son of God.

1[78]:2 For when you was weaker in the flesh, it was not declared unto you through an angel; but when you was enabled through the Spirit, and didst grow mighty in thy strength so that you could even see an angel, then at length was manifested unto you, through the Church, the building of the tower. In fair and seemly manner hast you seen all things, (instructed) as it were by a virgin; but now you see (being instructed) by an angel, though by the same Spirit;

1[78]:3 yet must you learn everything more accurately from me. For to this end also was I appointed by the glorious angel to dwell in thy house, that you might see all things mightily, in nothing terrified, even as before."

1[78]:4 And he took me away into Arcadia, to a certain rounded mountain, and set me on the top of the mountain, and showed me a great plain, and round the plain twelve mountains, the mountains having each a different appearance.

1[78]:5 The first was black as soot; the second was bare, without vegetation; the third was thorny and full of briars;

1[78]:6 the fourth had the vegetation half-withered, the upper part of the grass green, but the part by the roots withered, and some of the grass became withered, whenever the sun had scorched it;

1[78]:7 the fifth mountain had green grass and was rugged; the sixth mountain was full with clefts throughout, some small and some great, and the clefts had vegetation, but the grass was not very luxuriant, but rather as if it had been withered;

1[78]:8 the seventh mountain had smiling vegetation, and the whole mountain was in a thriving condition, and cattle and birds of every kind did feed upon that mountain; and the more the cattle and the birds did feed, so much the more did the herbage of that mountain flourish. The eighth mountain was full of springs, and every kind of creature of the Lord did drink of the springs on that mountain.

1[78]:9 the ninth mountain had no water at all, and was entirely desert; and it had in it wild beasts and deadly reptiles, which destroy mankind. The tenth mountain had very large trees and was umbrageous throughout, and beneath the shade lay sheep resting and feeding.

1[78]:10 the eleventh mountain was thickly wooded all over, and the trees thereon were very productive, decked with divers kinds of fruits, so that one seeing them would desire to eat of their fruits. The twelfth mountain was altogether white and its aspect was cheerful; and the mountain was most beauteous in itself.

2[79]:1 And in the middle of the plain he showed me a great white rock, rising up from the plain. The rock was loftier than the mountains, being four-square, so that it could contain the whole world.

2[79]:2 Now this rock was ancient, and had a gate hewn out of it; but the gate seemed to me to have been hewed out quite recently. And the gate glistened beyond the brightness of the sun, so that I marveled at the brightness of the gate.

2[79]:3 And around the gate stood twelve virgins. The four then that stood at the corners seemed to me to be more glorious (than the rest); but the others likewise were glorious; and they stood at the four quarters of the gate, and virgins stood in pairs between them.

2[79]:4 And they were clothed in linen tunics and girt about in seemly fashion, having their right shoulders free, as if they intended to carry some burden. Thus were they prepared, for they were very cheerful and eager.

2[79]:5 After I had seen these things, I marveled in myself at the greatness and the glory of what I was seeing And again I was perplexed concerning the virgins, that delicate as they were they stood up like men, as if they intended to carry the whole heaven.

2[79]:6 And the shepherd said unto me; "Why question you within yourself and art perplexed, and bring sadness on yourself? For whatsoever things you can not comprehend, attempt them not, if you art prudent; but entreat the Lord, that you may receive understanding to comprehend them.

2[79]:7 What is behind you you can not see, but what is before you you behold. The things therefore which you can not see, let alone, and trouble not yourself (about them; but the things which you see, these master, and be not over curious about the rest; but I will explain unto you all things whatsoever I shall show you. Have an eye therefore to what remains."

3[80]:1 I saw six men come, tall and glorious and alike in appearance and they summoned a multitude of men. And the others also which came were tall men and handsome and powerful. And the six men ordered them to build a tower above the gate. And there arose a great noise from those men who had come to build the tower, as they ran hither and thither round the gate.

3[80]:2 For the virgins standing round the gate told the men to hasten to build the tower. Now the virgins had spread out their hands, as if they would take something from the men.

3[80]:3 And the six men ordered stones to come up from a certain deep place, and to go to the building of the tower. And there went up ten stones square and polished, [not] hewn from a quarry.

3[80]:4 And the six men called to the virgins, and ordered them to carry all the stones which should go unto the building of the tower, and to pass through the gate and to hand them to the men that were about to build the tower.

3[80]:5 And the virgins laid the first ten stones that rose out of the deep on each other, and they carried them together, stone by stone.

4[81]:1 And just as they stood together around the gate, in that order they carried them that seemed to be strong enough and had stooped under the corners of the stone, while the others stooped at the sides of the stone. And so they carried all the stones. And they carried them right through the gate, as they were ordered, and handed them to the men for the tower; and these took the stones and built.

4[81]:2 Now the building of the tower was upon the great rock and above the gate. Those ten stones then were joined together, and they covered the whole rock. And these formed a foundation for the building of the tower. And [the rock and] the gate supported the whole tower.

4[81]:3 And, after the ten stones, other twenty-five stones came up from the deep, and these were fitted into the building of the tower, being carried by the virgins, like the former. And after these thirty-five stones came up. And these likewise were fitted into the tower. And after these came up other forty stones. and these all were put into the building of the tower. So four rows were made in the foundations of the tower.

4[81]:4 And (the stones) ceased coming up from the deep, and the builders likewise ceased for a little. And again the six men ordered the multitude of the people to bring in stones from the mountains for the building of the tower.

4[81]:5 They were brought in accordingly from all the mountains, of various colors, shaped by the men, and were handed to the virgins; and the virgins carried them right through the gate, and handed them in for the building of the tower. And when the various stones were placed in the building, they became all alike and white, and they lost their various colors.

4[81]:6 But some stones were handed in by the men for the building, and these did not become bright; but just as they were placed, such likewise were they found; for they were not handed in by the virgins, nor had they been carried in through the gate. These stones then were unsightly in the building of the tower.

4[81]:7 Then the six men, seeing the stones that were unsightly in the building, ordered them to be removed and carried [below] into their own place whence they were brought.

4[81]:8 And they say to the men who were bringing the stones in; "Abstain for your parts altogether from handing in stones for the building; but place them by the tower, that the virgins may carry them through the gate, and hand them in for the building. For if," [say they,] they be not carried in through the gate by the hands of these virgins, they cannot change their colors. Labor not therefore," [say they,] "in vain."

5[82]:1 And the building was finished on that day, yet was not the tower finally completed, for it was to be carried up [still] higher; and there was a cessation in the building. And the six men ordered the builders to retire for a short time [all of them], and to rest; but the virgins they ordered not to retire from the tower. And I thought the virgins were left to guard the tower.

5[82]:2 And after all had retired Land rested], I say to the shepherd; "How is it, Sir," say I, "that the building of the tower was not completed?" "The tower," he said, "cannot yet be finally completed, until its master come and test this building, that if any stones be found crumbling, he may change them; for the tower is being built according to His will."

5[82]:3 "I would fain know, Sir," say I, "what is this building of this tower, and concerning the rock and gate, and the mountains, and the virgins, and the stones that came up from the deep, and were not shaped, but went just as they were into the building;

5[82]:4 and wherefore ten stones were first placed in the foundations, then twenty-five, then thirty-five, then forty, and concerning the stones that had gone to the building and were removed again and put away in their own place--concerning all these things set my soul at rest, Sir, and explain them to me."

5[82]:5 "If," said he, "you be not found possessed of an idle curiosity, you shall know all things. For after a few days we shall come here, and you shall see the sequel that overtakes this tower and shall understand all the parables accurately."

5[82]:6 And after a few days we came to the place where we had sat, and he said to me, "Let us go to the tower; for the owner of the tower cometh to inspect it." And we came to the tower, and there was no one at all by it, save the virgins alone.

5[82]:7 And the shepherd asked the virgins whether the master of the tower had arrived. And they said that he would be there directly to inspect the building.

6[83]:1 And, behold, after a little while I see an array of many men coming, and in the midst a man of such lofty stature that he overtopped the tower.

6[83]:2 And the six men who superintended the building walked with him on the right hand and on the left, and all they that worked at the building were with him, and many other glorious attendants around him. And the virgins that watched the tower ran up and kissed him, and they began to walk by his side round the tower.

6[83]:3 And that man inspected the building so carefully, that he felt each single stone; and he held a rod in his hand and struck each single stone that

701

was built in.

6[83]:4 And when he smote, some of the stones became black as soot, others mildewed, others cracked, others broke off short, others became neither white nor black, others rough and not fitting in with the other stones, and others with many spots; these were the varied aspects of the stones which were found unsound for the building.

6[83]:5 So he ordered all these to be removed from the tower, and to be placed by the side of the tower, and other stones to be brought and put into their place.

6[83]:6 And the builders asked him from what mountain he desired stones to be brought and put into their place. And he would not have them brought from the mountains, but ordered them to be brought from a certain plain that was nigh at hand.

6[83]:7 And the plain was dug, and stones were found there bright and square, but some of them too were round. And all the stones which there were anywhere in that plain were brought every one of them, and were carried through the gate by the virgins.

6[83]:8 And the square stones were hewed, and set in the place of those which had been removed; but the round ones were not placed in the building, because they were too hard to be shaped, and to work on them was slow. So they were placed by the side of the tower, as though they were intended to be shaped and placed in the building; for they were very bright.

7[84]:1 So then, having accomplished these things, the glorious man who was lord of the whole tower called the shepherd to him, and delivered unto him all the stones which lay by the side of the tower, which were cast out from the building, and said unto him;

7[84]:2 "Clean these stones carefully, and set them in the building of the tower, these, I mean, which can fit with the rest; but those which will not fit, throw far away from the tower."

7[84]:3 Having given these orders to the shepherd, he departed from the tower with all those with whom he had come. And the virgins stood round the tower watching it.

7[84]:4 I say to the shepherd, "How can these stones go again to the building of the tower, seeing that they have been disapproved?" He said unto me in answer; "See you", said he, "these stones ?" I see them, Sir," say I. "I myself," said he, "will shape the greater part of these stones and put them into the building, and they shall fit in with the remaining stones."

7[84]:5 "How, Sir," say I, "can they, when they are chiseled, fill the same space?" He said unto me in answer, "As many as shall be found small, shall be put into the middle of the building; but as many as are larger, shall be placed nearer the outside, and they will bind them together."

7[84]:6 With these words he said to me, "Let us go away, and after two days let us come and clean these stones, and put them into the building; for all things round the tower must be made clean, lest haply the master come suddenly and find the circuit of the tower dirty, and he be wroth, and so these stones shall not go to the building of the tower, and I shall appear to be careless in my master's sight."

7[84]:7 And after two days we came to the tower, and he said unto me; "Let us inspect all the stones, and see those which can go to the building." I say to him, "Sir, let us inspect them."

8[85]:1 And so commencing first we began to inspect the black stones; and just as they were when set aside from the building, such also they were found. And the shepherd ordered them to be removed from the tower and to be put on one side.

8[85]:2 Then he inspected those that were mildewed, and he took and shaped many of them, and ordered the virgins to take them up and put them into the building. And the virgins took them up and placed them in the building of the tower in a middle position. But the rest he ordered to be placed with the black ones; for these also were found black.

8[85]:3 Then he began to inspect those that had the cracks; and of these he shaped many, and he ordered them to be carried away by the hands of the virgins for the building. And they were placed towards the outside, because they were found to be sounder. But the rest could not be shaped owing to the number of the cracks. For this reason therefore they were cast aside from the building of the tower.

8[85]:4 Then he proceeded to inspect the stunted (stones), and many among them were found black, and some had contracted great cracks; and he ordered these also to be placed with those that had been cast aside. But those of them which remained he cleaned and shaped, and ordered to be placed in the building So the virgins took them up, and fitted them into the middle of the building of the tower; for they were somewhat weak.

8[85]:5 Then he began to inspect those that were half white and half black, and many of them were (now) found black; and he ordered these also to be taken up with those that had been cast aside. But all the rest were [found white, and were] taken up by the virgins; for being white they were fitted by [the virgins] them[selves] into the building. But they were placed towards the outside, because they were found sound, so that they could hold together those that were placed in the middle; for not a single one of them was too short.

8[85]:6 Then he began to inspect the hard and rough; and a few of them were cast away, because they could not be shaped; for they were found very hard. But the rest of them were shaped [and taken up by the virgins] and fitted into the middle of the building of the tower; for they were somewhat weak.

8[85]:7 Then he proceeded to inspect those that had the spots, and of these some few had turned black and were cast away among the rest; but the remainder were found bright and sound, and these were fitted by the virgins into the building; but they were placed towards the outside, owing to their strength.

9[86]:1 Then he came to inspect the white and round stones, and he said unto me; "What shall we do with these stones?" "How do I know, Sir?" say I [And he said to me,] "Perceives you nothing concerning them?"

9[86]:2 "I, Sir," say I, "do not possess this art, neither am I a mason, nor can I understand." See you not," said he, "that they are very round; and if I wish to make them square, very much must needs be chiseled off from them? Yet some of them must of necessity be placed into the building."

9[86]:3 "If then, Sir," say I, "it must needs be so, why distress yourself, and why not choose out for the building those you will, and fit them into it?" He chose out from them the large and the bright ones, and shaped them; and the virgins took them up, and fitted them into the outer parts of the building.

9[86]:4 But the rest, which remained over, were taken up, and put aside into the plain whence they were brought; they were not however cast away, "Because," said he, there remains still a little of the tower to be built And the master of the tower is exceedingly anxious that these stones be fitted into the building, for they are very bright."

9[86]:5 So twelve women were called, most beautiful in form, clad in black, [girded about and having the shoulders bare,] with their hair hanging loose. And these women, I thought, had a savage look. And the shepherd ordered them to take up the stones which had been cast away from the building, and to carry them off to the same mountains from which also they had been brought;

9[86]:6 and they took them up joyfully, and carried away all the stones and put them in the place whence they had been taken. And after all the stones had been taken up, and not a single stone still lay round the tower, the shepherd said unto me; "Let us go round the tower, and see that there is no defect in it." And I proceeded to go round it with him.

9[86]:7 And when the shepherd saw that the tower was very comely in the building, he was exceedingly glad; for the tower was so well built, that when I saw it I coveted the building of it; for it was built, as it were, of one stone, having one fitting in it. And the stone-work appeared as if hewn out of the rock; for it seemed to me to be all a single stone.

10[87]:1 And I, as I walked with him, was glad to see so brave a sight. And the shepherd said to me; "Go and bring plaster and fine clay, that I may fill up the shapes of the stones that have been taken up and put into the building; for all the circuit of the tower must be made smooth."

10[87]:2 And I did as he bade, and brought them to him. "Assist me," said he, "and the work will speedily be accomplished." So he filled in the shapes of the stones which had gone to the building, and ordered the circuit of the tower to be swept and made clean.

10[87]:3 And the virgins took brooms and swept, and they removed all the rubbish from the tower, and sprinkled water, and the site of the tower was made cheerful and very seemly.

10[87]:4 The shepherd said unto me, "All," said he, "has now been cleaned. If the lord come to inspect the tower, he has nothing for which to blame us." Saying this, he desired to go away.

10[87]:5 But I caught hold of his wallet, and began to adjure him by the Lord that he would explain to me [all] what he had showed me. He said to me; "I am busy for a little while, and then I will explain everything to you. Await me here till I come."

10[87]:6 I say to him; "Sir, when I am here alone what shall I do?" "You art not alone," said he; "for these virgins are here with you." "Commend me then to them," say I. The shepherd calls them to him and said to them; "I commend this man to you till I come," and he departed.

10[87]:7 So I was alone with the virgins; and they were most cheerful, and kindly disposed to Me especially the four of them that were the more glorious in appearance.

11[88]:1 The virgins say to me; "Today the shepherd cometh not here." "What then shall I do?" say I. "Stay for him," say they, "till eventide; and if he come, he will speak with you; but if he come not, you shall stay here with us till he cometh."

11[88]:2 I say to them; "I will await him till evening, and if he come not, I will depart home and return early in the morning." But they answered and said unto me; "To us you were entrusted; you can not depart from us."

11[88]:3 "Where then," say I, "shall I remain?" "You shall pass the night with us," say they as a brother, not as a husband; for you art our brother, and henceforward we will dwell with you; for we love you dearly." But I was ashamed to abide with them.

11[88]:4 And she that seemed to be the chief of them began to kiss and to embrace me; and the others seeing her embrace me, they too began to kiss me, and to lead me round the tower, and to sport with me.

11[88]:5 And I had become as it were a younger man, and I commenced myself likewise to sport with them. For some of them began to dance, [others to skip,] others to sing. But I kept silence and walked with them round the tower, and was glad with them.

11[88]:6 But when evening came I wished to go away home; but they would not let me go, but detained me. And I stayed the night with them, and I slept by the side of the tower.

11[88]:7 For the virgins spread their linen tunics on the ground, and made me lie down in the midst of them, and they did nothing else but pray; and I prayed with them without ceasing, and not less than they. And the virgins rejoiced that I so prayed. And I stayed there with the virgins until the morning till the second hour.

11[88]:8 Then came the shepherd, and said to the virgins; "Have you done him any injury?" "Ask him," say they. I say to him, "Sir, I was rejoiced to stay with them." "On what didst you sup?" said he "I supped, Sir," say I, "on the words of the Lord the whole night through." "Did they treat you well?" said he. "Yes, Sir," say I.

11[88]:9 "Now," said he, "what would you hear first?" "In the order as you showed to me, Sir, from the beginning," say I; "I request you, Sir, to explain to me exactly in the order that I shall enquire of you." According as you desire," said he, "even so will I interpret to you, and I will conceal nothing whatever from you."

12[89]:1 "First of all, Sir," say I, "explain this to me. The rock and the gate, what is it?" "This rock," said he, "and gate is the Son of God." "How, Sir," say I, "is the rock ancient, but the gate recent?" "Listen," said he, "and understand, foolish man.

12[89]:2 The Son of God is older than all His creation, so that He became the Father's adviser in His creation. Therefore also He is ancient." "But the gate, why is it recent, Sir?" say I.

12[89]:3 "Because," said he, "He was made manifest in the last days of the consummation; therefore the gate was made recent, that they which are to be saved may enter through it into the kingdom of God.

12[89]:4 Didst you see," said he, "that the stones which came through the gate have gone to the building of the tower, but those which came not through it were cast away again to their own place?" "I saw, Sir," say I. "Thus," said he, "no one shall enter into the kingdom of God, except he receive the name of His Son.

12[89]:5 For if you wish to enter into any city, and that city is walled all round and has one gate only, can you enter into that city except through the gate which it has?" "Why, how, Sir," say I, "is it possible otherwise?" "If then you can not enter into the city except through the gate itself, even so," said he, "a man cannot enter into the kingdom of God except by the name of His

Son that is beloved by Him.

12[89]:6 Didst you see," said he, "the multitude that is building the tower?" "I saw it, Sir," say I. "They," said he, are all glorious angels. With these then the Lord is walled around. But the gate is the Son of God; there is this one entrance only to the Lord. No one then shall enter in unto Him otherwise than through His Son.

12[89]:7 Didst you see," said he, "the six men, and the glorious and mighty man in the midst of them, him that walked about the tower and rejected the stones from the building?" "I saw him, Sir," say I.

12[89]:8 "The glorious man," said he, "is the Son of God, and those six are the glorious angels who guard Him on the right hand and on the left. Of these glorious angels not one," said he, "shall enter in unto God without Him; whosoever shall not receive His name, shall not enter into the kingdom of God."

13[90]:1 "But the tower," say I, "what is it?" "The tower," said he, "why, this is the Church.

13[90]:2 "And these virgins, who are they?" "They," said he, "are holy spirits; and no man can otherwise be found in the kingdom of God, unless these shall clothe him with their garment; for if you receive only the name, but receive not the garment from them, you profit nothing. For these virgins are powers of the Son of God. If [therefore] you bear the Name, and bear not His power, you shall bear His Name to none effect.

13[90]:3 And the stones," said he, "which you didst see cast away, these bare the Name, but clothed not themselves with the raiment of the virgins." "Of what sort, Sir," say I, "is their raiment?" "The names themselves," said he, "are their raiment. Whosoever bears the Name of the Son of God, ought to bear the names of these also; for even the Son Himself bears the names of these virgins.

13[90]:4 As many stones," said he, "as you saw enter into the building of the tower, being given in by their hands and waiting for the building, they have been clothed in the power of these virgins.

13[90]:5 For this cause you see the tower made a single stone with the rock.

So also they that have believed in the Lord through His Son and clothe themselves in these spirits, shall become one spirit and one body, and their garments all of one color. But such persons as bear the names of the virgins have their dwelling in the tower."

13[90]:6 "The stones then, Sir," say I, "which are cast aside, wherefore were they cast aside? For they passed through the gate and were placed in the building of the tower by the hands of the virgins." "Since all these things interest you," said he, "and you enquire diligently, listen as touching the stones that have been cast aside.

13[90]:7 These all," [said he,] "received the name of the Son of God, and received likewise the power of these virgins. When then they received these spirits, they were strengthened, and were with the servants of God, and they had one spirit and one body [and one garment]; for they had the same mind, and they wrought righteousness.

13[90]:8 After a certain time then they were persuaded by the women whom you saw clad in black raiment, and having their shoulders bare and their hair loose, and beautiful in form. When they saw them they desired them, and they clothed themselves with their power, but they stripped off from themselves the power of the virgins.

13[90]:9 They then were cast away from the house of God, and delivered to these (women). But they that were not deceived by the beauty of these women remained in the house of God. So you hast," said he, "the interpretation of them that were cast aside."

13[90]:1 What then, Sir," say I, "if these men, being such as they are, should repent and put away their desire for these women, and return unto the virgins, and walk in their power and in their works? Shall they not enter into the house of God?"

13[90]:2 "They shall enter," said he, "if they shall put away the works of these women, and take again the power of the virgins, and walk in their works. For this is the reason why there was also a cessation in the building, that, if these repent, they may go into the building of the tower; but if they repent not, then others will go, and these shall be cast away finally."

13[90]:3 For all these things I gave thanks unto the Lord, because He had compassion on all that called upon His name, and sent forth the angel of repentance to us that had sinned against Him, and refreshed our spirit, and, when we were already ruined and had no hope of life, restored our life.

13[90]:4 "Now, Sir," say I, "show me why the tower is not built upon the ground, but upon the rock and upon the gate." "Because you art senseless," said he, "and without understanding [you ask the question]." "I am obliged, Sir," say I, "to ask all questions of you, because I am absolutely unable to comprehend anything at all; for all are great and glorious and difficult for men to understand."

13[90]:5 "Listen," said he. "The name of the Son of God is great and incomprehensible, and sustains the whole world. If then all creation is sustained by the Son [of God], what think you of those that are called by Him, and bear the name of the Son of God, and walk according to His commandments?

13[90]:6 See you then what manner of men He sustains? Even those that bear His name with their whole heart. He Himself then is become their foundation, and He sustains them gladly, because they are not ashamed to bear His name."

15[92]:1 "Declare to me, Sir," say I, "the names of the virgins, and of the women that are clothed in the black garments." "Hear," said he, "the names of the more powerful virgins, those that are stationed at the corners.

15[92]:2 The first is Faith, and the second, Continence, and the third, Power, and the fourth, Long-suffering. But the others stationed between them have these names--Simplicity, Guilelessness, Purity, Cheerfulness, Truth, Understanding, Concord, Love. He that bears these names and the name of the Son of God shall be able to enter into the kingdom of God.

15[92]:3 Hear," said he, "likewise the names of the women that wear the black garments. Of these also four are more powerful than the rest; the first is Unbelief; the second, Intemperance; the third, Disobedience; the fourth, Deceit; and their followers are called, Sadness, Wickedness, Wantonness, Irascibility, Falsehood, Folly, Slander, Hatred. The servant of God that bears these names shall see the kingdom of God, but shall not enter into it."

15[92]:4 "But the stones, Sir," say I, "that came from the deep, and were fitted into the building, who are they?" "The first," said he, "even the ten, that were placed in the foundations, are the first generation; the twenty-five are the second generation of righteous men; the thirty-five are God's prophets and His ministers; the forty are apostles and teachers of the preaching of the Son of God."

15[92]:5 "Wherefore then, Sir," say I, "did the virgins give in these stones also for the building of the tower and carry them through the gate?"

15[92]:6 "Because these first," said he, "bore these spirits, and they never separated the one from the other, neither the spirits from the men nor the men from the spirits, but the spirits abode with them till they fell asleep; and if they had not had these spirits with them, they would not have been found useful for the building of this tower."

15[92]:1 "Show me still further, Sir," say I. "What desire you to know besides?" said he. "Wherefore, Sir," say I, "did the stones come up from the deep, and wherefore were they placed into the building, though they bore these spirits?"

15[92]:2 "It was necessary for them," said he, "to rise up through water, that they might be made alive; for otherwise they could not enter into the kingdom of God, except they had put aside the deadness of their [former] life.

15[92]:3 So these likewise that had fallen asleep received the seal of the Son of God and entered into the kingdom of God. For before a man," said he, "has borne the name of [the Son of] God, he is dead; but when he has received the seal, he lays aside his deadness, and resumes life.

15[92]:4 The seal then is the water: so they go down into the water dead, and they come up alive. "thus to them also this seal was preached, and they availed themselves of it that they might enter into the kingdom of God."

15[92]:5 "Wherefore, Sir," say I, "did the forty stones also come up with them from the deep, though they had already received the seal?" "Because," said he, "these, the apostles and the teachers who preached the name of the Son of God, after they had fallen asleep in the power and faith of the Son of God, preached also to them that had fallen asleep before them, and themselves gave unto them the seal of the preaching.

15[92]:6 Therefore they went down with them into the water, and came up again. But these went down alive [and again came up alive]; whereas the others that had fallen asleep before them went down dead and came up

711

alive.

15[92]:7 So by their means they were quickened into life, and came to the full knowledge of the name of the Son of God. For this cause also they came up with them, and were fitted with them into the building of the tower and were built with them, without being shaped; for they fell asleep in righteousness and in great purity. Only they had not this seal. You hast then the interpretation of these things also." "I have, Sir," say I.

17[94]:1 "Now then, Sir, explain to me concerning the mountains. Wherefore are their forms diverse the one from the other, and various?" "Listen," said he. "These twelve mountains are [twelve] tribes that inhabit the whole world. To these (tribes) then the Son of God was preached by the Apostles."

17[94]:2 But explain to me, Sir, why they are various--these mountains--and each has a different appearance." "Listen," said he. "These twelve tribes which inhabit the whole world are twelve nations; and they are various in understanding and in mind. As various, then, as you saw these mountains to be, such also are the varieties in the mind of these nations, and such their understanding. And I will show unto you the conduct of each."

17[94]:3 "First, Sir," say I, "show me this, why the mountains being so various, yet, when their stones were set into the building, became bright and of one color, just like the stones that had come up from the deep."

17[94]:4 "Because," said he, "all the nations that dwell under heaven, when they heard and believed, were called by the one name of [the Son of] God. So having received the seal, they had one understanding and one mind, and one faith became theirs and [one] love, and they bore the spirits of the virgins along with the Name; therefore the building of the tower became of one color, even bright as the sun.

17[94]:5 But after they entered in together, and became one body, some of them defiled themselves, and were cast out from the society of the righteous, and became again such as they were before, or rather even worse."

18[95]:1 "How, Sir," say I, "did they become worse, after they had fully known God?" "He that knows not God," said he, "and commits wickedness, has a certain punishment for his wickedness; but he that knows God fully ought not any longer to commit wickedness, but to do good.

18[95]:2 If then he that ought to do good commits wickedness, does he not seem to do greater wickedness than the man that knows not God? Therefore they that have not known God, and commit wickedness, are condemned to death; but they that have known God and seen His mighty works, and yet commit wickedness, shall receive a double punishment, and shall die eternally. In this way therefore shall the Church of God be purified.

18[95]:3 And as you saw the stones removed from the tower and delivered over to the evil spirits, they too shall be cast out; and there shall be one body of them that are purified, just as the tower, after it had been purified, became made as it were of one stone. Thus shall it be with the Church of God also, after she has been purified, and the wicked and hypocrites and blasphemers and double-minded and they that commit various kinds of wickedness have been cast out.

18[95]:4 When these have been cast out, the Church of God shall be one body, one understanding, one mind, one faith, one love. And then the Son of God shall rejoice and be glad in them, for that He has received back His people pure." "Great and glorious, Sir," say I, "are all these things.

18[95]:5 Once more, Sir," [say I,] "show me the force and the doings of each one of the mountains, that every soul that trusts in the Lord, when it hears, may glorify His great and marvelous and glorious name." "Listen," said he, "to the variety of the mountains and of the twelve nations.

19[96]:1 "From the first mountain, which was black, they that have believed are such as these; rebels and blasphemers against the Lord, and betrayers of the servants of God. For these there is no repentance, but there is death. For this cause also they are black; for their race is lawless.

19[96]:2 And from the second mountain, the bare one, they that believed are such as these; hypocrites and teachers of wickedness. And these then are like the former in not having the fruit of righteousness. For, even as their mountain is unfruitful, so likewise such men as these have a name indeed, but they are void of the faith, and there is no fruit of truth in them. For these then repentance is offered, if they repent quickly; but if they delay, they will have their death with the former."

19[96]:3 "Wherefore, Sir," say I, "is repentance possible for them, but not for the former ? For their doings are almost the same." "On this account," he said, "is repentance offered for them, because they blasphemed not their Lord, nor became betrayers of the servants of God; yet from desire of gain they played the hypocrite, and taught each other [after] the desires of sinful men. But they shall pay a certain penalty; yet repentance is ordained for them, because they are not become blasphemers or betrayers.

20[97]:1 "And from the third mountain, which had thorns and briars, they that believed are such as these; some of them are wealthy and others are entangled in many business affairs. The briars are the wealthy, and the thorns are they that are mixed up in various business affairs.

20[97]:2 These [then, that are mixed up in many and various business affairs,] hold fast [not] to the servants of God, but go astray, being choked by their affairs, but the wealthy unwillingly hold fast to the servants of God, fearing lest they may be asked for something by them. Such men therefore shall hardly enter into the kingdom of God.

20[97]:3 For as it is difficult to walk on briars with bare feet, so also it is difficult for such men to enter the kingdom of God.

20[97]:4 But for all these repentance is possible, but it must be speedy, that in respect to what they omitted to do in the former times, they may now revert to (past) days, and do some good. If then they shall repent and do some good, they shall live unto God; but if they continue in their doings, they shall be delivered over to those women, the which shall put them to death.

20[97]:1 "And from the fourth mountain, which had much vegetation, the upper part of the grass green and the part towards the roots withered, and some of it dried up by the sun, they that believed are such as these; the double-minded, and they that have the Lord on their lips, but have Him not in their heart.

20[97]:2 Therefore their foundations are dry and without power, and their words only live, but their works are dead. Such men are neither alive nor dead. They are, therefore, like unto the double-minded; for the double-minded are neither green nor withered; for they are neither alive nor dead.

20[97]:3 For as their grass was withered up when it saw the sun, so also the double-minded, when they hear of tribulation, through their cowardice worship idols and are ashamed of the name of their Lord.

20[97]:4 Such are neither alive nor dead. Yet these also, if they repent quickly, shall be able to live; but if they repent not, they are delivered over already to the women who deprive them of their life.

22[99]:1 "And from the fifth mountain, which had green grass and was rugged, they that believed are such as these; they are faithful, but slow to learn and stubborn and self-pleasers, desiring to know all things, and yet they know nothing at all.

22[99]:2 By reason of this their stubbornness, understanding stood aloof from them, and a foolish senselessness entered into them; and they praise themselves as having understanding, and they desire to be self-appointed teachers, senseless though they are.

22[99]:3 Owing then to this pride of heart many, while they exalted themselves, have been made empty; for a mighty demon is stubbornness and vain confidence. Of these then many were cast away, but some repented and believed, and submitted themselves to those that had understanding, having learnt their own senselessness.

22[99]:4 Yea, and to the rest that belong to this class repentance is offered; for they did not become wicked, but rather foolish and without understanding. If these then shall repent, they shall live unto God; but if they repent not, they shall have their abode with the women who work evil against them.

23[100]:1 "But they that believed from the sixth mountain, which had clefts great and small, and in the clefts herbage withered, are such as these;

23[100]:2 they that have the small clefts, these are they that have aught against one another, and from their backbitings they are withered in the faith; but many of these repented Yea, and the rest shall repent, when they hear my commandments; for their backbitings are but small, and they shall quickly repent.

23[100]:3 But they that have great clefts, these are persistent in their backbitings and bear grudges, nursing wrath against one another. These then were thrown right away from the tower and rejected from its building. Such persons therefore shall with difficulty live.

23[100]:4 If God and our Lord, Who rules over all things and has the authority over all His creation, bears no grudge against them that confess their sins, but is propitiated, doth man, who is mortal and full of sins, bear a grudge against man, as though he were able to destroy or save him?

23[100]:5 I say unto you--I, the angel of repentance--unto as many as hold this heresy, put it away from you and repent, and the Lord shall heal your former sins, if you shall purify yourselves from this demon; but if not, you shall be delivered unto him to be put to death.

24[101]:1 " And from the seventh mountain, on which was herbage green and smiling, and the whole mountain thriving, and cattle of every kind and the fowls of heaven were feeding on the herbage on that mountain, and the green herbage, on which they fed, only grew the more luxuriant, they that believed are such as these;

24[101]:2 they were ever simple and guileless and blessed, having nothing against one another, but rejoicing always in the servants of God, and clothed in the Holy Spirit of these virgins, and having compassion always on every man, and out of their labors they supplied every man's need without reproach and without misgiving.

24[101]:3 The Lord then seeing their simplicity and entire childishness made them to abound in the labors of their hands, and bestowed favor on them in all their doings.

24[101]:4 But I say unto you that are such--I, the angel of repentance--remain to the end such as you are, and your seed shall never be blotted out. For the Lord has put you to the proof, and enrolled you among our number, and your whole seed shall dwell with the Son of God; for of His Spirit did you receive.

25[102]:1 "And from the eighth mountain, where were the many springs, and all the creatures of the Lord did drink of the springs, they that believed are such as these;

25[102]:2 apostles and teachers, who preached unto the whole world, and who taught the word of the Lord in soberness and purity, and kept back no part at all for evil desire, but walked always in righteousness and truth, even as also they received the Holy Spirit. Such therefore shall have their entrance with the angels.

26[103]:1 "And from the ninth mountain, which was desert, which had [the] reptiles and wild beasts in it which destroy mankind, they that believed are such as these;

26[103]:2 they that have the spots are deacons that exercised their office ill, and plundered the livelihood of widows and orphans, and made gain for themselves from the ministrations which they had received to perform. If then they abide in the same evil desire, they are dead and there is no hope of life for them; but if they turn again and fulfill their ministrations in purity, it shall be possible for them to live.

26[103]:3 But they that are mildewed, these are they that denied and turned not again unto their Lord, but having become barren and desert, because they hold fast not unto the servants of God but remain alone, they destroy their own souls.

26[103]:4 For as a vine left alone in a hedge, if it meet with neglect, is destroyed and wasted by the weeds, and in time becomes wild and is no longer useful to its owner, so also men of this kind have given themselves up in despair and become useless to their Lord, by growing wild.

26[103]:5 To these then repentance cometh, unless they be found to have denied from the heart; but if a man be found to have denied from the heart, I know not whether it is possible for him to live.

26[103]:6 And this I say not in reference to these days, that a man after denying should receive repentance; for it is impossible for him to be saved who shall now deny his Lord; but for those who denied Him long ago repentance seems to be possible. If a man therefore will repent, let him do so speedily before the tower is completed; but if not, he shall be destroyed by the women and put to death.

26[103]:7 And the stunted, these are the treacherous and backbiters; and the wild beasts which you saw on the mountain are these. For as wild beasts with their venom poison and kill a man, so also do the words of such men poison and kill a man.

26[103]:8 These then are broken off short from their faith through the conduct which they have in themselves; but some of them repented and were saved; and the rest that are of this kind can be saved, if they repent;

but if they repent not, they shall meet their death from those women of whose power they are possessed.

27[104]:1 "And from the tenth mountain, where were trees sheltering certain sheep, they that believed are such as these;

27[104]:2 bishops, hospitable persons, who gladly received into their houses at all times the servants of God without hypocrisy. [These bishops] at all times without ceasing sheltered the needy and the widows in their ministration and conducted themselves in purity at all times.

27[104]:3 These [all] then shall be sheltered by the Lord for ever. They therefore that have done these things are glorious in the sight of God, and their place is even now with the angels, if they shall continue unto the end serving the Lord.

27[104]:1 "And from the eleventh mountain, where were trees full of fruit, decked with divers kinds of fruits, they that believed are such as these;

27[104]:2 they that suffered for the Name [of the Son of God], who also suffered readily with their whole heart, and yielded up their lives."

27[104]:3 "Wherefore then, Sir," say I, "have all the trees fruits, but some of their fruits are more beautiful than others?" "Listen," said he; "all as many as ever suffered for the Name's sake are glorious in the sight of God, and the sins of all these were taken away, because they suffered for the name of the Son of God. Now here why their fruits are various, and some surpassing others.

27[104]:4 "As many," said he, "as were tortured and denied not, when brought before the magistracy, but suffered readily, these are the more glorious in the sight of the Lord; their fruit is that which surpasses. But as many as become cowards, and were lost in uncertainty, and considered in their hearts whether they should deny or confess, and yet suffered, their fruits are less, because this design entered into their heart; for this design is evil, that a servant should deny his own lord.

27[104]:5 See to it, therefore, you who entertain this idea, lest this design remain in your hearts, and you die unto God. But you that suffer for the Name's sake ought to glorify God, because God deemed you worthy that you should bear this name, and that all your sins should be healed.

27[104]:6 Reckon yourselves blessed therefore; yea, rather think that you have done a great work, if any of you shall suffer for God's sake. The Lord bestowed life upon you, and you perceived it not; for your sins weighed you down, and if you had not suffered for the Name [of the Lord], you had died unto God by reason of your sins.

27[104]:7 These things I say unto you that waver as touching denial and confession. Confess that you have the Lord, lest denying Him you be delivered into prison.

27[104]:8 If the Gentiles punish their slaves, if any one deny his lord, what think you the Lord will do unto you, He who has authority over all things? Away with these designs from your hearts, that you may live forever unto God."

27[104]:1 "And from the twelfth mountain, which was white, they that believed are such as these; they that are as very babes, into whose heart no guile entered, neither learned they what wickedness is, but they remained as babes forever.

27[104]:2 Such as these then dwell without doubt in the kingdom of God, because they defiled the commandments of God in nothing, but continued as babes all the days of their life in the same mind.

27[104]:3 As many of you therefore as shall continue," said he, "and shall be as infants not having guile, shall be glorious [even] than all them that have been mentioned before; for all infants are glorious in the sight of God, and stand first in His sight. Blessed then are you, as many as have put away wickedness from you, and have clothed yourselves in guilelessness: you shall live unto God cheifest of all."

27[104]:4 After he had finished the parables of the mountains, I say unto him, "Sir, now explain to me concerning the stones that were taken from the plain and placed in the building in the room of the stones that were taken from the tower, and concerning the round (stones) which were placed in the building, and concerning those that were still round".

27[104]:1 "Hear," said he, "likewise concerning all these things. The stones which were taken from the plain and placed in the building of the tower in the room of those that were rejected, are the roots of this white mountain.

27[104]:2 When then they that believed from this mountain were all found guiltless, the lord of the tower ordered these from the roots of the mountain to be put into the building of the tower. For He knew that if these stones should go into the building [of the tower], they would remain bright and not one of them would turn black.

27[104]:3 But if he added (stones) from other mountains, he would have been obliged to visit the tower again, and to purify it. Now all these have been found white, who have believed and who shall believe; for they are of the same kind. Blessed is this kind, for it is innocent!

27[104]:4 Hear now likewise concerning those round and bright stones. All these are from the white mountain. Now here wherefore they have been found round. Their riches have darkened and obscured them a little from the truth.

27[104]:5 When therefore the Lord perceived their mind, *that they could favor the truth,* and likewise remain good, He commanded their possessions to be cut off from them, yet not to be taken away altogether, so that they might be able to do some good with that which has been left to them, and might live unto God for that they come of a good kind. So therefore they have been cut away a little, and placed in the building of this tower".

27[104]:1 "But the other (stones), which have remained round and have not been fitted into the building, because they have not yet received the seal, have been replaced in their own possession, for they were found very round.

27[104]:2 For this world and the vanities of their possessions must be cut off from them, and then they will fit into the kingdom of God. For it is necessary that they should enter into the kingdom of God; because the Lord has blessed this innocent kind. Of this kind then not one shall perish. Yea, even though any one of them being tempted by the most wicked devil have committed any fault, he shall return speedily unto his Lord.

27[104]:3 Blessed I pronounced you all to be--I the angel of repentance-- whoever of you are guileless as infants, because your part is good and honorable in the sight of God.

27[104]a:4 Moreover I bid all of you, whoever have received this seal, keep guilelessness, and bear no grudge, and continue not in your wickedness nor in the memory of the offenses of bitterness; but become of one spirit, and heal these evil clefts and take them away from among you, that the owner of the flocks may rejoice concerning them.

27[104a]:5 For he will rejoice, if he find all things whole. But if he find any part of the flock scattered, woe unto the shepherds.

27[104a]:6 For if the shepherds themselves shall have been found scattered, how will they answer for the flocks? Will they say that they were harassed by the flock? No credence will be given them. For it is an incredible thing that a shepherd should be injured by his flock; and he will be punished the more because of his falsehood. And I am the shepherd, and it behooved me most strongly to render an account for you.

32[109]:1 "Amend yourselves therefore, while the tower is still in course of building.

32[109]:2 The Lord dwells in men that love peace; for to Him peace is dear; but from the contentious and them that are given up to wickedness He kept afar off. Restore therefore to Him your spirit whole as you received it.

32[109]:3 For suppose you hast given to a fuller a new garment whole, and desired to receive it back again whole, but the fuller give it back to you torn, wilt you receive it thus? Wilt you not at once blaze out and attack him with reproaches, saying; "The garment which I gave you was whole; wherefore hast you rent it and made it useless? See, by reason of the rent, which you hast made in it, it cannot be of use." Wilt you not then say all this to a fuller even about a rent which he has made in thy garment?

32[109]:4 If therefore you art thus vexed in the matter of thy garment, and complained because you received it not back whole, what think you the Lord will do to you, He, Who gave you the spirit whole, and you hast made it absolutely useless, so that it cannot be of any use at all to its Lord? For its use began to be useless, when it was corrupted by you. Will not therefore the Lord of this spirit for this thy deed punish [you with death]?"

32[109]:5 "Certainly," I said, "all those, whomsoever He shall find continuing to bear malice, He will punish." "Trample not," said he, "upon His mercy, but rather glorify Him, because He is so long-suffering with your sins, and is not like unto you. Practice then repentance which is expedient for you.

33[110]:1 "All these things which are written above I, the shepherd, the angel of repentance, have declared and spoken to the servants of God. If then you shall believe and hear my words, and walk in them, and amend your ways, you shall be able to live. But if you continue in wickedness and in bearing malice, no one of this kind shall live unto God. All things which were to be spoken by me have (now) been spoken to you."

33[110]:2 The shepherd said to me, "Hast you asked me all thy questions?" And I said, "Yes, Sir." "Why then hast you not enquired of me concerning the shape of the stones placed in the building, in that we filled up their shapes?" And I said, "I forgot, Sir."

33[110]:3 "Listen now," said he, "concerning them. These are they that have heard my commandments now, and have practiced repentance with their whole heart. So when the Lord saw that their repentance was good and pure, and that they could continue therein, he ordered their former sins to be blotted out. These shapes then were their former sins, and they have been chiseled away that they might not appear."

Parable 10

1[111]:1 After I had written out this book completely, the angel who had delivered me to the shepherd came to the house where I was, and sat upon a couch, and the shepherd stood at his right hand. Then he called me, and spoke thus unto me;

1[111]:2 "I delivered you," said he, "and thy house to this shepherd, that you might be protected by him." "True, Sir," I said "If therefore," said he, "you desire to be protected from all annoyance and all cruelty, to have also success in every good work and word, and all the power of righteousness, walk in his commandments, which I have given you, and you shall be able to get the mastery over all wickedness.

1[111]:3 For if you keep his commandments, all evil desire and the sweetness of this world shall be subject unto you; moreover success shall attend you in every good undertaking. Embrace his gravity and self-restraint, and tell it out unto all men that he is held in great honor and dignity with the Lord, and is a ruler of great authority, and powerful in his office. To him alone in the whole world has authority over repentance been assigned. Seemed he to you to be powerful? Yet you despise the gravity and moderation which he used towards you."

2[112]:1 I say unto him; "Ask him, Sir, himself, whether from the time that he has been in my house, I have done ought out of order, whereby I have offended him."

2[112]:2 "I myself know," said he, "that you hast done nothing out of order, nor art about to do so. And so I speak these things unto you, that you may persevere. For he has given a good account of you unto me. You therefore shall speak these words to others, that they too who have practiced or shall practice repentance may be of the same mind as you art; and he may give a good report of them to me, and I unto the Lord."

2[112]:3 "I too, Sir," I say, "declare to every man the mighty works of the Lord; for I hope that all who have sinned in the past, if they hear these things, will gladly repent and recover life."

2[112]:4 "Continue therefore," said he, "in this ministry, and complete it unto the end. For whosoever fulfill his commandments shall have life; yea such a man (shall have) great honor with the Lord. But whosoever keep not his commandments, fly from their life, and oppose him, and follow not his commandments, but deliver themselves over to death; and each one becomes guilty of his own blood. But I bid you obey these commandments, and you shall have a remedy for thy sins.

3[113]:1 "Moreover, I have sent these virgins unto you, that they may dwell with you; for I have seen that they are friendly towards you. You hast them therefore as helpers, that you may be the better able to keep his commandments; for it is impossible that these commandments be kept without the help of these virgins. I see too that they are glad to be with you. But I will charge them that they depart not at all from thy house.

3[113]:2 Only do you purify thy house; for in a clean house they will gladly dwell. For they are clean and chaste and industrious, and have favor in the sight of the Lord. If, therefore, they shall find thy house pure, they will continue with you; but if the slightest pollution arise, they will depart from thy house at once. For these virgins love not pollution in any form."

3[113]:3 I said unto him, "I hope, Sir, that I shall please them, so that they may gladly dwell in my house for ever; and just as he to whom you didst deliver me makes no complaint against me, so they likewise shall make no complaint."

3[113]:4 He said unto the shepherd, "I perceive," said he, "that he wishes to live as the servant of God, and that he will keep these commandments, and will place these virgins in a clean habitation."

3[113]:5 With these words he again delivered me over to the shepherd, and called the virgins, and said to them; "Inasmuch as I see that you are glad to dwell in this man's house, I commend to you him and his house, that you depart not at all from his house." But they heard these words gladly.

4[114]:1 He said then to me, "Quit you like a man in this ministry; declare to every man the mighty works of the Lord, and you shall have favor in this ministry. Whosoever therefore shall walk in these commandments, shall live and be happy in his life; but whosoever shall neglect them, shall not live, and shall be unhappy in his life.

4[114]:2 Charge all men who are able to do right, that they cease not to practice good works; for it is useful for them. I say moreover that every man ought to be rescued from misfortune; for he that has need, and suffered misfortune in his daily life, is in great torment and want.

4[114]:3 Whosoever therefore rescued from penury a life of this kind, wins great joy for himself. For he who is harassed by misfortune of this sort is afflicted and tortured with equal torment as one who is in chains. For many men on account of calamities of this kind, because they can bear them no longer, lay violent hands on themselves. He then who knows the calamity of a man of this kind and rescues him not, commits great sin, and becomes guilty of the man's blood.

4[114]:4 Do therefore good works, whoever of you have received (benefits) from the Lord, lest, while you delay to do them, the building of the tower be completed. For it is on your account that the work of the building has been interrupted. Unless then you hasten to do right, the tower will be completed, and you shut out."

4[114]:5 When then he had finished speaking with me, he rose from the couch and departed, taking with him the shepherd and the virgins. He said however unto me, that he would send the shepherd and the virgins back again to my house. . .

An Overview of Books.

1 Esdras

1 Esdras is a document that has been drawn from the materials now in 1 and 2 Chronicles, Ezra, and Nehemiah. The author seemed to want to conform the books of Ezra and Nehemiah to the ideology of the books of Chronicles by giving special emphasis to the centrality of David, the inclusive characteristics of Israel, the doctrine of retribution and the need to obey the prophets, and the Temple and its practices. With the exception of one section, this book appears to be nothing more than a parallel version of the history beginning with the Passover of Josiah (622 B.C.E.) in II Chronicles 35:1 and continuing through Ezra (except 4:6), including Nehemiah 7:73-8:12a . The story stops abruptly with Ezra's reading of the Law (c. 400 B.C.E.).

2 Esdras

The work known as 2 Esdras is in fact three separate compositions. Ezra's place in the story is that of a prophet. In 2 Esdras 1-2 (also known as 5 Ezra) Ezra prophesies about God's rejection of Israel as God's people and its replacement by the Church, making this section a Christian work , without question. It is composed in Greek around 150 C.E. In 2 Esdras 3-14 (also known as 4 Ezra) Ezra articulates the meaning of Israel's sufferings and reveals a vision of what God is going to do in the near future on Israel's behalf. This section of the text is a Jewish work written in Hebrew around 100 C.E.

1 Maccabees

Although the book presents the Jewish leaders Judas, Jonathan, and Simon as devout people and has little sympathy for people who favor hellenization, but it must be noted that he nowhere mentions divine intervention.
The contents of the book can be summarized as follows:

Chapter 1-2: The hellenization of Judah and the non-violent resistance by Mattathias;

Chapter 3-9: Military actions by Judas the Maccabaean ('battle hammer'): after 166, he defeats the Seleucid armies three times and liberates Jerusalem, where the temple is purified; more operations; Judas' defeat and death in 161;

Chapter 9-12: Continued warfare, led by Judas' brother Jonathan (160-

725

143), who, benefiting from wars of succession in the Seleucid
Empire, restores the fortunes of the Jewish nationalists and adds to
their territories;

Chapter 13-16: The third brother, Simon, achieves political independence,
and founds the Hasmonaean dynasty.

The author must have been a cultivated Jew living in Judah, and can be
dated to c.100 B.C.E. Although we assume there is a Hebrew or Aramaic
original, which is now lost. The Greek version has survived and was
accepted as canonical by the Christians. It must have been popular in the
Diaspora also. In the sixteenth century, the scholars of the Reformation
preferred to concentrate on those texts of the Jewish Bible that were written
in Hebrew. It was at this time that the final decision was made by church
fathers that if a book was not written in Hebrew it would not be considered
canon for the Old Testament.

2 Maccabees

2 Maccabees has a much greater interest in theology than I Maccabees. 2
Maccabees is not as well written and has a less polished form. The pagans
are defined as 'blasphemous and barbarous nations' in 10.4, but there are
also severe censures of apostate Jews, of whom there must therefore have
been considerable numbers. We find a theological features in 2 Maccabees
such as the resurrection of the body in 7.11; 14.46. This stand in stark
contrast first to Wisdom and Philo, both of which teach the immortality of
the soul. In 7.28 there appears for the first time in Hebrew thought the
doctrine which will later be called creatio ex nihilo, which is the belief that
creation, and thus all things created, was brought about out of nothing.
That is to say that God made the world not from things which were, which
is not identical with 'nothing' in the philosophical sense of the term. In 7.9,
14 (cf. 14.46; 12.43) we have concepts of eternal life and death, and in 12.43
the intercession of the living for the dead, an element on which the Catholic
church has sometimes sought to found the doctrine of Purgatory. Lastly,
there is a well-developed angelology (3.24-28; 5.2-4; 10.29ff.; 11.8, etc.)
Indeed, 2 Maccabees influenced the theology of certain churches more than
any apocryphal book.

3 Maccabees

The title of 3 Maccabees is a misnomer because the book has nothing to do
with the Maccabees, who are never mentioned in it. The book is a story
about a situation in which the Jewish people, this time in Egypt, were in
danger of being annihilated by a Hellenistic monarch, who was attempting

to top their religious convictions and practices. The book was composed in Greek and relates a story set in the time of Ptolemy IV Philopater (221-203 B.C.E).

4 Maccabees

4 Maccabees belongs to the Maccabees series only because it deals with the beginning of the persecution of Jews by Antiochus IV Epiphanes. It possibly was written during the reign of the emperor Caligula (C.E. 37.) The work's main religious theme is that the martyr's sufferings expunged the sins of the entire Jewish people through a type of propitiation. The Maccabees books were preserved only by the Christian church. Augustine wrote in The City of God that they were preserved for their accounts of the martyrs. This suggests that 4 Maccabees may have been the most highly regarded of the Maccabees series, although this is disputed by the fact that 3 Maccabees may have actually established the idea of Purgatory.

Letter (Epistle) of Jeremiah

Jeremiah is the 'author' of this text only insofar as Jeremiah provided the primary resource (Jer. 10:2-15) that the actual, anonymous author developed into a lengthier variation on the theme. With regard to the date of composition, Moore's caveat concerning the Additions to Daniel that one must distinguish this carefully from the time of translation into Greek is valid for the Additions to Jeremiah as well. The translation was accomplished before the end of the second century B.C.E, given the discovery of a Greek fragment of the Letter of Jeremiah at Qumran. The time of composition is less certain. Several scholars lay great stress on the peculiar internal indication of date: the prediction that the Jews would be in Babylon 'for a long time, up to seven generations' (v. 3) before God will bring them back to their ancestral land, which represents an alteration of Jeremiah's seventy years (Jer. 25:11; 29:10; an alteration also occurs in Daniel's 'seventy weeks of years' [Dan. 9:24; cf. 9:2]). (Ball 1913: 596; Moore 1977: 328; Mendels 1992: 722; Metzger 1957: 96). These scholars argue that the author must be writing before this period of time had elapsed, for it is difficult to imagine an author deliberately altering Jeremiah's prophecy in such a way that would already have proven false. A date between 317 and 306 B.C.E., or 280 years after either the first or second deportation to Babylon (597 and 586 B.C.E.), is taken as the latest date for the composition of the original Hebrew version. There is in fact no internal evidence to necessitate a later date, although the ambiguity of the length of time covered by a 'generation' should make us cautious about being overly precise about the range of dates."

The Prayer of Azariah

The original was in either Hebrew or Aramaic. Although not present in the MT, this so-called 'deuterocanonical fragment' has always been regarded as part of the canonical, inspired Scriptures. However, it is not part of the original story, but rather an addition made by an inspired author who took existing liturgical prayers, adapted them slightly, and inserted them here, with a few sentences of his own to make a smoother nexus. In both versions [LXX and Theodotian] this passage lies between MT Dan. 3:23 and 3:24 and consists of three unequal parts: first, the Prayer of Azariah, the Hebrew name of Abednego (vv. 1-22); second, a short prose account of the fate of the three Jews in the furnace (vv. 23-27); third, a hymn sung by the three youths while in the furnace (vv. 28-68). The relationship between MT Dan 3:23 and 3:24 is highly dramatic. The three Jewish youths are thrown into an incredibly hot furnace and presumably destroyed, when suddenly Nebuchadnezzar is perturbed and in astonishment claims to see four men in the fire, the fourth looking like a divine being. Nebuchadnezzar reacts to the miracle by praising the God of the Jews. The author of the addition must have found the transition too sudden and provided the details of the miracle to form a softer transitional path.

Baruch

There is some evidence that the work actually comes from at least three authors. The most obvious division occurs between the prose of 1:1-3:8 and the poetry in 3:9-5:9, but there appear also to be two distinct poems in this latter section: a celebration of Wisdom in 3:9-4:4 and a promise of restoration to Jerusalem in 4:5-5:9. The changes in style and the striking difference in the names for God ("Lord," "Lord God," "Lord Almighty, God of Israel" in 1:1-3:8; and "God," "the Holy One," "the Everlasting," "Everlasting Savior" in 3:9-5:9), makes the separate authorship of these two parts fairly certain. The poem on Wisdom, 3:9-4:4, may have been written at a later time based of the fact that it there is a sift of interest. Although the prose section, especially 1:14-3:8, shows considerable dependence on Jeremiah, the final poem of encouragement, 4:5-5:9, is highly reminiscent of II Isaiah. There is little to go on in attempting to fix a date. A good midpoint of dating would be 150 – 200 C.E.

Prayer of Manasseh (Manassas)

In II Chronicles 33:10-20 we are given an account of how the wicked king Manasseh, after being taken captive to Babylon by the Assyrians, repented and was restored to his kingdom, where he proceeded to undo much of the mischief he had done in his apostate days. Special mention is made in verses

18 and 19 of Manasseh's prayer. What were the words of Manasseh's prayer? Inquiring minds wanted to know. According to 2 Chronicles 33:18-19 the words were preserved in 'the Annals of the Kings of Israel' and in 'the records of the seers.' But neither of these books has been preserved. Since the prayer was not recorded by the Chronicler, an unknown writer of uncommon skill and piety has undertaken the task of supplying the lack by means of this prayer Although we have no solid evidence of date, the earliest evidence for the work's existence comes from the third century C.E., so it could have originated at any time between the composition of 2 Chronicles and then.

Bel and the Dragon

Daniel 14:23-42: "In the companion story the same motive of discrediting pagan deities is apparent. The issue is approached, however, from the opposite angle. Whereas Bel is nothing more than a man-made statue, a fact which is easily demonstrated by its inability to eat, the dragon is a living creature and does eat. To prove that the dragon also is no god, Daniel must somehow show that merely being alive and able to eat is not sufficient evidence to establish divinity. This he does by offering to perform the apparently impossible feat of slaying the dragon. This is done through poison. Cakes of pitch, fat, and hair, makes the witless beast explode.

Wisdom of Sirach

By far the longest book, comprising almost one third of the Deuterocanon, Ecclesiasticus, or by its Greek title, the Wisdom of Jesus (from the Hebrew, Joshua), the Son of Sirach, provides the reader with the unusual advantage of a translator's preface. The author himself, moreover, has obliged the reader with his signature along with a blessing upon those who concern themselves with wisdom (50:27-29). From these passages, therefore, we learn that the book was composed in Hebrew in Judea by an ardent collector of gnomic sayings whose Hebrew name was Joshua ben Sira and was brought to the Jewish community in Alexandria by his grandson and translated into Greek. In his reference to 'the thirty-eighth year of the reign of Euergetes,' the grandson provides us with a clue to the date. How long after his arrival in Egypt he made the translation, we are not told, but his arrival can be dated quite precisely as 132 B.C.E. Based on the dates of the high priest's term mentioned in the book as compared to the works of Josephus, the book can be fixed somewhere between 150-170 B.C.E.

Wisdom of Solomon

Several factors point to Alexandria in Egypt as the place of composition: the use of Greek, the philosophical concepts, the focus on the exodus, the polemic against Egyptian animal-worship, and so on. A date in the first century B.C.E.E. seems most likely. The terminus a quo is set by the author's use of the Greek translation of Isaiah, Job, and Proverbs, the first of which was probably available by 200 B.C.E.E. First, the description of the development of the ruler cult in 14:16-20 best describes not the cult of the Ptolemaic kings of Egypt, a cult that was organized and promoted from the center, but the spontaneous, decentralized development of the imperial cult under Augustus, who was also Egypt's first 'remote' ruler since Alexander. Considers the author's address in 6:1-2 to the 'judges of the ends of the earth' who 'rule over multitudes, and boast of many nations' to fit the Roman imperial period better than its predecessors.

Additions to Esther

The Greek version of the Hebrew Bible Book of Esther is designated, "Additions to Esther" and pre-serves many details of the Hebrew account. Its portrayal of Esther herself, however, is appreciably different, primarily because of Additions C and D (Add Esth 13:8–14:19; 15:1–16). The Additions to Esther consist of six extended passages (107 verses) that have no counterpart in the Hebrew version. They are numbered as chaps 11–16, designated A–F, and added to the Hebrew text at various places. Another important "addition" to Greek Esther is the mention of God's name over fifty times. This has the effect of making the story explicitly religious, in sharp contrast to the Hebrew text, which does not mention God at all. Addition C corrects all the "flaws" in the Hebrew version of Esther, which was rejected as authoritative by some Jews even as late as the third century C.E. because of its "inexcusable" omissions. It never mentioned God. Esther also confesses her hatred for every alien, the pomp and ceremony of her office, and her abhorrence at being married to a non-Jew, turning the book into an indictment against Gentiles. Thus, with the addition of God and hatred, we have an acceptable religious text.

Tobit

Since the law is known as 'the book of Moses' or 'the law of Moses' (6:13; 7:11-13), the work must certainly postdate the fifth century, when the formation of the Pentateuch was nearly complete. It seems reasonable to set the earliest date of composition as sometime during the third century B.C.E.E. The book reflects the same ethos as in Ben Sira and Judith with regard to dietary laws, burial of the dead, the custom of marrying within one's local area, and piety. The discovery of the fragments of Tobit at Qumran sets the earliest dates from 100 B.C.E.E. Tobit's failure to reflect any knowledge of the issues surrounding the Hellenization crisis and Maccabean Revolt suggests that the book was written sometime between

250 and 175 B.C.E.E.

Judith

Inconsistent historical facts run rampant through this text. The closest we can come to setting the book in any historical detail , which may be stretched enough to make it fit with exaggerations is to identify the generals, Holofernes and Bagoas, with the two generals sent against Phoenicia, Palestine and Egypt by Artaxerxes III towards 350. The names are certainly Persian, and are attested frequently, but there are many difficulties, unless we accept that Judith is a fictional account of one of the episodes in this campaign. Holofernes' itinerary in ch. 2 also seems impossible: he covers almost 300 miles in three days, passing through places which are either unknown or absurd when they are known. No account is taken of the fact that an average of 100 miles a day is in any case excessive for an army consisting of infanty as well as cavalry. As we have seen, the identity of Bethulia is also unknown.

Susanna

As the story goes, a fair Hebrew wife bathes in her garden, having sent her attendants away. Two overly sexed old men secretly observe the lovely Susanna. When she makes her way back to her house, they accost her, threatening to claim that she was meeting a young man in the garden unless she agrees to have sex with them. She refuses and they falsely accuse her. She is arrested and about to be put to death for promiscuity when a young man named Daniel interrupts the proceedings. After separating the two men, they are questioned about details of the incident. They claim to have seen her under a tree, but they name trees of different placement and size. In the Greek text, the names of the trees cited by the elders form puns with the sentence given by Daniel. The first says they were under a mastic (υπο σχινον, hupo schinon), and Daniel says that an angels stands ready to cut (σχισει, schisei) him in two. The second says they were under an evergreen oak tree (υπο πρινον, hupo prinon), and Daniel says that an angel stands ready to saw (πρισαι, prisai) him in two. The great difference in size between a mastic and an oak makes the elders' lie obvious to all, and the accusers are put to death instead.

Psalm 151

Psalm 151 is the name given to a short psalm that is found in most copies of the Septugint but not in the Masoretic text of the Hebrew Bible. The title given to this psalm in the Septuagint indicates that no number is affixed to it: "This Psalm is ascribed to David and is outside the number. The psalm was written when he slew Goliath in single combat". It is included also in some manuscripts of the Pershitta. The Eastern Orthodox Church accepts Psalm 151 as canonical. Psalm 151 appears along with a number of canonical and non-canonical psalms in the Dead Sea Scroll a first century CE scroll discovered in 1956.

Enoch

The patriarch Enoch is said to have "walked with God and was seen no more, because God took him". The mystery surrounding his departure from the world, made Enoch's name an apt one for the purposes of apocalyptic writers. In consequence there arose a literature attributed to him, which influenced not only later Jewish apocrypha, but has left its imprint on the New Testament and the works of the early Fathers. The canonical Epistle of St. Jude, in verses 14, 15, explicitly quotes from the Book of Enoch; the citation is found in the Ethopic version in verses 9 and 4 of the first chapter. However, in the fourth century the Enoch writings lost credit and ceased to be quoted. After an allusion by an author of the beginning of the ninth century, they disappear from view. So great was the oblivion into which they fell that only scanty fragments of Greek and Latin versions were preserved in the West. The complete text was thought to have perished when it was discovered by the traveler and archeologist Bruce in 1773 in Ethiopia. A complete text with commentary can now be found through Fifth Estate Publishers.

Jubilees

Imagine a book that took into account all of the Jewish rites according to calendar, seasons, ceremonies, and lunar occurrences, all toward the precise fulfilling of the law. The Book of Jubilees is in certain limited aspects the most important book in this volume for the student of religion. Without it we could of course have inferred from Ezra and Nehemiah, the Priests' Code, and the later chapters of Zechariah the supreme position that the law had achieved in Judaism, but without Jubilees we could hardly have imagined such an absolute supremacy of the law as finds expression in this book. This absolute supremacy is the place and power the law carried. Thus Jubilees represents the triumph of the movement, which had been at work for the past three centuries or more. It held the place until the next fixation came along. This element of course is apocalyptic thought, which was the source of the higher theology in Judaism, and subsequently was the parent of Christianity, wherein it seems to have become one with prophecy. The Book of Jubilees was written in Hebrew by a Pharisee between the year of the accession of Hyrcanus to the high priesthood in 135 B.C.E. and his breach with the Pharisees some years before his death in 105 B.C.E.

1 Clements

The epistle is customarily dated to the end of the reign of Domitian (95 or 96 C.E.). In the first sentence of the letter, the author explains that the Roman church has been delayed in turning its attention to the dispute at Corinth by "sudden and repeated misfortunes and hindrances which have befallen us" (1:1). This statement is usually interpreted as an allusion to a persecution through which the church at Rome has just been passing. The account of the deaths of Peter and Paul in chap. 5 is not that of an eye-witness. The presbyters installed by the apostles have died (44:2), and a second ecclesiastical generation has passed (44:3). The church at Rome is called "ancient" (47:6); and the emissaries from Rome are said to have lived "blamelessly" as Christians "from youth to old age" (63:3). Thus the epistle cannot have been written before the last decades of the 1st century. There are references to the letter by the middle of the next century in the works of Hegesippus and Dionysius of Corinth (apud Euseb. Hist. Eccl. 3.16; 4.22; 4.23). Thus one may place the composition of 1 Clement between C.E. 80 and 140 C.E..

Shepherd of Hermas

The early Christian document Hermas, or Shepherd of Hermas, was known to the early Church Fathers. The Muratorian canon, a list of canonical books from about the 3d century, says Hermas was written by the brother of Pius, Bishop of Rome, about 140-154 C.E.. It was written in Rome and involves the Roman church. The document was composed over a longer period of time. Visions I-IV were composed during a threatened persecution, probably under Trajan (the Clement of 8:3 could be Clement of Rome). Vision V - Similitude VIII and Similitude X were written perhaps by the same author to describe repentance to Christians who were wavering. Similitude IX was written to unify the entire work and to threaten those who had been disloyal. This last phase must have occurred before Irenaeus (ca. 175). A preferred date would be 140 C.E.

The text had a great vogue in orthodox circles and was even included in some copies of the New Testament (it is found in the Sinaitic Codex). The theology of the Church must have been very elastic at a time when such a book could enjoy popularity and implicit, if not explicit, ecclesiastical sanction, for its Christology does not seem to square with any of the Christologies of the New Testament, or with those of contemporary theologians whose occasional documents have reached us. The Shepherd speaks of a Son of God; but this Son of God is distinguished from Jesus.

"That Holy Spirit which was created first of all, God placed in a body, in which it should dwell, in a chosen body, as it pleased him and states, "God made His Holy Spirit, which pre-existed and created all creation, to enter and dwell in the flesh which He approved." In this text the Holy Spirit appears to be a divine substance. But we must not suspect Patripassionism, which assumes God the father took form and suffered on the cross. The "flesh" is spoken of as a person who "walked as pleased God, because it was not polluted on earth." "God, therefore, took into counsel the Son and the angels in their glory, to the end that this flesh might furnish, as it were, a place of tabernacling (for the Spirit), and might not seem to have lost the reward of its service. For all flesh shall receive the reward which shall be found without stain or spot, and in it the Holy Spirit shall have its home." This passage appears to make the "tabernacling" of the Holy Spirit in Jesus a reward for the purity of his life. Jesus then becomes divine through the power of God, after consultation with the Son of God, who elsewhere in The Shepherd is identified with the Holy Spirit. "The most venerable angel," "the glorious angel," "the holy angel" are titles that Hermas gives to Jesus in his allegory; but it is understood that the angelic status of Jesus is not his by nature. His labours on earth to save and to cleanse have gained him a co-inheritance with the Holy Spirit, God's primary Son, so that Jesus now is the second Son of God.